Computer Communications and Networks

T0156272

For other titles published in this series, go to
www.springer.com/series/4198

The **Computer Communications and Networks** series is a range of textbooks, monographs and handbooks. It sets out to provide students, researchers and non-specialists alike with a sure grounding in current knowledge, together with comprehensible access to the latest developments in computer communications and networking.

Emphasis is placed on clear and explanatory styles that support a tutorial approach, so that even the most complex of topics is presented in a lucid and intelligible manner.

Graham Cormode · Marina Thottan
Editors

Algorithms for Next Generation Networks

 Springer

Editors

Dr. Graham Cormode
AT&T Research
Florham Park
NJ, USA
graham@research.att.com

Dr. Marina Thottan
Bell Labs
Murray Hill
NJ, USA
marinat@alcatel-lucent.com

Series Editor
Professor A.J. Sammes, BSc, MPhil, PhD, FBCS, CEng
Centre for Forensic Computing
Cranfield University
DCMT, Shrivenham
Swindon SN6 8LA
UK

ISSN 1617-7975
ISBN 978-1-4471-2540-2   e-ISBN 978-1-84882-765-3
DOI 10.1007/978-1-84882-765-3
Springer London Dordrecht Heidelberg New York

British Library Cataloguing in Publication Data
A catalogue record for this book is available from the British Library

Cover design: SPi Publisher Services

Printed on acid-free paper

Springer is part of Springer Science+Business Media (www.springer.com)

Endorsements

"Understanding the science behind the networks of today is the necessary foundation for making significant contributions to the rapid evolution of next generation networks. This timely book comprised of chapters from authoritative experts provides an excellent overview of algorithms that form the basis of next generation communication networks. It covers problems ranging in scope from physical layer issues to the design of next generation applications. I strongly recommend this valuable book as essential reading for students, practitioners and researchers who are actively engaged in creating the emerging next generation communication networks."

Bell Laboratories   *Debasis Mitra*

"A few months ago a colleague at Georgia Tech asked me 'Which are the top-10 most significant algorithms that have been developed by networking research in the last decade?' This book would provide an excellent answer. Covering a wide range of topics from the entire spectrum of networking research, this book is highly recommended for anyone that wants to become familiar with the 'network algorithmics' state-of-the-art of the evolving Internet."

Georgia Institute of Technology   *Constantine Dovrolis*

Foreword

Over the past 20 years, computer networks have become a critical infrastructure in the global economy and have changed people's lives in ways that could not have been predicted in the early days of the Internet. Many technological advances contributed to these changes, including Moore's Law, the emergence of the World Wide Web, and concurrent advances in photonic transmission and disk storage capacity. These advances also relied on an economic climate that allowed innovation to flourish, in Silicon Valley and in other parts of the world. This story has been told many times. One part of the story that is not widely appreciated is the critical role that has been played by advances in algorithms research over this time. Advances in technology occur when engineers have both the theoretical understanding and the practical means to address an important technical problem. In this foreword, I will look briefly at a few of the major advances in algorithms that have fueled the growth of computer networks over the last 20 years. As we look ahead to the next generation of advances in networking, this book provides a survey of key areas in algorithms research that will be important to the researchers and architects working in our field.

The first graphical web browser, Mosaic, made its debut in 1993 – an event that is often associated with the beginning of the growth of the web. In the late 1990s, as the use of the web grew, few consumers had access to the Internet at speeds greater than 1 Megabit/s, and web page download times were slow. By placing web caches in ISP networks close to the end users, content delivery networks (CDNs) emerged to support "web acceleration". This situation led to a flurry of research in Internet mapping and the development of practical algorithms for DNS-based load balancing. Although broadband speeds have increased significantly since that time, CDNs are widely used to efficiently deliver web and multimedia content. Variants of the measurement tools and algorithms developed in the late 1990s are still in use by CDN providers today.

As the Internet grew, one of the challenges that might have limited the growth of the global Internet was scalable IP routing lookups. In the late 1990s, to better manage the utilization of the IPv4 address space the IETF published a new way of allocating IP addresses, called Classless Interdomain Routing (CIDR), along with a new method for routing IP packets based on longest prefix match. The need for longest prefix match routing forced the development of efficient hardware and software algorithms, which were developed during several years of vigorous research and subsequently implemented in routers and other network products. Variants of these algorithms continue to be used today.

The increase in the number of connected Internet users also led to the emergence of peer-to-peer (P2P) file sharing networks. P2P applications such as Napster and Gnutella emerged around 2000, and were used to exchange music and other forms of digital content. The rapid growth of distributed P2P applications inspired the invention of Distributed Hash Tables (DHTs). DHTs provide an efficient and very general distributed lookup service that is a fundamental building block in today's P2P applications such as the popular BitTorrent and in other overlay networks.

The rapid development of new Internet applications caused ISPs and businesses to need new tools to better understand the traffic on their networks. Router vendors developed mechanisms for exporting flow records that could be used for this purpose, but the huge volume of flow data required the invention of statistically robust methods for sampling flow data, such as "smart sampling". More generally, the vast amount of data transferred on the Internet has sparked a generation of research on algorithmic approaches to handling data streams.

The increasing amount of content on the web also led to the need for tools to search the web. While at Stanford University, Larry Page invented the original and now famous PageRank algorithm, which assigns a numerical weight to linked documents in a database based on the frequency of links to each document. The original PageRank algorithm has been enhanced over nearly a decade in an effort to improve web search. The combination of web search with online advertising created a dynamic online marketplace. This has led to a new industry focused on search engine optimization.

A discussion of the advances in computer networks over the past two decades would not be complete without mentioning the emergence of wireless data networks. The viral spread of 802.11-based WiFi networks and the more recent deployment of 3G cellular data services have made mobile access to information possible. Among the most important algorithmic advances, one must certainly list the invention of Multiple-Input-Multiple-Output (MIMO) antenna systems, and related work on Space-Time Coding. Since the first practical implementation of spatial multiplexing in the late 1990s, there has been over a decade of research aimed at improving the performance of wireless communication links that continues to this day.

Finally, optimization problems emerge in many aspects of computer networks. The results of decades of research in optimization are used daily in the design of large-scale networks. While optimization may not be as visible to users of the network as web search or wireless access, it is a critical tool in the network designer's toolkit.

It is likely that the next two decades will bring about continued advances in computer networks that will depend as much on sound algorithmic principles as the advances of the last two decades have. Efficient spectrum management and techniques for limiting interference will be critical to wireless networks. Overlay networks will be designed to operate efficiently in conjunction with the IP layer.

Techniques for packet processing and network monitoring will be developed to support the needs of large ISP networks. Network-based applications such as online gaming and social networks will continue to evolve, alongside new applications that have not yet been invented. Algorithms are at the heart of the networks that we use. This book offers a broad survey of algorithms research by leading researchers in the field. It will be a valuable tool for those seeking to understand these areas of work.

Vice President, Networking and Services Research   *Charles R. Kalmanek*
AT&T Labs
May 2009

Preface

Since the early 1990s coupled with the widespread deployment of broadband to the home, we have seen remarkable progress in the ease of Internet accessibility to end users. Both commercial and private sectors rely heavily on the availability of the Internet to conduct normal day-to-day functions. Underpinning this exponential growth in popularity of the Internet are the advances made in the applications of basic algorithms to design and architect the Internet. The most obvious example of these algorithms is the use of search engines to collect and correlate vast amounts of information that is spread throughout the Internet.

With the dawn of this new century, we are now on the verge of expanding the notion of what we mean to communicate. A new generation of netizens are poised to leverage the Internet for a myriad different applications that we have not envisioned thus far. This will require that the Internet be flexible and adapt to accommodate the requirements of next-generation applications. To address this challenge, in the United States, the National Science Foundation has initiated a large research project GENI. The goal of GENI is to perform a clean-slate design for a new Internet. In particular, the aim of this project is to rethink the basic design assumptions on which the current Internet is built, with the possibility that to improve flexibility for new services we may arrive at a radically different Internet, beyond what one might imagine from evolving the current network. Given this context of Internet research, the purpose of this book is to provide a comprehensive survey of present algorithms and methodologies used in the design and deployment of the Internet. We believe that a thorough understanding of algorithms used by the Internet today is critical to develop new algorithms that will form the basis of the future Internet.

The book is divided into three parts dealing with the application of algorithms to different aspects of network design, operations, and next-generation applications. Part I provides an algorithmic basis for the design of networks both at the physical and the service layer. This part is extensive since it considers different physical layer network technologies. The first chapter in this part outlines the goals for optimization in network design by considering both the optimizability of protocols and the optimum placement of network functionality. The general idea of Valiant load balancing, and its application in the context of efficient network design, is presented in Chapter 2.

Understanding the influence of physical network characteristics in the design of network services is critical to develop robust network services. The algorithms described in this part explicitly model physical and network level constraints while also discussing design tradeoffs made for practical implementation. Algorithms used for optimal capacity provisioning in optical networks and spectrum management in wireless networks are covered in Chapters 3 and 4. In order to maximize network throughput, it is necessary that design algorithms take into account the impact of physical network constraints such as interference on network performance. This awareness of the physical layer in the design of network level optimizations, also called cross-layer algorithms, is presented in Chapter 5. In Chapter 6 the constraint of radio interference is extended to the resource allocation problems of cellular networks. Chapter 7 considers several aspects that are involved in the definition of new network services such as addressing and traffic class definitions with a special emphasis on Ethernet-based services.

Several popular applications such as P2P file sharing applications employ overlay networks. Overlay networks are defined by the end user and constructed over the current Internet. As overlay network services become popular and make increasing demands on the network infrastructure it is becoming necessary to optimize network performance by considering the interactions of the different overlay networks. Overlay networks must also account for the coexistence of underlay services in the basic network infrastructure. Algorithms that are aimed at addressing these challenging issues are discussed in Chapter 8.

The second part of this book covers two important topics of network operations and management. As we know today, network providers have already completed field trials for the 100 Gbps network. It should not be long before these capacities become commonplace on the Internet. The challenge of processing packets at such high speeds imposes a tremendous significance on efficient and fast packet-processing algorithms. Chapter 9 surveys the area of Hash-based techniques for high-speed packet processing, and Chapter 10 goes into the next level of detail by surveying fast packet pattern matching algorithms. These techniques can be naturally extended to other network applications such as security and high-speed network monitoring.

In the face of ever-increasing heterogeneity in applications, services, and technologies, network management has been a difficult challenge for the Internet today. Quite often there is no clear picture of what the normal behavior of networks should be. In this book, we begin the discussion on network management in Chapter 11 with a survey of anomaly detection approaches with a special focus on unsupervised learning algorithms. There are a few instances when the model of the anomalous behavior is available and this is especially true in the case of physical networks. Chapter 12 discusses a model-based anomaly detection approach for the optical transmission system. We also present two different philosophies for network monitoring, the in-network monitoring in Chapter 13, and the end-to-end monitoring in Chapter 14.

Part III of this book discusses algorithmic techniques that form the basis of emerging applications. The part starts with the discussion in Chapter 15 on Network coding and its applications to communication networks. The algorithms that underlie the ubiquitous Internet search applications such as Yahoo and Google are surveyed in Chapter 16. However, as the nature and the modes of usage of this content on the Internet evolves the requirements of these search engine algorithms must also evolve. This chapter provides perspectives on how this evolution is taking place.

Until today the Internet has been used primarily for point-to-point and mostly for non-interactive communications. However, this is quickly changing as evidenced by the growing online gaming industry. Online gaming and the algorithms that implement these games at the client, server, and network are discussed in Chapter 17. Online gaming has opened up the possibility of exploring more real-time communications such as Telepresence on the Internet. It is expected that the next generation of communication services will leverage this interactively to make communications more content-rich. Social networking is one example of next-generation communications. Using online social networks, communities are being built across the world based on user group interests. Algorithms that attempt to describe the building and evolution of these online social networks are discussed in Chapter 18. These social networks also have the potential to evolve into interactive communication groups, therefore understanding their evolution patterns is critical from a network operations and management perspective.

In this book we have attempted to provide a flavor of how algorithms have formed the basis of the Internet as we know it today. It is our hope that this book will provide a useful overview of algorithms applied to communication networks, for any student who aspires to do research in network architecture as well as the application of algorithms to communication networks. We believe that for a robust design of the future Internet, it is essential that the architecture be founded on the basis of sound algorithmic principles.

Bell Labs, Murray Hill, NJ   *Marina Thottan*
AT&T Labs, Florham Park, NJ   *Graham Cormode*
May 2009

Acknowledgements

We first thank the authors who contributed directly to this book by their willingness to contribute a chapter in their areas of expertise. We would like to acknowledge the support of our respective managements at AT&T and Alcatel-Lucent Bell Labs, especially Divesh Srivastava at AT&T and T.V. Lakshman at Bell Labs. This book grew out of a workshop held at the DIMACS center in Rutgers University in 2007. We thank the DIMACS staff and leadership for their help in starting this project. We would like to thank Simon Rees and his team at Springer for their efforts to publish and market this book. Lastly, we thank all those who helped us by reviewing drafts of chapters and providing feedback to the authors to help them revise and improve their contributions. The reviewers include:

Matthew Andrews
Bell Labs

Tanya Berger-Wolf
University of Illinois

Manish Bhardwaj
Cisco Systems

Milind Buddhikot
Bell Labs

Wu-Cheng Feng
Portland State University

Christina Fragouli
EPFL

Ling Huang
Intel

Luigi Laura
Università di Roma

Li Li Bell Labs

Vahab Mirrokni
Google Research

Eugene Ng
Rice University

Rasmus Pagh
ITU Copenhagen

Irina Rozenbaum
Google

Shubho Sen
AT&T Labs

Yuval Shavitt
Tel Aviv University

Bruce Shepherd
McGill University

Mikkel Thorup
AT&T Labs

Shobha Venkataraman
AT&T Labs

Peter Winzer
Bell Labs

Graham Cormode
Marina Thottan

Contents

Part II   Network Operations

Part III   Emerging Applications

List of Contributors

David Amzallag BT

Grenville Armitage Swinburne University of Technology

Thomas Bengtsson Bell Labs

Li-Wei Chen Vanu

Yan Chen Northwestern University

Mung Chiang Princeton University

Chen-Nee Chuah UC Davis

Mads Dam KTH Royal Institute of Technology

Yanlei Diao University of Massachusetts

Debora Donato Yahoo! Research

Constantine Elster Qualcomm Israel

Aristides Gionis Yahoo! Research

Jiayue He Princeton University

Tin Kam Ho Bell Labs

Enrique Hernandez-Valencia Bell Labs

Chuanyi Ji Georgia Institute of Technology

Randy H. Katz UC Berkeley

Ram Keralapura Narus

Adam Kirsch Harvard University

V.S. Anil Kumar Virginia Tech

T.V. Lakshman Bell Labs

David Liben-Nowell Carleton College

Guanglei Liu Roane State Community College

Madhav V. Marathe Virginia Tech

Michael Mitzenmacher Harvard University

Eytan Modiano MIT

Srinivasan Parthasarathy IBM Research

Danny Raz Technion

Jennifer Rexford Princeton University

Todd Salamon Bell Labs

Alex Sprintson Texas A&M University

Rolf Stadler KTH Royal Institute of Technology

Marina Thottan Bell Labs

George Varghese UCSD

Sivarama Venkatesan Bell Labs

Harish Viswanathan Bell Labs

Christopher White Bell Labs

Fang Yu Microsoft Research

Rui Zhang-Shen Princeton University

Yao Zhao Northwestern University

Part I
Network Design

Chapter 1
Design for Optimizability: Traffic Management of a Future Internet

Jiayue He, Jennifer Rexford, and Mung Chiang

Abstract As networks grow in size and complexity, network management has become an increasingly challenging task. Many protocols have tunable parameters, and optimization is the process of setting these parameters to optimize an objective. In recent years, optimization techniques have been widely applied to network management problems, albeit with mixed success. Realizing that optimization problems in network management are induced by assumptions adopted in protocol design, we argue that instead of optimizing existing protocols, protocols should be designed with optimization in mind from the beginning. Using examples from our past research on traffic management, we present principles that guide how changes to existing protocols and architectures can lead to optimizable protocols. We also discuss the trade-offs between making network optimization easier and the overhead these changes impose.

1.1 Introduction

Network management is the continuous process of monitoring a network to detect and diagnose problems, and of configuring protocols and mechanisms to fix problems and optimize performance. Traditionally, network management has been largely impenetrable to the research community since many of the problems appear both complex and ill-defined. In the past few years, the research community has made tremendous progress casting many important network management problems as optimization problems. Network optimization involves satisfying network management objectives by setting the tunable parameters that control network behavior. Solving an optimization problem involves optimizing an *objective function* subject to a set of *constraints*. Unfortunately, while *convex* optimization problems are easier to solve, many problems that arise in data networks are non-convex. Consequently, they are computationally intractable, with many local optima that are suboptimal.

J. He (✉), J. Rexford, and M. Chiang
Princeton University, Princeton
e-mail: {jhe, jrex, chiangm}@princeton.edu

G. Cormode and M. Thottan (eds.), *Algorithms for Next Generation Networks*,
Computer Communications and Networks, DOI 10.1007/978-1-84882-765-3_1,
© Springer-Verlag London Limited 2010

In this paper, we argue that the difficulty of solving the key optimization problems is an indication that we may need to revise the underlying protocols, or even the architectures, that lead to these problem formulations in the first place. We advocate the design of *optimizable networks* – network architectures and protocols that lead to easy-to-solve optimization problems, and consequently, optimal solutions. Indeed, the key difference between "network optimization" and "optimizable networks" is that the former refers to solving a given problem (induced by the existing protocols and architectures) while the latter involves formulating the "right" problem (by changing protocols or architectures accordingly).

The changes to protocols and architectures can range from minor extensions to clean-slate designs. In general, the more freedom we have to make changes, the easier it would be to create an optimizable network. On the other hand, the resulting improvements in network management must be balanced against other considerations such as *scalability* and *extensibility*, and must be made *judiciously*. To make design decisions, it is essential to quantify the trade-off between making network management problems easier by changing the problem statement and the extra overhead the resulting protocol imposes on the network.

Network optimization has had a particularly large impact in the area of traffic management, which controls the flow of traffic through the network. Today, this spans across congestion control, routing, and traffic engineering. We start by introducing the notation used in this paper in Table 1.1. In Section 1.2, we describe how optimization is used in traffic management today. In Section 1.3, we illustrate *design principles* which we have uncovered through our own research experiences on traffic management. Traffic management is an extremely active area of research, but we will not address related work in this paper since these examples are included to serve as illustrations of general principles. In Section 1.4, we discuss other aspects of traffic management, such as interdomain routing and active queue management, where the problems are even more challenging. We also examine the trade-off between performance achieved and overhead imposed when designing optimizable protocols. We conclude and point to future work in Section 1.5.

Table 1.1 Summary of notation for Section 1.2.1

Symbol	Meaning
(i, j)	Pair of routers
$x^{(i,j)}$	Traffic demand between i and j
l	A single link
w_l	Link weight l
c_l	Capacity of link l
y_l	Traffic load on link l
$f(y_l/c_l)$	Penalty function as a function of link utilization
$r_l^{(i,j)}$	Portion of the traffic from router i to router j that traverses the link l

1.2   Traffic Management Today

In this section, we introduce how optimization is used in the context of traffic management inside a single Autonomous System (AS). Traffic management has three players: users, routers, and operators. In today's Internet, users run Transmission Control Protocol (TCP) congestion control to adapt their sending rates at the edge of the network based on packet loss. Congestion control has been reverse engineered to be implicitly solving an optimization problem [1–3]. Inside the network, operators tune parameters in the existing routing protocols to achieve some network-wide objective in a process called traffic engineering, see Figure 1.1.

1.2.1   Traffic Engineering

Inside a single AS, each router is configured with an integer weight on each of its outgoing links, as shown in Figure 1.2. The routers flood the link weights throughout the network and compute shortest paths as the sum of the weights. For example, i directs traffic to k though the links with weights (2,1,5). Each router uses this information to construct a table that drives the forwarding of each IP packet to the

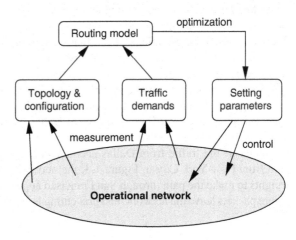

Fig. 1.1 Components of the route optimization framework

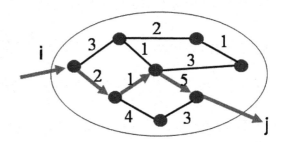

Fig. 1.2 Network topology with link weights for shortest-path routing

next hop in its path to the destination. These protocols view the network inside an AS as a graph where each router is a node $n \in N$ and each directed edge is a link $l \in L$ between two routers. Each unidirectional link has a fixed capacity c_l, as well as a configurable weight w_l. The outcome of the shortest-path computation can be represented as $r_l^{(i,j)}$: the proportion of the traffic from router i to router j that traverses the link l.

Operators set the link weights in intradomain routing protocols in a process called traffic engineering. The selection of the link weights w_l should depend on the offered traffic, as captured by a demand matrix whose entries $x^{(i,j)}$ represent the rate of traffic entering at router i that is destined to router j. The traffic matrix can be computed based on traffic measurements [4] or may represent explicit subscriptions or reservations from users. Given the traffic demand $x^{(i,j)}$ and link weights w_l, the volume of traffic on each link l is $y_l = \sum_{i,j} x^{(i,j)} r_l^{(i,j)}$, the proportion of traffic that traverses link l summed over all ingress–egress pairs. An objective function can quantify the "goodness" of a particular setting of the link weights. For traffic engineering, the optimization considers a network-wide objective of minimizing $\sum_l f(y_l/c_l)$. The traffic engineering penalty function f is a convex, non-decreasing, and twice-differentiable function that gives an increasingly heavy penalty as link load increases, such as an exponential function. The problem traffic engineering solves is to set link weights to minimize $\sum_l f(y_l/c_l)$, *assuming the weights are used for shortest-path routing.*

So far, we have covered the impact of link weights inside an AS. When a network, such as an Internet service provider (ISP) backbone, can reach a destination through multiple egress points, a routing change inside the AS may change how traffic leaves the AS. Each router typically selects the closest egress point out of a set of egress points which can reach a destination, in terms of the intradomain link weights w_l, in a practice known as early-exit or hot-potato routing [5]. In the example in Figure 1.3, suppose a destination is reachable via egress points in New York City and San Francisco. Then traffic from Dallas exits via New York City rather than San Francisco since the intradomain path cost from Dallas to New York City is smaller. If the traffic from Dallas encounters congestion along the downstream path from New York City in Figure 1.3, the network operators could tune the link weights to make the path through San Francisco appear more attractive. Controlling where packets leave the network, and preventing large shifts from one egress point to

Fig. 1.3 Traffic from Dallas exits via New York City (with a path cost of 10) rather than San Francisco (with a path cost of 11), due to hot-potato routing

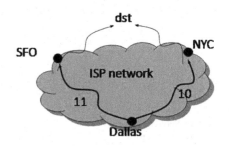

another, is an important part of engineering the flow of traffic in the network. Models can capture the effects of changing the link weights on the intradomain paths and the egress points, but identifying good settings of the weights is very difficult.

1.2.2 Pros and Cons of Traffic Management

Traffic management today has several strengths. First, routing depends on a very *small amount of state per link*, i.e., link weights. In addition, forwarding is done *hop-by-hop*, so that each router decides independently how to forward traffic on its outgoing links. Second, routers only disseminate information when link weights or topology change. Also, TCP congestion control is based only on *implicit feedback* of packet loss and delay, rather than explicit messages from the network. Third, the selection of link weights can depend on a wide variety of performance and reliability constraints. Fourth, hot-potato routing reduces internal resource usage (by using the closest egress point), adapts automatically to changes in link weights, and allows routers in the AS to do hop-by-hop forwarding towards the egress point. Last but not least, the decoupling of congestion control and traffic engineering reduces complexity through separation of concerns.

On the other hand, today's protocols also have a few shortcomings. To start with, optimizing the link weights in shortest-path routing protocols based on the traffic matrix is NP-hard, even for simplest of objective functions [6]. In practice, local-search techniques are used for selecting link weights [6]; however, the computation time is long and, while the solutions are frequently good [6], the deviation from the optimal solution can be large. Finding link weights which work well for egress point selection is even more challenging, as this adds even more constraints on how the weights are set.

There are other limitations to today's traffic management. The network operator can only *indirectly* influence how the routers forward traffic, through the setting of the link weights. Further, traffic engineering is performed assuming that the offered traffic is inelastic. In reality, end hosts adapt their sending rates to network congestion, and network operators adapt the routing based on measurements of the traffic matrix. Although congestion control and routing operate independently, their decisions are coupled. The joint system is stable, but often suboptimal [7]. Furthermore, traffic engineering does not necessarily adapt on a small enough timescale to respond to shifts in user demands. In addition to timescale alternatives, there are also choices as to geographically which part of traffic management work should be carried out inside the network, and which by the sources. These limitations suggest that revisiting architectural decisions is a worthy research direction.

1.3 Design Optimizable Protocols

In this section, we illustrate three design principles through proposed protocols. The three principles also correspond to the three parts of an optimization problem

Fig. 1.4 Convex and non-convex sets. A convex set S is defined as if $x, y \in S$, then $\theta x + (1 - \theta)y \in S$, for all $\theta \in [0, 1]$

Fig. 1.5 Convex and non-convex functions. A function g is a convex function if domain of g is a convex set and $f(\theta x + (1 - \theta)y) \leq \theta g(x) + (1 - \theta)g(y)$

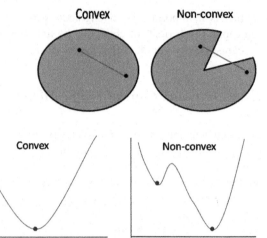

formulation: objective, variable and constraints. In a generic optimization problem formulation, the objective is to minimize $g(x)$ over the variable x, subject to constraints on x:

$$\text{Minimize } g(x)$$
$$\text{Subject to } x \in S \qquad\qquad (1.1)$$
$$\text{Variable } \quad x.$$

From optimization theory, it is well established that a local optimum of (1.1) is also a *global optimum*, which can be found in *polynomial time* and often very fast, if S is a convex set and g is a convex function. The intuition is as follows: searching for an optimum on a non-convex set is challenging as it would be difficult to "cross" any gaps as seen in Figure 1.4. In addition, a convex objective function is necessary for a global optimum to exist as seen in Figure 1.5.

In other words, a convex optimization problem leads to both *tractability* and *optimality*. Due to single-path routing, an artifact of the current system, the constraint set is not convex for most traffic management problems. In our first example, we tackle this problem head-on by changing the shape of the constraint set. In our second example, we avoid the problem because the particular problem formulation falls under a special class of integer programming problems. In our third example, we change the system to allow routing to be per path multicommodity flow, so that decomposition techniques can be applied to derive stable and fast-timescale interaction between routing and congestion control.

1.3.1 Changing the Shape of the Constraint Set

Some optimization problems involve *integer* constraints, which are not convex, making them intractable and their solutions suboptimal. Relaxing the integer constraint to approximate a convex constraint can lead to a more tractable problem and a smaller optimality gap. In the original link-weight setting problem where link weights are set to minimize $\sum_l f(y_l/c_l)$, assuming the weights are used for shortest-path routing, the constraints are non-convex. The network usually has a single shortest path from i to j, resulting in $r_l^{(i,j)} = 1$ for all links l along the path, and $r_l^{(i,j)} = 0$ for the remaining links (Notation for this section is summarized in Table 1.2). An OSPF or IS–IS router typically splits traffic evenly along one or more outgoing links along shortest paths to the destination, allowing for limited fractional values of $r_l^{(i,j)}$, but the constraint set is still highly non-convex. The ability to split traffic arbitrarily over multiple paths would make the constraints convex, i.e., $r_l^{(i,j)} \in [0,1]$. The downside in this approach would sacrifice the simplicity of OSPF and IS–IS, where routers compute paths in a distributed fashion based on link weights alone.

Rather than supporting arbitrary splitting, a recent proposal advocates small extensions to OSPF and IS–IS to split traffic over multiple paths [8]. Under this proposal, the routers forward traffic on multiple paths, with exponentially diminishing proportions of the traffic directed to the longer paths, as shown in Figure 1.6. The goal is still to minimize $\sum_l f(y_l/c_l)$, but allowing any routing protocol based on link weights instead of assuming only shortest-path routing.

Table 1.2 Summary of notation for Section 1.3.1

Symbol	Meaning
(i,j)	Pair of routers
$x^{(i,j)}$	Traffic demand between i and j
l	A link
$r_l^{(i,j)}$	Portion of the traffic from router i to router j that traverses the link l
k	A path between i and j
$w_k^{(i,j)}$	Path weight of path k between i and j
$x_k^{(i,j)}$	Traffic demand between i and j, that will be placed on path k

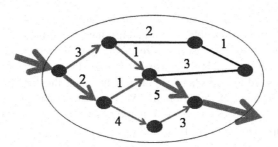

Fig. 1.6 Routers forwarding traffic with exponentially diminishing proportions of the traffic directed to the longer paths. Arrows indicate paths that make forward progress towards the destination, and the thickness of these lines indicates the proportion of the traffic that traverses these edges

More formally, given multiple paths between routers i and j, indexed by k, to keep the protocols simple, the constraint is to have $x_k^{(i,j)}/x^{(i,j)}$, the ratio of traffic placed on path k, be computable using only link weight information. At each router i, the following computation is performed:

$$\frac{x_k^{(i,j)}}{x^{(i,j)}} = \frac{e^{-w_k^{(i,j)}}}{\sum_m e^{-w_m^{(i,j)}}}, \tag{1.2}$$

where $w_k^{(i,j)}$ is the sum of the link weights on the kth path between router i and j. So as in OSPF and IS–IS today, each router would compute all the path weights for getting from i to j, there is just an extra step to compute the splitting ratios. For example, in Figure 1.6, consider the two lower paths of costs 8 (i.e., $2 + 1 + 5$) and 9 (i.e., $2 + 4 + 3$), respectively. The path with cost 8 will get $e^{-8}/(e^{-8} + e^{-9})$ of the traffic, and the path with cost 9 will get $e^{-9}/(e^{-8} + e^{-9})$ of the traffic.

Under this formulation, both link weights and the flow splitting ratios are variables. This enlarges the constraint set, and the resulting constraints are much easier to *approximate* with convex constraints. Consequently, the link-weight tuning problem is tractable, i.e., can be solved much faster than the local search heuristics today. In addition, the modified protocol is optimal, i.e., makes the most efficient use of link capacities, and is more robust to small changes in the path costs. The optimality result is unique to this particular problem where there is an intersection between the set of optimal protocols and protocols based on link weights. In general, the optimality gap is reduced by enlarging the constraint set, as seen in a similar proposed extension to OSPF and IS–IS [9]. By *changing the constraint set*, [8,9] retain the simplicity of link-state routing protocols and hop-by-hop forwarding, while inducing an optimization problem that is both faster to solve and leads to a smaller optimality gap.

1.3.2 Adding Variables to Decouple Constraints

Some optimization problems can involve many tightly-coupled constraints, making it difficult to find a feasible solution. Introducing extra variables can decouple the constraints, and increase the size of the feasible region. As an example, setting the link weights is highly constrained, since the weights are used to compute both the forwarding paths between the routers inside the domain and the egress points where the traffic leaves the domain. Weakening the coupling between intradomain routing and egress-point selection is the key to simplifying the optimization problem and improving network performance.

Rather than selecting egress points j from ingress router i based only on the intradomain path costs $w^{(i,j)}$ (sum of all link weights on the path from i to j), a variable $q_d^{(i,j)}$ is introduced for router i, across all destinations d and egress points j (Notation for this section is summarized in Table 1.3). To support flexible policy

Table 1.3 Summary of notation for Section 1.3.2

Symbol	Meaning
(i,j)	Ingress–egress pair
$w^{(i,j)}$	Path cost between i and j
d	Destination
$q_d^{(i,j)}$	Ranking metric for paths between i and j
$\alpha_d^{(i,j)}$	Tunable parameter to support automatic adaptation to topology changes
$\beta_d^{(i,j)}$	Tunable parameter to support static ranking of egress points j per ingress router i

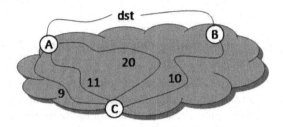

Fig. 1.7 Ingress router c can reach destination through egresses a and b

while adapting automatically to network changes, the metric $q_d^{(i,j)}$ includes both configurable parameters and values computed directly from a real-time view of the topology. In particular, $q_d^{(i,j)} = \alpha_d^{(i,j)} w^{(i,j)} + \beta_d^{(i,j)}$ where α and β are configurable values [10]. The first component of the equation supports automatic adaptation to topology changes, whereas the second represents a static ranking of egress points per ingress router. Providing separate parameters for each destination prefix allows even greater flexibility, such as allowing delay-sensitive traffic to use the closest egress point while preventing unintentional shifts in the egress points for other traffic.

Consider a scenario where α and β are tuned to handle failure scenarios. As seen in Figure 1.7, the ingress router c can reach a destination through egress routers a and b. There are three paths from c to a with paths costs 9, 11, and 20, respectively, the path cost from c to b is 11. The goal is to not switch the traffic from leaving egress router a if the path with cost of 9 fails, but do switch to egress B if the path with cost 11 fails also. This can be expressed as a set of conditions as in the following equation:

$$
\begin{aligned}
9\alpha_d^{c,a} + \beta_d^{c,a} &< 10\alpha_d^{c,b} + \beta_d^{c,b}, \\
11\alpha_d^{c,a} + \beta_d^{c,a} &< 10\alpha_d^{c,b} + \beta_d^{c,b}, \\
20\alpha_d^{c,a} + \beta_d^{c,a} &> 10\alpha_d^{c,b} + \beta_d^{c,b}.
\end{aligned}
\tag{1.3}
$$

One set of α and β values to achieve the conditions in (1.3) is $\alpha_d^{c,a} = 1$, $\beta_d^{c,a} = 1$, $\alpha_d^{c,b} = 1$, and $\beta_d^{c,b} = 0$.

In general, the resulting integer multicommodity flow problem is still non-convex and consequently intractable. This problem formulation happens to correspond to a very special subset of integer programming problems where relaxing the integrality constraints would still produce integer solutions [11], thus side-stepping the convexity issue. That is, the optimization problem becomes solvable in polynomial time if we allow an ingress point i to split traffic destined to d over multiple egress points e, rather than forcing all traffic from i to go to a single egress point; in practice, solving the relaxed problem produces integer solutions that do, in fact, direct all traffic from i to d via a single egress point e. Overall, by *increasing the degrees of freedom*, a management system can set the new parameters under a variety of constraints that reflect the operators' goals for the network [10]. Not only does the network become easier to optimize, but the performance improves as well, due to the extra flexibility in controlling where the traffic flows.

1.3.3   Combining Objectives to Derive Protocols

In a system, there can be multiple interacting optimization problems with different objectives. Combining the objectives of multiple problems can allow for a better solution to the overall problem. In today's traffic management system, congestion control and traffic engineering have different objectives. Congestion control tries to maximize aggregate user utility, and as a result tends to push traffic into the network so that multiple links are used at capacity. In contrast, traffic engineering uses a link cost function which heavily penalizes solutions with bottleneck links.

   User utility $U(x^{(i,j)})$ is a measure of "happiness" of router pair (i, j) as a function of the total sending rate $x^{(i,j)}$ (Notation for this section is summarized in Table 1.4). U is a concave, non-negative, increasing and twice differentiable function, e.g., logarithmic function, that can also represent the elasticity of the traffic or determine fairness of resource allocation. As mentioned earlier, the objective for traffic engineering is a convex function of link load. The objective function has two different practical interpretations. First, f can be selected to model M/M/1 queuing delay and thus the objective is to minimize average queuing delay. Second, network operators want to penalize solutions with many links at or near capacity and do

Table 1.4 Summary of notation for Section 1.3.3

Symbol	Meaning
(i, j)	Pair of routers
$x^{(i,j)}$	Traffic demand between i and j
$U(x^{(i,j)})$	Utility of traffic demand between i and j
l	A single link
c_l	Capacity of link l
$r_l^{i,j}$	Portion of the traffic from router i to router j that traverses the link l
$f(\sum_{i,j} x^{(i,j)} r_l^{(i,j)} / c_l)$	Penalty function as a function of link utilization
v	Weight between utility and penalty functions
k	A path between i and j
$x_k^{(i,j)}$	Traffic demand between i and j, that will be placed on path k
$H_{l,k}^{(i,j)}$	Matrix capturing the available paths between i and j

not care too much whether a link is 20% loaded or 40% loaded [6]. One way to combine the objectives of traffic engineering and congestion control is to construct a weighted sum of utility and link cost functions as the overall objective for traffic management [12], where v is the weight between the two objectives:

$$\text{Maximize } \sum_i U(x^{(i,j)}) - v \sum_l f(\sum_{i,j} x^{(i,j)} r_l^{(i,j)} / c_l)$$
$$\text{Subject to } \sum_{i,j} x^{(i,j)} r_l^{(i,j)} \leq c_l, \; \mathbf{x} \succeq \mathbf{0}. \tag{1.4}$$

In [12], we revisit the division of labor between users, operators, and routers. In this case, we allow for a per path multicommodity flow solution, hence resulting in a convex problem, and opens up many standard optimization techniques that derive distributed and iterative solutions. In its current form, (1.4) has a non-convex constraint set, which can be transformed into a convex set if the routing is allowed to be multipath. To capture multipath routing, we introduce $x_k^{(i,j)}$ to represent the sending rate of router i to router j on the kth path. We also represent available paths by a matrix $\mathbf{H}$ where

$$H_{l,k}^{(i,j)} = \begin{cases} 1, \text{ if path } k \text{ of pair } (i,j) \text{ uses link } l \\ 0, \text{ otherwise.} \end{cases}$$

$\mathbf{H}$ does not necessarily present all possible paths in the physical topology, but a subset of paths chosen by operators or the routing protocol. Using the new notation, the capacity constraint is transformed into $\sum_{i,j,k} x_k^{(i,j)} H_{l,k}^{(i,j)} \leq c_l$, which is convex.

Decomposition is the process of breaking up a single optimization problem into multiple ones that can be solved independently. As seen in Figure 1.8, decomposing the overall traffic management optimization problem, a distributed protocol is derived that splits traffic over multiple paths, where the splitting proportions depend on feedback from the links. The links send feedback to the edge routers in the form of a price s that indicates the local congestion level, based on local link load information. Although there are multiple ways to decompose the optimization problem, they all lead to a similar divisions of functions between the routers and the links [12].

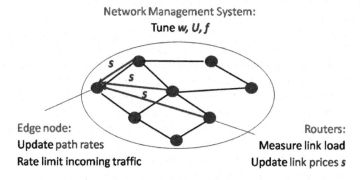

Fig. 1.8 A high-level view of how the distributed traffic-management protocol works

By *embedding the management objectives in the protocols*, the link-cost function is now automated incorporated by the links themselves as part of computing the feedback sent to the edge routers, rather than by the network management system. As seen in Figure 1.8, there are no link weights at all in this distributed protocol. As such, the network management system merely specifies U, f and v, instead of adapting the link weights over time.

1.4 Open Challenges in Traffic Management Optimization

The principles introduced in the previous section are a useful first step towards designing optimizable protocols, but are by no means comprehensive. The merits of proposed optimizable protocols should always be balanced with any extra overhead in practical implementation and robustness to changing network dynamics. In addition, the principles introduced in the previous section focus on intradomain traffic management, and do not address all the challenges in end-to-end traffic management. Finally, when deriving new architectures, the balance between performance and other factors is even more delicate.

1.4.1 Performance vs. Overhead Trade-Off

Characterizing a network architecture in terms of the tractability of network management problems is just one piece of a complex design puzzle. The design of optimizable networks introduces tension between the ease of network optimizability and the overhead on network resources. Some of the architectural decisions today make the resulting protocols simple. For example, protocols which rely on *implicit feedback*, e.g., TCP congestion control, do not have message passing overhead. Further, *hop-by-hop forwarding* does not depend on the upstream path, requiring less processing at the individual routers. It would be desirable to capture such notions of simplicity mathematically, so we can learn to derive optimizable protocols which retain them.

Our example in Section 1.3.1 manages to retain the simplicity of hop-by-hop forwarding while resulting in a tractable optimization problem. In this particular case, optimality gap was significantly reduced with very little extra overhead. However, some approaches make the protocol more optimizable at the expense of additional overhead. For example, adding flexibility in egress-point selection in Section 1.3.2 introduces more parameters that the network management system must set. Similarly, revisiting the division of functionalities in Section 1.3.3 leads to a solution that requires explicit feedback from the links. Imposing extra overhead on the network may be acceptable, if the improvement in performance is sufficiently large.

Furthermore, ensuring a completely tractable optimization problem is sometimes unnecessary. An NP-hard problem may be acceptable, if good heuristics are available. For striking the right trade-offs in the design of optimizable networks, it is important to find effective ways to quantify the acceptable amount of deviation from the optimal solution. There are also well-established, quantitative measures of the notions of how easily solvable an optimization is. These quantitative measures can help determine *how much* the protocols and architectures need to change to better support network management.

The protocols today are designed with certain assumptions in mind, e.g., single-path routing and hop-by-hop forwarding. Some of these assumptions cause the resulting optimization problem to be intractable, e.g., single-path routing, while others do not, e.g., hop-by-hop forwarding. By perturbing the underlying assumptions in today's protocols, we can achieve a different point in the trade-off space of optimality versus simplicity. Therefore, it is worth exploring the alternatives, even if at the end the decision is to keep the original protocol and architectures. In order to choose between protocol designs, the key is to gain a deeper understanding of the trade-offs. As such, we believe that *design for optimizability* can be a promising, new interdisciplinary area between the systems and theory communities.

1.4.2 End-to-End Traffic Management

Our examples thus far focused on optimization problems in intradomain traffic management. Routing within a single domain side-steps several important issues that arise in other aspects of data networking, for several reasons:

- A single domain has the authority to collect measurement data (such as the traffic and performance statistics) and tune the protocol configuration (such as the link weights).
- The routing configuration changes on the timescale of hours or days, allowing ample time to apply more computationally intensive solution techniques.
- The optimization problems consider highly aggregated information, such as link-level performance statistics or offered load between pairs of routers.

When these assumptions do not hold, the resulting optimization problems become even more complicated, as illustrated by the following two examples.

Optimization in interdomain traffic management: In the Internet, there are often multiple Autonomous Systems (AS) in the path between the sender and the receiver. Each AS does not have full view of the topology, only the paths which are made visible to it through the routing-protocol messages exchanged in the Border Gateway Protocol (BGP). In addition, each AS has a set of private policies that reflect its business relationships with other ASes. Without full visibility and control, it is difficult to perform interdomain traffic management. For example, to implement DATE in the Internet, the ASes would need to agree to provide explicit feedback from the links to the end hosts or edge routers, and trust that the feedback is an honest reflection of network conditions. Extending BGPs to allow for multiple paths would simplify the underlying optimization problem, but identifying the right incentives for ASes to deploy a multipath extension to BGP remains an open question.

Optimization in active queue management: A router may apply active queue management schemes like Random Early Detection [13] to provide TCP senders with early feedback about impending congestion. RED has many configurable parameters to be selected by network operators, e.g., queue-length thresholds and maximum drop probability. Unfortunately, predictive models for how the tunable parameters affect RED's behavior remain elusive. In addition, the appropriate parameter values may depend on a number of factors, including the number of active data transfers and the distribution of round-trip times, which are difficult to measure on high-speed links. Recent analytic work demonstrates that setting RED parameters to stabilize TCP is fundamentally difficult [14]. It is appealing to explore alternative active-queue management schemes that are easier to optimize, including self-tuning algorithms that do not require the network management system to adjust any parameters.

From these two examples, it is clear that there remain open challenges in end-to-end traffic management. Outside the context of traffic management, network optimization's role is even less understood. We argue for a principled approach in tackling these challenges so that, in time, protocol design can be less of an art and more of a science.

1.4.3 Placement of Functionality

The challenges are not just limited to protocols, but extend to architectural decisions regarding the placement of functionality. Architecturally, the DATE example represents one extreme where most of computation and coordination is moved into the distributed protocols that run in the routers. In the context of Figure 1.1, this means much of the measurement, control, and optimization is pushed down into the network. One can consider another extreme, where the network management systems bear all the responsibility for adapting to changes in network conditions, as in [15]. Both approaches redefine the division of labor between the management system and the routers, where one moves most of the control into the distributed protocols and the other has the management systems directly specify how the routers handle packets.

In some cases, having the management system bear more responsibility would be a natural choice. For example, where an optimization problem is fundamentally difficult, consequently leading to distributed solutions that are complicated or suboptimal, or both. Unlike the routers, a management system has the luxury of a global view of network conditions and the ability to run centralized algorithms for computing the protocol parameters. Today's traffic engineering uses the centralized approach and allows operators to tailor the objectives to the administrative goals of the network. This leads to a more evolvable system, where the objective function and constraints can differ from one network to another, and change over time.

In addition, the operators can capitalize on new advances in techniques for solving the optimization problems, providing an immediate outlet for promising research results.

The network management system can apply centralized algorithms based on a global view of network conditions, at the expense of a slower response based on coarse-grain measurements. Yet some parts of traffic management, such as detecting link failures and traffic shifts, must occur in real time. In order to understand which functions must reside in the routers to enable adaptation on a sufficiently small time-scale, it is important to quantify the loss in performance due to slower adaptation. For functions which require fast adaptation, an architecture where end user loads balance across multiple paths would be desirable. For functions that can operate on a slower timescale, the control of flow distribution can be left to operators. In general, determining the appropriate division of labor between the network elements and the management systems is an avenue for future research.

1.5 Conclusions and Future Work

In recent years, optimization has played an increasingly important role in network management. In this paper, we argue that, instead of just trying to optimize existing protocols, new protocols should be designed *for* the ease of optimization. If a set of architectures and protocols lead to intractable optimization problems for network management, we argue that, instead of trying to solve these problems by ad hoc heuristics, we should revisit some of the underlying assumptions in the architectures and protocols. Such explorations can lead to easier network optimization problems and may provide superior simplicity–optimality tradeoff curves.

Drawing from our own research experiences in traffic management, we propose three guiding principles for making optimizable protocols which correspond to three aspects of an optimization problem, i.e., constraints, variables, and objective. First, changing the constraint set can turn an NP-hard optimization problem into an easier problem and reduce the optimality gap. Second, increasing degrees of freedom (by introducing extra parameters) can break tightly coupled constraints. Finally, embedding management objectives in the protocol can lead to alternative architectures. Still, protocol changes must be made judiciously to balance the gain in performance with the extra consumption of network resources.

Ultimately, the design of manageable networks raises important architectural questions about the appropriate division of functionalities between network elements and the systems that manage them. This paper represents a first step towards identifying design principles that can guide these architectural decisions. The open challenges which remain suggest that the design of manageable networks may continue to be somewhat of an art, but hopefully one that will be guided more and more by design principles. We believe that providing a new, comprehensive foundation for the design of manageable networks is an exciting avenue for future research.

Acknowledgement We would like to thank Constantine Dovrolis, Nick Feamster, Renata Teixeira, and Dahai Xu for their feedback on earlier drafts. This work has been supported in part by NSF grants CNS-0519880 and CCF-0448012, and DARPA Seedling W911NF-07-1-0057.

References

1. F. P. Kelly, A. Maulloo, and D. Tan, "Rate control for communication networks: Shadow prices, proportional fairness and stability," *J. of Operational Research Society*, vol. 49, pp. 237–252, March 1998.
2. S. H. Low, "A duality model of TCP and queue management algorithms," *IEEE/ACM Trans. Networking*, vol. 11, pp. 525–536, August 2003.
3. R. Srikant, *The Mathematics of Internet Congestion Control*. Birkhauser, 2004.
4. M. Grossglauser and J. Rexford, "Passive traffic measurement for IP operations," in *The Internet as a Large-Scale Complex System*, pp. 91–120, Oxford University Press, 2005.
5. R. Teixeira, A. Shaikh, T. Griffin, and J. Rexford, "Dynamics of hot-potato routing in IP networks," in *Proc. ACM SIGMETRICS*, June 2004.
6. B. Fortz and M. Thorup, "Increasing Internet capacity using local search," *Computational Optimization and Applications*, vol. 29, no. 1, pp. 13–48, 2004.
7. J. He, M. Bresler, M. Chiang, and J. Rexford, "Towards multi-layer traffic engineering: Optimization of congestion control and routing," *IEEE J. on Selected Areas in Communications*, June 2007.
8. D. Xu, M. Chiang, and J. Rexford, "Link-state routing with hop-by-hop forwarding can achieve optimal traffic engineering," in *Proc. IEEE INFOCOM*, May 2008.
9. D. Xu, M. Chiang, and J. Rexford, "DEFT: Distributed exponentially-weighted flow splitting," in *Proc. IEEE INFOCOM*, May 2007.
10. R. Teixeira, T. Griffin, M. Resende, and J. Rexford, "TIE breaking: Tunable interdomain egress selection," *IEEE/ACM Trans. Networking*, August 2007.
11. A. Ozdaglar and D. P. Bertsekas, "Optimal solution of integer multicommodity flow problems with application in optical networks," *Frontiers in Global Optimization*, vol. 74, pp. 411–435, 2004.
12. J. He, M. Bresler, M. Chiang, and J. Rexford, "Rethinking Internet traffic management: From multiple decompositions to a practical protocol," in *Proc. CoNEXT*, December 2007.
13. S. Floyd and V. Jacobson, "Random early detection gateways for congestion avoidance," *IEEE/ACM Trans. Networking*, vol. 1, pp. 397–413, August 1993.
14. S. H. Low, F. Paganini, J. Wang, and J. C. Doyle, "Linear stability of TCP/RED and a scalable control," *Computer Networks*, vol. 43, pp. 633–647, December 2003.
15. A. Greenberg, G. Hjalmtysson, D. A. Maltz, A. Meyers, J. Rexford, G. Xie, H. Yan, J. Zhan, and H. Zhang, "A clean slate 4D approach to network control and management," *ACM SIGCOMM Computer Communication Review*, October 2005.

Chapter 2
Valiant Load-Balancing: Building Networks That Can Support All Traffic Matrices

Rui Zhang-Shen

Abstract This paper is a brief survey on how Valiant load-balancing (VLB) can be used to build networks that can efficiently and reliably support all traffic matrices. We discuss how to extend VLB to networks with heterogeneous capacities, how to protect against failures in a VLB network, and how to interconnect two VLB networks. For the readers' reference, included also is a list of work that uses VLB in various aspects of networking.

2.1 Introduction

In many networks the traffic matrix is either hard to measure and predict, or highly variable over time. In these cases, using Valiant load-balancing (VLB) to support all possible traffic matrices is an attractive option. For example, even though the traffic in the Internet backbone is extremely smooth due to high level of aggregation, it is still hard to measure. Accurately measuring the traffic matrix (e.g., using NetFlow) is too expensive to do all the time, and standard methods using link measurements give errors of 20% or more. Even if the current traffic matrix is satisfactorily obtained, extrapolating it to the future is fraught with uncertainty, due to the unpredictable nature of Internet traffic growth. Finally, since Internet traffic is dynamic, the traffic matrix can deviate from its normal values at any time, possibly causing congestion.

The traffic demand seen by a network can be represented by the *traffic matrix*, which indicates the rates at which each node initiates traffic to every other node. We say a network can *support* a traffic matrix if for every link in the network, the load caused by the traffic matrix is less than the capacity of the link. When a network cannot support the traffic matrix presented to it, at least one link in the network has a load higher than its capacity. Congestion occurs and backlog in the buffer builds up on the congested link(s), causing packet drops, increased delay, and high variations

R. Zhang-Shen (✉)
Google, Inc., New York, NY 10011
e-mail: ruizhangshen@gmail.com

G. Cormode and M. Thottan (eds.), *Algorithms for Next Generation Networks*, Computer Communications and Networks, DOI 10.1007/978-1-84882-765-3_2, © Springer-Verlag London Limited 2010

in delay. Ideally, we would like to design a network that can support a wide range of traffic matrices, so that congestion occurs only rarely or not at all.

In this paper, we discuss the use of VLB in building networks that can efficiently support *all* traffic matrices which do not over-subscribe any node. We first briefly survey the wide use of VLB in various aspects of networking, and describe the basic scenario of using VLB in a network. Section 2.2 extends VLB from a homogeneous setting to networks with arbitrary capacities, Section 2.3 describes how to protect against and recover quickly from failures in a VLB network, and Section 2.4 proposes to use VLB to route traffic between two networks. Finally Section 2.5 discusses possible future work.

2.1.1 The Wide Use of VLB

In the early 1980s, Valiant [19] first proposed the scheme of routing through a randomly picked intermediate node en route to a packet's destination. He showed that in an N-node binary cube network, given any permutation traffic matrix, the distributed two-phase randomized routing can route every packet to its destination within $O(\log N)$ time with overwhelming probability. This was the first scheme for routing arbitrary permutation in a sparse network in $O(\log N)$ time. Since then, such randomized routing has been used widely, and is often referred to as (VLB), *randomized load-balancing*, or *two-phase routing*. VLB has many good characteristics. It is decentralized, where every node makes local decisions. This also makes the scheme scalable. VLB is agnostic to the traffic matrix because the randomness erases the traffic pattern, and different traffic matrices can result in the same load on the links.

Soon after its invention, was used in other interconnection networks for parallel communication, to improve delivery time [1], and to relieve effects of adverse traffic patterns [13]. In recent years, it was adapted for routing in torus networks [17, 18] in order to provide worst-case performance guarantees without sacrificing average-case performance. The key is to use VLB adaptively, based on the observation that under low load, load-balancing only a small amount of traffic is sufficient to avoid congestion.

VLB is also used in building network switches with great scalability and performance guarantee, without the need of a centralized scheduler. It was used in ATM switches [7], routers [4, 5], optical routers [3, 9], and software routers [2]. In particular, the scheme was rediscovered for designing router switch fabrics [4] to mitigate routers' scaling challenges, because it was difficult for centralized schemes to keep up with the increasing link speed. In this context, it was shown that splitting traffic in a round-robin fashion has the same effect on link load as random splitting [4], and that is the most efficient in terms of the total required interconnection capacity for supporting all traffic matrices [8].

Almost simultaneously, several groups independently applied the idea of VLB to traffic engineering and network design for the Internet, in order to efficiently support all possible traffic matrices. Kodialam et al.'s two-phase routing [11, 12] is a traffic engineering method, where a full mesh of tunnels are set up over fixed capacity links and packets are sent in two phases (i.e., two hops) in the network. Winzer et al.'s selective randomized load-balancing [14, 16, 21] used VLB and its variants to design cost-effective optical networks. Their model assumes that a link's cost includes both the fiber and the terminating equipment, so there is incentive for having fewer links. In the optimal design, traffic is load-balanced only to a few intermediate nodes. Zhang-Shen and McKewon [23, 25] proposed using VLB over a logical full mesh in a backbone network to support all traffic matrices and to quickly recover from failures. In addition, VLB was used as an optical routing strategy in Ethernet LAN [20], for scheduling in metro area WDM rings [10], for circuit-switched networks [22], and for scaling and commoditizing data center networks [6].

A study on the queueing properties of a VLB network [15] found that VLB eliminates congestion in the network, and pseudo-random (e.g., round-robin) load-balancing reduces queueing delay. VLB was also shown to eliminate congestion on peering links when used to route traffic between networks [26].

2.1.2 A Simple VLB Network

Consider a network of N nodes, each with capacity r, i.e., a node can initiate traffic at the maximum rate of r, and can receive traffic at the same maximum rate. We assume that the network traffic satisfies such node aggregate constraint, because otherwise there is no way to avoid congestion. A logical link of capacity $\frac{2r}{N}$ is established between every pair of nodes over the physical links, as shown in Figure 2.1. We use the convention that a *flow* in the network is defined by the source node and the destination node, unless further specified. Every flow entering the network is equally split across N two-hop paths between ingress and egress nodes, i.e., a packet is forwarded twice in the network: In the first hop, an ingress node uniformly distributes each of its incoming flows to all the N nodes, regardless of

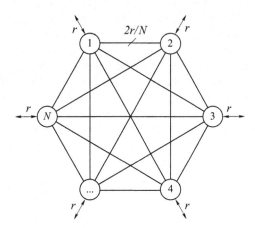

Fig. 2.1 VLB in a network of N identical nodes each having capacity r. A full mesh of logical links of capacity $2r/N$ connect the nodes

the destinations. In the second hop, all packets are sent to the final destinations by
the intermediate nodes. Load-balancing can be done packet-by-packet, or flow-by-
flow at the application flow level. The splitting of traffic can be random (e.g., to a
randomly picked intermediate node) or deterministic (e.g., round-robin).

Assume we can achieve perfect load-balancing, i.e., can split traffic at the exact proportions we desire, then each node receives exactly $\frac{1}{N}$ of *every* flow after
first-hop routing. This means, all the N nodes equally share the burden of forwarding traffic as the intermediate node. When the intermediate node happens to
be the ingress or egress node, the flow actually traverses one hop (the direct link
between ingress and egress) in the network. Hence, $\frac{2}{N}$ of every flow traverses the
corresponding one-hop path.

Such uniform load-balancing can guarantee to support all traffic matrices in this
network. Since the incoming traffic rate to each node is at most r, and the traffic is
evenly load-balanced to N nodes, the actual traffic on each link due to the first-hop
routing is at most $\frac{r}{N}$. The second-hop routing is the dual of the first-hop routing.
Since each node can receive traffic at a maximum rate of r and receives $\frac{1}{N}$ of the
traffic from every node, the actual traffic on each link due to the second-hop routing
is also at most $\frac{r}{N}$. Therefore, a full-mesh network where each link has capacity $\frac{2r}{N}$
is sufficient to support all traffic matrices in a network of N nodes of capacity r.

This is perhaps a surprising result – a network where any two nodes are connected
with a link of capacity $\frac{2r}{N}$ can support traffic matrices where a node can send traffic
to another node at rate r. It shows the power of load-balancing. In VLB, each flow
is carried by N paths, and each link carries a fraction of many flows; therefore any
large flow is averaged out by other small flows. In a static full-mesh network, if all
the traffic were to be sent through direct paths, we would need a full-mesh network
of link capacity r to support all possible traffic matrices; therefore load-balancing is
$\frac{N}{2}$ times more efficient than direct routing.

2.2 VLB in Heterogeneous Networks

Real-life networks are often heterogeneous, i.e., the nodes in a network can have
different capacities. In this section we discuss how to extend the result of uniform
load-balancing to heterogeneous networks [24].

We first introduce notations. In a network of N nodes, the traffic matrix $\Lambda =
\{\lambda_{ij}\}$ is an $N \times N$ matrix, where the entry λ_{ij} indicates the datarate at which Node
i initiates traffic destined to Node j. The traffic rate is typically averaged over a
long period of time so we consider it as constant. Typically in a network there are
buffers to absorb short-lived traffic fluctuations. Suppose Node i has capacity r_i,
i.e., the node can initiate traffic at the maximum rate of r_i, and can receive traffic at
the same maximum rate. So in order for the traffic matrix to not over-subscribe any
node, it must satisfy

$$\sum_j \lambda_{ij} \le r_i, \forall i \quad \text{and} \quad \sum_j \lambda_{ji} \le r_i, \forall i. \tag{2.1}$$

Without loss of generality, assume that the nodes have been sorted according to decreasing capacities, i.e., $r_1 \geq r_2 \geq \cdots \geq r_N$, so Node 1 is the largest node and Node N the smallest. Let R be the total node capacity, i.e., $R = \sum_{i=1}^{N} r_i$. We assume $r_1 \leq \sum_{i=2}^{N} r_i$ because even if $r_1 > \sum_{i=2}^{N} r_i$, Node 1 cannot send or receive traffic at a rate higher than $\sum_{i=2}^{N} r_i$, because that would over-subscribe some nodes.

Suppose that a full mesh of logical links are set up to connect these N nodes. Let c_{ij} represent the required link capacity from Node i to Node j and C the link capacity matrix $\{c_{ij}\}$. Having $c_{ij} = 0$ means that link (i, j) is not needed. The simple homogeneous network presented in Section 2.1.2 has that $c_{ij} = \frac{2r}{N}, \forall i \neq j$, and $r_i = r, \forall i$.

In a network with identical nodes, it is natural to load-balance uniformly. But uniform load-balancing seems too restrictive in a heterogeneous network because it does not take into account the difference in node capacities. A natural solution is to load-balance proportionally to the capacity of the intermediate node, i.e., Node i receives fraction $\frac{r_i}{R}$ of every flow. This is a direct generalization from uniform multicommodity flow in the homogeneous case to product multicommodity flow [16]. The required link capacity is $c_{ij} = 2r_i r_j / R$ [24].

We can further generalize VLB to allow *any* flow splitting ratio and let some external objective to determine the optimal ratios. We introduce a set of *load-balancing parameters* p_i such that $p_i \geq 0$, for all i, and $\sum_{i=1}^{N} p_i = 1$. An ingress node splits each flow according to $\{p_i\}$ and sends p_i of every flow to Node i. This gives us the freedom of, for example, letting the larger nodes forward more traffic than the smaller nodes, or not using some of the nodes as intermediates (by setting the corresponding p_i to zero). If there are some objectives to be optimized, there are N parameters ($p_i, i = 1, 2, \ldots, N$) that can be tuned, but if more freedom is needed, we can, for example, let each flow have its own set of load-balancing parameters.

We now find the required link capacity. The first-hop traffic on link (i, j) is the traffic initiated by Node i that is load-balanced to Node j, and the rate is at most $r_i p_j$. The second-hop traffic on the link is the traffic destined to Node j that is load-balanced to Node i, and the rate is at most $r_j p_i$. Therefore the maximum amount of traffic on link (i, j) is $r_i p_j + r_j p_i$, which is also the required capacity on link (i, j)

$$c_{ij} = r_i p_j + r_j p_i. \tag{2.2}$$

The required (outgoing) interconnection capacity of Node i is

$$l_i = \sum_{j:j \neq i} c_{ij} = r_i + Rp_i - 2r_i p_i,$$

and the total required interconnection capacity of the network is

$$L = \sum_{i=1}^{N} l_i = \sum_{i,j:i \neq j} c_{ij} = 2 \left(R - \sum_i r_i p_i \right). \tag{2.3}$$

Thus if we want to minimize the total required interconnection capacity of the network, we need to maximize $\sum_i r_i p_i$, subject to the constraints on p_i. The optimal solution has the form that $p_i > 0$ only if $r_i = \max_j r_j$, i.e., traffic is only load-balanced to the largest node(s). Thus we have

$$\min L = 2(R - \max_i r_i). \tag{2.4}$$

We can show that Equation (2.4) is also the minimum total interconnection capacity required by *any network* to support all traffic matrices [24], and hence is the necessary and sufficient condition. One network that minimizes the total required interconnection capacity is a "star" with Node 1 at the center, i.e., $p_1 = 1$, $p_i = 0$ for $i \geq 2$. In the case where all nodes have the same capacity, to achieve minimum L, p_i can take any non-negative values as long as they sum up to 1. Thus the uniform load-balancing presented in Section 2.1.2 is optimal in terms of total required interconnection capacity. Splitting flows proportional to node capacities, i.e., $p_i = r_i / R$, is not optimal when nodes have different capacities.

In order to use the minimum amount of interconnection capacity, only nodes with the largest capacity can act as intermediate nodes. This can be limiting, especially if only one node has the largest capacity, because a star network is not good for fault tolerance. A star network is efficient but not balanced, because the center node acts as the intermediate node for all traffic. We need a scheme that is not only efficient but also balanced, and we found one by minimizing the *network fanout*.

The *fanout* of node i is $f_i = \frac{l_i}{r_i}$, the ratio of node i's interconnection capacity to its node capacity. Since the interconnection capacity is used both for sending traffic originated from the node and for forwarding traffic for other nodes, the fanout measures the amount of responsibility the node has to forward other nodes' traffic relative to its size. If the fanouts of the two nodes are the same, then the larger node forwards more traffic, which is a desired property. Thus, to have a balanced network, we minimize the maximum fanout over all nodes, which results in all nodes having equal fanout. The resulting load-balancing parameters and fanout are

$$p_i = \frac{\frac{r_i}{R-2r_i}}{\sum_k \frac{r_k}{R-2r_k}}, \quad i = 1, 2, \ldots, N,$$

$$f_i = 1 + \frac{1}{\sum_{j=1}^{N} \frac{r_j}{R-2r_j}}, \quad \forall i.$$

The optimal load-balancing parameters are almost proportional to the node capacities: $p_i \propto \frac{r_i}{R-2r_i}$. The parameter p_i is a strictly increasing function of r_i. Therefore a larger node has greater responsibility for forwarding traffic. We can further show that the total interconnection capacity used in this scheme is no more than $\frac{1}{2}(\sqrt{2} + 1) = 1.207$ times the minimum total capacity [24]. Thus, the scheme of minimizing maximum fanout is not only balanced, but also efficient.

One can of course choose to optimize other criteria that are more suitable for the particular situation. Kodialam et al. [11] assume that the underlying physical links have fixed capacities, constraining the logical link capacities. They give efficient algorithms for calculating or approximating the optimal load-balancing ratios which allow the network to support the most traffic. Shepherd and Winzer [16] use a realistic cost model that takes into account both the fiber cost and the equipment cost. They opt to load-balance to only a subset of the nodes so that a full mesh is not needed.

2.3   Fault-Tolerance in a VLB Network

Most networks need to accommodate planned and unplanned interruptions. As we show in this section, VLB networks, due to their rich connectivity and path diversity, have many advantages in terms of tolerating failures, such as

- All of the working paths between a pair of nodes are used all the time, and flows are load-balanced across all working paths. Most other schemes require protection paths that are idle during normal operation.
- All paths are used all the time, so there is no need to set up new paths upon failure.
- In order to protect against k failures,[1] the fraction of extra capacity required is approximately $\frac{k}{N}$. This is extremely efficient compared to other fault tolerance schemes.
- VLB naturally protects against multiple failures. One can decide during design what failure scenarios the network should tolerate, such as k arbitrary link or node failures or a particular set of failure patterns.

When there are no failures, each flow is load-balanced over all the N paths according to some ratio. The same mechanism can be used when there are failures and some flows have fewer than N working paths. We assume that a node keeps track of the *available* paths for each flow originating from it, and load-balances each flow over the available paths, according to the same ratios. The network is self-healing because the paths are known prior to failures and traffic can be rerouted as soon as failure is detected.

We derive how much link capacity is needed so as to support all traffic matrices under k_n arbitrary node failures[2] and k_l arbitrary link failures. For simplicity, we assume the *simple* network model where all nodes have the same capacity r. Due to the symmetry of the topology, all links in the fault-tolerant network have the same capacity requirement, represented by $C(N, k_n, k_l)$. We first consider node failures and link failures separately and then combine them. By definition, $C(N, 0, 0) = \frac{2r}{N}$.

Node failures are relatively easy to analyze. When a node fails, it takes down all the links connecting to it and stops sending or receiving traffic. The network becomes an $(N-1)$-node full-mesh network, and a link capacity of $\frac{2r}{N-1}$ is sufficient

---

[1] We focus on failures in the logical topology, and since several logical links can share a physical link, a physical failure can correspond to multiple logical failures.

[2] If a node fails, we discard the traffic originating from or terminating at this node.

for supporting all traffic matrices. In general, when there are k node failures, the network becomes an $(N-k)$-node full mesh, so the link capacity required to tolerate k node failures is

$$C(N,k,0) = C(N-k,0,0) = \frac{2r}{N-k}. \tag{2.5}$$

Link failures are a little more complicated, as they can destroy the symmetry of the topology, so that it is no longer a full mesh. We only consider the worst-case failure scenarios (adversarial link failures) here. We omit the details and only give the final result. The amount of capacity required on each link to tolerate k arbitrary link failures, for $1 \le k \le N - 2$, is

$$C(N,0,k) = \begin{cases} \frac{r}{N-2} + \frac{r}{N} & k = 1 \\ \frac{r}{N-k-1} + \frac{r}{N-1} & k = 2 \text{ or } N-2, \text{ or } N \le 6 \\ \frac{2r}{N-k} & \text{otherwise.} \end{cases} \tag{2.6}$$

For $k \ge N - 1$, the network becomes disconnected in the worst-case failure scenario, therefore we cannot guarantee a congestion-free network. The significance of Equation (2.6) is that all entries on the right-hand side are very close to $\frac{2r}{N-k}$. Figure 2.2 plots Equation (2.6) for $N = 50$, and as we can see, the curve is very flat for small values of k.

Now assume that there are k_n node failures and k_l link failures. This is equivalent to having k_l link failures in a $(N - k_n)$-node network. So

$$C(N,k_n,k_l) \approx \frac{2r}{N-k_n-k_l} = \frac{2r}{N-k}, \tag{2.7}$$

where $k = k_n + k_l$. This means that the curve for Equation (2.7) is roughly the same as that for Equation (2.6), shown in Figure 2.2. So we conclude that in a VLB network, a small amount of over-provisioning goes a long way to make the network

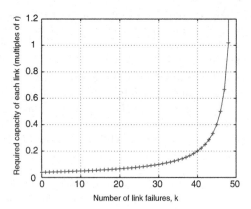

Fig. 2.2 The required link capacity vs. the number of link failures in a 50-node network

fault tolerant. For example, if the links in a 50-node network are over-provisioned by just about 11%, the network can tolerate any five (node or link) failures.

2.4 VLB for Peering Traffic

Today, most congestion in Internet backbone takes place on the peering links connecting them. When a link between two networks is congested, very likely some other peering links between these two networks are lightly loaded. That is, the peering links between two networks are usually not evenly utilized. We propose to use a technique similar to VLB to route peering traffic, so as to eliminate congestion on the peering links. We show that if traffic is load-balanced over all the peering links between two networks, there will be no congestion as long as the total peering capacity is greater than the total peering traffic. Even though the two networks using VLB to route their peering traffic do not need to use VLB internally, we assume they do and analyze how the peering scheme affects how the networks run VLB.

Suppose two VLB networks are connected by a subset of their nodes (the peering nodes), as shown in Figure 2.3. For the ease of description, we use the same numbering for the peering nodes in both networks. (Note that this convention is different from Section 2.2.) The traffic exchanged between the two networks is called *peering traffic* and assume the total amount is no more than R_p in each direction.

In the network of N nodes, we introduce the *peering load-balancing parameters* $q_i, i = 1, 2, \ldots, N$, such that a portion q_i of the peering traffic between the two networks is exchanged at node i. Naturally, $q_i = 0$ if i is not a peering node.

The peering load-balancing parameters, q_i, together with the maximum peering traffic between the two networks, R_p, determine the sizes of the peering links: the required capacity of the peering link at node i is $R_p q_i$. Suppose the peering links have the required capacities, then if the peering traffic is load-balanced across the peering links according to the proportions q_i, and the total amount of peering traffic between the two networks does not exceed R_p, there will be no congestion on the peering links.

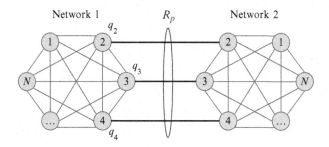

Fig. 2.3 Two VLB networks connect at a set of peering nodes. The total amount of traffic exchanged between the two networks is no more than R_p, and a portion q_i of the peering traffic is exchanged at node i.

The extra requirement of routing peering traffic may result in higher capacity requirements inside the networks. If we treat the peering traffic that originates from the network as traffic destined to the peering nodes, and the peering traffic that enters the network as traffic originated from the peering nodes, then the peering traffic may have to traverse two hops in each network.

Alternatively, we can load-balance peering traffic over the peering points only, instead of all the nodes. Thus, we require that peering traffic traverses at most one hop in each network, and at most two hops altogether.

Suppose the peering load-balancing parameters are fixed, for example, through negotiation between the two networks. Then we can vary p_i, i.e., how non-peering traffic is routed internally, to minimize the required link capacities. We observe that R_p is likely to be bigger than the node capacities r_i. R_p is the total amount of traffic the two network exchanges and can be a large portion of the network's total traffic R, while the node capacities are likely to make up only a small fraction of R, on the order of $\frac{R}{N}$.

If we assume that $R_p \geq r_i$ for all i, then we have

$$c_{ij} = r_i \max(p_j, q_j) + r_j \max(p_i, q_i),$$

and the minimum c_{ij} is achieved for all links when $p_i = q_i$ for all i. So the optimal capacity allocation in a network with peering traffic is

$$c_{ij} = r_i q_j + r_j q_i. \tag{2.8}$$

Since q_i is zero if node i is a non-peering node, $c_{ij} = 0$ if both Node i and Node j are non-peering nodes. The network is now a two-tiered one: in the center is a full mesh connecting the peering nodes, and on the edge are the non-peering nodes, each connected to all the center nodes.

Setting local load-balancing parameters to be the same as peering load-balancing parameters means that only the peering nodes will serve as intermediate nodes to forward traffic. Peering nodes are often the largest nodes in the network, so they should have larger responsibilities in forwarding traffic. The analysis shows that the optimal way is to *only* let the peering nodes forward traffic. This has the additional benefits of requiring fewer links and reducing network complexity.

2.5 Discussions

Using VLB to route traffic in a network has many advantages, such as efficiency and fast failure recovery. There are some open questions as well. Some examples are

- Sending packets through two hops may increase the propagation delay, while sending packets through the direct link may cause increased capacity requirement. There should be a tradeoff between packet delay and required capacity.

- Different paths that a flow traverses may have different delays, and hence packets in the flow may not arrive at the destination in the original order. This is usually not a problem in the Internet, since a flow may consist of many application-level flows, and can be split accordingly for load-balancing. But it can be a problem if a flow cannot be easily split.
- It is unclear whether VLB can be incrementally deployed in a network.

Despite the challenges, VLB is rapidly gaining popularity in networking research. This survey paper can be a starting point for those interested in applying VLB to other situations.

References

1. R. Aleliunas. Randomized parallel communication (preliminary version). In *PODC '82: Proceedings of the first ACM SIGACT-SIGOPS symposium on Principles of distributed computing*, pages 60–72, 1982.
2. K. Argyraki, S. Baset, B.-G. Chun, K. Fall, G. Iannaccone, A. Knies, E. Kohler, M. Manesh, S. Nedevschi, and S. Ratnasamy. Can software routers scale? In *PRESTO '08: Proceedings of the ACM workshop on Programmable routers for extensible services of tomorrow*, pages 21–26, 2008.
3. P. Bernasconi, J. Gripp, D. Neilson, J. Simsarian, D. Stiliadis, A. Varma, and M. Zirngibl. Architecture of an integrated router interconnected spectrally (IRIS). *High Performance Switching and Routing, 2006 Workshop on*, pages 8 pp.–, June 2006.
4. C.-S. Chang, D.-S. Lee, and Y.-S. Jou. Load balanced Birkhoff-von Neumann switches, Part I: One-stage buffering. *Computer Communications*, 25(6):611–622, 2002.
5. C.-S. Chang, D.-S. Lee, and C.-M. Lien. Load balanced Birkhoff-von Neumann switches, Part II: Multi-stage buffering. *Computer Communications*, 25(6):623–634, 2002.
6. A. Greenberg, P. Lahiri, D. A. Maltz, P. Patel, and S. Sengupta. Towards a next generation data center architecture: scalability and commoditization. In *PRESTO '08: Proceedings of the ACM workshop on Programmable routers for extensible services of tomorrow*, pages 57–62, 2008.
7. M. Henrion, K. Schrodi, D. Boettle, M. De Somer, and M. Dieudonne. Switching network architecture for ATM based broadband communications. *Switching Symposium, 1990. XIII International*, 5:1–8, 1990.
8. I. Keslassy, C.-S. Chang, N. McKeown, and D.-S. Lee. Optimal load-balancing. In *Proc. IEEE INFOCOM*, 2005.
9. I. Keslassy, S.-T. Chuang, K. Yu, D. Miller, M. Horowitz, O. Solgaard, and N. McKeown. Scaling Internet routers using optics. *Proceedings of ACM SIGCOMM '03, Computer Communication Review*, 33(4):189–200, October 2003.
10. I. Keslassy, M. Kodialam, T. Lakshman, and D. Stiliadis. Scheduling schemes for delay graphs with applications to optical packet networks. *High Performance Switching and Routing (HPSR)*, pages 99–103, 2004.
11. M. Kodialam, T. V. Lakshman, J. B. Orlin, and S. Sengupta. A Versatile Scheme for Routing Highly Variable Traffic in Service Overlays and IP Backbones. In *Proc. IEEE INFOCOM*, April 2006.
12. M. Kodialam, T. V. Lakshman, and S. Sengupta. Efficient and robust routing of highly variable traffic. In *HotNets III*, November 2004.
13. D. Mitra and R. A. Cieslak. Randomized parallel communications on an extension of the omega network. *J. ACM*, 34(4):802–824, 1987.
14. H. Nagesh, V. Poosala, V. Kumar, P. Winzer, and M. Zirngibl. Load-balanced architecture for dynamic traffic. In *Optical Fiber Communication Conference*, March 2005.

15. R. Prasad, P. Winzer, S. Borst, and M. Thottan. Queuing delays in randomized load balanced networks. In *Proc. IEEE INFOCOM*, May 2007.
16. F. B. Shepherd and P. J. Winzer. Selective randomized load balancing and mesh networks with changing demands. *Journal of Optical Networking*, 5:320–339, 2006.
17. A. Singh. *Load-Balanced Routing in Interconnection Networks*. PhD thesis, Department of Electrical Engineering, Stanford University, 2005.
18. A. Singh, W. J. Dally, B. Towles, and A. K. Gupta. Locality-preserving randomized oblivious routing on torus networks. In *SPAA '02: Proceedings of the fourteenth annual ACM symposium on parallel algorithms and architectures*, pages 9–13, 2002.
19. L. G. Valiant. A scheme for fast parallel communication. *SIAM Journal on Computing*, 11(2):350–361, 1982.
20. R. van Haalen, R. Malhotra, and A. de Heer. Optimized routing for providing Ethernet LAN services. *Communications Magazine, IEEE*, 43(11):158–164, Nov. 2005.
21. P. J. Winzer, F. B. Shepherd, P. Oswald, and M. Zirngibl. Robust network design and selective randomized load balancing. *31st European Conference on Optical Communication (ECOC)*, 1:23–24, September 2005.
22. R. Zhang-Shen, M. Kodialam, and T. V. Lakshman. Achieving bounded blocking in circuit-switched networks. *IEEE INFOCOM 2006*, pages 1–9, April 2006.
23. R. Zhang-Shen and N. McKeown. Designing a Predictable Internet Backbone Network. In *HotNets III*, November 2004.
24. R. Zhang-Shen and N. McKeown. Designing a predictable Internet backbone with Valiant Load-Balancing. *Thirteenth International Workshop on Quality of Service (IWQoS)*, 2005.
25. R. Zhang-Shen and N. McKeown. Designing a Fault-Tolerant Network Using Valiant Load-Balancing. *Proc. IEEE INFOCOM*, pages 2360–2368, April 2008.
26. R. Zhang-Shen and N. McKeown. Guaranteeing Quality of Service to Peering Traffic. *Proc. IEEE INFOCOM*, pages 1472–1480, April 2008.

Chapter 3
Geometric Capacity Provisioning for Wavelength-Switched WDM Networks

Li-Wei Chen and Eytan Modiano

Abstract In this chapter, we use an asymptotic analysis similar to the sphere-packing argument in the proof of Shannon's channel capacity theorem to derive optimal provisioning requirements for networks with both static and dynamic provisioning. We consider an N-user shared-link model where W_s wavelengths are statically assigned to each user, and a common pool of W_d wavelengths are available to all users. We derive the minimum values of W_s and W_d required to achieve asymptotically non-blocking performance as the number of users N becomes large. We also show that it is always optimal to statically provision at least enough wavelengths to support the mean of the traffic.

3.1 Introduction

Optical networking has established itself as the backbone of high-speed communication systems, incorporating both high bandwidth and low noise and interference characteristics into a single medium. Within optical networks, wavelength division multiplexing (WDM) technology has emerged as an attractive solution for exploiting the available fiber bandwidth to meet increasing traffic demands. WDM divides the usable bandwidth into non-overlapping frequency bands (usually referred to as *wavelengths* in the literature) and allows the same fiber to carry many signals independently by assigning each signal to a different wavelength.

L.-W. Chen
Vanu Inc., One Cambridge Center, Cambridge, MA 02142
e-mail: lwchen@alum.mit.edu

E. Modiano (✉)
Massachusetts Institute of Technology, 77 Massachusetts Ave, Cambridge, MA 02139
e-mail: modiano@mit.edu

Portions reprinted, with permission, from "A Geometric Approach to Capacity Provisioning in WDM Networks with Dynamic Traffic", *40th Annual Conference on Information Sciences and Systems*. ©2006 IEEE.

G. Cormode and M. Thottan (eds.), *Algorithms for Next Generation Networks*,
Computer Communications and Networks, DOI 10.1007/978-1-84882-765-3_3,
© Springer-Verlag London Limited 2010

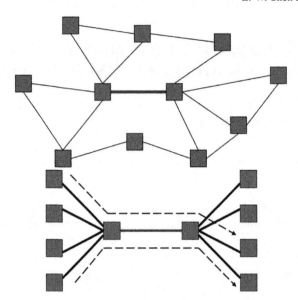

Fig. 3.1 An example of a mesh optical network consisting of numerous nodes and links, followed by a shared-link model based on the link. The dotted lines denote different users of the link. Since each pair of input–output fibers comprises a different user, and there are four input fibers and four output fibers, there are a total of $4 \cdot 4 = 16$ users in this example

In general, an optical WDM network can consist of a large number of nodes connected in some arbitrary fashion (see Figure 3.1) and can present the network architect with a complex wavelength provisioning problem over multiple links. For simplicity, in this chapter, we will focus on provisioning a single shared link on a backbone network. Figure 3.1 also shows a model for the shared link in the arbitrary network. We consider provisioning for traffic traveling from left to right along the link. Each wavelength on the link can be used to support one lightpath from one of the incoming fibers on the left side of the link to one of the outgoing fibers on the right side of the link.

Broadly speaking, wavelength provisioning can be done in one of two ways. One option is to *statically* provision a wavelength by hard-wiring the nodes at the ends of the link to always route the wavelength from a given input fiber to a given output fiber. The advantage to this is that the cost of the hardware required to support static provisioning is relatively low: no switching capability or intelligent decision-making ability is required. The downside is a lack of flexibility in using that wavelength – even if the wavelength is not needed to support a lightpath between the assigned input and output fibers, it cannot be assigned to support a lightpath between any other pair of fibers.

This shortcoming can be overcome by using *dynamic* provisioning. A dynamically provisioned wavelength is switched at the nodes on both sides of the link, allowing it to be dynamically assigned to support a lightpath between any source and destination fibers. Furthermore, this assignment can change over time as traffic demands change. This obviously imparts a great deal of additional flexibility. The downside is that the added switching and processing hardware makes it more expensive to dynamically provision wavelengths.

There has been much investigation of both statically provisioned and dynamically provisioned systems in the literature [1–4]. Such approaches are well suited for cases where either the traffic is known a priori and can be statically provisioned, or is extremely unpredictable and needs to be dynamically provisioned. However, in practice, due to statistical multiplexing, it is common to see traffic demands characterized by a large mean and a small variance around that mean. A hybrid system is well suited to such a scenario. In a hybrid system, a sufficient number of wavelengths are statically provisioned to support the majority of the traffic. Then, on top of this, a smaller number of wavelengths are dynamically provisioned to support the inevitable variation in the realized traffic. Such an approach takes advantage of the relative predicability of the traffic by cheaply provisioning the majority of the wavelengths, but retains sufficient flexibility through the minority of dynamic wavelengths that significant wavelength overprovisioning is not necessary.

After describing the system model used in this chapter, we will use the asymptotic analysis approach from information theory incorporated in the proof of Shannon's channel capacity theorem [5] to analyze hybrid networks: we allow the number of users to become large, and consider the minimum provisioning in static and dynamic wavelengths necessary to achieve non-blocking performance (i.e., to guarantee that the probability of any call in the snapshot being blocked goes to zero). We will show that it is always optimal to statically provision enough wavelengths to support the traffic mean. We also fully characterize the optimal provisioning strategy for achieving non-blocking performance with minimal wavelength provisioning.

3.1.1 System Model

In the shared link context, we can consider each incoming–outgoing pair of fibers to be a different *user* of the link. Each lightpath request (which we will henceforth term a *call*) can therefore be thought of as belonging to the user corresponding to the incoming–outgoing fiber pair that it uses. We can similarly associate each static wavelength with the corresponding user. Under these definitions, a call belonging to a given user cannot use a static wavelength belonging to a different user – it must either use a static wavelength belonging to its own user, or employ a dynamic wavelength.

Figure 3.2 gives a pictorial representation of the decision process for admitting a call. When a user requests a new call setup, the link checks to see if a static wavelength for that user is free. If there is a free static wavelength, it is used. If not, then the link checks to see if any of the shared dynamic wavelengths are free – if so, then a dynamic wavelength is used. If not, then no resources are available to support the call, and it is blocked.

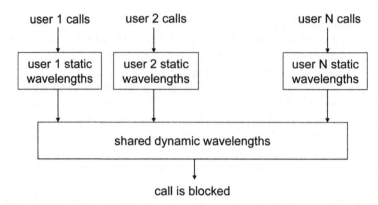

Fig. 3.2 Decision process for wavelength assignment for a new call arrival. A new call first tries to use a static wavelength if it is available. If not, it tries to use a dynamic wavelength. If again none are available, then it is blocked

There have been several approaches developed in the literature for blocking probability analysis of such systems under Poisson traffic models [6], including the Equivalent Random Traffic (ERT) model [7–9] and the Hayward approximation [10]. These approaches, while often able to produce good numerical approximations of blocking probability, are purely numerical in nature and do not provide good intuition for guiding the dimensioning of the wavelengths.

In this chapter, we adopt a snapshot traffic model that leads to closed-form asymptotic analysis and develop guidelines for efficient dimensioning of hybrid networks. We consider examining a "snapshot" of the traffic demand at some instant in time. The snapshot is composed of the vector $\mathbf{c} = [c_1, \ldots, c_N]$, where c_i is the number of calls that user i has at the instant of the snapshot, and N is the total number of users.

We model each variable c_i as a Gaussian random variable with mean μ_i and variance σ_i^2. This is reasonable since each "user" actually consists of a collection of source–destination pairs in the larger network that all use the link from the same source fiber to the same destination fiber. Initially we will assume that each user has the same mean μ and variance σ^2 and later extend the results to general μ_i and σ_i. Although the traffic for each individual source–destination pair for the user may have some arbitrary distribution, as long as the distributions are well behaved, the sum of each traffic stream will appear Gaussian by the Central Limit Theorem.

As a special case, consider the common model of Poisson arrivals and exponential holding times for calls. Then the number of calls that would have entered a non-blocking system at any instant in time is given by the stationary distribution of an $M/M/\infty$ queue – namely, Poisson with intensity equal to the load ρ in Erlangs. For a heavy load, this distribution is well approximated by a Gaussian random variable with mean ρ and variance ρ.

3.2   Wavelength-Granularity Switching

In this section, we consider a shared link, and assume that there are N users that are the source of calls on the link. Each user is statically provisioned W_s wavelengths for use *exclusively* by that user. In addition to this static provisioning, we will also provide a total of W_d dynamically switched wavelengths. These wavelengths can be shared by any of the N users.

As previously described, we will use a snapshot model of traffic. The traffic is given by a vector $\mathbf{c} = [c_1, \ldots, c_N]$, where each c_i is independent and identically distributed as $N(\mu, \sigma^2)$. We assume that the mean μ is sufficiently large relative to σ that the probability of "negative traffic" (where the realized value of a random variable representing the number of calls is negative, a physical impossibility) is low, and therefore does not present a significant modeling concern. We will primarily be concerned with a special blocking event that we call *overflow*. An overflow event occurs when there are insufficient resources to support all calls in the snapshot and at least one call is blocked. We will call the probability of this event the *overflow probability*.

From Figure 3.2, we see that an overflow event occurs if the total number of calls exceeds the ability of the static and dynamic wavelengths to support them. This can be expressed mathematically as

$$\sum_{i=1}^{N} \max\{c_i - W_s, 0\} > W_d, \tag{3.1}$$

where $\max\{c_i - W_s, 0\}$ is the amount of traffic from each user that exceeds the static provisioning; if the total amount of excess from each user exceeds the available pool of shared dynamic wavelengths, a blocking event occurs.

If we consider the N-dimensional vector space occupied by $\mathbf{c}$, the constraint given by (3.1) represents a collection of hyperplanes bounding the admissible traffic region:

$$c_i \leq W_s + W_d$$
$$c_i + c_j \leq 2W_s + W_d, \quad i \neq j,$$
$$c_i + c_j + c_k \leq 3W_s + W_d, \quad i \neq j \neq k$$
$$\vdots$$

Each constraint reflects the fact that the sum of the traffic from any subset of users clearly cannot exceed the sum of the static provisioning for those users plus the entire dynamic provisioning available. Note that there are a total of N sets of constraints, where the nth set consists of $C(N, n) = \frac{N!}{(N-i)!n!}$ equations, each involving the sum of n elements of the traffic vector $\mathbf{c}$. If the traffic snapshot $\mathbf{c}$ falls within the region defined by the hyperplanes, all calls are admissible; otherwise, an overflow event occurs. The bold lines in Figure 3.3 show the admissible region for $N = 2$ in two dimensions.

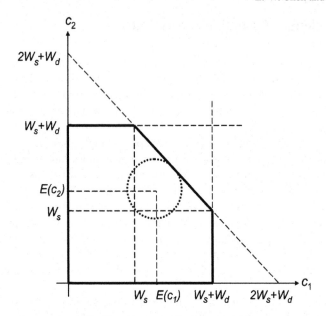

Fig. 3.3 The admissible traffic region, in two dimensions, for $N = 2$. Three lines form the boundary constraints represented by (3.1). There are two lines each associated with a single element of the call vector $\mathbf{c}$, and one line associated with both elements of $\mathbf{c}$. The traffic sphere must be entirely contained within this admissible region for the link to be asymptotically non-blocking

3.2.1 Asymptotic Analysis

We will consider the case where the number of users N becomes large, and use the law of large numbers to help us draw some conclusions. We can rewrite the call vector in the form

$$\mathbf{c} = \mu \cdot \mathbf{1} + \mathbf{c}',$$

where μ is the (scalar) value of the mean, $\mathbf{1}$ is the length-N all-ones vector, and $\mathbf{c}' \sim \mathbf{N}(\mathbf{0}, \sigma^2 \mathbf{1})$ is a zero-mean Gaussian random vector with i.i.d. components. Conceptually, we can visualize the random traffic vector as a random vector $\mathbf{c}'$ centered at $\mu \mathbf{1}$. The length of this random vector is given by

$$\|\mathbf{c}'\| = \sqrt{\sum_{i=1}^{N} c_i'^2}.$$

We use an approach very similar to the sphere packing argument used in the proof of Shannon's channel capacity theorem in information theory [5]. We will show that asymptotically as the number of users becomes large, the traffic vector falls onto a sphere centered at the mean, and the provisioning becomes a problem of choosing the appropriate number of static and dynamic wavelengths so that this traffic sphere is completely contained within the admissible region.

From the law of large numbers, we know that

$$\frac{1}{N} \sum_{i=1}^{N} c_i'^2 \to \sigma^2$$

as $N \to \infty$. This implies that asymptotically, as the number of users becomes large, the call vector $\mathbf{c}$ becomes concentrated on a sphere of radius $\sqrt{N}\sigma$ centered at the mean $\mu\mathbf{1}$. (This phenomenon is known in the literature as *sphere hardening*.) Therefore, in order for the overflow probability to converge to zero, a necessary and sufficient condition is that the hyperplanes described by (3.1) enclose the sphere entirely. This is illustrated in Figure 3.3.

3.2.2   Minimum Distance Constraints

Next, we will derive necessary and sufficient conditions for the admissible traffic region to enclose the traffic sphere. Our goal is to ensure that we provision W_s and W_d such that the minimum distance from the center of the traffic sphere to the boundary of the admissible region is at least the radius of the sphere, therefore ensuring that all the traffic will fall within the admissible region.

Due to the identical distribution of the traffic for each user, the mean point $\mu\mathbf{1}$ will be equidistant from all planes whose description involves the same number of elements of $\mathbf{c}$. We define a *distance function* $f(n)$ such that $f(n)$ is the minimum distance from the mean $\mu\mathbf{1}$ to any hyperplane whose description involves n components of $\mathbf{c}$.

Lemma 3.1. *The distance function $f(n)$ from the traffic mean to a hyperplane involving n elements of the traffic vector $\mathbf{c}$ is given by*

$$f(n) = \sqrt{n} \left(W_s + \frac{W_d}{n} - \mu \right), \quad n = 1, \ldots, N \tag{3.2}$$

Proof. This is essentially a basic geometric exercise. For a fixed n, the hyperplane has a normal vector consisting of n unity entries and $N - n$ zero entries. Since by symmetry the mean of the traffic is equidistant from all hyperplanes with the same number of active constraints, without loss of generality, assume the first n constraints that are active. Then the closest point on the hyperplane has the form

$$[\mu + x, \ldots, \mu + x, \mu, \ldots, \mu]$$

where the first n entries are $\mu + x$, and the remainder are μ. The collection of hyperplanar constraints described by (3.1) can then be rewritten in the form

$$\sum_{i=1}^{n} c_i \leq nW_s + W_d \qquad (3.3)$$

The value of x for which $\mathbf{c}$ lies on the hyperplane is obtained when the constraint in (3.3) becomes tight, which requires that

$$\sum_{i=1}^{n} (\mu + x) = nW_s + W_d$$
$$\Rightarrow nx = nW_s + W_d - n\mu$$
$$x = W_s + \frac{W_d}{n} - \mu$$

The distance from the point $[\mu, \ldots, \mu]$ to this point on the hyperplane is

$$\| [\mu + x, \ldots, \mu + x, \mu, \ldots, \mu] - [\mu, \ldots, \mu] \|$$
$$= \sqrt{nx^2}$$
$$= \sqrt{n}\, x$$

where, after substituting for x, we obtain

$$f(n) = \sqrt{n}\left(W_s + \frac{W_d}{n} - \mu\right)$$

which proves the theorem.   □

We define the *minimum boundary distance* to be

$$F_{\min} = \min_{n=1,\ldots,N} f(n)$$

A necessary and sufficient condition for the overflow probability to go to zero asymptotically with the number of users is

$$F_{\min} \geq \sqrt{N}\sigma$$

We would like to determine the index n such that $f(n)$ is minimized. Unfortunately, this value of n turns out to depend on the choice of provisioning W_s. Let us consider the derivative of the distance function $f'(n)$:

$$f'(n) = \frac{1}{2\sqrt{n}}\left(W_s + \frac{W_d}{n} - \mu\right) + \sqrt{n}\left(-\frac{W_d}{n^2}\right)$$
$$= \frac{1}{2\sqrt{n}}\left(W_s - \frac{W_d}{n} - \mu\right)$$

We can divide W_s into three regimes of interest, corresponding to different ranges of values for W_s and W_d, and characterize $f(n)$ in each of these regions:

Regime 1: If $W_s \leq \mu$

In this region, $f'(n) < 0$ for all n. This implies that $f(n)$ is a decreasing function of n, and $F_{min} = f(N)$, giving a minimum distance of

$$F_{min} = \sqrt{N} \left(W_s + \frac{W_d}{N} - \mu \right)$$

Regime 2: If $\mu < W_s \leq \mu + W_d$

In this region, $f'(n)$ starts out negative and ends up positive over $1 \leq n \leq N$. This implies that $f(n)$ is convex and has a minimum. Neglecting integrality concerns, this minimum occurs when $f'(n) = 0$, or

$$n^* = \frac{W_d}{W_s - \mu}$$

Therefore $F_{min} = f(n^*)$ in this regime. Substituting the appropriate values, it can be shown that the minimum distance is given by

$$F_{min} = 2\sqrt{W_d(W_s - \mu)}$$

Regime 3: If $W_s > \mu + W_d$

In this region, $f'(n) > 0$ for all n. This implies that $f(n)$ is an increasing function of n, and $F_{min} = f(1)$, giving a minimum distance of

$$F_{min} = W_s + W_d - \mu$$

3.2.3 Optimal Provisioning

In the preceding section, we derived the minimum distance criteria for the hybrid system. Given a fixed number of statically allocated wavelengths W_s, we can use the equation $F_{min} \geq \sqrt{N}\sigma$ to calculate the minimum number of dynamic wavelengths W_d to achieve asymptotically non-overflow performance. We can also draw a few additional conclusions about provisioning hybrid systems.

Theorem 3.1. *A minimum of μ static wavelengths should always be provisioned per user.*

Proof. For $W_s \leq \mu$, we know from Case 1 above that the minimum distance constraint is

$$F_{min} = \sqrt{N} \left(W_s + \frac{W_d}{N} - \mu \right) \geq \sqrt{N} \sigma$$

$$W_s + \frac{W_d}{N} \geq \mu + \sigma$$

$$\Rightarrow W_{tot} = N W_s + W_d \geq (\mu + \sigma) N$$

Note that the total number of wavelengths $W_{tot} = N W_s + W_d$ is independent of W_s and W_d in this regime, suggesting that the same total number of wavelengths is required regardless of the partitioning between static and dynamic wavelengths. Since static wavelengths are less expensive to provision than dynamic wavelengths, this shows that there is never any reason to provision less than $W_s = \mu$ wavelengths.   □

An interesting corollary to this theorem follows from the observation that the case where $W_s = 0$ (i.e., all wavelengths are dynamic) also falls in this regime (i.e., Regime 1). Since fully dynamic provisioning is obviously the least-constrained version of this system, we can use it as a bound on the minimum number of wavelengths required by *any* asymptotically overflow-free system.

Corollary: For non-overflow operation, a lower bound on the number of wavelengths is given by

$$W_{tot} \geq (\mu + \sigma) N \tag{3.4}$$

We can also consider a system that is fully static, with no dynamic provisioning. This is the most inflexible wavelength partitioning, and provides us with an upper bound on the number of wavelengths required by any hybrid system.

Theorem 3.2. *For a fully static system with no dynamic provisioning, the minimum number of wavelengths required is given by*

$$W_{tot} = (\mu + \sigma) N + \left(\sqrt{N} - 1 \right) N \sigma$$

Proof. Let $W_d = 0$. Then, for overflow-free operation, we obviously need $W_s > \mu$. This puts us in Regime 3 where $W_s > \mu + W_d$, and the minimum distance condition gives us

$$F_{min} = W_s + W_d - \mu \geq \sqrt{N} \sigma$$

$$W_s \geq \mu + \sqrt{N} \sigma$$

$$= \mu + \sigma + \left(\sqrt{N} - 1 \right) \sigma$$

$$W_{tot} = N W_s = (\mu + \sigma) N + \left(\sqrt{N} - 1 \right) N \sigma$$

□

Note that this exceeds the lower bound on the minimum number of wavelengths by $(\sqrt{N} - 1)N\sigma$. We can therefore regard this quantity as the *maximum switching gain* that we can achieve in the hybrid system. This gain is measured in the maximum number of wavelengths that could be saved if all wavelengths were dynamically switched.

Combining the upper and lower bounds, we can make the following observation:

Corollary: For efficient overflow-free operation, the total number of wavelengths required by any hybrid system is bounded by

$$(\mu + \sigma)N \le W_{tot} \le (\mu + \sigma)N + (\sqrt{N} - 1)N\sigma$$

3.2.4 Numerical Example

We examine the following numerical example to illustrate the application of the provisioning results described. Consider a system with some number of users N. Under the snapshot model each user generates traffic that is Gaussian with mean $\mu = 100$ and standard deviation $\sigma = 10$. We would like to provision the system to be asymptotically non-blocking as N becomes large. This is equivalent to provisioning the system so that the probability of an overflow event goes to zero.

From Theorem 3.1 we know that a minimum of $W_s = \mu$ static wavelengths should always be provisioned. From (3.4), we have

$$W_{tot} = N W_s + W_d \ge (\mu + \sigma)N$$
$$\Rightarrow W_d = N\mu + N\sigma - N W_s$$
$$= N\sigma$$

Figure 3.4 shows the overflow probability as N increases for a system provisioned with W_s and W_d wavelengths according to the equations given above as obtained through simulation. The rapidly descending curve shows that if the theoretical minimum of $W_{tot} = (\mu + \sigma)N$ wavelengths is provisioned with $W_s = \mu$, then as N increases, the overflow probability drops off quickly and eventually the system becomes asymptotically non-blocking. The second curve shows overflow probability when the pool of dynamic wavelengths has been reduced to bring W_{tot} down by 5%. We see that in this case, the overflow probability remains flat and no longer decreases as a function of the number of users.

Next suppose that we would like to provision additional static wavelengths to reduce the number of dynamic wavelengths required. Consider a provisioning scheme where $W_s = 1.1\mu$. For reasonably large N, this puts us in the region where $\mu < W_s \le \mu + W_d$. In this regime,

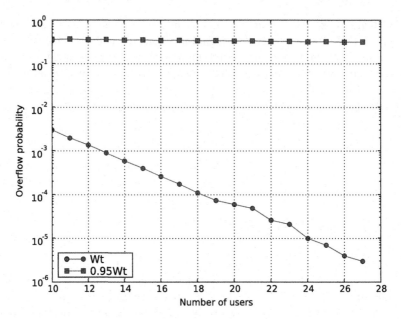

Fig. 3.4 Curves show decrease in overflow probability with increasing number of users N. Note that if significantly fewer than W_{tot} wavelengths are provisioned, the overflow probability no longer converges to zero as the number of users increases

$$F_{\min} = 2\sqrt{W_d(W_s - \mu)} \geq \sqrt{N}\sigma$$
$$4W_d(W_s - \mu) \geq N\sigma^2$$
$$W_d \geq \frac{N\sigma^2}{4(W_s - \mu)}$$
$$= \frac{N\sigma^2}{0.4\mu}$$

The first curve in Figure 3.5 shows the decrease in the overflow probability both when W_s and W_d are provisioned according to these equations. In the second curve, both the static and dynamic pools have been reduced in equal proportions such that the total number of wavelengths has decreased by 5%. We again see that the overflow probability no longer decreases as N increases.

Finally, Table 3.1 illustrates the tradeoff between provisioning more wavelengths statically versus the total number of wavelengths required in this example. We see that in the minimally statically provisioned case, the total number of wavelengths is small, at the cost of a large number of dynamic wavelengths. By overprovisioning the mean statically, as in the second case, the number of dynamic wavelengths can be significantly reduced, at the cost of increasing the total number of wavelengths. The optimal tradeoff in a specific case will depend on the relative cost of static versus dynamic wavelengths.

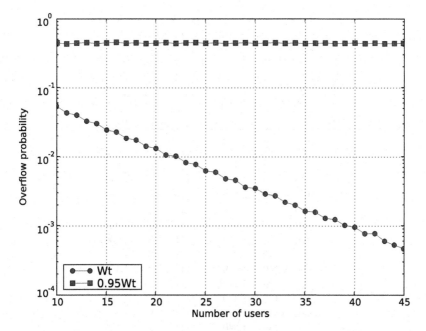

Fig. 3.5 Curves show decrease in overflow probability with increasing number of users N. Again note that if fewer than W_{tot} wavelengths are provisioned, the overflow probability no longer converges to zero as the number of users increases

3.2.5 Non-IID Traffic

The majority of this chapter has dealt with the case of independent identically distributed user traffic: we have assumed that $\mu_i = \mu$ and $\sigma_i^2 = \sigma^2$ for all users i. In many scenarios this will not be the case. Depending on the applications being served and usage profiles, users could have traffic demands that differ significantly from each other. In this section, we discuss how to deal with non-IID traffic scenarios.

We now consider each user i to be characterized by traffic c_i, where $c_i \sim N(\mu_i, \sigma_i^2)$. It now makes sense to allow for a different number of static wavelengths $W_s^{(i)}$ to be provisioned per user. As before, an overflow occurs if

$$\sum_{i=1}^{N} \max \left\{ c_i - W_s^{(i)} , 0 \right\} > W_d \qquad (3.5)$$

We next define a set of new random variables $\hat{c}_i$, where

$$\hat{c}_i = \frac{c_i - \mu_i}{\sigma_i}$$

Table 3.1 Wavelength requirements for two provisioning scenarios. In the first scenario, only the mean is statically provisioned, resulting in fewer overall wavelengths but more dynamic wavelengths. In the second scenario, fewer dynamic wavelengths and more static wavelengths are provisioned, at a higher cost in total wavelengths

Users	Min. static provisioning			Static overprovisioning		
	W_s	W_d	W_{tot}	W_s	W_d	W_{tot}
1	100	10	110	111	2	113
2	100	20	220	111	4	226
3	100	30	330	111	6	339
4	100	40	440	111	9	453
5	100	50	550	111	11	566
6	100	60	660	111	13	679
7	100	70	770	111	15	792
8	100	80	880	111	18	906
9	100	90	990	111	20	1,019
10	100	100	1,100	111	22	1,132
11	100	110	1,210	111	25	1,246
12	100	120	1,320	111	27	1,359
13	100	130	1,430	111	29	1,472
14	100	140	1,540	111	31	1,585
15	100	150	1,650	111	34	1,699
16	100	160	1,760	111	36	1,812
17	100	170	1,870	111	38	1,925
18	100	180	1,980	111	40	2,038
19	100	190	2,090	111	43	2,152
20	100	200	2,200	111	45	2,265
21	100	210	2,310	111	47	2,378
22	100	220	2,420	111	50	2,492
23	100	230	2,530	111	52	2,605
24	100	240	2,640	111	54	2,718
25	100	250	2,750	111	56	2,831

Note that each $\hat{c}_i$ is now an IID standard Gaussian random variable with mean 0 and variance 1. We can rewrite (3.5) in the form

$$\sum_{i=1}^{N} \max \left\{ \sigma_i \hat{c}_i + \mu_i - W_s^{(i)} , 0 \right\} > W_d$$

Again consider the nth set of boundary constraints, and suppose that the first n elements of **c** are active. Then we require

$$\sum_{i=1}^{n} \sigma_i \hat{c}_i + \mu_i - W_s^{(i)} \leq W_d$$

Rearranging terms, we obtain

$$\sum_{i=1}^{n} \sigma_i \hat{c}_i \le W_d + \sum_{i=1}^{n} \left(W_s^{(i)} - \mu_i \right) \tag{3.6}$$

Note that the equations in (3.6) again describe sets of hyperplanes that form the admissible region for the traffic vector $\hat{\mathbf{c}} = [\hat{c}_1, \ldots, \hat{c}_N]$. As the number of users becomes large, the traffic vector will concentrate itself on a sphere of radius $\sqrt{N}$ centered at the origin. Therefore, a necessary and sufficient condition for the system to be asymptotically non-blocking is simply for the minimum distance from the origin to each of the hyperplanes to be at least $\sqrt{N}$.

3.3 Conclusion

In this chapter, we examined wavelength provisioning for a shared link in a backbone network. We considered networks with both static and dynamically provisioned wavelengths. Using a geometric argument, we obtained asymptotic results for the optimal wavelength provisioning on the shared link. We proved that the number of static wavelengths should be sufficient to support at least the traffic mean. We derived in closed form expressions for the optimal provisioning of the shared link given the mean μ and variance σ^2 of the traffic. We show how to extend these results for users with asymmetric statistics.

Acknowledgement This work was supported in part by NSF grants ANI-0073730, ANI-0335217, and CNS-0626781.

References

1. R. Ramaswami and K. N. Sivarajan, *Optical Networks: A Practical Perspective*, Morgan Kaufmann, 1998.
2. L. Li and A. K. Somani, "Dynamic wavelength routing using congestion and neighborhood information," *IEEE/ACM Trans. Networking*, vol. 7, pp. 779–786, October 1999.
3. A. Birman, "Computing approximate blocking probabilities for a class of all-optical networks," *IEEE J. Select. Areas Commun.*, vol. 14, no. 5, pp. 852–857, June 1996.
4. O. Gerstel, G. Sasaki, S. Kutten, and R. Ramaswami, "Worst-case analysis of dyanmic wavelength allocation in optical networks," *IEEE/ACM Trans. Networking*, vol. 7, pp. 833–845, December 1999.
5. T. Cover and J. Thomas, *Elements of Information Theory*, Wiley-Interscience, 1991.
6. R. Guerin and L. Y.-C. Lien, "Overflow analysis for finite waiting-room systems," *IEEE Trans. Commun.*, vol. 38, pp. 1569–1577, September 1990.
7. R. I. Wilkinson, "Theories of toll traffic engineering in the U.S.A.," *Bell Syst. Tech. J.*, vol. 35, pp. 412–514, March 1956.
8. R. B. Cooper, *Introduction to Queueing Theory, 2nd Ed.*, North Holland, New York, 1981.

9. D. A. Garbin M. J. Fischer and G. W. Swinsky, "An enhanced extension to wilkinson's equivalent random technique with application to traffic engineering," *IEEE Trans. Commun.*, vol. 32, pp. 1–4, January 1984.
10. A. A. Fredericks, "Congestion in blocking systems - a simple approximation technique," *Bell Syst. Tech. J.*, vol. 59, pp. 805–827, July-August 1980.

Chapter 4
Spectrum and Interference Management in Next-Generation Wireless Networks

Harish Viswanathan and Sivarama Venkatesan

Abstract Further advances in cellular system performance will likely come from effective interference management techniques. In this chapter we focus on two emerging interference management methods, namely fractional frequency reuse (FFR) and Network MIMO, that transcend the limits of existing interference management techniques in cellular systems. FFR achieves interference avoidance between sectors through intelligent allocation of power, time and frequency resources that explicitly takes into account the impact on the neighbor sector performance of interference that is created as result of the allocation. Network MIMO is aimed at interference cancellation through joint coding and signal processing across multiple base stations. We present an overview of these techniques along with example simulation results to show the benefits that can be achieved. These techniques vary in complexity and the magnitude of the performance benefit achieved.

4.1 Introduction

Next-generation cellular systems are currently being developed and will be deployed in a few years time. These systems target significantly higher aggregate capacities and higher per-user data rates compared to existing systems [1, 2]. In particular, one of the goals of these systems is to boost the performance of users at the cell edge that typically suffer from significant out-of-cell interference. A variety of innovations, including multiple-input multiple-output (MIMO) multi-antenna techniques and use of wider signaling bandwidths, are being adopted to achieve the desired level of performance.

H. Viswanathan (✉)
Bell Labs, Alcatel Lucent 600-700 Mountain Avenue, Murray Hill, NJ 07974
e-mail: harish.viswanathan@alcatel-lucent.com

S. Venkatesan
Bell Labs, Alcatel Lucent R-207, 791 Holmdel Road, Holmdel, NJ 07733
e-mail: venkat.venkatesan@alcatel-lucent.com

G. Cormode and M. Thottan (eds.), *Algorithms for Next Generation Networks*,
Computer Communications and Networks, DOI 10.1007/978-1-84882-765-3_4,
© Springer-Verlag London Limited 2010

Having approached the information-theoretic limits of point-to-point communication through coding and MIMO techniques, further advances in cellular performance require focusing attention on eliminating interference efficiently. In particular, users at the cell edge will benefit significantly from interference reduction techniques. Two broad classes of techniques for interference mitigation are interference cancellation and interference avoidance. Interference cancellation relies on coding and signal processing at the transmitter or receiver to suppress interference. On the other hand, interference avoidance relies on intelligent resource allocation to eliminate interference.

While interference cancellation and interference avoidance are targeted at improving the spectral efficiency, i.e., the data rate or capacity that can be achieved using a given amount of spectrum, simply using more spectrum continues to remain an inexpensive option for increasing system capacity and data rates. With improvements in radio technologies, signaling over larger bandwidths has become not only feasible but also cost-effective. However, finding new spectrum within the prime spectrum band of 300 MHz to 3 GHz where signal propagation loss is most benign is difficult. Nevertheless, it has become quite clear through numerous studies [3] that the spectrum that has been licensed for various services is significantly under-utilized. Dynamic spectrum access (DSA), a technique for harvesting unused spectrum dynamically at particular locations and times using spectrum sensing, offers a method for essentially creating more spectrum.

DSA is akin to interference avoidance in the sense that the choice of what spectrum to use for communication is guided by the need to avoid intersystem interference. DSA can thus be viewed as interference avoidance across uncoordinated systems (possibly using different air interfaces, and operating over very different spatial scales), while traditional interference mitigation techniques of interference cancellation and interference avoidance are within the same system. We believe that the next wave of spectral efficiency enhancements to wireless systems will come about through a combination of interference management techniques, both intrasystem and intersystem. We are thus motivated to bring together some of the main techniques and associated algorithms for interference management in the context of cellular systems in this chapter. Although we do not explicitly discuss DSA-related algorithms in this chapter, the interference avoidance algorithms discussed here can be considered for DSA. We describe our algorithms in the context of cellular systems.

It should be noted that existing cellular systems already have a number of features that serve the end goal of interference management. For example, power control minimizes the interference caused by each user to all other users while attaining some desired signal-to-noise-plus-interference ratio (SINR). Similarly, handoff between base stations allows each user to be connected to the base station(s) to/from which it requires the least power to attain a target SINR, which again minimizes interference to other users. Finally, transmit beamforming helps focus transmitted energy in desired directions, and receive beamforming helps reject interference energy coming from undesired directions. Our focus in this chapter is on techniques that transcend the interference management limits of such existing features.

We specifically consider two techniques that have been proposed recently in the context of cellular networks, namely, *fractional frequency reuse* (FFR) [4–7] and *Network MIMO* [11–20]. FFR has been standardized in OFDM-based fourth-generation cellular systems such as the Third Generation Partnership Project's (3GPP) Long Term Evolution (LTE) standard and 3GPP2 Ultra Mobile Broadband (UMB) standard. Network MIMO is being considered for standardization in the next generation standards, namely LTE-Advanced and IEEE 802.16 m, for IMT-advanced.

4.2 Review of Enabling Technologies

In this section we provide a brief overview of some of the key building blocks upon which the interference management techniques discussed in this chapter are built.

4.2.1 Contiguous and Non-contiguous Orthogonal Frequency Division Multiple Access

In an orthogonal frequency division multiple access (OFDMA) system the transmission band is divided into a number of sub-carriers and information is transmitted by modulating each of the sub-carriers. The sub-carriers are closely spaced and overlapping with no guard-band between them. Nevertheless, the sub-carriers are orthogonal to each other at the receiver when demodulated using an appropriate set of samples. Thus there is minimal interference between information symbols on the different sub-carriers. Furthermore, the sub-carriers remain orthogonal under multipath channel propagation. Since each sub-carrier undergoes flat fading, the receiver processing in a frequency-selective channel is simplified.

One of the key advantages of OFDMA is the flexibility that it offers for resource allocation, which can be exploited for interference mitigation. The sub-carriers can be divided into sub-sets called sub-bands. Different transmit power levels can be assigned to different sub-bands in different sectors creating the so-called "soft" fractional reuse patterns resulting in superior performance through interference avoidance.

Another advantage of OFDMA for dynamic spectrum access is the ability to transmit only portions of the band by transmitting zero power on a set of sub-carriers. When the set of sub-carriers used for transmission is not contiguous, the transmission technique is referred to as non-contiguous OFDM.

4.2.2 MIMO Signal Processing

MIMO techniques based on multiple transmitting and receiving antennas have proven to be a fruitful area of research in the last 10 years or so. In the context of point-to-point communication links operating in rich-scattering environments, MIMO techniques have been shown to increase the achievable spectral efficiency (i.e., the data rate per unit of bandwidth) in proportion to the number of antennas deployed. This increase is obtained by sending multiple independent information streams from the antennas at the transmitter, and resolving them at the receiver by exploiting their distinct spatial signatures (in a highly scattering environment).

In the context of multiuser systems, simply deploying multiple receiving antennas on each link is a powerful method of mitigating interference between links, since the resulting array gain allows each link to operate with lower transmit power, thereby lowering the interference caused to other links. In addition, the diversity against fading obtained through multiple transmit and receive antennas (in conjunction with appropriate space–time coding schemes) reduces the required link margin, which again has the effect of reducing interference.

More recently, multi-user MIMO (MU-MIMO) techniques have been proposed as a way to obtain the spectral efficiency benefits of single-user MIMO (SU-MIMO) in cellular systems without requiring multiple antennas at the terminals. This can be regarded as space division multiple access (SDMA).

In both SU-MIMO and MU-MIMO, the signal processing at the receiver can be restricted to linear, e.g., based on zero-forcing (ZF) or minimum mean squared error (MMSE) criteria. Optionally, non-linear interference cancellation techniques can be included, as in the V-BLAST algorithm [21, 22].

4.3 Fractional Frequency Reuse

4.3.1 Concept Overview

OFDMA systems supporting FFR for interference mitigation divide frequency sub-carriers into several sub-bands or more generally frequency and time resources into *resource sets*. Frequency hopping of sub-carriers is restricted to be within the sub-carriers of a resource set so that users scheduled on a certain resource set experience interference only from users scheduled in neighboring sectors in the same resource set. Typically, each resource set is reserved for a certain reuse factor and is associated with a particular transmission power profile. For example, suppose we have three sectors covering a certain area, and there are four resource sets. Then, resource set 4 can be reserved for "good geometry" users (those close to their base station, with less interference from other sectors) in all sectors, and resource sets 1, 2, 3, for "bad geometry" users (further from their base station, more interference from other sectors) in sectors 1, 2, 3, respectively. As a result, we have 1/3 reuse for bad geometry users and 1/1 (i.e., universal) reuse for good geometry users. This is an example of a fractional frequency reuse. The FFR concept is illustrated in Figure 4.1 where example resource allocations for integer reuse and fractional reuse are shown. Note that FFR can also be "soft" reuse in the sense that although all resource sets

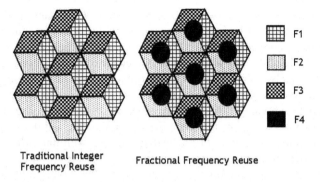

Traditional Integer
Frequency Reuse

Fractional Frequency Reuse

Fig. 4.1 Illustration of integer frequency reuse and fractional frequency reuse resource allocations in three sector cells

are utilized in all cells, a reuse pattern is created through non-uniform transmission of power across the different resource sets – most of the power is transmitted on a subset of the resource sets while a small portion of the power is transmitted on the remaining resource sets.

Fixed FFR does not adapt to traffic dynamics in the sense that the frequency reuse achieved is not adjusted based on interference conditions experienced by the users. Instead of a fixed partition of the available bandwidth leading to fixed frequency reuse it is possible to achieve dynamic frequency reuse through prioritized use of sub-carriers in the adjacent sectors. Interference avoidance is achieved by assigning different priority orders in the neighboring sectors so that when transmitting to cell edge users using sub-channelization, the neighboring interfering sectors transmit on different sub-carriers. Such a scheme was described in [4]. For such an approach it is necessary to do some a priori frequency planning to determine the priorities and also to dynamically adjust the thresholds under which users are assigned to different resource sets.

It is also possible for the FFR patterns to be obtained "automatically" without any prior frequency planning. One such approach is described in [5] where each sector constantly performs a "selfish" optimization of the assignment of its users to re-source sets, with the objective of optimizing its own performance. The optimization is done based on the interference levels reported by users for different resource sets, and is performed "continuously" via a computationally efficient *shadow scheduling algorithm*. This approach is shown to achieve efficient frequency reuse patterns that dynamically adapt to the traffic distribution.

4.3.2 Algorithm Overview

We present a brief overview of the algorithm from [5]. The reader is referred to [5] for the details.

Consider one of the cells, which needs to support N constant bit rate (CBR)-type flows, say VoIP. Similar ideas can be applied to develop algorithms for elastic, best effort traffic. For each user $i \in \mathcal{I} = \{1, \ldots, N\}$, the cell's base station (BS) can choose which sub-band j to assign it to. Given the other-cell interference levels, *currently observed* by user i, the BS "knows" (i.e., can estimate from user feedback) that it would need to allocate m_{ij} sub-carriers and average power p_{ij}, if this user is to be assigned to sub-band j. Since other-cell interference is not constant in time (it depends on the user-to-sub-band assignments in other cells, and the actual powers those users require), the values of m_{ij} and p_{ij} change with time. However, these "parameters" depend on time-averaged interference levels (over the intervals of the order of 1 second), and therefore they do not change "fast" (i.e., from slot to slot). Any user-to-sub-band assignment the cell employs at a given time should be such that sub-band capacities are not exceeded:

$$\sum_{i \in A(j)} m_{ij} \leq c, \ \forall j, \tag{4.1}$$

where $A(j)$ is the set of users assigned to sub-band j, and the total power used in all sub-bands is below the maximum available level p^*:

$$\sum_{j} \sum_{i \in A(j)} p_{ij} \leq p^*. \tag{4.2}$$

A good user-to-sub-band assignment strategy, from the overall system performance point of view, would be one "producing" user-to-sub-band assignments in the cells, allowing the system to support as many users as possible with the constraints (4.1)–(4.2) being satisfied in each cell.

Assume the typical situation when it is the power constraints (4.2) that limit system capacity. Then, a natural "selfish" strategy for each cell is to try to minimize its own total power usage, given the current values of m_{ij} and p_{ij} for its current users:

$$\min \sum_{j} \sum_{i \in A(j)} p_{ij}, \tag{4.3}$$

subject to (4.1)–(4.2). (The minimization in (4.3) is over all possible assignments $\{A(j), \ j \in \mathcal{I}\}$.)

Suppose that each cell does try to minimize its own total power usage, as described by (4.3) and as illustrated in Figure 4.2. Then, we expect the following to happen. "Edge users" in a cell (those further away from their own BS) will have generally larger requirements m_{ij} and p_{ij}, and – more importantly – m_{ij} and p_{ij} will be relatively smaller in those "good" sub-bands j where neighboring cells happen to allocate less power. "Inner users" of the cell (those close to their own BS) generally have smaller requirements m_{ij} and p_{ij}; in addition, they are less affected by the interference from neighboring cells and, consequently, the inner users' values of m_{ij} and p_{ij} are much less dependent on the sub-band j. As a result, the cell (trying to solve (4.3), will have a tendency to put its edge users into its good

Fig. 4.2 Flow chart of steps
in an FFR algorithm

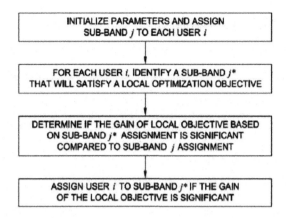

sub-bands j. Therefore, the cell will allocate larger powers to its good sub-bands, thus making those sub-bands "bad" for the neighboring cells. Neighboring cells then (while trying to minimize their own total powers) will "avoid" putting their edge user into those sub-bands, making them even "better" for the cell under consideration, and so on. It is intuitive that the system "settles" into a user-to-sub-band allocation pattern, generally requiring less power in all cells, because neighboring cells will automatically "separate" their edge users into different sub-bands.

How each BS is going to solve problem (4.3), (4.1), (4.2) is of crucial importance, because, to make the approach practical, the following requirements need to be observed:

- The algorithm has to be computationally very efficient.
- It should *not* result in a large number of users being re-assigned from sub-band to sub-band in each time slot.
- We want an algorithm which adapts automatically to "evolving" set of users $\mathscr{I}$ and their "evolving" parameters m_{ij} and p_{ij}.

Such an algorithm that is run separately in each cell can be devised using the greedy primal-dual algorithm described in [8]. We refer the reader to [5] for the details.

4.3.3 Algorithm Performance

We present some simulation results from [5] to illustrate how the algorithm performs in a simple setting. We do not provide all the detailed simulation assumptions here but refer the reader to the original above source.

A three sector network (as shown in Figure 4.3), with the sectors facing each other is used to study the behavior of the algorithm under a variety of traffic distribution scenarios. The site-to-site distance is set to 2.5 km. Users are distributed in the triangular region covered by the three sectors. Standard propagation parameters

Fig. 4.3 Three sector
network used in simulations

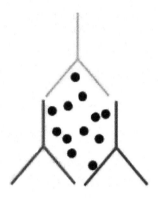

[9] are used to determine the received signal power level for a given transmit power level. The propagation parameters result in a cell edge SNR (signal to thermal noise ratio) of 20 dB, when there is no interference from surrounding cells, and the total available power is distributed over the entire bandwidth.

A constant bit rate traffic model in which, for all users in the active state, fixed length packets of size 128 bits arrive once every 20 slots is adopted. Users transition between active and inactive states according to exponentially distributed waiting times in each state. No packets arrive when a user is in the inactive state. The mean time in each state is 200 slots.

In the simulations, an OFDMA system with 48 sub-carriers divided into a number of sub-bands with the same number of sub-carriers in each sub-band is considered. Typically, we consider three sub-bands with 16 sub-carriers in each sub-band. Random frequency hopping is implemented from slot to slot by permuting the sub-carrier indices independently across the different sub-bands and sectors.

A key requirement for the algorithm is the feedback of channel quality in the form of data rate that can be supported within each of the sub-bands. Average channel quality is assumed to be fed back every slot in the simulations. Transmission rates achieved are computed using the Shannon formula and idealized incremental redundancy is also simulated.

When the activity state for user i changes from inactive to active and the first packet arrives at the sector, p_{ij}, m_{ij} are calculated for each sub-band j to meet the target data rate requirement. For this computation the channel quality indicator fed back by each user on a per sub-band level is used. Among the various combinations of p_{ij}, m_{ij} that result in the same rate, the one that requires the least number of sub-carriers is used. Determining the optimal combination of p_{ij} and m_{ij} is non-trivial.

We compare the performance of the shadow algorithm for three sub-bands to that of universal reuse with a single sub-band and no interference coordination. Users are distributed uniformly in all three sectors in all of the results in this section. Comparison is performed on the basis of the maximum number of users that can be supported in each sector. This maximum number is obtained from the cumulative distribution functions (CDFs) of the total sector transmit power and the mean queue size.

Figure 4.4 shows the complementary cumulative distribution functions of the total sector power normalized by the maximum available sector power and the mean

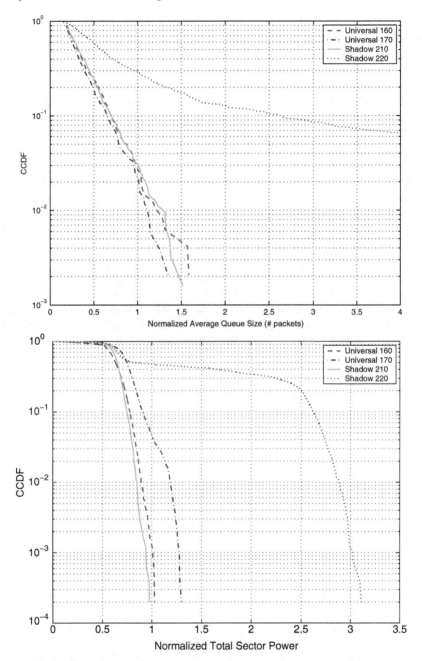

Fig. 4.4 Complementary cumulative distribution functions of the total sector power and mean queue size for 20 dB cell edge SNR

queue size over the duration of the simulation normalized by the packet size for the different users. The criteria for determining if a given number of users can be supported by the system are (a) the one-percentile point in normalized total sector power plot should not exceed 1 for valid system operation and (b) the one-percentile point in the normalized mean queue size plot should not exceed about 2. The latter is because of the fact that for real-time traffic such as VoIP traffic, over the air one way delay of up to 80 ms may be tolerated. This translates to a maximum delay of about four packets. Since we are using mean delay, two packets delay has been used as the criterion. From these plots we conclude that the gain for the shadow algorithm over universal reuse in this case is about 30%

In Figure 4.5 we show the total number of users across the three sectors that require re-assignment to a different band to make the allocation more efficient as a function of the index slot. This number is important because reassigning a user to a different band incurs additional signaling overhead. Thus, the smaller the number of reassignments the better. From the figure it is clear that the number of users reassigned is a small fraction, less than 3%, of the total number of users.

In Figure 4.6 we show the relative power spectral density across the three sub-bands. This is calculated as follows. First the average transmit power level in each sub-band is normalized by the average number of sub-carriers assigned in that sub-band. The resulting power spectral densities are then normalized by the smallest of the three power spectral density values to obtain the relative values which are

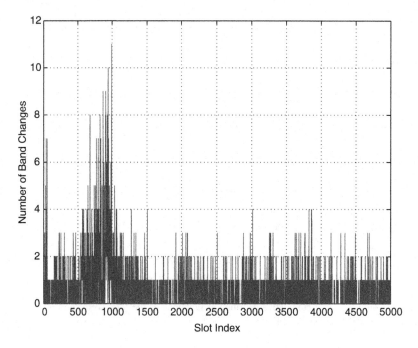

Fig. 4.5 Number of band changes

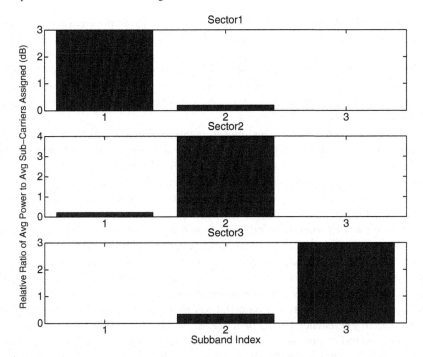

Fig. 4.6 Relative transmit power ratios (in dB) in the different bands in the three sectors

then plotted in dB. This shows that there is a significant difference in the transmit power spectral densities across the three sub-bands demonstrating that automatic soft fractional frequency reuse is indeed taking place.

In the case of non-uniform traffic higher gains are achieved with the proposed algorithm as illustrated in [5].

4.4 Network MIMO

As pointed out in Section 4.1, the spectral efficiency achievable in today's cellular networks (i.e., the overall system throughput per unit of bandwidth) is fundamentally limited by cochannel interference, i.e., the interference between users sharing the same time-frequency channel. While intracell interference can be eliminated by orthogonal multiple access and multiplexing techniques, intercell interference still remains. Consequently, increasing the signal-to-noise-ratio (SNR) on individual links does not increase the spectral efficiency of the network appreciably beyond a point, because the signal-to-interference-plus-noise ratio (SINR) on each link begins to saturate.

Within the SINR limits imposed by this cochannel interference environment, link performance is already close to optimal, thanks to the use of sophisticated error correcting codes, adaptive modulation, incremental redundancy, etc. [10] While the SINR distribution can be improved (especially in terms of helping cell-edge users) by means of the fractional frequency reuse techniques described earlier in this chapter, the resulting spectral efficiency gains are typically modest, as seen in the results of Section 4.3.

It is therefore clear that major improvements in spectral efficiency for future generations of cellular networks will require more ambitious approaches to mitigate cochannel interference. "Network MIMO" [11–20] is one such approach, which can be regarded as an extension to the network level of traditional link-level MIMO concepts. The basic idea behind Network MIMO is to coordinate several base stations in the transmission and reception of user signals and to suppress interference between such users by joint beamforming across the antennas of all the base stations (possibly augmented by non-linear interference cancellation techniques).

Suppose that the network has several "coordination clusters", each consisting of a base station and one or more rings of its neighbors, and that the antennas of all the base stations in each cluster can act as a single coherent antenna array. It is envisaged that such coordination between base stations in a cluster would be facilitated by a high-speed, low-latency (wired or wireless) backhaul network. Each user in the network is served by one such cluster. The interference affecting each user can then be suppressed quite effectively by means of coherent linear beamforming at the antennas of all the base stations in its assigned cluster (transmit beamforming on the downlink, and receive beamforming on the uplink), thereby greatly increasing the attainable spectral efficiency [11–20].

It should be noted that Network MIMO on the downlink requires downlink channel state information at the base stations. In a frequency-division duplexing (FDD) system, this calls for accurate and timely feedback of such information from the users, at a significant cost in terms of uplink bandwidth. With time-division duplexing (TDD), however, channel reciprocity can be exploited to obtain downlink channel state information directly from uplink channel estimates. In contrast, Network MIMO on the uplink does not require any over-the-air exchange of information beyond what is customary, making it potentially amenable to a standards-free implementation.

Some thought shows that cochannel interference mitigation through Network MIMO should have a greater impact on spectral efficiency in a higher-SNR environment, since the level of cochannel interference relative to receiver noise is then higher. The SNR distribution in the network is determined by the transmitter power available to each user, bandwidth of operation, propagation characteristics of the environment, antenna gains, amplifier noise figures, etc. Also, it is intuitively clear that, for a given SNR distribution, there is a diminishing benefit in coordinating farther and farther base stations.

4.4.1 Algorithms

To illustrate Network MIMO concepts and algorithms, we will focus here on the uplink [18–20]. Following [18], suppose that the network is populated with one user per base station antenna (i.e., one user per spatial dimension), and that all these users, but for a small fraction consigned to outage due to unfavorable channel conditions, must be served at a common data rate. Results on power control from [23–25] can be used to develop algorithms for identifying the subset of users that must be declared in outage, as well as the powers at which the remaining users must transmit and the coordination clusters at which they must be received. The largest common data rate that is consistent with the desired user outage probability can then be determined by simulation, for coordination clusters of different sizes.

Several idealizing assumptions are made in [18] in order to get a sense of the potential payoff without getting bogged down in details. For example, channel estimation issues are ignored by assuming the availability of perfect channel state information wherever necessary. Also, the bandwidth, latency, and synchronization requirements on the backhaul network connecting the base stations in each cluster are not dealt with. All such issues will need to be solved before Network MIMO can be deployed in real-world networks.

In the interest of simplicity, all user-to-sector links in the network are assumed flat-fading and time-invariant in [18], with perfect symbol synchronization between all users at each sector (i.e., the symbol boundaries in all the user signals are assumed to be aligned at each sector). Further, each user in the network has a single omnidirectional transmitting antenna. Accordingly, the complex baseband signal vector $\mathbf{y}_s(t) \in \mathbb{C}^N$ received at the N antennas of sector s during symbol period t is modeled as

$$\mathbf{y}_s(t) = \sum_{u=1}^{U} \mathbf{h}_{s,u} x_u(t) + \mathbf{z}_s(t). \tag{4.4}$$

Here, U is the total number of users in the network; $x_u(t) \in \mathbb{C}$ is the complex baseband signal transmitted by user u during symbol period t; $\mathbf{h}_{s,u} \in \mathbb{C}^N$ is the vector representing the channel from user u to sector s; and $\mathbf{z}_s(t) \in \mathbb{C}^N$ is a circularly symmetric complex Gaussian vector representing additive receiver noise, with $E[\mathbf{z}_s(t)] = \mathbf{0}$ and $E[\mathbf{z}_s(t)\mathbf{z}_s^*(t)] = \mathbf{I}$. Each user is subject to a transmitted power constraint of 1, i.e., $E[|x_u(t)|^2] \leq 1$.

A *coordination cluster* is defined to be a subset of base stations that jointly and coherently process the received signals at the antennas of all their sectors. The network is postulated to have a predefined set of coordination clusters, and each user can be assigned to any one of these clusters. Further, each cluster uses a linear minimum-mean-squared-error (MMSE) beamforming receiver to detect each user assigned to it, in the presence of interference from all other users in the network (more generally, receivers based on interference cancellation could also be considered).

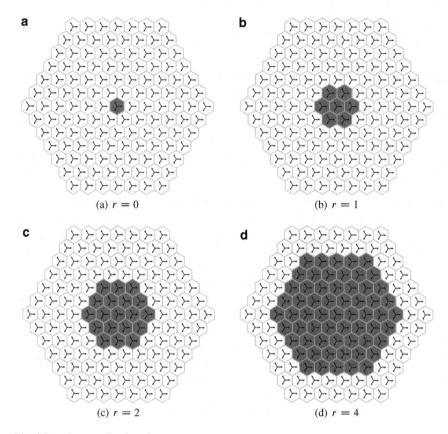

Fig. 4.7 *r*-ring coordination clusters

To highlight the dependence of the spectral efficiency gain on the number of rings of neighbors with which each base station is coordinated, coordination clusters with a specific structure are of interest. For any integer $r \geq 0$, an *r-Ring coordination cluster* is defined to consist of any base station and the first r rings of its neighboring base stations (accounting for wraparound), and $\mathscr{C}_r$ is defined to be the set of all r-ring coordination clusters in the network. Figure 4.7 illustrates r-ring clusters for $r = 0, 1, 2, 4$.

With $\mathscr{C}_0$ as the set of coordination clusters in the network, there is in fact no coordination between base stations. This case serves as the benchmark in estimating the spectral efficiency gain achievable with sets of larger coordination clusters. With some abuse of notation, let $\mathbf{h}_{C,u} \in \mathbb{C}^{3N|C|}$ denote the channel from user u to the antennas of all the base stations in the coordination cluster C (here $|C|$ denotes the number of base stations in C). Then, with user u transmitting power p_u, the SINR attained by user u at cluster C is $\mathbf{h}_{C,u}^* \left(\mathbf{I} + \sum_{v \neq u} p_v \mathbf{h}_{C,v} \mathbf{h}_{C,v}^* \right)^{-1} \mathbf{h}_{C,u} \, p_u$. Note that this expression assumes perfect knowledge at cluster C of the channel vector $\mathbf{h}_{C,u}$ and the composite interference covariance $\sum_{v \neq u} p_v \mathbf{h}_{C,v} \mathbf{h}_{C,v}^*$.

Let the target rate for each user in the network be R bits/sym. Since there are $3N$ users per cell, the offered load to the network is then $3NR$ bits/sym/cell. Assuming Gaussian signaling and ideal coding, the target rate of R bits/sym translates to a target SINR of $\rho \triangleq 2^R - 1$ for each user.

To begin with, suppose that the target SINR ρ is small enough for all the users to achieve it, given the power constraint on each user and the interference between users. This means that there exists a feasible setting of each user's transmitted power, and an assignment of users to coordination clusters, such that each user attains an SINR of ρ or higher at its assigned cluster, with an SINR-maximizing linear MMSE receiver. In this situation, the following iterative algorithm from [23] (also see [24, 25]) can be used to determine the transmitted powers and cluster assignments for all the users:

1. Initialize all user powers to 0: $p_u^{(0)} = 0$ for all u.
2. Given user powers $\{p_u^{(n)}\}$, assign user u to the cluster $C_u^{(n)}$ where it would attain the highest SINR:

$$C_u^{(n)} = \arg\max_{C \in \mathscr{C}_r} \mathbf{h}_{C,u}^* \mathbf{Q}_{C,u}^{(n)} \mathbf{h}_{C,u}, \tag{4.5}$$

$$\mathbf{Q}_{C,u}^{(n)} \triangleq \left(\mathbf{I} + \sum_{v \neq u} p_v^{(n)} \mathbf{h}_{C,v} \mathbf{h}_{C,v}^* \right)^{-1}. \tag{4.6}$$

Let $p_u^{(n+1)}$ be the power required by user u to attain the target SINR of ρ at the cluster $C_u^{(n)}$, assuming every other user v continues to transmit at the current power level:

$$p_u^{(n+1)} = \rho \left(\mathbf{h}_{C_u^{(n)},u}^* \mathbf{Q}_{C_u^{(n)},u}^{(n)} \mathbf{h}_{C_u^{(n)},u} \right)^{-1}. \tag{4.7}$$

3. Iterate until convergence.

In [23], the above iteration is shown to converge to transmitted powers $\{\tilde{p}_u\}$ that are optimal in the following strong sense: if it is possible for every user to attain the target SINR of ρ with transmitted powers $\{p_u\}$, then $p_u \geq \tilde{p}_u$ for every u. In other words, the iteration minimizes the power transmitted by *every* user, subject to the target SINR of ρ being achieved by all users.

In general, however, it might be impossible for all the users to achieve the target SINR simultaneously. It is then necessary to settle for serving only a subset of the users, declaring the rest to be in outage. In principle, the largest supportable subset of users could be determined by sequentially examining all subsets of users in decreasing order of size, but this approach is practical only when the number of users is small.

Instead, in [18], the iterative algorithm of [23] is modified slightly to obtain a suboptimal but computationally efficient algorithm for determining which subset of users should be served. After each iteration, the modified algorithm declares users whose updated powers exceed the power constraint of 1 to be in outage, and eliminates them from consideration in future iterations. This progressive elimination of users eventually results in a subset of users that can all simultaneously achieve the target SINR ρ. For this subset of users, the algorithm then finds the optimal transmitted powers and cluster assignments. However, the user subset itself need not be the largest possible; essentially, this is because a user consigned to outage in some iteration cannot be resurrected in a future iteration.

4.4.2 Simulation Results

Figures 4.8–4.10 illustrate the spectral efficiency gain achievable with different coordination cluster sizes, for $N = 1$, $N = 2$, and $N = 4$, respectively. Specifically, each figure shows the ratio of the spectral efficiency achievable with $\mathscr{C}_1$ (1-ring coordination), $\mathscr{C}_2$ (2-ring coordination), and $\mathscr{C}_4$ (4-ring coordination) to that achievable with $\mathscr{C}_0$ (no coordination), for a different value of N. Note that:

1. The coordination gain increases with the reference SNR η in each case, because interference mitigation becomes more helpful as the level of interference between users goes up relative to receiver noise.
2. At the low end of the η range, most of the spectral efficiency gain comes just from 1-ring coordination. This is because most of the interferers that are significant relative to receiver noise are within range of the first ring of surrounding base stations. However, as η is increased, interferers that are further away start to become significant relative to receiver noise, and therefore it pays to increase the coordination cluster size correspondingly.
3. The coordination gain values are not very sensitive to N, the number of antennas per sector as well as the number of users per sector, suggesting that it is the ratio of users to sector antennas (1 in all our results) that matters.

The results from the simulations indicate that, in a high-SNR environment, the uplink spectral efficiency can potentially be doubled with 1-ring coordination, and nearly quadrupled with 4-ring coordination. When the user-to-sector-antenna ratio is smaller than 1, the coordination gain will be somewhat lower since, even without coordination, each base station can then use the surplus spatial dimensions to

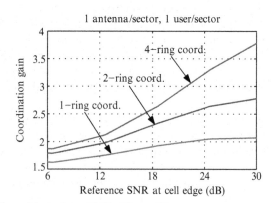

Fig. 4.8 Coordination gain: 1 antenna/sector, 1 user/sector

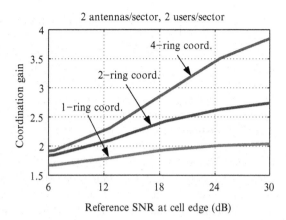

Fig. 4.9 Coordination gain: 2 antennas/sector, 2 users/sector

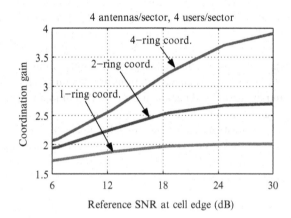

Fig. 4.10 Coordination gain: four antennas/sector, four users/sector

suppress a larger portion of the interference affecting each user it serves. The co-ordination gain with a user-to-sector-antenna ratio larger than 1 will also be lower, because the composite interference affecting each user at any coordination cluster will then tend towards being spatially white, making linear MMSE beamforming less effective at interference suppression.

4.5 Challenges in Taking Theory to Practice

The FFR algorithm for the CBR case presented here is fairly simple to implement. Additional computational resources would of course be required to perform the computations required. One of the challenges common to all interference manage-ment techniques is the need for appropriate feedback from the mobile. Because interoperability between mobiles and base stations from different vendors is re-quired, the quantity that is fed back has to be standardized.

The FFR algorithm presented applies only to the CBR case. In practice, a mixture of different traffic types will be involved. A hard separation of resources between

CBR and best effort type traffic will be suboptimal. Thus an algorithm that seams together the CBR and best effort solution in an adaptive manner is required in practice.

As far as Network MIMO goes, several issues will need to be addressed before the large spectral efficiency gains hinted at by theoretical results can be realized in practice. For example, techniques must be developed to estimate the channel from a user to a faraway base station without excessive overhead for training signals, especially in a highly mobile environment (data-aided channel estimation methods could be investigated for this purpose).

Perhaps, most importantly, a high-bandwidth, low-latency backhaul network will be required for several base stations to jointly process transmitted and received signals in a timely manner (coherent processing also requires a high degree of synchronization between the base stations). To get a rough idea of the required increase in backhaul bandwidth, consider the downlink. Without Network MIMO, the data to be transmitted to a user is routed to a single base station. Now, with Network MIMO, if the average user is served by B base stations, then the overall backhaul bandwidth required for user data dissemination will increase by a factor of B (since the average user's bits must be routed to B base stations instead of 1). In addition, the exchange of channel state and beamforming weight information between base stations (or between base stations and a central Network MIMO processor) will also require additional backhaul bandwidth, but this will typically be small compared to what the user data requires.

The costs associated with such a network must be considered in relation to the savings from the greater efficiency in the use of scarce spectrum. More generally, Network MIMO must be compared in economic terms with alternative approaches to increasing spectral efficiency.

4.6 Summary

Interference management techniques will be a vital part of future cellular systems. The techniques vary in complexity and the magnitude of the performance benefit achieved. Fractional frequency reuse (FFR) is a technique that is based on intelligent interference avoidance, providing modest gains with manageable implementation complexity. It is likely to be deployed in scenarios where the Network MIMO technique is found too complex to implement. The latter provides significantly higher gains in spectral efficiency through interference suppression, but at the expense of considerably greater complexity.

References

1. 3GPP Specification TR 36.913: Requirements for further advancements for E-UTRA (LTE-Advanced). Available from http://www.3gpp.org/ftp/Specs/html-info/36913.htm (2008)
2. IEEE 802.16m-07/002r7: IEEE 802.16m System Requirements. Available from http:// wirelessman.org/tgm/ (2008)

3. Buddhikot, M.: Understanding dynamic spectrum access: models, taxonomy and challenges. Proc. IEEE DYSPAN. (March 2007)
4. Das, S., Viswanathan, H.: Interference mitigation through intelligent scheduling. Proc. Asilomar Conference on Signals and Systems. (November 2006)
5. Stolyar, A. L., Viswanathan, H.: Self-organizing Dynamic Fractional Frequency Reuse in OFDMA Systems. Proc of INFOCOM. (April 2008)
6. Third Generation Partnership Project 2: Ultra Mobile Broadband Technical Specifications. http://www.3gpp2.org (March 2007)
7. Third Generation Partnership Project: Radio Access Network Work Group 1 Contributions. http://www.3gpp.org (September 2005)
8. Stolyar, A. L.: Maximizing queueing network utility subject to stability: greedy primal-dual algorithm. Queueing Systems (2005) 401–457
9. Stolyar, A. L., Viswanathan. H.: Self-organizing dynamic fractional frequency reuse in OFDMA Systems. Bell-Labs Alcatel-Lucent Technical Memo (June 2007) http://cm.bell-labs.com/who/stolyar/dffr.pdf
10. Huang, H., Valenzuela, R. A.: Fundamental Simulated Performance of Downlink Fixed Wireless Cellular Networks with Multiple Antennas. Proc. IEEE PIMRC (2005) 161–165
11. Shamai, S., Zaidel, B. M.: Enhancing the cellular downlink capacity via co-processing at the transmitting end. Proc. IEEE Veh. Tech. Conf. (Spring 2001) 1745–1749
12. Karakayali, K., Foschini, G. J., Valenzuela, R. A., Yates, R. D.: On the maximum common rate achievable in a coordinated network. Proc. IEEE ICC (2006) 4333–4338
13. Karakayali, K., Foschini, G. J., Valenzuela, R. A.: Network coordination for spectrally efficient communications in cellular systems. IEEE Wireless Commun. Mag. **13:4** (2006) 56-61
14. Foschini, G. J., Karakayali, K., Valenzuela, R. A.: Coordinating multiple antenna cellular networks to achieve enormous spectral efficiency. Proc. IEEE **153:4** (2006) 548-555
15. Somekh, O., Simeone, O., Bar-Ness, Y., Haimovich, A. M.: Distributed Multi-Cell Zero-Forcing Beamforming in Cellular Downlink Channels. Proc. IEEE Globecom (2006) 1–6
16. Jing, S., Tse, D. N. C., Soriaga, J. B., Hou, J., Smee, J. E., Padovani, R.: Downlink Macro-Diversity in Cellular Networks. Proc. Int'l Symp. Info. Th. (2007)
17. Ng, B. L., Evans, J., Hanly, S.: Distributed Downlink Beamforming in Cellular Networks. Proc. Int'l Symp. Info. Th. (2007)
18. Venkatesan, S.: Coordinating Base Stations for Greater Uplink Spectral Efficiency in a Cellular Network. Proc. PIMRC (2007)
19. Venkatesan, S.: Coordinating Base Stations for Greater Uplink Spectral Efficiency: Proportionally Fair User Rates. Proc. PIMRC (2007)
20. Venkatesan, S., Lozano, A., Valenzuela, R. A.: Network MIMO: Overcoming Intercell Interference in Indoor Wireless Systems. Proc. Asilomar Conf. on Signals, Systems and Computers (2007)
21. Wolniansky, P. W., Foschini, G. J., Golden, G. D., Valenzuela, R. A.: V-BLAST: an architecture for realizing very high data rates over the rich-scattering wireless channel. Proc. 1998 URSI International Symposium on Signals, Systems and Electronics (1998) 295–300
22. Golden, G. D., Foschini, G. J., Valenzuela, R. A., Wolniansky, P. W.: Detection algorithm and initial laboratory results using V-BLAST space-time communication architecture. IEEE Electronics Letters **35** (1999) 14–16
23. Rashid-Farrokhi, F., Tassiulas, L., Liu, K. J. R.: Joint optimal power control and beamforming in wireless networks using antenna arrays. IEEE Trans. Commun. **46** (1998) 1313–1324
24. Hanly, S.: An algorithm for combined cell-site selection and power control to maximize cellular spread spectrum capacity. IEEE J. Sel. Areas. Commun. **13** (1995) 1332–1340
25. Yates, R., Huang, C. Y.: Integrated power control and base station assignment. IEEE Trans. Veh. Tech. **44** (1995) 638–644

Chapter 5
Cross-Layer Capacity Estimation and Throughput Maximization in Wireless Networks

V.S. Anil Kumar, Madhav V. Marathe, and Srinivasan Parthasarathy

Abstract In this chapter, we explore techniques for capacity estimation and throughput maximization in multi-hop wireless networks. The specific problem we investigate is the following: how can we characterize the set of all feasible end-to-end connection throughput rate vectors which can be supported by the network (i.e., what is the network capacity), and how can we design cross-layer algorithms at the scheduling, routing, and transport layers which are guaranteed to operate the network close to its capacity? We approach this problem from three distinct perspectives which have greatly influenced research in this field: (1) throughput scaling in random geometric graphs whose nodes are distributed uniformly in space, (2) geometric packing and linear programming-based techniques for arbitrary networks, and (3) the dynamic back-pressure scheme based on queueing theoretic principles for achieving network stability. A recurring theme throughout this chapter is the role of geometric insights into the design and analysis of provably good algorithms for multi-hop wireless networks. We also include a brief survey of related developments in the field of cross-layer algorithms for multi-hop wireless networks.

5.1 Introduction

With rapid advances in wireless radio technology, there has been a significant growth of interest in various types of large-scale multi-hop wireless networks such as mesh networks, sensor networks, and mobile ad hoc networks. Effective deployment and operation of these multi-hop wireless networks demands a thorough

V.S. Anil Kumar (✉) and M.V. Marathe
Department of Computer Science and Virginia BioInformatics Institute, Virginia Tech, Blacksburg, VA 24061
e-mail: vsakumar@vt.edu; mmarathe@vbi.vt.edu

S. Parthasarathy
T. J. Watson Research Center, IBM, Hawthorne, NY 10532
e-mail: spartha@us.ibm.com

G. Cormode and M. Thottan (eds.), *Algorithms for Next Generation Networks*,
Computer Communications and Networks, DOI 10.1007/978-1-84882-765-3_5,
© Springer-Verlag London Limited 2010

grasp over the following fundamental issues: What is the rate at which data can be transferred across a multi-hop wireless network (this is also known as the throughput capacity)? How can the network communication protocols be designed in order to achieve the maximum possible rate? The throughput capacity is a function of a number of factors including the topology of the network, the traffic pattern, and, most significantly, the specific communication protocols employed for data transfer. Network communication protocols are commonly structured in a *layered* manner – this is a fundamental architectural principle that has guided the design of protocols for data networks in general, and the Internet in particular since their inception. Each layer in the protocol stack performs a collection of related functions, with the goal of providing a specific set of services to the layer above it and receiving a set of services from the layer below it. The task of characterizing and maximizing the throughput capacity of a network involves the joint analysis and optimization of several layers of the protocol stack.

It is well understood that imposing a strict separation between various layers of the protocol stack by treating them as isolated units leads to a significantly suboptimal performance in wireless networks [16]. As a result, there is a considerable amount of emphasis on the *cross-layer* protocol design, which is characterized by tighter coupling between various layers: information associated with a specific layer could be exposed across other layers if such sharing could potentially lead to increased efficiency of some network functions. The main goal here is to determine how best to *jointly* control various parameters associated with all the layers, and how to operate the layers in synergy in order to optimize some global network objective of interest. There are two key factors at work behind the shift towards cross-layer design in the domain of wireless networking as opposed to the Internet. First, the complexity of the wireless communication channel, its unreliability, and temporal changes (due to fading, mobility, multipath, and other wireless propagation effects) as well as the phenomenon of wireless interference necessitates a holistic and a global, optimization-centric view of protocols. Second, the baggage of legacy systems does not pose as much of an issue in ad hoc wireless networks as it does in the Internet. This permits a clean-slate approach to network design and control which is not an option in the present-day Internet.

There has been considerable amount of theoretical research on cross-layer formulations to characterize the set of traffic rates (also referred to as the *rate region*) that can be supported by the network, as well as the design of cross-layer protocols motivated by such analysis. This research has witnessed a confluence of diverse perspectives which have their bearings in convex optimization theory [22,23,25,44,80], queueing theory [61, 62, 64, 74, 76], geometric insights [4, 13, 48–50, 79], graph theory [68], and systems research [28,29,82] (these references indicate a small sample; see also the references therein). The potential benefits due to cross-layer design have been demonstrated in the context of several central network performance measures including end-to-end throughput related objectives [4, 44, 49, 50, 76, 79, 80], energy minimization [26, 27, 53], end-to-end latency [19, 41, 48, 70], and network longevity [59, 77].

In this chapter, we focus our attention on the problem of characterizing the achievable rate region of wireless networks and describe some of the key techniques that have been developed in this area. The research related to this problem can be broadly classified into various threads based on the assumptions made about node distributions, physical and MAC layers, and the exogenous (application-level) packet generation process. We discuss three specific results in detail in this chapter, which lie at various points of the above spectrum. In all these results, as explained in Section 5.2, wireless link interference is modeled either using geometric or conflict-graph-based constraints.

1. Suppose n nodes are distributed uniformly at random within a unit square, and there are n connections whose origins and destinations are randomly chosen nodes within the network. What is the expected value of the maximum end-to-end throughput which we can simultaneously support across each connection in this setting? This question was investigated by Gupta and Kumar [36], who showed that the expected per-connection throughput in a random network is $\Theta\left(\frac{1}{\sqrt{n\log n}}\right)$, where n is the number of network nodes. In other words, the per-connection throughput within a random wireless network vanishes asymptotically as the number of network nodes increases – a fact which points to the scalability limitations of large-scale ad hoc networks with a flat architecture. This result has subsequently resulted in a large body of throughput scaling laws for random ad hoc networks [14, 32, 35, 46, 57, 66, 67] under power constraints, mobility, multiple channels, directional antennas, infrastructure support, and other variations. The basic result due to Gupta and Kumar [36] is the subject of our discussion in Section 5.3.

2. Suppose we are given an arbitrary wireless network whose node locations are specified arbitrarily (as opposed to chosen uniformly at random). We are also given a set of end-to-end network connections whose end points are chosen arbitrarily. Our problem is to assign the end-to-end rate for each connection, and design a joint routing and scheduling scheme which can support the end-to-end connection rates, in order to maximize the total (weighted) connection throughput. This is a fundamental wireless network flow problem which has been the focus of significant research efforts [39, 42–44, 49, 71, 79]; in Section 5.4, we will present a solution due to Kumar et al. [49] under a geometric model of wireless interference which yields a provably good near-optimal polynomial time strategy. This result is derived under the assumption that the packet arrivals at the connections are spaced uniformly in time (i.e., CBR or constant bit-rate traffic).

3. We consider an extension of the previous result in which we are given an arbitrary network, an arbitrary set of connections, and a rate vector $\mathscr{A}$, which specifies the rate at which each connection injects data, according to a broadly defined stochastic arrival process. We study the following question: is it possible to construct a joint routing and scheduling scheme that is guaranteed to support every possible feasible rate vector $\mathscr{A}$ for the given setting. We answer this question in the affirmative in Section 5.5 by presenting the network stabilizing dynamic back-pressure scheme due to Tassiulas and Ephremides [76]. The back-pressure

scheme has been generalized in several ways [61, 64, 73, 75] and is an essential component of many other policies that optimize other performance objectives. While this algorithm is valid in a very general setting, it requires computing a maximum weight interference free set from among a given set of links, which is NP-complete in general; however, polynomial time (approximate) extensions of the algorithm are known for several geometric interference models including the one described in Section 5.2.

The field of cross-layer design and control is a vast and rapidly expanding research area and we acknowledge our inability to survey all the developments in this field, let alone dive into them in depth. Our afore-mentioned choice of the three topics for detailed exploration was guided by the fact that, in addition to influencing much subsequent research in the field of cross-layer design, the specific algorithms we present are also relatively simple to present and demand little other than a knowledge of basic probability as a prerequisite. We present a brief survey of several other major developments in the field of cross-layer design in Section 5.6 and conclude in Section 5.7 by presenting a set of open problems for future research. Several excellent tutorials on cross-layer design are now available which present diverse perspectives on the field. Especially notable are the tutorials due to Chiang et al. [25] and Lin et al. [56] which present an optimization based perspective on cross-layer network design and architecture, and the tutorial due to Georgiadis et al. [33] which presents a queueing theoretic perspective on cross-layer resource allocation. The role of geometric insights into the design of provably good analytical and algorithm design techniques for cross-layer design is an important perspective which has received relatively little attention in the above tutorials. We hope to redress this imbalance through this work.

5.2 Network Model

In this section, we define the basic models and concepts used in this chapter. We consider ad hoc wireless networks. The network is modeled as a directed graph $G = (V, E)$. The nodes of the graph correspond to individual transceivers and a directed edge (link) (u, v) denotes that node u can transmit to node v directly. A link (u, v) is said to be active at time t if there is an ongoing transmission from u to v at time t. Link e in $G = (V, E)$ has a capacity $c(e)$ bits/sec and denotes the maximum data that can be carried on e in a second. We assume that the system operates synchronously in a time slotted mode. For simplicity, we will assume that each time slot is 1 s in length. Therefore, if a link e is active in a time slot, then $c(e)$ bits of information can be transmitted over that link during the slot. The results we present are not affected if the length of each slot is an arbitrary quantum of time instead of one unit.

5.2.1 Interference Models

Since the medium of transmission is wireless, simultaneous transmissions on proximate links may *interfere* with each other resulting in collisions. Formally, we say
that links $e_1, e_2 \in E$ interfere with each other if links e_1 and e_2 cannot both transmit successfully during the same time slot. Let $I(e)$ denote the set of links which
interfere with link e, i.e., e cannot transmit successfully whenever a link $f \in I(e)$
is transmitting. An *interference model* defines the set $I(e)$ for each link e in the
network. For instance, the set $I(e)$ of links that interfere with a given link e could
be specified as an arbitrary subset of the network links. While this assumption leads
to the most general interference model, wireless interference in reality tends to be
governed by the properties of radio propagation in space. This consideration, along
with variations in the underlying transmission technology, physical and link-layer
protocols, has resulted in a variety of *geometric* interference models that have been
studied in the literature. In this chapter, particularly in Sections 5.3 and 5.4, the
results we present are under the transmitter model (Tx-model) of interference, a
simple geometric model which is defined as follows.

We assume that the network nodes are embedded in a two-dimensional plane.
Each node u has a maximum transmission range associated with it which is denoted
by *maxRange(u)*. A necessary condition for a node v to hear a transmission from
node u is that v be within a distance of *maxRange(u)* from u. Suppose this condition
holds and u chooses to transmit to v; then, we assume that node u adjusts its transmission power, and in turn the transmission range for this specific transmission as
follows: $range(u) = ||u, v||$. In other words, transmitters tune their ranges in order
to just be able to reach the receivers. This transmission from u is successful (i.e., received by v without interference related losses) if and only if any other simultaneous
transmitter w in the network is such that $||u, w|| \geq (1 + \Delta) \cdot (range(u) + range(w))$.
Here, Δ is a non-negative constant, which specifies a *guard zone* around the transmitters, and is specified as part of the model. Further, a node can either receive a
message or transmit a message (and not both) at the same time. Thus for any link
$e = (u, v)$, all other links which are incident on u or v are also included in the
set $I(e)$ (See Figure 5.1).

The Tx-model was introduced by Yi *et al.* [83] to analyze the capacity of
randomly distributed ad hoc wireless networks. We note that the Tx-model is a simplification of reality, as it is a sender-based interference model while interference is
inherently a receiver-based phenomenon. Further, the Tx-model stipulates that the
senders must be spatially far apart in order to avoid collisions which is a conservative
assumption. Despite these limitations, we adopt the Tx-model here as it lends itself
to easier and simpler analysis while retaining the basic spirit of the impact of interference on the cross-layer capacity of wireless networks. We emphasize that all the
results we present in this chapter can also be recovered under more realistic models
of interference such as the protocol model and the SINR (or physical) model [36].

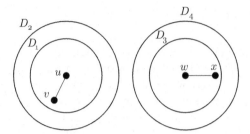

Fig. 5.1 An example illustrating the Tx-model. D_1 and D_2 are disks centered at u of radii $range(u)$ and $(1 + \Delta)range(u)$, respectively. Similarly, D_3 and D_4 are disks centered at w of radii $range(w)$ and $(1 + \Delta)range(w)$, respectively. The transmissions (u, v) and (w, x) can be scheduled simultaneously because $\|u, w\| \geq (1 + \Delta) \cdot (range(u) + range(w))$ (since the disks D_2 and D_4 do not intersect)

5.2.2 Network Flows

Two of the fundamental network wide throughput optimization problems which we will be concerned with are the maximum multi commodity flow problem (MFP), and the maximum concurrent flow problem (MCFP). In both these problems, we are given a network $G(V, E)$ and a set of data connections where the ith connection originates at node s_i and terminates at node t_i. In MFP, each connection also has a non-negative weight w_i. The goal in MFP is to find the data rate(s) at which the source(s) s_i can inject data into the network, the routes that are used to transport the data for each connection, and a feasible link schedule which supports the routing, in such a way that the *total* weighted rate of data injection across all the connections is maximized. This formulation does not consider any notion of fairness across per-connection throughput but is concerned only with the aggregate throughput. In contrast, the goal in MCFP is to maximize the minimum throughput which we support across all the connections.

We note that both MFP and MCFP are special cases of the MAXFLOW problem which we define now. The central notion in MAXFLOW is the *fairness index* $\lambda \in [0, 1]$, which denotes the ratio between the minimum and maximum connection rates: $\lambda = \frac{\min_i r_i}{\max_i r_i}$, where r_i denotes the throughput for the ith connection. MAXFLOW seeks a choice of (i) per-connection throughput such that the fairness index is at least λ (specified as part of the input), which is captured by linear constraints of the form $r_i \leq r_j/\lambda$, for all $i \neq j$; (ii) routing which determines how the data for each connection is transported across the network, and (iii) a feasible link schedule which can support the end-to-end data flows, with the objective of maximizing the aggregate weighted connection throughput. The setting where λ equals 0 corresponds to MFP (since the constraints $r_i \leq \infty$ which result in this case do not place any limits on the individual rates), while the setting where λ and the weights associated with the connections equal 1 corresponds to MCFP.

MFP, MCFP, and MAXFLOW are variations of classical multicommodity flow problems that have been studied in the context of *wired* networks [2], with the added constraint that transmissions on links that interfere with each other cannot be scheduled simultaneously. Thus the task of finding optimal multicommodity flows in wireless networks becomes considerably more complicated. In any such problem involving dynamic packet injections, a central question is that of *stability*: a protocol is said to be stable if every packet incurs a bounded delay and, consequently, all buffers have bounded sizes. We seek stable cross-layer protocols that jointly optimize the end-to-end rate allocation, routing, and the scheduling components in order to maximize the throughput objective of interest to us.

5.3   Capacity of Random Wireless Networks

In this section, we focus our analysis on randomly distributed wireless networks. The specific setting we will investigate is as follows. The wireless network is constructed by placing n nodes uniformly at random within a unit square.[1] The *maxRange* for each node is sufficiently large so that any node in the network is capable of directly communicating with any other node through a suitable choice of transmission range. Link capacities are uniform, and $c(e) = W$ for all links e in the network; here W is a fixed positive constant. There are n network connections with each of the n nodes being the source for exactly one of the connections. Source s_i for connection i is paired with a destination t_i, which is a randomly chosen network node; further, the choice of the destination nodes is made such that each node is a destination for exactly a single connection. Thus, we may view the vector of destinations as a random permutation of the corresponding vector of sources. Let $MCF(n)$ be the random variable which denotes the maximum rate at which the n connections can simultaneously inject data into the network, while maintaining network stability (i.e., $MCF(n)$ denotes the maximum multicommodity flow value). The main question which we seek to answer is the following: how does $\mathbf{E}[MCF(n)]$ evolve[2] as a function of n; i.e., how does the expected per-connection throughput which can be supported by a random network evolve asymptotically, as the number of nodes grows to ∞.

Gupta and Kumar [36] answered this question by proving that in a random ad hoc network, the expected per-connection throughput is $\Theta\left(\sqrt{\frac{1}{n\log n}}\right)$. This is one of the earliest results in the field of wireless network capacity and has influenced much subsequent work in this area [14, 32, 35, 46, 57, 66, 67, 83]. The key intuition behind this result is as follows. A specific transmission creates an interference zone which prohibits other transmissions from occurring in the vicinity of this region; the greater the distance between the transmitter and receiver, the larger the interference zone. There is thus an incentive for multi-hop transmissions and for lowering

---

[1] Note that the size of the square does not vary with n. The results discussed here will change if the size of the square varies with n.

[2] $\mathbf{E}[\cdot]$ denotes expectation over a distribution which is usually clear from the context.

the ranges of individual transmissions as much as possible. However, smaller individual transmission ranges lead to an increased number of hops traversed by the data from its source to the destination. This in turn leads to an increase in the fraction of the time each node needs to spend in relaying the traffic of other connections which it is not a part of. At the optimal point which balances these two considerations, the per-connection throughput delivered by the network turns out to be $\Theta\left(\sqrt{\frac{1}{n\log n}}\right)$ in expectation.

Our presentation of this result deviates significantly from the analysis of Gupta and Kumar [36]. In Section 5.3.1, we establish an upper bound of $O\left(\frac{1}{\sqrt{n}}\right)$ on the per-connection throughput in a random wireless network – a slightly weaker upper bound than the $O\left(\frac{1}{\sqrt{n\log n}}\right)$ bound derived in [36]; here, we make use of the analysis techniques developed by Yi et al. [83]. In Section 5.3.2, using the techniques developed by Kulkarni and Viswanath [47], we describe a joint routing and scheduling protocol which achieves a per-connection throughput of $\Omega\left(\frac{1}{\sqrt{n\log n}}\right)$. The analysis techniques of both [47, 83] are significantly simpler than [36], while they retain much of the geometric flavor and analytical insights that underlie the results of [36].

5.3.1 Capacity Upper Bound

Let us start with the following assumptions.

(A1) The network supports a per-connection throughput of λ. Thus, there is a T-second window during which it transports λnT bits across all the connections.

(A2) The average distance between the source and destination of a connection is $\overline{L}$.

(A3) Let the transport rate of a connection be defined as the product of its connection throughput and the distance between its source and destination. Define the transport capacity of the network to be the sum of the per-connection transport rates. (A1) and (A2) imply that a transport capacity of $\lambda n\overline{L}$ bit-meters per second is achieved.

Consider the bth bit, where $1 \le b \le \lambda nT$. Suppose it moves from its source to its destination in a sequence of $h(b)$ hops, where the hth hop covers a distance of r_b^h units. From (A2) we have

$$\sum_{b=1}^{\lambda nT}\sum_{h=1}^{h(b)} r_b^h \ge \lambda nT\overline{L}. \tag{5.1}$$

Let $\Gamma(h, b, s)$ be the binary indicator variable which is set to one if the hth hop of bit b occurs during slot s. Since at most half the network nodes can act as a transmitter during any slot, we have

$$\sum_{b=1}^{\lambda nT}\sum_{h=1}^{h(b)} \Gamma(h, b, s) \le \frac{Wn}{2} \quad \text{(since } \tau\text{, the slot length, is 1 s).} \tag{5.2}$$

Summing over all slots over the T-second period, we have:

$$H \doteq \sum_{b=1}^{\lambda n T} h(b) \leq \frac{WTn}{2}. \tag{5.3}$$

From the definition of the Tx-model of interference, disks of radius $(1+\Delta)$ times the lengths of hops centered at the transmitters are disjoint. Ignoring edge effects, all these disks are within the unit square. Since at most W bits can be carried in slot s from a transmitter to a receiver, we have:

$$\sum_{b=1}^{\lambda n T} \sum_{h=1}^{h(b)} \Gamma(h,b,s)\pi(1+\Delta)^2 (r_b^h)^2 \leq W \cdot 1. \tag{5.4}$$

Note that the unit on each side of the above Equation is bit-meter^2. Summing over all the slots gives

$$\sum_{b=1}^{\lambda n T} \sum_{h=1}^{h(b)} \pi(1+\Delta)^2 (r_b^h)^2 \leq WT \tag{5.5}$$

$$\Rightarrow$$

$$\sum_{b=1}^{\lambda n T} \sum_{h=1}^{h(b)} \frac{1}{H}(r_b^h)^2 \leq \frac{WT}{\pi(1+\Delta)^2 H}. \tag{5.6}$$

Since the quadratic function in Equation (5.6) is convex, we have

$$\left(\sum_{b=1}^{\lambda n T} \sum_{h=1}^{h(b)} \frac{1}{H}(r_b^h) \right)^2 \leq \sum_{b=1}^{\lambda n T} \sum_{h=1}^{h(b)} \frac{1}{H}(r_b^h)^2.$$

Hence,

$$\sum_{b=1}^{\lambda n T} \sum_{h=1}^{h(b)} \frac{1}{H}(r_b^h) \leq \sqrt{\frac{WT}{\pi(1+\Delta)^2} \cdot H}. \tag{5.7}$$

Combing Equation (5.7) with Equation (5.1) yields

$$\lambda n T \overline{L} \leq \sqrt{\frac{WTH}{\pi(1+\Delta)^2}}. \tag{5.8}$$

Combining Equation (5.3) with the above yields:

$$\lambda n \overline{L} \leq \frac{1}{\sqrt{2\pi}} \frac{1}{(1+\Delta)} W \sqrt{n} \quad \text{bit-meters / second} \tag{5.9}$$

$\overline{L}$, which is the average distance between a source and the destination of a connection is easily seen to be a constant independent of n. This implies that $\lambda = O(\frac{1}{\sqrt{n}})$, which is the requisite upper-bound.

5.3.2 Lower Bound

We will show that the per-connection throughput achievable in a random wireless network is $\Omega(\sqrt{\frac{1}{n\log n}})$ with high probability, following the two-step approach of Kulkarni and Viswanath [47]. First, we will consider the closely related problem of permutation routing problem in a *mesh*. Next, we will establish a correspondence between the problem of throughput maximization in a random wireless network to the mesh routing problem.

Reduction to mesh routing (step 1): We begin by dividing the unit square which contains the wireless network into $\frac{1}{s_n^2}$ squares of area s_n^2 each by drawing equi-spaced horizontal and vertical lines of spacing s_n. We will use the term *squarelets* to denote the smaller squares in the mesh. We will also assume that each squarelet has at least one node (later, we will show that this event happens with high probability in a random wireless network for a suitably chosen value of s_n). We define *crowding factor*, c_n, to be the maximum number of nodes in any squarelet.

We now describe a few key elements of our scheduling strategy. First, when a specific node transmits a packet, it will do so only to a node in its own squarelet or to a node in one of the four squarelets adjacent to itself. The reason for localizing the transmissions in such a manner is that other squarelets that are sufficiently far away can transmit simultaneously without interference. This naturally leads to "equivalence classes" of squarelets such that nodes within the same class can transmit simultaneously.

Specifically, for each squarelet s, its equivalence class is defined to be those squarelets whose vertical and horizontal separation from s is an integral multiple of K squarelets, where the integer K will be defined below. The value of the parameter K can be computed in terms of Δ as follows. Since transmissions are either within a squarelet or between neighboring squarelets only, the maximum distance between the endpoints of a transmission is $\sqrt{5}s_n$. By our construction, the minimum distance between two transmitters in the same equivalence class is $(K-2)s_n$. By our interference condition, we require $(K-2)s_n > 2(1+\Delta)\sqrt{5}s_n$, or $K > 4+2\sqrt{5}\Delta$. Thus, we could set $K = 5 + \lceil 2\sqrt{5}\Delta \rceil$. We observe that the number of equivalence classes is K^2, a fixed constant dependent only on Δ.

We are almost ready to describe our scheduling strategy. As a prelude, we first discuss the closely related problem of routing in mesh networks. Consider a square grid whose lattice points are occupied by ℓ^2 processors; thus, there are ℓ processors in each row and column. Each processor can communicate with its adjacent vertical and horizontal neighbors in a single slot simultaneously (with one *packet* being a unit of communication with any neighbor during a slot). Suppose each processor is the source and destination of exactly k packets. The $k \times k$ *permutation routing* problem is that of routing all the $k\ell^2$ packets to their destinations. The following result characterizes the achievable performance of $k \times k$ permutation routing algorithms.

Lemma 5.1. *([40, 52]) $k \times k$ permutation routing in a $\ell \times \ell$ mesh can be performed deterministically in $\frac{k\ell}{2} + o(k\ell)$ steps with maximum queue size at each processor equal to k.*

We are ready to describe the scheduling strategy for our random wireless network by reducing it to a permutation routing problem on an $\ell \times \ell$ mesh. We first map the nodes in each specific squarelet in the random wireless network onto a particular processor in the mesh by letting $\ell = \frac{1}{s_n}$. Next, we let each node have m packets and since a squarelet has a maximum of c_n nodes, we set $k = mc_n$. By fixing the buffer size of each node to be $k = mc_n$, we are ready to map the routing and scheduling algorithm of Lemma 5.1 to the wireless network.

Each processor in the mesh can transmit and receive up to four packets in the same slot. However, in the wireless network, communication is restricted between users in neighboring squarelets and only nodes in the same equivalence class of squarelets can transmit simultaneously during a slot. Further, a user can either transmit or receive at most one packet in each slot. We now *serialize* the routing protocol on the mesh network to meet the above constraints. First, we serialize the transmissions of the processors that are not in the same equivalence class. Since there are K^2 equivalence classes in all, this expands the total number of steps in the mesh routing algorithm by a factor of K^2. Next, we serialize the transmissions of a single processor. Since there are no more than four simultaneous transmissions of any processor, this increases the total number of steps in the mesh routing by a further factor of 4.

Thus, we can map the mesh routing algorithm to the wireless network and conclude that m packets of each of the $\frac{n}{2}$ nodes reach their destination in number of slots equal to $4K^2 \frac{k\ell}{2} = \frac{2K^2 mc_n}{s_n}$. This yields the following proposition.

Proposition 5.1. *Assuming each squarelet has at least one node, the per-connection throughput for a network with squarelet size s_n and crowding factor c_n is $\Omega\left(\frac{s_n}{c_n}\right)$.*

We now conclude our proof by showing that, if we set $s_n = \sqrt{\frac{3\log n}{n}}$, then with high probability, no squarelet is empty and $c_n \leq 3e \log n$. We begin by proving the non-empty squarelets claim. The probability that any fixed squarelet is empty is equal to $(1 - s_n^2)^n$. From a simple union bound and using the fact that there are $\frac{1}{s_n^2}$ squarelets, we conclude that the probability that at least one squarelet is empty is upper-bounded by $\frac{(1-s_n^2)^n}{s_n^2}$. Combining this with the fact that $1 - x \leq e^{-x}$, and $s_n = \sqrt{\frac{3\log n}{n}}$, we see that the probability of at least one squarelet being empty is at most $\frac{1}{n^2}$, which yields a high probability of $1 - \frac{1}{n^2}$ for the complementary event.

We now prove the bound on the crowding factor. Fix a specific squarelet. The number of nodes in this squarelet is a binomial random variable (say, Z_n) with parameters (s_n^2, n). By Chernoff–Hoeffding bounds [24, 38], for any $a > 0$ and $\theta > 0$, we have

$$\Pr[Z_n > a \log n] \leq \frac{\mathrm{E}[e^{\theta Z_n}]}{e^{\theta a \log n}},$$

$$\mathrm{E}[e^{\theta Z_n}] = (1 + (e^{\theta} - 1) \cdot s_n^2)^n$$

$$\leq n^{3(e^{\theta} - 1)},$$

$$\Pr[Z_n > 3e \log n] \leq \frac{1}{n^3} \quad \text{(setting } \theta = 1 \text{ and } a = 3e\text{)},$$

$$\Pr[c_n \geq 3e \log n] \leq \frac{1}{n^2} \quad \text{(by a simple union bound)}.$$

The above bound on the crowding factor, along with the value of s_n and Proposition 5.1, yields the requisite result.

5.4 Capacity of Arbitrary Wireless Networks

In this section, we will investigate the MAXFLOW problem in the context of a given wireless network which is specified as part of the input. Recall the definition of MAXFLOW from Section 5.2.2. In Section 5.3, we derived closed-form analytical bounds on the asymptotic capacity of a random wireless network as a function of the number of network nodes. In general, such closed-form asymptotic bounds do not exist for arbitrary networks whose node locations and traffic requirements are specified as part of the input (rather than chosen at random). Instead, our focus will be on the algorithmic aspects of network capacity; specifically, we seek to design a polynomial time algorithm for optimally solving MAXFLOW. Unfortunately, as shown in [65], this is unlikely to be the case as MAXFLOW is NP-Hard when we consider the problem under the Tx-model of interference. Given that MAXFLOW is NP-Hard, we are instead forced to ask if there exists a near-optimal (polynomial time) approximation algorithm[3] for MAXFLOW? We answer this question in the affirmative by developing a 5-approximation for MAXFLOW under the Tx-model. The techniques developed here can be suitably adopted to derive near-optimal approximation algorithms for a variety of other geometric interference models as well.

5.4.1 An Approximation Algorithm for MAXFLOW

In this section, we present a 5-approximation algorithm for the MAXFLOW problem under the Tx-model of interference, which is due to Kumar et al. [49]. A novel link-scheduling mechanism namely inductive scheduling underlies this

---

[3] Recall that an α-approximation algorithm for a maximization problem is one which is always guaranteed to produce a solution whose value is within a factor of α from that of the optimal solution.

approximation algorithm. The basic idea behind the inductive scheduling scheme is to first perform a total ordering of the links according to a precedence function, and schedule the links sequentially according to this order. By suitably changing the precedence function defined on the links, Kumar et al. [49, 50] show how the inductive scheduling scheme leads to provably good algorithms for a variety of geometric interference models. We begin by establishing certain necessary conditions which must be satisfied by the link-rate vector in order for it to be scheduled by any link-scheduling algorithm. This also highlights the geometric underpinnings of the inductive scheduling scheme.

5.4.1.1   Geometric Packing Based Necessary Conditions for Link Scheduling

Recall that for a link $e = (u, v) \in E$, $I(e)$ denotes the set of links which interfere with e. Let $I_{\geq(e)}$ be defined as follows.

Definition 5.1. $I_{\geq}(e) = \{(p, q) : (p, q) \in I(e) \text{ and } ||p, q|| \geq ||u, v||\}$.

$I_{\geq}(e)$ is the subset of links in $I(e)$ which are greater than or equal to e in length. Let $X_{e,t}$ be the indicator variable which is defined as follows:

$$X_{e,t} = \begin{cases} 1 \text{ if } e \text{ transmits successfully at time } t \\ 0 \text{ otherwise.} \end{cases} \tag{5.10}$$

The following claim holds.

Claim. In any link schedule,

$$\forall e \in E, \quad \forall t \quad X_{e,t} + \sum_{f \in I_{\geq}(e)} X_{f,t} \leq \kappa, \tag{5.11}$$

where κ is a fixed constant that depends only on the interference model. In particular, for the Tx-model of interference, $\kappa = 5$.

Proof. We first note that in the Tx-model of interference, we may treat interference as occurring between transmitting nodes rather than links, since the interference condition depends solely on the transmission ranges of the transmitters and the distance between them. For any node u, define $I(u)$ and $I_{\geq}(u)$ analogous to the definition for links as follows: $I(u) = \{w : ||u, w|| < (1 + \Delta) \cdot (range(u) + range(w))\}$. $I_{\geq}(u) = \{w : range(w) \geq range(u) \text{ and } w \in I(u)\}$. For any link $e = (u, u')$, $I(e)$ is now defined as follows: $I(e) = \{e' = (w, v) : w \in I(u)\}$. Similarly, $I_{\geq}(e) = \{e' = (w, v) : w \in I_{\geq}(u)\}$. In order to complete the proof of the claim, we only need to show that for any node u, at most five nodes in $I_{\geq}(u)$ can simultaneously transmit in any time slot without interfering with each other.

Consider any node u and a large disk centered at u which contains all the nodes in the network. Consider any sector which subtends an angle of $\frac{\pi}{3}$ at u. Let $w, w' \in I_{\geq}(u)$ be two nodes in this sector. Without loss of generality, assume that $||u, w'|| \geq ||u, w||$. It is easy to see that $||w, w'|| \leq ||u, w'||$. Further, we have $range(w') \geq range(u)$. Thus, w' has a bigger range than u and is closer to w than u. Since u and w interfere with each other, clearly, w and w' also each interfere with each other and hence cannot transmit simultaneously. Thus the angle subtended at u by any two simultaneous transmitters in the set $I_{\geq}(u)$ is strictly greater than $\frac{\pi}{3}$. Hence, there can be at most five successful transmitters from this set which proves the claim.

Let $\mathbf{f}(e)$ denote a link-flow vector which specifies the rate $f(e)$ which must be supported on each link e. Define the utilization of link e to be $\frac{f(e)}{c(e)}$: this is the *fraction of the time* link e is successfully transmitting data in order to meet its rate requirement. Let $\mathbf{x}$ denote the corresponding link-utilization vector whose components are the $x(e)$-values. Taking a time-average of Equation (5.11) yields the following lemma which imposes a simple necessary condition for link-flow stability.

Lemma 5.2. *Let κ be the constant in Claim 5.4.1.1. $\mathbf{x}$ is a stable link-utilization vector only if the following holds:*

$$\forall e \in E, \quad x(e) + \sum_{f \in I_{\geq}(e)} x(f) \leq \kappa.$$

5.4.1.2 Inductive Scheduling Algorithm

In this section we present the inductive scheduling algorithm for scheduling a link-flow vector, whose corresponding link-utilization vector is $\mathbf{x}$. In Section 5.4.1.3, we analyze conditions under which this algorithm yields a stable schedule (and hence sufficient conditions for link-flow stability). The algorithm works as follows: time is divided into uniform and contiguous windows or *frames* of length w, where w is a sufficiently large positive integer such for all e, $w \cdot x(e)$ is integral. The algorithm employs a subroutine called *frame-scheduling* which specifies a schedule for each link e within each frame. This schedule is repeated periodically for every frame to obtain the final schedule. We now present the details of the frame-scheduling algorithm whose pseudo-code is presented in Algorithm 1 (referred to as INDUCTIVE SCHEDULER).

```
1: for all e ∈ E do
2:     s(e) = Φ
3: Sort E in decreasing order of length of the links.
4: for i = 1 to |E| do
5:     e = E[i]
6:     s'(e) = ⋃_{f∈I(e)} s(f)
7:     s(e) = any subset of W \ s'(e) of size w · x(e)
```

Algorithm 1: INDUCTIVE SCHEDULER$(\mathbf{x}, w)$

Consider a single frame W whose time slots are numbered $\{1, \ldots, w\}$. For each link e, the subroutine assigns a subset of slots $s(e) \subseteq W$ such that the following hold:

1. $|s(e)| = w \cdot x(e)$, i.e., each link receives a fraction $x(e)$ of time slots.
2. $\forall f \in I(e), s(f) \cap s(e) = \Phi$, i.e., two links which interfere with each other are not assigned the same time slot.

The pseudo-code for sequential frame-scheduling is provided in Algorithm INDUC-TIVE SCHEDULER. For all links $e \in E$, the set $s(e)$ (set of time slots in W which are currently assigned to e) is initialized to Φ. Links in E are processed sequentially in the decreasing order of their lengths. Let the current link being processed be e. Let $s'(e)$ denote the set of time slots in W which have already been assigned to links in $I(e)$ (and hence cannot be assigned to e): $s'(e) = \bigcup_{f \in I_{\geq}(e)} s(f)$. In the remaining slots $W \setminus s'(e)$, we choose any subset of $w \cdot x(e)$ time slots and assign them to $s(e)$. The running time of this algorithm depends on w, and if the $x(e)$'s are arbitrarily small, w could become exponential in n in order to satisfy this condition (this still does not affect the stability of the scheduling algorithm). However, as we discuss in Section 5.4.1.3, this issue can be addressed through a simple flow scaling technique which ensures that the link utilizations are not "too small"; this allows us to bound w by a polynomial in n and consequently the INDUCTIVE SCHEDULER algorithm runs in polynomial time.

5.4.1.3   Link-Flow Stability: Sufficient Conditions

In this section, we analyze conditions under which INDUCTIVE SCHEDULER achieves stability; hence this also yields sufficient conditions for link-flow stability. Recall that $s(e)$ is the set of time slots assigned to link e within a single frame. It is easy to see that INDUCTIVE SCHEDULER produces a conflict-free schedule.

The following lemma proposes a sufficient condition for which INDUCTIVE SCHEDULER yields a *valid* schedule, i.e., appropriate number of slots are chosen for each link within a frame.

Lemma 5.3. *The link-flow scheduling algorithm produces a valid schedule for* **x** *if the following holds:*

$$\forall e \in E, \quad x(e) + \sum_{f \in I_{\geq}(e)} x(f) \leq 1.$$

Proof. The schedule produced by Algorithm INDUCTIVE SCHEDULER is stable if step 8 is well defined, i.e., there are always $w \cdot x(e)$ slots available in the set $W \setminus s'(e)$. We now show that this is the case for all links. Assume otherwise, i.e., there exists a link e such that $|W \setminus s'(e)| < w \cdot x(e)$. Hence,

$$|W| < |s'(e)| + w \cdot x(e)$$
$$\leq |\bigcup_{f \in I_{\geq}(e)} s(f)| + w \cdot x(e)$$

$$\leq \sum_{f \in I_{\geq}(e)} |s(f)| + w \cdot x(e)$$

$$\leq \sum_{f \in I_{\geq}(e)} w \cdot x(f) + w \cdot x(e).$$

Dividing both sides above by w and rearranging the terms, we have

$$x(e) + \sum_{f \in I_{\geq}(e)} x(f) > 1.$$

which contradicts our assumption. This completes the proof of the lemma. $\square$

Suppose we have a set of end-to-end connections with rates r_i between each s_i, t_i pair. Let $r_i(e)$ denote the amount of connection i flow that is carried by link e. For each $e \in E$, let $f(e) = \sum_i r_i(e)$ denote the total flow on link e, and let $x(e) = \frac{f(e)}{c(e)}$ denote its utilization. Assuming that the packet injections by the connections into the network are uniform over time, if $\mathbf{x}$ satisfies the conditions of Lemma 5.3, the following result shows that we get a stable schedule, i.e., each packet is delivered in a bounded amount of time to its destination.

Observation 5.1 *If the vector $\mathbf{x}$ above satisfies the conditions of Lemma 5.3, each packet is delivered in at most Wn steps.*

Proof. Assume that W is such that $W \cdot \frac{r_i(e)}{c(e)}$ is integral for each i and e. Consider any connection i. The number of packets injected for this connection during the window of W is exactly $r_i \cdot W$. For each link e, partition the $Wx(e)$ slots into $\frac{r_i(e)}{c(e)} \cdot W$ slots for each connection i. Then, clearly, for each connection i, each packet can be made to move along one link in W steps. This completes the proof. $\square$

5.4.1.4 Scheduling End-to-End Flows

We now combine the ideas presented thus far in this section in the form of the INDUCTIVELP. The solution to this linear program, along with the inductive scheduling algorithm, yields a provably good solution to the MAXFLOW problem. The INDUCTIVELP formulation is presented below.

In the formulation, $\mathscr{P}_i$ denotes the set of all paths between source s_i and destination t_i of connection i. For any $p \in \mathscr{P}_i$, $r(p)$ denotes the data rate associated with the path p: this is the rate at which data is transferred from s_i to t_i along p. Recall that r_i denotes the total rate at which source s_i injects data for destination t_i: i.e., thus $r_i = \sum_{p:\, p \in \mathscr{P}_i} r(p)$; for any link $e \in E$, $x(e)$ denotes the total utilization of e.

$$\max \qquad \sum_{i \in C} w_i \cdot r_i \qquad \text{subject to}$$

$$\forall i \in C, \qquad r_i = \sum_{p \in \mathscr{P}_i} r(p)$$

$$\forall i \in C, \forall j \in C \setminus \{i\}, \quad r_i \geq \lambda r_j,$$

$$\forall e \in E, \quad x(e) = \frac{\sum_{p:\, e \in p} r(p)}{c(e)},$$

$$\forall e \in E, \quad x(e) + \sum_{f \in I_{\geq}(e)} x(f) \leq 1,$$

$$\forall i \in C, \forall p \in \mathscr{P}_i, \quad r(p) \geq 0.$$

We make the following observations about the above LP. First, we observe that the size of this program may not be polynomial in the size of the network G as there could be exponentially many paths $\mathscr{P}_i$. However, using standard techniques, the same program could be equivalently stated as a polynomial-size network flow formulation [2]; we choose to present this standard formulation here for ease of exposition. Next, we note that the stability conditions derived in Lemmas 5.2 and 5.3 are crucial for modeling the effect of interference in the LP and still guarantee a constant-factor performance ratio. Specifically, in the INDUCTIVELP, the fourth set of constraints capture wireless interference. These constraints along with the INDUCTIVE SCHEDULER algorithm ensure that the data flows computed by the LP can be feasibly scheduled. Further, the objective value of this LP is at most a constant factor away from an optimal solution because of the following reason: suppose the optimal schedule induces a utilization $x^*(e)$ on each link e; these rates need to satisfy the conditions of Lemma 5.3. Hence, scaling down the optimal end-to-end rates and hence the optimal link rates by a factor κ (the constant which appears in Lemma 5.2) results in a feasible solution to the INDUCTIVELP. These observations lead to the following theorem.

Theorem 5.1. *The* INDUCTIVELP *formulation always results in a solution which can be stably scheduled. Further, the value of the objective function computed by the* INDUCTIVELP *is within a constant factor from the optimal solution to the corresponding flow problem. In particular, the value of this constant factor is 5 for the Tx-model of interference.*

We now address the time complexity of the INDUCTIVE SCHEDULER algorithm. Recall from the discussion in Section 5.4.1.2 that the INDUCTIVE SCHEDULER algorithm could potentially run in exponential time if some of the $x(e)$'s are very small (e.g., inverse exponential). We now discuss a polynomial time implementation of INDUCTIVE SCHEDULER. For ease of exposition, we restrict ourselves to a simpler version of the INDUCTIVELP formulation where the third set of constraints (which capture fairness) are absent, and where $c(e) = 1.0$ for all e; Kumar et al. [51] show how these assumptions can be relaxed. Let $(\mathbf{x}, \mathbf{r})$ be an optimum *basic feasible* solution to the INDUCTIVELP formulation, and let $\mathscr{Q}_i = \{p \in \mathscr{P}_i : r(p) > 0\}$ be the set of paths for connection i which have positive rate. Then, by definition of a basic feasible solution, we have $|\mathscr{Q}_i| = O(k^2 + m)$ (which is the number of constraints in the LP), where k and m are the number of connections and edges respectively [69]. In other words, there are at most $O(k^2 + m)$ paths per connection carrying positive flow in this solution, leading to a total of $O(k^3 + km)$ such paths. Let $m' = \max\{k, m\}$. Next, define $(\mathbf{x}', \mathbf{r}')$ where $r'(p) = \max\{r(p), 1/m'^5\}$, i.e., this solution is obtained by rounding up the flow on paths which carry very low flow (i.e., less than $1/m'^5$) to $1/m'^5$. This rate vector could be such that $x'(e) + \sum_{f \in I_{\geq}(e)} x'(f)$ exceeds 1 for some edges e. However, we can show that for each $e \in E$, we have $x'(e) + \sum_{f \in I_{\geq}(e)} x'(f) \leq 1 + O(1/m')$. This is because there are at most $O(m'^3)$ paths in all, and even if all of these paths are rounded up, they would still carry a total flow of at most $O(1/m'^2)$. This implies that $x'(f) \leq x(f) + 1/m'^2$. Therefore $x'(e) + \sum_{f \in I_{\geq}(e)} x'(f) \leq x(e) + \sum_{f \in I_{\geq}(e)} x(f) + m' \cdot O(1/m'^2) \leq 1 + O(1/m')$. It now follows that the solution $(\mathbf{x}'', \mathbf{r}'')$ defined by $r''(p) = r'(p)/(1 + O(1/m'))$ is feasible, which leads to a total throughput of at least $\sum_i w_i r_i/(1 + O(1/m'))$. Since $x''(e) \geq 1/m'^5$, it follows from our discussion in Section 5.4.1.2 that the algorithm INDUCTIVE SCHEDULER runs in polynomial time.

5.5 Dynamic Control for Network Stability

In Section 5.4, we showed how to formulate and approximately solve MAXFLOW – a global optimization problem for determining the end-to-end connection rates, routing, and link scheduling, with the objective of maximizing a global throughput objective. Our focus in this section is the *dynamic back-pressure algorithm* – a joint scheme for network routing and link scheduling. The basic guarantee provided by the dynamic back-pressure algorithm is as follows: assuming that the per-connection arrival rates are within the network layer capacity region,[4] the algorithm will provide a routing and scheduling strategy which will maintain network stability. The dynamic back-pressure algorithm is grounded in queuing theory and has a very different flavor when compared with the inductive scheduling algorithm of Section 5.4. The stability guarantee in Section 5.4 implicitly assumed that data arrivals at each connection are uniformly spaced over time. In contrast, the dynamic back-pressure scheme handles a broad class of arrival processes. Further, one of the key strengths of this algorithm is its ability to seamlessly handle time variant arrival rates as well as link capacity values.[5] The objective of the back-pressure scheme we present is global end-to-end throughput optimization; instead, it is best viewed as a mechanism for stabilizing the network whenever the end-to-end connection rate vector is within the network capacity region (this needs to be guaranteed through possibly *out-of-band* flow control mechanisms).

Our description in this section is a simplified version of the description of the back-pressure algorithm by Georgiadis et al. [33]. We begin with a rigorous

---

[4] The network layer capacity region consists of all connection rate vectors that can be stably scheduled by *any* routing and scheduling strategy. This notion is made rigorous in Section 5.5.1.

[5] For ease of exposition, we will not consider the time varying aspects of the algorithm in this chapter.

description of the network layer capacity region in Section 5.5.1. We then describe
the dynamic back-pressure scheme in Section 5.5.2 and prove its stability property
in Section 5.5.3.

5.5.1 Network Layer Capacity Region

Consider a system comprising of a single queue. Let $A(t)$ denote its arrival process:
i.e., $A(t)$ denotes the amount of new data entering the queue at slot t; we assume
that this data arrives at the end of slot t and hence cannot be serviced during that
slot. Let μ denote the transmission rate of the queue (this is the amount of data that
the queue can service during each slot). Let $U(t)$ represent the backlog of the queue
at the beginning of slot t. This process evolves according to the following equation:

$$U(t + 1) = \max\{U(t) - \mu(t), 0\} + A(t). \tag{5.12}$$

Definition 5.2. A queue is *strongly stable* if

$$\limsup_{t \to \infty} \frac{1}{t} \sum_{\tau=0}^{t-1} \mathbf{E}[U(\tau)] < \infty.$$

In the setting of our wireless network, let the *exogenous* arrival process $A^i(t)$
denote the amount of data generated by connection i at the source s_i at slot t; in
order to analyze network capacity, we assume that the $A^i(t)$ processes satisfy the
following properties for *admissible inputs*.

Definition 5.3. An arrival process $A(t)$ is admissible with rate λ if

1. The time averaged expected arrival rate satisfies

$$\lim_{t \to \infty} \frac{1}{t} \sum_{\tau=0}^{t-1} \mathbf{E}[A(\tau)] = \lambda.$$

2. Let $H(t)$ represent the history until time t, i.e., all events that take place during
   slots $\{0, \ldots, t-1\}$. There exists a finite value $A_{\max}$ such that $\mathbf{E}[A^2(t) \mid H(t)] \leq A_{max}^2$ for all slots t and all possible events $H(t)$.
3. For any $\delta > 0$, there exists an interval size T, possibly dependent on δ, such that
   for any initial time t_0:

$$\mathbf{E}\left[\frac{1}{T} \sum_{k=0}^{T-1} A(t_0 + k) \mid H(t_0)\right] \leq \lambda + \delta.$$

We will find it convenient to view the network as being operated by a *network controller*. The network controller determines the routing and scheduling decisions made by the network elements (nodes and links) at each time step. Specifically, the network controller chooses the set of (mutually conflict-free) links which are allowed to transmit during each slot, as well as the fraction of the link capacity for each link which is allocated to various connections.

Recall that $A^i(t)$ represents the exogenous arrival process for connection i. Suppose the $A^i(t)$ processes are admissible with average rates λ_i; let $\lambda = \langle \lambda_i \rangle$ denote the arrival rate vector. We now define the network layer capacity region.

Definition 5.4. The network layer capacity region Λ is the closure of the set of all arrival rate vectors $\langle \lambda_i \rangle$ that can be stably serviced by the network, considering all possible strategies available for the network controller to perform routing and scheduling, including those strategies with perfect knowledge of future arrivals.

In order to construct the network layer capacity region, we first consider the capacity region of a *wired* network with no interference constraints. A wired network is characterized by a constant matrix $G_{(u,v)}$ where $G_{(u,v)}$ is the fixed rate at which data can be transferred over link (u, v) of the network. The network capacity region in this scenario is described by the set of all arrival rate vectors $\langle \lambda_i \rangle$ which satisfy the following constraints [2]:

$$\forall i, \qquad \lambda_i = \sum_{p \in \mathscr{P}_i} r(p),$$

$$\forall e \in E, \qquad y(e) = \sum_{p:\, e \in p} r(p),$$

$$\forall e \in E, \qquad y(e) \le G_e,$$

$$\forall i, \forall p \in \mathscr{P}_i, \quad r(p) \ge 0.$$

In the above linear program, $\mathscr{P}_i$ denotes the set of all paths between s_i and t_i in the network, and $r(p)$ where $p \in \mathscr{P}_i$ denotes the amount of traffic carried by path p for connection i. In the language of network flows, the above program merely states that there is a feasible multicommodity flow to support the connection rate vector $\langle \lambda_i \rangle$. The crucial distinction between a wired network and a wireless network with interference constraints is that the achievable link rates during each time slot in a wireless network are not fixed, but depend on the network controller's actions which decide the set of links to be activated during each slot. Thus, instead of characterizing the wireless network using a single link rate matrix G, we use a collection of link-rate matrices Γ. The set Γ can be thought of as the set of all long-term link transmission rate matrices G that can be achieved by the network through a suitable choice of the network control policy. Γ can be characterized as follows.

Let $I \subseteq E$ denote a subset of links in the network. We will call I a conflict-free link set if *no* link within I interferes with any other link in I. Let $\mathscr{I}$ denote the set of all conflict-free link sets within the network. Suppose the network controller chooses to activate the set of links $I \in \mathscr{I}$ during a particular slot; then, the link transmission rates during this slot are given by the vector $\mu(I)$, each of whose components correspond to a specific link in the network; further, the component $\mu(e) = 0$ if $e \notin I$ and $\mu(e) = c(e)$ if $e \in I$. The set Γ can now be described as follows:

$$\Gamma \doteq Conv(\{\mu(I) \mid I \in \mathscr{I}\})$$

where $Conv(\mathscr{A})$ denotes the convex hull of set $\mathscr{A}$. Specifically, $Conv(\mathscr{A})$ is defined as the set of all convex combinations $\sum_i p_i \cdot a_i$ of elements $a_i \in \mathscr{A}$, where the co-efficients p_i are non-negative and add up to one.

Intuitively, we may think of Γ as the set of all long-term link transmission rate matrices G which are achievable through a randomized control policy and vice versa. Specifically, consider any matrix G such that $G = \sum_j p_j \cdot \mu(I_j)$, where the I_j's belong to $\mathscr{I}$, p_j's are non-negative and $\sum_j p_j = 1$. The randomized control policy, which selects a single conflict-free link set I_j during each slot at random with probability equal to p_j, achieves the rate matrix G in expectation. The above discussions lead to the following characterization of the network layer capacity region, which is proved formally in [61, 64]. Let $\mu^i_{(u,v)}(t)$ denote the data rate allocated to commodity i during slot t across the link (u, v) by the network controller.

Theorem 5.2. *The connection rate vector $\langle \lambda_i \rangle$ is within the network layer capacity region Λ if and only if there exists a randomized network control algorithm that makes valid $\mu^i_{(u,v)}(t)$ decisions, and yields*

$$\forall i, \; \mathbf{E}\left[\sum_{v:(s_i,v) \in E} \mu^i_{(s_i,v)}(t) - \sum_{u:(u,s_i) \in E} \mu^i_{(u,s_i)}(t) \right] = \lambda_i,$$

$$\forall i, \; \forall w \notin \{s_i, t_i\}, \; \mathbf{E}\left[\sum_{v:(w,v) \in E} \mu^i_{(w,v)}(t) - \sum_{u:(u,w) \in E} \mu^i_{(u,w)}(t) \right] = 0.$$

Observe that although the exogenous arrival processes are assumed to be admissible in Theorem 5.2, the capacity region captures all possible network control strategies, including those that result in non-admissible arrival processes at the individual network queues.

5.5.2 Dynamic Back-Pressure Algorithm

We now present the dynamic back-pressure algorithm. At every slot t, the network controller observes the queue backlog matrix $\mathbf{U}(t) = \langle U^i_v(t) \rangle$, where $U^i_v(t)$ denotes the amount of connection i data backlogged at node v, and performs the following action. For each link (v, w), let $i^*_{(v,w)}(t)$ denote the connection which maximizes the differential backlog (with ties broken arbitrarily): i.e., $i^*_{(v,w)}(t) = \arg\max_i \{U^i_v(t) - U^i_w(t)\}$. Let $W^*_{(v,w)}(t) = U^{i^*_{(v,w)}(t)}_v(t) - U^{i^*_{(v,w)}(t)}_w(t)$ denote the corresponding differential backlog. The network controller first chooses a conflict-free set I^* of links during time t by solving the following optimization program:

Choose conflict-free link set $I^* \in \mathscr{I}$ to maximize $\sum_{(u,v) \in I^*} W^*_{(u,v)}(t) \cdot c(u,v)$ (5.13)

The solution to the above program is a set I^* of mutually conflict-free links; these are the links that will be scheduled for transmission during slot t. For each link $(u,v) \in I^*$ such that $W^*_{(u,v)}(t) > 0$, the network controller schedules connection $i^*_{(u,v)}(t)$ to be transmitted on link (u,v) during slot t. If there is not enough backlogged data belonging to this connection (i.e., $U^{i^*_{(u,v)}(t)}_{(u,v)}(t) < c(u,v)$), dummy bits are used during the transmission to make up for the deficit. We emphasize that this is a joint scheduling and routing scheme, as both these aspects are addressed by the network control decisions made during each slot.

Before we begin the analysis of the back-pressure algorithm, we present an important property satisfied by it. Consider any valid resource allocation policy during slot t; suppose this policy assigns a rate of $\tilde{\mu}^i_{(u,v)}(t)$ to commodity i across link (u,v) at time t. Let $\mu^i_{(u,v)}(t)$ denote the corresponding values for the dynamic back-pressure algorithm. By the construction of the back-pressure algorithm, we have

$$\sum_{(u,v)} \sum_i \tilde{\mu}^i_{(u,v)}(t)[U^i_u(t) - U^i_v(t)] \leq \sum_{(u,v)} \sum_i \tilde{\mu}^i_{(u,v)}(t) W^*_{(u,v)}(t)$$

$$\leq \sum_{(u,v)} W^*_{(u,v)}(t) \cdot \mu(u,v).   (5.14)$$

Further, we have

$$\sum_i \sum_v U^i_v(t) \cdot \left[\sum_w \mu^i_{(v,w)}(t) - \sum_u \mu^i_{(u,v)}(t) \right] = \sum_{(u,v)} \sum_i \mu^i_{(u,v)}(t)[U^i_u(t) - U^i_v(t)]$$

Combining the simple identity above with Equation (5.14) yields the following important property of the back-pressure algorithm:

$$\sum_v \sum_i U^i_v(t) \left[\sum_w \tilde{\mu}^i_{(v,w)}(t) - \sum_u \tilde{\mu}^i_{(u,v)}(t) \right] \leq \sum_v \sum_i U^i_v(t) \left[\sum_w \mu^i_{(v,w)}(t) - \sum_u \mu^i_{(u,v)}(t) \right]$$

$$(5.15)$$

5.5.3 Analysis

We begin our analysis of the back-pressure algorithm with a brief introduction to the Lyapunov function framework. The Lyapunov function framework is an important queuing theoretic tool for proving stability results for networks and for designing stable network control algorithms [8,58,76]. The essential idea in this framework is to define the *Lyapunov function*, a non-negative function that is an aggregate measure of the lengths of all the queues within the system. The resource allocation choices made by the network controller are evaluated in terms of how they affect the Lyapunov function over time. The specific function which we will use in our analysis is defined as follows. Recall that $U(t)$ denotes the queue backlog matrix whose rows correspond to network nodes, columns correspond to connections, and the (u, i)th entry in the matrix corresponds to the backlog at node u for connection i. We define the Lyapunov function $L(U(t))$ as follows:

$$L(U(t)) = \sum_i \sum_v (U_v^i(t))^2. \tag{5.16}$$

Note that $L(U(t)) = 0$ only when all the queue backlogs are zero and $L(U(t))$ is large when one or more components in the backlog matrix is large. The following theorem, which is proved in [33], holds for the specific Lyapunov function described above. We note that claims similar to the following theorem can be made for a broader class of Lyapunov functions as well. Intuitively, the theorem ensures that the Lyapunov function incurs a non-negative *decrement* whenever the sum of queue backlogs is sufficiently large.

Theorem 5.3. *If there exist constants $B > 0$ and $\epsilon > 0$ such that for all slots t:*

$$E[L(U(t + 1)) - L(U(t)) \mid U(t)] \le B - \epsilon \sum_v \sum_i U_v^i(t) \tag{5.17}$$

then, the network is strongly stable.

We are now ready to prove the stability of the dynamic back-pressure algorithm, specifically, Theorem 5.4.

Theorem 5.4. *Let λ denote the vector of arrival rates; if there exists an $\epsilon > 0$ such that $\lambda + \varepsilon \in \Lambda$ (where ε is the vector such that $\varepsilon_i = 0$ if $\lambda_i = 0$, and $\varepsilon_i = \varepsilon$ otherwise), then the dynamic back-pressure algorithm stably services the arrivals.*

Proof. Let $A_v^i(t) = A^i(t)$ if $v = s_i$ and $A_v^i(t) = 0$ otherwise. For simplicity, we will assume in our proof that the arrivals $A_v^i(t)$ are i.i.d. over slots. We start with the following simple inequality. If $V, U, \mu, A \ge 0$ and $V \le \max\{U - \mu, 0\} + A$, then,

$$V^2 \le U^2 + \mu^2 + A^2 - 2U(\mu - A) \tag{5.18}$$

Combining Equation (5.18) with Equation (5.12), we get

$$U_v^i(t + 1)^2 \le U_v^i(t)^2 + \left(\sum_w \mu_{(v,w)}^i(t)\right)^2 + \left(A_v^i(t) + \sum_u \mu_{(u,v)}^i(t)\right)^2$$

$$- 2U_v^i(t) \cdot \left(\sum_w \mu_{(v,w)}^i(t) - A_v^i(t) - \sum_u \mu_{(u,v)}^i(t)\right)$$

Summing the above over all indices (v, i) (say, N in number) and combining it with the fact that sum of squares of non-negative real numbers is less than or equal to the square of the sum, it follows that

$$L(U(t + 1)) - L(U(t)) \le 2BN - 2\sum_v \sum_i U_v^i(t) \cdot \left(\sum_w \mu_{(v,w)}^i(t) - A_v^i(t) - \sum_u \mu_{(u,v)}^i(t)\right)$$

where $B \doteq \frac{1}{2N} \cdot \sum_v [(\max_w \mu(v, w))^2 + (\max_i A^i + \max_u \mu(u, v))^2]$. Taking conditional expectation yields the following

$$\mathbf{E}[L(U(t + 1)) - L(U(t)) \mid U(t)] \le 2BN + 2 \cdot \sum_i U_{s_i}^i(t) \cdot \mathbf{E}[A_{s_i}^i(t) \mid U(t)]$$

$$-2\mathbf{E}\left[\sum_v \sum_i U_v^i(t) \cdot \left(\sum_w \mu_{(v,w)}^i(t) - \sum_{(u,v)} \mu_{(u,v)}(t)\right) \mid U(t)\right] \quad (5.19)$$

Since the arrivals are i.i.d. over slots, we have $\mathbf{E}[A_{s_i}^i(t) \mid U(t)] = \lambda_i$ for all commodities i. Hence, we can rewrite Equation (5.19) as

$$\mathbf{E}[L(U(t + 1)) - L(U(t)) \mid U(t)] \le 2BN + 2 \cdot \sum_i U_{s_i}^i(t)\lambda_i$$

$$-2\mathbf{E}\left[\sum_v \sum_i U_v^i(t) \cdot \left(\sum_w \mu_{(v,w)}^i(t) - \sum_{(u,v)} \mu_{(u,v)}(t)\right) \mid U(t)\right] \quad (5.20)$$

Equation (5.15) guarantees that the dynamic back-pressure algorithm minimizes the last term on the R.H.S. of the above inequality over all possible alternatives. Noting that the randomized control strategy of Theorem 5.2 is one such alternative which handles the connection rate vector $\lambda + \varepsilon$, we obtain the following inequality:

$$\mathbf{E}[L(U(t + 1)) - L(U(t)) \mid U(t)] \le 2BN - 2\epsilon \sum_v \sum_i U_v^i(t) \quad (5.21)$$

Combing Eqn. (5.21) with Theorem 5.3 proves the stability of the back-pressure algorithm. $\square$

5.5.4 Complexity Issues

Recall from Section 5.4 that MAXFLOW is an NP-Hard optimization problem. A basic consequence of this fact is that given a collection of end-to-end connection rates, the problem of deciding if this end-to-end connection rate vector is within the network layer capacity region is also NP-Complete. However, in Section 5.5.3, we essentially proved that whenever an end-to-end connection rate vector is within the network layer capacity region, the dynamic back-pressure algorithm can stably support it, an apparent contradiction! The key to this paradox lies in the solution

to the optimization problem (5.13). In general, in the presence of interference constraints (for instance, under the Tx-model), the solution to this optimization problem
is itself NP-Hard. Thus, the dynamic back-pressure algorithm is not a polynomial
time scheme in its most general form. This, however, is not a serious setback in
practice. As shown in [61, 63, 76], we can plug in any approximation algorithm for
solving (5.13) into the dynamic back-pressure algorithm, as long as the approximate
solution value is guaranteed to be $\gamma OPT - D$, where $\gamma \leq 1$ and D are fixed constants
(which depend on the specific interference models), and OPT is the optimal solution
value. In this scenario, the back-pressure algorithm is guaranteed to achieve at least
a γ-fraction of the network layer capacity region. An interesting consequence of this
fact is that full network capacity can be achieved by using queue length *estimates*,
as long as the difference between the estimates and the actual values is bounded
by a constant [21, 55, 61, 81]. This allows queue updates to be arbitrarily infrequent
without affecting network stability.

5.6   Survey of Cross-Layer Throughput Estimation and Optimization in Wireless Networks

We now discuss some of the main threads of research in the area of cross-layer
capacity estimation and throughput maximization in wireless networks.

5.6.1   Scaling Laws for Random Networks

Over the last few years, the capacity of random wireless ad hoc networks has been a
subject of active research. A key result in this area is that of Gupta and Kumar [36],
who studied how the total throughput capacity of an ad hoc wireless network formed
by n nodes distributed randomly in the unit square scales with n – as discussed in
Section 5.3, this quantity scales as $\sqrt{n/\log n}$ in the protocol model of interference.
An important consequence of this result is that the throughput capacity of a wireless
network does not scale linearly with the system size unlike wireline networks, where
the capacity can be increased by adding more network elements. We discussed this
result in detail in Section 5.3 of this chapter. This result has been extended in a
number of directions, building on the techniques introduced in [36].

For the physical (or SINR) model of interference, Agarwal and Kumar [1] show
that the throughput capacity is $\Theta(\sqrt{n})$. Several papers have shown that the results
of [36] can be obtained by significantly simpler techniques [47, 66, 83] – in particular, the upper bound of [36] on the throughput capacity can be obtained much
more easily by just examining the minimum multicut separating the connection endpoints. The capacity of networks with directional antennas has been explored in
[66, 83]. These results have shown that directional antennas increase the capacity
under omnidirectional antennas roughly by a factor of $\frac{1}{\sqrt{\alpha\beta}}$, where α and β are the

beam widths for the transmitter and receiver, respectively; therefore, the throughput capacity can increase significantly only when the beam widths become very small, at which point the network starts behaving like a wired network.

A natural way to augment the capacity of wireless networks is to consider hybrid networks containing base stations connected by high capacity wired links. Liu et al. [57] show that in this model, there is a significant improvement in the capacity only if $\Omega(\sqrt{n})$ hybrid nodes are added. See [1, 34, 45] for further work in this direction.

When nodes are mobile, the estimation of the capacity becomes even more non-trivial. In a surprising result, Grossglauser and Tse [35] show that in fact the throughput capacity can be increased significantly when nodes are mobile by a novel packet relaying scheme; see [15, 31, 34, 60, 78] on other results in this direction.

5.6.2 Estimating the Throughput Capacity

A central issue in the research on characterizing the rate region is that of stability. The techniques for proving stability are closely related to the nature of arrival processes, and this gives a natural way of classifying the literature on this area. Three broad classes of arrival processes have been studied – constant bit rate, adversarial processes, and admissible stochastic arrival processes (as discussed in Section 5.5). The first two processes have been usually studied using multicommodity flow techniques, while control theoretic techniques have been used for the third class of processes.

5.6.2.1 Linear Programming Techniques for Arrival Processes with Constant Bit Rate

There has been much research on determining the optimal rates to maximize throughput via linear programming (LP) formulations, e.g., [4, 12, 18, 37, 39]. The first attempts can be traced back to Hajek and Sasaki [37], and to Baker et al. [12]. Jain et al. [39] propose LP-formulations for max-flow and related problems in a wireless network; in fact, they formulate their constraints in terms of arbitrary conflict graphs which can incorporate any interference model. Kodialam and Nandagopal [42] propose similar LP-formulations and a scheduling algorithm for determining the maximum transmission rates for a given network with primary interference models. This is extended to incorporate secondary interference and non-uniform power levels in [49], as described in Section 5.4. Buraagohain et al. [18] show that for the Tx-Rx model, the bounds of [49] can be improved by a factor of 2 by a more careful ordering of the edges during scheduling. Alicherry et al. [4] extend these techniques to the case of multiradio wireless networks. Chafekar et al. [19] extend the inductive scheduling technique to the case where interference is modeled by SINR constraints, and obtain a logarithmic approximation to the throughput capacity in this model. There is also interest in estimating the capacity for other protocol models, and Chafekar et al. [20] study this question for the random access model.

5.6.2.2 Techniques for Admissible Stochastic Arrival Processes

The Lyapunov drift technique discussed in the analysis of the Dynamic Backpressure algorithm in Section 5.5.2 is one of the most commonly employed techniques for proving stability. There is a large body of work that extends [76] – Lin and Shroff [55] show that under primary interference constraints, this approach guarantees 50% of the throughput capacity; Chaporkar et al. [21] extend this to the case of secondary interference. Zussman et al. [84] identify a large class of graphs that satisfy "Local Pooling" conditions, for which the algorithm of [76] achieves the optimal throughput.

The back-pressure technique of [76] combines routing and scheduling decisions at the packet level. There has been a lot of work on extending this to layered crosslayer aware protocols, along with other objectives such as fairness or general utility maximization (see, e.g., [22, 23, 25, 54, 59, 81]) – these papers use convex optimization techniques and interpret lagrangian multipliers as layer specific quantities. In addition to the Lyapunov analysis technique, methods based on fluid models (e.g., [30, 72]) have also been used for stability analysis in wireless networks.

5.6.2.3 Techniques for Adversarial Queuing Models

Simple stochastic arrival processes are not adequate for some applications involving very bursty traffic. Borodin et al. [17] develop a new model of arrival processes called an *Adversarial Queuing Model*. Here, it is convenient to think of the packet arrivals to be determined by an adversary. Let $c_e(t)$ denote the capacity of edge e at time slot t; $c_e(t)$ can either vary according to a stochastic model, or be chosen by the adversary. The adversary determines the time at which a packet p is injected, its size ℓ_p, its source s_p, and destination d_p. Let $I[t, t']$ denote the set of packets injected by the adversary during the time slots $t, \ldots, t'$. Clearly, an unrestricted adversary can completely flood the network, making it impossible to achieve stability. This motivates the following notion of a restricted adversary.

Definition 5.5. ([3, 6]). An adversary injecting packets is said to be an $A(w, \epsilon)$ adversary for some $\epsilon \geq 0$ and some integer $w \geq 1$ if the following condition holds for every time step t: the adversary can associate a simple path Γ_p from s_p to d_p for each $p \in I[t, t + w - 1]$ so that for each edge $e \in E$

$$\sum_{p \in I[t,t+w-1]} \sum_{e \in \Gamma_p} \ell_p \leq (1 - \epsilon) \sum_{t'=t}^{t+w-1} c_e(t')$$

With the exception of [6], all other work on adversarial queueing models [3,5,7,9, 17] has focused on static networks, in which $c_e(t)$ is not a function of time. Andrews et al. [5] showed that several well-known simple greedy queuing protocols, such as Farthest-to-Go (FTG), Longest-in-System (LIS), and Shortest-in-System (SIS), are stable, but can have exponentially sized queues; they develop a randomized protocol with polynomially bounded queues. Aiello et al. [3] show that the dynamic back-pressure algorithm discussed in Section 5.5.2 is stable. In fact, this algorithm was developed independently by Awerbuch and Leighton [10, 11] for computing multicommodity flows around the same time as Tassiulas and Ephremides [76]. Andrews et al. [6] show that in fact the same algorithm, which they refer to as MAX-WEIGHT, is stable even for the adversarially controlled traffic and network model of Definition 5.5.

5.7 Open Problems

Despite the enormous strides in the throughput capacity problem under several general settings, many significant open questions remain. Most of the results yielding polynomial time algorithms for approximating the throughput capacity in arbitrary networks assume simplified conflict-graph based interference models, and extending this to more realistic interference models, e.g., those based on SINR/generalized-SINR constraints is an important class of problems. It would seem that a first step towards this goal would be to extend the results of Section 5.4 to stochastic and adversarial packet arrival processes. SINR based models do not have the feature of simple spatial decomposition, making them much harder to analyze.

An important direction of future research in throughput capacity estimation is to predict the capacity of a realistic wireless network in which communication protocols have been *plugged into* certain layers of the protocol stack and other layers are open to design. This would require extending the current results to the setting where common routing and scheduling protocols are abstracted in a realistic manner. One step in this direction is the work on estimating the network capacity under random access MAC protocols, e.g., [20, 80]. Further, there is limited work on combining power control along with aspects of the other layers, because these formulations become non-convex. Developing techniques to jointly optimize the overall throughput capacity, along with the total power usage, is an interesting direction.

Finally, an important step in translating the algorithmic research on achieving the rate region into practical protocols would be to develop realistic distributed algorithms. Most current cross-layer algorithms which have provably good guarantees are either centralized, or require a significant amount of information sharing, making them expensive to implement in a distributed manner. Further, existing distributed algorithms do not suitably exploit the broadcast nature of wireless medium, and do not provide useful non-trivial guarantees on their time and message complexity, which lends tremendous scope for future investigation.

Acknowledgements V.S. Anil Kumar and Madhav Marathe are partially supported by the following grants from NSF: CNS-0626964, SES-0729441, CNS-0831633, and CNS CAREER 0845700.

References

1. A. Agarwal and P. Kumar. Capacity bounds for ad hoc and hybrid wireless networks. In *ACM SIGCOMM Computer Communications Review*, volume 34(3), 2004.
2. R. Ahuja, R. Magnanti, and J. Orlin. *Network Flows: Theory, Algorithms, and Applications*. Prentice Hall, 1993.
3. W. Aiello, E. Kushilevitz, R. Ostrovsky, and A. Rosén. Adaptive packet routing for bursty adversarial traffic. *J. Comput. Syst. Sci.*, 60(3):482–509, 2000.
4. M. Alicherry, R. Bhatia, and L. E. Li. Joint channel assignment and routing for throughput optimization in multi-radio wireless mesh networks. In *MobiCom '05: Proceedings of the 11th annual international conference on Mobile computing and networking*, pages 58–72, New York, NY, USA, 2005. ACM Press.
5. M. Andrews, B. Awerbuch, A. Fernández, F. T. Leighton, Z. Liu, and J. M. Kleinberg. Universal-stability results and performance bounds for greedy contention-resolution protocols. *J. ACM*, 48(1):39–69, 2001.
6. M. Andrews, K. Jung, and A. Stolyar. Stability of the max-weight routing and scheduling protocol in dynamic networks and at critical loads. In *STOC*, pages 145–154, 2007.
7. E. Anshelevich, D. Kempe, and J. M. Kleinberg. Stability of load balancing algorithms in dynamic adversarial systems. In *STOC*, pages 399–406, 2002.
8. S. Asmussen. *Applied Probability and Queues*. New York: Springer-Verlag, 2 edition, 1993.
9. B. Awerbuch, P. Berenbrink, A. Brinkmann, and C. Scheideler. Simple routing strategies for adversarial systems. In *FOCS*, pages 158–167, 2001.
10. B. Awerbuch and F. T. Leighton. A simple local-control approximation algorithm for multi-commodity flow. In *FOCS*, pages 459–468, 1993.
11. B. Awerbuch and T. Leighton. Improved approximation algorithms for the multi-commodity flow problem and local competitive routing in dynamic networks. In *STOC*, pages 487–496, 1994.
12. D. J. Baker, J. E. Wieselthier, and A. Ephremides. A distributed algorithm for scheduling the activation of links in self-organizing mobile radio networks. In *IEEE Int. Conference Communications*, pages 2F6.1–2F6.5, 1982.
13. H. Balakrishnan, C. Barrett, A. Kumar, M. Marathe, and S. Thite. The Distance 2-Matching Problem and Its Relationship to the MAC Layer Capacity of Adhoc Wireless Networks. *special issue of IEEE J. Selected Areas in Communications*, 22(6):1069–1079, 2004.
14. N. Bansal and Z. Liu. Capacity, Delay and Mobility in Wireless Ad-Hoc Networks. In *IEEE INFOCOM 2003*, San Francisco, CA, April 1–3 2003.
15. N. Bansal and Z. Liu. Capacity, Delay and Mobility in Wireless Ad-Hoc Networks. In *IEEE INFOCOM 2003*, San Francisco, CA, April 1–3 2003.
16. C. L. Barrett, A. Marathe, M. V. Marathe, and M. Drozda. Characterizing the interaction between routing and mac protocols in ad-hoc networks. In *MobiHoc*, pages 92–103, 2002.
17. A. Borodin, J. M. Kleinberg, P. Raghavan, M. Sudan, and D. P. Williamson. Adversarial queuing theory. *J. ACM*, 48(1):13–38, 2001.
18. C. Buraagohain, S. Suri, C. Tóth, and Y. Zhou. Improved throughput bounds for interference-aware routing in wireless networks. In *Proc. Computing and Combinatorics Conference*, 2007.
19. D. Chafekar, V. A. Kumar, M. Marathe, S. Parthasarathy, and A. Srinivasan. Approximation algorithms for computing of wireless networks with sinr constraints. In *Proc. of IEEE INFO-COM*, 2008.
20. D. Chafekar, D. Levin, V. A. Kumar, M. Marathe, S. Parthasarathy, and A. Srinivasan. Capacity of asynchronous random-access scheduling in wireless networks. In *Proc. of IEEE INFOCOM*, 2008.

21. P. Chaporkar, K. Kar, and S. Sarkar. Throughput guarantees through maximal scheduling in multi-hop wireless networks. In *Proceedings of 43rd Annual Allerton Conference on Communications, Control, and Computing*, 2005.
22. L. Chen, S. H. Low, M. Chiang, and J. C. Doyle. Cross-layer congestion control, routing and scheduling design in ad hoc wireless networks. In *INFOCOM*, pages 1–13, 2006.
23. L. Chen, S. H. Low, and J. C. Doyle. Joint congestion control and media access control design for ad hoc wireless networks. In *INFOCOM*, pages 2212–2222, 2005.
24. H. Chernoff. A measure of asymptotic efficiency for tests of a hypothesis based on the sum of observations. *Annals of Mathematical Statistics*, 23:493–509, 1952.
25. M. Chiang, S. H. Low, A. R. Calderbank, and J. C. Doyle. Layering as optimization decomposition: A mathematical theory of network architectures. *Proceedings of the IEEE*, 95(1): 255–312, 2007.
26. S. Cui and A. J. Goldsmith. Cross-layer design of energy-constrained networks using cooperative mimo techniques. *Signal Processing*, 86(8):1804–1814, 2006.
27. S. Cui, R. Madan, A. J. Goldsmith, and S. Lall. Cross-layer energy and delay optimization in small-scale sensor networks. *IEEE Transactions on Wireless Communications*, 6(10): 3688–3699, 2007.
28. D. S. J. De Couto, D. Aguayo, J. Bicket, and R. Morris. A High-Throughput Path Metric for Multi-Hop Wireless Routing. In *Proceedings of Mobicom*, pages 134–146. ACM Press, 2003.
29. R. Draves, J. Padhye, and B. Zill. Routing in multi-radio, multi-hop wireless mesh networks. In *MobiCom '04: Proceedings of the 10th annual international conference on Mobile computing and networking*, pages 114–128, 2004.
30. A. Eryilmaz and R. Srikant. Fair resource allocation in wireless networks using queue-length-based scheduling and congestion control. In *Proc. of IEEE INFOCOM*, 2005.
31. A. E. Gamal, J. P. Mammen, B. Prabhakar, and D. Shah. Throughput-delay trade-off in wireless networks. In *IEEE INFOCOM*, 2004.
32. M. Gastpar and M. Vetterli. On The Capacity of Wireless Networks: The Relay Case. In *IEEE INFOCOM 2002*, New York, NY, June 23–27 2002.
33. L. Georgiadis, M. J. Neely, and L. Tassiulas. Resource allocation and cross-layer control in wireless networks. *Found. Trends Netw.*, 1(1):1–144, 2006.
34. M. Gerla, B. Zhou, Y.-Z. Lee, F. Soldo, U. Lee, and G. Marfia. Vehicular grid communications: the role of the internet infrastructure. In *WICON '06: Proceedings of the 2nd annual international workshop on Wireless internet*, page 19, New York, NY, USA, 2006. ACM.
35. M. Grossglauser and D. N. C. Tse. Mobility increases the capacity of ad hoc wireless networks. *IEEE/ACM Trans. Netw.*, 10(4):477–486, 2002.
36. P. Gupta and P. R. Kumar. The Capacity of Wireless Networks. *IEEE Transactions on Information Theory*, 46(2):388–404, 2000.
37. B. Hajek and G. Sasaki. Link scheduling in polynomial time. *IEEE Transactions on Information Theory*, 34:910–917, 1988.
38. W. Hoeffding. Probability inequalities for sums of bounded random variables. *American Statistical Association Journal*, 58:13–30, 1963.
39. K. Jain, J. Padhye, V. N. Padmanabhan, and L. Qiu. Impact of interference on multi-hop wireless network performance. In *Proceedings of the 9th annual international conference on Mobile computing and networking*, pages 66–80. ACM Press, 2003.
40. M. Kaufmann, J. F. Sibeyn, and T. Suel. Derandomizing algorithms for routing and sorting on meshes. In *SODA '94: Proceedings of the fifth annual ACM-SIAM symposium on Discrete algorithms*, pages 669–679, Philadelphia, PA, USA, 1994. Society for Industrial and Applied Mathematics.
41. S. A. Khayam, S. Karande, M. Krappel, and H. Radha. Cross-layer protocol design for real-time multimedia applications over 802.11 b networks. In *ICME '03: Proceedings of the 2003 International Conference on Multimedia and Expo*, pages 425–428, 2003.
42. M. Kodialam and T. Nandagopal. Characterizing achievable rates in multi-hop wireless networks: the joint routing and scheduling problem. In *Proceedings of the 9th annual international conference on Mobile computing and networking*, pages 42–54. ACM Press, 2003.

43. M. Kodialam and T. Nandagopal. Characterizing thanks, rates in multi-hop wireless mesh networks with orthogonal channels. *IEEE/ACM Trans. Netw.*, 13(4):868–880, 2005.
44. M. Kodialam and T. Nandagopal. Characterizing the capacity region in multi-radio multi-channel wireless mesh networks. In *MobiCom '05: Proceedings of the 11th annual international conference on Mobile computing and networking*, pages 73–87, New York, NY, USA, 2005. ACM Press.
45. U. Kozat and L. Tassiulas. Throughput capacity in random ad-hoc networks with infrastructure support. In *Proc. 9th Annual ACM International Conference on Mobile computing and networking*, 2003.
46. U. C. Kozat and L. Tassiulas. Throughput capacity of random ad hoc networks with infrastructure support. In *MobiCom '03: Proceedings of the 9th annual international conference on Mobile computing and networking*, pages 55–65, New York, NY, USA, 2003. ACM Press.
47. S. R. Kulkarni and P. Viswanath. A deterministic approach to throughput scaling in wireless networks. *IEEE Transactions on Information Theory*, 50(6):1041–1049, 2004.
48. V. S. A. Kumar, M. V. Marathe, S. Parthasarathy, and A. Srinivasan. End-to-end packet-scheduling in wireless ad-hoc networks. In *SODA '04: Proceedings of the fifteenth annual ACM-SIAM symposium on Discrete algorithms*, pages 1021–1030, Philadelphia, PA, USA, 2004. Society for Industrial and Applied Mathematics.
49. V. S. A. Kumar, M. V. Marathe, S. Parthasarathy, and A. Srinivasan. Algorithmic aspects of capacity in wireless networks. In *SIGMETRICS '05: Proceedings of the 2005 ACM SIGMETRICS International Conference on Measurement and Modeling of Computer Systems*, pages 133–144, 2005.
50. V. S. A. Kumar, M. V. Marathe, S. Parthasarathy, and A. Srinivasan. Provable algorithms for joint optimization of transport, routing and mac layers in wireless ad hoc networks. In *Proc. DialM-POMC Workshop on Foundations of Mobile Computing*, 2007. Eight pages.
51. V. S. A. Kumar, M. V. Marathe, S. Parthasarathy, and A. Srinivasan. Throughput maximization in multi-channel multi-radio wireless networks. Technical report, Virginia Tech, 2009.
52. M. Kunde. Block gossiping on grids and tori: Deterministic sorting and routing match the bisection bound. In *ESA '93: Proceedings of the First Annual European Symposium on Algorithms*, pages 272–283, London, UK, 1993. Springer-Verlag.
53. Q. Liang, D. Yuan, Y. Wang, and H.-H. Chen. A cross-layer transmission scheduling scheme for wireless sensor networks. *Comput. Commun.*, 30(14-15):2987–2994, 2007.
54. X. Lin and S. Rasool. A distributed and provably efficient joint channel-assignment, scheduling and routing algorithm for multi-channel multi-radio wireless mesh networks. In *Proc. of IEEE INFOCOM*, 2007.
55. X. Lin and N. B. Shroff. The impact of imperfect scheduling on cross-layer congestion control in wireless networks. *IEEE/ACM Trans. Netw.*, 14(2):302–315, 2006.
56. X. Lin, N. B. Shroff, and R. Srikant. A tutorial on cross-layer optimization in wireless networks. *IEEE Journal on Selected Areas in Communications*, 24(8):1452–1463, 2006.
57. B. Liu, Z. Liu, and D. Towsley. On the Capacity of Hybrid Wireless Networks. In *IEEE INFOCOM 2003*, San Francisco, CA, April 1–3 2003.
58. S. Meyn and R. Tweedie. *Markov Chains and Stochastic Stability*. Springer-Verlag, London, 1993.
59. H. Nama, M. Chiang, and N. Mandayam. Utility lifetime tradeoff in self regulating wireless sensor networks: A cross-layer design approach. In *IEEE ICC*, jun 2006.
60. M. Neely and E. Modiano. Capacity and delay tradeoffs for ad hoc mobile networks. *IEEE Transactions on Information Theory*, 51(6):1917–1937, 2005.
61. M. J. Neely. *Dynamic power allocation and routing for satellite and wireless networks with time varying channels*. PhD thesis, Massachusetts Institute of Technology, LIDS, 2003.
62. M. J. Neely, E. Modiano, and C.-P. Li. Fairness and optimal stochastic control for heterogeneous networks. In *INFOCOM*, pages 1723–1734, 2005.
63. M. J. Neely, E. Modiano, and C. E. Rohrs. Tradeoffs in delay guarantees and computation complexity for $n \times n$ packet switches. In *Conference on Information Sciences and Systems*, 2002.

64. M. J. Neely, E. Modiano, and C. E. Rohrs. Dynamic power allocation and routing for time-varying wireless networks. *IEEE Journal on Selected Areas in Communications*, 23(1):89–103, 2005.
65. S. Parthasarathy. *Resource Allocation in Networked and Distributed Environments*. PhD thesis, Department of Computer Science, University of Maryland at College Park, 2006.
66. C. Peraki and S. D. Servetto. On the maximum stable throughput problem in random networks with directional antennas. In *MobiHoc '03: Proceedings of the 4th ACM international symposium on Mobile ad hoc networking & computing*, pages 76–87, New York, NY, USA, 2003. ACM Press.
67. A. Rajeswaran and R. Negi. Capacity of power constrained ad-hoc networks. In *INFOCOM*, 2004.
68. S. Ramanathan and E. L. Lloyd. Scheduling algorithms for multihop radio networks. *IEEE-ACM Transactions on Networking (ToN)*, 1:166–177, 1993.
69. A. Schrijver. *Theory of Linear and Integer Programming*. Wiley, 2001.
70. E. Setton, T. Yoo, X. Zhu, A. Goldsmith, and B. Girod. Cross-layer design of ad hoc networks for real-time video streaming. *Wireless Communications, IEEE*, 12(4):59–65, 2005.
71. G. Sharma, R. R. Mazumdar, and N. B. Shroff. On the complexity of scheduling in wireless networks. In *MobiCom '06: Proceedings of the 12th annual international conference on Mobile computing and networking*, pages 227–238, New York, NY, USA, 2006. ACM Press.
72. A. Stolyar. Maximizing queueing network utility subject to stability: Greedy primal-dual algorithm. *Queueing Systems*, 50:401–457, 2005.
73. A. L. Stolyar. Maxweight scheduling in a generalized switch: State space collapse and workload minimization in heavy traffic. *Annals of Applied Probability*, 14(1):1–53, 2004.
74. L. Tassiulas. *Dynamic link activation scheduling in multihop radio networks with fixed or changing topology*. PhD thesis, University of Maryland, College Park, 1991.
75. L. Tassiulas. Scheduling and performance limits of networks with constantly changing topology. *IEEE Transactions on Information Theory*, 43(3):1067–1073, 1997.
76. L. Tassiulas and A. Ephremides. Stability properties of constrained queueing systems and scheduling policies for maximum throughput in multihop radio networks. *IEEE Trans. Aut. Contr.*, 37:1936–1948, 1992.
77. Y. Tian and E. Ekici. Cross-layer collaborative in-network processing in multihop wireless sensor networks. *IEEE Transactions on Mobile Computing*, 6(3):297–310, 2007.
78. S. Toumpis and A. Goldsmith. Large wireless networks under fading, mobility, and delay constraints. In *Proc. of the IEEE INFOCOM*, 2004.
79. W. Wang, X.-Y. Li, O. Frieder, Y. Wang, and W.-Z. Song. Efficient interference-aware TDMA link scheduling for static wireless networks. In *MobiCom '06: Proceedings of the 12th annual international conference on Mobile computing and networking*, pages 262–273, New York, NY, USA, 2006. ACM Press.
80. X. Wang and K. Kar. Cross-layer rate optimization for proportional fairness in multihop wireless networks with random access. *IEEE Journal on Selected Areas in Communications*, 24(8):1548–1559, 2006.
81. X. Wu and R. Srikant. Regulated maximal matching: A distributed scheduling algorithm for multi-hop wireless networks with node-exclusive spectrum sharing. In *IEEE Conf. on Decision and Control*, 2005.
82. Y. Yang, J. Wang, and R. Kravets. Designing routing metrics for mesh networks. In *First IEEE Workshop on Wireless Mesh Networks (WiMesh)*, 2005.
83. S. Yi, Y. Pei, and S. Kalyanaraman. On the capacity improvement of ad hoc wireless networks using directional antennas. In *Proceedings of the 4th ACM International Symposium on Mobile Ad Hoc Networking and Computing (MobiHoc)*, pages 108–116, 2003.
84. G. Zussman, A. Brzezinski, and E. Modiano. Multihop local pooling for distributed throughput maximization in wireless networks. In *Proc. of IEEE INFOCOM*, 2008.

Chapter 6
Resource Allocation Algorithms for the Next Generation Cellular Networks

David Amzallag and Danny Raz

Abstract This chapter describes recent results addressing resource allocation problems in the context of current and future cellular technologies. We present models that capture several fundamental aspects of planning and operating these networks, and develop new approximation algorithms providing provable good solutions for the corresponding optimization problems. We mainly focus on two families of problems: cell planning and cell selection. Cell planning deals with choosing a network of base stations that can provide the required coverage of the service area with respect to the traffic requirements, available capacities, interference, and the desired QoS. Cell selection is the process of determining the cell(s) that provide service to each mobile station. Optimizing these processes is an important step towards maximizing the utilization of current and future cellular networks.

6.1 Introduction

The forthcoming fourth generation (4G) cellular systems are expected to provide a wide variety of new services, from high quality voice and high-definition video to very high bit rate data wireless channels. With the rapid development of wireless communication networks, it is expected that fourth-generation mobile systems will be launched around 2012–2015. 4G mobile systems focus on seamlessly integrating the existing wireless technologies including GSM, wireless LAN, and Bluetooth.

D. Amzallag (✉)
British Telecommunications plc,
81 Newgate Street, London EC1A 7AJ,
e-mail: david.amzallag@bt.com

D. Raz
Computer Science Department,
Technion – Israel Institute of Technology,
Haifa 32000, Israel,
e-mail: danny@cs.technion.ac.il

G. Cormode and M. Thottan (eds.), *Algorithms for Next Generation Networks*,
Computer Communications and Networks, DOI 10.1007/978-1-84882-765-3_6,
© Springer-Verlag London Limited 2010

This contrasts with third-generation (3G) systems, which focused on developing new standards and hardware. 4G systems are expected to support comprehensive and personalized services, providing stable system performance and quality service. The migration of current systems into 4G and the integration of the different technologies into a single framework present enormous challenges (see, e.g., the excellent survey of [23]). In this chapter, we focus on selected resource allocation challenges, discussing new techniques, and emphasizing algorithmic aspects which address 4G characterizations[1].

Second-generation (2G) mobile systems were very successful in the previous decade. Their success prompted the development of 3G mobile systems. While 2G systems such as GSM, IS-95, and CDMA1 were designed to carry voice and low-bit-rate data, 3G systems were designed to provide higher data- rate services. During the evolution from 2G to 3G, a range of wireless systems, including GPRS, WCDMA, Bluetooth, WLAN, and HiperLAN, have been developed. All these systems were designed independently, targeting different service types, data rates, and users. As all these systems have their own merits and shortcomings, there is no single system that is good enough to replace all the other technologies. At the time of writing this chapter, there is no formal definition of 4G, yet, there is a clear consensus regarding some of the important aspects of the technologies to be implemented in these systems (see, for instance, pages 12–13 in [26]).

First, 4G networks are all-IP based heterogeneous networks that allow users to use any system at any time and anywhere. Users carrying an integrated terminal can use a wide range of applications provided by multiple wireless technologies.

Second, 4G systems provide not only "traditional" telecommunications services, but also data and multimedia services. To support multimedia services, high-data-rate services with good system reliability will be provided. Most likely, 4G systems will be designed to offer bit rates of 100 Mbit/s (peak rate in mobile environment) to 1 Gbit/s (fixed indoors). The system capacity is expected to be at least 10 times larger than current 3G systems. These objectives should be met together with a drastic reduction in the cost (1/10 to 1/100 per bit) [34, 36].

Third, personalized service will be provided by this new-generation network. It is expected that when 4G services are launched, users in widely different locations, occupations, and economic classes will use the services. In order to meet the demands of these diverse users, service providers should design personal and customized services for them.

Finally, 4G systems also provide facilities for integrated services. Users could use multiple services from any service provider at the same time. Just imagine a 4G mobile user, Sarah, who is looking for information on movies shown in nearby cinemas. Her mobile may simultaneously connect to different wireless systems. These wireless systems may include a Global Positioning System (GPS) (for tracking her current location), a wireless LAN (for receiving previews of the movies

---

[1] We assume that the reader is familiar with the most well-known notions in cellular networks. An excellent introduction can be found in [36]

in nearby cinemas), and an orthogonal frequency-division multiplexing access (OFDMA) (for making a telephone call to one of the cinemas). In this example (based on [23]), Sarah is actually using multiple wireless services that differ in quality of service (QoS) levels, security policies, device settings, charging methods, and applications.

The convergence of the different wireless technologies is a contiguous process. With each passing day, the maturity level of the mobile user and the complexity level of the cellular network reach a new high. Current networks are no longer "traditional" GSM networks, but a complex mixture of 2G, 2.5G, and 3G technologies. Furthermore, new technologies beyond 3G (e.g., HSPA, WiMAX, LTE) are being utilized in these cellular networks (see [24] for excellent introduction and further reading). The very existence of all these technologies in one cellular network has brought the work of design and optimization of the networks to be viewed from a different perspective. We no longer *need* to plan GSM, GPRS, or WCDMA networks individually. The cellular network business is actually about dimensioning for new and advanced technologies, planning and optimizing 4G networks, while upgrading 3G/3.5G networks.

A good example for such a planning problem is the *cell planning problem*, one of the most important resource allocation problem in the design and planning of cellular networks. Cell planning deals with finding optimal *configurations* for base stations (or antennas) in order to serve a given set J of client locations (or mobile-users). By a configuration we mean not just the geographical location (as provided by the operator), but also the antenna type, azimuth, tilt, height, and more. Each configuration $i \in I$ has bandwidth capacity w_i, installation cost c_i, and every client $j \in J$ has a (bandwidth) demand d_j. This means that a base station configuration $i \in I$ cannot satisfy more than w_i demand units of the served clients. The objective here is to find a feasible subset $I' \subseteq I$ of configurations of minimum cost that can satisfy the demands of all clients.

Obviously, there is an exponential number of possible subsets of configurations and hence checking all possible solutions for the best one is not a practical option. In fact, one needs to find a much faster way to reach the optimal solution. Unfortunately, finding a polynomial-time optimal solution is very unlikely, since this problem, like many other network optimization problems, is NP-hard. The most common approaches to address such NP-hard optimization problems are the following:

1. **Easy special cases** Identify properties of the input instances that make the problem easier (or even tractable), and design an algorithm that makes use of these properties.
2. **Somewhat efficient exponential algorithms** Design an algorithm that always solves the problem whose running time is not polynomial, but still much faster than exhaustive search. This approach may be useful for inputs of moderate size.
3. **Heuristics** Design algorithms that work well on many practical instances, though not on all instances. This is perhaps the most commonly used approach in practice (e.g., local search, simulated annealing, genetic algorithms).

4. **Approximation algorithms**   Sacrifice the quality of the solution so as to obtain
more efficient algorithms. Instead of finding the optimal solution, settle for a near
optimal solution that can be done in polynomial time. Hopefully, this solution
works well for the specific input of interest.

Examples of coping with NP-hardness of cellular optimization problems can be
found in [7] (and also [19]). With respect to cell planning, previous works dealt with
a wide variety of special cases (e.g., cell planning without interference, frequency
planning, uncapacitated models, antenna-type limitations, and topological assumptions regarding coverage) and the objectives are mostly of minimum-cost type. The
techniques used in these works range from meta-heuristics (e.g., genetic algorithms,
simulated annealing, etc.) and greedy approaches, through exponential-time algorithms that compute an optimal solution, to approximation algorithms for special
cases of the problem. A comprehensive survey of various works on cell planning
problems appears in [4, 5] and a comparison between optimization methods for cell
planning of 3G systems appears in Chapter 14 of [28].

We dedicate the next section to study this problem (and its generalizations) using
approximation algorithms. A δ-*approximation algorithm* is a polynomial-time algorithm that always finds a feasible solution for which the objective function value is
within a proven factor of δ of the optimal solution.

The main goal of this chapter is to present new approaches specifically addressing
several fundamental resource allocation problems associated with the upcoming future cellular networks. This chapter rigorously studies algorithmic aspects of these
optimization problems, incorporates the anticipated future new technologies into
the studied framework, and presents new methods for solving these problems. The
discussed techniques are based on novel modeling of technology dependent characterizations and using approximation algorithms in order to provide provable good
solutions.

We start, in Section 6.2, by studying several variants if the cell planning problem
includes both the *budget limited cell planning problem* and the *minimum-cost cell
planning problem*. Motivated by algorithmic characterizations of the new OFDMA
multiple access technique standard (as defined by the IEEE 802.16e–2005), we
present, in Section 6.3, a new approach for the cell selection mechanism. Cell selection is the process of determining the cell(s) that provide service to each mobile
station. Optimizing these processes is an important step towards maximizing the
utilization of current and future cellular networks.

6.2   Cell Planning Problems

As described above, cell planning is an important step in the design, deployment,
and management of cellular networks. Cell planning includes planning a network of
base stations that provides a (full or partial) coverage of the service area with respect
to current and future traffic requirements, available capacities, interference, and the
desired QoS. Cell planning is employed not only when a new network is built or

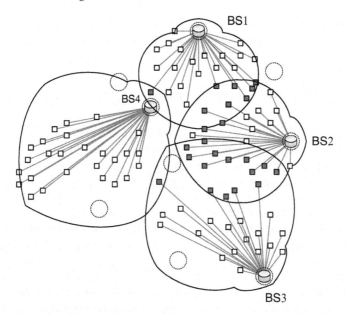

Fig. 6.1 A cell planning example

when a modification to a current network is made, but also (and mainly) when there are changes in the traffic demand, even within a small local area (e.g., building a new mall in the neighborhood or opening new highways). Cell planning that is able to respond to local traffic changes and/or to make use of advanced technological features at the planning stage is essential for cost-effective design of future systems.

Figure 6.1 depicts a typical example of a cell planning instance. Each square in the picture represents either a single mobile station (associated with its bandwidth demand) or a cluster of mobile stations (associated with their aggregated demand). The dotted circles represent potential places to locate base stations (with their corresponding installation/opening costs), and the corresponding drawn patterns are the coverage area of the configuration (depending on the height, azimuth, tilt, antenna type, etc.). The outcome of the minimum-cost cell planning problem (CPP) is a minimum-cost subset of places for positioning base stations (in the figure BS1–BS4) that covers all the demand of the mobile stations. Mobile stations in an overlapped area (e.g., the marked mobile stations in the overlapped area of BS1 and BS2) can be served (or satisfied) by each of these base stations. A mutual interference occurs between the overlapped base-stations (exact type of interference depends on the deployed technology) as described later in this chapter.

This section studies algorithmic aspects of cell planning problems, incorporates the anticipated future technologies into the cell planning, and presents new methods for solving these problems. These techniques are based on novel modeling of technology dependent characterizations and approximation algorithms that provide provable good solutions. Clearly, methods presented in this chapter are also applicable to current networks and various radio technologies.

6.2.1 The Main New Factors in Planning Future Networks

As introduced earlier, future systems will be designed to offer very high bit rates with a high frequency bandwidth. Such high frequencies yield a very strong signal degradation and suffer from significant diffraction resulting from small obstacles, hence forcing the reduction of cell size (in order to decrease the amount of degradation and to increase coverage), resulting in a significantly larger number of cells in comparison to previous generations. Future systems will have cells of different sizes: *picocells* (e.g., an in-building small base station with antenna on the ceiling), *microcells* (e.g., urban street, up to 1 km long with base stations above rooftops at 25 m height), and *macrocells* (e.g., non-line-of-sight urban macro-cellular environment). Each such cell is expected to service users with different mobility patterns, possibly via different radio technologies. Picocells can serve slow mobility users with relatively high traffic demands. They can provide high capacity coverage with hot-spot areas coverage producing local solutions for these areas. Even though these cells do not have a big RF impact on other parts of the network, they should be taken into consideration during the cell planning stage since covering hot-spot areas may change the traffic distribution. At the same time, microcells and macrocells can be used to serve users with high mobility patterns (highway users) and to cover larger areas. Hence, it is important to be able to choose appropriate locations for potential base stations and to consider different radio technologies, in order to achieve maximum coverage (with low interference) at a minimum cost.

The increased number of base stations, and the variable bandwidth demand of mobile stations, will force operators to optimize the way the *capacity* of a base station is utilized. Unlike in previous generations, the ability of a base station to successfully satisfy the service demand of all its mobile stations will be highly limited and will mostly depend on its infrastructure restrictions, as well as on the service distribution of its mobile stations. To the best of our knowledge, no cell planning approach, known today, is taking the base station ("bandwidth") capacity into account.

Base stations and mobile terminals are expected to make substantial use of adaptive antennas and smart antennas. In case the system will have the ability to distinguish between different users (by their RF positions, or by their channel estimation), adaptive antennas will point a narrow lobe to each user, reducing interference while at the same time, maintaining high capacity. Smart antenna systems combine an antenna array with a digital signal-processing capability, enabling base stations to transmit and receive in an adaptive, spatially sensitive manner. In other words, such a system can automatically change the directionality of its radiation patterns in response to its signal environment. This can dramatically increase the performance characteristics (such as capacity) of a wireless system. Hence, future methods for cell planning should be able to include a deployment of smart antennas and adaptive antennas in their optimization process. Note that current advanced tools for cell planning already contain capabilities for electrical modifications of tilt and azimuth.

6.2.2   On Discrete Location Problems in Combinatorial Optimization

The theoretical models for cell planning are closely related to a family of combinatorial optimization problems called facility location problems. The facility location problem is one of the most well-studied problems in combinatorial optimization (see [35] for an excellent survey). In the traditional *facility location problem* we wish to find optimal locations for facilities (or base stations) in order to serve a given set of client locations; we are also given a set of locations in which facilities may be built, where building a facility in location $i \in I$ incurs a cost of c_i; each client $j \in J$ must be assigned to one facility, thereby incurring a cost of c_{ij}, proportional to the distance between locations i and j; the objective is to find a solution of minimum total (assignment + opening) cost. In the k-*median problem*, facility costs are replaced by a constraint that limits the number of facilities to be k and the objective is to minimize the total assignment costs. These two classical problems are min-sum problems, in that the sum of the assignment costs goes into the objective function. The k-*center problem* is the min–max analogue of the k-median problem: one builds facilities at k locations out of a given number of locations, so as to minimize the maximum distance from a given location to the nearest selected location.

Theoretically speaking, the minimum-cost cell planning problem (CPP) is a "new" type of discrete location problem. In a cell planning problem, every client $j \in J$ has a positive demand d_j and every facility (or base station) $i \in I$ has also a hard capacity w_i and a subset $S_i \subseteq J$ of clients admissible to be satisfied by it. Two interesting situations can happen when satisfying the demand of a client. The first case is when multiple coverage is possible, meaning that several facilities are allowed to participate in the satisfaction of a single client, while in the second case clients can be satisfied only by a single facility. In addition, a *penalty* function is introduced, capturing the "interference" between radio channels of neighboring base stations (or facilities). In this model, for example, when the demand of a client is satisfied by two facilities, their "net" contribution is less than or equal the sum of their supplies. The *minimum-cost cell planning problem* is to find a subset $I' \subseteq I$ of minimum cost that satisfies the demands of all the clients (while taking into account interference for multiple satisfaction).

It is important to note that this new problem is not a special case of any of the known min-sum discrete location problems (e.g., there is no connection cost between base stations and clients) nor a "special NP-hard case" of a minimum-cost flow problem.

6.2.3 Formulation and Background

Consider a set $I = \{1, 2, \ldots, m\}$ of possible configurations of base stations and a set $J = \{1, 2, \ldots, n\}$ of clients[2]. Each *base station configuration* (abbreviated *base stations*) containing the geographical location, typical antenna pattern (as well as its adopted model for propagation), azimuth, tilt, height and any other relevant parameters of a base station antenna that together with the technology determine the coverage area of the antenna and the interference pattern. Each base station $i \in I$ has capacity w_i, installation cost c_i, and every client $j \in J$ has a demand d_j. The demand is allowed to be simultaneously satisfied (i.e., by at least d_j units of demands) by more than one base station.

Each base station i has a *coverage area* represented by a set $S_i \subseteq J$ of clients admissible to be covered (or satisfied) by it; this base station can satisfy at most w_i demand units of the clients in S_i. Computing S_i, as a preprocessing stage to the cell planning itself, is based on the physical properties of the antenna, the power setting, terrain information, and the corresponding area-dependent propagation models. One optional way to build the S_i's collection is to list the set of clients who "see" base station i as their "best" server (or either "best" or "secondary"). Such computations are usually done using simulators and are outside the scope of this chapter.

When a client belongs to the coverage area of more than one base station, interference between the servicing stations may occur. These interferences are modeled by a penalty-based mechanism and may reduce the contribution of a base station to a client. We denote by $Q(i, j)$ the net contribution of base station i to client j, for every $j \in J$, $i \in I$, after incorporating all relevant interference. We formulate cell planning problems using the abstract notation of $Q(i, j)$ to be *independent* of the adopted model of interference. Interference models are discussed in the next section.

Using this formulation, we define two cell planning problems. The *minimum-cost cell planning problem* (CPP) is to find a subset $I' \subseteq I$ of minimum cost that satisfies the demands of all the clients. The *budgeted cell planning problem* (BCPP) asks for a subset of base stations $I' \subseteq I$ whose cost does not exceed a given budget B and the total number of satisfied clients is maximized. That is, an optimal solution to BCPP needs to maximize the number of clients for which $\sum_{i \in I} Q(i, j) \geq d_j$.

6.2.4 The Interference Model

Interference handling is an important issue in planning and management of cellular networks. Basically, interference is caused by simultaneous signal transmissions in

---

[2] Notice that when planning cellular networks, the notion of "clients" sometimes means mobile stations and sometimes it represents the total traffic demand created by a cluster of mobile stations at a given location. In this chapter we support both forms of representations.

different cells (inter-cell). In this section we model interference for the forthcoming cellular systems and present a new approach of incorporating interference in cell planning.

Interference is typically modeled, for cell planning purposes, by an *interference matrix* which represents the impact of any base station on other base stations, as a result of simultaneous coverage of the same area (see Appendix 6B in [12]). Next we generalized this behavior to also include the geographic position of this (simultaneous) coverage.

Let P be an $m \times m \times n$ matrix of *interference*, where $p(i_1, i_2, j) \in [0, 1]$ represents the fraction of i_1's service which client j loses as a result of interference with i_2 (defining $p(i, i, j) = 0$ for every $i \in I$, $j \in J$, and $p(i, i', j) = 0$ for every $j \notin S_{i'})^3$. This means that the interference caused as a result of a coverage of a client by more than one base station depends on the geographical position of the related "client" (e.g., in-building coverage produces a different interference than a coverage on highways using the same set of base stations). As defined above, $Q(i, j)$ is the contribution of base station i to client j, taking into account the interference from all relevant base stations. We describe here two general models for computing $Q(i, j)$.

Let x_{ij} be the fraction of the capacity w_i of base station i that is supplied to client j. Recall that $I' \subseteq I$ is the set of base stations selected to be opened, the contribution of base station i to client j is defined to be

$$Q(i, j) = w_i x_{ij} \cdot \prod_{i' \neq i : i' \in I'} \left(1 - p(i, i', j)\right). \tag{6.1}$$

Notice that, as defined by the above model, it is possible that two distinct base stations, say α and β, interfere with each other "in" a place j (i.e., $p(\alpha, \beta, j) > 0$) although $j \notin S_\beta$. In general, each of these base stations "interferes" base station i to service j and reduces the contribution of $w_i x_{ij}$ by a factor of $p(i, i', j)$.

Since (6.1) is a high-order expression we use the following first-order approximation, while assuming that the p's are relatively small:

$$\prod_{i' \in I'} \left(1 - p(i, i', j)\right) = \left(1 - p(i, i'_1, j)\right)\left(1 - p(i, i'_2, j)\right) \cdots \approx 1 - \sum_{i' \in I'} p(i, i', j). \tag{6.2}$$

Combining (6.1) and (6.2) we get

$$Q(i, j) \approx \begin{cases} w_i x_{ij}\left(1 - \sum_{i' \neq i \in I'} p(i, i', j)\right), & \sum_{i' \in I'} p(i, i', j) < 1 \\ 0, & \text{otherwise.} \end{cases} \tag{6.3}$$

---

[3] For simplicity, we do not consider here interference of higher order. These can be further derived and extended from our model.

Consider, for example, a client j belonging to the coverage areas of two base stations i_1 and i_2, and assume that just one of these base stations, say i_1, is actually participating in j's satisfaction (i.e., $x_{i_1 j} > 0$ but $x_{i_2 j} = 0$). According to the above model, the mutual interference of i_2 on i_1's contribution ($w_1 x_{i_1 j}$) should be considered, although i_2 is not involved in the coverage of client j.

In most cellular wireless technologies, this is the usual behavior of interference. However, in some cases a base station can affect the coverage of a client *if and only if* it is participating in its demand satisfaction. The contribution of base station i to client j in this case is defined by

$$Q(i, j) \approx \begin{cases} w_i x_{ij} \left(1 - \sum_{i' \neq i \in I_j} p(i, i')\right), & \sum_{i' \neq i \in I_j} p(i, i') < 1 \\ 0, & \text{otherwise.} \end{cases} \quad (6.4)$$

where I_j is the set of base stations that participate in the coverage of client j, i.e., $I_j = \{i \in I : x_{ij} > 0\}$. Notice that in this model the interference function does not depend on the geographic position of the clients.

6.2.5 The Budgeted Cell-Planning Problem

In many cases, the engineering process of designing cellular network is a part of business process which also determines a budget constraint. In such cases we want to find the "best" possible plan under the given budget constraint. How can we evaluate the quality of this planning and define this "best" plan? One way to do this is to measure the number of satisfied clients (i.e., whose bandwidth demand was fully supplied by one or more base stations). A major difference between the problems of minimum-cost cell planning (CPP) and the budgeted cell planning (BCPP) is that the first is motivated by *coverage* (i.e., all, or a pre-defined part of the clients, are fully satisfied), while the second addressing the required *capacity* in order to maximize the number of satisfied clients. Speaking from an optimization viewpoint, the first is a minimization problem while the second is a maximization one. Surprisingly enough, addressing planning cellular network under budget constraint is not common in both literature and the industry (in particular, in the market of wireless optimization tools) as the minimum-cost cell planning problem. This section will study the problem of cell planning under budget constraint.

6.2.6 How Well the Budgeted Cell Planning Problem (BCPP) Can Be Approximated?

At first sight we must admit that the answer is not so encouraging. BCPP is closely related to the well-known budgeted maximum coverage problem. Given a budget B and a collection of subsets $\mathscr{S}$ of a universe U of elements, where each element in U

has a specified weight and each subset has a specified cost. The *budgeted maximum coverage problem* asks for a subcollection $\mathscr{S}' \subseteq \mathscr{S}$ of sets, whose total cost is at most B, such that the total weight of elements covered by $\mathscr{S}'$ is maximized. This problem is the "budgeted" version of the set cover problem in which one wishes to cover all the elements of U using a minimum number of subsets of $\mathscr{S}$. The budgeted maximum coverage problem is a special case of BCPP in which elements are clients with unit demand, every set $i \in I$ corresponds to a base station i containing all clients in its coverage area $S_i \subseteq J$, and $w_i \geq |S_i|$ for all base stations in I. In this setting, budgeted maximum coverage is precisely the case (in the sense that a solution to BCPP is optimal if and only if it is optimal for the budgeted maximum coverage) when there is no interference (i.e., P is the zero matrix). For the budgeted maximum coverage problem, there is a $(1 - \frac{1}{e})$-approximation algorithm [1,25], and this is the best approximation ratio possible unless NP=P [18,25].

BCPP is also closely related to the budgeted unique coverage version of set cover. In the *budgeted unique coverage problem* elements in the universe are uniquely covered, i.e., appear in exactly one set of S'. As with the budgeted maximum coverage problem, this problem is a special case of BCPP. In this setting, budgeted unique coverage is when the interference is taken to be the highest. For the budgeted unique coverage problem, there is an $\Omega(1/\log n)$-approximation algorithm [17] and, up to a constant exponent depending on ε, $O(1/\log n)$ is the best possible ratio assuming NP $\nsubseteq$ BPTIME (2^{n^ε}) for some $\varepsilon > 0$. This means that in case of very strong interference one might get an arbitrary bad solution (i.e., far from the optimal solution).

Finally, another similar problem to BCPP is the *all-or-nothing demand maximization problem* (AoNDM). In this problem, we are given a set of basestations that *already* opened (or exists), each has its own capacity, and a subset of clients that are admissible to be serviced by it. Given a set of clients, each associated with a demand, we wish to find a way to "share" the base stations' capacity among the clients in order to maximize the number of satisfied clients. This problem is not a special case of BCPP, and the only two differences between these two problems are that there is no interference in AoNDM, and the identity of the opened base stations is unknown in BCPP (moreover, this problem is trying to decide which base stations are the best for opening). "Surprisingly", AoNDM was showed [3] to be unable to obtain a reasonable approximation algorithm under standard complexity assumptions (to be precise, AoNDM is hard to approximate as the maximum independent set problem). We will devote Section 6.3 to AoNDM and its important role in solving resource allocation problem in future cellular networks.

As expected from these similarities, one can prove that it is NP-hard even to find a feasible solution to BCPP [4,6].

6.2.7   The *k4k*-Budgeted Cell Planning Problem

In light of the above inapproximability result, we turn to define a restrictive version of BCPP which is nevertheless general enough to capture interesting practical cases.

To this end we use the fact that typically the number of base stations in cellular networks is much smaller than the number of clients. Moreover, when there is a relatively large cluster of antennas in a given location, this cluster is usually designed to meet the traffic requirements of a high-density area of clients. Thus, for both interpretations of "clients", the number of satisfied clients is always much bigger than the number of base stations. Followed by the above discussion, we define the *k4k-budgeted cell planning problem* (*k4k*-BCPP) to be BCPP with the additional property that every set of k base stations can fully satisfy at least k clients, for every integer k (and we refer to this property as the "*k4k* property"). Using this property it was shown [4, 6] that *k4k*-BCPP is NP-hard but no longer NP-hard to approximate (i.e., the problem to approximate the problem within *any* performance guarantee is polynomial-time solvable).

In the remainder of this section we assume that the interference model is the one defined in Equation (6.4).

6.2.8   An $\frac{e-1}{3e-1}$-Approximation Algorithm

The following approximation algorithm is based on a combinatorial characterization of the solution space of BCPP (and also of *k4k*-BCPP). The following lemma describes this characterization and is a key component in the analysis of the approximation algorithm [4, 6].

Lemma 6.1. *Every solution to the budgeted cell planning problem (or to k4k-BCPP) can be transformed to a solution in which the number of clients that are satisfied by more than one base station is at most the number of opened base stations. Moreover, this transformation leaves the number of fully satisfied clients as well as the solution cost unchanged.*

Proof sketch. Consider a solution $\Delta = \{I', J', \mathbf{x}\}$ to BCPP, where $I' \subseteq I$ is the set of base stations selected for opening, $J' \subseteq J$ is the set of satisfied clients, x_{ij}'s are the base station–client service rates, and $J'' \subseteq J'$ is the set of clients that are satisfied by more than one base station. Without loss of generality we may assume that every client has a demand greater than zero, since there is no need for serving clients with zero demand. We associate the weighted bipartite graph $G_\Delta = (I' \cup J', E)$ with every such a solution. In this graph, $(i, j) \in E$ has weight $w(i, j) = w_i x_{ij}$ if and only if $x_{ij} > 0$, and $w(i, j) = 0$, otherwise. In Figure 6.2 base stations are represented by the black nodes while clients are the whites. Base station i' has a bandwidth capacity of 12, client j' has a demand of 9 and, by the solution presented at left, client j' get only 2 bandwidth units from base station i' (and the rest from base station i'', or from base stations outside this cycle). Two cases need to be considered:

1. If G_Δ is acyclic then we are done (i.e., no transformation is needed); in this case $|J''| < |I'|$. To see this, let T be a forest obtained from G_Δ by fixing an arbitrary

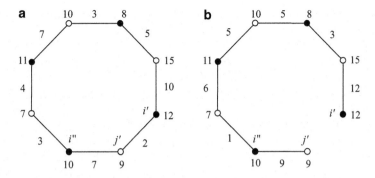

Fig. 6.2 Cycle canceling algorithm on G_Δ

base station vertex as the root (in each of the connected components of G_Δ) and trimming all client leaves. These leaves correspond to clients who are covered, in the solution, by a single base station. Since the distance, from the root, to every leaf of each tree is even, the number of internal client vertices is at most the number of base station vertices, hence $|J''| < |I'|$.

2. Otherwise, we transform $G_\Delta = (I' \cup J', E)$ into an acyclic bipartite graph $G_{\Delta'} = (I' \cup J', E')$ using the following cycle canceling algorithm.

Cycle canceling algorithm   As long as there are cycles in G_Δ, identify a cycle C and let θ be the weight of a minimum-weight edge on this cycle ($\theta = 2$ in Figure 6.2 (right)). Take a minimum-weight edge on C and, starting from this edge, alternately, in clockwise order along the cycle, decrease and increase the weight of every edge by θ.

Two important invariants are maintained throughout the cycle-canceling procedure. The first is that $w'(i, j) \geq 0$ for every edge (i, j) of the cycle. The second is that there exists at least one edge $e = (i, j)$ on the cycle for which $w'(i, j) = 0$. Therefore the number and the identity of the satisfied clients are preserved and $G_{\Delta'}$ is also a solution to the problem. Since at each iteration at least one edge is removed, $G_{\Delta'}$ is acyclic and $|J''| < |I'|$ as before.   □

The main difference between $k4k$-BCPP and other well-studied optimization problems is the existence of interferences. Overcoming this difficulty is done using Lemma 6.1. Although $k4k$-BCPP is still NP-hard, we show how to approximate it using the greedy approach, similar to the ideas presented in [25].

6.2.8.1   The Client Assignment Problem

Prior to using the greedy approach to solve the $k4k$-BCPP it turns out that one must answer the next question: how many clients can be covered by a set S of opened base stations, and how many more can be covered if an additional base station i is to be opened next? Formally, for a given set of base stations, I', let $N(I')$ be the number of clients that can be satisfied, each by exactly one base station (hence we assume that there is no interference here, or interference of the second kind). We refer to the problem of computing $N(\cdot)$ as the *Client Assignment Problem* (CAP).

Algorithmically speaking, at first sight CAP has two important properties [4]. The first (which is straightforward, can be obtained from a reduction from the PARTITION problem) is that CAP is NP-hard. The second, and the non-intuitive one, is that the function $N(\cdot)$ is not submodular (a set function is submodular if $f(S) + f(T) \geq f(S \cup T) + f(S \cap T)$ for all $S, T \subseteq U$).

To see this, consider the following example: $J = \{1, 2, 3, 4, 5, 6, 7, 8, 9, 10\}$, $I = \{1, 2, 3\}$, $S_1 = J$, $S_2 = \{1, 2, 3\}$, $S_3 = \{4, 5, 6\}$. The demands are: $d_1 = d_2 = d_3 = d_4 = d_5 = d_6 = 4$, $d_7 = 3$, $d_8 = d_9 = d_{10} = 9$, and the capacities are: $w_1 = 30$, $w_2 = w_3 = 12$.

Let $S = \{1, 2\}$ and $T = \{1, 3\}$. One can verify that $N(S) = N(T) = 8$, $N(S \cap T) = 7$, and $N(S \cup T) = 10$.

These two properties indicate the difficulty in applying a greedy approach for solving $k4k$-BCPP. Informally speaking, submodularity guarantees that a greedy choice made at some point stays a greedy choice even when taking into account subsequent steps. Without submodularity it is not clear whether greediness is the right approach. Moreover, the NP-hardness of CAP implies that we cannot efficiently compute the best (in the greedy sense) base station to open in a single step. These two difficulties prevent us from using the generalization of [25] proposed by Sviridenko [32] to approximate $k4k$-BCPP, as the algorithm of Sviridenko can be used to approximate only submodular (that is polynomial-time computable) functions.

In order to overcome these problems, we present Algorithm 2 as an approximation algorithm for CAP. The algorithm gets as an input an *ordered* set of base stations $I' = \{i_1, \ldots, i_k\}$, and is a 1/2-approximation for CAP, as proven in [4].

6.2.8.2 The Budgeted Maximum Assignment Problem

In this section we present an approximation algorithm for the budgeted "generalization" of CAP. Consider the following problem: find a subset I' of base stations whose cost is at most the given budget and that maximizes $N(I')$. We refer to this problem as the *budgeted maximum assignment problem* (BMAP). Algorithm 3 and its analysis generalize the ideas of [25] to include both capacities and non-uniform

---

1: **for all** clients in a non-decreasing order of their demand **do**
2:      Let j be the current client.
3:      Find the first base station in the given order that can cover j.
4:      **if** it exists **then**
5:          Assign j to this base station.
6:      **else** {all base stations cannot cover j due to capacity constraints}
7:          Leave client j uncovered.

Algorithm 2: GREEDY APPROXIMATION FOR CAP

1: For every ordered $I' \subseteq I$, $c(I') \leq B$ and $|I'| < 3$, compute $N_A(I')$. Let I_1 be the
   subset with the highest value of N_A computed.
2: **for** every ordered $I' \subset I$, $c(I') \leq B$ and $|I'| = 3$ **do**
3:     $U \leftarrow I \setminus I'$
4:     **repeat**
5:         Select $i \in U$ such that maximizes $\frac{N_A(I',i)-N_A(I')}{c_i}$.
6:         **if** $c(I') + c_i \leq B$ **then**
7:             $I' \leftarrow (I', i)$
8:         $U \leftarrow U \setminus \{i\}$.
9:     **until** $U = \emptyset$
10:    **if** $N_A(I') > N_A(I_1)$ **then**
11:        $I_1 \leftarrow I'$
12: Output I_1.

Algorithm 3: BUDGETED MAXIMUM ASSIGNMENT

demands. Moreover, Algorithm 3 is a $\frac{e-1}{2e}$-approximation for BMAP [4]. Notice that we use here Algorithm 2 to compute $N_A(\cdot)$, and hence all subsets of base stations are ordered.

If the optimal solution has fewer than three base stations, we will consider it in the first step of the algorithm, and get at least $\frac{1}{2}$ of its value. It is left to take care of the case that the optimal solution has at least three base stations. In this case, we order the base stations in OPT by selecting at each step the set in OPT that maximizes the difference in the value of $N_A(\cdot)$. In other words, we greedily pick the base station that has the best ratio between the number of new satisfied clients its selection can contribute and its opening cost.

6.2.8.3   Approximating $k4k$-BCPP

Based on the above discussion, we are ready to present a $\frac{e-1}{3e-1}$-approximation algorithm for $k4k$-BCPP. We distinguish between two cases according to whether or not the optimal solution has the following property: there are many clients that are covered by more than one base station. If the optimal solution has this property, then by opening the maximum number of base stations and applying the $k4k$ property, we get a good approximation. Otherwise, we reduce the problem to the problem of finding a feasible set of base stations such that the number of clients that can be covered, each by exactly one base station, is maximized.

Theorem 6.1. *Algorithm 4 is a $\frac{e-1}{3e-1}$-approximation algorithm for the $k4k$-budgeted cell planning problem.*

Proof. Let $\tilde{n}$ be the number of covered clients in the solution obtained by Algorithm 4, and let n^* be the maximum number of satisfied clients as obtained by the optimal solution. In the latter, let n_1^* denote the number of clients that are satisfied by a single base station, and n_2^* denote the number of clients satisfied by more than one base station. Let I^* denote the set of base stations opened (by the optimal solution) for satisfying these $n^* = n_1^* + n_2^*$ clients.

1: Let I_1 be the output of Algorithm 3.
2: Let I_2 be a set of base stations of maximum size having a total opening cost less than or equal to B.
3: **if** $N_A(I_1) < |I_2|$ **then**
4:     Output I_2 and a set of $|I_2|$ clients that can be covered using the oracle.
5: **else**
6:     Output I_1 and the clients covered by Algorithm 2 for these base stations.

Algorithm 4: $k4k$-BUDGETED CELL PLANNING

Let $N(\text{OPT})$ denote the value of the optimal solution for the BMAP instance. It holds that $N(\text{OPT}) \geq n_1^*$. For the solution I_1 we know that

$$\tilde{n} \geq N_A(I_1) \geq \frac{e-1}{2e} N(\text{OPT}) \geq \frac{e-1}{2e} n_1^* . \tag{6.5}$$

We get:

$$\frac{3e-1}{2e}\tilde{n} = \tilde{n} + \frac{e-1}{2e}\tilde{n} \tag{6.6}$$

$$\geq \tilde{n} + \frac{e-1}{2e}|I^*| \tag{6.7}$$

$$\geq \frac{e-1}{2e}n_1^* + \frac{e-1}{2e}n_2^* \tag{6.8}$$

$$= \frac{e-1}{2e}n^*, \tag{6.9}$$

where inequality (6.7) follows from the fact that $\tilde{n} \geq |I_2| \geq |I^*|$ and the $k4k$ property, and inequality (6.8) is based on (6.5) and Lemma 6.1.   □

It is important to understand that in case of $N_A(I_1) < |I_2|$, Algorithm 4 outputs only an integer number. This number, using the $k4k$-property, provides us a lower bound for the maximum number of satisfied clients in this problem. However, we have no information about the identity of these satisfied clients nor the way these clients are satisfied by the selected set of base stations (i.e., x_{ij}'s). This problem is the main resource allocation problem behind many networks applications. One important example is the cell selection mechanism in future cellular networks. Section 6.3 is devoted to this problem.

6.2.9 The Minimum-Cost Cell Planning Problem

Recall that the minimum-cost cell planning problem (CPP) asks for a subset of base stations $I' \subseteq I$ of minimum cost that satisfies the demands of all the clients using the available base station capacity.

Let z_i denote the indicator variable of an opened base station, i.e., $z_i = 1$ if base station $i \in I$ is selected for opening, and $z_i = 0$ otherwise. Consider the following integer program for this problem (IP$_1$):

$$\min \sum_{i \in I} c_i z_i \qquad \text{(IP}_1)$$

$$\text{s.t.} \sum_{i: j \in S_i} Q(i, j) \geq d_j, \qquad \forall\, j \in J, \qquad (6.10)$$

$$\sum_{j \in J} x_{ij} \leq z_i, \qquad \forall\, i \in I, \qquad (6.11)$$

$$0 \leq x_{ij} \leq 1, \qquad \forall\, i \in I, j \in S_i, \qquad (6.12)$$

$$x_{ij} = 0, \qquad \forall\, i \in I, j \notin S_i,$$

$$z_i \in \{0, 1\}, \qquad \forall\, i \in I. \qquad (6.13)$$

In the first set of constraints (6.10), we ensures that the demand d_j of every client j is satisfied, while the second set (6.11) ensure that the ability of every open base station to satisfy the demands of the clients is limited by its capacity (and that clients can be satisfied only by opened base stations). The contribution $Q(i, j)$ of base station i to client j, taking into account interference from other base stations, can be modeled as in (6.3) or (6.4), or any other predefined behavior of interference. However, because of the way $Q(i, j)$'s are computed, the integer program (IP$_1$) is not linear when interference exists. Without loss of generality we may assume that every client in the input has demand at least 1, as the used units can be scaled accordingly and there is no need for "covering" the clients with zero demand. Lastly, we use the *integrality* assumption that the values $\{w_i\}_{i \in I}$ and $\{d_j\}_{j \in J}$ are integers.

When there are no interference, IP$_1$ becomes much simpler. (LP$_2$) is its linear programming relaxation, in which the last set of integrality constraints (6.13) is relaxed to allow the variables z_i to take rational values between 0 and 1:

$$\min \sum_{i \in I} c_i z_i \qquad \text{(LP}_2)$$

$$\text{s.t.} \sum_{i \in I} w_i x_{ij} \geq d_j, \qquad \forall\, j \in J, \qquad (6.14)$$

$$\sum_{j \in J} x_{ij} \leq z_i, \qquad \forall\, i \in I, \qquad (6.15)$$

$$0 \leq x_{ij} \leq 1, \qquad \forall\, i \in I, j \in S_i, \qquad (6.16)$$

$$x_{ij} = 0, \qquad \forall\, i \in I, j \notin S_i,$$

$$0 \leq z_i \leq 1, \qquad \forall\, i \in I. \qquad (6.17)$$

In fact, LP_2 is a minimum-cost flow problem. To see that, consider the network (G, u, c'), which is defined as follows:

– The graph $G = (V, E)$, where $V = I \cup J \cup \{s\}$ and $E = \{(i, j) \mid i \in I, j \in S_i\} \cup \{(s, i) \mid i \in I\} \cup \{(j, s) \mid j \in J\}$
– The vertex capacity function u, where $u(s) = \infty$, $u(i) = w_i$ for $i \in I$ and $u(j) = d_j$ for $j \in J$
– The vertex cost function c', where $c'(i) = \frac{c_i}{w_i}$ for $i \in I$, $c'(j) = 0$ for $j \in J$ and $c'(s) = -1 - \max_{i \in I} c'(i)$

Accordingly, the integrality assumption yields that there is an optimal solution to the above flow problem, in which the flow in every edge is integral (specifically, any open base station i that serves a client j contributes at least one unit of the client's demand). Moreover, this solution can be computed efficiently using the known algorithms for minimum-cost flow [2]. We denote the solution to LP_2 which corresponds to that flow by $\{\bar{z}, \bar{x}\}$. Let $\bar{I}_j = \{i \in I : \bar{x}_{ij} > 0\}$, for every client $j \in J$. Note that by this definition it follows that for every $i \in \bar{I}_j$ we have that

$$w_i \bar{x}_{ij} \geq 1 . \tag{6.18}$$

Next we introduce an approximation algorithm for CPP with no interference. The algorithm is based on the greedy approach and achieves an approximation of $O(\log W)$, where $W = \max_{i \in I}\{w_i\}$. Unlike the criterion used by other known greedy heuristics, this greedy algorithm chooses to open a base station which maximizes the increase in the maximum demand that can be satisfied by the entire set of the opened base stations.

6.2.10 A Greedy $O(\log W)$-Approximation Algorithm

The algorithm generalizes the one of Chuzhoy and Naor [15] for set cover with hard capacities. In this section we use their notation.

For a subset of base stations, $H \subseteq I$, let $f(H)$ denote the maximum total demand (in demand units, where the clients need *not* be fully covered) that can be satisfied by the base stations in H. For $i \in I$, define $f_H(i) = f(H \cup \{i\}) - f(H)$. Note that when the is no interference, we can calculate $f(H)$ using the following linear program:

$$\text{Max} \sum_{j \in J} \sum_{i \in H} w_i x_{ij} \tag{LP$_3$}$$

$$\text{S.t.} \sum_{i \in H} w_i x_{ij} \leq d_j, \qquad \forall j \in J, \tag{6.19}$$

$$\sum_{j \in J} x_{ij} \leq 1, \qquad \forall i \in H, \tag{6.20}$$

$$0 \le x_{ij} \le 1, \qquad \forall i \in H, j \in S_i, \tag{6.21}$$
$$x_{ij} = 0, \qquad \forall i \in H, j \notin S_i.$$

We need the following lemma.

Lemma 6.2. *Let $H \subseteq I$ be a subset of the base stations, and let H_1 and H_2 be a partition of H into two disjoint sets. Then, there exists a solution to IP_1 in which the base stations in H_1 satisfy a total of $f(H_1)$ demand units.*

Proof. Assume that we are given a solution to IP_1, $\{\tilde{z}\}, \{\tilde{x}\}$, such that the base stations in H_1 satisfy a total of less than $f(H_1)$ demand units. Let $\mathbf{x}$ be an optimal solution to LP_2 for H_1. Iteratively, update $\{\tilde{z}\}, \{\tilde{x}\}$ as follows: while $\sum_{i \in H_1} \sum_{j \in J} w_i \tilde{x}_{ij} < f(H_1)$,

1. Let $i \in H_1$ be a base station such that $\sum_{j \in J} \tilde{x}_{ij} < \sum_{j \in J} x_{ij}$ (notice there must exist such i).
2. Let $j \in J$ be a client such that $\tilde{x}_{ij} < x_{ij}$.
3. Let $\Delta = w_i \cdot \min \{x_{ij} - \tilde{x}_{ij}, \sum_{j \in J} x_{ij} - \sum_{j \in J} \tilde{x}_{ij}\}$.
4. If there exists a base station $i' \in H_2$ such that $\tilde{x}_{i'j} > 0$, let $\delta = \min \{w_{i'} \tilde{x}_{i'j}, \Delta\}$ and set $\tilde{x}_{ij} \leftarrow \tilde{x}_{ij} + \frac{\delta}{w_i}$ and $\tilde{x}_{i'j} \leftarrow \tilde{x}_{i'j} - \frac{\delta}{w_{i'}}$.
5. Else, there exists a base station $i' \in H_1$ such that $\tilde{x}_{i'j} > x_{ij}$.
   Let $\delta = \min \{w_{i'} \cdot (\tilde{x}_{i'j} - x_{i'j}), \Delta\}$ and set $\tilde{x}_{ij} \leftarrow \tilde{x}_{ij} + \frac{\delta}{w_i}$ and $\tilde{x}_{i'j} \leftarrow \tilde{x}_{i'j} - \frac{\delta}{w_{i'}}$.

One can easily verify that the above process halts with a feasible solution with the desired property. □

Let $i_1, i_2, \ldots, i_k$ be the base stations that were chosen by Algorithm 4 to the solution, in the order they were chosen. Let I'_ℓ be the solution at the end of iteration ℓ of the algorithm. Let OPT be a set of base stations that comprise an optimal solution, $\{\bar{z}, \bar{x}\}$.

Next, we inductively define for each iteration ℓ and $i \in \text{OPT} \setminus I'_\ell$ a value $a_\ell(i)$, so that the following invariant holds: it is possible to cover all the clients using the base stations in $\text{OPT} \cup I'_\ell$ with the capacities $a_\ell(i)$ for $i \in \text{OPT} \setminus I'_\ell$ and w_i for $i \in I'_\ell$.

Let $a_0(i) = \sum_{j \in J} w_i \bar{x}_{ij}$. The invariant holds trivially. Consider the ℓth iteration. By the induction hypothesis and Lemma 6.2, there exists a solution $\{z, x\}$ of IP_1 such that the base stations in I'_ℓ satisfy a total of exactly $f(I'_\ell)$ demand units and each base station $i \in \text{OPT} \setminus I'_\ell$ satisfies at most $a_{\ell-1}(i)$ demand units. For each $i \in \text{OPT} \setminus I'_\ell$ let $a_\ell(i) = \sum_{j \in J} w_i x_{ij}$.

1: $I' \leftarrow \emptyset$.
2: **while** $f(I') < \sum_{j \in J} d_j$ **do**
3:     Let $i = \arg \min_{i \in I : f_{I'}(i) > 0} \frac{c_i}{f_{I'}(i)}$.
4:     $I' \leftarrow I' \cup \{i\}$.
5: **return** I'.

Algorithm 5: MINIMUM-COST CELL PLANNING (GREEDY)

In what follows, we charge the cost of the base stations that are chosen by Algorithm 5 to the base stations in OPT. If $i_\ell \in$ OPT, we do not charge any base station for its cost, since OPT also pays for it. Otherwise, we charge each $i \in$ OPT $\setminus I'_\ell$ with $\frac{c_{i_\ell}}{f_{I'_{\ell-1}}(i_\ell)} \cdot (a_{\ell-1}(i) - a_\ell(i))$. Notice that the total cost of i_ℓ is indeed charged.

Consider a base station $i \in$ OPT. If $i \in I'$, let h denote the iteration in which it was added to the solution. Else, let $h = k + 1$. For $\ell < h$, it follows from the definition of $a_{\ell-1}(i)$ that $f_{I'_{\ell-1}}(i) \geq a_{\ell-1}(i)$. By the greediness of Algorithm 4 it holds that:

$$\frac{c_{i_\ell}}{f_{I'_{\ell-1}}(i_\ell)} \leq \frac{c_i}{f_{I'_{\ell-1}}(i)} \leq \frac{c_i}{a_{\ell-1}(i)},$$

and the total cost charged upon i is

$$\sum_{\ell=1}^{h-1} \frac{c_{i_\ell}}{f_{I'_{\ell-1}}(i_\ell)} \cdot (a_{\ell-1}(i) - a_\ell(i)) \leq c_i \sum_{\ell=1}^{h-1} \frac{(a_{\ell-1}(i) - a_\ell(i))}{a_{\ell-1}(i)}$$

$$= c_i \cdot H(a_0(i))$$

$$= c_i \cdot O(\log a_0(i))$$

$$= c_i \cdot O(\log w_i),$$

where $H(r)$ is the rth harmonic number. This completes the analysis.

An additional approximation algorithm for CPP can be found in [4, 8]. This algorithm is based on solving the LP-relaxation (LP$_2$), and randomly rounding the fractional solution to an integer solution. The integer solution it produces is within a factor of $O(W \sqrt{\log n})$ of the optimum, where as before, $W = \max_{i \in I}\{w_i\}$.

Practically speaking, two different simulation sets were conducted with scenarios relevant to 4G technologies in [4, 8]. Each of these simulations has the goal of minimizing the total cost and minimizing the total number of antennas (sectors). In both simulation sets results indicate that the practical algorithms derived from the theoretical scheme can generate solutions that are very close to the optimal solutions and much better than the proved worst-case theoretical bounds. Moreover, the algorithms presented in this section achieve a significantly better lower bound on the solution cost than that achieved by the commonly used greedy approaches [28, 33].

6.2.11 Challenges and Open Problems

The main open problem is a development of an approximation algorithm for CPP (while taking into account also the interference). Unlike the approach presented in this chapter for the no-interference version of the problem (Section 6.2.9), the solution for the full version of the problem most likely cannot be based on LP-based techniques. When considering the formulation of CPP (IP$_1$) one may notice that this non-linear program is not convex, in general. This means that when given two solutions to an instance of the CPP, a convex combination of these two solutions *is not necessarily* a solution for this instance. Solving non-convex non-linear programs is a long-standing open problem, in general.

A fully combinatorial greedy algorithm that generalizes the approach for solving CPP (Section 6.2.10) seems also as a challenge. The analysis for the greedy algorithm makes use of the fact that the objective function is submodular. Unfortunately, in this case the objective functions are not submodular, in general, when interference is involved.

Thus combinatorial algorithms seem to be the correct approach for this purpose. Moreover, we believe that sophisticated analysis of a greedy algorithm is a promising avenue in this direction. A further advantage of a combinatorial approach for CPP is the possibility to achieve a performance guarantee that is independent of W. As shown in [8], it is impossible to design a better than $\Omega(W)$-approximation algorithm for this problem based solely on its LP formulation (i.e., the LP relaxation of IP_1).

Another open problem is the minimum-cost site planning problem. In this problem, in addition to the CPP input, we also have a set of potential geographic locations (sites) for installing a cluster of antennas (or base stations). Usually, such a cluster comprises of antennas of different pattern, power, and direction, and these are addressed to service a large area with several relatively different behavior subareas (e.g., a close high-density mall on one side and a farther low-density neighborhood, on the other side). The problem is motivated by the operator's need to reduce the number of geographical sites in which its equipment is installed since their rental cost is relatively high. Followed by the above discussion, we can define the *minimum-cost site planning problem* as the problem of finding a subset of sites and a subset of base stations in such a way that the demands of all the clients are satisfied, and the total cost of installing sites and base stations (on open sites) is minimized.

The minimum-cost site planning problem can be seen as two-level CPP, where selecting the "sites" is the first level and selecting the base stations configurations to be installed in these sites is the second level. Since this problem is a natural generalization of CPP, we believe that solving CPP will be an important first step towards a solution for the former.

6.3   Cell Selection Problems

The ability to provide services in a cost-effective manner is an important building block of competitive modern cellular systems. Usually, an operator would like to have a maximal utilization of the installed equipment, that is, an operator would like to maximize the number of satisfied customers at any given point in time. This section addresses a basic resource allocation problems in this domain, the cell selection mechanism – see Figure 6.3. Cell selection determines the base station (or base stations) that provides the service to a mobile station – a process that is performed

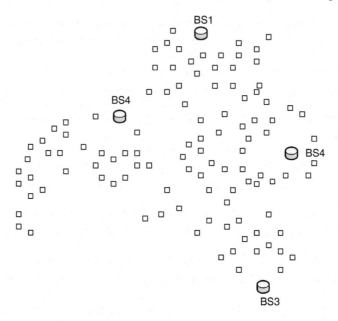

Fig. 6.3 The cell selection problem. Unlike the previous cell planning situation, we are given a set of base stations that are *already* selected for opening. The question now is how to best connect the mobile stations to these base stations in order to maximize the number of mobile stations that fully satisfy their bandwidth demands

when a mobile station joins the network (called *cell selection*), or when a mobile station is on the move in idle mode (called *cell reselection*, or *cell change*, in HSPA).

In most current cellular systems the cell selection process is done by a local procedure initialized by a mobile device according to the best detected SNR. In this process the mobile device measures the SNR to several base stations that are within radio range, maintains a "priority queue" of those that are best detected (those whose pilots are comprised the active set), and sends an official service request to subscribe to base stations by their order in that queue. The mobile station is connected to the first base station that positively confirmed its request. Reasons for rejecting service requests may be handovers or drop calls areas, where the capacity of the base station is nearly exhausted.

Consider for example the settings depicted in Figure 6.4. Assume that the best SNR for Mobile Station 1 (MS1) is detected from microcell A, and thus MS1 is being served by this cell. When Mobile Station 2 (MS2) arrives, its best SNR is also from microcell A, which is the only cell able to cover MS2. However, after serving MS1, microcell A does not have enough capacity to satisfy the demand of MS2 who is a heavy data client. However, if MS1 could be served by picocell B then both MS1 and MS2 could be served. Note that MS1 and MS2 could represent a cluster of clients. The example shows that the best-detected-SNR algorithm can be a

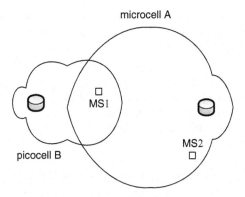

Fig. 6.4 Bad behavior of the *best detected SNR* algorithm in high-loaded capacitated network

factor of $\max\{\tilde{d}\}/\min\{\tilde{d}\}$ from an optimal cell assignment, where $\tilde{d}$ is the demand of any mobile station in the coverage area. Theoretically speaking, this ratio can be arbitrarily large.

This simple example illustrates the need for a global, rather than a local, cell selection solution that tries to maximize the global utilization of the network, and not just the SNR of a single user. In voice only networks, where base station capacities are considered to be high, sessions have limited duration, and user demands are uniform, this may not be a big barrier. That is, the current base station selection process results, in most cases, in a reasonable utilization of the network. However, in the forthcoming future cellular networks this may not be the case.

Another interesting aspect is the support for different QoS classes for the mobile stations (e.g., *gold*, *silver*, or *bronze*). In such a case, the operator would like to have as many satisfied "gold" customers as possible, even if this means several unsatisfied "bronze" customers.

In this section we follow [3] and study the potential benefit of a new global cell selection mechanism, which should be contrasted with the current local mobile SNR-based decision protocol. In particular, we rigorously study the problem of maximizing the number of mobile stations that can be serviced by a given set of base stations in such a way that each of the serviced mobile station has its minimal demand fully satisfied. We differentiate between two coverage paradigms: The first is *cover-by-one* where a mobile station can receive service from at most one base station. The second is *cover-by-many*, where we allow a mobile station to be simultaneously satisfied by more than one base station. This means that when a mobile stations has a relatively high demand (e.g., video-on-demand) in a sparse area (e.g., sea-shore), several base stations from its active set can participate in its demand satisfaction. This option is not available in third-generation networks (and not even in HSPA networks) since these networks have universal frequency reuse and the quality of a service a mobile station receives will be severely damaged by the derived co-channel interference. However, OFDMA-based technology systems and their derivatives are considered to be among the prime candidates for future cellular communication networks. The ability to satisfy the demand of a mobile station by more than one base station (whose pilot is part of the active set) is *possible* in these systems, as defined by the IEEE 802.16e-2005 standard. An important question in this context is whether cover-by-many is indeed more powerful than cover-by-one, in the sense that it improves the ability of the network to satisfy more clients.

Cell selection has received much attention in recent years (e.g., [22, 27, 30, 31]) where research focused mainly on multiple-access techniques, as well as on power control schemes and handoff protocols [22, 30, 31].

In [22] a cell selection algorithm is presented where the goal is to determine the power allocations to the various users, as well as a cover-by-one allocation, so as to satisfy per-user SINR constraints. An HSPA-based handoff/cell-site selection technique is presented in [30, 31], where the objective is to maximize the number of connected mobile stations (very similar to our objective), and reaching the optimality of this objective is done via a new scheduling algorithm for this cellular system. All the above results did not take into account variable base station capacities nor mobile station bandwidth demands. In the case of [30, 31], this enables the authors to reduce their corresponding optimization problem to a polynomial-time solvable matching problem. As shown in our paper, when base station capacities and/or mobile stations' demands are incorporated, this approach is no longer feasible.

An integrated model for optimal cell-site selection and frequency allocation is shown in [27], where the goal is to maximize the number of connected mobile stations, while maintaining quasi-independence of the radio based technology. The optimization problem in this model is shown to be NP-hard.

Another closely related problem is the *all-or-nothing multicommodity flow problem* discussed in [13, 14]. In this problem we are given a capacitated undirected graph $G = (V, E, u)$ (where u is the edge-capacity function) and set of k pairs $(s_1, t_1), \ldots, (s_k, t_k)$. Each pair has a unit demand. The objective is to find a largest subset S of $\{1, \ldots, k\}$ such that one can simultaneously route for every $i \in S$ one unit of flow between s_i and t_i. It is straightforward to verify that the unit profit version of AoNDM is a special case of this problem. It was shown that the all-or-nothing multicommodity flow problem can be approximated within an $O(\log^2 k)$ factor of the optimum [14]. On the other hand, for any $\epsilon > 0$, the problem cannot be approximated to within a factor of $O(\log^{\frac{1}{3}-\epsilon} |E|)$ of the optimum, unless $NP \subseteq ZPTIME\,(|V|^{\text{poly}\log|V|})$ [9]. However, no special attention is given to specific network topologies (e.g., bipartite graphs, as in our case), and other special instances.

Finally, cell selection is strongly related to the well-known family of *generalized assignment problems* (GAP) discussed, among others, in [20]. In its basic form, there are a number of "agents" and a number of "tasks". Any agent can be assigned to perform any task, incurring some cost and profit that may vary depending on the agent–task assignment. Moreover, each agent has a budget and the sum of the costs of task assigned to it cannot exceed this budget. It is required to find an assignment in which all agents do not exceed their budget and total profit of the assignment is maximized.

6.3.1   Model and Definitions

We capture cell selection mechanism by the following *all-or-nothing demand maximization problem* (AoNDM). An instance of the AoNDM consists of the following components:

- A bipartite graph $G = (I, J, E)$ where $I = \{1, 2, \ldots, m\}$ is a set of base stations and $J = \{1, 2, \ldots, n\}$ is a set of clients. An edge (i, j) represents the fact that client j can receive service from base station i.
- A *demand* function d that associate every client j a non-negative integer $d(j)$ called the demand of j.
- A *capacity* function c that associate every base station i a non-negative integer $c(i)$ called the capacity of i (measured in the same unit of the clients' demand).
- A *profit* function p that map each base station i to a non-negative integer $p(j)$ called the profit of j.

The output of AoNDM is a partial assignment of clients to base stations in which a client may be assigned by two possible paradigms. This depends if a client may be assigned only to one of its neighboring base stations (cover-by-one), or to get a service simultaneously by more than one base station (cover-by-many), as described above. In any case, the demand assigned to a base station should not exceed its capacity, and a restriction of $\sum_{i \,:\, (i,j) \in E} x(i, j) \geq d(j)$, for every $j \in S$, is also known as *all-or-nothing*-type of coverage. This means that clients that are partially satisfied are not considered to be covered (such a model appears, for example, in OFDMA-based networks where mobile stations have their slot requirements over a frame and these are not useful if not fulfilled). The goal is to maximize the sum of profits of assigned (or satisfied) clients.

Given any constant $0 < r < 1$, we say an instance is *r-restricted* if for every $(i, j) \in E$, $d(j) \leq r \cdot c(i)$. We further define the problem of *r-AoNDM* as the AoNDM problem limited to r-restricted instances.

6.3.2   Approximating AoNDM and r-AoNDM Problems

The important goal of efficient solution to AoNDM is beyond our reach since this problem is NP-hard. Moreover, it is not even possible to design a close-to-optimal polynomial-time approximation algorithm for AoNDM, unless NP=ZPP[4]. To be precise, since a solution for the general version of AoNDM can be used to solve the Maximum Independent Set Problem in graphs (Problem GJ20 in [21]), and since the latter cannot be approximated within a factor better than $|J|^{1-\varepsilon}$, unless NP=ZPP, for any $\varepsilon > 0$, this hardness of approximation can be used as a lower bound for AoNDM.

---

[4] The class ZPP is equal to the intersection of the computational complexity classes RP and Co-RP

Motivated by practical scenarios where the network satisfies the condition that $d(j) \leq r$, a restricted version of AoNDM, the r-AoNDM problem was defined in the previous section [3].

Two approximation algorithms for the r-AoNDM problem are presented in [3]. The algorithms are *local-ratio*-fashion based [10, 11] and based on a decomposition of the profit obtainable from every client into two non-negative terms; one part is proportional to the demand of the client, while the other part is the remaining profit. A family of feasible solutions is defined, which we dub "maximal" (see the formal definition later in this section), and prove that any such "maximal" solution is an approximate solution when considering a profit function which is proportional to the demand. The approximation algorithms generate such maximal solutions recursively, and an inductive argument is applied in order to prove that the solution generated by the algorithm is also an approximate solution w.r.t. the original profit function. We focus here only on one of these two approximation algorithms, the one that guarantees a solution whose value is within a factor of $\frac{1-r}{2-r}$ from the value of an optimal solution. This algorithm follows the cover-by-one paradigm, and thus every mobile station is covered by at most one base station.

The second algorithm is obtained by a careful refinement of this algorithm and an appropriate change to the notion of maximality. This algorithm uses the cover-by-many paradigm, and as shown in [3] is guaranteed to produce a solution whose value is within a factor of $(1-r)$ from the value of an optimal solution, while the complexity increases by a polynomial factor.

6.3.3 A Cover-by-one $\frac{1-r}{2-r}$-Approximation Algorithm

An approximate solution for the r-AoNDM problem is described in Algorithm 6. The idea of this simple greedy algorithm is to compute, for each client, its profit-to-demand ratio; then to scan clients in decreasing order of this ratio, and for each client in turn, to assign it to a base station if possible, or discard it and continue. However, to facilitate the analysis, we present this algorithm in recursive form (Algorithm 6).

```
 1: if J = ∅ then
 2:     Return empty assignment
 3:  J' = {j ∈ J | p(j) = 0}
 4: if J' ≠ ∅ then
 5:     Return r-AoNDM (I, J \ J', c, d, p)
 6: else
 7:      δ = min_{j∈J} { p(j)/d(j) }
 8:      For every j ∈ J, set p₁(j) = δ · d(j)
 9:      x ← r-AoNDM (I, J, c, d, p − p₁)
10:      Using clients from J', extend x to an α-cover w.r.t. J
11:      Return x
```

Algorithm 6: r-AoNDM (I, J, c, d, p)

Let $(I, J, E, c, d.p)$ be an instance of AoNDM. For every base station i we by $N(i) \subseteq J$ the set of clients that can be covered by i, and for every client j we denote $N(j) \subseteq I$ to be the set of base stations that potentially may serve j. For any set of clients or base stations A, we define $N(A) = \bigcup_{v \in A} N(v)$. Given any function f (e.g., the demand, profit, or capacity), we denote $f(A) = \sum_{v \in A} f(v)$. Given any subset of clients $S \subseteq J$, we define $\bar{S} = J \setminus S$.

Let x be a mapping that assigns clients to base stations, and let clients(x) denote the set of clients assigned by x to some base station. In addition, for a base station $i \in I$ we denote load$_x(i) = \sum_{j:x(j)=i} d(j)$, i.e., load$_x(i)$ is the sum of all demands assigned to i. Finally, for any client $j \in J \setminus$ clients(x) and a base station $i \in N(j)$ we say that j is *eligible for i* if $c(i) -$ load$_x(i) \geq d(j)$.

To specify the algorithm, we need the following concept. Given an assignment x, let $J' \subseteq J$ be a set of clients such that clients$(x) \subseteq J'$. We say that x is an α-*cover* w.r.t. J' if the following condition holds:

If load$_x(i) < \alpha \cdot c(i)$, for a base station i, then $N(i) \cap J' \subseteq$ clients(x).

In other words, a client from J' may not be assigned by an α-cover only if the load of each of its neighbors is at least an α fraction of its capacity. Notice that in terms of r-restricted instances, $\alpha = 1 - r$.

The key step in Algorithm 6 (Step 10) is to extend the assignment returned by the recursive call of Step 9. The algorithm maintains the invariant that returned assignment is an α-cover w.r.t. J. Whenever the recursive call of Step 9 returns, the assignment is extended using the clients in J' to ensure that the invariant holds true.

The key to the analysis of the algorithm is the following result (see also [3, 16]).

Lemma 6.3. *Assume there exists some $\delta \in \mathbb{R}^+$ such that $p(j) = \delta \cdot d(j)$ for every client j. Consider any assignment x. If x is an α-cover w.r.t. J, then $p(\text{clients}(x)) \geq \left(\frac{\alpha}{1+\alpha}\right) \cdot p(\text{clients}(y))$ for any feasible assignment y.*

Proof. Let $S = $ clients(x), and let $Y = $ clients(y). Then

$$
\begin{aligned}
p(Y) &= p(Y \cap S) + p(Y \cap \bar{S}) \\
&= \delta \left[d(Y \cap S) + d(Y \cap \bar{S}) \right] \\
&\leq \delta \left[d(S) + c(N(\bar{S})) \right] \\
&\leq \delta \left[d(S) + d(S)/\alpha \right] \\
&= \frac{\alpha + 1}{\alpha} \cdot p(S),
\end{aligned}
$$

where the first inequality follows from the feasibility of y and the definition of $N(\bar{S})$, while the second follows from our assumption that x is an α-cover w.r.t. J.   □

We note that the above lemma actually bounds the profit of an α-cover even with respect to *fractional* assignment as in the case of cover-by-many.

The following theorem shows that Algorithm 6 produces an $\frac{\alpha}{\alpha+1}$-approximation, assuming one can extend a given solution to an α-cover.

Theorem 6.2. *Algorithm 6 produces an $\frac{\alpha}{\alpha+1}$-approximate (or $\frac{1-r}{2-r}$-approximate) solution.*

Proof. The proof is by induction on the number of recursive calls. The base case is trivial. For the inductive step, we need to consider two cases. For the cover returned in Step 5, by the induction hypothesis, it is an $\frac{\alpha}{\alpha+1}$-approximation w.r.t. $J \setminus J'$, and since all clients in J' have zero profit, it is also an $\frac{\alpha}{\alpha+1}$-approximation w.r.t. J. For the cover returned in Step 11, note that by the induction hypothesis, the solution returned by the recursive call in Step 9 is an $\frac{\alpha}{\alpha+1}$-approximation w.r.t. profit function $p - p_1$. Since every client $j \in J'$ satisfies $p(j) - p_1(j) = 0$, it follows that any extension of this solution is also $\frac{\alpha}{\alpha+1}$-approximation w.r.t. $p - p_1$. Since the algorithm extends this solution to an α-cover by adding clients from J', and p_1 is proportional to the demand, by Lemma 6.3 we have that the extended α-cover is an $\frac{\alpha}{\alpha+1}$-approximation w.r.t. p_1. By the Local-Ratio Lemma (see, e.g., [11]), it follows that this solution is an $\frac{\alpha}{\alpha+1}$-approximation w.r.t. p, thus completing the proof. $\square$

A closer examination of the local-ratio framework presented above shows that what the algorithm essentially does is to traverse the clients in non-decreasing order of their profit-to-demand ratio, while ensuring that at any point, the current solution is an α-cover w.r.t. clients considered so far. Note that the solution x produced by Algorithm 6 is a cover-by-one plan. It therefore follows that the ratio between the *optimal* cover-by-one solution and the optimal cover-by-many solution is at most $\frac{1-r}{2-r}$ as well.

In order to evaluate the practical differences between a global and a local mechanism for cell selection in future networks, an extensive simulation has been conducted [3]. The authors compared between global mechanisms that are based on the two approximation algorithms and the current best-SNR greedy cell selection protocol. The relative performance of these three algorithms under different conditions has been studied. In particular, they showed that in a high-load capacity-constrained 4G-like network, where clients' demands may be large with respect to cell capacity, global cell selection can achieve up to 20% better coverage than the current best-SNR greedy cell selection method.

A distributed version of the above algorithm is recently described by Patt-Shamir et al. [29]. In their $O(\varepsilon^{-2} \log^3 n)$-running time algorithm clients and base stations communicate locally, and after a polylogarithmic number of rounds of communication agree upon an assignment, without resorting to a centralized algorithm with global knowledge (as described in Algorithm 6). They showed that their algorithm guarantees, with high probability, an assignment with overall profit that is at least $\frac{1-r}{2-r}(1-\varepsilon)$ fraction of the optimal profit possible, for any $0 < \varepsilon < 1$.

6.3.4 Challenges and Open Problems

There are several interesting problems that arise from this section. The first is whether or not one can devise a constant-factor approximation algorithm to the

r-AoNDM *that is independent of r*. In this respect it seems that a primary starting point for answering such a question is determining the complexity of r-AoNDM in the case where $r = 1$. A more general question is whether or not there exists a polynomial-time approximation scheme (PTAS) for the problem, and under which conditions. We note that by the reduction presented in [3], the general case is proven to be hard to approximate for instances in which the demand of every client is strictly greater than the capacity of the base stations which can contribute to its coverage. Abusing the notation adopted in this section, it is unclear whether such a phase transition occurs in $r = 1$, or is there some $r > 1$ for which the r-AoNDM problem still adheres to good approximation algorithms.

6.4 Concluding Remarks

This chapter describes approximation algorithms for several planning and control problems in the context of advanced wireless technology. It seems that this area provides many very interesting optimization problems. Moreover, theoretical computer science based approaches and especially approximation algorithm techniques have been shown to provide, in many cases, very good practical algorithms. We believe that these approaches can and should be further used to address the diverse challenges in the design and planning of future cellular networks.

References

1. A. Ageev and M. Sviridenko. Approximation algorithms for maximum coverage and max cut with given sizes of parts. In *Proceedings of the Conference on Integer Programming and Combinatorial Optimization* (IPCO), volume 1610 of *Lecture Notes in Computer Science*, pages 17–30. Springer-Verlag, 1999.
2. R. K. Ahuja, T. L. Magnanti, and J. B. Orlin. *Network Flows (Theory, Algorithms, and Applications)*. Prentice Hall, 1993.
3. D. Amzallag, R. Bar-Yehuda, D. Raz, and G. Scalosub. Cell Selection in 4G Cellular Networks. In *Proceedings of the Annual IEEE 27th INFOCOM*, pages 700–708, 2008.
4. D. Amzallag, R. Engelberg, J. Naor, and D. Raz. Cell planning of 4G cellular networks. Technical Report CS-2008-04, Computer Science Department, Technion - Israel Institute of Technology, 2008.
5. D. Amzallag, M. Livschitz, J. Naor, and D. Raz. Cell planning of 4G cellular networks: Algorithmic techniques, and results. In *Proceedings of the 6th IEE International Conference on 3G & Beyond* (3G'2005), pages 501–506, 2005.
6. D. Amzallag, J. Naor, and D. Raz. Coping with interference: From maximum coverage to planning cellular networks. In *Proceedings of the 4th Workshop on Approximation and Online Algorithms* (WAOA), volume 4368 of *Lecture Notes in Computer Science*. Springer-Verlag, 2006.
7. D. Amzallag, J. Naor, and D. Raz. Algorithmic aspects of radio access network design in B3G/4G cellular networks. In *Proceedings of the Annual IEEE 26th INFOCOM*, pages 991–999, 2007.

8. David Amzallag. *Approximation Algorithms for Optimization Problems in Future Cellular Networks*. PhD thesis, Department of Computer Science, Technion - Israel Institute of Technology, 2008.

9. M. Andrews and L. Zhang. Hardness of the undirected edge-disjoint path problem. In *Proceedings of the 37th Annual ACM Symposium on Theory of Computing* (STOC), pages 276–283, 2005.

10. A. Bar-Noy, R. Bar-Yehuda, A. Freund, J. Naor, and B. Schieber. A unified approach to approximating resource allocation and scheduling. In *Proceedings of the 32th ACM Symposium on Theory of Computing* (STOC), pages 735–744, 2000.

11. R. Bar-Yehuda. One for the price of two: A unified approach for approximating covering problems. *Algorithmica*, 27(2):131–144, 2000.

12. M. F. Cátedra and J. Pérez-Arriaga, editors. *Cell Planning for Wireless Communications*. Mobile Communications Series. Atrech House Publishers, Norwood, MA, 1999.

13. C. Chekuri, S. Khanna, and F. B. Shepherd. The all-or-nothing multicommodity flow problem. In *Proceedings of the 36th Annual ACM Symposium on Theory of Computing* (STOC), pages 156–165, 2004.

14. C. Chekuri, S. Khanna, and F. B. Shepherd. Multicommodity flow, well-linked terminals, and routing problems. In *Proceedings of the 37th Annual ACM Symposium on Theory of Computing* (STOC), pages 183–192, 2005.

15. J. Chuzhoy and J. Naor. Covering problems with hard capacities. In *Proceedings of the 43th Annual IEEE Symposium on Foundations on Computer Science* (FOCS), pages 481–489, 2002.

16. M. Dawande, J. Kalagnanam, P. Keskinocak, F.S. Salman, and R. Ravi. Approximation algorithms for the multiple knapsack problem with assignment restrictions. *Journal of Combinatorial Optimization*, 4(2):171–186, 2000.

17. E. D. Demaine, U. Feige, M. Hajiaghayi, and M. R. Salavatipour. Combination can be hard: Approximability of the unique coverage problem. In *Proceedings of the 17th Annual ACM-SIAM Symposium on Discrete Algorithms* (SODA), pages 162–171, 2006.

18. U. Feige. A threshold of $\ln n$ for approximating set cover. *J. ACM*, 45:634–652, 1998.

19. U. Feige. Coping with NP-hardness of the graph bandwidth problem. In *Proceedings of the 7th Scandinavian Workshop on Algorithm Theory* (SWAT), pages 10–19, 2000.

20. L. Fleischer, M.X. Goemans, V.S. Mirrokni, and M. Sviridenko. Tight approximation algorithms for maximum general assignment problems. In *Proceedings of the 17th ACM-SIAM Symposium on Discrete Algorithms* (SODA), pages 611–620, 2006.

21. M. R. Garey and D. S. Johnson. *Computers and Intractability: A Guide to the Theory of NP-Completeness*. W. H. Freeman and Co., San Francisco, 1979.

22. S. V. Hanly. An algorithm for combined cell-site selection and power control to maximize cellular spread spectrum capacity. *IEEE Journal on Selected Areas in Communications*, 13(7):1332–1340, 1995.

23. S. Y. Hui and K. H. Yeung. Challenges in the migration to 4G mobile systems. *IEEE Communications Magazine*, 41:54–59, December 2003.

24. N. Johnston and H. Aghvami. Comparing WiMAX and HSPA: A guide to the technology. *BT Technology Journal* (BTTJ), 25(2):191–199, 2007.

25. S. Khuller, A. Moss, and J. Naor. The budgeted maximum coverage problem. *Information Processing Letters*, 70:39–45, 1999.

26. Y. K. Kim and R. Prasad. *4G Roadmap and Emerging Communication Technologies*. Artech House Publishers, Boston, MA, 2006.

27. R. Mathar and M. Schmeink. Optimal base station positioning and channel assignment for 3G mobile networks by integer programming. *Annals of Operations Research*, 107:225–236, 2002.

28. M. J. Nawrocki, M. Dohler, and A. Hamid Aghvami, editors. *Understanding UMTS Radio Network: Modelling, Planning and Automated Optimisation*. John Wiley & Sons, Ltd., 2006.

29. B. Patt-Shamir, D. Rawitz, and G. Scalosub. Distributed approximation of cellular coverage. In *Proceedings of the 12th International Conference on Principles of Distributed Systems* (OPODIS), pp. 331–345, 2008.

30. A. Sang, X. Wang, M. Madihian, and R. D. Gitlin. A Load-aware handoff and cell-site se-
    lection scheme in multi-cell packet data systems. In *Proceedings of the IEEE 47th Global
    Telecommunications Conference* (GLOBECOM), volume 6, pages 3931–3936, 2004.
31. A. Sang, X. Wang, M. Madihian, and R. D. Gitlin. Coordinated load balancing, handoff/
    cell-site selection, and scheduling in multi-cell packet data systems. In *Proceedings of the 10th
    Annual International Conference on Mobile Computing and Networking* (MOBICOM), pages
    302–314, 2004.
32. M. Sviridenko. A note on maximizing a submodular set function subject to knapsack con-
    straint. *Operations Research Letters*, 32:41–43, 2004.
33. K. Tutschku. Demand-based radio network planning of cellular mobile communication sys-
    tems. In *Proceedings of the IEEE 17th INFOCOM*, pages 1054–1061, 1998.
34. N. Umeda, T. Otsu, and T. Masamura. Overview of the fourth-generation mobile com-
    munication system. *NTT DoCoMo Technical Review*, 2(9):12–31, 2004. Available at http:
    //www.ntt.co.jp/tr/0409/special.html.
35. J. Vygen. Approximation algorithms for facility location problems. Technical report 05950-
    OR, Research Institute for Discrete Mathematics, University of Bonn, 2005. Available at http:
    //www.or.uni-bonn.de/~vygen/fl.pdf.
36. D. Wisely. Cellular mobile–the generation game. *BT Technology Journal* (BTTJ), 25(2):27–41,
    2007.

Chapter 7
Ethernet-Based Services for Next Generation Networks

Enrique Hernandez-Valencia

Abstract Over the last few years, Ethernet technology and services have emerged as an indispensable component of the broadband networking and telecommunications infrastructure, both for network operators and service providers. As an example, Worldwide Enterprise customer demand for Ethernet services by itself is expected to hit the $30B US mark by year 2012. Use of Ethernet technology in the feeder networks that support residential applications, such as "triple play" voice, data, and video services, is equally on the rise. As the synergies between packet-aware transport and service oriented equipment continue to be exploited in the path toward transport convergence. Ethernet technology is expected to play a critical part in the evolution toward converged Optical/Packet Transport networks. Here we discuss the main business motivations, services, and technologies driving the specifications of so-called carrier Ethernet and highlight challenges associated with delivering the expectations for low implementation complexity, easy of use, provisioning and management of networks and network elements embracing this technology.

7.1 Introduction

Over the last few years, Ethernet technology and services have emerged as an indispensable component of the broadband networking and telecommunications infrastructure, both for network operators and service providers. As an example, Worldwide Enterprise customer demand for Ethernet services by itself is expected to hit the $30B US mark by year 2012 [47]. Use of Ethernet technology in the feeder networks that support residential applications, such as "triple play" voice, data, and video services, is equally on the rise. As the synergies between packet-aware transport and service oriented equipment continue to be exploited in the path toward transport convergence, [40]. Ethernet technology is expected to play a critical part in the evolution toward converged Optical/Packet Transport networks. Here we discuss the main business motivations, services, and technologies driving the specifications

E. Hernandez-Valencia (✉)
Bell Labs, Alcatel-Lucent, 600 Mountain Avenue, Murray Hill, NJ 07974,
e-mail: enrique.hernandez@alcatel-lucent.com

G. Cormode and M. Thottan (eds.), *Algorithms for Next Generation Networks*,
Computer Communications and Networks, DOI 10.1007/978-1-84882-765-3_7,
© Springer-Verlag London Limited 2010

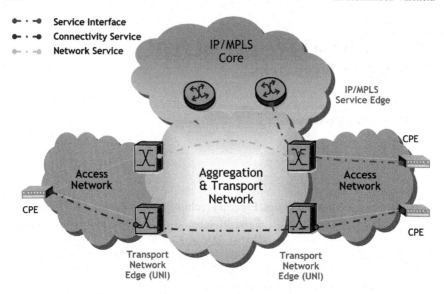

Fig. 7.1 Ethernet roles in a Carrier Ethernet Network

of so-called carrier Ethernet and highlight challenges associated with delivering the expectations for low implementation complexity, easy of use, provisioning and management of networks and network elements embracing this technology.

Ethernet, as the defined by the IEEE 802.1 Working Group [11–13,15], has a vertically integrated architecture framework with physical and data link (MAC) layers modeled after the OSI reference model. This layered architecture framework allows Ethernet technology to be exploited in a variety of data networking and telecommunications roles, as illustrated in Figure 7.1, in support of Carrier Ethernet centric packet services:

- As a network infrastructure service used as one of the building blocks of a network operator, or service provider, transport infrastructure (similar in scope to WDM, SDH/SONET [18], or OTN [17] transport services)
- As a connectivity service used to provide a high bandwidth alternative to Private Lines, Frame Relay, ATM connectivity services for Enterprise site interconnection or to provide a service interface used to enable business or residential access to L3+ data services and associated applications (e.g., Internet Access, IP VPNs, etc.)

In most applications, digital centric (TDM or Packet) approaches tend to be preferred in scenarios with high subscriber density; broad interconnect granularity (in terms of bandwidth demand) and fluid service demand. Conversely, photonic centric approaches tend to be preferred in scenarios with coarser interconnect granularity and more predictable service demand. Here we present the evolving framework for Carrier Ethernet services and discuss transport technologies required to support what we refer to as Ethernet Transport capabilities.

7.2   Carrier Ethernet Services Architecture

The concept of Carrier Ethernet differs from enterprise Ethernet in both the service models and their associated reference architectures. Enterprise Ethernet technology is optimized for deployment on a private network scenario, with a highly uniform user base, a high degree of trust on user behavior, and a strong appreciation for plug-and-play functionality. Carrier Ethernet technology on the other hand is intended to support a public network service, with strong requirements on formal demarcation between subscriber and provider roles, high user heterogeneity, weak subscriber-to-subscriber and subscriber-to-provider trust, and a pay-to-play service model. In practicality, there is limited formal work on service model specifications. From a network infrastructure perspective most of the ITU-T work is based on the concept of functional modeling [45] which attempts to characterize network technologies according to its forwarding paradigm (Circuit vs Packet and Connection-oriented vs. Connectionless/Datagram) and the intrinsic information elements associated with them. More recently, work has focused on the concept of context aware services particularly as ambient networks [1].

The reference network model for Carrier Ethernet Services follows a traditional architecture model for telecom public networking services [34, 36]. Figure 7.2 depicts such a reference model as defined by the MEF and ITU-T. This model follows an emerging industry practice to partition networks along administrative boundaries between subscribers, network operators, and service providers. A Service Provider (SP) network, referred to as a Carrier Ethernet Network (CEN), is demarked by a number of well-defined External Interfaces. Key among these interfaces is the User-to-Network Interface (UNI), which is used to demark the boundary between the CEN and its service subscribers. Another important external interface, the External Network-to-Network Interface (E-NNI), is used to demark the boundaries between CENs.

Subscribers attach their Customer Equipment (CE) to the CEN's provider edge (PE) equipment via such UNIs. The UNI is purposely specified to define the expected forwarding behavior for the service frames, both on ingress (toward the

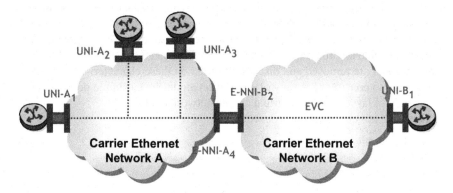

Fig. 7.2 Reference Ethernet Services Architecture

CEN) and egress (toward the CE) in terms of capabilities typically associated with enterprise Ethernet technology. The format for the service frame is expected to comply with the IEEE-defined Ethernet MAC frame format and allows for the use of virtual LAN tags, also referred to as customer tags (C-Tags), as a means to classify various kinds of customer frames and flows. Ethernet services are then defined as a set of processing and forwarding rules for the service frames across a number of UNIs.

7.2.1 Ethernet Virtual Connection

The basic service creation construct is referred to as an Ethernet Virtual Connection (EVC). An EVC is defined by the MEF as "an association of two or more UNIs". In terms of the service architecture reference model, the association is in terms of the network side of the interface (UNI-N) rather than the client side of the interface (UNI-C). Hence, the EVC exists completely within the scope of the service provider network. This approach gives the service provider the ability to virtualize the service interface and the freedom to choose their preferred technology to deploy within their network boundary at the cost of slightly higher complexity in providing service frame transition from one network domain to another. An EVC performs two main functions:

- Associates two or more subscriber sites (UNIs) to enable the transfer of Ethernet service frames between them.
- Establishes the rules for service frame transfer between the subscriber sites, whether they are part or not of the same EVC.

The EVC construct is intended to emulate the same kind of service capabilities associated with other existing data networking connection services, such as for a Frame Relay data link connection identifiers (DLCI) or ATM Virtual Circuit/virtual Path connection (VCC/VPC). Two basic rules govern delivery of Ethernet service frames over an EVC. First, a service frame must never be delivered back to the UNI from which it originated (to avoid traffic looping back and forth between the CE and the PE). Second, service frames must be delivered with the Ethernet MAC addresses and frame payload unchanged unless otherwise negotiated between the subscriber and the SP, i.e., the Ethernet frame remains intact from source to destination(s). This forwarding behavior differs from a typical routed Ethernet model where the Ethernet frame headers are removed and discarded. Based on these characteristics, an EVC can be used to construct a variety of connection models from simple point-to-point to a variety of layer 2 oriented virtual private networks (VPN).

The MEF has defined three types of EVCs:

- Point-to-point
- multipoint
- Rooted-multipoint

These EVC types are the current basis for the Ethernet services so far defined by both the MEF and the ITU-T [19, 35].

7.2.2   Defining Ethernet Services

Ethernet services may vary in many ways. For instance, there are the so-called "retail" services which are typically services intended to be sold to individual subscribers. These services are based on "open" UNI service models and, as such, tend to be defined from a subscriber perspective. There are also the so-called "wholesale" services which are typically sold between service providers or service operators themselves. These services may be based on "open" or private E-NNI implementation agreements, and hence, tend to be described from a network operators perspective.

A variety of transport technologies, and associated management and control plane protocols, may be used to implement Ethernet service on a given CE. For instance, SONET/SDH and DWDM/OTN technology use GFP[27] to support point-to-point transport and services for Ethernet frames. Packet oriented technologies such as Provider Bridging [13], Provider Backbone Bridging [14] and MPLS [43, 44] /PWE3 [33] may also be used to natively support, or emulate multipoint LAN-like services. Next we discuss different types of Ethernet services and some of the important characteristics that distinguish them from other packet service offerings.

7.2.3   Ethernet Service Definitions

Table 7.1 gives the names of the connectivity services so far specified by the MEF and the ITU-T and the relationship between them.

Next we provide a short description of the main characteristics of these services as defined by the MEF and ITU-T.

7.2.3.1   Ethernet Line (E-Line) Services

The E-Line Services are intended to provide point-to-point connectivity between two UNIs via a point-to-point EVC. An E-Line service is referred as an Ethernet Private Line (EPL) service when only one service instance can be associated with the two UNIs. This service is intended for applications where the endpoints need to communicate over a dedicated, or "leased line", channel. Hence, EPL is well suited

Table 7.1   MEF Ethernet services Definitions

Service type	Port-based	VLAN-based
E-line	Ethernet Private Line	Ethernet Virtual Private Line
E-LAN	Ethernet Private Lan	Ethernet Virtual Private Lan
E-Tree	Ethernet Private Tree	Ethernet Virtual Private Tree

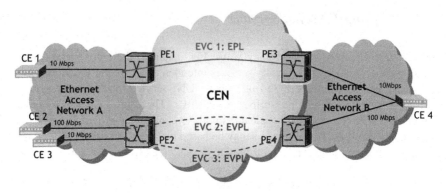

Fig. 7.3 Examples of E-Line services

for transparent Ethernet LAN interconnects as well as for circuit emulation applications over Ethernet. An E-Line service is referred as an Ethernet Virtual Private
Line (EVPL) service when multiple service instance (i.e., service multiplexing) can
be associated with at least one of the UNIs participating in the given point-to-point
service instance. This service is intended for applications that can communicate over
a shared point-to-point communications channel. Hence, EVPL can provide similar
connectivity capabilities as point-to-point Frame Relay and ATM data services.

As in the example illustrated in Figure 7.3, an E-Line Service instance, EVC 1,
can be used to provide point-to-point connectivity to transfer Ethernet frames between symmetric ports with very strict performance commitments, e.g., a premium
circuit-like service between the 10 Mbps UNIs at CE 1 and CE 4. Another set of
E-Line Service instances may be used to provide point-to-point statistical access
to network resources. For instance, EVC 2 interconnects symmetric UNIs at 100
Mbps between CE 2 and CE 4 and provides committed network resources (including bandwidth or frame delay commitments) as long as the traffic complies with
a contracted traffic descriptor. At the same time, EVC 3 interconnects two asymmetric UNIs, at 10 Mbps on CE 3 and at 100 Mbps on CE 4, but may deliver no
performance assurances. In this case, the UNI port on PE4 would be configured as
a service multiplexing interface while the UNI ports on PE1 and PE3 are dedicated
to the given service instance.

Note that since E-Line only provides point-to-point connectivity it does not require support of Ethernet MAC bridging capability and associated Ethernet MAC
learning for frame forwarding purposes. Hence, service scaling in terms of switching and storage complexity is on par to Frame Relay and ATM switching.

7.2.3.2 Ethernet LAN Services

The Ethernet LAN Services are intended to provide multipoint connectivity between
two or more UNIs via multipoint EVCs. An E-LAN service is referred as an Ethernet
Private LAN (EP-LAN) service when only one service instance can be associated

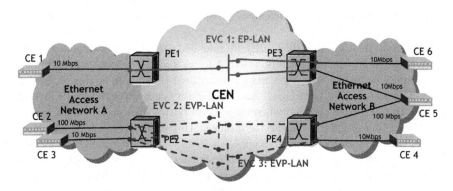

Fig. 7.4 Examples of E-LAN services

with the UNIs using the given service instance. This service is intended for applications where the endpoints need to appear to communicate over a dedicated LAN. Hence, the network provides what is typically referred as a bridge LAN service as endpoints communicate as if connected to an IEEE 802.1 VLAN bridge [11]. An E-LAN service is referred as an Ethernet Virtual Private LAN (EV-PLAN) service when multiple service instances (i.e., service multiplexing) can be associated with at least one of the UNIs participating in the given multipoint service instance. This service is intended for applications that can communicate over a shared multipoint communications channel such as IP routers communicating over a shared Ethernet LAN or for the interconnection of IEEE 802.1 VLAN bridges.

As in the example illustrated in Figure 7.4, an E-LAN service instance, EVC 1, can be used to provide multipoint connectivity to transfer Ethernet frames among a set of symmetric access ports (i.e., connecting CE 1, CE 5, and CE 6), say, with either statically or statistically allocated transport resources for the interconnected ports. Similarly, another set of E-LAN service instances may be used to provide shared multipoint access to network resources. For instance, CE 2 and CE 3 can use their UNI port to access either CE 4 or CE 5. EVC 2 may provide committed network resources (including bandwidth or frame delay commitments), as long as the traffic complies with a contracted traffic descriptor. EVC 3 may deliver no performance assurances, e.g., Best Effort quality of service.

Since an E-LAN service provides multipoint connectivity it does require either direct support of Ethernet MAC bridging capability and associated Ethernet MAC learning for frame forwarding purposes or emulation of such capabilities by some other means, e.g., VPLS [31, 32]. Hence, service scaling in terms of switching and storage complexity is higher than E-LINE but still lower than equivalent emulations capabilities via Frame Relay and ATM switching as there is no native multipoint forwarding mechanism in those technologies.

7.2.3.3   Ethernet E-TREE Services

The Ethernet Tree Services (E-TREE) are intended to provide multipoint connectivity between two or more UNIs, referred to as Root UNIs, and point-to-point connectivity between a Root UNI and a number Leaf UNIs, with no direct connectivity between any two Leaf UNIs. An E-TREE service is referred as an Ethernet Private Tree (EP-Tree) service when only one service instance can be associated with the UNIs using the given service instance. This service is intended for applications where the endpoints need to appear to communicate over a dedicated LAN but wish to restrict connectivity between certain sites. Hence, the network provides what is typically referred as a "hub-and-spoke". An E-TREE service is referred as an Ethernet Virtual Private Tree (EVP-Tree) service when multiple service instance (i.e., service multiplexing) can be associated with at least one of the UNIs participating in the given multipoint service instance. This service is intended for applications where communications with certain devices need must occur over a given set of sites (the Root UNIs) nut communications to other devices may occur over a shared point-to-point or multipoint communications channel.

As in the example illustrated in Figure 7.5, an E-TREE service instance, EVC 1, can be used to provide rooted multipoint connectivity to transfer Ethernet frames among a set of symmetric access ports (i.e., connecting CE 1, CE 5, and CE 6), say, with either statically or statistically allocated transport resources for the interconnected ports. But unlike E-LAN, CE 5 and CE 6 can only communicate directly with CE 1, but not directly with each other. Also similarly to E-LAN, another set of E-TREE service instances may be used to provide shared rooted multipoint access to network resources. For instance, CE 2 and CE 3 can use their UNI port to access either CE 4 or CE 5 via their (Root) UNIs on PE4. EVC 2 may provide committed network resources (including bandwidth or frame delay commitments), as long as the traffic complies with a contracted traffic descriptor. EVC 3 may deliver no performance assurances, e.g., Best Effort quality of service. But, unlike E-LAN, CE 2 and CE 3 cannot communicate directly among themselves as their EVCs are provided over Leaf UNIs.

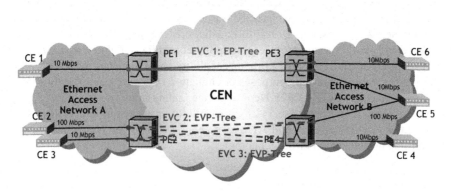

Fig. 7.5 Examples of E-TREE services

Since an E-TREE service provides rooted multipoint connectivity it does require direct or emulated support of Ethernet MAC bridging capability, and associated Ethernet MAC learning, for frame forwarding purposes at the Root UNI. Yet, it does not require Ethernet bridging or Ethernet MAC address learning at Leaf UNIs. Neither IEEE Ethernet nor its emulated versions support native means to provide rooted multipoint connectivity. This is an open area for future standardization. Service scaling in terms of switching and storage complexity could be expected to be higher than the combination of an equivalent E-LAN service among the UNI roots and E-LINE service instances between root and leaf UNIs.

7.3 Ethernet Service Attributes

The Ethernet Service Attributes are the service constructs within the MEF Ethernet Service Definition Framework[37] provided to allow further customization of Ethernet service categories, hence, further characterizing the forwarding treatment to be expected by the subscriber. Currently, Ethernet Service Attributes are arranged into three groups:

1. UNI SA: apply to all services instances created on a specific UNI, hence they can be set to a different value only on each UNI location. Attributes in this group cover most physical media parameters, such as link speed, or port aggregation capabilities. Table 7.2 provides a short description of the service attributes in the UNI SA group.
2. EVC Endpoint SA: or UNI per EVC SA in MEF terminology, apply to a specific service instance at a given UNI. EVC Endpoint SA, they can be set to different values on each end of the EVC. Attributes in this group include most of the direction-specific parameters such as packet filtering rules and traffic descriptors. Table 7.3 provides a short description of the service attributes in the EVC Endpoint SA group.
3. EVC SA: apply to the entire connection irrespective of direction. Attributes in this group include most of the performance affecting parameters, such as connection protection model and performance objectives. Table 7.4 provides a short description of the service attributes in the EVC SA group.

Below we discuss some of the more critical service attributes for service differentiation.

7.3.1 Ethernet Virtual Connection Type (EVC Type)

The EVC type service attribute indicates the kind of connectivity to be established among the relevant UNIs. Three EVC types are currently specified:

1. Point-to-Point: The EVC associates exactly two UNIs and there are not restrictions on the bi-directional connectivity between them.

Table 7.2 UNI Service Attribute

UNI Service Attribute	Description
UNI Identifier	An arbitrary text string to identify the UNI
Physical Medium	The physical medium or media type supported by this UNI. Most of the media types covered are specified in the IEEE 802.3-WG and intended for business applications (i.e., no EPON media types are currently specified)
Speed	The UNI link speed. Based on the traditional Ethernet data rate hierarchy: 10 Mbps, 100 Mbps, 10/100 Mbps Auto-negotiation, 10/100/1,000 Mbps Auto-negotiation, 1 Gbps, or 10 Gbps
Mode	The transmission mode of the interface. Only Full Duplex transmission is currently specified
MAC Layer	The Ethernet MAC as per IEEE 802.3-2005
UNI MTU Size	The maximum transmission unit at the UNI. It must be large enough to accommodate up to 1522 bytes, the standard maximum frame size for Ethernet
Service Multiplexing	An indicator that multiple service instances are supported from the given UNI. It must be set to No if the All to One Bundling SA is set to Yes
Bundling	An indicator that aggregation of Customer VLANs into a single EVC is supported at the given UNI. It must be set to No if the All to One Bundling SA is set to Yes
All to One Bundling	An indicator that all Customer VLANs must be aggregated into a single EVC. It must be set to No if Bundling or Service Multiplexing SA is set to Yes
CE-VLAN ID for untagged and priority tagged Service Frames	Specifies the Customer VLAN ID (VID) number to be used for untagged and priority tagged Service Frames (in the range of 1-4094)
Maximum number of EVCs	The maximum number of EVCs supported by the UNI
Ingress Bandwidth Profile Per UNI	An optional capability to specify an Ingress traffic descriptor, or bandwidth profile, applicable to all service frames into the UNI
Egress Bandwidth Profile Per UNI	An optional capability to specify an egress traffic descriptor, or bandwidth profile, applicable to all service frames out of the UNI
Layer 2 Control Protocols Processing	A list that specifies, for each Ethernet control protocol, whether the PE needs to Peer (process), Discard, Pass, or Peer and Pass the control traffic to EVC

2. Multipoint: The EVC associates two or more UNIs and there are not restrictions on the bi-directional connectivity between them.
3. Rooted-Multipoint: The EVC associates two or more UNIs. One or more UNIs are declared Roots and the rest are declared Leafs. There are not restrictions on the bi-directional connectivity between the Root UNIs. Leaf UNIs can only communicate directly with the Root UNIs.

Notice that in practicality Ethernet services can be delivered from a combination of the above connection types, i.e., some portions of an E-LAN EVC may be supported via point-to-point connections.

Table 7.3 EVC Endpoint Service Attributes

EVC per UNI Service Attribute	Description
UNI EVC ID	A string formed by the concatenation of the UNI ID and the EVC ID to identify the EVC endpoint
CE-VLAN ID/EVC Map	A mapping table that specifies the Customer VLAN IDs to be associated with the EVC
Ingress Bandwidth Profile Per EVC	An optional capability to specify an ingress traffic descriptor per EVC for service frames into the UNI
Ingress Bandwidth Profile Per CoS Identifier	An optional capability to specify an ingress traffic descriptor per CoS ID. A variety of CoS IDs are also specified
Egress Bandwidth Profile Per EVC	An optional capability to specify an egress traffic descriptor per EVC for service frames out of the UNI
Egress Bandwidth Profile Per CoS Identifier	An optional capability to specify an egress traffic descriptor per CoS ID

Table 7.4 EVC Service Attribute

EVC Service Attribute	Description
EVC Type	The type of EVC (Point-to-Point, multipoint or Rooted Multipoint)
EVC ID	An arbitrary string unique across the CEN that identifies the EVC supporting the service instance
UNI List	The list of UNI Identifiers associated with the EVC
Maximum Number of UNIs	The maximum number of UNIs on the EVC. It must be 2 for P2P EVCs and grater for others
EVC MTU size	The maximum frame size for the EVC. It must be greater or equal to the minimum of the UNI MTU sizes associated with the EVC
CE-VLAN ID Preservation	An indicator of whether Customer VLAN IDs values are required to be preserved
CE-VLAN CoS Preservation	An indicator of whether Customer Priority Code Point (PCP) values are required to be preserved
Unicast Service Frame Delivery	The set of delivery rules associated with Unicast service frames
Multicast Service Frame Delivery	The set of delivery rules associated with Multicast service frames
Broadcast Service Frame Delivery	The set of delivery rules associated with Broadcast service frames
Layer 2 Control Protocol Processing	A list that specifies, for each Ethernet protocol passed to the EVC, whether to Tunnel or Discard them
EVC Performance	The performance objective for each CoS ID specified for the EVC

Also, as noted before, rooted multipoint forwarding is not natively supported by either IEEE Ethernet or any its emulation mechanisms. Destination based traffic filtering is one common approach to emulate this service but that scales poorly when connectivity does not follow a "hub-and-spoke" logical topology.

7.3.2 Class of Service Identifier (CoS ID)

The MEF service framework allows for one or more CoS instances (or set of service frames to which a CoS commitment may apply) to be associated with a single EVC. A minimum number of traffic classification mechanisms are currently identified for the purpose of CoS instance determination via the CoS ID service attribute:

- Physical Port
- User Priority/Priority Code Point (as per IEEE P802.1ad [13])
- IP/MPLS DiffServ/IP TOS (as per IETF RFC 2475 [3])
- Ethernet (Layer 2) Control Protocols

The service provider will then enforce different traffic descriptors for each CoS instance. Each CoS instance will offer different levels of performance as specified in the performance parameters per class of service, e.g., delay, jitter, and loss. The following subsections will explore each of the aforementioned CoS identifiers.

7.3.2.1 Physical Port

In this case a single CoS instance is associated with all service frames across the physical port irrespective of the number of EVCs that may be configured on the UNI. The port based CoS ID provides the simplest form to specify a CoS instance using the minimum amount of subscriber information. Port-based CoS indications are well-suited for "hose" or "point-to-cloud" service models. Yet, it provides the highest challenge for network resource allocation to the service provider [5].

7.3.2.2 Priority Code Point/User Priority

In this case up to eight CoS instances can be associated with non-overlapping set of service frames of a given EVC by looking into the Ethernet MAC Priority Code Point (PCP) field as per clause 9 IEEE 802.1Q [13] (ex User_Priority filed in IEEE 802.1p). This option is only applicable when the subscriber Ethernet frames are tagged either with a Priority tag or a VLAN tag as per IEEE 802.1 Q [11]. The PCP based CoS ID provides a means for customers to indicate QoS commitments, including frame delay and frame loss precedence, for its service frames. Either relative (i.e., as in IETF DiffServ) or strict QoS commitments can be offered under this CoS ID by encoding both the service frame priority and drop precedence in the PCP field, using the IEEE defined 8P0D, 7P1D, 6P2D, or 5P3D CoS encoding model. Here, the digit before P indicates the number of distinct frame delay priority levels and the digit before D the number of frame drop precedence levels being communicated. UPC-based CoS indications are to traditional connection-oriented QoS model such as in ATM, Frame Relay and IP Integrated Service/Differentiated service models [2].

7.3.2.3   IP/MPLS DiffServ/IP TOS

In this case information from either an IPv4/IPv6 TOS field or DiffServ fields can be used to associate a CoS instance to a non-overlapping set of service frame on a given EVC. IP TOS, in general, can be used to provide up to eight CoS instances to a given EVC. The IP ToS precedence model is similar to the 8P0D QoS precedence model in IEEE 802.1Q. DiffServ, by contrast, defines several per-hop behaviors (PHBs) that can be used to provide more granular QoS capabilities when compared to the simple forwarding precedence based on the IP TOS field. DiffServ can be used to specify up to 64 QoS encodings (called DiffServ codepoints or DSCPs) that can be used to define, theoretically, up to 64 CoS instances per EVC (note that CoS instance identification is not allowed on a per IP address basis).

Standardized DiffServ PHBs include Expedited Forwarding (EF) for a low delay, low loss service, four classes of Assured Forwarding (AF) for bursty real-time and non-real-time services, Class Selector (CS) for some backward compatibility with IP TOS, and Default Forwarding (DF) for best effort services. Unlike the port and PCP COS ID indicators the DiffServ and IP TOS based CoS ID indicators require the subscriber CE and provider PE to inspect and classify the service frames as per the IP/MPLS packet header in the Ethernet frames payload. Hence, the price to be paid for the additional CoS granularity is increased configuration complexity when establishing the EVC.

7.3.2.4   Ethernet Control Protocols

In this case a single CoS instance can be associated with all service frames conveying IEEE 802 based control protocols such as PAUSE messages and Link Aggregation Control Protocol in IEEE 802.3 or Spanning Tree Protocols or GARP/GVRP in IEEE 802.1Q. The Layer 2 Control Protocol based CoS ID provides the simplest form to specify QoS differentiation to user control traffic over user data frames. Note that uses of PCP values for this purpose would require careful configuration on the frame classification rules in the subscriber networks as Ethernet control protocols are typically carried untagged in IEEE 802 based networks.

7.3.3   Bandwidth Profile (BWP)

The configuration of a CoS ID goes hand-in-hand with the specification of traffic profile for the set of service frame associated with the CoS instance. The set of traffic descriptors and associated bandwidth profile is referred to the Bandwidth Profile service attribute. An ingress bandwidth profile can be configured on a per CoS ID basis, i.e., a CoS instance. Egress bandwidth profiles are typically not applicable to point-to-point EVCs unless service multiplexing is enabled at the relevant UNI.

The Bandwidth Profile service attribute consists of six parameters. Four of the parameters are used to specify a two-rate traffic descriptor:

- The Committed Information Rate (CIR)
- The Committed Burst Size (CBS)
- The Excess Information Rate (EIR)
- The Excess Burst Size (EIR)

CIR and EIR are typically expressed in bits/sec. CBS and EBS are typically expressed in bits although it is typically allocated as an integer number of the MTU for the particular interface and/or the EVC. Two additional parameters, the Color Mode and the Coupling Flag (CF), are used to govern the rules to allocate excess unused transmission opportunities. The actual bandwidth allocation algorithm, or Bandwidth Profile (BWP) algorithm, is provided in Figure 7.6.

The main purpose of the BWP algorithm is to determine the compliance of a particular Ethernet frame flow to the two-rate traffic descriptor. The actual algorithm can be interpreted as two "leaky buckets" containing a number of tokens allocated for transmission of arriving frames, one for frames to be checked for conformance to the specified CIR (the "green" token bucket) and one for frames to be checked for conformance to the specified EIR (the "yellow" token bucket). "Green" tokens are added to the "green" token bucket at rate CIR while "yellow" tokens are added to the "yellow" buckets at rate EIR. Hence, it is a common practice to refer to the frames that draw from the "green" token bucket as "green" frames while the frames that draw from the "yellow" token are referred to as "yellow" frames. Below we further discuss the interpretation of the behavior of the MEF BWP.

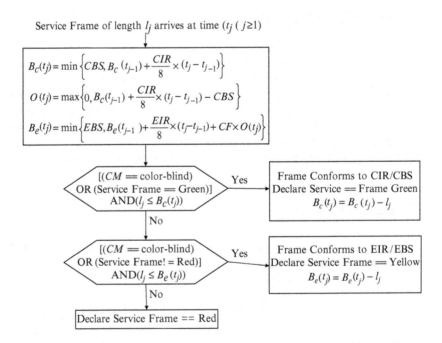

Fig. 7.6 MEFs two-rate Bandwidth Profile Algorithm

7.3.4   Traffic Descriptors

As noted before, the pair or parameters CIR/CBS and EIR/EBS characterize the behavior of the two-rate bandwidth profile specified by the MEF. The CIR parameter indicates the long-term average rate allocated to the frames that draw their transmission opportunity from the presence of sufficient credits from the "green" token bucket. The CBS actually indicates the maximum number of tokens that can be accumulated in the "green" token bucket, or the maximum frame burst size if multiple frames could arrive at the same time. Similarly, the EIR parameter indicates the long-term average rate allocated to the frames that draw their transmission opportunity from the presence of sufficient credits from the "yellow" token bucket. The EBS indicates the maximum number of tokens that can be accumulated in the "yellow" token bucket, or the maximum frame burst size if multiple frames could arrive at the same time.[1]

7.3.4.1   Frame Color and Token Disposition

The parameters CF and CM determine how tokens are drawn and disposed. CF is a binary parameter that determines whether unused frame transmission opportunities lost from a full "green" token bucket can be used to replenish the "yellow" token bucket. Lost transmission opportunities from the "yellow" token are never reused. The CM parameter indicates whether the Ethernet service provider recognizes frame coloring on the incoming frames, prior to the application of the BWP algorithm. CM is said to be Color-Blind if the service provider always deems the initial color of any arriving frame to be "green". On the other hand, CM is said to be Color-Aware if the service provider recognizes the incoming color of the frame.

7.3.4.2   Frame Coloring and Frame Disposition

The frame color is used to determine the set of frames that qualifies for QoS commitments. Frames colored "green" qualify for any of the performance objective specified for the relevant CoS. Frames colored "yellow" qualify for "Best Effort" treatment (up to the committed EIR). Frames can be colored by either the subscriber or the service provider. Frame coloring by the subscriber is relevant only if the subscriber shapes the relevant CoS instance to conform to the negotiated CIR and service provider recognizes the frame colors generated by the subscriber. Frame coloring by the subscriber happens as an outcome of applying the BWP algorithm.

---

[1] Note that the actual maximum burst size at the UNI, for instance, would be a function of the UNI link rate, the CIR and the CBS (for the "green" token bucket) or the EIR and the EBS (for the "yellow" token bucket). The Optical Transport Hierarchy encompasses integrated photonic and digital transmission and switching capabilities for next-generation transport systems.

Frames conforming to its intended token bucket retain their color as they traverse the CEN. Frames that fail to conform to its intended token bucket are re-colored: non-conforming "green" frames are re-colored "yellow" and non-conforming "yellow" frames are re-colored "red". "Red" frames are not required to be transported across the CEN.

7.3.5 Performance Service Attribute

The performance service attribute conveys the committed quality of service associated with the identified CoS Instance. There are three parameters currently specified:

- Frame delay
- Frame jitter
- Frame loss

7.3.5.1 Frame Loss

Frame loss is the most elemental performance metric for most packet service as it determines the actual throughput delivered by the service. Frame loss is defined the percentage of CIR-conformant (green) service frames not delivered between an ordered pair of UNIs over the sampling interval. Hence, let TX_{ij} denote the total number of green service frames received by UNIi and intended to UNIj and let RXij the number of green service frame received from UNI_i by UNI_j then FL_{ij}, the Frame Loss between UNI_i and UNI_j can be expressed as

$$FL_{ij} = (1 - RX_{ij}/TX_{ij}) \times 100$$

Not all applications can be expected to be affected in similar manner by the Frame Loss level delivered by a service. For instance, let us consider the broad class of "inelastic" applications (those that have limited control over their packet rate). Sample inelastic applications such as packet voice (e.g., Voice over IP – VoIP) tend to be resilient to packet loses in the range of 1–5% of the total packet stream [26]. Yet, others such as Circuit Emulation would suffer significant performance degradation even with an FL level of 0.1%. A similar situation can be observed for the broad class of "elastic" applications (those that can adjust their transmission rate to the channel conditions). TCP-based applications, for instance, will gracefully recover from low to moderate levels of packet loss showing no significant impact to the application throughput. Yet, their throughput can degrade substantially once the FL objective increases above moderate levels, say above 5%. Interaction between the BWP policing mechanism, which determines in part the service frame color, and the FL objective can further complicate the overall application level performance.

Matching applications to performance objectives is still an area of research. Hence, it is expected that service providers will craft multiple CoS with different levels of FL objectives.

7.3.5.2 Frame Delay

Frame delay is a critical performance parameter for many interactive applications that require timely delivery of information, such as IP telephony and video gaming. Frame Delay for Ethernet services has been defined as a percentile of the frame delay distribution where frame delay is measured as the time elapsed from the reception of the last bit of a green service frame at the ingress UNI to the transmission of the first bit of the green service frame at the egress UNI. Let S_T denote the set of the N collected frame delay samples representing all the successfully delivered Green Service Frames whose first bit arrived at its ingress UNI_i during the sampling interval T. S_T can be expressed as $S_T = \{d_{ij}^1, d_{ij}^2, \ldots, d_{ij}^N\}$, where d_{ij}^k represents the Frame Delay of the kth Green Service Frame in the set. Then the frame delay performance between UNI_i and UNI_j, d_{ij}^P, can be expressed as

$$\bar{d}_{ij}^P = \begin{cases} \min\{d \,|\, P \le \frac{100}{N} \sum_{k=1}^{N} I(d, d_{ij}^k)\} & \text{if } N \ge 1 \\ 0 & \text{otherwise}, \end{cases}$$

where,

$$I(x, y) = \begin{cases} 1 & \text{if } x \ge y \\ 0 & \text{otherwise}, \end{cases}$$

A limitation of defining frame delay metric in term of percentiles of the frame delay distribution is the difficulty allocation delay budgets to network components or network domains in order to achieve a given end-to-end delay objective.

7.3.5.3 Frame Delay Variation

Frame delay variation (FDV), also referred to as frame delay jitter, is a critical performance parameter for real-time applications such as IP telephony, Circuit Emulation, or broadband video distribution. These real-time applications require a low and predictable delay variation to ensure timely play-out of the transferred information. Unfortunately there is no universal agreement on metric for frame delay variation. The dominant concern is applicability to application requirements vs. computation complexity. One metric for FDV, used by the MEF, defines FDV in terms of a high-percentile of the distribution between the sample frame delay and the minimum frame delay for the target set of UNIs over a target sampling period.

Let $V_T = \{\Delta d_{ij}^{kl} \,|\, \forall i, j$ such that $a_l - a_k = \Delta t, a_k \in T$, and $a_{lj} \in T\}$ be the set of all delay variations for all eligible pairs of Green Service Frames where a_k

represents the arrival time of the kth Green Service Frame in the set. Let N be the number of samples in V_T. Define $\Delta \tilde{d}_{ij}^P$ to be the P-percentile of the set V_T. Thus

$$\Delta \tilde{d}_{ij}^P = \begin{cases} \min\{d \mid P \leq \frac{100}{K} \sum I(d, \Delta d_{ij})\} \text{ if } K \geq 1 \\ 0 \text{ otherwise,} \end{cases}$$

where:

$$I(d, \Delta d_{ij}) = \begin{cases} 1 \text{ if } d \geq \delta_{ij} \\ 0 \text{ otherwise,} \end{cases},$$

and the sum is carried out over all the values in the set V_T. An alternative definition of FDV is as the percentile of the difference vs. the observed delay and some fixed component, such as the minimum or average delay.

7.3.5.4 Ethernet Quality of Service

Delivering Quality of Service (QoS) expectations to Ethernet service subscribers poses similar challenges as delivering performance commitments to IP flows. Both technologies share a datagram oriented forwarding model, not to mention that IP is the most common traffic type carried via Ethernet technology. Hence, most research on IP traffic characterization is relevant to Ethernet flows [4, 9, 49], except for Ethernet specific control and forwarding behaviors such as Address Resolution Protocol (ARP) and broadcasting of unknown destination for unicast flows, which are a source of broadcast "storms" in any large bridged network and require a different type of characterization. Yet, given the preponderance of client/server based applications in enterprise networks it should not be assumed that IP traffic models are equally applicable to Ethernet services.

Performance characterization for Ethernet services is currently focused around point-to-point connectivity models, and hence, similar in scope to the service model for frame relay and other virtual leased line approaches. The frame loss, frame delay, and delay variation performance metrics specified above are consistent with this forwarding paradigm. Ideally, based on the service performance objectives specified as a Service Level Agreement (SLA) and the associated traffic descriptors, a service provider can allocate network resources to fulfill the service needs. Traffic descriptors for Ethernet services share a similar "leaky bucket" based frameworks as those for ATM and IP. Hence, as many of the performance bounds to provide guaranteed or statistical services objectives carry over to E-Line type services [2, 29, 42]. Yet, mapping traffic descriptors to the actual traffic characteristics and then deriving relevant traffic engineering statistics is not always straightforward [39, 48].

The frame loss, frame delay, and delay variation performance metrics specified for point-to-point services are not the ideal performance metric for multicast and rooted-multipoint connections. The SLA of a LAN service can be specified using the hose model [5], which is well matched to the MEF port-based bandwidth profile model. In this model only the ingress and egress capacities are specified for each interface, not the specific traffic demands between every pair of interfaces. Yet, given the multipoint nature and uncertainty in the actual traffic flow between the multiple connection points it is extremely difficult to provision the network to meet all traffic demand without potentially wasting substantial network resources. Techniques as dual-hop load balancing, also named Valiant Load Balancing (VLB) [30,50], could be used as a forwarding approach robust to traffic fluctuations for E-LAN emulation using full mesh connectivity. Yet, the scheme increases transport delays and it is unfriendly to specific Ethernet specific forwarding functions (such as unknown traffic replication). Handling resource allocation as a multicommodity flow problem [10] can be impractical for very large networks [1].

7.4 Implementing Ethernet Transport Services

In a telecommunications environment IEEE Ethernet technology can be used by itself or in conjunction with other transport centric technologies, e.g., WDM, SDH/SONET, OTH, or (T)MPLS [23,24], to deliver a full complement of carrier-grade forwarding, OA&M, survivability and management features. These so-called Ethernet Transport Services address network operator and service provider needs for carrier-grade packet transport solutions based on Ethernet technology. For instance, survivability approaches such as PESO [8] reuse components of Enterprise grade Ethernet with other well-established transport mechanisms as defined by the ITU-T [21, 22]. Yet, researchers are also looking at extensions to native Ethernet networking [16, 38, 41]. For instance, work from Elmeleegy et al. [7] investigates approaches to mitigate native Ethernet forwarding behavior such as Rapid Spanning Tree infamous slow convergence to forwarding topology changes or network congestion from broadcast/unknown unicast packet duplication [6]. Kim et al. work on SEATTLE [28] and Sharma et al. work on Viking [46] look to design, implement, and evaluate practical replacement for Ethernet bridging that scales to large and dynamic networks. The section below describes the application space for the various existing technologies.

7.4.1 Addressing Ethernet as Dedicated Network Infrastructure

Solutions in this application space deliver "virtual fiber" based connections required to implement an Ethernet-oriented transport network infrastructure. The functional blocks used to implement these services are modeled after ITU-T requirements for network transport equipment [22]. Note that use of IEEE 802.3 physical layer interfaces to interconnect network equipment also falls into this application space. A "virtual fibre" Ethernet Network Service is intended to emulate a physical medium or "wire". It is typically realized as a point-to-point constant-bit rate (CBR) transport capability that extends the reach of a defined Ethernet PHY (IEEE 802.3). It may be complemented with networking mechanisms from an under optical layer network for switching, OA&M and trail protection, including PHY layer extensions

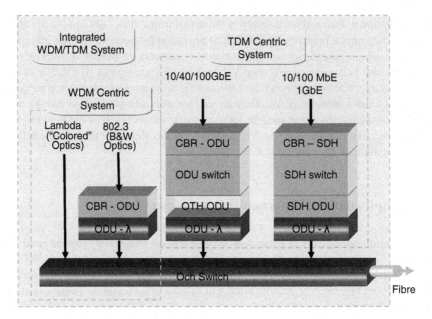

Fig. 7.7 Ethernet Transport over WDM and TDM

for link fault detection, performance management, and client signal fail (when the emulated PHY lacks such features). Network elements for this application space are expected to be managed consistent with established architectural and operational models for transport network operators [20, 21]. Products that address this application space fall within what is referred to as Multi-Service Transport Platforms (MSTP)/Multi-Service Provisioning Platforms (MSPP) market segment and they include network elements based on:

- Ethernet-over-WDM (EoW)
- Ethernet-over-SDH/SONET (EoS) – Type 1 Services
- Ethernet-over-OTH (EoP)[2]

Figure 7.7 illustrates the functional framework for WDM and TDM solutions addressing the "virtual fibre" application space.

7.4.2 Addressing Ethernet as Switched Network Infrastructure

Network elements in this application space deliver "virtual circuit" based connections required to implement an Ethernet-oriented transport network infrastructure.

---

[2] The Optical Transport Hierarchy encompasses integrated photonic and digital transmission and switching capabilities for next-generation transport systems.

The functional blocks used to implement these services are modeled after ITU-T requirements for network transport equipments [19] and the functional model for the
Ethernet MAC [22]. A "virtual circuit" Ethernet Transport Services is intended to
emulate a "shared" or "fractional" link. It is typically realized as a point-to-point or
point-to-multipoint variable-bit rate (VBR) packet-oriented transport capability that
provides differentiable level of services independent of the access media speed). It
may be complemented with networking mechanisms from an under optical layer
network, mostly for OA&M and trail protection (when the emulated data link lacks
such features). Network elements for this application space are also expected to
be managed consistent with established architectural and operational models for
transport network operators. Yet, they must also incorporate best-in class data networking procedures that allow for forwarding and control plane independence, and
packet-oriented OAM. Products that address this application space fall within what
is referred to as the Next Generation Multi-Service Provisioning Platforms (NG
MSPP)/ Optical Packet Transport System (OPTS) market segments and they include
network elements based on:

• Ethernet-over-Fibre (EoF) a.k.a. Carrier Ethernet
• Ethernet-over-SDH/SONET (EoS) – Type 2 Services
• Ethernet-over-(T)MPLS (EoM)

Figure 7.8 illustrates the functional framework for the hybrid WDM/TDM/Packet
solutions addressing this application space.

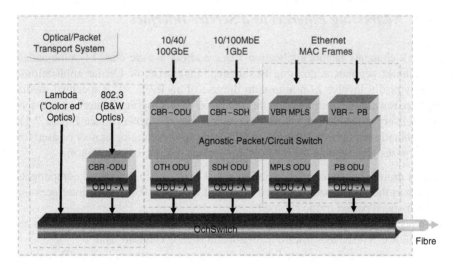

Fig. 7.8 Transport over an Optical/Packet Transport System

7.4.3 Addressing Ethernet Connectivity Service

Solutions in this application space may be based on either "virtual fibre" or "virtual circuit" interconnect capabilities in order to be optimized for Enterprise data networking applications. Ethernet connectivity services are based on Metro Ethernet Forums E-Line and E-LAN service definitions and they use the IEEE 802.1 MAC as the basis for their services attributes.

Ethernet connectivity services allow for a variety of enterprise data networking applications. Specifically:

- Ethernet Private Lines and Private LANs may be delivered through CBR-oriented, "virtual fibre" transport solutions addressing mission-critical Enterprise services. They are managed consistently with established operational models for private managed networks (a subset of the network operation model in [20, 21]).
- Ethernet Virtual Private Lines and Virtual Private LANs may be delivered through VBR-oriented, "virtual circuit" transport solutions addressing public/private Enterprise data networking services. They are managed consistently with operation models for public data networks [22, 25] (either via vendor specific EMS/NMS or Web/SNMP based 3rd party management tools).

The solution space is addressed by products designed for the Optical Packet Transport Systems (OPTS) market segment with integrated Packet, TDM, and WDM fabrics.

7.4.4 Addressing Ethernet as a Service Interface

Network elements in this application space address a wide class of value-added interconnect services addressing Residential, Enterprise, or Carrier applications. They typically involve as a minimum the use of an IEEE 802.3 specified media interface toward the customer and the extension of this "service" interface to a service delivery point deeper within the service provider network (see Figure 7.1). A combination or optical, Ethernet or MPLS transport technologies may be used for the purposes of extending the reach of this service interface. For instance,

- In a mobile backhaul application where 3G radio access network components such as the BTS/NodeB and their BSC/RNCs support IEEE 802.3 interfaces for high-speed packet traffic off-load,
- In residential triple play scenarios where the broadband access node supports an IEEE 802.3 interfaces toward it Broadband Access Gateway, and
- In enterprise services where Ethernet is used as a means to access an IP-enabled services, such as Internet access or an IP-VPN.

In those applications the basic Ethernet connectivity service is typically complemented with additional content-specific technologies, most commonly from IP/MPLS. Network elements that address this application space include products

in the OPTS market segment complemented with Layer 3 (IP/MPLS) functionality intended to facilitate Interworking with the service-aware Network Edge
Routers/Switches.

References

1. F. Belqasmi, R. Glitho, and R. Dssouli. Ambient network composition. *IEEE Network Maga-zine*, Jul/Aug 2008.
2. J. C. R. Bennett, K. Benson, A. Charny, W. F. Courtney, and J. Y. Le-Boudec. Delay jitter bounds and packet scale rate guarantee for expedited forwarding. *IEEE/ACM Transactions on Networking*, 10(4), August 2002.
3. S. Blake, D. Black, M. Carlson, E. Davies, Z. Wang, and W. Weiss. An Architecture for Differentiated Service. RFC 2475 (Informational), December 1998.
4. N. Brownlee and K.C Claffy. Understanding internet traffic streams: Dragonflies and tortoises. *IEEE Communications Magazine*, 40(10), August 2002.
5. N.G. Duffield, P. Goyal, A. Greenberg, P. Mishra, K.K. Ramakrishnan, and J.E.V.D. Merwe. Resource management with hoses: Point-to-cloud services for virtual private networks. *IEEE/ACM Transactions on Networking*, 10(5):679–692, 2002.
6. K. Elmeleegy, A. L. Cox, and T. S. Ng. Etherfuse: An ethernet watchdog. In *ACM SIGCOMM*, 2007.
7. K. Elmeleegy, A L. Cox, and T. S. Ng. Understanding and mitigating the effects of count to in-finity in ethernet networks. *IEEE/ACM Transactions on Networking*, 17(9):186–199, February 2009.
8. S. Acharya et al. PESO: Low overhead protection for ethernet over SONET transport. In *IEEE Infocom*, 2004.
9. A. Feldmann, A. Greenberg, C. Lund, N. Reingold, J. Rexford, and F. True. Deriving traffic demands for operational ip networks: Methodology and experience. *IEEE/ACM Transactions on Networking*, 9(3), June 2001.
10. A. Gupta, J. Kleinberg, A. Kumar, R. Rastogi, and B. Yener. Provisioning a virtual private network: A network design problem for multicommodity flow. In *ACM Symposium on Theory of Computing (STOC)*, 2001.
11. IEEE standard 802.1Q – IEEE standards for local and metropolitan area networks – virtual bridged local area networks. Institute of Electrical and Electronics Engineers, May 2003.
12. IEEE standard 802.1d – IEEE standard for local and metropolitan area networks: Media access control (MAC) bridges. Institute of Electrical and Electronics Engineers, June 2004.
13. IEEE standard 802.1ad – IEEE standard for local and metropolitan area networks – virtual bridged local area networks – amendment 4: Provider bridges. Institute of Electrical and Elec-tronics Engineers, May 2006.
14. IEEE project 802.1ah – provider backbone bridging. Institute of Electrical and Electronics Engineers, June 2008. See http://www.ieee802.org/1/pages/802.1ah.html.
15. IEEE standard 802.3 – 2005, information technology – telecommunications and information exchange between systems – local and metropolitan area net-works – specific requirements – part 3: Carrier sense multiple access with collision detection (CSMA/CD) access method and physical layer specifications. Institute of Electrical and Electronics Engineers, December 2005.
16. IETF TRILL working group. Internet Engineering Task Force, http://www.ietf.org/html. charters/trill-charter.html, 2009.
17. ITU-T recommendation G.707 network node interface for the synchronous digital hierarchy (SDH). International Telecommunication Union, December 1998.
18. ITU-T recommendation G.709. interfaces for the optical transport network (OTN). Interna-tional Telecommunication Union, March 2003.

19. ITU-T recommendation G.8011 ethernet over transport – ethernet services framework. International Telecommunication Union, August 2005.
20. ITU-T G.798. characteristics of optical transport network hierarchy equipment functional blocks. International Telecommunication Union, December 2006.
21. ITU-T recommendation G.783. characteristics of synchronous digital hierarchy (SDH) equipment functional blocks. International Telecommunication Union, March 2006.
22. ITU-T recommendation G.8021 characteristics of ethernet transport network equipment functional blocks. International Telecommunication Union, June 2006.
23. ITU-T recommendation G.8110.1, architecture of transport MPLS layer network. International Telecommunication Union, 2006.
24. ITU-T recommendation G.8113, requirements for operation & maintenance functionality in t-mpls networks. International Telecommunication Union, 2006.
25. ITU-T draft recommendation G.8114, operation & maintenance mechanism for T-MPLS layer networks. International Telecommunication Union, 2007.
26. ITU-T Y.1540. internet protocol data communication service – IP packet transfer and availability performance parameters. International Telecommunication Union, 2007.
27. ITU-T Recommendation G.7041. Generic Framing Procedure (GFP), 2008.
28. C. Kim, M. Caesar, and J. Rexford. Floodless in SEATTLE: A scalable ethernet architecture for large enterprises. In *ACM SIGCOMM*, 2008.
29. E. Knightly and N.B. Shroff. Admission control for statistical QoS: theory and practice. *IEEE Network Magazine*, 13(2), 1999.
30. M. Kodialam, T.V. Lakshman, and S. Sengupta. Efficient and robust routing of highly variable traffic. In *HotNets III*, 2004.
31. K. Kompella and Y. Rekhter. Virtual Private LAN Service (VPLS) Using BGP for Auto-Discovery and Signaling. RFC 4761 (Proposed Standard), January 2007.
32. M. Lasserre and V. Kompella. Virtual Private LAN Service (VPLS) Using Label Distribution Protocol (LDP) Signaling. RFC 4762 (Proposed Standard), January 2007.
33. L. Martini, E. Rosen, N. El-Aawar, and G. Heron. Encapsulation Methods for Transport of Ethernet over MPLS Networks. RFC 4448 (Proposed Standard), April 2006.
34. MEF4: Metro ethernet network architecture framework - part 1: Generic framework. Metro Ethernet Forum, May 2004.
35. MEF6.1: Ethernet services definitions - phase 1. Metro Ethernet Forum, June 2004.
36. MEF12: Metro ethernet network architecture framework: Part 2: Ethernet services layer. Metro Ethernet Forum, April 2005.
37. MEF10.1: Ethernet services attributes - phase 2. Metro Ethernet Forum, November 2006.
38. A. Myers, T. S. Ng, and H. Zhang. Rethinking the service model: Scaling ethernet to a million nodes. In *Third Workshop on Hot Topics in Networks (HotNets-III)*, 2004.
39. I. Norros. On the use of fractional brownian motion in the theory of connectionless networks. *IEEE Journal of Selected Areas in Communications*, 13(6), August 1995.
40. Market alert: 4Q07 and global 2007 optical networking. Ovum, March 2008.
41. R. Perlman. Rbridges: Transparent routing. In *IEEE Infocom*, 2004.
42. H. Ren and K. Park. Towards a theory of differentiated services. In *Proceedings of Quality of Service, Eighth International Workshop*, 2000.
43. E. Rosen, D. Tappan, G. Fedorkow, Y. Rekhter, D. Farinacci, T. Li, and A. Conta. MPLS Label Stack Encoding. RFC 3032 (Proposed Standard), January 2001.
44. E. Rosen, A. Viswanathan, and R. Callon. Multiprotocol Label Switching Architecture. RFC 3031 (Proposed Standard), January 2001.
45. M. Sexton and A. Reid. *Broadband Networking: ATM, SDH, and SONET*. Artech House Publishing, 1997.
46. S. Sharma, K. Gopalan, S. Nanda, and T. Chiueh. Viking: A multi-spanning-tree ethernet architecture for metropolitan area and cluster networks. In *IEEE Infocom*, 2004.
47. Business ethernet services: Worldwide market update (MEF). Vertical System Group, January 2008.

48. D. Wischik and N. McKeown. Part I: Buffer sizes for core routers. *ACM SIGCOMM Computer Communication Review*, 35(2), July 2005.
49. L. Yao, M. Agapie, J. Ganbar, and M. Doroslovacki. Long range dependence in internet backbone traffic. In *IEEE International Conference on Communications*, 2003.
50. R. Zhang-Shen and N. McKeown. Designing a predictable internet backbone network. In *Hot-Nets III*, 2004.

Chapter 8
Overlay Networks: Applications, Coexistence with IP Layer, and Transient Dynamics

Chen-Nee Chuah and Ram Keralapura

Abstract Overlay networks have emerged as a promising paradigm for providing customizable and reliable services at the application layer, such as fault-resilient routing, multicast, and content delivery. This chapter focuses on infrastructure-based overlay networks, where pre-selected nodes (located in one or multiple network domains) are connected to one another through application-layer routing. Overlay routing allows individual flows to optimize route selection based on specific metrics like delay, loss rate, or throughput. When different overlays are simultaneously and independently conducting routing control, they may unintentionally interfere with each other, leading to traffic oscillations. Similarly, problematic interactions can occur between IP and overlay networks. For example, traffic matrices become more dynamic and ambiguous, making them harder to estimate, and load-balancing policies at IP layer can be undermined. We will review existing works that model such interactions and provide guidelines to circumvent these problems.

8.1 Introduction

Despite the ease of deploying new applications in the Internet, the network layer in the current Internet fails to provide the flexibility and stringent quality-of-service (QoS) guarantees required by some delay and/or loss sensitive applications like Voice-over-IP and real-time multimedia streaming. There are several reasons for this. First, link failures are a commonplace occurrence in today's Internet [30, 31], and trouble shooting routing problems is extremely challenging. While intra-domain routing protocols can take several seconds to reconverge after a failure [20], inter-domain path restorations can take several minutes due to the slow convergence of

C.-N. Chuah (✉)
Electrical and Computer Engineering, University of California, Davis, One Shields Avenue,
CA 95616
e-mail: chuah@ucdavis.edu

R. Keralapura
Narus, Inc., 500 Logue Avenue, Mountain View, CA 94043
e-mail: rkeralapura@Narus.com

G. Cormode and M. Thottan (eds.), *Algorithms for Next Generation Networks*,
Computer Communications and Networks, DOI 10.1007/978-1-84882-765-3_8,
© Springer-Verlag London Limited 2010

BGP, resulting in poor performance of real time applications. Many studies have contributed to a better understanding of the root causes of BGP anomalies (e.g., failures, misconfigurations, malicious hijacking, etc.) [17, 25, 26, 29, 41, 43]. However, given the tremendous volume of BGP routing updates, it is difficult to detect BGP anomalies in real time, let alone fix them. Secondly, applications are constrained by the network layer routing and peering policies of the Internet service providers (ISPs). As shown in [36], the paths provided by ISPs based on their routing and peering policies are usually much longer than the shortest possible path. Thirdly, strategic techniques such as multihoming [38] or hot-potato routing result in asymmetric inter-domain paths, making it more challenging for applications to predict their end-to-end routing performance. Fourthly, network layer support for new services such as multicast, mobility, and efficient content distribution to a large number of users, to name but a few, requires a large-scale infrastructure change in all ISPs. Such a change is impractical (although not impossible) considering the cost and effort involved to support each of the new services.

To address these issues in the Internet, application developers and service providers have started using application-layer networks, more popularly known as *overlay networks*. An overlay network typically consists of nodes located in one or more network domains that communicate with one another at the application layer. Application traffic can be routed from one overlay node to another solely on the default network layer paths or by using an intermediate overlay node as a forwarding agency, thereby forming paths that are not readily provided by the native layer. An overlay network typically monitors multiple paths between pairs of nodes and selects one based on its own requirements of end-to-end delay, loss rate, and/or throughput. By doing so, it gives applications more control over routing decisions, instead of being constrained by the network layer.

In other words, an overlay network adds an additional layer of *indirection* on top of one or more physical networks. As a result, it can provide additional routing services to applications and, in some cases, processing resources to overlay users. For example, overlay nodes can forward data traffic onto other overlay nodes, forming an "indirect" overlay path that can be drastically different from the default network layer path chosen by the specific intra-domain or inter-domain protocols. Overlay nodes typically encapsulate the application-layer data that now include information regarding overlay routing control. Note that the network layer is oblivious to the routing performed at the application layer. Once an overlay node receives a packet, it decapsulates the application-layer data and decides how to handle the packet (i.e., forward the packet to one or more overlay nodes, spawn other processes on the overlay node, etc.). Therefore, overlay traffic from different source–destination pairs will share bandwidth and processing resources at the same overlay node that they traverse. From the perspective of overlay users/flows, they are now sharing (and competing for) the physical resources of the underlying nodes and links.

8.1.1   Overlay Network Architecture

Overlay networks can be classified into two broad categories based on their design: *infrastructure-based* and *noninfrastructure-based* overlay networks. Infrastructure-based overlays rely on a preselected set of nodes (i.e., regular infrastructure) to provide overlay services, while noninfrastructure-based networks do not have a fixed infrastructure, but depend on nodes that frequently enter and leave the network. In the rest of this chapter, we refer to noninfrastructure-based overlays as *peer-to-peer* (P2P) overlays. Some of the popular infrastructure-based overlay networks are Detour [36], RON [12], Akamai [1], OPUS [13], PlanetLab [9], etc. Similarly BitTorrent [2], Napster [7], Kazaa [6], Gnutella [4], Chord [40], and Bamboo [34] are examples of popular P2P overlays.

Infrastructure-based overlay networks require an organization to own the complete application-layer network and administer it. For example, consider the Akamai network that provides a fast delivery mechanism between content providers and their customers. This overlay network spans several different autonomous systems (ASes) in different continents. However, the entire infrastructure of the overlay network is owned and administered by Akamai. Detour [36] and RON [12] also fall into this category and provide generic routing services to achieve reliability and fault tolerance that are not guaranteed by the IP layer. On the other hand, P2P overlay networks are built dynamically based on participating end hosts. Popular file sharing services like BitTorrent form application-layer networks using the nodes of the users who login and use this network to exchange audio, video, and data files among themselves. Notice that the current users can leave the network at anytime and new users can join the network frequently. Hence these overlay networks do not have a fixed topology or connectivity, but depend on the number of users logged in, their locations, and the files that they own.

While different overlay networks designed for a wide range of applications may differ in their implementation details (e.g., choice of topologies or performance goals), most of them provide the following common set of functionalities: path/performance monitoring, failure detection, and restoration. Most overlay routing strategies select a path between a source–destination pair with the best performance in terms of delay, throughput, and/or packet loss. Overlay networks monitor the actively used paths by sending frequent probes to check if the paths adhere to acceptable performance bounds. If a problem is detected (e.g., failures or congestion), the overlay network will select an alternate path to use.

Figure 8.1 illustrates how overlay networks operate and provide the intended functionality to the end users. It shows two example overlays built on top of the same physical network. Nodes A, B, C, D, E, F, G, H, and Q belong to the underlying IP network. Endnodes A_1, B_1, C_1, and D_1 belong to the first overlay network whereas A_2, E_2, F_2, and D_2 belong to the second overlay network. Note that the overlay nodes sit on top of the corresponding IP layer node. Let us consider A-D source–destination pair. The default path selected by the IP layer is $A - G - H - Q - D$. Now suppose that link $G - H$ is congested, resulting in poor performance. The overlay networks will detect this and reroute the traffic through

Fig. 8.1 Two overlays built on top of the same physical networks

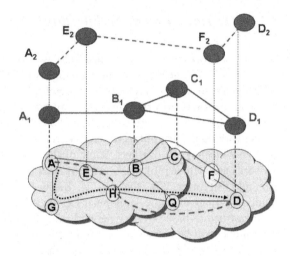

another path (that avoids link $G - H$) that offers better performance. For example, in the first overlay, endnode A_1 can forward all the traffic to node B_1 and B_1 can in turn forward all the traffic to D_1. Thus the overlay path taken by the traffic is now $A_1 - B_1 - D_1$, which translates to the IP layer path $A - E - B - C - F - D$. Similarly, the overlay and IP layer paths for the second overlay network can be $A_2 - E_2 - D_2$ and $A - E - H - Q - D$, respectively.

Thus the actual IP layer path taken by the traffic is now $A - E - B - C - F - D$. Similarly, the second overlay can use the path $A - E - H - Q - D$.

8.1.2 Challenges and Design Issues

The overlay approach has its own advantages and disadvantages. The main benefit of overlay networks is its ease of deployment without having to add new equipment or modifying existing software/protocols in the existing Internet infrastructure. Instead, the required modifications are introduced at the end hosts in the application layer. This allows bootstrapping and incremental deployment, since not every node needs or wants the services provided by a specific overlay network. On the other hand, adding an additional layer of indirection does add overhead in terms of additional packet headers and processing time. Additional layer of functionality also introduces complexity that can be hard to manage and may lead to unintended interactions with other existing layers.

We will focus our discussion on infrastructure-based overlays that aim to provide fault-resilient routing services to circumvent the performance problems of the IP layer routing. In particular, we will explore how allowing routing control at two independent layers, i.e., the application and the IP layers, could lead to short-term or long-term traffic oscillations. As pointed out in our previous work [24], such unintended interactions have profound implications on how ISPs design, maintain, and run their networks. Given the increasing popularity of overlay networks, it is critical to address issues that arise from the interaction between the two layers to ensure healthy and synergistic coexistence. As more overlays are deployed, the volume of traffic that they carry is increasing [39]. We show in [22] that since most overlay networks are designed independently with different target applications in mind, their routing decisions may also interfere with each other. This article surveys existing work that attempts to seek a better understanding of the dynamic interactions between overlay and IP layer, as well as across multiple overlays.

The rest of the article is organized as follows. Section 8.2 contains an overview of various applications of overlay networks. In Section 8.3, we explore the problematic interactions that can occur between IP and overlay networks. For example, traffic matrices become more dynamic and ambiguous, making them harder to estimate, and load-balancing policies at IP layer can be undermined. We will discuss existing works that apply game theory to study such interactions both in equilibrium and during the transient period. We examine interactions across multiple layers in Section 8.4 and determine the conditions under which they occur, model the synchronization probability, and seek solutions to avoid those problematic scenarios. We summarize our findings and outline lessons learned in Section 8.5.

8.2   Applications of Overlay Networks

One of the earliest designs for application-layer networks was proposed in Detour [36], where the authors identify the problems in Internet routing. They highlight the fact that the paths that applications traverse are typically not ideal in terms of various performance metrics like end-to-end delay, loss, and throughput. They identify two main reasons for this: (i) policy-based BGP routing restricts the use of the best inter-AS path between different source–destination pairs that span multiple domains, and (ii) proprietary traffic engineering policies determine the shortest-path routing within a domain. The authors go on to suggest that instead of using default Internet routing, overlay networks can be used to provide better paths and thus improve the performance of various applications.

The main focus in RON [12] is to build an overlay network that can provide resiliency to applications. The paper identifies that failures in the Internet could take a long time to recover. For example, a BGP reconvergence after a failure takes more than 10 min. The paper proposes an overlay network that recovers from a failure in the order of seconds instead of minutes. With the help of an experimental test bed, the authors show that they achieve significant improvement in performance.

One other popular application of infrastructure-based overlay networks is in the distribution of content in the Internet. Popular Web sites (like Yahoo! [11] and CNN [3]) that get millions of hits everyday and need to stream video and audio to several people at the same time face the problem of congestion, server overload, and performance degradation. One approach to avoid these problems is to store multiple copies of the content in strategic locations on the Internet, and dynamically redirect requests to different servers to avoid congestions, server overload, and performance degradation. This requires that the servers at various locations on the Internet are always up to date. To accomplish this, content delivery networks (like Akamai) build application-layer networks that provide services to various Web sites in replicating their data in different places on the Internet.

Another well-known use of overlay networks is in distributed hash tables (DHTs) like Chord [40], Pastry [35], Tapestry [45], Scribe [15], and Bamboo [34]. DHTs are self-organizing, structured peer-to-peer networks that are used to locate objects and route messages in a group of nodes. Typically, the nodes and objects in a DHT are assigned identifiers (called *nodeID* and *keys*, respectively). The node identifiers and object keys have a certain length (e.g., 128 bits long in Pastry) and are derived from a 2^b id space, where b is typically a large value. Given a message and key, DHTs route the messages through the system of nodes such that the number of hops taken by the message to reach the destination object is minimized. The approach is to continually route the message in such a way that the next hop is numerically closer to the destination than the current node.

Implementing multicast in the Internet has been explored for a long time. Many schemes (like [16]) that were proposed required changes to the IP routing plane and hence did not find widespread deployment. Hence the focus shifted to application-layer networks to accomplish multicast. SplitStream [14] was one such scheme that proposed the use of overlay networks to achieve multicast. The authors propose to use distributed hash tables (like Pastry [35] or Scribe [15]) to build multicast trees that are used to distribute audio/video to different hosts in a reward-based approach.

Another use of overlay networks is in coordinating peer-to-peer applications such as file sharing on the Internet. Popular applications such as BitTorrent, KaZaa, and EDonkey have designed application-layer protocols where the computers of users are the endnodes, and these endnodes can share audio, video, and data files amongst themselves. This concept of peer-to-peer communication is now being extended to include applications like live TV (e.g., Joost [5]), video streaming, multicast, voice over IP (e.g., Skype [10]), etc.

8.3   Coexistence of Overlay and IP Layers

ISPs manage the performance of their networks in the presence of failures or congestion by employing common traffic engineering (TE) techniques such as link weight settings, load balancing, and routing policies. On the other hand, overlay networks attempt to provide delay and loss sensitive applications with more control in choosing end-to-end paths (hence bypassing ISP-dictated paths) to achieve better performance in the presence of failures or high loads. The question arises as to whether the two independent routing control layers will inadvertently interact with each other and hamper each layer from achieving their respective goals.

8.3.1   Equilibrium Behavior

The interaction between the overlay networks and the IP layer was first identified by the work of Qiu et al. [33], where the authors investigate the performance of selfish overlay routing in Internet-like environments. The approach in this paper was to model overlay routing and IP routing as a game theoretic problem. In this game, overlay networks and IP network take turns in playing the game before they reach the Nash equilibrium point (when network-level routing is static). The authors evaluate the performance of the network only after the system reaches equilibrium. This approach is based on two assumptions: (i) The system has a Nash equilibrium point and it is reachable, and (ii) overlay networks and the IP network take turns at playing the game. Also, the work ignores a wide variety of dynamics (due to events like link/node failures, congestions, and software bugs) that occur in the real-world networks. Zhang et al. [44] and Liu et al. [28] model the interaction between overlay routing and traffic engineering (TE) as a two-player game, where the overlay attempts to minimize its delay and the TE tries to minimize network cost. They argue that the lack of common objective for the overlay and IP networks could result in poor performance. In summary, selfish overlay routing can degrade the performance of the network as a whole. Overlay routing never improves TE performance. The average cost inflation suffered by TE depends on the fraction of overlay traffic in the network. Studies show that the maximum cost and variation occurs when half of the network demand is overlay traffic. On the other hand, the impact on TE cost is reduced when link capacity increases.

8.3.2   Transient Behavior

In [24], we examined the interaction between the two layers of control from an ISP's view, with emphasis on system dynamics before it reaches the equilibrium state. Instead of static network layer routing, we are interested in what happens when both the overlay and the IGP protocols dynamically recompute routes in response to external triggers such as link/router failures, flash crowds, and network congestion. We will briefly summarize the problematic interactions that can occur between IP and overlay networks in this context (as identified in [24])

- **Increased dynamism in traffic matrices**. A traffic matrix (TM) specifies the traffic demand from origin nodes to destination nodes in a network, and hence is a critical input for many traffic engineering tasks (e.g., capacity planning and link weight setting). Conventionally, overlay nodes typically encapsulate the next hop information in the packet header and hence the IP layer is unaware of the true final destination. Therefore, overlay routing dynamics can introduce big *shifts* and *duplications* of TM entries in a very short timescale, making TM more dynamic and ambiguous, and harder to estimate. This is illustrated in Figure 8.2(a) and (b), which shows an overlay network spanning single and multiple domains, re-

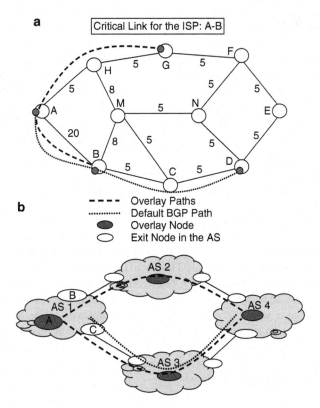

Fig. 8.2 (**a**) Overlay network contained within an AS and (**b**) overlay network spanning multiple
AS domains. (Same illustration is used in [24])

spectively. In Figure 8.2(a), the TM entry for the source–destination pair $A--D$
is 10 as a result of IP-routing decisions. However, if overlay routing intervenes
and redirects traffic through an overlay path (say, $A-B-D$), then the TM entry
for the pair $A--D$ is *duplicated* as two entries of 10 units each, one for $A-B$
and another for $B-D$, while the value for the entry $A--D$ is 0. This change
could happen at the time instant when the overlay network decides to change the
traffic path. Given that ISPs typically estimate their TM at coarser timescales (in
the order of several minutes or hours), such a sudden shift in TM could introduce
errors in the ISP's estimated TM, resulting in poor network management policies.
In the example shown in Figure 8.2(b), suppose that the path from $AS1$ to $AS4$
dictated by the IP layer is through $AS3$. If the overlay network redirects traffic
through $AS2$, the traffic will appear to leave $AS1$ via a different exit point. The
TM entry in $AS1$ for $A-C$ now *shifts* to $A-B$.

- **Bypassing the ISP's load balancing policies**. A common practice for ISPs to
manage the traffic is changing the IGP link weights. ISPs make two assumptions
while using this technique: (i) traffic demands do not vary significantly over short
timescales, and (ii) changes in the path within a domain do not impact traffic

demands. Overlay network routing defeats these assumptions. For example, in Figure 8.2(a), the ISP may assign a high link metric to link $A - B$ (link weight of 20, compared to 5 on all other links) to discourage the use of this link by other node pairs and reserve the resources for customers connected to nodes A and B. The IP layer path from D to A would be $D - N - M - H - A$. However, overlay node D can choose to reach A by forwarding through another overlay node, such as B. Hence, path $D - C - B - A$ is used. This undermines the ISPs intent and its load balancing policies. The impact could be magnified in the presence of multiple overlays making independent routing decisions.

- **Coupling of multiple ASes**. Through an overlay network that spans multiple ASes, the network state of an AS domain can impact how traffic flows through its surrounding AS neighbors. This defeats the purpose of the original two-tier Internet routing hierarchy (with IGP and BGP) to decouple different domains so that events in one domain do not affect another domain. For example, in Figure 8.2(b), the default BGP path from $AS1$ to $AS4$ is through $AS3$ via exit point C. However, the overlay network may react to some internal failure events in $AS1$ and redirect traffic to a different exit point B, and follow inter-domain path $AS1 - AS2 - AS4$ instead.

8.3.3   Coping with Cross-Layer Interactions

Clearly, an uncoordinated effort of the two layers or multiple overlays to recover from failures may cause performance degradation for both overlay and non-overlay traffic. Other works have studied the overlay network probing process, a crucial component of overlay routing. Nakao et al. [32] proposed a shared routing underlay that exposes large-scale, coarse-grained static information (e.g., topology and path characteristics) to overlay services through a set of queries. They advocate that the underlay must take cost (in terms of network probes) into account and be layered so that specialized routing services can be built from a set of basic primitives. However, sharing network layer path information may induce synchronized routing decisions in overlay networks and unintentionally lead to route/traffic oscillations, an aspect not addressed in [32]. The authors in [19] explore the problem of oscillations due to intelligent route control (IRC) systems deployed by networks that multihome to different ISPs. The objective of IRC systems is to probe all the available alternate paths and determine the best path for a network to route traffic. Similar to the findings in [24], the authors show that IRC systems, like overlay networks, do not consider *self-load effects* while moving traffic to alternate paths, resulting in oscillations.

The interactions between the overlay and IP layers are often caused by mismatch of routing objectives and misdirection of traffic matrix estimation. In recent work [37], Seetharam et al. attempt to derive preemptive strategies to resolve conflicts between native and overlay layers. Their goal is to obtain the best possible performance for a particular layer while maintaining a stable state. They propose to designate a leader and a follower role to the two layers, such that the leader will act after "predicting" or "counteracting" the subsequent reaction of the follower. For example, given that the native layer optimizes route selection to balance traffic load across the network, an overlay network (the leader) can improve latency of overlay routes while retaining the same load pressure on the native network. As a result, there will be no incentive for the native layer to make any further route changes. An alternate solution to this friendly approach is a hostile strategy where the overlay layer can send dummy traffic on unused overlay links to thwart TE's effort to reroute overlay traffic. Results show that the friendly preemptive strategies adopted by the leader cause minimal cost inflation for the follower. However, it is unclear if such preemptive strategies will work in practice with multiple coexisting overlays, multiple competing ISPs, and incomplete information about the selfish objective of each party.

Recently there has been an effort to help P2P overlay networks and ISPs to cooperate with each other to provide the best possible performance to the end user. This project is called P4P [8]. The main objectives of this project are to provide ISPs with the ability to optimize utilization of network resources while enhancing service levels for P2P traffic, and improve P2P overlay performance while enhancing efficient usage of ISP bandwidth. The idea is for both P2P overlay networks and ISPs to share limited information with each other. P4P proposes that ISPs should set up servers that are publicly accessible by P2P overlays, and P2P nodes can query these servers to find out the best possible neighbors to download data from. Based on the current network conditions, the server will respond with a weight for each of the possible neighbors and the P2P node can then decide which neighbors to connect to. With this strategy, P4P allows the P2P networks to optimize traffic within each ISP, which not only reduces the volume of data traversing the ISP's infrastructure, but also creates a more manageable flow of data [8]. Such cooperation between overlays and ISPs could help improve the performance of both overlays and ISPs.

8.4 Interactions Between Multiple Coexisting Overlay Networks

The simplicity and feasibility of designing overlay networks has attracted several service providers to adopt this approach to deliver new services. As a consequence, several new overlay networks are getting deployed on top of the same underlying IP networks in the Internet. These overlay networks are typically unaware of the existence of other overlay networks (i.e., their node locations, routing and failover strategies, optimization metrics, etc.). By allowing end hosts in these overlay networks to make independent routing decisions at the application level, different overlay networks may unintentionally interfere with each other. These interactions could lead to suboptimal states in all of the involved overlay networks. In this section we explore two kinds of such interactions. The first kind of interactions are those interactions between overlay networks that result in suboptimal and unexpected equilibrium conditions in all of the involved overlay networks. The second kind of interactions are transient interactions that capture how different protocols in different overlay networks can interfere with each other resulting in oscillations (in both route selection and network load) and cascading reactions, thus affecting the performance of the overlay network traffic.

8.4.1 Interactions Leading to Suboptimal Equilibrium Point

Traditional overlay routing has been selfish in nature, i.e., most overlay networks try to find the best path (in terms of delay, loss, and/or throughput) and route their traffic along this best path. As we discussed earlier, such an approach will result in performance degradation in all the overlays involved. In [21], the authors examine if there is an optimal overlay routing strategy that can provide better performance than the traditional selfish routing. In fact, the authors propose a routing strategy called *optimal overlay routing*, where every overlay network decides to route its own traffic along one or more paths in its network by minimizing an objective function (e.g., the weighted average delay along the paths). They model this as a non-cooperative strategic game and show that there always exists a Nash equilibrium point. They also show that such an equilibrium point is not Pareto optimal.[1] Such an optimal routing scheme will provide significant performance improvement over traditional selfish routing, but overlays could encounter fairness issues (one overlay network getting a bigger share of resources than the others). The work proposes two pricing models to fix this issue, and shows that if overlay networks adopt this strategy it could be beneficial to all the overlay networks.

8.4.2 Transient Overlay Network Protocol Interactions

In this section, we highlight how multiple overlay network protocols can interact with each other and the corresponding dynamics during the *transient* period. We begin by describing the generic overlay routing mechanism that we consider in the rest of our discussion.

Most overlay routing strategies select a path between a source–destination pair with the best performance based on end-to-end delay, throughput, and/or packet loss. Similar to our previous studies [22, 23], we assume that the overlay path with the shortest end-to-end delays will be selected (but this can be extended to include other metrics). Overlay networks monitor the actively used paths by sending frequent probes to check if the paths adhere to acceptable performance bounds. If the probing event detects a problematic path (due to failures, congestion, etc. at the IP

---

[1] An outcome of a game is Pareto optimal if there is no other outcome that makes every player at least as well off and at least one player strictly better off. That is, a Pareto Optimal outcome cannot be improved upon without hurting at least one player.

layer), then the overlay network sends probes at a higher rate to confirm the problem before selecting an alternate path. We assume that regular probes are sent out every P seconds. If a probe does not receive a response within a given *timeout* (or T) value, then the path is probed at a higher rate (every Q seconds). If a path remains bad after N such high-frequency probes, the overlay will find an alternate path (or the next best path) between the source and destination nodes. For instance, RON [12] can be modeled with $P = 12$s, $Q = 3$s, and $N = 3$, while the Akamai network can be modeled with much smaller values of P, Q, and N [27]. As soon as an alternate path is found, the traffic is moved to the alternate path, which is now probed every P seconds to ensure that it is healthy.[2]

Using this generic overlay routing model described above, different overlay networks with different routing strategies can be simulated. Our previous studies [22, 23] based on a realistic ISP topology have shown that transient interactions between multiple overlays could result in two types of race conditions: traffic oscillations and cascading reactions. In the remainder of this section, we will briefly summarize our findings, in particular, on how interactions lead to traffic oscillations, an analytical model for the synchronization probability between two overlays and insights gained through it, and the various strategies for reducing the impact of race conditions.

8.4.2.1 Conditions for Traffic Oscillations

Traffic oscillations refer to the network state where the traffic load between certain source–destination pairs in different overlay networks start oscillating between two or more alternate paths. From the perspective of the underlying IP network, the loads on some of the IP links constantly change, affecting the non-overlay traffic on these links. This constant fluctuation of traffic load occurs at small timescales resulting in unstable network conditions. Figure 8.3 shows one of our simulation results from [22] that illustrate traffic oscillations on some of the links in a realistic tier-1 ISP backbone topology. These oscillations continue until a *stop trigger* stops these oscillations. These stop triggers could be events like IGP protocol convergence, a link failure, link recovery after a failure, etc. However, an important observation here is that certain events that act as stop triggers for oscillations at some point in time might not affect the oscillations at another point in time. Also, most of the events that act as stop triggers are heavily dependent on the network conditions at the IP layer. The order of occurrence of these stop triggers is not deterministic, thus introducing unpredictability in the duration of the oscillations. In essence, the end of oscillations depends on numerous factors, thus making it non-trivial to accurately estimate the impact of oscillations on overlay or non-overlay traffic.

---

[2] As long as the current path adheres to the performance bounds, an overlay does not shift traffic to an alternate path even if the alternate path starts to exhibit better performance.

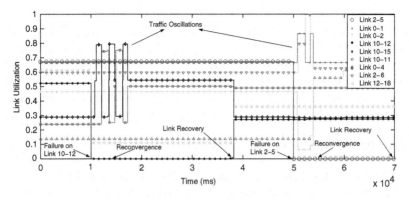

Fig. 8.3 Link utilization as a function of time (source from [22])

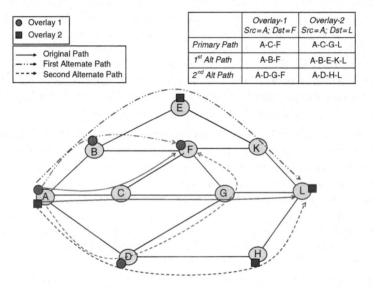

Fig. 8.4 Two overlay networks that partially share primary and alternate paths [22]

Traffic oscillations are initiated when the following conditions are satisfied [22]:

- **Presence of External Trigger**   A network event that perturbs the network state will trigger overlay networks to search for alternate paths. This event can be a link/node failure or sudden increase in traffic demand that leads to performance degradation on the original path.
- **Sharing Primary and Backup Paths**   The topologies of coexisting overlay networks determine how the different overlay paths overlap in terms of the underlying physical resources. Synchronization between two overlays occurs when there is a pair of overlay nodes in two different overlay networks, such that they share bottleneck link/s in both their first and second alternate path choices. Figure 8.4 illustrates this case with overlays on top on an IP network. The node

pair $A - F$ in *Overlay-1* and pair $A - L$ in *Overlay-2* share the link $A - C$ on their primary paths. Assume, for simplicity of discussion, that the "top" path is their first alternate choice. If link $A - C$ fails, then the first alternate path for $A - F$ and that for $A - L$ would share link $A - B$. If this link becomes a bottleneck, forcing the overlay networks to move their traffic again, then the overlay source–destination pairs $A - F$ and $A - L$ would now move to the "bottom" path. However, they would still share link $A - -D$ that could itself now become a bottleneck.

- **Periodic Probing Process**   Consider the two overlays in Figure 8.4 and a failure on *link A-C* that is common to their primary paths ($A - F$ in *Overlay-1* and $A - L$ in *Overlay-2*). If the last high-frequency probes for both overlays expire within a short time window of one another, then both overlays will reroute their traffic to their first alternate path at the same time. The time window is so short that the overlay that moves second does not have time to re-probe its path to realize that some traffic load from the other overlay has already moved. As a result, the two overlays get *synchronized*. If the traffic load on the first alternate path becomes high, then the overlays could react again by rerouting their traffic to the second alternate path. Such reactions can continue and overlays move their traffic in a lock-step fashion between the two alternate paths until the distance between the probes grows large enough to end the synchronization. When this happens we say that the two overlays *disentangle* themselves.

An event in one overlay network can trigger a series of events in other overlay networks. Such a domino effect is called *cascading reactions* [23]. For example, a route change in overlay network could result in congesting paths in a second overlay network. The second overlay network could react to this congestion and change its route to an alternate path. Now this alternate path could overlay with a third overlay network, resulting in a route change event in the third overlay network. As the number of coexisting overlay networks increases, the possibility of such cascading reactions also increases. Cascading reactions tend to occur when there are a large number of overlays that coexist.

Since a particular overlay network cannot know whether its paths overlap with those of another overlay, and since it cannot predict performance failures, avoiding these conditions is beyond its control. However, an overlay can control its own probing process, thus our previous analyses [22,23] focus on modeling the impact of the path probing process on race conditions. In particular, we focus on traffic oscillations and derive an analytic formulation to predict the probability of synchronization of two overlay networks that coexist on the same IP network.

8.4.2.2 Analyzing Traffic Oscillations

Here, we will give the intuition for the analytical model derived in [22]. As described earlier, overlay networks probe their paths at regular intervals of P seconds. If the path is healthy, the probe should return in one round trip time, with a measure of the path delay (or an assessment of another chosen metric). If the probe does not return before the timeout T expires, then the overlay starts sending its high-frequency probes (N will be sent) every Q seconds. Thus, the probing procedure for each overlay i on path j is specified by five parameters: the probe interval P_i, the high-frequency probe interval Q_i, the timeout T_i, the number of high-frequency probes N_i, and the round trip time R_{ij} over path j. Note that T_i is the same for low- and high-frequency probes. By definition $P_i \geq Q_i \geq T_i \geq R_{ij}$.

The probing procedure implies that (under normal circumstances) on a given path there will be exactly one probe in every time period of length P. Now suppose that an event (e.g., a link failure) occurs at time t_l. We assume that a probe sent on path j in overlay i at time t_0 "senses" the state of the path at $t_0 + R_{ij}/2$, i.e., the probe is dropped if the path is not operational at that time.[3] Hence, the overlay network will detect the failure event with the probe sent at t_0 if $t_0 \in [t_l - R_{ij}/2, t_l - R_{ij}/2 + P_i]$. We call this period the *detection period*. The overlay will then react at time $t_0 + T_i$ sending the high-frequency probes as discussed above.

Consider two overlay networks, O_1 and O_2. Let t_1 and t_2 be the actual times at which the initial probes are sent during the detection period. We assume that t_1 and t_2 are equally likely to occur anywhere in their detection period and hence are uniformly distributed in their detection period. Once an overlay network detects the failure, it begins sending the high-frequency probes every Q_i time units. The final high-frequency probe will be sent out at $f_i = t_i + N_i Q_i$ for $i = 1, 2$. There are two cases for synchronization – in one case O_1 moves its traffic first and O_2 moves shortly thereafter, or vice versa. We can mathematically express this as

$$0 < f_2 - f_1 < T_1, \tag{8.1}$$
$$0 < f_1 - f_2 < T_2. \tag{8.2}$$

Since the above two conditions are independent of each other, we can combine them as follows:

$$-T_1 < f_1 - f_2 < T_2,$$
$$-T_1 < (t_1 + N_1 Q_1) - (t_2 + N_2 Q_2) < T_2,$$
$$b < t_1 - t_2 < a. \tag{8.3}$$

where $a = N_2 Q_2 - N_1 Q_1 + T_2$; $b = N_2 Q_2 - N_1 Q_1 - T_1$.

Assuming that t_1 and t_2 can occur anywhere in their detection period with a uniform probability, we can represent the system as a two-dimensional graph with the x-axis representing probe t_1 and the y-axis representing probe t_2. This geometric representation allows us to compute the probability of synchronization, $P(S)$, of two overlays in an intuitively simple way. We define *region of conflict* to be the portion of this rectangle in which synchronization will occur, i.e., the region that satisfies the two constraints specified in Equation 8.3. The boundaries of the *region of*

---

[3] To simplify our analysis during failures we ignore the exact values of propagation delays between the source, the failed spot, and destination. Thus we approximate the instant at which a probe is dropped by $R_{ij}/2$.

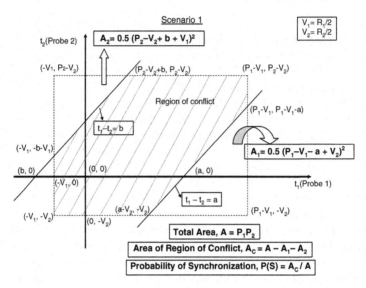

Fig. 8.5 Scenario 1 ($V_1 = R_1/2$ and $V_2 = R_2/2$) [22]

conflict are thus determined by the boundaries of the rectangle and their intersection with the two parallel lines of slope 1 (i.e., $t_1 - t_2 = a$ and $t_1 - t_2 = b$). The probability of synchronization of two overlays, $P(S)$, can be defined to be the ratio of the area of the region of conflict to the total area of the rectangle. We can see one specific scenario of this geometric representation in Figure 8.5. This two-dimensional representation captures the influence of all the parameters (P_i, Q_i, N_i, T_i, R_i) since these quantities ultimately define all the corners and line intersection points needed to compute the relevant areas. We can clearly see that the area A of the rectangle is composed of three distinct regions: A_1 (area of the region below *Line-1*: $t_1 - t_2 = a$ and the rectangle boundaries), A_2 (area of the region above *Line-2*: $t_1 - t_2 = b$ and the rectangle boundaries), and the *region of conflict*. Hence, the *region of conflict*, A_C, can be expressed as $A_C = A - A_1 - A_2$.

Thus we can express the probability of synchronization as

$$P(S) = Probability(b < t_1 - t_2 < a) = \frac{A_C}{A} \tag{8.4}$$

There are a number of ways in which the two lines can intersect the boundaries of the rectangle [22], but are not shown here. Although this model results in nine different scenarios, each of them with a different equation for $P(S)$, it is still attractive since it is conceptually very simple. Our formulation indicates that the probability of synchronization is non-negligible across a wide range of parameter settings (P, Q, T, and N), thus implying that the ill-effects of synchronization should not be ignored.

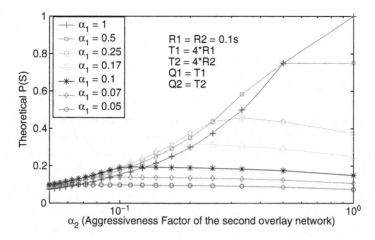

Fig. 8.6 Proportional parameter overlays with mixed aggressiveness and a chosen value of RTT [22]

For illustration purposes, let us consider a scenario where two overlay networks use identical probing parameters, and $R_1 = R_2 = R$. In this case probability of synchronization collapses to the simple equation $P(S) = T(2P - T)/P^2$. If our model is correct, this implies that $P(S)$ depends only on the probe interval and time out value, which was confirmed through simulation [22]. The maximum value of $P(S) = 1$ occurs when $T = P$, i.e., the overlay networks will definitely synchronize. To decrease the probability of synchronization to less than 0.05 (i.e., 5% chance of synchronization) we need to set $P \approx 40T$. This observation motivated us to characterize an overlay network based on its *aggressiveness factor*, α, defined as the ratio of the timeout and probe interval, $\alpha_i = T_i/P_i$. We consider overlays that probe frequently and move their traffic quickly as *aggressive*. Note that $RTT \leq T \leq P$, hence $0 < \alpha \leq 1$. For two identical overlay networks we have $P(S) = 2\alpha - \alpha^2$, which shows that as the networks increase their aggressiveness (i.e., as $\alpha \to 1$), $P(S)$ increases.

Figure 8.6 [22] shows how $P(S)$ varies as a function of the aggressiveness factors of the two overlays. Each curve in the graph represents the value of $P(S)$ for a fixed value of T_1/P_1 but different values of T_2/P_2. We can clearly see that as the aggressiveness of both the overlays increases, there is a higher chance of synchronization. $P(S)$ decreases significantly when the overlays are non-aggressive. This confirms that as long as one of the overlays is non-aggressive, the probability of synchronization is low. In other words, setting a high value of P is critical to reducing $P(S)$. However, we wish to point out that there could be fairness issues when one overlay is very aggressive, and exploits the non-aggressive parameter settings of the other overlay. Even in the case of one aggressive and one non-aggressive overlay network, we found that $P(S)$ can still be non-negligible for a wide range of relative RTT values.

8.4.3 Coping with Interactions Between Coexisting Overlays

As the number of overlays in the Internet increases, the possibility of their inter-actions also increases. Similar to the work in [21], the authors in [42] also try to address the problem of performance degradation when multiple overlays coexist by modeling it as a dynamic auction game. The problem that the authors address is the following: when multiple overlay streams contend for resources at the same peer, then the performance of all the streams deteriorates. The approach that the authors propose is to let the downstream peer play a dynamic auction game with the up-stream peer to decide the bandwidth allocation for each of the flows.

To limit the impact of interactions highlighted earlier in this section, in particular the problem of synchronization among multiple overlay networks, we can take two approaches: (i) reduce the probability of synchronization among overlays, and/or (ii) reduce the number of oscillations once the overlays get synchronized.

Intuitively, one way to make it less likely that two overlays actually get syn-chronized is to increase the probing intervals to a large value (i.e., probe less aggressively). But this would defeat the purpose of overlay networks to react quickly to performance degradation events. A second approach would be to add randomness into the probing procedure. The idea of adding randomness was illustrated to help in several cases like periodic routing protocols [18]; however, in the case of overlay networks, the probability of synchronization depends on the difference terms (like $N_1 Q_1 - N_2 Q_2$) and randomness added to the same parameters in two overlays could either increase or decrease the probability of synchronization [23]. Hence, adding randomness does not always ensure that two overlays are less likely to synchronize.

In order to reduce the number of oscillations after a synchronization event, an approach similar to the well-known behavior of TCP can be used. Whenever a flow using TCP experiences a packet loss due to congestion the protocol backs off from using an aggressive packet transfer rate. Typically this back-off occurs at an expo-nential rate to reduce the impact of congestion. In the case of multiple overlays, a similar back-off technique can be used where an overlay network successively in-creases the reaction time each time it decides to switch routes between the same source and destination nodes (if the reactions occur in a small time interval). This is similar in spirit to damping i.e., slow down the reaction time of a protocol to avoid responding too quickly. Note that the back-off technique is also similar to the idea of non-aggressive probing. The main difference is that while using non-aggressive probing, the parameter (or timer) values are always large, but while using back-off strategy the parameter values are increased only when oscillations are detected. A more comprehensive analysis of all the above techniques can be found in [23].

8.5 Summary

Over the past few years, application service providers have started using the Internet as a medium to deliver their applications to consumers. For example, Skype [10] and Joost [5], among others, are now using the Internet to provide voice and video services to users. There are two main reasons for this popularity: (i) Internet is becoming more and more pervasive, a much larger audience can be reached, and (ii) It is much more economical to use the shared IP networks as the transport medium than the traditional dedicated telephone lines. With this popularity, service providers find it necessary to provide QoS guarantees for their applications. Given the problems in IGP and BGP convergence, and the lack of stringent QoS metrics by ISPs, application service providers started building application-layer overlay networks that guaranteed certain performance. These overlay networks have several attractive features: (i) very simple to design, (ii) flexible enough to be used for several different applications, (iii) cheaper than installing an IP layer infrastructure, (iv) easy to deploy and manage, and (v) gives more control over application performance (routing, failure resiliency, etc.). In this chapter, we highlight how overlay networks work along with a brief taxonomy, and describe several applications for which they are currently being used.

The attractive features of overlay networks come with several disadvantages as well. As described in this chapter, overlay networks could interact with the underlying IP networks leading to problems both in the equilibrium state and during transient convergence. The equilibrium state can be analyzed by modeling the interactions as non-cooperative game. Several works in the literature show that the equilibrium is not optimal, and could affect the performance of both overlay and IP networks. We also discussed in detail how multiple coexisting overlay networks could interact with each other, resulting in traffic oscillations, and possible remedies for these interactions.

Acknowledgements The research on the interactions between overlay and IP layer routing was supported by NSF CAREER Award No. 0238348. We also thank our collaborators, Dr. Nina Taft and Dr. Gianluca Iannaccone, at Intel Research Berkeley for their invaluable technical input.

References

1. Akamai. http://www.akamai.com.
2. Bittorrent. http://www.bittorrent.com/.
3. CNN. http://www.cnn.com.
4. Gnutella. http://www.gnutella.com.
5. Joost. http://www.joost.com/.
6. Kazaa. http://www.kazaa.com.
7. Napster. http://www.napster.com.
8. P4P Working Group. http://www.pandonetworks.com/p4p.
9. Planetlab. http://www.planet-lab.org/.
10. Skype. http://www.skype.com/.
11. Yahoo Inc. http://www.yahoo.com.
12. D. Anderson, H. Balakrishna, M. Kaashoek, and R. Morris. Resilient Overlay Networks. In *Proceedings of ACM Symposium on Operating Systems Principles*, Oct. 2001.
13. R. Braynard, D. Kostic, A. Rodriguez, J. Chase, and A. Vahdat. Opus: An Overlay Peer Utility Service. In *Proceedings of IEEE Open Architectures and Network Programming (OpenArch)*, June 2002.

14. M. Castro, P. Druschel, A. Kermarrec, A. Nandi, A. Rowstron, and A. Singh. SplitStream: High-Bandwidth Multicast in Cooperative Environments. In *Proceedings of ACM Symposium on Operating Systems Principles*, Oct. 2003.
15. M. Castro, P. Druschel, A. Kermarrec, and A. Rowstron. SCRIBE: A Large-Scale and Decentralized Application-Level Multicast Infrastructure. *IEEE Journal on Selected Areas in Communication*, Oct. 2002.
16. S. Deering. Host Extensions for IP Multicasting. RFC 1112, Aug. 1989.
17. A. Feldmann, O. Maennel, Z. M. Mao, A. Berger, and B. Maggs. Locating Internet Routing Instabilities. In *Proc. SIGCOMM'04*, Portland, Oregon, USA, Aug 2004.
18. S. Floyd and V. Jacobson. The Synchronization of Periodic Routing Messages. In *Proceedings of ACM Sigcomm*, Sept. 1993.
19. R. Gao, C. Dovrolis, and E. Zegura. Avoiding Oscillations due to Intelligent Route Control Systems. In *Proceedings of IEEE Infocom*, Apr. 2006.
20. G. Iannaccone, C. Chuah, R. Mortier, S. Bhattacharyya, and C. Diot. Analysis of Link Failures in an IP Backbone. In *Proceedings of ACM Sigcomm Internet Measurement Workshop*, Nov. 2002.
21. J. Jiang, D. Chiu, and J. Lui. On the Interaction of Multiple Overlay Routing. In *Journal of Performance Evaluation*, 2005.
22. R. Keralapura, C. N. Chuah, N. Taft, and G. Iannaccone. Can overlay networks inadvertently step on each other? In *IEEE ICNP*, Nov. 2005.
23. R. Keralapura, C.-N. Chuah, N. Taft, and G. Iannaccone. Race Conditions in Multiple Overlay Networks. *IEEE/ACM Transactions on Networking*, Mar. 2008.
24. R. Keralapura, N. Taft, C. N. Chuah, and G. Iannaccone. Can ISPs take the heat from overlay networks? In *Proceedings of ACM Sigcomm Workshop on Hot Topics in Networks*, Nov. 2004.
25. C. Labovitz, R. Wattenhofer, S. Venkatachary, and A. Ahuja. The Impact of Internet Policy and Topology on Delayed Routing Convergence. In *Proceedings of IEEE Infocom*, Apr. 2001.
26. M. Lad, X. Zhao, B. Zhang, D. Massey, and L. Zhang. Analysis of BGP Update Burst during Slammer Attack. In *Proceedings of the 5th International Workshop on Distributed Computing*, December 2003.
27. T. Leighton. The Challenges of Delivering Content and Applications on the Internet. In *NSDI Keynote*, May 2005.
28. Y. Liu, H. Zhang, W. Gong, and D. Towsley. On the Interaction Between Overlay Routing and Traffic Engineering. In *Proceedings of IEEE Infocom*, Mar. 2005.
29. R. Mahajan, D. Wetherall, and T. Anderson. Understanding bgp misconfiguration. *ACM Sigcomm Computer Communication Review*, 32(4):3–16, 2002.
30. A. Markopulou, G. Iannaccone, S. Bhattacharyya, C.-N. Chuah, and C. Diot. Characterization of failures in an IP backbone. In *Proceedings of IEEE Infocom*, Mar. 2004.
31. A. Markopulu, G. Iannaccone, S. Bhattacharya, C.-N. Chuah, Y. Ganjali, and C. Diot. Characterization of failures in an operational IP backbone network. *IEEE/ACM Transactions on Networking*, 16(5), Oct. 2008.
32. A. Nakao, L. Peterson, and A. Bavier. A Routing Underlay for Overlay Networks. In *Proceedings of ACM Sigcomm*, Aug. 2003.
33. L. Qiu, Y. Yang, Y. Zhang, and S. Shenker. On Selfish Routing in Internet-Like Environments. In *Proceedings of ACM Sigcomm*, Aug. 2003.
34. S. Rhea, D. Geels, T. Roscoe, and J. Kubiatowicz. Handling Churn in a DHT. In *USENIX ATC*, June 2004.
35. A. Rowstron and P. Druschel. Pastry: Scalable, distributed object location and routing for large-scale peer-to-peer systems. In *IFIP/ACM Middleware*, Nov. 2001.
36. S. Savage, A. Collins, E. Hoffman, J. Snell, and T. Anderson. The End-to-End Effects of Internet Path Selection. In *Proceedings of ACM Sigcomm*, Aug. 1999.
37. S. Seetharaman, V. Hilt, M. Hofmann, and M. Ammar. Preemptive strategies to improve routing performance of native and overlay layers. In *IEEE INFOCOM*, 2007.
38. P. Smith. BGP Multihoming Guide. In *North American Network Operators Group (NANOG) 23*, Oct. 2001.

39. K. Sripanidkulchai, B. Maggs, and H. Zhang. An Analysis of Live Streaming Workloads on the Internet. In *Proceedings of ACM Sigcomm Internet Measurement Conference*, Oct. 2004.

40. I. Stoica, R. Morris, D. Karger, M. F. Kaashoek, and H. Balakrishnan. Chord: A scalable peer-to-peer lookup service for internet applications. In *Proceedings of ACM Sigcomm*, August 2001.

41. R. Teixeira, T. Griffin, G. Voelker, and A. Shaikh. Network sensitivity to hot-potato disruptions. In *Proceedings of ACM Sigcomm*, Aug. 2004.

42. C. Wu and B.Li. Strategies of Conflict in Coexisting Streaming Overlays. In *Proceedings of IEEE Infocom*, 2007.

43. J. Wu, Z. M. Mao, J. Rexford, and J. Wang. Finding a needle in a haystack: pinpointing significant BGP routing changes in an IP network. In *Proc. 2nd conference on Symposium on Networked Systems Design & Implementation (NSDI'05)*, Boston, MA, USA, May 2005.

44. H. Zhang, Y. Liu, D. Towsley, and W. Gong. Understanding the Interaction between Overlay Routing and Traffic Engineering. In *ACM Sigcomm Poster Session*, Aug. 2004.

45. B. Zhao, L. Huang, J. Stribling, and J. Kubiatowicz. Exploiting Routing Redundancy via Structured Peer-to-Peer Overlays. In *ICNP*, Nov. 2003.

Part II
Network Operations

Chapter 9
Hash-Based Techniques for High-Speed Packet Processing

Adam Kirsch, Michael Mitzenmacher, and George Varghese

Abstract Hashing is an extremely useful technique for a variety of high-speed packet-processing applications in routers. In this chapter, we survey much of the recent work in this area, paying particular attention to the interaction between theoretical and applied research. We assume very little background in either the theory or applications of hashing, reviewing the fundamentals as necessary.

9.1 Introduction

This chapter surveys recent research on hash-based approaches to high-speed packet processing in routers. In this setting, it is crucial that all techniques be amenable to a hardware implementation, as high-performance routers typically must operate at *wire speed*, meaning that the time that a router can operate on a packet is at most the time that it takes the link to process a packet of some minimal size (e.g., 40 bytes, corresponding to a TCP acknowledgement with no payload). Software-based approaches are simply inadequate for this task.

Since this topic is quite broad, we start by specifying some boundaries for our coverage. There is a very large and growing body of work on the more general theme of algorithmic approaches to important packet-processing applications. The most comprehensive reference for these techniques is the text by Varghese [70], published in 2004. We therefore focus our attention on work done since then. Even limiting ourselves to the relevant research in the last few years, however, would leave an enormous amount of work to cover! We therefore further focus our attention

A. Kirsch (✉) and M. Mitzenmacher
Harvard School of Engineering and Applied Sciences, Harvard University, 33 Oxford Street
Cambridge, MA 02138
e-mail: kirsch@eecs.harvard.edu; michaelm@eecs.harvard.edu

G. Varghese
Department of Computer Science and Engineering, University of California, San Diego,
9500 Gilman Drive, La Jolla, CA 92040
e-mail: varghese@cs.ucsd.edu

G. Cormode and M. Thottan (eds.), *Algorithms for Next Generation Networks*,
Computer Communications and Networks, DOI 10.1007/978-1-84882-765-3_9,
© Springer-Verlag London Limited 2010

on two key application areas for high-speed routers: hash tables and related data structures, and hash-based schemes for network measurement. While we aim to be comprehensive, given the huge recent growth of interest in this area, this survey should be considered a guide to the literature rather than a full account.

Before diving into the literature, we offer some of our high-level perspective that guides this survey. First, as will become apparent in the body of this chapter, there is an enormous amount of potential for interplay between theoretical and applied techniques. It follows that the relevant literature spans the spectrum from very theoretical to very applied. We aim our attention on the middle of this range, but we emphasize that any particular piece of work must be considered relative to its place in the spectrum. For instance, when we discuss hash table designs for high-speed routers, we consider several theoretical papers that focus on the design of hash tables generally, rather than on some particular application. In such work, the primary goal is often to present and evaluate general data structure design principles that appear to have broad potential to impact the implementation of practical systems. The evaluation in these works usually takes the form of establishing various guarantees on the data structure outside the context of any particular application. For example, a work in this vein that proposes a novel hash table design may place significant emphasis on the sorts of theoretical and numerical guarantees that can be obtained under the new design, with simulations serving in a mostly supporting role. Naturally, then, a major challenge in this area is to design data structures that are amenable to a compelling evaluation of this sort. Of course, since this approach is very general, it typically does not speak directly to how such a data structure might perform when appropriately adjusted and implemented in a real application. When properly interpreted, however, the results of these more theoretical works can be highly suggestive of increased performance for a broad range of settings.

Similarly, very applied works should be considered with respect to the concrete results that they demonstrate for the specific application of interest. Works in the middle of the spectrum typically should be considered with respect to some combination of these goals, for instance showing that a particular theoretical intuition seems to lead to compelling results for some class of related applications.

In the rest of the survey, we first give the necessary background and history in Section 9.2. We then consider three fairly broad application settings: hash table lookups for various hardware memory models (Sections 9.3 and 9.4), Bloom filter-type applications (Section 9.5), and network measurement (Section 9.6).

9.2 Background

We review some of the key concepts underlying the hash-based data structures commonly proposed for high-speed packet processing. We describe the performance measures relevant to these applications and the resulting hardware models, and also give a brief history of the earlier literature on these applications.

9.2.1 Hash-Based Data Structures

We begin with a brief review of the relevant history, constructions, and issues in the design of hash-based data structures. We describe some of the tension between the theory and practice of hash functions that informs our analyses, review the standard Bloom filter data structure and its variants, and discuss multiple-choice hash tables.

9.2.1.1 Hash Functions

Intuitively, a hash function $h : U \to V$ is a function that maps every item $u \in U$ to a hash value $h(u) \in V$ in a fashion that is somehow random. The most natural mathematical model for a hash function is that it is *fully random*; that is, it is a random element of V^U, the set of functions with domain U and codomain V. Under this assumption, the hash values $\{h(x) : x \in U\}$ corresponding to the items in U are independent random variables that are each uniformly distributed over V. Clearly, this is a very appealing scenario for probabilistic analysis.

Unfortunately, it is almost always impractical to construct fully random hash functions, as the space required to store such a function is essentially the same as that required to encode an arbitrary function in V^U as a lookup table. From a theoretical perspective, this sort of thinking quickly leads to compromises between the randomness properties that we desire in a hash function and the computational resources needed to store and evaluate such a function. The seminal work along these lines is the introduction of *universal hash families* by Carter and Wegman [10, 75], which introduces the idea of choosing a hash function h randomly (and efficiently) from a set $\mathcal{H}$ of potential hash functions, chosen so that the joint distribution of the random variables $\{h(x) : x \in U\}$ satisfies limited but intuitively powerful properties. As a matter of terminology, the terms *hash functions* and *hash families* are often used interchangeably when the meaning is clear.

Specifically, a family of hash functions $\mathcal{H}$ with domain U and codomain V is said to be *2-universal* if, for every pair of distinct items $x, y \in U$, we have for a properly sampled hash function $h \in \mathcal{H}$

$$\mathbf{Pr}(h(x) = h(y)) \le \frac{1}{|V|}.$$

That is, the probability of a collision between any pair of items after being hashed is at most what it would be for a fully random hash function, where this probability is taken over the choice of hash function. A family of hash functions is said to be *strongly 2-universal*, or more commonly in modern terminology *pairwise independent*, if, for every pair of distinct items $x, y \in U$ and any $x', y' \in V$, we have

$$\mathbf{Pr}(h(x) = x' \text{ and } h(y) = y') = \frac{1}{|V|^2}.$$

That is, the behavior for any pair of distinct items is the same as for a fully random hash function. Historically, in some cases, the term *universal* is used when *strongly universal* is meant. Pairwise independence generalizes naturally to k-wise independence for collections of k items, and similarly one can consider k-universal hash functions, although generally k-wise independence is more common and useful. More information can be found in standard references such as [52].

Since Carter and Wegman's original work [10], there has been a substantial amount of research on efficient constructions of hash functions that are theoretically suitable for use in data structures and algorithms (e.g., [21, 54, 62] and references therein). Unfortunately, while there are many impressive theoretical results in that literature, the constructed hash families are usually impractical. Thus, at least at present, these results do not seem to have much potential to directly impact a real implementation of hash functions.

Fortunately, it seems that in practice simple hash functions perform very well. Indeed, they can be implemented very efficiently. For example, Dietzfelbinger et al. [20] exhibit a hash function that can be implemented with a single multiplication and a right shift operation and is almost universal. For scenarios where multiplications are undesirable, Carter and Wegman's original work [10] provides a universal hash function that relies on XOR operations. Some practical evaluations of these hash functions and others, for both hardware and software applications (including Bloom filters, discussed in Section 9.2.1.2), are given in [26, 59–61, 67]. Overall, these works suggest that it is possible to choose very simple hash functions that work very well in practical applications.

There is also theoretical work that strives to explain why simple hash functions seem to perform well in practice. One common approach is to examine a particular theoretical analysis that uses the assumption of fully random hash functions, and then attempt to modify the analysis to obtain a comparable result for a class of simple hash functions (e.g., universal hash functions), or a particular family of hash functions. For instance, partitioned Bloom filters (described in Section 9.2.1.2) can be implemented with any universal hash function, albeit with a small increase in the false positive probability. As an example of this technique that works only for a specific hash family, Woelfel [76] shows that one can implement d-left hashing (described in Section 9.2.1.3) using a particular type of simple hash function. In a different direction, Mitzenmacher and Vadhan [53] show that for certain applications, if one is willing to assume that the set of items being hashed satisfies certain randomness properties, then any analysis based on the assumption that the hash functions are fully random is also valid with universal hash functions (up to some small, additional error probability). From a practical perspective, this work shows that it may be possible to construct some sort of statistical test that would provide a theoretical explanation for how well applications built on simple hash functions will work on a particular source of real data. Alternatively, if one is willing to assume that the set of items being hashed has a certain amount of entropy, then one can expect the same performance as derived from an analysis with fully random hash functions.

Having reviewed the approaches to hashing most related to this work, we now articulate our perspective on hash functions. This is essentially just the standard view in the networking literature, but it bears repeating. Since we are primarily concerned with real-world systems, and since it is usually possible to choose a simple, practical hash function for an application that results in performance similar to what we would expect for a fully random hash function, we allow ourselves to assume that our hash functions are fully random in our theoretical analyses. Thus, we take the perspective of *modeling* the hash functions for the sake of predicting performance in a statistical sense, as opposed to explicitly constructing the hash functions to satisfy concrete theoretical guarantees. Furthermore, since we assume that simple hash functions work well, we generally do not think of the cost of hashing as a bottleneck, and so we often allow ourselves to use hash functions liberally.

9.2.1.2 Bloom Filters and Their Variants

A *Bloom filter* [2] is a simple space-efficient randomized data structure for representing a set in order to support membership queries. We begin by reviewing the fundamentals, based on the presentation of the survey [8], which we refer to for further details. A Bloom filter for representing a set $S = \{x_1, x_2, \ldots, x_n\}$ of n items from a large universe U consists of an array of m bits, initially all set to 0. The filter uses k independent (fully random) hash functions $h_1, \ldots, h_k$ with range $\{1, \ldots, m\}$. For each item $x \in S$, the bits $h_i(x)$ are set to 1 for $1 \leq i \leq k$. (A location can be set to 1 multiple times.) To check if an item y is in S, we check whether all $h_i(y)$ are set to 1. If not, then clearly y is not a member of S. If all $h_i(y)$ are set to 1, we assume that y is in S, and hence a Bloom filter may yield a *false positive*.

The probability of a false positive for an item not in the set, or the *false positive probability*, can be estimated in a straightforward fashion, given our assumption that the hash functions are fully random. After all the items of S are hashed into the Bloom filter, the probability that a specific bit is still 0 is

$$p' = (1 - 1/m)^{kn} \approx e^{-kn/m}.$$

In this section, we generally use the approximation $p = e^{-kn/m}$ in place of p' for convenience.

If ρ is the proportion of 0 bits after all the n items are inserted in the Bloom filter, then conditioned on ρ the probability of a false positive is

$$(1 - \rho)^k \approx (1 - p')^k \approx (1 - p)^k = \left(1 - e^{-kn/m}\right)^k.$$

These approximations follow since $\mathbf{E}[\rho] = p'$, and ρ can be shown to be highly concentrated around p' using standard techniques [52]. It is easy to show that the expression $\left(1 - e^{-kn/m}\right)^k$ is minimized when $k = \ln 2 \cdot (m/n)$, giving a false positive probability f of

$$f = \left(1 - e^{-kn/m}\right)^k = (1/2)^k \approx (0.6185)^{m/n}.$$

In practice, k must be an integer, and a smaller, suboptimal k might be preferred since this reduces the number of hash functions that have to be computed.

This analysis provides us (roughly) with the probability that a single item $z \notin S$ gives a false positive. We would like to make a broader statement, that in fact this gives a false positive *rate*. That is, if we choose a large number of *distinct* items not in S, the fraction of them that yield false positives is approximately f. This result follows immediately from the fact that ρ is highly concentrated around p', and for this reason, the false positive probability is often referred to synonymously as the *false positive rate*. (However, note that if we choose a large number of items not in S that may contain repeats, the repeated items may cause the number of false positives to exceed the predicted rate.)

Before moving on, we note that sometimes Bloom filters are described slightly differently, with each hash function having a disjoint range of m/k consecutive bit locations instead of having one shared array of m bits. We refer to this variant as a *partitioned* Bloom filter. The partitioned Bloom filter can be easier to parallelize than our original non-partitioned variation. Repeating the analysis above, we find that in this case the probability that a specific bit is 0 is

$$\left(1 - \frac{k}{m}\right)^n \approx e^{-kn/m},$$

and so, asymptotically, the performance is the same as the original scheme. In practice, however, the partitioned Bloom filter tends to perform slightly worse than the non-partitioned Bloom filter. This is explained by the observation that

$$\left(1 - \frac{1}{m}\right)^{kn} > \left(1 - \frac{k}{m}\right)^n,$$

when $k > 1$, so partitioned filters tend to have more 1's than non-partitioned filters, resulting in larger false positive probabilities.

We also point out that, in some cases, memory considerations may make alternative approaches for setting the bits of a Bloom filter more attractive. If one must bring in a page or a cache line to examine the bits in a Bloom filter, then examining k random bits may be too expensive. One can instead associate with an item k random bits from a page or a smaller number of cache lines. This idea originated with work of Manber and Wu [49], but variations are commonly explored (e.g., [58]).

The standard Bloom filter naturally supports insertion operations: to add a new item x to the set represented by the filter, we simply set the corresponding bits of the filter to 1. Unfortunately, the data structure does not support deletions, since changing bits of the filter from 1 to 0 could introduce false negatives. If we wish to support deletions, we can simply replace each bit of the filter with a counter, initially set to 0. To insert an item x into the filter, we now increment its corresponding counters $h_1(x), \ldots, h_k(x)$, and to delete an item known to be in the set represented by the filter, we decrement those counters. To test whether an item y is in S, we can simply check whether all the counters $h_1(y), \ldots, h_k(y)$ are positive, obtaining a false positive if $y \notin S$ but none of the counters are 0.

This Bloom filter variant is called a *counting Bloom filter* [26]. Clearly, all of our prior analysis for standard Bloom filters applies to counting Bloom filters. However, there is a complication in choosing the number of bits to use in representing a counter. Indeed, if a counter overflows at some point, then the filter may yield a false negative in the future. It is easy to see that the number of times a particular counter is incremented has distribution Binomial$(nk, 1/m) \approx$ Poisson$(nk/m) =$ Poisson$(\ln 2)$, by the Poisson approximation to the binomial distribution (assuming $k = (m/n) \ln 2$ as above). By a union bound, the probability that some counter overflows if we use b-bit counters is at most $m\mathbf{Pr}($Poisson$(\ln 2) \geq 2^b)$. As an example, for a sample configuration with $n = 10{,}000, m = 80{,}000, k = (m/n) \ln 2 = 8 \ln 2$, and $b = 4$, we have $f = (1/2)^k = 2.14\%$ and $m\mathbf{Pr}($Poisson$(\ln 2) \geq 2^b) = 1.78 \times 10^{-11}$, which is negligible. (In practice k must be an integer, but the point is clear.) This sort of calculation is typical for counting Bloom filters.

One could also use counting Bloom filters to represent multisets. Again, when a copy of an element x in inserted, we increment its corresponding counters $h_1(x), \ldots, h_k(x)$, and to delete a copy of an item known to be in the set represented by the filter, we decrement those counters. We can test whether an item y occurs in S with multiplicity at least $\ell \geq 1$ by testing whether the counters $h_1(y), \ldots, h_k(y)$ are at least ℓ, with some probability of a false positive.

We now describe a variant of counting Bloom filters that is particularly useful for high-speed data stream applications. The data structure is alternately called a *parallel multistage filter* [24] or a *count-min sketch* [13] (the paper [24] applies the data structure to network measurement and accounting, while Cormode and Muthukrishnan [13] show how it can be used to solve a number of theoretical problems in calculating statistics for data streams). The input is a stream of *updates* (i_t, c_t), starting from $t = 1$, where each *item* i_t is a member of a universe $U = \{1, \ldots, n\}$, and each *count* c_t is an integer. The state of the system at time T is given by a vector $\mathbf{a}(T) = (a_1(T), \ldots, a_n(T))$, where $a_j(T)$ is the sum of all c_t for which $t \leq T$ and $i_t = j$. The input is typically guaranteed to satisfy the condition that $a_j(T) > 0$ for every j and T. We generally drop the T when the meaning is clear.

The structures consist of a two-dimensional array Count of counters with width w and depth d: Count$[1, 1], \ldots,$ Count$[d, w]$. Every entry of the array is initialized to 0. In addition, there are d independent hash functions $h_1, \ldots, h_d : \{1, \ldots, n\} \rightarrow \{1, \ldots, w\}$. (Actually, it is enough to assume that the hash functions are universal, as shown in [13]; the argument below also holds with this assumption.) To process an update (i, c), we add c to the counters Count$[1, h_1(i)], \ldots,$ Count$[d, h_d(i)]$. Furthermore, we think of $\hat{a}_i = \min_{j \in \{1, \ldots, d\}}$ Count$[j, h_j(i)]$ as being an estimate of a_i. Indeed, it is easy to see that $\hat{a}_i \geq a_i$ (using the assumption that $a_j > 0$ for every j).

We now derive a probabilistic upper bound on $\hat{a}_i$. For $j \in \{1, \ldots, d\}$, let

$$X_{i,j} = \sum_{i' \neq i : h_j(i') = h_j(i)} a_{i'}.$$

Since the hash functions are fully random, $E[X_{i,j}] \leq \|\mathbf{a}\|/w$, where $\|\mathbf{a}\| = \sum_k a_k$ (the L_1 norm of $\mathbf{a}$, assuming all of the entries in $\mathbf{a}$ are non-negative). Markov's inequality [52] then implies that for any threshold value $\theta > 0$, we have $\Pr(X_{i,j} \geq \theta) \leq \|\mathbf{a}\|/w\theta$. Now we note that $\hat{a}_i = a_i + \min_{j\in 1,\dots,d} X_{i,j}$ and use independence of the h_j's to conclude that

$$\Pr(\hat{a}_i \geq a_i + \theta) \leq \left(\frac{\|\mathbf{a}\|}{w\theta}\right)^d.$$

In particular, if we fix some parameters $\epsilon, \delta > 0$ and set $w = \lceil e/\epsilon \rceil$, $d = \lceil \ln(1/\delta) \rceil$, and $\theta = \epsilon\|\mathbf{a}\|$, then we obtain

$$\Pr(\hat{a}_i \geq a_i + \epsilon\|\mathbf{a}\|) \leq \left(\frac{1}{e}\right)^{\ln(1/\delta)} = \delta.$$

In essence, we have that $\hat{a}_i$ is likely to be a fairly good estimate of a_i as long as a_i is not too small.

Under the assumption that all c_t are non-negative, we can optimize this data structure further using a technique called *conservative updating* [24]. The basic idea is to never increment a counter more than is strictly necessary in order to guarantee that $\hat{a}_i \geq a_i$. Formally, to process an update (i, c), we let $c' = \min_{j\in\{1,\dots,d\}} \text{Count}[j, h_j(i)]$ and then set $\text{Count}[j, h_j(i)] = \max(c + c', \text{Count}[j, h_j(i)])$ for $j = 1, \dots, d$. In particular, a counter is not updated if it is already larger than the count associated with the item, which is c' (the minimum over all the counters associated with i before the update) plus the update value c. We define the estimate $\hat{a}_i$ of a_i as before. It is easy to see that we still have $\hat{a}_i \geq a_i$ under this approach, but now the counters are not incremented as much. Intuitively, this technique further reduces the impact of small items on the estimates for large items. Experiments show that the improvement can be substantial [24].

A further variant of a Bloom filter extending the paradigm in a different direction is the *Bloomier filter*, which keeps a function value associated with each of the set items, thereby offering more than set membership [11]. More specifically, for each item x in a set S, there can be an associated fixed r-bit value $f(x) \in \{1, \dots, 2^r - 1\}$; the 0 value is meant for items not in S. Given any item $x \in S$, the Bloomier filter correctly returns $f(x)$, and for any item $y \notin S$, the Bloomier filter should return 0. Here, a false positive occurs when $y \notin S$ but the Bloomier filter returns a non-zero value. As shown in [11], a Bloomier filter can be implemented near-optimally using a cascade of Bloom filters, although there are somewhat more complex constructions with better asymptotic performance.

We emphasize that the performance of a Bloom filter does not depend at all on the size of the items in the set that it represents (except for the additional complexity required for the hash functions for larger items). Thus, although Bloom filters allow false positives, the space savings over more traditional data structures for set membership, such as hash tables, often outweigh this drawback. It is therefore not surprising that Bloom filters and their many variations have proven increasingly important for many applications (see, for instance, the survey [8]). As just a partial listing of additional examples of the proliferation of Bloom filter variations, *compressed Bloom filters* are optimized to minimize space when transmitted [50], *retouched Bloom filters* trade off false positives and false negatives [22], and *approximate concurrent state machines* extend the concept of a Bloomier filter by tracking the dynamically changing state of a changing set of items [3]. Although recently more complex but asymptotically better alternatives have been proposed (e.g., [4, 55]), the Bloom filter's simplicity, ease of use, and excellent performance make it a standard data structure that is, and will continue to be, of great use in many applications.

9.2.1.3   Hash Tables

The canonical example of a hash table is one that uses a single hash function (which is assumed to be fully random) with chaining to deal with collisions. The standard analysis shows that if the number of buckets in the table is proportional to the number of items inserted, the expected number of items that collide with a particular item is constant. Thus, on average, lookup operations should be fast. However, for applications where such average case guarantees are not sufficient, we also need some sort of probabilistic worst-case guarantee. Here, the qualifier that our worst-case guarantees be *probabilistic* excludes, for instance, the case where all items in the table are hashed to the same bucket. Such situations, while technically possible, are so ridiculously unlikely that they do not warrant serious consideration (at least from a theoretical perspective). As an example of a probabilistic worst-case guarantee, we consider throwing n balls independently and uniformly at random into n bins. In this case, a classical result (e.g., [52, Lemmas 5.1 and 5.12] or the original reference by Gonnet [32]) shows that the maximum number of balls in a bin is $\Theta((\log n)/\log\log n)$ with high probability. This result translates directly to a probabilistic worst-case guarantee for a standard hash table with n items and n buckets: while the expected time to look up a particular item is constant, with high probability the longest time that *any* lookup can require is $\Theta((\log n)/\log\log n)$. Similar results hold for other hashing variations, such as *linear probing*, where each item is hashed to a bucket, each bucket can hold one item, and if a bucket already contains an item, successive buckets are searched one at a time until an empty bucket is found [39]. A standard result is that when αn items are placed into n buckets, the expected time to look up a particular item is constant, but with high probability the longest time that *any* lookup can require is $\Theta(\log n)$. It is worth pointing out that, for certain memory layouts, where several buckets can fit on a single cache line, the locality offered by linear probing may offer performance advantages beyond what is suggested by these asymptotics.

The chained hashing example illustrates a connection between hashing and *balanced allocations*, where some number of balls is placed into bins according to some probabilistic procedure, with the implicit goal of achieving an allocation where the balls are more-or-less evenly distributed among the bins. In a seminal work,

Azar et al. [1] strengthened this connection by showing a very powerful balanced allocation result: if n balls are placed sequentially into $m \geq n$ bins for $m = O(n)$, with each ball being placed in one of a constant $d \geq 2$ randomly chosen bins with minimal load at the time of its insertion, then with high probability the maximal load in a bin after all balls are inserted is $(\ln \ln n)/\ln d + O(1)$. In particular, if we modify the standard hash table with chaining from above to use d hash functions, inserting an item into one of its d hash buckets with minimal total load, and performing a lookup for an item by checking all d of its hash buckets, then the expected lookup time is still constant (although larger than before), but the probabilistic worst-case lookup time drops exponentially. This scheme, usually called d-*way chaining*, is arguably the simplest instance of a *multiple choice hash table*, where each item is placed according to one of several hash functions.

Unsurprisingly, the impact of [1] on the design of randomized algorithms and data structures, particularly hash tables and their relatives, has been enormous. For details and a more complete list of references, we refer to the survey [51]. Before moving on, however, we mention an important improvement of the main results in [1] due to Vöcking [73]. That work exhibits the d-*left* hashing scheme, which works as follows. There are n items and m buckets. The buckets are partitioned into d groups of approximately equal size, and the groups are laid out from left to right. There is one hash function for each group, mapping the items to a randomly chosen bucket in the group. The items are inserted sequentially into the table, with an item being inserted into the least loaded of its d hash buckets (using chaining), with ties broken to the left. Vöcking [73] shows that if $m = n$ and $d \geq 2$ is constant, then the maximum load of a bucket after all the items are inserted is $(\ln \ln n)/d \ln \phi_d + O(1)$, where ϕ_d is the asymptotic growth rate of the dth order Fibonacci numbers. (For example, when $d = 2$, ϕ_d is the golden ratio $1.618\ldots$.) In particular, this improves the factor of $\ln d$ in the denominator of the $(\ln \ln n)/\ln d + O(1)$ result of Azar et al. [1]. Furthermore, Vöcking [73] shows that d-left hashing is optimal up to an additive constant. Interestingly, both the partitioning and the tie-breaking together are needed to obtain this improvement.

Both d-way chaining and d-left hashing are practical schemes, with d-left hashing being generally preferable. In particular, the partitioning of the hash buckets into groups for d-left hashing makes that scheme more amenable to a hardware implementation, since it allows for an item's d hash locations to be examined in parallel. For high-speed packet-processing applications, however, hashing schemes that resolve collisions with chaining are often undesirable. Indeed, for these applications, it is often critical that almost everything be implemented cleanly in hardware, and in this case the dynamic memory allocation requirements of hashing schemes that use chaining are problematic. Thus, we prefer *open-addressed* hash tables where each bucket can store a fixed constant number of items (typically determined by the number of items that can be conveniently read in parallel). Of course, we can simulate a hashing scheme that uses chaining with an open-addressed hash table as long as no bucket overflows, and then we just need to ensure that it is highly unlikely for a bucket to overflow. Alternatively, we can work directly with open-addressed hashing schemes that are explicitly designed with a limit on the number of items that can be stored in a bucket. In this case, for the sake of simplicity, we typically assume that each bucket can hold at most one item. The results can usually be generalized for larger buckets in a straightforward way. The potential expense of using open-addressed hash tables in these ways is that many buckets may be far from full, wasting significant space.

The standard open-addressed multiple choice hash table is the multilevel hash table (MHT) of Broder and Karlin [7]. This is a hash table consisting of d sub-tables $T_1, \ldots, T_d$, with each T_i having one hash function h_i. We view these tables as being laid out from left to right. To insert an item x, we find the minimal i such that $T_i[h_i(x)]$ is unoccupied, and place x there. As above, we assume that each bucket can store at most one item; in this case the MHT is essentially the same as a d-left hash table with the restriction that each bucket can hold at most one item, but the correspondence disappears for larger bucket sizes. If $T_1[h_1(x)], \ldots, T_d[h_d(x)]$ are all occupied, then we declare a *crisis*. There are multiple things that we can do to handle a crisis. The approach in [7] is to resample the hash functions and rebuild the entire table. That work shows that it is possible to insert n items into a properly designed MHT with $O(n)$ total space and $d = \log \log n + O(1)$ in $O(n)$ expected time, assuming only 4-wise independent hash functions.

In Section 9.3, we discuss more recent work building on [7] that describes ways to design MHTs so that no rehashings are necessary in practice. Essentially, following [7], the idea is that if the T_i's are (roughly) geometrically decreasing in size, then the total space of the table is $O(n)$. If the ratio by which the size of T_{i+1} is smaller than T_i is, say, twice as large as the expected fraction of items that are not stored in $T_1, \ldots, T_i$, then the distribution of items over the T_i's decreases doubly exponentially with high probability. This double exponential decay allows the choice of $d = \log \log n + O(1)$. For a more detailed description of this intuition, see [7] or [36].

We defer the details of the various ways to construct MHTs to Sections 9.3 and 9.4, where MHTs play a critical role. For the moment, however, we simply note that MHTs naturally support deletions, as one can just perform a lookup on an item to find its location in the table, and then mark the corresponding item as deleted. Also, MHTs appear well suited to a hardware implementation. In particular, their open-addressed nature seems to make them preferable to approaches that involve chaining, and their use of separate sub-tables allows for the possibility that all of the hash locations for a particular item can be accessed in parallel. Indeed, these considerations are part of the original motivation from [7].

There is also a substantial amount of work in the theory literature on open-addressed multiple choice hashing schemes that allow items in the table to be moved during an insertion in order to increase space utilization [15, 21, 30, 38, 56, 57]. The most basic of these schemes is *cuckoo hashing* [30, 56], which works as follows. There are d sub-tables $T_1, \ldots, T_d$, with each T_i having one hash function h_i. When attempting to insert an item x, we check if any of its hash locations $T_1[h_1(x)], \ldots, T_d[h_d(x)]$ are unoccupied, and place it in an unoccupied bucket if that is the case. Otherwise, we choose a random $I \in \{1, \ldots, d\}$ and evict the item y in $T_I[h_I(x)]$, replacing y with x. We then check if any of y's hash locations are unoccupied, placing it in the leftmost unoccupied bucket if this is the case. Otherwise, we choose a random $J \in \{1, \ldots, d\} - \{I\}$ and evict the item z in $T_J[h_J(y)]$, replacing it with y. We repeat this procedure until an eviction is no longer necessary.

Cuckoo hashing allows for a substantial increase in space utilization over a standard MHT with excellent amortized insertion times (even for small d, say, $d = 4$). Unfortunately, however, in practice a standard cuckoo hash table occasionally experiences insertion operations that take significantly more time than the average. This issue is problematic for high-speed packet-processing applications that have very strict worst-case performance requirements. We address this issue further in Section 9.4.

9.2.2 Application Performance Measures and Memory Models

Roughly speaking, the quality of the algorithms and data structures in this chapter can be measured by their space requirements and speed for various operations. In conventional algorithm analysis, speed is measured in terms of processing steps (e.g., instructions). However, as a first approximation, we count only memory accesses as processing steps. In a hardware design, this approximation is usually justified by the ability to perform multiple complex processing steps in a single cycle in hardware (using combinatorial logic gates, which are plentiful). In a software design, we can often ignore processing steps because instruction cycle times are very fast compared to memory access times.

Thus our main application performance measures are usually the amount of memory required and the number of memory accesses required for an operation of interest. Unfortunately, these measures are more complicated than they may first appear because there are different types of memories: *fast memory* (cache in software, Static Random Access Memory (SRAM) in hardware), and *slow memory* (main memory in software, Dynamic Random Access Memory (DRAM) in hardware). The main space measure is typically the amount of fast memory required for a technique. If a design only uses slow memory, then the amount of memory used is often irrelevant because such memory is typically cheap and plentiful. Similarly, if a design uses both fast and slow memory, the main speed measure is typically the number of slow memory accesses (because fast memory accesses are negligible in comparison). If a design uses only fast memory, then the speed measure is the number of fast memory accesses.

To make this abstraction more concrete, we give a brief description and comparison of SRAM and DRAM. Typical SRAM access times are 1–2 ns for on-chip SRAM and 5–10 ns for off-chip SRAM; it is possible to obtain on-chip SRAMs with 0.5 ns access times. On-chip SRAM is limited to around 64 Mbits today. The level 1 and level 2 caches in modern processors are built from SRAM.

In order to refresh itself, an SRAM bit cell requires at least five transistors. By comparison, a DRAM cell uses only a single transistor connected to an output capacitance that can be manufactured to take much less space than the transistors in an SRAM. Thus SRAM is less dense and more expensive (per bit) than memory technology based on DRAM. However, the compact design of a DRAM cell has an important negative consequence: a DRAM cell requires higher latency to read or write than the SRAM cell. The fastest off-chip DRAMs take around 40–60 ns to access (latency) with longer times such as 100 ns between successive reads (throughput). It seems clear that DRAM will always be denser but slower than SRAM.

Moving on, three major design techniques are commonly used in memory subsystem designs for networking chips and can be used for the algorithms and data structures in this chapter. While we will not dwell on such low-level issues, it is important to be aware of these techniques (and their limitations).

- **Memory Interleaving and Pipelining**   Many data structures can be split into separate banks of an interleaved memory, where each bank is a DRAM. Memory accesses can then be interleaved and pipelined to facilitate parallelism. For example, consider a binary search tree data structure, and suppose that it is split into separate banks based on nodes' locations in the tree. If we wish to perform multiple lookups on the tree, we can boost performance by allowing operations at different nodes of the tree to occur in parallel.
- **Wide Word Parallelism**   A common theme in many networking designs is to use wide memory words that can be processed in parallel. This can be implemented using DRAM and exploiting the *page mode*, or by using SRAM and making each memory word wider. In software designs, wide words can be exploited by aligning data structures to the cache line size. In hardware designs, one can choose the width of memory to fit the problem (up to say 5,000 bits or so, after which electrical issues may become problematic).
- **Combining DRAM and SRAM**   Given that SRAM is expensive and fast, and DRAM is cheap and slow, it makes sense to combine the two technologies to attempt to obtain the best of both worlds. The simplest approach is to simply use some SRAM as a cache for a DRAM database. While this technique is classical, there are many more creative applications of the use of non-uniform memory models; we will see some in this chapter.

We must also point out that routers often make use of content-addressable memories (CAMs), which are fully associative memories, usually based on SRAM technology (so that improvements in SRAM technology tend to translate into improvements in CAM technology), that support a lookup of a data item in a single access by performing lookups on all memory locations in parallel. There are also ternary CAMs (TCAMs) that support wildcard bits, which is an extremely useful feature for prefix match lookups, a critical router application discussed in Section 9.2.3. This specialty hardware is much faster than any data structure built with commodity SRAM, such as a hash table, could ever be. However, the parallel lookup feature of CAMs causes them to use a lot more power than comparable SRAMs. Furthermore, the smaller market for this sort of technology results in CAMs being much more expensive, per bit, than SRAMs. For both peak power consumption and cost per bit, an order of magnitude difference between a CAM and a comparable SRAM would not be surprising.

In this chapter, we regard CAMs as being expensive, special-purpose hardware for table lookups that are practical only when storing small sets of items. Thus, we do not think of CAMs as being a replacement for hash tables, but we do advocate their use for parts of our hash-based data structures. In particular, in Section 9.4, we describe MHTs from which some small number of items are expected to overflow. There, a CAM is used to store those items (but not all items, which is prohibitively expensive), allowing excellent worst-case lookup times for the entire data structure.

9.2.3 History of Hash-Based Techniques

As mentioned in the introduction, the primary purpose of this chapter is to survey the major recent developments in the literature on hash-based techniques for high-speed packet processing. In this section, we give a brief overview of the relevant history covered by the text [70], published in 2004. We refer the reader to [70] and the references below for further details.

Historically, hashing based on flow IDs has been used for load-balancing packets across network paths (see, for example, RFC 2991[66]) instead of schemes like round-robin that do not preserve FIFO ordering. This chapter, however, concentrates on packet-processing tasks such as lookups and measurement.

The earliest directly relevant application of a hash-based technique is probably the implementation of bridge lookups in the DEC GIGAswitch system [68]. The GIGAswitch was a switch designed in the early 1990s to connect up to 32 100 Mbps FDDI links, with the main technical challenge being the need for wire-speed forwarding. This requirement made the earlier bridge lookup algorithms, which were based on binary search and designed to work at lower speeds, impractical. Ultimately, the issue was addressed by using a hash table, where the particular hash function used was multiplication by a random polynomial modulo a particular irreducible polynomial over a finite field of characteristic two. To ensure that the hash function was suitable (i.e., that it did not hash too many items to the same bucket), the hash function was simply resampled until all items were suitably accommodated in the table. For the sake of completeness, we note that there was a small content-addressable memory (CAM) that could store some overflow from the table, which was checked in parallel with the table; the hash function was actually resampled only when an item could not be inserted into its bucket in the table and the CAM was full. While this use of a CAM is common in networking applications, it is only recently being considered in the theory literature on hashing; we discuss this more in Section 9.4. From a theoretical perspective, this implementation of hashing was not particularly novel, but it has been enormously influential in the design of real networking products. (Like many great ideas, it seems obvious in retrospect.)

The next major application of hashing-based techniques in networking hardware described in the literature was the scheme of Waldvogel et al. [74] for longest prefix match for fast IP lookups. (The *longest prefix match* problem is essentially the task of building a data structure for a set of strings that, for a query string, finds a longest string in the data structure that is a prefix of the query string; see [70] for details.) The basic idea was to keep hash tables for all possible prefix lengths and then perform the longest prefix match by a binary search over those tables. Many optimizations were needed to make this approach practical [9, 69, 74]. For our purposes, the most significant observation was that the scalability of the scheme was basically determined by the space utilization achievable by the hash tables. Indeed, the scheme required that no hash bucket receive more than a certain number of items, and the hash function was resampled until that condition was satisfied. Thus, improving the space utilization of hash tables became a problem of direct interest for implementing networking hardware.

In particular, Srinivisan and Varghese [69] pointed out that using wide memory words (easily done in hardware) ameliorated the problems of resampling the hash function and improved space utilization. However, Broder and Karlin [7] had earlier shown that the use of parallelism via multiple hash functions was also a powerful tool for this purpose. The next logical development was to combine parallelism and wide words. This was done through an application of d-left hashing [73] by Broder and Mitzenmacher [9], increasing the space utilization considerably. It appears that d-left hashing is the "state of the art" way to implement a hash table in hardware; many current products use this scheme.

While Bloom filters have for some time been proposed for networking applications [8], only recently have they been considered for speeding up core networking hardware. For example, Dharmapurikar et al. [17] appear to have been the first to suggest utilizing Bloom filters to speed up longest prefix matching algorithms. They keep hash tables for all possible prefix lengths in slow memory as in [74], but with the addition that a Bloom filter corresponding to each hash table is also stored in fast memory so that the hardware can quickly find the length of the longest matching prefix. Assuming no false positives, the hardware then has to do only 1 more lookup to slow memory to confirm the match. Similar ideas are applied to packet classification and string matching in [16, 18, 19].

Another early suggestion for using Bloom filters in network hardware appears in the IP traceback schemes of Snoeren et al. [64], where the Bloom filters are used not for speed but to save memory. Essentially, the set of packets passing through a router over some interval is stored using a Bloom filter, rather than storing a hash value for each packet, to keep the size of the set representation manageable.

A further development beyond lookups for networking hardware was the introduction by Estan and Varghese [24] of hashing-based data structures specifically designed to facilitate network measurement and accounting. The main contribution of that work is the count-min sketch (there called a *parallel multistage filter*) and the accompanying conservative update heuristic described in Section 9.2.1.2. The analysis presented in Section 9.2.1.2 is essentially taken from the more theoretical paper [13] for generality, although it is important to note that [24] contains a significant amount of analysis for the specific applications of interest. In particular, [24] contains a detailed evaluation of how count-min sketches perform for the task of identifying large network flows in real data.

Later, Singh et al. [63] used the methods of [24] for extracting worm signatures at high speeds. The basic premise of [63] is that if hashing methods are useful for measurement, then they can also be used to measure patterns indicative of network security attacks. This theme is continued in later work. Examples include hash-based algorithms to detect denial-of-service attacks based on detecting so-called *superspreaders* [72] and algorithms to detect sources that send control packets to start sessions without corresponding end control packets [40].

We also note that there are likely countless applications of innovative hashing-based techniques in networking hardware that are not described in the literature. Unfortunately, few concrete aspects of these designs are discussed openly, primarily because the actual implementations of these techniques are widely considered to be trade secrets by router manufacturers. Broadly speaking, though, hash tables and related data structures are considered generally useful for a variety of packet classification, network monitoring, and lookup applications.

Finally, we note that while it is common for a high-speed packet-processing application to be amenable (at least in principle) to a hash-based approach, there is something of a historical bias against these techniques. The issue is that hash tables and related data structures can only offer probabilistic guarantees, as opposed to the more commonly accepted deterministic worst-case performance bounds offered by classical algorithmic approaches. For instance, for the longest prefix match problem described above, a hardware designer may prefer (simply as a matter of philosophy) a trie-based approach (see, for example, [70]) to a variant of the scheme of Waldvogel et al. [74], whose effectiveness ultimately relies on the efficiency of hash table lookups, which can be difficult to quantify. While this attitude may be changing, it is important to remember that the sorts of probabilistic guarantees offered by hash-based solutions always depend strongly on certain randomness assumptions (i.e., the assumption that hash functions are fully random), and so convincingly evaluating the performance of such a scheme requires extensive analysis and experimentation.

9.3   Lookups in a Non-uniform Memory Model: On-Chip Summaries of Off-Chip Hash Tables

We start by examining a problem first addressed by Song et al. [65]. Recall that in a multiple choice hashing scheme with d hash functions, one performs a lookup for an item x by examining (in the worst case) all d hash locations corresponding to x. In a hardware application, it may be reasonable to implement this procedure by examining all d locations in parallel, particularly if the hash table memory is stored on the chip that is performing the lookup. However, if the hash table must be stored off-chip (due to its size), then performing all d of these lookups in parallel may introduce a prohibitively expensive cost in terms of chip I/O, particularly the number of pins on the chip that are needed to access the hash table. It then becomes natural to ask whether we can design some sort of on-chip *summary* that can reduce the number of worst-case (off-chip) memory accesses to the hash table from d to, say, 1. This is the question addressed in [65].

More formally, the summary answers questions of the following form, "Is item x in the hash table, and if so, in which of its d hash locations is it?" The summary is allowed some small false positive probability (e.g., 0.5%) for items not in the hash table, since these are easily detected and so do not significantly impact performance as long as they are infrequent. However, if a queried item x is in the hash table, the summary should always correctly identify the hash location used to store x, unless some sort of unlikely failure condition occurs during the construction of the summary. (In particular, if the summary is successfully constructed, then it does not generate false negatives and the worst-case number of off-chip memory accesses is 1.) The objective is now to design a summary data structure and the corresponding hash table so that they are efficient and the summary data structure is successfully constructed with overwhelming probability.

The basic scheme proposed by Song et al. [65] is as follows. (Essentially, it is a combination of a counting Bloom filter variant for the summary with a variant of d-way chaining for the hash table.) For simplicity, we start by describing the variant where the hash table is built by inserting n items, and after that it is never modified. Here, the hash table consists of m buckets and d hash functions, and the summary consists of one b-bit counter for each bucket. When an item is inserted into the hash table, it is placed in all of its d hash buckets and all of the corresponding counters are incremented. Then the hash table is *pruned*; for each item in the table, the copy in the bucket whose corresponding counter is minimal (with ties broken according to the ordering of the buckets) is kept, and the rest are deleted. A query to the summary for an item x is now answered by finding the smallest of its d counters (again with ties broken according to the ordering of the buckets). If the value of this counter is 0, then x cannot be in the table, and otherwise x is presumed to be in the corresponding bucket.

Song et al. [65] give several heuristic improvements to this basic scheme in order to reduce collisions in the underlying hash table and optimize performance for various applications. The heuristics appear effective, but they are only analyzed through simulations, and do not appear to be amenable to theoretical or numerical analyses. Insertions can be handled, but can necessitate moving items in the hash table. Deletions are significantly more challenging in this setting than in most hash table constructions. In particular, it may be necessary to keep a copy of the entire hash table (or a smaller variant called a shared-node fast hash table) before pruning; see [65] for details.

Kirsch and Mitzenmacher [36] build on [65], offering alternative approaches more amenable to analysis. They propose the use of an MHT as the underlying hash table. This gives a worst case bound on the number of items in a bucket, although it introduces the possibility of a crisis, which must be very unlikely in order for the MHT to give good performance. Furthermore, since the distribution of items over the sub-tables of an MHT decays doubly exponentially with high probability, it suffices to design summaries that perform well under the assumption that most of the items in the MHT are in the first sub-table, most of the rest are in the second, etc.

Kirsch and Mitzenmacher [36] propose two summary design techniques based on this observation, both based on Bloom filter techniques. We review the one that is easier to describe and motivate here. As before, for simplicity we start by assuming that we are only interested in building a hash table and corresponding summary for n items by inserting the n items sequentially, and then the data structures are fixed for all time. If the MHT consists of d sub-tables $T_1, \ldots, T_d$, then the summary consists of d Bloom filters $F_1, \ldots, F_d$. Each filter F_i represents the set of all items stored in $T_i, \ldots, T_d$. To perform a query for an item x, we first check whether F_1 yields a positive for x; if not, then x cannot be in the MHT. Otherwise, we find the largest i where F_i returns a positive for x, and declare that x is in T_i.

The first important observation here is that F_1 is simply a standard Bloom filter for the set of items stored in the MHT. Thus, false positives for F_1 merely yield false positives for the summary. As before, such false positives are acceptable as long as they are sufficiently infrequent (e.g., the false positive probability of F_1 is 0.5%). However, if an item x is in T_i, then it will be inserted into $F_1, \ldots, F_i$ but not F_{i+1}. If F_{i+1} gives a false positive for x, then querying the summary for x yields an incorrect answer, which is unacceptable to us because x is actually in the MHT. Thus, $F_2, \ldots, F_d$ must have extremely small false positive probabilities.

The second important observation is the effect of the distribution of the items over the sub-tables of the MHT on the quality of the summary. Recall that for a typical MHT, with high probability, most of the items are stored in T_1, most of the rest are stored in T_2, etc. In fact, the distribution of items over the sub-tables decays doubly exponentially. In particular, if S_i is the set of items stored in $T_i, \ldots, T_d$, then S_i is almost surely small for $i \geq 2$. Thus, for $i \geq 2$, since F_i is just a standard Bloom filter for S_i, we can achieve an extremely small false probability for F_i without using too much space. Since we only need a moderate false positive probability for F_1 (as described above), we can adequately construct it in a reasonable amount of space.

A further advantage of the approach of [36] is that one can obtain fairly precise estimates of the probabilities that the relevant hash-based data structures fail using numerical techniques. This property is very useful, as purely theoretical techniques often obscure constant factors and simulation results can be computationally expensive to obtain (especially when the probabilities being estimated are very small, as they should be for the sorts of failure probabilities that we are interested in bounding). Numerical techniques offer the potential for very accurate and predictive results for only a moderate computational cost.

For the summary approach described above, it is fairly easy to see that if we can obtain numerical information about the distributions of the sizes of the S_i's, then the standard Bloom filter analysis can be directly applied to estimate the failure probability of the summary. The primary issue then becomes obtaining this numerical information (note that the probability of a crisis is just $\mathbf{Pr}(|S_1| < n)$, and so it too follows from this information). Now, if $m_1, \ldots, m_d$ are the sizes of $T_1, \ldots, T_d$, then it is fairly easy to see that the distribution of the number of items that are stored in T_1 is the same as the number of bins that are occupied if we throw n balls at random into m_1 buckets. Furthermore, for $i > 1$, the conditional distribution of the number of items in T_i given that N_{i-1} items are stored in $T_1, \ldots, T_{i-1}$ is the same as the number of bins that are occupied if we throw $n - N_{i-1}$ balls into m_i buckets. These balls-and-bins probabilities are easy to compute and manipulate to obtain the desired information about the distribution of the S_i's; for details, see [36]. As an example of the improvement, for 10,000 items these techniques allow for a hash table that uses 50% of the space as the hash table in [65] and an accompanying summary that uses about 66% of the space of the corresponding summary from [65], for a comparable false positive probability and a failure probability of about 5×10^{-12}; different tradeoffs are possible (e.g., a larger hash table to get more skew in the distribution of the items, allowing for a smaller summary).

As is usually the case for hash-based data structures, it is more difficult to measure the effectiveness of these techniques when deletion operations are allowed. However, we do note that the summary construction above can be modified to handle deletions by replacing the Bloom filters with counting Bloom filters. Unfortunately, while the MHT supports deletions in the natural way (an item can simply be removed from the table), intermixing deletion and insertion operations can have a major impact on the distribution of the S_i's, which is critical for the failure probability guarantees. Thus, while the approach of [36] seems adaptable to deletions, understanding and mitigating the impact of deletions on these sorts of data structures remains an important open problem.

In more practical work, Kumar et al. [42, 43] use similar ideas to construct alternative high-performance hash tables. The paper [42] presents a variant of a multiple choice hash table. A hash table is broken into multiple segments, each of which can be thought of as a separate hash table; each item chooses a bucket in each segment. If an item cannot be placed without a collision, a standard collision-resolving technique, such as double hashing, is applied to the segment where the item is placed. To avoid searching over all segments when finding an item, a Bloom filter is used for each segment to record the set of items placed in that segment. When an item is placed, the first priority is to minimize the length of the collision chain, or the search time, for that item. Often, however, there will be ties in the search length, in which case priority is given to a segment where the new item will introduce the fewest new 1's into the Bloom filter; this reduces the chances of false positives. (Some related theory is presented in [48].)

The paper [43] introduces *peacock hashing*, which takes advantage of the skewed construction developed for MHTs. The main innovation of [43] appears to arise from using more limited hash functions in order to improve rebalancing efforts in case of deletion. In sub-tables beyond the first, the possible locations of an item depend on its location in the previous table. Because of this, when an item is deleted, there are only a very small number of possible locations in the subsequent sub-tables that need to be checked to see if an item from a later, smaller table can be moved to the now empty position in the larger, earlier table, potentially reducing the probability of a crisis. In exchange, however, one gives up some of the power of hashing each item independently to multiple locations. Also, currently peacock hashing lacks a complete mathematical analysis, making it hard to compare to other schemes except by experiment. Some analysis and alternative schemes are suggested in [34].

9.4 Lookups in a Uniform Memory Model: Hardware Hash Tables with Moves

We now turn our attention to the setting where it is feasible to examine all of an item's hash locations in a multiple choice hash table in parallel. In this case, our goal becomes to increase space utilization of our hash table constructions, while ensuring that they are amenable to hardware implementations for high-speed applications. For instance, one can think of these techniques as potentially enabling us to take an off-chip hash table and decrease its space overhead enough so that it can be effectively implemented on-chip, thus eliminating the chip I/O problem from Section 9.3 and replacing it with a very restrictive memory constraint.

As discussed in Section 9.2.1.3, there are a number of hashing schemes in the theory literature that allow items to be moved in the table during the insertion of a new item in order to increase the space utilization of the table. Unfortunately, while these schemes have excellent amortized performance, they occasionally allow for insertion operations that take a significant amount of time. For high-speed packet-processing applications, such delays may be unacceptable.

We discuss two approaches to this problem. First, we consider new hashing schemes that are designed to exploit the potential of moves while ensuring a reasonable worst-case time bound for a hash table operation. Second, we consider a more direct adaptation of an existing scheme from the theory literature (specifically, cuckoo hashing) to this setting, striving for a de-amortized performance guarantee.

9.4.1 The First Approach: The Power of One Move

The first approach is taken by Kirsch and Mitzenmacher in [35]. That work proposes a number of modifications to the standard MHT insertion scheme that allow at most one move during an insertion operation. The opportunity for a single move demonstrates that the space utilization of the standard MHT can be significantly increased without a drastic increase in the worst-case time of a hashing operation. The proposed schemes are all very similar in spirit; they differ primarily in the tradeoffs between the amount of time spent examining potential moves during an insertion and the resulting increases in space utilization.

The core idea behind these schemes is best illustrated by the following procedure, called the *second chance scheme*. Essentially, the idea is that as we insert items into a standard MHT with sub-tables $T_1, \ldots, T_d$, the sub-tables fill up from left to right, with items cascading from T_i to T_{i+1} with increasing frequency as T_i fills up. Thus, a natural way to increase the space utilization of the table is to slow down this cascade at every step.

This idea is implemented in the second chance scheme in the following way. We mimic the insertion of an item x using the standard MHT insertion procedure, except that if we are attempting to insert x into T_i, if the buckets $T_i[h_i(x)]$ and

$T_{i+1}[h_{i+1}(x)]$ are occupied, rather than simply moving on to T_{i+2} as in the standard scheme, we check whether the item y in $T_i[h_i(x)]$ can be moved to $T_{i+1}[h_{i+1}(y)]$. If this move is possible (i.e., the bucket $T_{i+1}[h_{i+1}(y)]$ is unoccupied), then we perform the move and place x at $T_i[h_i(x)]$. Thus, we effectively get a *second chance* at preventing a cascade from T_{i+1} to T_{i+2}. (We note that this basic idea of relocating items to shorten the length of hash chains appears to have originated with the work of Brent on double-hashing [6].)

Just as in the standard MHT insertion scheme, there may be items that cannot be placed in the MHT during the insertion procedure. Previously, we considered this to be an extremely bad event and strived to bound its probability. Here we take a different perspective and say that if an item x is not successfully placed in the MHT during its insertion, then it is placed on an overflow list L, which, in practice, would be implemented with a CAM. (A similar idea is found in [30], where it is dubbed a filter cache, and the implementation of the overflow list is different.) To perform a lookup, we simply check L in parallel with the MHT.

It turns out that since the second chance scheme only allows moves from left to right, it is analyzable by a *fluid limit* or *mean-field* technique, which is essentially a way of approximating stochastic phenomena by a deterministic system of differential equations. The technique also applies to the standard MHT insertion procedure, as well as a wide variety of extensions to the basic second chance scheme. This approach makes it possible to perform very accurate numerical analyses of these systems, and in particular it allows for some interesting optimizations. We refer to [35] for details, but as an example, we note that when both the standard MHT insertion scheme and second chance insertion scheme are optimized to use as little space as possible with four hash functions so that no more than 0.2% of the items are expected to overflow from the table under either scheme, then the second chance scheme requires 72% of the space of the standard scheme, with about 13% of insertion operations requiring a move.

The second chance scheme is also much more amenable to a hardware implementation than it may at first seem. To insert an item x, we simply read all of the items $y_1 = T_1[h_1(x)], \ldots, y_d = T_d[h_d(x)]$ in parallel. Then we compute the hashes $h_2(y_1), \ldots, h_d(y_{d-1})$ in parallel. (Here, for notational simplicity, we are assuming that all of $T_1[h_1(x)], \ldots, T_d[h_d(x)]$ are occupied, so that the y_i's are well defined; it should be clear how to handle the general case.) At this point, we now have all of the information needed to execute the insertion procedure without accessing the hash table (assuming that we maintain a bit vector indicating which buckets of the table are occupied).

The second chance scheme and its relatives also support deletions in the natural way: an item can simply be removed from the table. However, as in Section 9.3, the intermixing of insertions and deletions fundamentally changes the behavior of the system. In this case, the differential equation approximations become much more difficult and heuristic, but still useful. For details, see [35]; for further experimental analysis of schemes that make one move on either an insertion or a deletion, see [34].

9.4.2   The Second Approach: De-amortizing Cuckoo Hashing

We now discuss some possible adaptations of the standard cuckoo hashing scheme, proposed by Kirsch and Mitzenmacher [37], to obtain better de-amortized performance. Recall that in standard cuckoo hashing, the insertion of an item x corresponds to a number of *sub-operations* in the following way. First, we attempt to insert x into one of its hash locations. If that is unsuccessful, then we choose one of x's hash locations at random, evict the item y in that place, and replace it with x. We then attempt to place y into one of its hash locations, and, failing that, we choose one of y's hash locations other than the one from which it was just evicted at random, evict the item z in that location, and replace it with y. We then attempt to place z similarly.

We think of each of these attempts to place an item in its hash locations as a sub-operation. In a hardware implementation of cuckoo hashing, it is natural to consider an *insertion queue*, implemented in a CAM, which stores sub-operations to be processed. To process a sub-operation, we simply remove it from the queue and execute it. If the sub-operation gives rise to another sub-operation, we insert the new sub-operation into the queue. Generally speaking, the queue is implemented with some policy for determining the order in which sub-operations should be processed. For the standard cuckoo hashing algorithm, this policy would be for sub-operations coming from newly inserted items to be inserted at the back of the queue, and a sub-operation arising from a sub-operation that was just executed to be inserted at the front of the queue.

The key feature of this approach is that we can efficiently perform insertions, lookups, and deletions even if we reorder sub-operations. Indeed, an insertion can be performed by inserting a single sub-operation into the queue, and a lookup can be performed by examining all of the items' hash locations in the table and the entire queue in parallel (since the queue is implemented with a CAM). To perform a deletion, we check whether the item is in the table, and if so we mark the corresponding bucket as deleted so that the item is overwritten by a future sub-operation. If the item is in the queue, we remove the corresponding sub-operation from the queue.

Since the queue must actually fit into a CAM of modest size (at least under ordinary operating conditions), the main performance issue is the size of the queue when it is equipped with a particular policy. For instance, the problem with standard cuckoo hashing policy is that it can become "stuck" attempting to process an unusually large number of sub-operations arising from a particularly troublesome insertion operation, allowing new insertion operations to queue up in the mean time. A natural first step towards fixing this problem is to insert the sub-operations corresponding to newly inserted items on the front of queue, rather than on the back. In particular, this modification exploits the fact that a newly inserted item has a chance of being placed in any of its d hash locations, whereas an item that was just evicted from the table has at most $d - 1$ unoccupied hash locations (assuming that the item responsible for the eviction has not been deleted).

Another useful observation comes from introducing the following notion of the *age* of a sub-operation. If a sub-operation corresponds to the initial attempt to insert an item, then that sub-operation has age 0. Otherwise, the sub-operation results from the processing of another sub-operation with some age a, and we say that the new sub-operation has age $a + 1$. The previous queuing policy can then be thought of as a modification of the standard policy to give priority to sub-operations with age 0. More generally, we can introduce a policy in which insertion operations are prioritized by their ages. Intuitively, this modification makes sense because the older a sub-operation is, the more likely the original insertion operation that gave rise to it is somehow troublesome, which in turn makes it more likely that this sub-operation will not give a successful placement in the table, resulting in a new sub-operation.

While it may not be practical to implement the insertion queue as a priority queue in this way, since sub-operations with large ages are fairly rare, we should be able to approximate the performance of the priority queue with following approach. As before, sub-operations corresponding to an initial insertion of an item are placed on the front of the queue. Furthermore, whenever the processing of a sub-operation yields a new sub-operation, the new sub-operation is placed on the back of the queue.

All of these policies are evaluated and compared empirically in [37]. (It does not seem possible to conduct a numerical evaluation here, due to the complexity of mathematically analyzing cuckoo hashing.) Overall, the results indicate that all of the intuition described above is accurate. In particular, the last queuing policy is extremely practical and performs substantially better than the standard policy over long periods of time. More specifically, the size of the queue under the standard policy is much more susceptible to occasional spikes than the last policy. In practice, this observation means that when the insertion queue is implemented with a CAM that should hold the entire queue almost all of the time, the last policy is likely to perform much better than the original one.

9.5 Bloom Filter Techniques

This section describes some additional improvements and applications of Bloom filters for high-speed packet processing that have been proposed in recent work. We start by describing some improvements that can be made to the standard Bloom filter and counting Bloom filter data structures that are particularly well suited to hardware-based networking applications. Then we describe the *approximate concurrent state machine*, which is a Bloom filter variant that makes use of these ideas to efficiently represent state information for a set of items, as opposed to membership, as in a standard Bloom filter. Finally, we review a number of additional applications of Bloom filters to a wide variety of high-speed networking problems.

9.5.1 Improved (Counting) Bloom Filters

Standard counting Bloom filters, by their very nature, are not particularly space-efficient. Using the standard optimization for false positives for a Bloom filter from

Section 9.2.1.2, the value for a particular counter in a counting Bloom filter is 0 with probability approximately $1/2$. Using multiple bits (e.g., 4, which is the usual case) to represent counters that take value 0 roughly half the time is an inefficient use of space. Some space gains can be made in practice by introducing additional lookups; counters can be kept to two bits and a secondary table can be used for counters that overflow. More sophisticated approaches exist, but their suitability for hardware implementation remains untested (see, e.g., [12, 55]).

To address this issue, Bonomi et al. [5] develop new constructions with the same functionality as a Bloom filter and counting Bloom filter, based on d-left hashing. These schemes are designed particularly for hardware implementation. In particular, they generally reduce the number of hashes and memory accesses required by the standard data structures. The idea behind these constructions actually first appears in another work by Bonomi et al. [3], where an extension to the Bloomier filter dubbed *approximate concurrent state machines*, or ACSMs, are developed. Here we describe the Bloom filter and counting Bloom filter variants, and discuss ACSMs in Section 9.5.2.

The starting point for these constructions is the folklore result that one can obtain the same functionality as a Bloom filter for a static set S with near-optimal performance using a perfect hash function. (A *perfect* hash function is an easily computable bijection from S to an array of $|S|$ hash buckets.) One finds a perfect hash function P, and then stores at each hash location an $f = \lceil \log 1/\varepsilon \rceil$ bit fingerprint, computed according to some other hash function H. A query on z requires computing $P(z)$ and $H(z)$, and checking whether the fingerprint stored at $P(z)$ matches $H(z)$. When $z \in S$ a correct response is given, and when $z \notin S$ a false positive occurs with probability at most ε; this uses $n\lceil \log 1/\varepsilon \rceil$ bits for a set S of n items.

The problem with this approach is that it does not cope with changes in the set S – either insertions or deletions – and perfect hash functions are generally too expensive to compute in many settings. To deal with this, we make use of the fact, recognized by Broder and Mitzenmacher [9] in the context of designing hash-based approaches to IP lookup (along the lines of the work by Waldvogel et al. [74] discussed in Section 9.2.3), that using d-left hashing provides a natural way to obtain an "almost perfect" hash function. The resulting hash function is only almost perfect in that instead of having one set item in each bucket, there can be several (there are d possible locations for each item), and space is not perfectly utilized.

An example demonstrates the idea behind the approach; details are presented in [5]. Suppose we wish to handle sets of n items. We utilize a d-left hash table with $d = 3$ choices per item, so that on insertion each item chooses one bucket from each of three sub-tables uniformly at random, and the fingerprint for the item is then stored in the least loaded of the three choices. Each sub-table will have $n/12$ buckets, for $n/4$ buckets in total, giving an average of 4 items per bucket. The maximum number of items in a bucket will be 6 with high probability (for large n, the probability converges to a value greater than $1 - 10^{-30}$). Hence we can implement the hash table as a simple array, with space for 6 fingerprints per bucket, and be guaranteed a very small probability of a failure due to bucket overflow. As with the folklore perfect hashing result, to check if an item is in the set, one checks for the fingerprint, but here one now has to check all three sub-tables.

Unfortunately, while this approach only uses three hashes and memory accesses for a lookup, analysis shows that as presented it gives a larger false positive probability for a given amount of space than a properly configured standard Bloom filter. Some additional manipulations are necessary to improve performance. The most important idea is to make use of the empty space; we are giving buckets space for six fingerprints, but on average they only hold four, leaving significant empty space throughout the hash table. To better use this space, we utilize variable-length fingerprints and a technique called *dynamic bit reassignment* [4]. That is, suppose we use 64-bit buckets, and give 60 bits to the fingerprints. (The remaining 4 bits are useful for various additional accounting.) This yields 10 bits per fingerprint. But if there are only 3 items in the bucket, we could use as many as 20 bits per fingerprint; if there are 4 items, as many as 15; and if there are 5 items, as many as 12. To improve performance, we dynamically change the fingerprint length in the bucket according to the number of items, shrinking fingerprints as the bucket load increases. This requires reading an entire bucket and processing it to extract the fingerprint, and rewriting an entire bucket when an item is inserted, but this can all be done easily in hardware.

The same idea can be used to construct a counting Bloom filter variant based on a d-left hash table [3, 5]. With a counting Bloom filter, the standard construction is quite wasteful of space, so even without using dynamic bit reassignment, one can gain a factor of 2 or more in space quite easily. (Indeed, using variable-length fingerprints is more problematic in this setting, since one may not be able to increase the fingerprint size naturally when an item is deleted from the set.) Some care needs to be taken, however, to handle deletions properly; if one is not careful, the fingerprint corresponding to an item could appear in more than one bucket, if some other item shares the same fingerprint and one of the buckets. This is not a problem for the Bloom filter setting, where there are no deletions, but is a problem for the counting Bloom filter setting – which copy of the fingerprint do we delete? This problem can be avoided by using a hash function combined with permutations, instead of several hash functions.

Briefly, we can think of the hashing as being done in two phases. First, we hash an item with a hash function $h : U \to [B] \times [R]$ (where for an integer n, the notation $[n]$ denotes the set $\{0, \ldots, n-1\}$). Then, to obtain the d locations, we make use of additional (pseudo)-random permutations $P_1, \ldots, P_d$, so that

$$P_1(h(x)) = (b_1, r_1), P_2(h(x)) = (b_2, r_2), \ldots, P_d(h(x)) = (b_d, r_d),$$

where (b_i, r_i) are the bucket and fingerprint for the ith sub-table. Now, two items x and y will share a fingerprint and bucket if and only if they have the same hash $h(x) = h(y)$, so that a small counter (generally 2 bits) can be used to keep track of collisions for items under the hash function h.

9.5.2 Approximate Concurrent State Machines

Approximate concurrent state machines (ACSMs), introduced by Bonomi et al. [3], are a generalization of Bloom filters and Bloomier filters designed for router applications. In many such applications, a router may be handling a collection of flows, where a flow is determined by a source–destination pair or the standard IP 5-tuple. Each flow may have an associated state that changes over time, according to transitions over a well-defined finite state machine, usually with a small number of states. We desire a method that allows us to track the state of flows over time, as both the state of flows change and as the set of flows being tracked change over time, using smaller space than an explicit listing. Specifically, in [3], four operations are suggested for an ACSM data structure: insert a new flow with a given state, look up the state of a flow, modify the state of a flow, and delete an existing flow. In the spirit of Bloom filters, it makes sense to consider data structures that may return a state value for flows not currently extant, or that may return an incorrect state value for an extant flow. In practice there are several practical challenges to consider, such as handling situations where flows do not terminate correctly or are not initialized properly.

There are multiple possible ways to construct ACSM data structures, with several suggested in [3]. The best in experiments is based upon the d-left hashing approach. For each flow a fingerprint is stored, along with its associated state, in the d-left hash table. (This technique is intuitively similar to the techniques for improving the space utilization of Bloom filters and counting Bloom filters discussed in Section 9.5.1.) Interestingly, if fingerprints collide, it may be appropriate in some cases for the data structure to return a "don't know" response; such a response may be significantly less damaging than an incorrect response. The idea of allowing a "don't know" response, found also in [46], appears potentially quite powerful and worthy of further study.

Perhaps the simplest example of a use for an ACSM is to keep a small counter for each flow; the count represents the state of an item. Additional monitoring or other functionality could be required if the count for a flow reached a threshold value. A further example application considered in [3] is for specialized congestion control mechanisms for MPEG-based video streams. By tracking the frame type as the state of an MPEG-video flow, one can implement non-trivial congestion mechanisms based on the frame type, including tail-dropping mechanisms, where all packets are dropped until the next important frame (generally an I-Frame).

9.5.3 More Applications of Bloom Filters

Bloom filters have also recently been employed for more sophisticated packet processing and packet classification tasks in hardware. A useful example design is given in [16, 18], where the question being tackled is how to find specific substrings, commonly called signatures, in packets at wire speeds. A common current use of signatures is to scan for byte sequences particular to Internet worms, allowing malicious packets to be dropped. However, other natural uses arise in a variety of settings.

If we think of a collection of signatures as being a set of strings, then a natural approach is to represent this set with a Bloom filter. More specifically, it makes sense to separate signatures by length, and use a Bloom filter for each length, allowing the Bloom filters to be considered in parallel as the bytes of the packet are shifted through as a data stream. In order to obtain a suitable hardware implementation, however, there are further details to consider. For example, to handle the possible deletion and insertion of signature strings, one can use an associated counting Bloom filter. As insertions and deletions are likely to be rare, these counting Bloom filters can be kept separately in slower memory [16]. To avoid costly hashing overhead for longer signatures, such strings can be broken into smaller strings, and a small amount of state is kept to track how much of the string has been seen. In such a setting, the Bloom filter can also be used to track the state (in a manner similar to one of the approaches suggested for approximate concurrent state machines [3]).

Using Bloom filters allows a large database of signature strings to be effectively represented with a small number of bits, making use of fast memory in hardware feasible. Thousands and even tens of thousands of strings can be effectively dealt with while maintaining wire speed [16].

Bloom filters have also been proposed for use in various longest prefix matching implementations [17, 19]. Many variations of IP lookup algorithms, for example, create hash tables consisting of prefixes of various lengths that have to potentially be matched against a given input IP address, with the goal of finding the longest possible match. The number of accesses to the hash tables can potentially be reduced by using a Bloom filter to record the set of prefixes in each hash table [17]. By checking the Bloom filter, one can avoid an unnecessary lookup into a hash table when the corresponding prefix does not exist in the table. Notice, though, that because of false positives, one cannot simply take the longest match suggested by the Bloom filters themselves; the hash table lookup must be done to check for a true match. The average number of hash table lookups, however, is reduced dramatically, so under the assumption that hash table lookups are dramatically slower or more costly than Bloom filter lookups, there are substantial gains in performance.

Bloom filters can also be used in multi-dimensional longest prefix matching approaches for packet classification, potentially giving a cheaper solution than the standard TCAM approach [19]. The solution builds on top of what is known as the cross-product algorithm: find the longest prefix match on each field, and hash the resulting vector of longest matches into a hash table that will provide the packet classification rules associated with that vector. Unfortunately, straightforward implementations of the cross-product rule generally lead to very large hash tables, because the cross-product approach leads to a large number of prefix vectors, roughly corresponding to the product of the number of prefixes in each field. This creates a significant overhead. An alternative is to split the rules into subsets and perform the cross-product algorithm on each subset, in order to reduce the overall size for hash tables. To keep the cost of doing longest prefix matchings reasonable, for each field, the longest prefix match is performed just once, over all subsets. The problem with this approach is now that for each subset of rules, for each field, there are multiple prefix lengths that might be possible; conceivably, any subprefix of the longest prefix match over all subsets of rules could apply to any specific subset of rules. To avoid hash table lookups for all possible combinations of prefixes over all subsets of rules, a Bloom filter of valid prefix vectors for each subset of rules can be maintained, reducing the number of necessary lookups in the hash table in a spirit similar to [17].

Results based on this approach yield a solution that requires at most $4+r$ memory accesses on average when r rules can match a packet; this can be further reduced with pipelining. Memory costs range on the order of 32 to 45 bytes per rule, allowing reasonably large rule sets to be effectively handled in SRAM.

Another recently proposed approach makes use of multiple choice hashing in order to reduce memory usage for IP lookup and packet classification algorithms, as well as other related algorithms. The setting here revolves around the fact that many algorithms for these types of problems reduce to directed graph traversal problems. Longest prefix matching structures are often represented by a trie, where one finds the longest prefix match by walking down the trie. Similarly, regular expression matching structures are often represented by finite automata, where one finds the match by a walk on the corresponding automata graph.

Kumar et al. [44] describe an approach for compressing the representation of tries and other directed graphs, by avoiding using pointers to name nodes. Instead, the history of the path used to reach a node is used as a key for that node, and a multiple-choice hash structure stores the graph information associated with the node, such as its neighbors, in a format that allows continued traversal. For this approach to be successful, there should be no collisions in the hash table. This is best accomplished with low space overheads using cuckoo hashing, which works well even in the face of updates to the underlying graph that change the set of keys being stored. By avoiding the use of expensive node identifiers, a factor of 2 or more in space can be saved over standard representations with minimal additional processing.

Another recent methodology for longest prefix matching problems based on hash-based approaches was described as part of the Chisel architecture [33]. Here the underlying technology used is a Bloomier filter. Prefixes correspond to keys, which are stored in the filter. One issue with this approach is that Bloomier filters do not support updates; insertions, in particular, can require the Bloomier filter to be reconstructed, which can take time linear in the number of keys. (See related lower bounds in [14].) The trace analysis in [33] suggests that updates can be done quickly without reconstruction in most cases, but it is not clear whether this holds more generally, and there is not currently a theoretical justification for this finding. The authors also develop other techniques to handle issues particular to the longest prefix matching problem in this context, such as how to cope with wildcard bits in the keys.

9.6   Measurement Applications Using Hash-Based Algorithms

Today's routers provide per-interface counters that can be read by the management protocol SNMP, and/or a much more expensive solution that involves sampling packets using the NetFlow protocol [23]. The problem with this state of affairs is that SNMP counters are extremely coarse, while NetFlow is extremely expensive. Indeed, for the SNMP approach, there is only a single counter for all packets received and sent on an interface. In particular, there is no way to find how much a particular source is sending over the interface. Sampling packets with NetFlow addresses such issues, but often with prohibitive cost. For instance, even if we only sample one in a thousand packets, the wire speed may be such that gigabits of data are collected every minute. Much of this data is lost, and the rest (which is still substantial) must be transferred to a measurement station, where it is logged to disk and eventually post-processed. Furthermore, despite its cost, NetFlow does not provide accurate answers to natural questions, such as the number of distinct source addresses seen in packets [25]. In this section, we describe hash-based measurement algorithms that can be implemented in hardware and can answer questions that SNMP counters cannot in a way that is much more direct and less expensive than NetFlow. The setting for all of these algorithms is a single interface in a router, and the algorithm is implemented by some logic or software associated with the link.

9.6.1   Finding Heavy-Hitters and Flow Size Distributions

In networking terminology, a *flow* is any collection of packets that pass through a given link and have some common header fields. For example, we could partition packets into flows based upon their destination addresses. In a hardware design, the exact definition of a flow can be left flexible in the interface logic by using simple mask registers on the IP and TCP fields so that network managers can change the definition to ask different questions in a running network.

For some types of flows, such as TCP flows, there are measurements that indicate millions of concurrent flows on a link [27]. Measuring these flows directly is prohibitively expensive (as is measuring them with NetFlow). Fortunately, a network manager may not need direct measurements of all flows on a link, but instead require knowledge of the flows that consume the most bandwidth. This problem is often called finding *heavy-hitters*. More precisely, the heavy-hitters problem can be defined as finding all flows that consume more than some fixed fraction of the bandwidth of the link.

We have already seen that the count-min sketch (or parallel multistage filter) with conservative updating is a natural solution to this problem (for details, see Section 9.2.1.2 or the original references [13, 24]). Indeed, the data structure is essentially designed for this task. Unlike a direct measurement approach like NetFlow, this data structure only requires memory proportional to the number of heavy-hitters and simultaneously provides accurate probabilistic estimates of their bandwidth consumption.

Estan and Varghese [24] also describe a sampling-based technique called *sample-and-hold* for heavy-hitters estimation in which each packet is sampled independently with some very low probability and all subsequent occurrences of a sampled packet's flow are counted exactly in a CAM. A problem with this approach is that the CAM may be polluted with small flows. To address this issue, Lu et al. [47] propose *elephant traps* that, in essence, enhance sample-and-hold by periodically removing small flows from the CAM using a Least Recently Used-like algorithm that can be efficiently implemented in hardware. Since this chapter concentrates on hash-based algorithms, we do not describe this approach any further.

A general approach to measurement using hash-based counters is described by Kumar et al. [41]. The idea is that, over some time interval, all flows are hashed in parallel to several counters as in the count-min sketch. At the end of the interval, the counters are sent to software to be estimated for the measures of interest. For example, Kumar et al. [41] describe how to estimate the flow size distribution (i.e., the number of packets sent by each flow). For simplicity, assume that each counter is incremented by one for each packet and not by the number of bytes. The main idea is to use *expectation maximization* to iteratively estimate the flow size distribution. We first estimate the current vector of flow sizes coarsely using the hardware counters. Then we calculate expectations from the estimates, replace the original estimates with these expectations, and iterate the process until convergence.

The idea of using more complex iterative estimators in software at the end of the time interval is also applied in later work on *counter braids* by Lu et al. [45]. The hardware setup generalizes the earlier work on count-min sketches in that it allows different levels of counters (two seems to suffice), with each level having a smaller number of counters than the previous levels. A flow is hashed in parallel to some number of counters in a table at the first level. If these counters overflow, the flow is then hashed to some number of counters in a table at the next level (again the mapping is done using a hash function), and so on. At the end of the interval an iterative estimate of the counts for each flow is provided, similar to the technique of [41]. However, the authors use tools inspired by coding theory (in particular, turbo-code decoding) rather than expectation maximization.

One problem with both techniques in [41, 45] is that since estimates are found only at the end of certain time intervals, the techniques lose information about flows. By contrast, a standard count-min sketch uses a simple estimator that can be computed in real time. Indeed, at the instant that a flow's estimator crosses a threshold, the flow ID can be logged. The techniques of [41, 45], however, lose all information about flow IDs. This is acceptable in [41] because the measure (flow size distribution) does not require any flow IDs (while heavy-hitters clearly do). This problem is addressed in [45] by assuming that either the flows to be measured are already known (in which case a simple CAM suffices to determine whether a packet should be processed) or that all flow IDs are logged in slow memory. In the latter case, the real gain of [45] is to log all flows in slow and large DRAM, but to *update* flow size information in a much smaller randomized structure in SRAM. Despite this problem, the general technique of using sophisticated iterative estimators, whether directed by expectation maximization or decoding techniques, seems like a promising direction for future work.

9.6.2 Measuring the Number of Flows on a Link

The number of flows on a link is a useful indicator for a number of security applications. For example, the Snort intrusion detection tool detects port scans by counting all the distinct destinations sent to by a given source, and sounding an alarm if this amount is over a threshold. Similarly, to detect a denial of service attack, one might want to count the number of sources sending to a destination because many such attacks use multiple forged addresses. In both examples, it suffices to count flows, where a flow identifier is a destination (for detecting port scans) or a source (for detecting denial of service attacks).

A naive method to count, say, source–destination pairs would be to keep a counter together with a hash table that stores all of the distinct 64 bit source–destination address pairs seen thus far. When a packet arrives with source–destination address pair (s, d), the algorithm searches the hash table for (s, d); if there is no match, the counter is incremented and (s, d) is added to the hash table. Unfortunately, this solution requires memory proportional to the total number of observed source–destination pairs, which is prohibitively expensive.

An algorithm due to Flajolet and Martin based on *probabilistic counting* [29] can considerably reduce the memory needed by the naive solution at the cost of some accuracy in counting flows. The intuition behind the approach is to compute a metric of how rare a certain pattern is in a random hash of a flow ID, and define the *rarity* $r(f)$ of a flow ID f to be the rarity of its corresponding hash. We then keep track of the largest value X of $r(f)$ ever seen over all flow IDs f that pass across the link. If the algorithm sees a very large value for X, then by our definition of rarity, it stands to reason that there is a large number of flows across the link.

More precisely, for each packet seen the algorithm computes a hash function on the flow ID. It then counts the number of consecutive zeroes starting from the least significant position of the hash result: this is the measure $r(\cdot)$ of rarity used. The tracked value X now corresponds to the largest number of consecutive zeroes seen (starting from the least significant position) in the hashed flow ID values of all packets seen so far.

At the end of some time interval, the algorithm converts X into an estimate 2^X for the number of flows. Intuitively, if the stream contains two distinct flows, on average one flow will have the least significant bit of its hashed value equal to zero; if the stream contains eight flows, on average one flow will have the last three bits of its hashed value equal to zero – and so on. Thus, 2^X is the natural estimate of the number of flows corresponding to the tracked value X.

Hashing is essential for two reasons. First, implementing the algorithm directly on the sequence of flow IDs itself could make the algorithm susceptible to flow ID assignments where the traffic stream contains a flow ID f with many trailing zeroes. If f is in the traffic stream, even if the stream has only a few flows, the algorithm without hashing will wrongly report a large number of flows. Notice that adding multiple copies of the same flow ID to the stream will not change the algorithm's final result, because all copies hash to the same value.

A second reason for hashing is that accuracy can be boosted using multiple independent hash functions. The basic idea with one hash function can guarantee at most 50% accuracy. By using n independent hash functions in parallel to compute n separate estimates $X_1, \ldots, X_n$, we can greatly reduce the error by calculating the mean M of the X_i's and returning 2^M as the estimated number of flows. (Note that M should be represented as a floating point number, not an integer.)

More modular algorithms for flow counting (again hash-based) for networking purposes are described by Estan et al. in [25]. Suppose we wish to count up to 64,000 flows. Then it suffices to hash each flow into a single bit in a 64,000 bit map (initially zeroed), and then estimate the number of flows accounting for hash collisions by counting the number of ones.

However, just as Hubble estimated the number of stars in the universe by sampling the number of stars in a small region of space, one could reduce memory to, say, 32 bits but still hash flows from 1 to 64,000. In this case, flows that hash to values beyond 32 would not set bits but flows that hash from 0 to 31 would. At the end of some time interval the number of bits set to 1 are counted, an estimate is found by correcting for collisions, and then the estimate is scaled up by $64,000/32 = 2,000$ to account for the flows that were lost. Unfortunately, the accuracy of this estimator depends critically on the assumption that the number of flows is within some constant factor of 64,000. If the number of flows is much smaller (e.g., 50), the error is considerable.

The accuracy can be greatly improved in two ways. In a parallel approach, an array of, say, 32 counters are used, each responsible for estimating the number of flows in different ranges (e.g., 1–10, 10–100, 100–1,000) using a logarithmic scale. Thus, at least one counter will be accurate. The counter used for the final estimate is the one which has neither too many bits set or too few bits set. The precise algorithm is in [25].

In some cases, even this memory can be too much. An algorithm proposed by Singh et al. [63] addresses this issue by using only one counter and adapting sequentially to reduce memory (at the cost of accuracy). The algorithm has a bit map of say 32 bits. The algorithm initially hashes all flows to between 0 and 31. If all the bits fill up, the number of flows is clearly greater than 32, so the algorithm clears the bitmap, and now hashes future flows (all memory is lost of older flows) from 0 to 64. It keeps doubling the range of the hash function until the number of bits stops overflowing. The range of the hash function is tracked in a small scale factor register. The net result is that flow counting can be done for up to a million flows using a bit map of size 32 and a 16-bit scale factor register at a cost of a factor of 2 loss in accuracy (better tradeoffs are described in [63]).

Singh et al. [63] also describe how both the heavy-hitters and flow size estimators can be used together to extract worm signatures. Any string of some pre-specified fixed size in a packet payload is considered to be a possible worm signature. If the string occurs frequently (measured using a heavy-hitters estimator) and has a large number of associated unique source and destination IP addresses (measured by the sequential flow size estimator in [63]) the string is considered as a possible worm signature and is subjected to further offline tests. The sequential hash-based estimator is crucial to the efficiency of worm detection in [63] as the algorithm often tracks 100,000 potential signatures at the same time. Further, the accuracy of the flow size estimator is less of a concern because a "large" number of sources is used as a rough indicator of worm-like activity.

Finally, the problem with probabilistic counting and the techniques in [25] is that the definition of a flow must be predefined before measurement begins. In other words, the estimator must be programmed in advance to determine whether it is counting, say, source IP addresses, destination IP addresses, or TCP flows. On the other hand, managers may want a more flexible estimator that can be queried for a count of any definition of flows that the analyst might think of after measurements are taken (e.g., the number of TCP flows from Harvard to MIT).

The paper [25] shows how a beautiful algorithm due to Wegman (analyzed by Flajolet) [28] can be used to allow a flow size estimator that can be sliced-and-diced after the fact. (See a similar idea in [31].) The idea is useful in general because it allows a way to compute a random sample from the set of all unique flows. To allow slicing later, the definition of flows used is the most specific definition the analyst can specify in advance of the measurements (e.g., TCP flows).

The idea is to start by recording all unique flows in a hash table with hash function h. If the hash table size exceeds some fixed size s, then all flows f such that $h(f)$ has low order bit 1 are discarded from the existing table and in the future. If the hash table size exceeds s, then only flows f such that $h(f)$ has low order bits 00 are retained, and so on. This is similar to the reservoir sampling algorithm of Vitter [71], but it does not seem to have received as much attention. After the measurement interval is over, the analyst can compute an estimate of the number of flows, for any more specific definition of a flow than was used during the sampling phase (such as TCP flows with some specific source), by simply counting the number of such flows in the random sample.

9.7 Conclusion

We have surveyed the recent literature on hash-based approaches to high-speed packet processing in routers, with a particular focus on how theoretical and applied ideas can often interact to yield impressive results. However, we admit that we have only scratched the surface. We could have presented many more results, or given much more detail on the results we have presented. We strongly encourage interested readers to read the original works. We believe that this trend of applying hash-based approaches to these problems will continue, and that there is an enormous potential for designing hash-based approaches that are both theoretically interesting and practically significant for these very demanding and increasingly important applications.

Indeed, we see two important high-level directions for future work. The first is to increase the already existing connections between the theoretical and applied work in this general area. Many new and potentially interesting ideas have been consistently produced in recent years on the theoretical side; finding the right applications and proving the value of these ideas could be extremely beneficial. Also, those building applications need to be able to understand and predict the behavior of schemes they wish as well as evaluate tradeoffs between schemes they wish to implement in advance, based on sound theoretical principles. On the other side, those working at a more theoretical level need to pay attention to the needs and requirements of applications, including possibly some details of hardware implementation.

A second high-level direction, more speculative and far-reaching, is to consider whether a hashing infrastructure could be developed to support hash-based approaches for high-speed packet processing. Hash-based approaches offer great value, including relative simplicity, flexibility, and cost-effectiveness. While not every packet-processing task can naturally be placed in a hashing framework, as this survey shows, a great many can. One could imagine having some standardized, flexible, programmable hashing architecture for Internet devices, designed not for a specific task or algorithm, but capable of being utilized for many hash-based data structures or algorithms. The goal of such an infrastructure would not only be to handle issues that have already arisen in today's network, but also to provide a general framework for handling additional, currently unknown problems that may arise in the future. Additionally, a potential key value in a standardized hashing infrastructure lies in not only its potential use for monitoring or measuring individual routers, links, or other components, but the network as a whole.

Acknowledgements Adam Kirsch and Michael Mitzenmacher received support for this work from NSF grant CNS-0721491 and a research grant from Cisco Systems, Inc. George Varghese received support from NSF grant 0509546 and a grant from Cisco Systems, Inc.

References

1. Y. Azar, A. Broder, A. Karlin, and E. Upfal. Balanced Allocations. *SIAM Journal on Computing*, 29(1):180–200, 1999.
2. B. Bloom. Space/Time Tradeoffs in Hash Coding with Allowable Errors. *Communications of the ACM*, 13(7):422–426, 1970.
3. F. Bonomi, M. Mitzenmacher, R. Panigrahy, S. Singh, and G. Varghese. Beyond Bloom Filters: From Approximate Membership Checks to Approximate State Machines. In *Proceedings of ACM SIGCOMM*, pp. 315–326, 2006.
4. F. Bonomi, M. Mitzenmacher, R. Panigrahy, S. Singh, and G. Varghese. Bloom Filters via d-left Hashing and Dynamic Bit Reassignment. In *Proceedings of the Allerton Conference on Communication, Control and Computing*, 2006.
5. F. Bonomi, M. Mitzenmacher, R. Panigrahy, S. Singh, and G. Varghese. An Improved Construction for Counting Bloom Filters. In *Proceedings of the 14th Annual European Symposium on Algorithms* (ESA), pp. 684–695, 2006.
6. R. Brent. Reducing the Retrieval Time of Scatter Storage Techniques. *Communications of the ACM*, 16(2), pp. 105–109, 1973.
7. A. Broder and A. Karlin. Multilevel Adaptive Hashing. In *Proceedings of the 1st ACM-SIAM Symposium on Discrete Algorithms* (SODA), pp. 43–53, 1990.

8. A. Broder and M. Mitzenmacher. Network Applications of Bloom Filters: A Survey. *Internet Mathematics*, 1(4):485–509, 2004.
9. A. Broder and M. Mitzenmacher. Using Multiple Hash Functions to Improve IP Lookups. *Proceedings of the 20th IEEE International Conference on Computer Communications* (INFOCOM), pp. 1454–1463, 2001.
10. J. L. Carter and M. N. Wegman. Universal Classes of Hash Functions. *Journal of Computer and System Sciences*, 18(2):143–154, 1979.
11. B. Chazelle, J. Kilian, R. Rubinfeld, and A. Tal. The Bloomier Filter: An Efficient Data Structure for Static Support Lookup Tables. In *Proceedings of the Fifteenth Annual ACM-SIAM Symposium on Discrete Algorithms* (SODA), pp. 30–39, 2004.
12. S. Cohen and Y. Matias. Spectral Bloom Filters. In *Proceedings of the 2003 ACM SIGMOD International Conference on Management of Data* (SIGMOD), pp. 241–252, 2003.
13. G. Cormode and S. Muthukrishnan. An Improved Data Stream Summary: The Count-Min Sketch and Its Applications. *Journal of Algorithms*, 55(1):58–75, 2005.
14. E. Demaine, F. Meyer auf der Heide, R. Pagh, and M. Patrascu. De Dictionariis Dynamicis Pauco Spatio Utentibus (lat. On Dynamic Dictionaries Using Little Space). In *7th Latin American Theoertical Informatics Symposium*, pp. 349–361, 2006.
15. L. Devroye and P. Morin. Cuckoo Hashing: Further Analysis. *Information Processing Letters*, 86(4):215–219, 2003.
16. S. Dharmapurikar, P. Krishnamurthy, T. S. Sproull, and J. W. Lockwood. Deep Packet Inspection Using Parallel Bloom Filters. *IEEE Micro*, 24(1):52–61, 2004.
17. S. Dharmapurikar, P. Krishnamurthy, and D. E. Taylor. Longest Prefix Matching Using Bloom Filters. *IEEE/ACM Transactions on Networks*, 14(2):397–409, 2006.
18. S. Dharmapurikar and J. W. Lockwood. Fast and Scalable Pattern Matching for Network Intrusion Detection Systems. *IEEE Journal on Selected Areas in Communications*, 24(10):1781–1792, 2006.
19. S. Dharmapurikar, H. Song, J. Turner, and J. Lockwood. Fast Packet Classification Using Bloom Filters. In *Proceedings of the 2006 ACM/IEEE Symposium on Architecture For Networking and Communications Systems* (ANCS), pp. 61–70, 2006.
20. M. Dietzfelbinger, T. Hagerup, J. Katajainen, and M. Penttonen. A Reliable Randomized Algorithm for the Closest-Pair Problem. *Journal of Algorithms*, 25(1):19–51, 1997.
21. M. Dietzfelbinger and C. Weidling. Balanced Allocation and Dictionaries with Tightly Packed Constant Size Bins. *Theoretical Computer Science*, 380(1–2):47–68, 2007.
22. B. Donnet, B. Baynat, and T. Friedman. Retouched Bloom Filters: Allowing Networked Applications to Flexibly Trade Off False Positives Against False Negatives. *arxiv, cs.NI/0607038*, 2006.
23. C. Estan, K. Keys, D. Moore, and G. Varghese. Building a Better NetFlow. In *Proceedings of ACM SIGCOMM*, pp. 245–256, 2004.
24. C. Estan and G. Varghese. New Directions in Traffic Measurement and Accounting: Focusing on the Elephants, Ignoring the Mice. *ACM Transactions on Computer Systems*, 21(3):270–313, 2003.
25. C. Estan, G. Varghese, and M. E. Fisk. Bitmap Algorithms for Counting Active Flows on High-Speed Links. *IEEE/ACM Transactions on Networks*, 14(5):925–937, 2006.
26. L. Fan, P. Cao, J. Almeida, and A. Z. Broder. Summary Cache: A Scalable Wide-Area Web Cache Sharing Protocol. *IEEE/ACM Transactions on Networking*, 8(3):281–293, 2000.
27. W. Fang and L. Peterson. Inter-AS Traffic Patterns and Their Implications. In *Proceedings of the Global Telecommunications Conference, 1999* (GLOBECOM), 1999.
28. P. Flajolet. On Adaptive Sampling. *Computing*, 43(4):391–400, 1990.
29. P. Flajolet and G. N. Martin. Probabilistic Counting Algorithms for Data Base Applications. *Journal of Computer and System Sciences*, 31(2):182–209, 1985.
30. D. Fotakis, R. Pagh, P. Sanders, and P. Spirakis. Space Efficient Hash Tables With Worst Case Constant Access Time. *Theory of Computing Systems*, 38(2):229–248, 2005.
31. P. Gibbons and Y. Matias. New sampling-based summary statistics for improving approximate query answers. In *Proceedings of the ACM SIGMOD International Conference on Management of Data*, pp. 331–342, 1998.

32. G. Gonnet. Expected Length of the Longest Probe Sequence in Hash Code Searching. *Journal of the Association for Computing Machinery*, 28(2):289–304, 1981.

33. J. Hasan, S. Cadambi, V. Jakkula, and S. Chakradhar. Chisel: A Storage-efficient, Collision-free Hash-based Network Processing Architecture. In *Proceedings of the 33rd International Symposium on Computer Architecture* (ISCA), pp. 203–215, 2006

34. A. Kirsch and M. Mitzenmacher. On the Performance of Multiple Choice Hash Tables with Moves on Deletes and Inserts. In *Proceedings of the Forty-Sixth Annual Allerton Conference*, 2008.

35. A. Kirsch and M. Mitzenmacher. The Power of One Move: Hashing Schemes for Hardware. In *Proceedings of the 27th IEEE International Conference on Computer Communications* (INFOCOM), 2008.

36. A. Kirsch and M. Mitzenmacher. Simple Summaries for Hashing with Choices. *IEEE/ACM Transactions on Networking*, 16(1):218–231, 2008.

37. A. Kirsch and M. Mitzenmacher. Using a Queue to De-amortize Cuckoo Hashing in Hardware. In *Proceedings of the Forty-Fifth Annual Allerton Conference on Communication, Control, and Computing*, 2007.

38. A. Kirsch, M. Mitzenmacher, and U. Wieder. More Robust Hashing: Cuckoo Hashing with a Stash. To appear in *Proceedings of the 16th Annual European Symposium on Algorithms*, 2008.

39. D. Knuth. *Sorting and Searching*, vol. 3 of The Art of Computer Programming (2nd edition), Addison-Wesley Publishing Company, 1998.

40. R. R. Kompella, S. Singh, and G. Varghese. On Scalable Attack Detection in the Network. In *Proceedings of the 4th ACM SIGCOMM Conference on Internet Measurement*, pp. 187–200, 2004.

41. A. Kumar, M. Sung, J. Xu, and J. Wang. Data Streaming Algorithms for Efficient and Accurate Estimation of Flow Size Distribution. In *Proceedings of the Joint International Conference on Measurement and Modeling of Computer Systems* (SIGMETRICS/Performance), pp. 177–188, 2004.

42. S. Kumar and P. Crowley. Segmented Hash: An Efficient Hash Table Implementation for High Performance Networking Subsystems. In *Proceedings of the 2005 ACM Symposium on Architecture for Networking and Communications Systems* (ANCS), pp. 91–103, 2005.

43. S. Kumar, J. Turner, and P. Crowley. Peacock Hash: Fast and Updatable Hashing for High Performance Packet Processing Algorithms. In *Proceedings of the 27th IEEE International Conference on Computer Communications* (INFOCOM), 2008.

44. S. Kumar, J. Turner, P. Crowley, and M. Mitzenmacher. HEXA: Compact Data Structures for Faster Packet Processing. In *Proceedings of the Fifteenth IEEE International Conference on Network Protocols* (ICNP), pp. 246–255, 2007.

45. Y. Lu, A. Montanari, B. Prabhakar, S. Dharmapurikar, and A. Kabbani. Counter Braids: A Novel Counter Architecture for Per-Flow Measurement. *Proceedings of the 2008 ACM SIGMETRICS International Conference on Measurement and Modeling of Computer Systems* (SIGMETRICS), 2008.

46. Y. Lu, B. Prabhakar, and F. Bonomi. Perfect Hashing for Networking Algorithms. In *Proceedings of the 2006 IEEE International Symposium on Information Theory* (ISIT), pp. 2774–2778, 2006.

47. Y. Lu, M. Wang, B. Prabhakar, and F. Bonomi. ElephantTrap: A Low Cost Device for Identifying Large Flows. In *Proceedings of the 15th Annual IEEE Symposium on High-Performance Interconnects* (HOTI), pp. 99–108, 2007.

48. S. Lumetta and M. Mitzenmacher. Using the Power of Two Choices to Improve Bloom Filters. To appear in *Internet Mathematics*.

49. U. Manber and S. Wu. An Algorithm for Approximate Membership checking with Application to Password Security. *Information Processing Letters*, 50(4), pp. 191–197, 1994.

50. M. Mitzenmacher. Compressed Bloom Filters. *IEEE/ACM Transactions on Networking*, 10(5):613–620, 2002.

51. M. Mitzenmacher, A. Richa, and R. Sitaraman. *The Power of Two Choices: A Survey of Techniques and Results*, edited by P. Pardalos, S. Rajasekaran, J. Reif, and J. Rolim. Kluwer Academic Publishers, Norwell, MA, 2001, pp. 255–312.

52. M. Mitzenmacher and E. Upfal. *Probability and Computing: Randomized Algorithms and Probabilistic Analysis*. Cambridge University Press, 2005.
53. M. Mitzenmacher and S. Vadhan. Why Simple Hash Functions Work: Exploiting the Entropy in a Data Stream. In *Proceedings of the Nineteenth Annual ACM-SIAM Symposium on Discrete Algorithms* (SODA), pp. 746–755, 2008.
54. A. Östlin and R. Pagh. Uniform Hashing in Constant Time and Linear Space. In *Proceedings of the Thirty-Fifth Annual ACM Symposium on Theory of Computing* (STOC), pp. 622–628, 2003.
55. A. Pagh, R. Pagh, and S. S. Rao. An Optimal Bloom Filter Replacement. In *Proceedings of the Sixteenth Annual ACM-SIAM Symposium on Discrete Algorithms* (SODA), pp. 823-829, 2005.
56. R. Pagh and F. Rodler. Cuckoo Hashing. *Journal of Algorithms*, 51(2):122–144, 2004.
57. R. Panigrahy. Efficient Hashing with Lookups in Two Memory Accesses. In *Proceedings of the Sixteenth Annual ACM-SIAM Symposium on Discrete Algorithms* (SODA), pp. 830–839, 2005.
58. F. Putze, P. Sanders, and J. Singler. Cache-, Hash-and Space-Efficient Bloom Filters. In *Proceedings of the Workshop on Experimental Algorithms*, pp. 108–121, 2007. Available as Springer Lecture Notes in Computer Science, volume 4525.
59. M. V. Ramakrishna. Hashing Practice: Analysis of Hashing and Universal Hashing. In *Proceedings of the 1988 ACM SIGMOD International Conference on Management of Data*, pp. 191–199, 1988.
60. M. V. Ramakrishna. Practical Performance of Bloom Filters and Parallel Free-Rext Searching. *Communications of the ACM*, 32(10):1237–1239, 1989.
61. M.V. Ramakrishna, E. Fu, and E. Bahcekapili. Efficient Hardware Hashing Functions for High Performance Computers. *IEEE Transactions on Computers*, 46(12):1378–1381, 1997.
62. A. Siegel. On Universal Classes of Extremely Random Constant-Time Hash Functions. *Siam Journal on Computing*, 33(3):505–543, 2004.
63. S. Singh, C. Estan, G. Varghese, and S. Savage. Automated Worm Fingerprinting. In *Proceedings of the 6th ACM/USENIX Symposium on Operating System Design and Implementation* (OSDI), 2004.
64. A. Snoeren, C. Partridge, L. Sanchez, C. Jones, F. Tchakountio, B. Schwartz, S. Kent, and W. Strayer. Single-Packet IP Traceback. *IEEE/ACM Transactions on Networks*, 10(6):721–734, 2002.
65. H. Song, S. Dharmapurikar, J. Turner, and J. Lockwood. Fast Hash Table Lookup Using Extended Bloom Filter: An Aid to Network Processing. In *Proceedings of ACM SIGCOMM*, pp. 181–192, 2005.
66. D. Thaler and C. Hopps. Multipath Issues in Unicast and Multicast Next-Hop Selection. RFC 2991, 2000. Available at ftp://ftp.rfc-editor.org/in-notes/rfc2991.txt.
67. M. Thorup. Even Strongly Universal Hashing is Pretty Fast. In *Proceedings of the Eleventh Annual ACM-SIAM Symposium on Discrete Algorithms* (SODA), pp. 496–497, 2000.
68. GIGAswitch System: A High-Performance Packet-Switching Platform. R. J. Souza, P. G. Krishnakumar, C. M. Özveren, R. J. Simcoe, B. A. Spinney, R. E. Thomas, and R. J. Walsh. *Digital Technical Journal*, 6(1):9–22, 1994.
69. V. Srinivasan and G. Varghese. Fast Address Lookups Using Controlled Prefix Expansion. *ACM Transactions on Computer Systems*, 17(1):1–40, 1999.
70. G. Varghese. *Network Algorithmics: An Interdisciplinary Approach to Designing Fast Networked Devices*. Morgan Kaufmann Publishers, 2004.
71. J. S. Vitter. Random Sampling with a Reservoir. *ACM Transactions on Mathematical Software*, 11(1):37–57, 1985.
72. S. Venkataraman, D. Song, P. B. Gibbons, and A. Blum. New Streaming Algorithms for Fast Detection of Superspreaders. In *Proceedings of the 12th ISOC Symposium on Network and Distributed Systems Security* (SNDSS), 149–166, 2005.
73. B. Vöcking. How Asymmetry Helps Load Balancing. *Journal of the ACM*, 50(4):568–589, 2003.
74. M. Waldvogel, G. Varghese, J. Turner, and B. Plattner. Scalable High Speed IP Routing Lookups. *ACM SIGCOMM Computer Communication Review*, 27(4):25–36, 1997.

75. M. N. Wegman and J. L. Carter. New Hash Functions and Their Use in Authentication and Set Equality. *Journal of Computer and System Sciences*, 22(3):265–279, 1981.
76. P. Woelfel. Asymmetric Balanced Allocation with Simple Hash Functions. In *Proceedings of the Seventeenth Annual ACM-SIAM Symposium on Discrete Algorithm* (SODA), pp. 424–433, 2006.

Chapter 10
Fast Packet Pattern-Matching Algorithms

Fang Yu, Yanlei Diao, Randy H. Katz, and T.V. Lakshman

Abstract Packet content scanning at high speed has become extremely important due to its applications in network security, network monitoring, HTTP load balancing, etc. In content scanning, the packet payload is compared to a set of patterns specified as regular expressions. In this chapter, we first describe the typical patterns used in packet-scanning applications and show that for some of these patterns the memory requirements can be prohibitively high when traditional matching methods are used. We then review techniques for efficient regular expression matching and explore regular expression rewrite techniques that can significantly reduce memory usage. Based on new rewrite insights, we propose guidelines for pattern writers to make matching fast and practical. Furthermore, we discuss deterministic finite automaton (DFA) link compression techniques and review algorithms and data structures that are specifically designed for matching regular expressions in networking applications.

10.1 Motivation

Packet content scanning (also known as Layer-7 filtering or payload scanning) is crucial to network security and network monitoring applications. It is useful for detecting and filtering packets containing worms and other attack code, and also for

F. Yu (✉)
Microsoft Research Silicon Valley, 1065 La Avenida, Mountain View, CA 94043
e-mail: fangyu@microsoft.com

Y. Diao
Department of Computer Science, University of Massachussets Amherst,
140 Governors Drive Amherst, MA 01003
e-mail: yanlei@cs.umass.edu

R.H. Katz
Electrical Engineering and Computer Science Department, University of California Berkeley,
Berkeley, CA 94720
e-mail: randy@eecs.berkeley.edu

T.V. Lakshman
Bell-Labs, Alcatel-Lucent, 600 Mountain Avenue, Murray Hill NJ 07974
e-mail: lakshman@research.bell-labs.com

G. Cormode and M. Thottan (eds.), *Algorithms for Next Generation Networks*,
Computer Communications and Networks, DOI 10.1007/978-1-84882-765-3_10,
© Springer-Verlag London Limited 2010

newly emerging edge network services. Examples of the emerging edge network services include high-speed firewalls, which protect end hosts from security attacks; HTTP load balancing, which smartly redirects packets to different servers based on their HTTP requests and Extensible Markup Language (XML) processing, which facilitates the sharing of data across different systems.

In packet-scanning systems, the payload of packets in a traffic stream is matched against a given set of patterns to identify specific classes of applications, viruses, protocol definitions, and so on. When viruses and worms were simple, patterns could be expressed using *simple strings* format, e.g., *"GetInfo\x0d"* is the signature for a back door attack [3]. However, as viruses and worms became more complex, they rendered simple pattern-matching approaches inadequate for sophisticated payload scanning. For example, polymorphic worms make it impossible to enumerate all the possible signatures using explicit strings. *Regular expressions* appear to be a suitable choice for these patterns due to their rich expressive power. Consider a regular expression, *"^Entry/file/[0−9.]{71,}//.∗\x0Aannotate\x0A"*, for detecting a Concurrent Versions System (CVS) revision overflow attack [12]. This pattern first searches for a fixed string pattern *"Entry/file/"* followed by 71 or more digits or dots, then a fixed pattern *"//"* followed by some arbitrary characters (.∗), and finally the pattern *"\x0Aannotate\x0A"*. Obviously, it is very hard to enumerate this type of attack using fixed string patterns.

As a result, regular expressions are replacing explicit string patterns as the pattern-matching language of choice in packet-scanning applications. In the Linux Application Protocol Classifier (L7-filter) [12], all protocol identifiers are expressed as regular expressions. Similarly, the SNORT [3] intrusion detection system has evolved from no regular expressions in its rule set in April 2003 (Version 2.0) to 1131 out of 4867 rules using regular expressions as of February 2006 (Version 2.4). Another intrusion detection system, Bro [1], also uses regular expressions as its pattern language.

In this chapter, we present a number of regular expression pattern-matching schemes. We begin with a brief introduction to regular expressions with simple examples in Section 10.2. We briefly survey traditional regular expression matching methods in Section 10.3. We then analyze the special characteristics of typical regular expression patterns used in network scanning applications in Section 10.4. We show that some of the complex patterns lead to exponential memory usage or low matching speed when using the traditional methods. Based on this observation, we propose rewrite rules for two common types of complex regular expressions in Section 10.5. The rewrite rules can dramatically reduce the sizes of resulting deterministic finite automatons (DFAs), making them small enough to fit in high-speed memory. In Section 10.6, we review DFA compression techniques that can further reduce memory consumption. Finally, in Section 10.7, we discuss some advanced DFA processing techniques developed specifically for high-speed router implementation.

10.2 Introduction to Regular Expressions

A regular expression describes a set of strings without explicitly enumerating them. Table 10.1 lists the regular expression operators used to describe patterns within packets. An anchor ('^') is used when a pattern must be matched at the beginning of the input. The '|' operator denotes the OR relationship. The '.' operator is a single-character wildcard; in other words, any character can be matched using '.'. The '?' operator is a quantifier representing zero or one instance of the previously specified pattern, '+' operator stands for at least one, whereas '*' denotes zero or more. "{}" can be used to define more specific occurrence restrictions. For example, "{3, 5}" stands for repeating three to five times. We can also use "[]" to define a class; characters inside the brackets form a class with OR relationships between them. When '^' appears in "[]", it has the special meaning of exception. For example, "[^\n]" denotes anything but the return key.

Let us now consider a more complex regular expression that is used for detecting Yahoo messenger traffic: "^(ymsg|ypns|yhoo).?.?.?.?.?.?.?[lwt]. * \xc0\x80". According to the analysis by Venkat [15], Yahoo messenger commands start with ymsg, ypns, or yhoo. Therefore, this pattern first identifies any of these three strings "(ymsg|ypns|yhoo)". The next seven or fewer bytes contain command length and Version information that varies among packets. So this pattern ignores those by using ".?.?.?.?.?.?.?". Then it identifies a letter l, w, or t using [lwt]. l stands for "Yahoo service verify", w denotes "encryption challenge command", and t represents "login command". This pattern ends with ASCII letters c0 and 80 in the hexadecimal form because \xc0\x80 is the standard argument separator in hexadecimal notation.

10.3 Traditional Regular Expression Matching Schemes

Regular expression matching is a well-studied subject in Computer Science. In this section, we briefly review the traditional approaches to the general regular expression matching problem.

Table 10.1 Features of regular expressions

Syntax	Meaning	Example
^	Pattern to be matched at the start of the input	^AB means the input starts with AB. A pattern without '^', e.g., AB, can be matched anywhere in the input
|	OR relationship	A|B denotes an occurrence of either A or B
.	A single-character wildcard	A. matches any two-character string starting with A
?	A quantifier denoting one or less	A? denotes A or an empty string
+	A quantifier denoting one or more	A+ denotes at least one letter A
*	A quantifier denoting zero or more	A* means an arbitrary number of As
{}	Repeat	A{100} denotes a sequence of 100 As
[]	A class of characters	[lwt] denotes a letter l, w, or t
[^]	Anything but	[^ \n] denotes any character except \n

Finite automata are a natural formalism for regular expression matching. There are two main categories: deterministic finite Automaton (DFA) and Nondeterministic Finite Automaton (NFA). This section provides a brief survey of existing methods using these two types of automata.

10.3.1 DFA

A DFA consists of a finite set of input symbols, denoted as Σ, a finite set of states, and a transition function δ [8]. In networking applications, Σ contains the 2^8 symbols from the extended ASCII code. Among the states, there is a single start state and a set of accepting states. The transition function δ takes a state and an input symbol as arguments and returns a state. A key feature of DFA is that at any time there is *at most one* active state in the DFA.

Figure 10.1 shows a simple DFA for regular expression $((A|B)C|(A|D)E)$, which matches string AC, BC, AE, or DE. If the given string is BC, it will first go to State 1 based on character B, then it will arrive at the final accept state (State 2) based on character C. Given another input starting with A, the DFA will first go to State 5. Depending on whether the next input is B or E, it will transition to the corresponding accept state, that is, State 2 or State 4. If the next input is neither B nor E, DFA will report the result of no-match for the given string.

10.3.2 NFA

An NFA is similar to a DFA except that the δ function maps from a state and a symbol to a *set* of new states. Therefore, *multiple* states can be active simultaneously in an NFA.

Figure 10.2 shows the NFA for the previous example $((A|B)C|(A|D)E)$. Unlike a DFA, for the NFA given an input starting with A, two states will be active at the same time (State 1 and State 3). State 1 means we have already seen the prefix

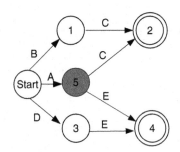

Fig. 10.1 A DFA example

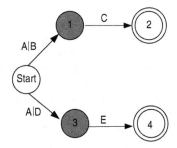

Fig. 10.2 An NFA example

Table 10.2 Worst-case comparisons of DFA and NFA

	One regular expression of length n		m regular expressions compiled together	
	Processing complexity	Storage cost	Processing complexity	Storage cost
NFA	$O(n^2)$	$O(n)$	$O(n^2 m)$	$O(nm)$
DFA	$O(1)$	$O(\Sigma^n)$	$O(1)$	$O(\Sigma^{nm})$

pattern $(A|B)$, now waiting for the character C. State 3 means we have seen $(A|D)$, now waiting for the character E. Depending on the next input character, the NFA will go to State 2 if given C, go to State 4 if given E, or fail to match the regular expression if given any other character.

Using automata to recognize regular expressions introduces two types of complexity: automata storage and processing costs. A theoretical worst-case study [8] shows that a single regular expression of length n can be expressed as an NFA with $O(n)$ states. When the NFA is converted into a DFA, it may generate $O(\Sigma^n)$ states, where Σ is the set of symbols. The processing complexity for each character in the input is $O(1)$ in a DFA, but is $O(n^2)$ for an NFA when all n states are active at the same time.

To handle m regular expressions, two choices are possible: processing them individually in m automata, or compiling them into a single automaton. The former is used in Snort [3] and Linux L7-filter [12]. The latter is proposed in recent studies [5,6] so that the single composite NFA can support shared matching of common prefixes of those expressions. Despite the demonstrated performance gains over using m separate NFAs, in practice this approach still experiences large numbers of active states. This has the same worst-case complexity as the sum of m separate NFAs. Therefore, this approach on a serial processor can be slow, as given any input character, each active state must be serially examined to obtain new states.

In DFA-based systems, compiling m regular expressions into a composite DFA provides guaranteed performance benefit over running m individual DFAs. Specifically, a composite DFA reduces processing cost from $O(m)$ (cost of $O(1)$ for each automaton) to $O(1)$, i.e., a single lookup to obtain the next state for any given character. However, the number of states in the composite automaton grows to $O(\Sigma^{mn})$ in the theoretical worst case as listed in Table 10.2.

10.3.3 Lazy DFA

There is a middle ground between DFA and NFA, called lazy DFA. Lazy DFAs are designed to reduce the memory consumption of conventional DFAs [7, 14]: a lazy DFA keeps a subset of the DFA states that match the most common strings in memory; for uncommon strings, it extends the subset from the corresponding NFA at runtime. As such, a lazy DFA is usually much smaller than the corresponding fully compiled DFA and provides good performance for common input strings. The Bro intrusion detection system [1] adopts this approach. However, malicious senders can easily construct packets with uncommon strings to keep the system busy and slow down the matching process. As a result, the system will start dropping packets and malicious packets can sneak through.

10.4 Regular Expression Matching in Network Scanning Applications

The previous section surveyed the most representative traditional approaches to regular expression matching. In this section, we show that these techniques do not always work efficiently for some of the complex patterns that arise in networking applications. To this end, we first enumerate the pattern structures that are common in networking applications in Section 10.4.1. We then show that certain pattern-structures that occur in networking applications are hard to match using traditional methods – they incur either excessive memory usage or high computation cost. In particular, we show two categories of regular expressions in Section 10.4.2 that lead to quadratic and exponential numbers of states, respectively.

10.4.1 Patterns Used in Networking Applications

We study the complexity of DFAs for typical patterns used in real-world packet payload scanning applications such as Linux L7-filter (as of Feb 2006), SNORT (Version 2.4), and Bro (Version 0.8V88). Table 10.3 summarizes the results.[1]

- Explicit strings generate DFAs of size linear in the number of characters in the pattern. Twenty-five percent of the networking patterns, in the three applications we studied (Linux L7-filter, SNORT, and Bro), fall into this category and they generate relatively small DFAs with an average of 24 states.
- If a pattern starts with '^', it creates a DFA of polynomial complexity with respect to the pattern length k and the length restriction j on the repetition of a class of

---

[1] This study is based on the use of exhaustive matching and one-pass search defined in [16].

Table 10.3 An analysis of patterns in network scanning applications

Pattern features	Example	Number of states	Percent of patterns	Average # of states
Case 1: Explicit strings with k characters	^ABCD .*ABCD	$k+1$	25.1	23.6
Case 2: Wildcards	^AB.*CD .*AB.*CD	$k+1$	18.8	27.2
Case 3: Patterns with ^, a wildcard, and a length restriction j	^AB{j+}CD ^AB{0, j}CD ^AB{j}CD	$O(k*j)$	44.7	180.3
Case 4: Patterns with ^, a class of characters overlaps with the prefix, and a length restriction j	^A+[A-Z]{j}D where [A-Z] overlaps with prefix A+	$O((k+j^2))$ $j \sim 370$	5.1	136,903
Case 5: Patterns with a length a wildcard restriction j, where or a class of characters overlaps with the prefix	.*AB.{j}CD .*A[A-Z]{j+}D	$O((k+2^j))$ $j \sim 344$	6.3	$>2^{344}$

characters in the pattern. Our observation from the existing payload scanning rule sets is that the pattern length k is usually limited. The length restriction j is usually small too, unless it is for buffer overflow attempts. In that case, j will be more than 300 on average and sometimes even reaches thousands. Therefore, Case 4 in Table 10.3 can result in a large DFA because it has a factor quadratic in j. Although this type of pattern only constitutes 5.1% of the total patterns, they create DFAs with an average of 136,903 states.

- There are also a small percent (6.8%) of patterns starting with ".*" and having length restrictions (Case 5). These patterns create DFAs of exponential sizes. We will address Cases 4 and 5 in detail in Section 10.4.2.

We compare the regular expressions used in three networking applications, namely, SNORT, Bro, and the Linux L7-filter, against those used in emerging Extensible Markup Language (XML) filtering applications [5, 6] where regular expressions are matched over text documents encoded in XML. The results are shown in Table 10.4. We observe three main differences:

(1) While both types of applications use wildcards ('.', '?', '+', '*'), the patterns for packet-scanning applications contain larger numbers of them. Many such patterns use multiple wildcard metacharacters (e.g., '.', '*'). For example, the pattern for identifying the Internet radio protocol, "membername.*session.*player", has two wildcard fragments ".*". Some even contain over 10 such wildcard fragments. As regular expressions are converted into state machines for pattern matching, large numbers of wildcards bring multiple matching choices to the matching process, causing the corresponding DFAs to grow exponentially.

Table 10.4 Comparison of regular expressions in networking applications against those in XML filtering

	SNORT	Bro	L7-filter	XML filtering
Number of regular expressions analyzed	1555	2780	70	1,000–100,000
Percent of patterns starting with "^"	74.4%	2.6%	72.8%	0.80%
Percent of patterns with wildcards ".,+, ?, *	74.9%	98.8%	75.7%	50%–100%
Average Number of wildcards per pattern	4.7	4.3	7.0	1–2
Percent of patterns with class "[]"	31.6%	65.8%	52.8%	0
Average number of classes per pattern	8.0	3.4	4.8	0
Percent of patterns with length restrictions on classes or wildcards	56.3%	23.8%	21.4%	≈0

(2) Classes of characters ("[]") are used in packet-scanning applications, but not in XML processing applications. In addition, the class of characters may intersect with other classes or wildcards. For example, the pattern for detecting buffer overflow attacks to the Network News Transport Protocol (NNTP) is "$^\wedge SEARCH \backslash s + [^\wedge \backslash n]\{1024\}$", where a class of character "$[^\wedge \backslash n]$" interacts with its preceding white space characters "$\backslash s+$". When given an input with SEARCH followed by a series of white spaces, there is ambiguity whether these white spaces match $\backslash s+$ or the non-return class "$[^\wedge \backslash n]$". As we will show later in Section 10.4.2.1, such interaction can result in a highly complex state machine.

(3) A high percentage of patterns in packet payload scanning applications have length restrictions on some of the classes or wildcards, while such length restrictions usually do not occur in XML filtering. For example, the pattern for detecting Internet Message Access Protocol (IMAP) email server buffer overflow attack is as follows "$. * AUTH \backslash s[^\wedge \backslash n]\{100\}$". This pattern contains the restriction that there would be 100 non-return characters "$[^\wedge \backslash n]$" after matching of keyword *AUTH* and any number of white spaces "$\backslash s$". As we shall show in Section 10.4.2.2, such length restrictions can increase the resource needs for regular expression matching.

10.4.2 Analysis of Regular Expressions That Generates Large DFAs

We mentioned previously that some patterns generate DFAs of quadratic size (Case 4 of Table 10.3) and some others generate exponential-sized DFAs (Case 5 of Table 10.3). Next, we explain these two cases in more detail.

10.4.2.1 DFAs of Quadratic Size

A common misconception is that patterns starting with '^' create simple DFAs. In fact, even in the presence of '^', classes of characters that overlap with the prefix

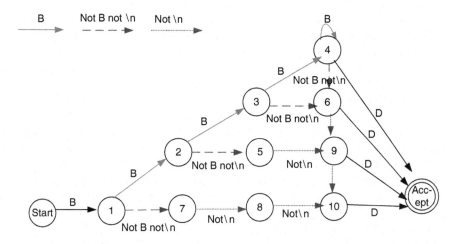

Fig. 10.3 A DFA for pattern ^B+[^\n]3D that generates quadratic number of states

pattern can still yield a complex DFA. Consider the pattern "^B+[^\n]{3}D", where the class of character [^\n] denotes any character but the return character '\n'.

Figure 10.3 shows that the corresponding DFA has a quadratic number of states. The quadratic complexity comes from the fact that the letter B overlaps with the class of character [^\n] and, hence, there is inherent ambiguity in the pattern: the second B letter can be matched either as part of B+, or as part of [^\n]{3}. Therefore, if an input contains multiple Bs, the DFA needs to remember the number of Bs it has seen and their locations i to make a correct decision with the next input character. If the class of characters has length restriction of j bytes, DFA needs $O(j^2)$ states to remember the combination of distance to the first B and the distance to the last B.

Seventeen patterns in the SNORT rule set fall into this quadratic state category. For example, the regular expression for the NNTP rule is "^$SEARCH$\s+[^\n]{1024}". Similar to the example in Figure 10.3, \s overlaps with ^[\n]. White space characters cause ambiguity of whether they should match \s+ or be counted as part of the 1024 non-return characters [^\n]{1024}. For example, an input of *SEARCH* followed by 1024 white spaces and then 1024 'A's will have 1024 ways of matching strings, i.e., one white space matches \s+ and the rest as part of [^\n]{1024}, or two white spaces match \s+ and the rest as part of [^\n]{1024}, and so on. By using 1024^2 states to remember all possible sequences of these white spaces, the DFA accommodates all the ways to match the substrings of different lengths. Note that all these substrings start with *SEARCH* and hence are overlapping matches.

This type of quadratic state problem cannot be solved by an NFA-based approach. Specifically, the corresponding NFA contains 1042 states; among these, the first six are for the matching of *SEARCH*, the next one for the matching of \s+, and the rest of the 1024 states for the counting of [^\n]1024 with one state for each count. An intruder can easily construct an input as *SEARCH* followed by 1024 white spaces. With this input, both the \s+ state and all the 1023 non-return states would be active at the same time. Given the next character, the NFA needs to check these 1024 states sequentially to compute a new set of active states, hence significantly slowing down the pattern-matching speed.

10.4.2.2 DFAs of Exponential Size

In real life, many payload scanning patterns contain an *exact distance* requirement. Figure 10.4 shows the DFA for an example pattern ". $* A..CD$". An exponential number of states (2^{2+1}) are needed to represent these two wildcard characters. This is because we need to remember all possible effects of the preceding As as they may yield different results when combined with subsequent inputs. For example, an input AAB is different from ABA because a subsequent input BCD forms a valid pattern with AAB ($AABBCD$), but not so with ABA ($ABABCD$). In general, if a pattern matches exactly j arbitrary characters, $O(2^j)$ states are needed to handle the requirement that the distance exactly equals j. This result is also reported in [6]. Similar results apply to the case where the class of characters overlaps with the prefix, e.g., ". $* A[A - Z]\{j\}D$".

Similar structures exist in real-world pattern sets. In the intrusion detection system SNORT, 53.8% of the patterns (mostly for detecting buffer overflow attempts) contain a fixed length restriction. Around 80% of the rules start with '^'; hence, they will not cause exponential growth of DFA. The remaining 20% of the patterns do suffer from the state explosion problem. For example, consider the rule for detecting IMAP authentication overflow attempts, which uses the regular expression ". $* AUTH\backslash s[^\backslash n]\{100\}$". This rule detects any input that contains $AUTH$, then a white space, and no return character in the following 100 bytes. If we directly compile this pattern into a DFA, the DFA will contain more than 10,000 states because

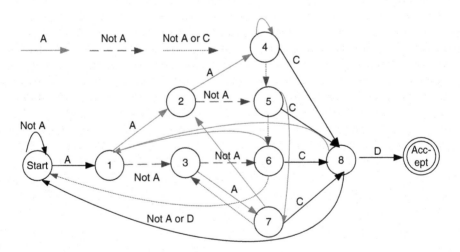

Fig. 10.4 A DFA for pattern . $* A..CD$ that generates exponential number of states

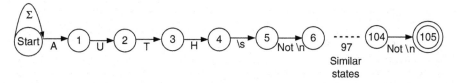

Fig. 10.5 NFA for the pattern . $* AUTH \backslash s[^\wedge \backslash n]\{100\}$

it needs to remember all the possible consequences that an $AUTH \backslash s$ subsequent to the first $AUTH \backslash s$ can lead to. For example, the second $AUTH \backslash s$ can either match $[^\wedge \backslash n]\{100\}$ or be counted as a new match of the prefix of the regular expression.

It is obvious that the exponential blow-up problem cannot be mitigated by using an NFA-based approach. The NFA for the pattern ". $* AUTH \backslash s[^\wedge \backslash n]\{100\}$" is shown in Figure 10.5. Because the first state has a self-loop marked with Σ, the input "$AUTH \backslash sAUTH \backslash sAUTH \backslash s \ldots$" can cause a large number of states to be simultaneously active, resulting in significantly degraded system performance, as demonstrated in [16].

In the next three sections, we review existing technologies that aim to resolve these problems and speed up regular expression matching in networking applications. In particular, we begin with regular expression rewriting techniques that can significantly reduce DFA sizes (Section 10.5). We next review a DFA compression techniques to further reduce DFA sizes (Section 10.6). Since the fast memory on routers is limited, we also discuss techniques that split DFAs and only keep a compact representation of frequently visited portions in fast memory (Section 10.7).

10.5   Regular Expression Rewriting Techniques

Having identified the typical patterns that yield large DFAs, in this section we investigate possible rewriting of some of those patterns to reduce the DFA size. Such rewriting is enabled by relaxing the requirement of exhaustive matching to that of non-overlapping matching (Section 10.5.1). With this relaxation, we propose pattern rewriting techniques that explore the potential of trading off exhaustive pattern matching for memory efficiency for quadratic patterns (Section 10.5.2) and exponential patterns (Section 10.5.3). Finally, we offer guidelines to pattern writers on how to write patterns amenable to efficient implementation (Section 10.5.4).

10.5.1   Rationale Behind Pattern Rewriting

Most existing studies of regular expressions focus on a specific type of evaluation, that is, checking if a fixed length string belongs to the language defined by a regular expression. More specifically, a fixed length string is said to be in the language of a regular expression, if the string is matched from start to end by a DFA corresponding to that regular expression. In contrast, in packet payload scanning, a regular expression pattern can be matched by the entire input or specific substrings of the input[2] . Without a priori knowledge of the starting and ending positions of those substrings (unless the pattern starts with '^' that restricts it to be matched at the beginning of the line, or ends with '$' that limits it to be matched at the end of the line), the DFAs created for recognizing all substring matches can be highly complex. This is because the DFA needs to remember all the possible subprefixes it has encountered. When there are many patterns with a lot of wildcards, they can be simultaneously active (recognizing part of the pattern). Hence, a DFA needs many states to record all possible combinations of partially matched patterns.

For a better understanding of the matching model, we next present a few concepts pertaining to the completeness of matching results and the DFA execution model for substring matching. Given a regular expression pattern and an input string, a complete set of results contains all substrings of the input that the pattern can possibly match. For example, given a pattern "$ab*$" and an input $abbb$, four possible matches can be reported, a, ab, abb, and $abbb$. We call this style of matching *Exhaustive Matching*. It is formally defined as below:

Exhaustive Matching Consider the matching process M as a function from a pattern P and a string S to a power set of S, such that $M(P, S) =$ {substring S' of S |, S' is accepted by the DFA of P}.

In practice, it is expensive and often unnecessary to report all matching substrings, as most applications can be satisfied by a subset of those matches. For example, if we are searching for the Oracle user name buffer overflow attempt, the pattern may be "$^{\wedge}$ $USR\backslash s[\ ^{\wedge}\ \backslash n]\{100, \}$", which searches for packets starting with "$USR\backslash s$" and followed by 100 or more non-return characters. An incoming packet with "$USR\backslash s$" followed by 200 non-return characters may have 100 ways of matching the pattern because each combination of the "$USR\backslash s$" with the sequential 100 to 200 characters is a valid match of the pattern. In practice, reporting just one of the matching results is sufficient to detect the buffer overflow attack. Therefore, we propose a new concept, *Non-overlapping Matching*, that relaxes the requirements of exhaustive matching.

Non-overlapping Matching Consider the matching process M as a function from a pattern P and a string S to a set of strings, specifically,

$$M(P, S) = \{\text{substring } S_i \text{ of } S \,|\, \forall S_i, S_j \text{ accepted by the DFA of } P, S_i \cap S_j = \emptyset\}.$$

If a pattern appears in multiple locations of the input, this matching process reports all non-overlapping substrings that match the pattern. We revisit our example above. For the pattern $ab*$ and the input $abbb$, the four matches overlap by sharing

---

[2] The techniques presented in this chapter assume packets are reassembled into a stream before checking for patterns. For pattern matching on out of order packets, please refer to [9].

the prefix a. If we assume non-overlapping matching, we only need to report one match instead of four.

For most payload scanning applications, we expect that non-overlapping matching would suffice, as those applications are mostly interested in knowing if certain attacks or application layer patterns appear in a packet. In fact, most existing scanning tools like grep [2] and flex [13] and systems like SNORT [3] and Bro [1] implement special cases of non-overlapping matches such as left-most longest match or left-most shortest match. As we show later in this section, by restricting the solutions for non-overlapping matches, we can construct more memory-efficient DFAs.

10.5.2 Rewrite Rules for DFAs with Quadratic Size

Section 10.4.2.1 showed an example pattern, "^SEARCH\s+[^\n]{1024}", that can generate DFAs of quadratic size with respect to the length restriction. Below, we explain the intuition behind the pattern rewrite using the above example and then address more general cases.

When identifying non-overlapping patterns, "^SEARCH\s+[^\n] {1024}" can be rewritten to "^SEARCH\s[^\n]{1024}". The new pattern specifies that after matching string *SEARCH* and a single white space \s, it starts counting non-return characters for [^\n]{1024} regardless of the content. In this way, the ambiguity of matching \s is removed. It is not hard to see that for every matching substring s that the original pattern reports, the new pattern produces a substring s that is either identical to s or is a prefix of s. In other words, the new pattern essentially implements non-overlapping left-most shortest match. It is also easy to see that the new pattern requires a number of states linear in the length restriction j (1024 in the example).

This rewrite rule can be applied to a more general case where the suffix of a pattern contains a class of characters overlapping with its prefix and a length restriction, e.g., "^A+[A−Z]{j}". It is proved in [16] that this type of patterns can be rewritten to "^A[A − Z]{j}" with equivalence guaranteed under the condition of non-overlap matching. This rewrite rule can also be extended to patterns with various types of length restriction such as "^A + [A − Z]{j+}" and "^A + [A − Z]{j, k}".

10.5.3 Rewrite Rule for DFAs of Exponential Size

As discussed in Section 10.4.2.2, patterns like ". ∗ AUTH\s[^\n]{100}" generate exponential numbers of states to keep track of all the *AUTH*\s subsequent to the first *AUTH*\s. If non-overlapping matching is used, the intuition of our rewriting is that after matching the first *AUTH*\s, we do not need to keep track of the second *AUTH*\s. This is because:

- If there is a '\n' character within the next 100 bytes, the return character must also be within 100 bytes to the second $AUTH\backslash s$.
- If there is no '\n' character within the next 100 bytes, the first $AUTH\backslash s$ and the following characters have already matched the pattern.

The intuition is that we can rewrite the pattern such that it only attempts to capture one match of the prefix pattern. Following the intuition, we can simplify the DFA by removing the states that deal with the successive $AUTH\backslash s$. As shown in Figure 10.6, the simplified DFA first searches for $AUTH$ in the first four states, then looks for a white space, and after that starts to count and check whether the next 100 bytes contains a return character. After rewriting, the DFA only contains 106 states.

The rewritten pattern can be derived from the simplified DFA shown in Figure 10.6. We can transform this DFA to an equivalent NFA in Figure 10.7 using standard automaton transform techniques [8]. The transformed NFA can be directly described using the following regular expression:

$$([^A]|A[^U]|AU[^T]|AUT[^H]|AUTH[^\backslash s]|AUTH\backslash s[^\backslash n]\{0, 99\}\backslash n) * AUTH \backslash s[^\backslash n]\{100\}$$

This pattern first enumerates all the cases that do not satisfy the pattern and then attaches the original pattern to the end of the new pattern. In other words,

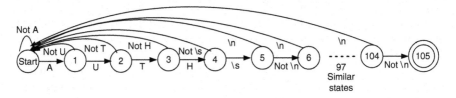

Fig. 10.6 DFA for rewriting the pattern $. * AUTH\backslash s[^\backslash n]\{100\}$

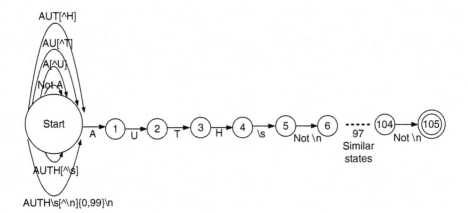

Fig. 10.7 Transformed NFA for rewriting

".*" is replaced with the cases that do not match the pattern, represented by
$([\hat{}A]|A[\hat{}U]|AU[\hat{}T]|AUT[\hat{}H]|AUTH[\hat{}\backslash s]|AUTH\backslash s[\hat{}\backslash n]\{0, 99\}\backslash n)*$

Then, when the DFA comes to the states for $AUTH\backslash s[\hat{}\backslash n]\{100\}$, it must be able to match the pattern. Since the rewritten pattern is directly obtained from a DFA of size $j + 5$, it generates a DFA of a linear number of states rather than an exponential number before applying the rewrite.

More generally, it is proven in [16] that pattern ".$* AB[A - Z]\{j\}$" can be rewritten as "$([\hat{}A]|A[\hat{}B]|AB[A - Z]\{j - 1\}[\hat{}(A - Z)])*AB[A - Z]\{j\}$" for detecting non-overlapping strings. Similar rewrite rules apply to patterns in other forms of length restriction, e.g., ".$ * AB[A - Z]\{j+\}$".

In [16], these two rewriting rules are applied to the Linux L7-filter, SNORT, and Bro pattern sets. While the Linux L7-filter pattern set does not contain any pattern that needs to be rewritten, the SNORT pattern set contains 71 rules that need to be rewritten and the Bro pattern set contains 49 such patterns (mostly imported from SNORT). For both types of rewrite, the DFA size reduction rate is over 98%.

10.5.4   Guidelines for Pattern Writers

From the analysis, we can see that patterns with length restrictions can sometimes generate large DFAs. In typical packet payload scanning pattern sets including Linux L7-filter, SNORT, and Bro, 21.4–56.3% of the length restrictions are associated with classes of characters. The most common of these are "[^\n]", "[^\]]" (not ']'), and "[^\"]" (not ''), used for detecting buffer overflow attempts. The length restrictions of these patterns are typically large (233 on the average and reaching up to 1024). For these types of patterns, we highly encourage the pattern writer to add "^" so as to avoid the exponential state growth. For patterns that cannot start with "^", the pattern writers can use the techniques shown in Section 10.5.3 to generate patterns with linear numbers of states to the length restriction requirements.

Even for patterns starting with '^', we need to avoid the interactions between a character class and its preceding character, as shown in Section 10.5.2. One may wonder why a pattern writer uses $\backslash s+$ in the pattern "^SEARCH$\backslash s+[\hat{}\backslash n]\{1024\}$", when it can be simplified as $\backslash s$. Our understanding is that, in reality, a server implementation of a search task usually interprets the input in one of the two ways: either skips a white space after SEARCH and takes the following up to 1024 characters to conduct a search, or skips all white spaces and takes the rest for the search. The original pattern writer may want to catch intrusion into systems of either implementation. However, the way the original pattern is written, it generates false positives if the server does the first type of implementation (skipping all the white spaces). This is because if an input is followed by 1024 white spaces and then some non-whitespace regular command of less than 1024 bytes, the server can skip these white spaces and take the follow-up command successfully. However, this legitimate input will be caught by the original pattern as an intrusion because these white spaces themselves can trigger the alarm. To catch attacks to this type of server implementation, while not generating false positives, we need the following pattern:

$$\text{``}\hat{}\text{SEARCH}\backslash s+[\hat{}\backslash s][\hat{}\backslash n]\{1023\}\text{''}$$

In this pattern, $\backslash s+$ matches all white spaces and $[\hat{}\backslash s]$ means the first non-white space character. If there are more than 1023 non-return characters following the first non-white space character, it is a buffer overflow attack. By adding $[\hat{}\backslash s]$, the ambiguity in the original pattern is removed; given an input, there is only one way to match each packet. As a result, this new pattern generates a DFA of linear size. To generalize, we recommend pattern writers to avoid all the possible overlaps between the neighboring segments in the pattern. Here, overlap denotes an input can match both segments simultaneously, e.g., $\backslash s+$ and $[\hat{}\backslash n]$. Overlaps will generate a large number of states in a DFA because the DFA needs to enumerate all the possible ways to match the pattern.

10.6 D²FA: Algorithms to Reduce DFA Space

The pattern rewriting schemes presented in the previous section reduce the DFA storage overhead by reducing the number of DFA states. Besides the states, the DFA storage overhead is also affected by the links between states. This section discusses link compression techniques.

If no link compression is applied, each state in the DFA has $2^8 = 256$ possible outgoing links, one for each ASCII alphabet input. Usually not all outgoing links are distinct. Therefore, table compression techniques can be used to efficiently represent the identical outgoing links [4]. However, these techniques are reported to be inefficient when applied to networking patterns because on the average one state has more than 50 distinct next states [11].

Kumar et al. proposed Delayed Input DFA (D²FA), a new representation of regular expressions for reducing the DFA storage overhead. Instead of compressing identical links originated from the one state, it compresses links across states based on the observation that multiple states in a DFA can have identical outgoing links. Therefore, linking these states together through *default transitions* can remove the need of storing outgoing links in each state separately. For a concrete example, consider three states s_1, s_2, and s_3 and their outgoing links in Table 10.5. States s_1 and

Table 10.5 Three states in a DFA and their transitions for different input characters

	A	B	C	D
State s_1	s_2	s_3	s_4	s_5
State s_2	s_2	s_7	s_4	s_5
State s_3	s_2	s_7	s_8	s_5

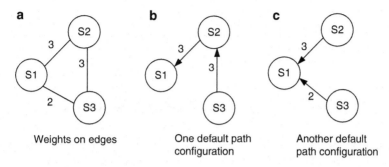

Fig. 10.8 The default link selection example

s_2 have identical next states on inputs A, C, and D. Only character B leads to different next states. Similarly, s_2 and s_3 have identical next states except for character C. Instead of these three states storing next states separately, D^2FA only stores one outgoing link for s_2 (for character B), and one for s_3 (for character C). For other states, s_2 can have a default link to s_1 and s_3 has a default link to s_2, where identical links are stored. In this way, the storage overhead of D^2FA can be significantly smaller than the original DFA.

To construct D^2FA from DFA, one can check the number of identical outgoing links between any two states and use that as a weight function. The weight indicates the number of links that can be eliminated in D^2FA. Figure 10.8(a) shows weights in the previous example. The goal of default link selection is to pick default links between states that shared the highest weights. Note that a default path must not contain cycles because otherwise it may bring the D^2FA into an infinite loop at some given input. Therefore, the default paths can create a tree or forests. Figure 10.8(b) and (c) are two example selections and (b) has a higher weight than (c). In [11], maximum weight spanning tree algorithms are used to create the default paths and consequently convert DFA to D^2FA.

The storage savings of D^2FA come at the cost of multiple memory lookups. In the previous example, if using the DFA, given an input A at current state s_2, we can obtain the next states with one table lookup. With D^2FA, Figure 10.8(b), two memory lookups are necessary. First, we perform one lookup to find out that s_2 has no stored outgoing link for character A and we obtain the default link to s_1. Next, we perform another lookup into s_1 to retrieve the next state for A, which is s_2. Default links can be connected to form a default path. With a default path, multiple memory lookups are needed. For example, given an input A at state s_3 in Figure 10.8(b), we need two extra memory lookups, one following the default link from s_3 to s_2 and the other from s_2 to s_1. To generalize, given an input, the number of memory lookups is the number of default links followed plus one. In the worst case, the longest default path becomes the system bottleneck. Therefore, when constructing D^2FA from DFA, it is critical to bound the maximum default paths lengths. A spanning tree-based heuristic algorithm is used in [11] for this purpose.

D^2FA is very effective when applied to networking pattern sets. It was able to remove more than 95% of the transitions between states [11], which greatly reduces the memory consumption.

10.7 Bifurcated, History-Augmented DFA Techniques

The previous sections presented rewrite and compression techniques to reduce the storage overhead of DFAs for fast packet pattern processing. DFA sizes can be further reduced by using data structures and algorithms particularly suitable for these packet patterns. In particular, Kumar et al. [10] identified several limitations of traditional DFA-based approaches to packet pattern processing and proposed techniques to overcome these limitations, resulting in compact representations of multiple patterns for high-speed packet content scanning.

A foremost limitation of traditional DFA-based approaches is that they employ complete patterns to parse the packet content. These approaches fail to exploit the fact that normal packet streams rarely match more than the first few symbols of any pattern. As a result, the automata unnecessarily explode in size as they attempt to represent the patterns in their entirety even if the tail portions of the patterns are rarely visited. To overcome this limitation, a key idea in [10] is to isolate frequently visited portions of the patterns, called pattern prefixes, from the infrequent portions, called pattern suffixes. Another important observation of common packet patterns is that the prefixes are generally simpler than the suffixes. Hence, such prefixes can be implemented using a compact DFA representation and stored in a fast memory, expediting the critical path of packet scanning. On the other hand, the suffixes can be implemented using DFAs if they fit in memory, or even using NFAs since they are expected to be executed only infrequently. Such a prefix and suffix-based architecture is referred to as a bifurcated pattern-matching architecture.

There is an important tradeoff in such a bifurcated pattern-matching architecture: On the one hand, we want to make the prefixes small so that the automaton that is active all the time is compact and fast. On the other hand, very small prefixes can be matched frequently by normal data streams, causing frequent invocations of the slow processing of the complex suffixes. Hence, a good solution must strike an effective balance between the two competing goals. The solution proposed in [10] is sketched below with some simplification:

1. Construct an NFA for each packet pattern and execute all those NFAs against typical network traffic. For each NFA, compute the probability with which each state of the NFA becomes active and the probabilities with which the NFA makes its various transitions. The NFAs for two example patterns and their transition probabilities are illustrated in Figure 10.9.
2. Once these probabilities are computed, determine a cut in the NFA graph such that (i) there are as few nodes as possible on the left-hand side of the cut and (ii) the probability that the states on the right-hand side of the cut are active is sufficiently small. Such a cut is illustrated in Figure 10.9(b).

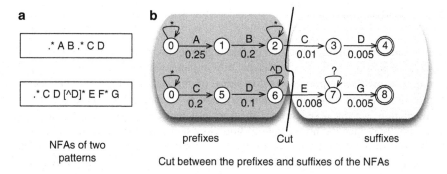

Fig. 10.9   Example NFAs and the cut between their prefixes and suffixes

3. After the cut is determined, a composite DFA is constructed for all the prefixes
   of the NFAs on the left-hand side of the cut. A DFA or NFA is chosen for each
   suffix on the right-hand side depending on the available memory.

Experimental results in [10] show that more than 50% reduction of memory usage
can be achieved for a spectrum of pattern sets used in network intrusion detection
systems, when the DFAs for entire patterns are replaced with the DFAs for the prefixes of those patterns obtained using the above technique.

   A second limitation of traditional DFA-based approaches is that given a set of
patterns to be matched simultaneously with the input data, a composite DFA maintains a single state of execution, which represents the combination of all the partial
matches of those patterns. As a result, it needs to employ a large number of states
to remember various combinations of the partial matches. In particular, an exponential blowup of the DFA can occur when multiple patterns consist of a simple
sequence of characters followed by a Kleene closure [8] over a class of characters,
e.g., the two prefixes on the left-hand side of the cut in Figure 10.9(b). In this scenario, the DFA needs to record the power set of the matching results of such prefixes
using individual states, hence the exponential size of the machine [10, 16].

   To mitigate the combinatorial effect of partial matches of multiple patterns, a
history-augmented DFA [10], H-FA, equips the composite DFA with a small auxiliary memory that uses a set of history flags to register the events of partial matches.
H-FA further identifies the fragments of the composite DFA that perform similar
processing of the input data and only differ in the True/False values of a history flag.
In many cases, these DFA fragments can be merged with additional conditions imposed on the DFA transitions and appropriate set and reset operations of the history
flag. As reported in [10], such H-FAs can result in more than 80% space reduction
for most common pattern sets used in network intrusion detection systems.

10.8 Summary

We considered the implementation of fast regular expression matching for packet-payload scanning applications. Naive DFA implementations can result in exponentially growing memory costs for some of the patterns used in networking applications. Since reducing this memory cost is critical for any high-speed implementation, we discussed several memory-efficient DFA-based approaches that substantially reduce memory usage. While these techniques do not handle all possible cases of dramatic DFA growth, they do cover those patterns that are present in common payload scanning rulesets like SNORT and Bro. Hence, fast DFA-based pattern matching is feasible for today's payload-scanning applications.

References

1. Bro intrusion detection system. http://bro-ids.org/Overview.html.
2. Gnu grep tool. http://www.gnu.org/software/grep/.
3. Snort network intrusion detection system. http://www.snort.org.
4. A. V. Aho, R. Sethi, and J. D. Ullman. *Compilers: principles, techniques, and tools*. Addison-Wesley Longman Publishing Co., Inc., Boston, MA, USA, 1986.
5. Y. Diao, M. Altinel, M. J. Franklin, H. Zhang, and P. Fischer. Path sharing and predicate evaluation for high-performance xml filtering. *ACM Trans. Database Syst.*, 28(4):467–516, 2003.
6. T. J. Green, A. Gupta, G. Miklau, M. Onizuka, and D. Suciu. Processing xml streams with deterministic automata and stream indexes. *ACM Trans. Database Syst.*, 29(4):752–788, 2004.
7. T. J. Green, A. Gupta, G. Miklau, M. Onizuka, and D. Suciu. Processing xml streams with deterministic automata and stream indexes. *ACM Trans. Database Syst.*, 29(4):752–788, 2004.
8. J. E. Hopcroft, R. Motwani, and J. D. Ullman. *Introduction to Automata Theory, Languages, and Computation (3rd Edition)*. Addison-Wesley Longman Publishing Co., Inc., Boston, MA, USA, 2006.
9. T. Johnson, S. Muthukrishnan, and I. Rozenbaum. Monitoring regular expressions on out-of-order streams. In *ICDE*, 2007.
10. S. Kumar, B. Chandrasekaran, J. Turner, and G. Varghese. Curing regular expressions matching algorithms from insomnia, amnesia, and acalculia. In *ANCS '07: Proceedings of the 2007 ACM/IEEE Symposium on Architecture for networking and communications systems*, pages 155–164, 2007.
11. S. Kumar, S. Dharmapurikar, F. Yu, P. Crowley, and J. Turner. Algorithms to accelerate multiple regular expressions matching for deep packet inspection. In *SIGCOMM '06: Proceedings of the 2006 conference on Applications, technologies, architectures, and protocols for computer communications*, pages 339–350, 2006.
12. J. Levandoski, E. Sommer, and M. Strait. Application layer packet classifier for linux. http://l7-filter.sourceforge.net/.
13. V. Paxson. Flex: A fast scanner generator. http://dinosaur.compilertools.net/flex/index.html.
14. R. Sommer and V. Paxson. Enhancing byte-level network intrusion detection signatures with context. In *CCS '03: Proceedings of the 10th ACM conference on Computer and communications security*, pages 262–271, 2003.
15. Venkat. Yahoo messenger protocol. http://www.venkydude.com/articles/yahoo.htm/.
16. F. Yu, Z. Chen, Y. Diao, T. V. Lakshman, and R. H. Katz. Fast and memory-efficient regular expression matching for deep packet inspection. In *ANCS '06: Proceedings of the 2006 ACM/IEEE symposium on Architecture for networking and communications systems*, pages 93–102, 2006.

Chapter 11
Anomaly Detection Approaches for Communication Networks

Marina Thottan, Guanglei Liu, and Chuanyi Ji

Abstract In recent years, network anomaly detection has become an important area for both commercial interests as well as academic research. Applications of anomaly detection typically stem from the perspectives of network monitoring and network security. In network monitoring, a service provider is often interested in capturing such network characteristics as heavy flows, flow size distributions, and the number of distinct flows. In network security, the interest lies in characterizing known or unknown anomalous patterns of an attack or a virus.

In this chapter we review two main approaches to network anomaly detection: streaming algorithms, and machine learning approaches with a focus on unsupervised learning. We discuss the main features of the different approaches and discuss their pros and cons. We conclude the chapter by presenting some open problems in the area of network anomaly detection.

11.1 Introduction

Network anomaly detection has become an important research area for both commercial interests as well as academic research. Applications of anomaly detection methods typically stem from the perspectives of network monitoring and network security. In network monitoring, a service provider is interested in capturing such

M. Thottan (✉)
Bell Labs, Alcatel-Lucent, 600-700 Mountain Avenue, Murray Hill, NJ 07974, USA
e-mail: marinat@alcatel-lucent.com

G. Liu
Division of Mathematics and Sciences, Roane State Community College, 276 Patton Lane, Harriman, TN 37748, USA
e-mail: liug@roanestate.edu

C. Ji
School of Electrical and Computer Engineering, Georgia Institute of Technology, 777 Atlantic Drive, Atlanta, GA 30332, USA
e-mail: jic@ece.gatech.edu

G. Cormode and M. Thottan (eds.), *Algorithms for Next Generation Networks*, Computer Communications and Networks, DOI 10.1007/978-1-84882-765-3_11,
© Springer-Verlag London Limited 2010

network characteristics such as heavy flows that use a particular link with a given capacity, flow size distributions, and the number of distinct flows in the network. In network security, the interest lies in characterizing known or unknown anomalous patterns of misbehaving applications or a network attack or even a virus in the packet payload.

A general definition for a network anomaly describes an event that deviates from normal network behavior. However, since known models for normal network behavior are not readily available, it is difficult to develop an anomaly detector in the strictest sense. Based on the inherent complexity in characterizing normal network behavior, the problem of anomaly detection can be categorized as model-based and non-model-based. In model-based anomaly detectors, it is assumed that a known model is available for the normal behavior of certain specific aspects of the network and any deviation from the norm is deemed an anomaly. For network behaviors that cannot be characterized by a model, non-model-based approaches are used. Non-model-based approaches can be further classified according to the specific implementation and accuracy constraints that have been imposed on the detector.

In network monitoring applications, where a statistical characterization of network anomalies is required, a known model is not a must. Nevertheless, a statistical anomaly detector must have access to large volumes of data that can provide the required samples, from which one can accurately learn the normal network behavior. However, with increasing speeds of network links, the frequency of sampling that is necessary for achieving a desired accuracy may be infeasible to implement. For example, on an OC-768 link, packets arrive every 25 ns. Online monitoring of these packets requires per packet processing along with a large of amount of state information that must be kept in memory. This is a heavy burden on the limited memory (SRAM) that is available on the router line cards. The sampling rates are therefore heavily resource-constrained. Under these circumstances it is more appropriate to use anomaly detection that can process long streams of data with small memory requirements and limited state information. Consequently, an online detection of anomalies with processing resource constraints corresponds to making some specific queries on the data and this is better handled by discrete algorithms that can process streaming data. In comparison with statistical sampling, streaming inspects every piece of data for the most important information while sampling processes only a small percentage of the data and absorbs all the information therein [56].

Machine learning approaches can be used when computational constraints are relaxed. Machine learning can be viewed as adaptively obtaining a mapping between measurements and network states, normal or anomalous. The goal is to develop learning algorithms that can extract pertinent information from measurements and can adapt to unknown network conditions and/or unseen anomalies. In a broad sense, statistical machine learning is one class of statistical approaches. The choice of the learning scenario depends on the information available in the measurements. For example, a frequent scenario is where there are only raw network measurements available, and thus unsupervised learning methods are used. If additional information is available, e.g., if network operators can provide examples of known anomalies or normal network behaviors, then learning can be done with supervision. The choice of mapping depends on the availability of a model, the amount and the type of measurements, and the complexity of the learning algorithms.

In this chapter we focus on network anomaly detection using streaming algorithms and machine learning approaches with a focus on unsupervised learning. We discuss the main features of the two approaches and discuss their pros and cons. We conclude the chapter by presenting some open problems in the area of network anomaly detection.

11.2 Discrete Algorithms for Network Anomaly Detection

In many cases, network anomaly detection involves tracking significant changes in traffic patterns such as traffic volume or the number of flows. Due to the high link speeds and the large size of the Internet, it is usually not scalable to track the per-flow status of traffic. In [14], Duffield et al. propose packet sampling to monitor flow-level traffic. The authors show that by limiting the number of flows that need to be monitored, sampling can partially solve the scalability problem. This scalability is attained at the expense of the accuracy in the performance of anomaly detection systems. Thus one important issue to investigate is the tradeoff between the amount of sampled information and the corresponding performance. In [4], Androulidakis and Papavassiliou investigate selective flow-based sampling to find a good balance between the volume of sampled information and the anomaly detection accuracy. The authors suggest that selective sampling that focuses on small flows can achieve improved anomaly detection efficiency with fewer flows selected. This work assumes that the majority of flows on the network are small flows, which may not be an accurate assessment for all networks.

Simple sampling cannot fully solve the scalability problem as packets or flows that are not sampled may contain important information about anomalies. Furthermore, it is likely that this information can only be recovered if these packets or flows are sampled and stored. Thus, sometimes a large number of flows (up to 2^{64} flows based on different combinations of source and destination IP addresses) may need to be sampled to achieve an anomaly detector with good performance [29].

To address the disadvantages of sampling approaches, there has been extensive research in data streaming algorithms for anomaly detection especially for high-speed networks. A key difference between streaming and sampling is that streaming looks at every piece of data for the most important information while sampling digests a small percentage of the available data or packets and absorbs all the information contained in those data [56].

Specifically, using streaming techniques, anomaly detection problems can generally be formulated as heavy-hitter detection problems or heavy-change detection problems. In the heavy-hitter detection problem, the goal is to identify the set of flows that represent a significantly large proportion of the ongoing traffic or the capacity of the link [17]. In the heavy-change detection problem, the goal is to detect the set of flows that have a drastic change in traffic volume from one time period to another [29].

11.2.1 Heavy-Hitter Detection

In the context of network anomaly detection, the goal of heavy-hitter detection is to efficiently identify the set of flows that represent a significantly large proportion of the link capacity using very small memory requirements and limited state information. Specifically, it can be formulated as follows [29].

Consider streams of data $\alpha_1, \alpha_2, \ldots$ that arrive sequentially, where each item $\alpha_i = (a_i, u_i)$ consists of a key $a_i \in \{0, 1, \ldots, n-1\}$ and an update $u_i \in \mathfrak{R}$. Associated with each key a_i is a time-varying signal $A[a_i]$, i.e., the arrival of each new data item updates the signal $A[a_i]$ such that $A[a_i] = A[a_i] + u_i$. In network anomaly detection, the key can be defined as the source and destination IP addresses, source and destination port numbers, protocol numbers, and so on [29]. Thus n can be a very large number, e.g., $n = 2^{64}$ considering all possible source and destination IP address pairs. The updates can be viewed as sizes of packets in traffic flows. The problem of heavy-hitter detection is to find those items (keys) satisfying the following:

$$\frac{A[a_i]}{\sum_{l=0}^{n-1} A[a_l]} > \varepsilon \quad \text{or} \quad A[a_i] > \phi,$$

where ε and ϕ are predetermined thresholds.

The challenge with heavy-hitter detection is that data processing cannot be done on a per-flow basis due to the high speed of network links in the Internet. Thus, streaming algorithms based on summary structures are used to solve this problem with guaranteed error bounds. In data mining, there has been extensive research on algorithms for heavy-hitter detection. The application of these algorithms to heavy-hitter detection in computer networks was first made in [17, 39].

In [17], Estan and Varghese initiate a new direction in traffic measurement by recommending that algorithms concentrate only on large flows, i.e., flows whose volumes are above certain thresholds. The authors also propose two algorithms for detecting large flows: sample and hold algorithm and multistage filter algorithm. Theoretical results show that the errors of these two algorithms are inversely proportional to the memory available. Furthermore, in [17], the authors note that network measurement problems bear a lot of similarities to measurement problems in other research areas such as data mining, and thus initiate the application of data streaming techniques to network anomaly detection.

In [39], Manku and Motwani propose the Sticky Sampling algorithm and the Lossy Counting algorithm to compute approximate frequency counts of elements in a data stream. The proposed algorithms can provide guaranteed error bounds and require very small memory. Thus, these algorithms also provide powerful tools for solving the heavy-hitter detection problem in high-speed networks.

Cormode, Muthukrishnan and other authors introduce the Count-Min sketch method to heavy-hitter detection. A sketch is a probabilistic summary data structure based on random projections. In [7], the authors note that it is an open problem to develop extremely simple and practical sketches for data streaming applications. In [8], Cormode and Muthukrishnan extend the study of heavy-hitter detection algorithms by identifying performance bottlenecks and tradeoffs in order to make these algorithms useful in practice. Using generated and actual IP packet data, the authors find that approximate complex aggregates are effective in providing accuracy guarantees with less processing load. In addition, adaptive implementations of "heavy-weight" approximations such as sketches are beneficial. The work in [8] provides excellent insights on how to make these heavy-hitter detection algorithms fast and space-efficient so that they can be used in high-speed data stream applications.

In many data stream applications such as traffic anomaly detection, the data have hierarchical attributes. For instance, IP addresses can be aggregated based on the prefixes. Another example is that TCP/UDP port numbers can be categorized based on different types of services. Sometimes it is important to find a hierarchical aggregate that corresponds to a heavy hitter. For instance, one may want to find whether traffic from sources with certain IP prefixes corresponds to volume anomalies. Thus, an item at a certain level of detail made up by aggregating many small frequency items may be a heavy-hitter item although its individual constituents are not [11]. In [11], Cormode et al. formally define the notion of a hierarchical heavy hitter (HHH) on a single dimension, i.e., on one data attribute such as source IP address or source port number. Basically, given a hierarchy and a fraction ϕ, HHHs are nodes in the hierarchy that have a total number of descendant elements in the data stream no smaller than ϕ of the total number of elements in the data stream, after discounting descendant nodes that are HHHs themselves [6].

In practice, data may be associated with multiple attributes at the same time such as the IP addresses and port numbers discussed above. Therefore, in [11], the definition of single-dimensional HHHs is extended to multi-dimensional HHHs. One major challenge in defining multi-dimensional HHHs is that each item may belong to multiple parents due to the multiple attributes that it is associated with. Consequently the definition of multiple-dimension HHHs depends on how to allocate the count of each item to each of its parents. Specifically, in [11], two counting rules are applied. The first "overlap rule" allocates the full count of an item to each of its parents and therefore is counted multiple times in nodes that overlap. The second "split rule" divides the count of each item between its parents in some way such as an even split. Similar to single-dimensional HHH problems, the multi-dimensional hierarchical heavy-hitter problem is to find all multi-dimensional HHHs and their associated values. For a more formal definition of multi-dimensional HHHs, refer to [11].

There has been a lot of research in finding efficient algorithms for the HHH problem. In [11], the authors extend the study in [6, 9] and propose different online algorithms to solve the HHH problems, e.g., the *PartialAnces* algorithm for multi-dimensional HHH problems. In addition, experiments based on live IP traffic streams are conducted to confirm the quality of the proposed algorithms. In a separate work [59], Zhang et al. also consider the problem of HHH detection, where the definition of HHHs is simplified such that counts from heavy-hitter items are not excluded for their parents. The work in [59] establishes a connection between multi-dimensional HHH detection problems and packet classification problems. Furthermore, dynamic algorithms based on adaptive synopsis data structures are shown to be efficient tools for HHH detection and can serve as promising building blocks for network anomaly detection.

Closely related to the heavy-hitter problem is the heavy distinct-hitter problem, which can be defined as in [52]: Given a stream of (x, y) pairs, the heavy distinct-hitter problem is to find all the xs that are paired with a large number of distinct ys. For instance, in the case of worm propagation, a compromised host may scan a large number of distinct destinations in a short time. Such a compromised host can be considered as a heavy distinct-hitter. Please note that a heavy distinct-hitter might not be a heavy hitter. For example, the compromised host in the worm propagation example may only create a limited amount of network traffic and is not considered a heavy hitter based on traffic volume. On the other hand, a heavy hitter may not be a heavy distinct-hitter if it is only connected to a limited number of hosts even though its traffic volume is significantly large. To detect heavy distinct-hitter is meaningful in many network applications such as identification of Distributed Denial-Of-Service (DDOS) attacks. In [52], Venkataraman et al. propose one-level and two-level filtering algorithms for heavy distinct-hitter detection. Both theoretical and experimental results show that these algorithms can provide accurate detection in a distributed setting with limited memory requirements for data storage.

There has been much progress in heavy-hitter problems as discussed above. Nevertheless, as indicated in [29], heavy hitters are flows that represent a significantly large proportion of the ongoing traffic or the capacity of the link, but they do not necessarily correspond to flows experiencing significant changes. In terms of network anomaly detection, heavy-change detection is usually more informative than heavy-hitter detection. In addition, the solutions for heavy-hitter detection discussed here usually use data structures that do not have linearity property. Thus, it is difficult to perform the more general task of query aggregations [45].

11.2.2 Heavy-Change Detection

In the context of network anomaly detection, the goal of heavy-change detection is to efficiently identify the set of flows that have drastic changes in traffic volume from one time period to another with small memory requirements and limited state information. Specifically, the Heavy-change detection problem can be formulated similarly to the heavy-hitter detection problem [10, 29].

Consider streams of data $\alpha_1, \alpha_2, \ldots$ that arrives sequentially, where each item $\alpha_i = (a_i, u_i)$ consists of a key $a_i \in \{0, 1, \ldots, n - 1\}$ and an update $u_i \in \Re$. Associated with each key a_i is a time varying signal $A[a_i]$, i.e., the arrival of each new data item updates signal $A[a_i]$ such that $A[a_i] = A[a_i] + u_i$. We break time into discrete intervals, $I_1, I_2, \ldots$, and define the value of $A[a_i]$ at time interval k, $k = 1, 2, \ldots, t$ as $s_{i,k}$. The problem of heavy-change detection is to find those items (keys) satisfying the following condition:

$$|s_{i,j} - s_{i,k}| > \varepsilon \quad \text{or} \quad \frac{|s_{i,j}|}{max\{|s_{i,k}|, 1\}} > \phi,$$

where ε and ϕ are predetermined thresholds. Note that in this case changes can be defined using different measures of differences such as absolute difference, relative difference and so on [10].

Clearly heavy-change detection is a harder problem than heavy-hitter detection. In heavy-change detection, the sketch method has shown great potential. The basic idea is to summarize the input streams so that per-flow analysis can be avoided. In [29], Krishnamurthy et al. first apply sketches to the heavy-change detection problem. With sketch-based change detection, input data streams are summarized using k-ary sketches. After the sketches are created, different time series forecast models can be implemented on top of the summaries. Then the forecast errors are used to identify whether there are significant changes in the data stream. The sketch-based techniques use a small amount of memory and has constant per-record update and reconstruction costs, thus it can be used for change detection in high-speed networks with a large number of flows. However, the k-ary sketch-based change detection has one main drawback: the k-ary sketch is irreversible, thus making it impossible to reconstruct the desired set of anomalous keys without querying every IP address or querying every address in the stream if the IP addresses have been saved.

To address these problems, in [45, 46], Schweller et al. develop change detection schemes based on reversible sketch data structures. The basic idea is to hash intelligently by modifying the input keys and hashing functions so that keys with heavy changes can be recovered [46]. Using reverse hashing schemes, the authors can efficiently identify the set of all anomalous keys in the sketch. In addition, the authors introduce the bucket index matrix algorithm for accurate multiple heavy-change detection. Empirical results show that the reverse hashing is capable of detecting heavy changes and identifying the anomalous flows in real time. In [18], Gao et al. extend the work in [29,45,46] by considering an optimal small set of metrics and building two-dimensional sketches for flow-level traffic anomaly detection. The authors also implement a high-speed online intrusion detection system based on two-dimensional sketches, which is shown to be capable of detecting multiple types of attacks simultaneously with high accuracy.

In a separate work [10], Cormode et al. introduce the deltoid concept for heavy-change detection, where a deltoid is defined as an item that has a large difference. The authors propose a framework based on a structure of Combinational Group Testing to find significant deltoids in high-speed networks. It is also shown that the proposed algorithms are capable of finding significant deltoids with small memory and update time, and with guaranteed pre-specified accuracy. As commented in [45], deltoids can be considered as an expansion of k-ary sketch with multiple counters for each bucket in the hash table at the cost of memory requirements for data storage.

Sketch-based schemes are capable of detecting significant changes efficiently with high accuracy. Nevertheless, there still remain important challenges before the wide deployment of sketch-based network anomaly detection schemes. For instance, given the wide variety of attacks and anomalies exhibited in the Internet, one challenge for sketch-based schemes is to identify a minimal set of metrics for network monitoring.

11.3   Statistical Approaches for Network Anomaly Detection

In this section, we review statistical approaches for anomaly detection. Fig. 11.1 illustrates the general steps involved in statistical anomaly detection. The first step is to preprocess or filter the given data inputs. This is an important step as the types of data available and the timescales in which these data are measured can significantly affect the detection performance [50]. In the second step, statistical analysis and/or data transforms are performed to separate normal network behavior from anomalous behavior and noise. A variety of statistical techniques can be applied here, e.g., wavelet analysis, covariance matrix analysis, and principal component analysis. The main challenge is to find computationally efficient techniques for anomaly detection with low false alarm rate. In the final step, decision theories such as Generalized Likelihood Ratio (GLR) test can be used to determine whether there is a network anomaly based on the deviations observed in the input data.

In a broader context, statistical anomaly detection can also be viewed from a machine learning perspective, where the goal is to find the appropriate discriminant function that can be used to classify any new input data vector into the normal or anomalous region with good accuracy for anomaly detection. One subtle difference between statistical anomaly detection and machine learning based methods is that statistical approaches generally focus on statistical analysis of the collected data,

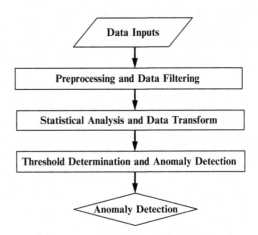

Fig. 11.1 Statistical Learning Approach for network anomaly detection

whereas machine learning methods focus on the "learning" aspect. Thus based on the availability of models or on the strength of the assumptions that can be made regarding the normal and anomalous models we can classify learning approaches under two broad categories: model-based and non-model-based learning.

11.3.1 Model-Based Detection

When the anomaly detection can safely assume a known model for the behavior of normal and anomalous data we can employ model-based learning approaches. The assumed models may be actual statistical models defined on the input data and/or system specific information.

11.3.1.1 Change-Point Detection

Statistical sequential change-point detection has been applied successfully to network anomaly detections. In statistical change-point analysis, abrupt changes can be modeled using a stochastic process such as the auto-regressive (AR) process. In addition, if there is an understanding on the system level behavior in the event of an anomaly, such as a mechanism for how the detected change points may propagate through the network then they can be traced as correlated events among different input data streams.

Using the change-point detection approach, in [50, 51], Thottan and Ji characterize network anomalies using the Management Information Base (MIB) variables as input data. Anomaly detection is accomplished by detecting change points that occur in a temporally correlated fashion across the different input variables. Given a set of MIB variables sampled at a fixed time interval as inputs, the authors compute a network health function by combining the anomaly indicators of each individual MIB variable. The anomaly indicators are obtained by assuming that the normal data within the time window of consideration can be modeled using an AR process of order 2. The network health function is then obtained by temporally correlating the anomaly indicators across the different input variables. The network health function is then used to determine the presence of an anomaly in the network.

In [55], Wang et al. detect SYN flooding attacks based on the dynamics of the differences between the number of SYN and FIN packets, which is modeled as a stationary ergodic random process. The non-parametric Cumulative Sum (CUSUM) method is then used to detect change points in the observed time series of the SYN and FIN packets and thus detect SYN flooding attacks.

The work in both [51, 55] models network dynamics as a quasi-stationary or stationary process. However, it is well known that under certain network scenarios the traffic dynamics exhibit non-stationary behavior [36]. Thus better traffic modeling methods that can capture the non-stationary behavior could lead to improved anomaly detection with lower false alarm rates. In addition, not all detected change points correspond to network anomalies. Therefore, accurate characterization of anomalies in terms of change points in network dynamics is essential for effective anomaly detection [51].

11.3.1.2 Kalman Filter

In the past the Kalman filter has been applied successfully to a wide variety of problems involving the estimation of dynamics of linear systems from incomplete data. A Kalman filter generally consists of two steps: the prediction step and the estimation step. In the prediction step, the state at time $t + 1$ is predicted based on all the observed data up to time t. In the estimation step, the state at time $t + 1$ is estimated by comparing the prediction from the previous step with the new observations.

In [47], Soule et al. develop a traffic anomaly detection scheme based on a Kalman filter. The authors assume that per-link statistics on byte counts are easily available, but the traffic matrix that includes all pairs of origin-destination flows are not directly observable. The authors process the link data using a Kalman filter to predict the traffic matrix one step into the future. After the prediction is made, the actual traffic matrix is estimated based on new link data. Then the difference between the prediction and the actual traffic matrix is used to detect traffic volume anomalies based on different thresholding methods. Kalman filter is a promising tool for network anomaly detection together with other more complicated models of non-linear dynamics.

11.3.2 Model-Based Learning – Approximating an Assumed Model

When the anomaly detection problem is presented such that there is no clarity on the type and specifics of a model that can be assumed one can still use the model-based learning approaches. The methods used in this case allow for the uncertainty of the model to co-exist in the detection methods used.

11.3.2.1 Covariance Matrix Analysis

In [58], Yeung et al. develop a covariance matrix method to model and detect flooding attacks. Each element in the covariance matrix corresponds to the correlation between two monitored features at different sample sequences. The profile of the normal traffic can then be described by the mathematical expectation of all covariance matrices constructed from samples of the normal class in the training dataset. Anomalies can be detected with threshold-based detection schemes. The work in [58] uses second-order statistics of the monitored features for anomaly detection and is independent of assumptions on prior data distribution.

In [49], the covariance matrix method is extended, where the signs in the covariance matrices are used directly for anomaly detection. Detecting anomalies by comparing the sign of the covariance matrices saves computation costs while maintaining low false alarm rates. In a separate work [38], Mandjes et al. consider anomaly detection in a voice over IP network based on the analysis of the variance of byte counts. The authors derive a general formula for the variance of the cumulative traffic over a fixed time interval, which can be used to determine the presence of a load anomaly in the network.

By employing second-order features, covariance matrix analysis has been shown to be a powerful anomaly detection method. One interesting direction in this area is to find what variables best characterize network anomaly and improve detection performance.

11.3.2.2   Wavelet Analysis

Wavelet analysis has been applied to modeling non-stationary data series because it can characterize the scaling properties both in the temporal and frequency domains. Wavelet analysis generally consists of two steps [5, 27]: decomposition and reconstruction. The goal of the decomposition process is to extract from the original signal a hierarchy of component signals. The reconstruction process aims to perform the inverse of the decomposition and recapture the original signal. When wavelet analysis is applied to network anomaly detection, a decomposition process can be performed first on different input data such as IP packet headers. Afterwards, the decomposed signals can be reconstructed across different timescales, which are then used for anomaly detection. In the reconstruction stage, some signals derived from the decomposition stage may be suppressed so that one can focus on signals of interest. For instance, in anomaly detection of network traffic, one may choose to ignore the day and night variation in the traffic volume and suppress the corresponding signals in the reconstruction stage. One advantage of the wavelet approach is that by constructing the wavelet basis at different timescales, the signatures of anomalies at different timescales are preserved. The success of the wavelet analysis techniques depends on selecting a suitable wavelet transform for a given application [5].

In [41], Miller and Willsky apply wavelet transform techniques to anomaly detection in geophysical prospecting. Although in a different setting, the anomaly detection problem considered in [41] has some similarities to the problem of network anomaly detection. In both cases, one seeks to detect anomalous situations using limited and/or partial measurements. For example, in geophysical prospecting, the data available for anomaly detection are usually scattered radiation collected at medium boundaries [41], while in network anomaly detection, limited data is a common scenario. In addition, there is the stringent requirement for computationally efficient anomaly detection with low alarm rate in both cases.

In [5], Barford et al. successfully apply wavelet techniques to network traffic anomaly detection. The authors develop a wavelet system that can effectively isolate both short- and long-lived traffic anomalies. The wavelet analysis in [5] mainly focuses on aggregated traffic data in network flows. In [27], Kim and Reddy extend the work in [5] by studying IP packet header data at an egress router through wavelet analysis for traffic anomaly detection. Their approach is motivated by the observation that the out-bound traffic from an administrative domain is likely to exhibit strong correlation with itself over time. Thus, in [27], the authors study the correlation among addresses and port numbers over multiple timescales with discrete wavelet transforms. Traffic anomalies are detected if historical thresholds are exceeded in the analyzed signal.

Wavelet analysis is an effective anomaly detection method when dealing with aggregate flow data. However, when applied to modeling the time series corresponding to volume counts in a time window, Soule et al. [47] find that wavelet-based methods do not perform as well compared to the simple Generalized Likelihood Ratio (GLR) test method. The GLR method is used to test the likelihood of an occurrence of an anomaly by comparing the effectiveness of an assumed traffic model over two time windows of input data [50].

11.3.2.3 Information Theoretic Approaches

Information theoretic measures can be used to characterize the performance of anomaly detections. For example, in [35], Lee and Xiang provide several information theoretic measures for detecting network attacks. The information theoretic measures include entropy and conditional entropy as well as information gain/cost. Entropy is used to measure the regularity of a dataset of unordered records. Conditional entropy can be used to measure the regularity on sequential dependencies of a dataset of ordered records. The information gain of a feature describes its power in classifying data items, while the information cost measures the computational cost of processing the audit by an anomaly detection model [35]. Entropy measures have been applied to several datasets including call data and "tcpdump" data for detecting network security attacks. They have also been used to assist in selecting parameters for detection algorithms. The study in [35] is limited to anomaly detection models based on classification algorithms, but it provides useful theoretical understanding for developing improved anomaly detectors.

In [19], Gu et al. apply information theoretic measures in behavior-based anomaly detection. First, the maximum entropy principle is applied to estimate the distribution for normal network operation using raw data. The maximum entropy framework produces a "uniform" probability distribution to describe the normal behavior using raw data and a set of given constraints describing the network model. Next, a measure related to the relative entropy of the measured network traffic with respect to the estimated distribution of the normal behavior is computed. This measure is then applied to detect different kinds of network anomalies. Experiments show that the relative entropy detection algorithm can effectively detect anomalies that cause both abrupt and gradual changes in network traffic such as SYN attacks and port scans. The detection algorithm in [19] requires a computation time that is proportional to the traffic bandwidth.

Information theoretic measures such as entropy characterize the regularity in measured data and thus guide the model building and performance evaluation process for anomaly detection [35]. However, entropy measures are usually calculated based on complex algorithms using a relatively large dataset. This limits their application to anomaly detection in high-speed networks. To realize the potential of this approach in practice, in [30], Lall et al. investigate the problem of entropy estimation in a streaming computation model. The authors provide two efficient algorithms for randomly approximating the entropy. One basic idea is to improve the performance of the streaming algorithms by separating the high-frequency items from the low-frequency items. Evaluations on multiple packet traces show that the proposed techniques can be applicable to routers with gigabit per second link speeds. Nevertheless, finding entropy estimation algorithms that are practically viable has remained an important research topic.

11.3.3 Statistical Learning for Anomaly Detection

Statistical learning is in the general context of statistical approaches but with greater emphasis on techniques that adapt to the measured data. In particular, statistical machine learning approaches perform anomaly detection and continue to adapt to new measurements, changing network conditions, and unseen anomalies. A general formulation of this type of network anomaly detection algorithms is as follows:

Let $X(t) \in \Re$ (X in short) be an n-dimensional random feature vector drawn from a distribution at time $t \in [0, t]$. Consider the simplest scenario that there are two underlying states of a network, $\omega_i, i = 0, 1$, where ω_0 corresponds to normal network operation, and ω_1 corresponds to "unusual or anomalous" network state. An anomaly detection can be considered as determining whether a given observation x of the random feature vector X is a symptom of an underlying network state ω_0 or ω_1. That is, a mapping needs to be obtained between X and ω_i for $i = 0, 1$. Note that an anomalous network state may or may not correspond to an abnormal network operation. For example, flash crowd, which is a surge of user activities, may result from users' legal requests for new software or from DDOS or Worm attacks.

Due to the complexity of networks, such a mapping is usually unknown but can be learned from measurements. Assume that a set D of m measurements is collected from a network as observations on X, i.e., $D = \{x_i(t)\}_{i=1}^{m}$, where $x_i(t)$ is the ith observation for $t \in [0, t]$. $x_i(t)$ is called a training sample in machine learning. In addition, another set $D_l = \{y_q\}_{l=1}^{k}$ of k measurements is assumed to be available in general that are samples ($y_q = 0, 1$) on ω_i's. y_q's are called labels in machine learning. A pair $(x_i(t), y_i)$ is called a labeled measurement, where observation $x_i(t)$ is obtained when a network is in a known state. For example, if measurement $x_i(t)$ is taken when the network is known to operate normally, $y_i = 0$ and $(x_i(t), 0)$ is considered as a sample for normal network operation. If $x_i(t)$ is taken when the network is known to operate abnormally, $y_i = 1$ and $(x_i(t), 1)$ is considered as a "signature" in anomaly detection. In general $x_i(t)$ is considered as an unlabeled measurement, meaning the observation $x_i(t)$ occurs when the network state is unknown. Hence, network measurements are of three types:

(a) normal data $D_n = \{x_i(t), 0\}_{i=1}^{k-u}$,
(b) unlabeled data $D = \{x_j(t)\}_{j=1}^{m}$, and
(c) anomalous data $D_l = \{x_r(t), 1\}_{r=1}^{u}$.

A training set consists of all three types of data in general although a frequent scenario is that only D and D_n are available. Examples of D include raw measurements on end-to-end flows, packet traces, and data from Management Information Base (MIB) variables. Examples of D_n and D_l can be such measurements obtained under normal or anomalous network conditions, respectively.

Given a set of training samples, a machine learning view of anomaly detection is to learn a mapping $f(\cdot)$ using the training set, where

$$f(\cdot) : Network\ Measurements \rightarrow \omega_i,$$

so that a desired performance can be achieved on assigning a new sample x to one of the two categories. Figure 11.2 illustrates the learning problem.

A training set determines the amount of information available, and thus categorizes different types of learning algorithms for anomaly detection. Specifically, when D and D_n are available, learning/anomaly detection can be viewed as unsupervised. When D, D_l, and D_n are all available, learning/anomaly detection becomes supervised, since we have labels or signatures. $f(\cdot)$ determines the architecture of a "learning machine", which can either be a model with an analytical expression or a computational algorithm. When $f(\cdot)$ is a model, learning algorithms for anomaly detection are parametric, i.e., model-based; otherwise, learning algorithms are non-parametric, i.e., non-model-based.

11.3.3.1 Unsupervised Anomaly Detection

We now focus on unsupervised learning for anomaly detection, where D_l is not available, a mapping $f(\cdot)$ is learned using raw measurements D and normal

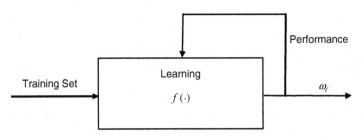

Fig. 11.2 Machine learning view of anomaly detection

data D_n. Unsupervised learning is the most common scenario in anomaly detection due to its practicality: Networks provide a rich variety and a huge amount of raw measurements and normal data.

One unsupervised learning approach for anomaly detection is *behavioral-based*. That is, D_n together with D is learned to characterize a normal network behavior. A deviation from the normal is considered as an anomaly.

11.3.3.1.1 Adaptive Threshold-Based Anomaly Detection

Early work [23, 40, 50] in this area begins with a small network, e.g., interface ports at a router, and chooses aggregated measurements, e.g., Management Information Base (MIB) variables that are readily available from a network equipment. Measurements are made within a moving window across a chosen time duration [23, 50]. Both off-line and online learning have been considered, and simple algorithms have been evaluated on the measured data. For example, in [23, 50], the authors select model-based learning, where $X((t)$ from normal operations is modeled as a second-order AR process, i.e., $f(X) = a_0 + a_1 X + a_2 X^2 + \varepsilon \cdot a_i, i = 0, 1, 2$ are parameters and learned using measurements collected from a moving window of a chosen time-duration, and ε is assumed to be Gaussian residual noise. A likelihood ratio test is applied. If the sample variance of the residual noise exceeds a chosen threshold, an observation x is classified as an anomaly. The model has been successful in detecting a wide-range of anomalies such as flash-crowds, congestion, broadcast storms [50], and worm attacks [12]. In addition, these anomalies have been detected proactively before they cause catastrophic network failures [23, 50]. One disadvantage of such an approach is the difficulty of choosing an appropriate timescale where AR processes can accurately characterize normal behavior of the MIB variables. The AR model with Gaussian noise is also not applicable to more complex temporal characteristics, e.g., bursty and non-Gaussian variables.

More recently a broader class of raw measurements has been selected for anomaly detection. For example, IP packet traces are used to detect faults/anomalies related to load changes (see [5] and references therein). The number of TCP SYN and FIN (RST) per unit time has been used to detect DDOS attacks [55]. Route update measurements have been used to understand routing anomalies and/or BGP routing instability [25, 60, 61]. Aggregated rates are used to detect bottlenecks in 3G networks [42]. These measurements are of different types but are all aggregated data (counts) rather than individual packets. Aggregated measurements facilitate scalable detection but do not contain detailed information, such as in packet headers that are available from end-to-end flow-based measurements.

More general algorithms have also been developed that go beyond simple models. One type of algorithm aims at better characterizing temporal characteristics in measurements. For example, wavelets are applied to BGP routing updates in [60], and four other types of measurements (outages, flash crowds, attacks, and measurement errors) in [5]. In this case, wavelets can better characterize anomalies across different timescales. Another example of this type of algorithm is non-parametric hypothesis-testing which is used to accommodate non-Gaussian statistics in DDOS attacks in [55]. The Generalized likelihood ratio test is applied to BGP measurements to detect anomalies such as worm attacks [12].

11.3.3.1.2 Clustering

Clustering is another class of algorithms in unsupervised anomaly detection. Clustering algorithms [13] characterize anomalies based on dissimilarities. The premise is that measurements that correspond to normal operations are similar and thus cluster together. Measurements that do not fall in the "normal clusters" are considered as anomalies.

The similarity measure is a key parameter of clustering algorithms that distinguish between normal and anomalous clusters. "Similarity" measures the distance among the input x_i's. The Euclidean distance is a commonly used similarity measure for numerical network measurements. Another frequently used measure is the Mahalanobis distance, which unlike the Euclidean distance, takes into consideration the variance of different feature components and does not depend on the scale of the measurements. When samples lie with distances below a chosen threshold, they are grouped into one cluster [13]. Such an approach has been applied in the following examples: (a) to cluster network flows from the Abilene network [2] to detect abrupt changes in the traffic distribution over an entire network, and (b) to cluster BGP update messages and detect unstable prefixes that experience frequent route changes [60]. More complex algorithms, e.g., hierarchical clustering algorithms, are applied to group BGP measurements based on coarse-to-fine distances [3]. An advantage of hierarchical clustering is computational efficiency, especially when applied to large network datasets [3]. In addition, fuzzy-k-mean and swarm-k-mean algorithms have been applied to detecting network attacks [15].

Mixture models provide a model-based approach for clustering [13]. A mixture model is a linear combination of basis functions. Gaussian basis functions with different parameters are commonly used to represent individual clusters. The basis functions are weighted and combined to form the mapping. Parameters of the basis functions and the weighting coefficients can be learned using measurements [13]. For example, in [21], Hajji uses Gaussian mixture models to characterize utilization measurements. Parameters of the model are estimated using the Expectation-Maximization (EM) algorithm and anomalies are detected corresponding to network failure events.

In [54], Xie et al. propose the pointillist approach for anomaly detection. The idea is that many host state transitions of interest have both temporal and spatial locality. Some of these abnormal state changes may be hard to detect in isolation, but become apparent when they are correlated with similar changes on other hosts. In [54], both wavelet-based methods and PCA-based methods are used for efficient feature selection. Then a simple iterative algorithm is utilized for clustering. The detection of a new cluster may indicate an abnormal event and raise an alarm. The prototype in [54] called Seurat shows great promise in attack detection involving file system changes.

One limitation of clustering algorithms is that they do not provide an explicit representation of the statistical dependence exhibited in raw measurements. Such a representation is important for correlating multiple variables in detection and diagnosis of anomalies.

11.3.3.1.3 Bayesian Belief Networks

Bayesian Belief Networks are used to capture the statistical dependence or causal-relations that map a set of input variables to a set of anomalies.

In an early work [23], Hood and Ji applied Bayesian Belief Networks to MIB variables in proactive network fault detection. The premise is that many variables in a network may exhibit anomalous behavior upon the occurrence of an event, and can be combined to provide a network-wide view of anomalies that may be more robust and result in more accurate detection. Specifically, the Bayesian Belief Network [23] first combines MIB variables within a protocol layer, and then aggregates intermediate variables of protocol layers to form a network-wide view of anomalies. Combinations are done through conditional probabilities in the Bayesian Belief Network. The conditional probabilities were determined a priori.

In a recent work [28], Kline et al. use Bayesian Belief Networks to combine and correlate different types of measurements such as traffic volumes, ingress/egress packets, and bit rates. Parameters in the Bayesian Belief Network are learned using measurements. The performance of the Bayesian Belief Network compares favorably with that of wavelet models and time-series detections, especially in lowering false alarm rates [28].

In [26], Ide and Kashima provide an example of Bayesian Networks in unsupervised anomaly detection at the application layer. In this work a node in a graph represents a service and an edge represents a dependency between services. The edge weights vary with time, and are estimated using measurements. Anomaly detection is conducted from a time sequence of graphs with different link weights. The paper shows that service-anomalies are detected with little information on normal network-behaviors.

Hidden Markov Models are related to Belief Networks, and other probabilistic graphical models, when certain internal states are unobservable. In [57], Yang et al. use a Hidden Markov Model to correlate observation sequences and state transitions so that the most probable intrusion sequences can be predicted. The approach is applied to intrusion detection datasets and shown to reduce false alarm rates effectively.

Belief networks are also related to representations of rules. In [34], Lee et al. describe a data mining framework for building intrusion detection models. The approach first extracts an extensive set of features that describe each network connection or host session using the audit data. Several types of algorithms such as classification, link analysis, and sequence analysis are then used to learn rules that can accurately capture intrusions and normal activities. To facilitate adaptability and extensibility, meta-learning is used as a means to construct an integrated model that can incorporate evidence from multiple models. Experiments show that frequent patterns mined from audit data can serve as reliable anomaly detection models.

11.3.3.1.4 Principal Component Analysis

Principal Component Analysis (PCA) is a dimensionality-reduction approach of mapping a set of data points onto new coordinates. Given a data matrix $\mathbf{Y}_{n \times m}$, $n \geq m$, PCA returns a set of k ($k \leq m$) ortho-normal vectors that defines a k-subspace. The k-subspace in theory characterizes the maximum variance in the original data matrix [31]. The spirit of PCA-based anomaly detection is to separate the normal behavior from anomalies through dimensionality-reduction, which as discussed earlier can also be viewed from a machine learning perspective.

Lakhina et al. pioneered the application of PCA to network-wide anomaly detection [31–33]. The basic idea of using PCA for traffic anomaly detection is that: the k-subspace obtained through PCA corresponds to the normal behavior of the traffic, whereas the remaining $(n - k)$ subspace corresponds to either anomalies or anomalies plus noise. Each new traffic measurement vector is projected on to the normal subspace and the anomalous subspace. Afterwards, different thresholds can be set to classify the traffic measurement as normal or anomalous. The source of the anomalous traffic can then be pinpointed by determining the ingress and egress points of different traffic flows. In the series of works [31–33], Lakhina et al. show that PCA can serve as a powerful method for network-wide anomaly detection with low false alarm rates.

The work in [31] assumes that all the data is processed off-line for anomaly detection, which cannot scale for large networks and may not detect anomalies in real time. This motivates the work in [24], where Huang et al. consider online network anomaly detection based on PCA techniques. In [24], Huang et al. propose detection architectures based on distributed tracking and approximate PCA analysis. The idea is that only limited/partial data is transmitted through the network to a coordinator and anomaly detection is done at the coordinator with limited/partial view of the global states. Furthermore, using stochastic matrix perturbation theory, the authors develop a theoretical formulation on how to trade off quantization due to limiting the frequency and size of data communications against the overall detection accuracy.

In [1], Ahmed et al. consider another online anomaly detection method based on the kernel version of the recursive least squares algorithm. The basic idea is that, given the low dimensionality of network traffic, regions occupied by the traffic features can be represented with a relatively small dictionary of linearly independent feature vectors. In addition, the size of the dictionary is much smaller than the size of the traffic measurements, thus facilitating the implementation of online anomaly detection. It has been demonstrated in [1] that the proposed algorithm can achieve similar detection performance to that in [32], but has the advantages of faster detection time and lower computational complexity.

In [25], Huang et al. propose to use network-wide analysis to improve detection of network disruptions. By studying the BGP update messages across a backbone network, the authors find that nearly 80% of the network disruptions exhibit some level of correlation across multiple routers in the network. Then Huang et al. apply PCA analysis techniques to the BGP updates and successfully detect all node and link failures and two-thirds of the failures on the network periphery. The work in [25] also demonstrates that it is possible to combine the analysis of routing dynamics with static configuration analysis for network fault localization. Thus network-wide analysis techniques could be applied to online anomaly detection. However, as indicated in [25], one remaining open issue is to understand what information best enables network diagnosis and to understand the fundamental tradeoffs between the information available and the corresponding performance.

Although PCA-based approaches have been shown to be an effective method for network anomaly detection, in [43], Ringberg et al. point out the practical difficulty in tuning the parameters of the PCA-based network anomaly detector. In [43], the authors perform a detailed study of the feature time series for detected anomalies in two IP backbone networks (Abilene and Geant). Their investigation shows that the false positive rate of the detector is sensitive to small differences in the number of principal components in the normal subspace and the effectiveness of PCA is sensitive to the level of aggregation of the traffic measurements. Furthermore, a large anomaly may contaminate the normal subspace, thus increasing the false alarm rate. Therefore, there remains one important open issue which is to find PCA-based anomaly detection techniques that are easy to tune and robust in practice.

11.3.3.2 Learning with Additional Information

When additional information is available, other learning scenarios can be considered to learning the mapping $f(\cdot)$. For example, in [22], He and Shayman apply reinforcement learning in proactive network fault detection based on partially observable Markov Decision Processes. This scenario corresponds to the situation that contains reinforcement signals that guide the learning process (see [13] for details).

When labeled anomalous data D_l is available, supervised learning can be used to learn the mapping for anomaly detection. Probe-measurements can be used to provide a source of such data during anomalous events since they gain direct information on network status upon failures/attacks. In [44], Rish et al. use probe measurements to develop a dynamic Bayesian Belief Network for adaptive network failure diagnosis. In [48], Steinder and Seti use simulated failure data to build a Bayesian Belief Network for fault-localization. Recently, in [20], Haffner et al. show that labeled measurements from known applications can be used in supervised learning to extract features for other applications.

In [16], Erjongmanee and Ji use a large number of BGP updates together with a small number of human inputs in semi-supervised learning. The approach resulted in efficient inferences of large-scale network-service disruptions that occurred during Hurricane Katrina.

11.4 Challenges and Deployment Issues

From the above study of the different anomaly detection approaches that are available today, it is clear that a black box anomaly detector may indeed be a utopian dream [53] for two main reasons: (1) the nature of the information that is fed to the anomaly detector could be varied both in format and range, and (2) the nature of the anomaly, its frequency of occurrence and resource constraints clearly dictates the detection method of choice. In [53] the authors propose an initial prototype anomaly detector that transforms the input data into some common format before choosing the appropriate detection methodology. This is clearly an area where further research is an important contribution, especially for deployment in service provider environments where it is necessary to build multiple anomaly detectors to address the myriad monitoring requirements.

Some of the challenges encountered when employing machine learning approaches or statistical approaches is the multiple timescales in which different network events of interest occur. Capturing the characteristics of multi-time-scale anomalies is difficult since the timescale of interest could be different for different anomaly types and also within an anomaly type depending on the network conditions. In [40], Maxion and Tan describe the influence of the regularity of data on the performance of a probabilistic detector. It was observed that false alarms increase as a function of the regularity of the data. The authors also show that the regularity of the data is not merely a function of user type or environments but also differs within user sessions and among users. Designing anomaly detectors that can adapt to the changing nature of input data is an extremely challenging task. Most anomaly detectors employed today are affected by the inherent changes in the structure of the data that is being input to the detector and therefore does affect performance parameters such as probability of hits and misses, and false alarm rates.

Sampling strategies for multi-time-scale events with resource constraints is another area where there is a need for improved scientific understanding that will aid the design of anomaly detection modules. In [37], the authors discovered that most sampling methods employed today introduce significant bias into measured data, thus possibly deteriorating the effectiveness of the anomaly detection. Specifically, Mai et al. use packet traces obtained from a Tier-1 IP-backbone using four sampling methods including random and smart sampling. The sampled data is then used to detect volume anomalies and port scans in different algorithms such as wavelet models and hypothesis testing. Significant bias is discovered in these commonly used sampling techniques, suggesting possible bias in anomaly detection.

Often, the detection of network anomalies requires the correlation of events across multiple correlated input datasets. Using statistical approaches it is challenging to capture the dependencies observed in the raw data. When using streaming algorithms also it is impossible to capture these statistical dependencies unless there are some rule-based engines that can correlate or couple queries from multiple streaming algorithms. Despite the challenges, the representation of these dependencies across multiple input data streams is necessary for the detailed diagnosis of network anomalies.

To sum up, there still remain several open issues to improve the efficiency and feasibility of anomaly detection. One of the most urgent issues is to understand what information can best facilitate network anomaly detection. A second issue is to investigate the fundamental tradeoffs between the amount/complexity of information available and the detection performance, so that computationally efficient real-time anomaly detection is feasible in practice. Another interesting problem is to systematically investigate each anomaly detection method and understand when and in what problem domains these methods perform well.

References

1. Ahmed T., Coates M., Lakhina A.: Multivariate Online Anomaly Detection Using Kernel Recursive Least Squares. Proc. of 26th IEEE International Conference on Computer Communications (2007)
2. Ahmed T., Oreshkin B., Coates M.: Machine Learning Approaches to Network Anomaly Detection. Proc. of International Measurement Conference (2007)
3. Andersen D., Feamster N., Bauer S., Balaskrishman H.: Topology inference from BGP routing dynamics. Proc. SIGCOM Internet Measurements Workshop, Marseille, France (2002)
4. Androulidakis G., Papavassiliou S.: Improving Network Anomaly Detection via Selective Flow-Based Sampling. Communications, IET. Vol. 2, no. 3, 399–409 (2008)
5. Barford P., Kline J., Plonka D., Ron A.: A Signal Analysis of Network Traffic Anomalies. Proc. of the 2nd ACM SIGCOMM Workshop on Internet Measurements, 71–82 (2002)
6. Cormode G., Korn F., Muthukrishnan S. D., Srivastava D.: Finding Hierarchical Heavy Hitters in Data Streams. Proc. of VLDB, Berlin, Germany (2003)
7. Cormode G., Muthukrishan S.: Improved Data Stream Summaries: The Count-Min Sketch and Its Applications. Tech. Rep. 03-20, DIMACS (2003)
8. Cormode G., Johnson T., Korn F., Muthukrishnan S. Spatscheck O., Srivastava D.: Holistic UDAFs at Streaming Speeds. Proc. of ACM SIGMOD, Paris, France (2004)
9. Cormode G., Korn F, Muthukrishnan S., Srivastava D.: Diamond in the Rough: Finding Hierarchical Heavy Hitters in Multi-Dimensional Data. Proc. of ACM SIGMOD, 155–166 (2004)
10. Cormode G., Muthukrishnan S.: What's New: Finding Significant Differences in Network Data Streams. IEEE/ACM Trans. Netw. 13(6):1219–1232 (2005)
11. Cormode G., Korn. F., Muthukrishnan S., Srivastava D: Finding Hierarchical Heavy Hitters in Streaming Data. ACM Trans. Knowledge Discovery from Data 1(4) (2008)
12. Deshpande S., Thottan M., Sikdar B.: Early Detection of BGP Instabilities Resulting From Internet Worm Attacks. Proc. of IEEE Globecom, Dallas, TX (2004)
13. Duda R. O., Hart P., Stork D.: Pattern Classification, 2nd edn. John Willy and Sons (2001)
14. Duffield N.G., Lund C., Thorup M.: Properties and Prediction of Flow Statistics from Sampled Packet Streams. Proc. of ACM SIGCOMM Internet Measurement Workshop (2002)
15. Ensafi R., Dehghanzadeh S., Mohammad R., Akbarzadeh T.: Optimizing Fuzzy K-Means for Network Anomaly Detection Using PSO. Computer Systems and Applications, IEEE/ACS International Conference, 686–693 (2008)
16. Erjongmanee S., Ji C.: Inferring Internet Service Disruptions upon A Natural Disaster. To appear at 2nd International Workshop on Knowledge Discovery from Sensor Data (2008)
17. Estan C., Varghese G.: New Directions in Traffic Measurement and Accounting. Proc. of ACM SIGCOMM, New York, USA (2002)
18. Gao Y., Li Z., Chen Y.: A DoS Resilient Flow-level Intrusion Detection Approach for High-speed Networks, Proc. of IEEE International Conference on Distributed Computing Systems (2006)

19. Gu Y., McCallum A., Towsley D.: Detecting Anomalies in Network Traffic Using Maximum Entropy Estimation. Proc. of IMC (2005)
20. Haffner P., Sen S., Spatscheck O., Wang D.: ACAS: Automated Construction of Application Signatures. Proc. of ACM SIGCOMM Workshop on Mining Network Data, Philadelphia, (2005)
21. Hajji H.: Statistical Analysis of Network Traffic for Adaptive Faults Detection. IEEE Trans. Neural Networks. Vol. 16, no. 5, 1053–1063 (2005)
22. He Q., Shayman M.A.: Using Reinforcement Learning for Pro-Active Network Fault Management. Proc. of Communication Technology. Vol. 1, 515–521 (2000)
23. Hood C.S., Ji C.: Proactive Network Fault Detection. IEEE Tran. Reliability. Vol. 46 3, 333–341 (1997)
24. Huang L., Nguyen X., Garofalakis M., Jordan M.I., Joseph A., Taft N.: Communication-Efficient Online Detection of Network-Wide Anomalies. Proc. of 26th Annual IEEE Conference on Computer Communications (2007)
25. Huang Y., Feamster N., Lakhina A., Xu J.: Diagnosing Network Disruptions with Network-Wide Analysis. Proc. of ACM SIGMETRICS (2007)
26. Ide T., Kashima H.: Eigenspace-Based Anomaly Detection in Computer Systems. Proc. of the tenth ACM SIGKDD international conference on Knowledge discovery and data mining, Seattle, 440–449 (2004)
27. Kim S.S., Reddy A.: Statistical Techniques for Detecting Traffic Anomalies Through Packet Header Data. Accepted by IEEE/ACM Tran. Networking (2008)
28. Kline K., Nam S., Barford P., Plonka D., Ron A.: Traffic Anomaly Detection at Fine Time Scales with Bayes Nets. To appear in the International Conference on Internet Monitoring and Protection (2008)
29. Krishnamurthy B., Sen S., Zhang Y., Chan Y.: Sketch-Based Change Detection: Methods, Evaluation, and Applications. Proc. of ACM SIGCOMM IMC, Florida, USA (2003)
30. Lall S., Sekar V., Ogihara M., Xu J., Zhang H.: Data Streaming Algorithms for Estimating Entropy of Network Traffic. Proc. of ACM SIGMETRICS (2006)
31. Lakhina A., Crovella M., Diot C.: Diagnosing Network-Wide Traffic Anomalies. Proc. of ACM SIGCOMM (2004)
32. Lakhina A., Papagiannaki K., Crovella M., Diot C., Kolaczyk E. N., Taft N.: Structural Analysis of Network Traffic Flows. Proc. of ACM SIGMETRICS (2004)
33. Lakhina A., Crovella M., Diot C.: Mining Anomalies Using Traffic Feature Distributions. Proc. of ACM SIGCOMM, Philadelphia, PA (2005)
34. Lee W., Stolfo F., Mok K.W.: A Data Mining Framework for Building Intrusion Detection Models. Proc. of In IEEE Symposium on Security and Privacy (1999)
35. Lee W., Xiang D.: Information-Theoretic Measures for Anomaly Detection. Proc. of IEEE Symposium on Security and Privacy (2001)
36. Leland W. E., Taqqu M. S., Willinger W., Wilson D. V.: On the Self-Similar Nature of Ethernet Traffic, Proc. of ACM SIGCOMM (1993)
37. Mai J., Chuah C., Sridharan A., Ye T., Zang H.: Is Sampled Data Sufficient for Anomaly Detection? Proc. of 6th ACM SIGCOMM conference on Internet measurement, Rio de Janeriro, Brazil. 165–176 (2006)
38. Mandjes M., Saniee I., Stolyar A. L.: Load Characterization and Anomaly Detection for Voice over IP traffic. IEEE Tran. Neural Networks. Vol.16, no. 5, 1019–1026 (2005)
39. Manku G. S., Motwani R.: Approximate Frequency Counts over Data Streams. Proc. of IEEE VLDB, Hong Kong, China (2002)
40. Maxion R. A., Tan K. M. C.: Benchmarking Anomaly-Based Detection Systems. Proc. International Conference on Dependable Systems and Networks (2000)
41. Miller E. L., Willsky A. S.: Multiscale, Statistical Anomaly Detection Analysis and Algorithms for Linearized Inverse Scattering Problems. Multidimensional Systems and Signal Processing. Vol. 8, 151–184 (1997)
42. Ricciato F., Fleischer W.: Bottleneck Detection via Aggregate Rate Analysis: A Real Case in a 3G Network. Proc. IEEE/IFIP NOMS (2004)

43. Ringberg H., Soule A., Rexford J., Diot C.: Sensitivity of PCA for Traffic Anomaly Detection. Proc. of ACM SIGMETRICS (2007)
44. Rish I., Brodie M., Sheng M., Odintsova N., Beygelzimer A., Grabarnik G., Hernandez K.: Adaptive Diagnosis in Distributed Systems. IEEE Tran. Neural Networks. Vol. 16, No. 5, 1088–1109 (2005)
45. Schweller R., Gupta A., Parsons E., Chen Y.: Reversible Sketches for Efficient and Accurate Change Detection over Network Data Streams. Proc. of IMC, Italy (2004)
46. Schweller R., Li Z., Chen Y., Gao Y., Gupta A., Zhang Y., Dinda P., Kao M., Memik G.: Reverse hashing for High-Speed Network Monitoring: Algorithms, Evaluation, and Applications. Proc. of IEEE INFOCOM (2006)
47. Soule A., Salamatian K., Taft N.: Combining Filtering and Statistical Methods for Anomaly Detection. Proc. of IMC Workshop (2005)
48. Steinder M., Sethi A.S.: Probabilistic Fault Localization in Communication Systems Using Belief Networks. IEEE/ACM Trans. Networking. Vol. 12, No. 5, 809–822 (2004)
49. Tavallaee M., Lu W., Iqbal S. A., Ghorbani A.: A Novel Covariance Matrix Based Approach for Detecting Network Anomalies. Communication Networks and Services Research Conference (2008)
50. Thottan M., Ji C.: Anomaly Detection in IP Networks. IEEE Trans. Signal Processing, Special Issue of Signal Processing in Networking, Vol. 51, No. 8, 2191–2204 (2003)
51. Thottan M., Ji C.: Proactive Anomaly Detection Using Distributed Intelligent Agents. IEEE Network. Vol. 12, no. 5, 21–27 (1998)
52. Venkataraman S., Song D., Gibbons P., Blum A.: New Streaming Algorithms for Fast Detection of Superspreaders. Proc. of Network and Distributed Systems Security Symposium (2005)
53. Venkataraman S., Caballero J., Song D., Blum A., Yates J.: Black-box Anomaly Detection: Is it Utopian?" Proc. of the Fifth Workshop on Hot Topics in Networking (HotNets-V), Irvine, CA (2006)
54. Xie Y., Kim H.A., O'Hallaron D. R., Reiter M. K., Zhang H.: Seurat: A Pointillist Approach to Anomaly Detection. Proc. of the International Symposium on Recent Advances in Intrusion Detection (RAID) (2004)
55. Wang H., Zhang D., Shin K. G.: Detecting SYN flooding attacks. Proc. of IEEE INFOCOM (2002)
56. Xu J.: Tutorial on Network Data Streaming. SIGMETRICS (2007)
57. Yang Y., Deng F., Yang H.: An Unsupervised Anomaly Detection Approach using Subtractive Clustering and Hidden Markov Model. Communications and Networking in China. 313–316 (2007)
58. Yeung D. S., Jin S., Wang X.: Covariance-Matrix Modeling and Detecting Various Flooding Attacks. IEEE Tran. Systems, Man and Cybernetics, Part A, vol. 37, no. 2, 157–169 (2007)
59. Zhang Y., Singh S., Sen S., Duffield N., Lund C.: Online Identification of Hierarchical Heavy Hitters: Algorithms, Evaluation and Applications. Proc. of ACM SIGCOMM conference on Internet measurement. 101–114 (2004)
60. Zhang J., Rexford J., Feigenbaum J.: Learning-Based Anomaly Detection in BGP Updates. Proc. of ACM SIGCOMM MineNet workshop (2005)
61. Zhang Y., Ge Z., Greenberg A., Roughan M.: Network Anomography. Proc. of ACM/USENIX Internet Measurement Conference (2005)

Chapter 12
Model-Based Anomaly Detection for a Transparent Optical Transmission System

Thomas Bengtsson, Todd Salamon, Tin Kam Ho, and Christopher A. White

Abstract In this chapter, we present an approach for anomaly detection at the physical layer of networks where detailed knowledge about the devices and their operations is available. The approach combines physics-based process models with observational data models to characterize the uncertainties and derive the alarm decision rules. We formulate and apply three different methods based on this approach for a well-defined problem in optical network monitoring that features many typical challenges for this methodology. Specifically, we address the problem of monitoring optically transparent transmission systems that use dynamically controlled Raman amplification systems. We use models of amplifier physics together with statistical estimation to derive alarm decision rules and use these rules to automatically discriminate between measurement errors, anomalous losses, and pump failures. Our approach has led to an efficient tool for systematically detecting anomalies in the system behavior of a deployed network, where pro-active measures to address such anomalies are key to preventing unnecessary disturbances to the system's continuous operation.

12.1 Introduction

Transparent optical networks offer a number of advantages over more traditional networks that rely on optical–electrical–optical (OEO) conversion in the backbone of the network [8]. These advantages include improved operations, better scalability, smaller footprint, and reduced cost [9] associated with the elimination of OEO conversion sites. However, minimizing OEO conversion sites also reduces the ability to isolate degradations and failures facilitated by detailed knowledge of the quality of the electronic (e.g., digital) signal at these locations [2, 9]. In this chapter, we discuss several model-based approaches to anomaly detection that facilitate fault

T. Bengtsson, T. Salamon, T.K. Ho (✉), and C.A. White
Bell Laboratories, Alcatel-Lucent, Murray Hill, NJ 07974
e-mail: Bengtsson.Thomas@gene.com; Todd.Salamon@alcatel-lucent.com;
Tin-Ho@alcatel-lucent.com; Chris.White@alcatel-lucent.com

G. Cormode and M. Thottan (eds.), *Algorithms for Next Generation Networks*,
Computer Communications and Networks, DOI 10.1007/978-1-84882-765-3_12,
© Springer-Verlag London Limited 2010

localization and characterization in a transparent optical network. This represents one methodology for building intelligence into the transport layer and extending fault management and Quality-of-Service (QoS) monitoring into the optical domain.

Anomaly detection in networks is often based on a characterization of expected behavior using manually designed rules or empirical models inferred from large quantities of observational data. These can be the only feasible approaches for systems featuring highly complex interactions of many components and algorithms that cannot be described analytically. At the physical layer, however, there are situations where detailed understanding and explicit models of the essential processes are available. In these cases, interesting methods can be developed using such process models. This study gives a specific example of what can be done using a model of the physics that governs the critical behavior of a network system.

The study is to build a monitoring and diagnostic tool for a large-scale, highly transparent optical network using dense wavelength division multiplexing (DWDM) [8]. The network uses primarily Raman amplification technology [7, 10, 13] for its substantial advantages in capacity and reach. The network is designed with highly automated control mechanisms that can adapt to and compensate for deviations from ideal operating conditions. Further reduction in deployment and operational costs can be achieved by providing capabilities for automatic real-time fault analysis and diagnostics. Detailed understanding of normal and anomalous system states also allows for proactive fault detection to avoid serious and large-scale failures. Such diagnostic capabilities can also provide significant product differentiation.

A network that uses Raman amplification can achieve high transparency and avoid expensive regeneration through many spans. However, this also means that detailed visibility of the signal behavior is not available between regeneration points. Many elaborate monitoring approaches [9], such as methods for checking bit error rates, are not applicable for the transparent spans. Despite this, detailed understanding of the internal states of the hardware devices and software settings is required to ensure adequate characterization of network health. Process models that encapsulate such understanding can thus offer an important advantage.

For the network of our concern, an important health indicator is the proper levels of signal powers and the corresponding levels of launched pump powers in the Raman amplifiers. Therefore our developments focus on detecting performance anomalies from near-real-time measurements of signal and pump powers taken along a specific network link. Although the diagnostic procedures are tailored to the network's system design, the methodology we followed, namely, a model-based approach combined with statistical estimation, is applicable to similar networks where a clear understanding and a detailed representation of the underlying data generation process are available.

We formulate the diagnostic problem as one of statistical anomaly detection. In a classical hypothesis testing framework, performance anomalies are detected by comparing field measurements to known baseline (i.e., null) distributions that describe the behavior of the measurements under normal variations. We construct the baseline distributions using a set of models that characterize the underlying processes, along with assumptions and observations of measurement noise. The process models that are available to us include a mathematical model that describes the transmission physics, and an algorithmic model that represents the interactions of the component devices and the control mechanisms. The models are integrated in a simulator [5] that predicts optimized signal and pump powers as would be determined by the real system given the conditions upstream to the network link.

We describe three ways for using these models to construct baseline distributions and derive the decision rules. Our first method uses large-scale virtual experiments to sample from the space of transmission link configurations and operating conditions and generate the distribution of values of a performance metric. The second method uses per-span, detailed simulations to match the exact operating conditions and generate the expected signal gain for comparison with observations. The last method uses a simplified mathematical model of the transmission physics together with a noise model to analytically derive a baseline distribution.

The discussion begins with a brief introduction to the Raman amplification physics. This is followed by a description of the diagnostic tool and data collection procedures along with a presentation of the three methods and the challenges involved. We conclude with suggestions for various ways such methods can be combined, and comments on the advantages of the model-based approach for anomaly detection.

12.2 Background on Raman-Amplified Transmission Systems

Raman amplification [7, 10, 13] uses the transmission (outside plant) fiber as the amplification medium. High-powered pumps can be coupled to the transmission fiber in both the forward (co-propagating) and backward (counter-propagating) directions (Figure 12.1). Energy from the pumps is transferred to lower-frequency signal channels following a characteristic gain function (Figure 12.2). The technology offers significant benefits for increasing network transparency due to improved

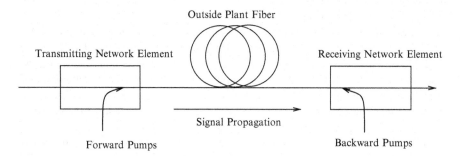

Fig. 12.1 Schematic diagram of a Raman amplifier using both forward and backward pumping

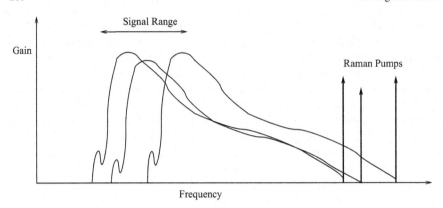

Fig. 12.2 Schematic diagram of Raman gain. Variable settings of pump levels are associated with variable gain at down-shifted frequencies. Pump levels are controlled to achieve a flat gain across the signal frequencies

noise characteristics associated with distributed amplification within the fiber span and the ability to provide gain flattening (ripple control) through the use of multiple Raman amplifier pumps (Figure 12.2).

To effectively assess the health of a Raman amplification system, measurements of signal and pump powers at different physical locations must be jointly collected and analyzed. Joint analysis of spatially non-local measurements can also provide better understanding of the propagation of potentially anomalous events. As mentioned, this can be especially useful when networks become more transparent, where greater reach, enhanced switching, and increased automation may result in anomalous effects which propagate far before being detected and corrected. As an example, consider the case of an amplifier with a hardware or software anomaly that results in undesirable noise amplification in an unused portion of the signal spectrum. If uncorrected, this can result in preferential amplification of the noise relative to the signals at each subsequent downstream amplifier node, and may eventually lead to a loss of signal several nodes away from the original fault. One key challenge in the analysis of such complex, interconnected networks is to break the system into spatially independent components.

In the remainder of this chapter we describe a novel, model-based approach for anomaly detection and monitoring within Raman-amplified systems. The proposed methodology assesses if the signal gain across a fiber span is consistent with the amplification level of the pumps being input to the span. Our approach combines models of the Raman gain physics with statistical estimation, and results in several methods that allow precise statements to be made regarding the state of the network, including detection of anomalous conditions. The methods focus on detecting network behavior that is inconsistent with Raman physics, and hence may capture more complex anomalies not readily recognized by an engineering-rule-based approach.

12.3 Establishing Baseline Distributions for Alarm Decision Rules

A model-based approach to anomaly detection requires an operational mathematical definition of network anomaly. Since the network spans many layers of both spatial and temporal variability, any definition of anomaly should be broad enough to capture errors at a wide range of scales. To be useful, the anomaly measure and its associated distribution under normal operating conditions must be computable in real time. This requires quick access to measurements and to relevant system information needed to predict the available measurements. We note that any notion of real time will be related to a specific network time- (and space) scale, and that the network operates across many scales. For instance, the Raman pump response times are $O(10^{-6}$ s) and local failures thus occur in the micro-second range, while a spectral analyzer may take up to $O(10^{-1}$ s) to produce a power spectral evaluation. Longer timescales are related to continent-wide signal propagation, which crosses the continental United States in $O(1$ s), as well as to network control algorithms which are $O(10^2$ s). A challenge in designing the monitoring tool is to select the appropriate scale to work with. For example, in our analysis, we have assumed that the system has reached a quasi-steady state when all the pumps are optimized, and that the signal has responded to the pump settings and remains stable over the period of data collection.

In a statistical anomaly detection framework, observations are matched with predictions and the differences are compared to a baseline (null) distribution, which depends on the underlying physical model and its parameters. To determine if a specific observation constitutes an anomaly, the residual difference between the observation and its associated prediction is compared to the null-distribution, and, if the residual falls in the tail of the distribution, the observation is classified as an anomaly. To make use of this paradigm for anomaly detection in our context, we need to be able to calculate the predicted (expected) observation. That is, with $E_c(\cdot)$ denoting expectation taken with respect to the conditional distribution of the observation given all a priori available information, we seek to calculate the residual measurement

$$residual = observation - E_c(observation). \tag{12.1}$$

Evaluating this difference requires knowledge of both the *a priori* conditional information set and the conditional probability distribution. In classical control theory (e.g., Kalman filter), the distribution of the residual measure in (12.1) can often be derived analytically from first principles, and can thus be used directly to determine if an observation is congruent with the past and the underlying physical system. However, in our setting, because the network operates across several physical and software layers, explicit knowledge of both the relevant information set and the conditional probability distribution represents a substantial challenge.

One way to estimate the variability for a chosen anomaly measure is to generate the range of values using simulation, and then empirically model the distribution of the measure using statistical techniques. In the remainder of this section, we describe one such analysis that focuses on a particular measure known as the "ripple" of the gain profile.

12.3.1 The Ripple Measure as a Performance Metric

With y_i and $y_i^\star$ being the observed and targeted channel powers at frequency λ_i, we define the observed ripple at a spatial location s, time t, and span configuration θ by

$$obs_{ripple}(s,t,\theta) = max_i\{y(s,t,\theta;i) - y^\star(s,t,\theta;i)\} - min_i\{y(s,t,\theta;i) - y^\star(s,t,\theta;i)\}. \tag{12.2}$$

The parameter θ represents a set of system parameters that fully define the configuration of the fiber span, including the fiber type, fiber length, connector losses, pump specifications, channel loading, etc. For channels with a flat amplification target, i.e., $y_i^\star \equiv y^\star, \forall i$, the observed ripple is equivalent to the range of channel powers, i.e.,

$$obs_{ripple}(s,t,\theta) = max_i\{y(s,t,\theta;i)\} - min_i\{y(s,t,\theta;i)\}.$$

To diagnose the system based on the observed ripple, we need to understand the distribution of $obs_{ripple}(s,t,\theta)$ for given s,t, and θ. As discussed previously, this baseline may be determined empirically by observing the system when the network is operating according to specification. However, to obtain the most precise decision rule, the baseline distribution should be derived given the specific network settings at spatial location s, time t, and with configuration θ. Hence, we seek a residual measure of the form (12.1), i.e.,

$$e_{ripple}(s,t,\theta) = obs_{ripple}(s,t,\theta) - pred_{ripple}(s,t,\theta), \tag{12.3}$$

where $pred_{ripple}(s,t,\theta)$ represents the predicted/expected ripple associated with $E_c(\cdot)$.

12.3.1.1 Prediction of Ripple via Simulation

One approach to determining the predicted ripple is by using a simulator[5]. To this end, define $\Psi(s,t,\theta)$ to be a set of upstream network conditions/setting associated with the measurement $obs_{ripple}(s,t,\theta)$. We have

$$pred_{ripple}(s,t,\theta) = E(obs_{ripple}(s,t,\theta)|\Psi(s,t,\theta)),$$

which represents the conditional expectation (i.e., the second term on the right-hand side) in (12.1).

Based on the conditions in $\Psi(s,t,\theta)$, we seek the baseline of $obs_{ripple}(s,t,\theta)$, or, more precisely, the probability density function $p(obs_{ripple}(s,t,\theta)|\Psi(s,t,\theta))$. Assuming an accurate simulator is available, we may approximate the distribution of $obs_{ripple}(s,t,\theta)$ as follows: for a given $\Psi(s,t,\theta)$, and a set of possible values for the remaining system parameters ς that may affect the observation, calculate $obs_{ripple}(s,t,\theta)$. Repeated simulations covering all variability in ς under the same $\Psi(s,t,\theta)$ would give the baseline distribution $p(obs_{ripple}(s,t,\theta)|\Psi(s,t,\theta))$. Then, referring to $p(obs_{ripple}(s,t,\theta)|\Psi(s,t,\theta))$, one can obtain the probability that an observed $obs_{ripple}(s,t,\theta)$ can occur under normal operating conditions. An exceptionally small value of the probability would signify an anomaly.

12.3.2 Issues in Using Simulation to Generate Null Distributions

A few issues are critical in using simulation to obtain a baseline distribution suitable for deriving decision rules regarding the network health:

1. Does the simulator "mimic" the network sufficiently close to warrant matching $obs_{ripple}(s,t,\theta)$ with $pred_{ripple}(s,t,\theta)$? Can we validate the "machine" approximation in a step prior to matching?
2. Can we easily define and obtain $\Psi(s,t,\theta)$?
3. How do we model the null-distribution of $obs_{ripple}(s,t,\theta)$?

As it turns out, signal powers in a concatenation of multiple Raman-amplified spans depend only on the conditions occurring at the entrance of and locally in the span. Once the input spectrum to the current span is fully specified, variations in upstream conditions are irrelevant. Thus, in our context, we are dealing with a one-step Markov process. The variations that remain to be studied then include variations in the input spectrum, plus the differences in the configuration parameters θ.

In the next section, we describe a designed experiment where we generate (simulate) the null-distribution of the "ripple" metric for one span by varying several key configuration parameters θ that are most relevant, assuming a fixed input spectrum. (A complete description of the distribution can be obtained by repeating the experiment over another set of parameters ς, here representing the upstream conditions that may cause changes in the input spectrum.)

12.3.3 Experimental Design

We present an analysis of variance (ANOVA) study that yields a compact representation of the response surface $E_c(obs_{ripple})$, and an approximation of the associated conditional distribution. In this experiment we analyze the effects of four independent variables from the set θ on the ripple metric: connector loss, channel loading, initial co-pump setting (for the forward, or co-propagating pumps), and fiber length. The reader is referred to [12] for a detailed description of the ANOVA techniques described herein.

A set of $n = 720$ ripple measurements are observed from simulation across these four variables. The connector losses and channel loadings are treated as categorical variables with two factor levels each [12]. The connector loss levels are "typical" and "worst case", and the levels of channel loading are 17 and 128 channels. The co-pump setting is varied across 20 levels including zero mW and then increments in 10 from 40 to 220 mW. The fiber length is varied across 9 levels from 40 to 120 km. The experimental design produces a mesh with $2 \times 2 \times 20 \times 9 = 720$ measurement nodes. In the analysis, both co-pump setting and fiber length are treated as quantitative variables, producing a 2×2 ANOVA design with two quantitative regressors at each of the four experimental levels.

Let α_i ($i = 1, 2$) and β_j ($j = 1, 2$) denote the (fixed) main effects of loss and loading at levels i and j, respectively, and let ξ and γ be the regression coefficients for co-pump setting and fiber length, respectively. With p and ℓ representing pump setting and fiber length, and with Y_{ijk}^{ripple} denoting the kth ripple measurement at levels i and j, we write the main-effects-only model as

$$Y_{ijk}^{ripple} = \mu + \alpha_i + \beta_j + \xi p + \gamma \ell + \epsilon_{ijk}, \tag{12.4}$$

where μ is an overall mean effect and ϵ_{ijk} corresponds to unmodeled effects and represents the discrepancy between the regression function and the data.

A regression model including higher-order interaction terms is also used to represent the data. With notation given in Tables 12.1 and 12.2, the full three-way interaction model is given by

$$Y_{ijk}^{ripple} = \mu + \alpha_i + \beta_j + \xi p + \gamma \ell \tag{12.5}$$

$$+ (\alpha\beta)_{ij} + (\alpha\xi)_i p + (\alpha\gamma)_i \ell + (\beta\xi)_j p + (\beta\gamma)_j \ell + (\xi\gamma) p\ell + \xi_Q p^2 + \gamma_Q \ell^2 + \tag{12.6}$$

$$+ (\alpha\beta\xi)_{ij} p + (\alpha\beta\gamma)_{ij} \ell + (\alpha\xi\gamma)_i p\ell + (\beta\xi\gamma)_j p\ell \tag{12.7}$$

$$+ (\alpha\xi_Q)_i p^2 + (\beta\xi_Q)_j p^2 + (\xi_Q\gamma) p^2\ell + (\alpha\gamma_Q)_i \ell^2 + (\beta\gamma_Q)_j \ell^2 + (\xi\gamma_Q) p\ell^2 + \xi_C p^3 + \gamma_C \ell^3 \tag{12.8}$$

$$+ \epsilon_{ijk}.$$

In the above equation (12.5) represents the main effects, (12.6) represents the two-way interactions, and (12.7) and (12.8) models all three-way interactions.

Table 12.1 Second-order interactions

Parameter	Interaction
$(\alpha\beta)_{ij}$	Connector loss and channel loading
$(\alpha\xi)_i$	Connector loss and co-pump setting
$(\alpha\gamma)_i$	Connector loss and fiber length
$(\beta\xi)_j$	Channel loading and co-pump setting
$(\beta\gamma)_j$	Channel loading and fiber length
$(\xi\gamma)$	Co-pump setting and fiber length
ξ_Q	Co-pump setting, quadratic
γ_Q	Fiber length, quadratic

Table 12.2 Third-order interactions

Parameter	Interaction
$(\alpha\beta\xi)_{ij}$	Connector loss, channel loading & co-pump setting
$(\alpha\beta\gamma)_{ij}$	Connector loss, channel loading & fiber length
$(\alpha\xi\gamma)_i$	Connector loss, co-pump setting & fiber length
$(\beta\xi\gamma)_j$	Channel loading, co-pump setting & fiber length
$(\alpha\xi_Q)_i$	Connector loss & co-pump setting (quadratic)
$(\beta\xi_Q)_j$	Channel loading & co-pump setting (quadratic)
$(\xi_Q\gamma)$	Co-pump setting (quadratic) & fiber length
$(\alpha\gamma_Q)_i$	Connector loss & fiber length (quadratic)
$(\beta\gamma_Q)_j$	Channel loading & fiber length (quadratic)
$(\xi\gamma_Q)$	Co-pump setting & fiber length (quadratic)
ξ_C	Co-pump setting (cubic)
γ_C	Fiber length (cubic)

Based on the experimental design and the above model, we next analyze data from simulation and provide graphical displays of the experimental response surface as well as the associated ANOVA results.

12.3.4 Simulation Results & ANOVA

Using the FROG/RATS simulator [5], we model several SSMF (standard single-mode fiber) spans of the lengths specified above. Each span also includes the connector losses and is loaded with the number of channels as specified above. The signal power is amplified by both forward and backward Raman pumping, with the forward (co-)pumps fixed at the above-specified levels. An additional stage of backward pumping is applied at a dispersion compensating module (DCM) that follows the transmission fiber. The simulator includes a control module that determines the optimal setting of the backward Raman pumps to provide a flat gain within a small tolerance around the power target [4, 5]. The ripple is measured at the endpoint of the dispersion compensating module, and is determined after all the pump settings are optimized for each configuration and channel load.

In Figure 12.3 the measured ripple is shown as a histogram and in Figure 12.4 as box-plots. The measured ripple distribution has a mean and standard deviation of 1.35 and 1.61, respectively, and a median value of 0.59. The first and third quartiles are 0.46 and 1.33. The histogram shown in Figure 12.3 depicts a right-skewed distribution for the ripple measurements. It should be noted that the depicted density is a marginal distribution estimate, where the data is collapsed across all experimental conditions. In principle, the marginal distribution can be used as a baseline distribution for anomaly detection. If this were the case, the cutoff point would be around 6.0 dB, which corresponds to the 95th quantile of the empirical, marginal distribution. Thus, we would classify an observed ripple as anomalous whenever the ripple exceeds 6.0 dB. This value does, however, represent a rather large ripple, and we seek a more precise value as a function of the parameters in θ. Indeed, as indicated

Fig. 12.3 Histogram of DCM power ripple (dB) calculated based on a flat signal target

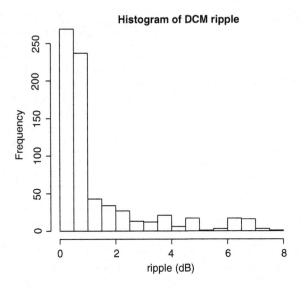

Fig. 12.4 Box-plot of ripple, split by connector loss (typical, worst case) and channel loading (17, 128 channels)

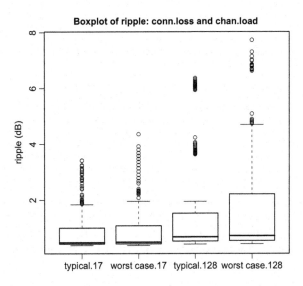

by the box-plots in Figure 12.4, the distribution of ripple measurements is clearly dependent on the experimental conditions. Additional descriptive statistics of each configuration and channel load are shown in Table 12.3. Again, as can be seen in the table, the 95th quantile is highly dependent on the experimental conditions, with values ranging from 2.91 to 6.81 dB. This indicates that the cutoff point for excess ripple should be conditional on θ.

Figures 12.5 and 12.6 show the mean ripple levels for the two-factor variables. As seen in Figure 12.5, the worst-case connector loss scenario produces only slightly higher ripples than the typical case, while a higher channel loading clearly produces

Table 12.3 Minimum, maximum, and sample quantiles of ripple split by channel loading and loss

Cell	Min.	5%	First quartile	Median	Mean	Third quartile	95%	Max.
17:typical	0.38	0.40	0.43	0.47	0.91	0.99	2.91	3.40
17:worst case	0.38	0.40	0.43	0.50	0.93	1.10	3.03	4.40
128:typical	0.42	0.43	0.53	0.68	1.60	1.50	6.15	6.40
128:worst case	0.43	0.44	0.55	0.72	1.90	2.20	6.81	7.70

Fig. 12.5 Mean level plot of ripple for connection loss and channel loading

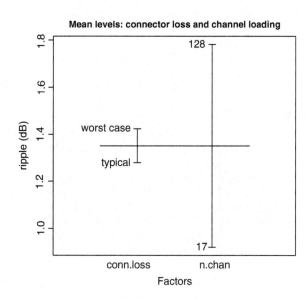

Fig. 12.6 Interaction plot for connection loss crossed with channel loading

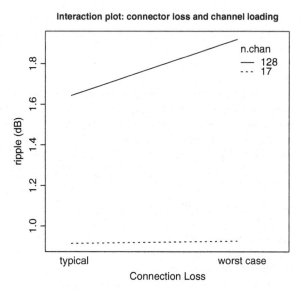

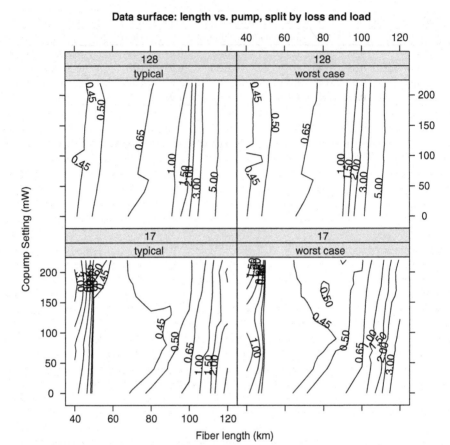

Fig. 12.7 Contour plot of ripple as a function of co-pump setting, fiber length, channel loading, and connector losses

larger ripples. Figure 12.6 depicts the mean levels for the four experimental conditions, and the near parallel lines indicate a lack of substantial interaction between connection loss and channel loading. Figure 12.7 further delineates the data using a contour plot of the (simulated) ripple surface across all combinations of the independent variables. As can be seen, the main effect due to channel load is clearly visible as a monotone increase in ripple from 17 to 128 channels. Moreover, in each of the four subplots, the surface appear bowl-shaped that higher-order interactions involving fiber length are present.

Although Figures 12.3–12.6 give a good indication of which factors are most crucial in determining ripple level, we now delineate more formally using ANOVA which factors and combinations (interactions) of independent variables contribute to the variability in ripple measurements.

To delineate which factors contribute most significantly to ripple using ANOVA, we apply a log transformation to the data. This transformation is necessary because

Table 12.4 ANOVA table for the reduced model. The overall F-statistic for this model is 1,157 on 7 numerator and 712 denominator degrees of freedom (p-value: < 2.2e-16). The residual standard error for the model is 0.2405 and the adjusted R-squared value is 0.918

Source, parameter	Df	Sum Sq	Mean Sq	F value	Pr($>F$)
Channel loading, β_j	1	32.191	32.191	556.457	<2.2e-16
Fiber length, γ	1	206.179	206.179	3564.061	<2.2e-16
Fiber length^2, γ_Q	1	146.512	146.512	2532.649	<2.2e-16
Connector loss*fiber length, $(\alpha\gamma)_i$	1	1.936	1.936	33.467	1.086e-08
Channel loading*fiber length, $(\beta\gamma)_j$	1	72.040	72.040	1245.297	<2.2e-16
Connector loss*fiber length, $(\xi\gamma)$	1	1.607	1.607	27.776	1.808e-07
Channel loading*fiber length^2, $(\beta\gamma_Q)_j$	1	8.009	8.009	138.439	< 2.2e-16
Residuals	712	41.189	0.058		

the data distribution is right-skewed (cf., Figure 12.4), and the transformation serves to approximately stabilize the variance across experimental conditions. Thus, Y_{ijk}^{ripple} represents the i, j, k:th ripple measurement in log scale, and the ANOVA study is performed on the transformed data. For the full model described by (12.5)–(12.8), which includes all main and interaction effects, the F-statistic equals 410.6 with 20 numerator and 699 denominator degrees of freedom (p-value $< 2.2e - 16$). Although the model is highly significant, not all terms in the full model are statistically significant. Table 12.4 shows a reduced model where only highly significant factors are retained. The reduced model fits the data well, and has an adjusted R^2 of 0.918.

As the ANOVA sums-of-squares represent independent sources of variation (since the experimental design is orthogonal), the relative importance of the retained factors can be obtained by considering the magnitude of the F-values in column 5. Inspection of the table shows that two variables, namely, fiber length and channel load, contribute most significantly to the variability in ripple. The estimated response surface (in log scale) is given in the upper panel of Figure 12.8.

12.3.5   Derivation of Alarm Decision Rules

The fitted log-surface gives a visualization of how the expected ripple varies smoothly across θ. From the fitted surface, along with an estimate of the average magnitude of the residual term, $\hat{\sigma} = 0.2405$ (cf., caption of Table 12.4), a simple anomaly detection rule for excess ripple is based on determining if $\log(obs_{ripple})$ is greater than the estimated log-surface plus $3 * \hat{\sigma}$. Equivalently, we may consider this cutoff point in the data scale. This quantity is depicted in the data scale in the lower panel of Figure 12.8. Thus, any ripple exceeding this surface is deemed anomalous.

We note that this classification rule is approximate, and is given as an example to illustrate our first anomaly detection method. More generally, we comment that the empirical distribution of residuals within each experimental condition can be used to define more exact cutoff points. When the response surface turns out to be less regular, one may consider using non-parametric models.

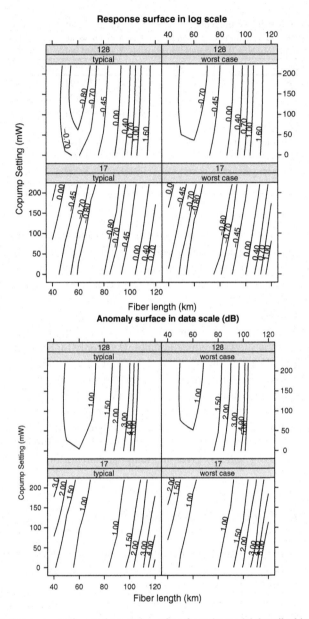

Fig. 12.8 Fitted response surface and anomaly surface from the model described in Table 12.4

The example illustrates that using a simulator we can compute the expected ripple measures as a function of a variety of system parameters, and that statistical models of the response surfaces can give simplified rules to guide anomaly detection in real time. These include rules on the expected values together with measures of variability under different operational configurations. This adds significant understanding to the nominal values estimated from the engineering design.

To tailor such an analysis to the design of a particular system, one may use only a subset of values for the concerned parameters that are optimized for the system. The simulation may be extended to include a larger set of potential variability, such as variations in the input spectrum at the entrance to the span, or changes in the initial pump configurations that may lead to different optimized settings.

Batch simulations are useful for generating baseline distributions and gross decision rules. While this can provide the first level of alarms for severe deviations from normality, subtle differences between expected and observed performances could be missed if the deviations fall within the expected range of variability. To provide detailed diagnostic information on a per-span basis, we explore two other uses of the physics-based models that can provide other characterizations of the system behavior [6]. We will refer to these two methods as: (i) forward simulation using the **detailed physical model**, which includes, in addition, signal–signal Raman amplification, spontaneous Raman amplification (noise), Rayleigh back-scattering, connector loss effects, and direct correlation with launch pump powers; and (ii) back projection using the **R-Beta model**, which approximates the span behavior as comprising two dominant physical effects, namely fiber attenuation and pump-signal Raman amplification. The following sections describe the two methods in detail.

12.4   Anomaly Detection Using the Detailed Physical Model

In this section, we present the use of a detailed model that describes the interaction of pump and signal powers in a Raman amplifier as depicted in Figures 12.1 and 12.2. We first give the mathematical description of the physical effects. This is followed by the device model of a Raman repeater node that contains additional loss elements. The losses are an important concern in calibrating the model predictions (Section 12.4.1). We then describe the use of calibrated predictions in detecting poor fit to observed gain profile (Section 12.4.2), premature signal degradation, and pump failure (Section 12.4.3).

The following equation [3] represents a more comprehensive model for power propagation on a Raman-amplified fiber span of length L that includes signal–signal pumping, noise generation and Rayleigh back-scattering effects:

$$\frac{\partial \rho^+(z, v)}{\partial z} = -\alpha(v)\rho^+(z, v) + \gamma(v)\rho^-(z, v) - 4hv\rho^+(z, v)\int_\zeta b_T(v, \zeta)d\zeta \quad (12.9)$$

$$+ 2hv\int_\zeta b_T(v, \zeta)[\rho^+(z, \xi) + \rho^-(z, \xi)]d\zeta$$

$$+ \rho^+(z, v)\int_\zeta a(v, \zeta)[\rho^+(z, \xi) + \rho^-(z, \xi)]d\xi,$$

where

$$a(v, \zeta) := \begin{cases} g(v, \zeta) & \text{if } \zeta \geq v, \\ -\dfrac{v}{\zeta} g(\zeta, v) & \text{if } \zeta < v, \end{cases}$$

$$b_T(v, \zeta) := \begin{cases} (1 + n_T(v, \zeta)) g(v, \zeta) & \text{if } \zeta \geq v, \\ n_T(v, \zeta) g(\zeta, v) & \text{if } \zeta < v, \end{cases}$$

$$n_T(v, \zeta) := \frac{1}{\exp(h |v - \zeta| / (k_B T)) - 1}.$$

Here, $\rho^{(+/-)}(z, v)$ represents the power spectral density at fiber position z and frequency v propagating in the $(+/-)$ forward/backward direction, $\alpha(v)$ is the fiber attenuation coefficient, $\gamma(v)$ is the Rayleigh back-scattering coefficient, $g(v, \zeta)$ is the Raman gain for a pump at frequency ζ and a signal at v, h is Planck's constant, k_B is Boltzmann's constant, and T is the absolute temperature. Equation 12.9 describes the power propagation on a Raman fiber span. Note that the power $p(z, v_i)$ at position z and in a signal band located at frequency v_i and with channel width dv_i is given by

$$p(z, v_i) = \int_{v_i - dv_i/2}^{v_i + dv_i/2} \rho(z, v) dv. \tag{12.10}$$

For further descriptions of the relevant physical effects, readers are referred to [1, 11, 14].

Equation 12.9 is completed by specifying launch conditions for the forward-propagating signals and co-pumps and the backward-propagating counter-pumps, i.e., $\rho^+(0, v)$ and $\rho^-(L, v)$. The equations are solved by using a Galerkin-type discretization in the frequency space and by use of higher-order predictor–corrector methods in physical space [5].

The propagation model for a Raman repeater node is given in Figure 12.9, and includes the S-Office and R-Office connector losses Δ^S, Δ^R. The office losses

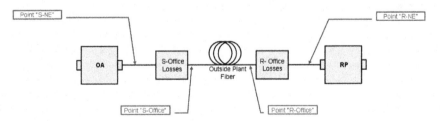

Fig. 12.9 Diagram of elements comprising a Raman repeater node. The direction of signal propagation is from left to right in the diagram

are constant values given in dB that degrade the power spectra going through the connector, i.e., $\rho_{out}^{(+/-)}(v) = \rho_{in}^{(+/-)}(v)10^{-\frac{A}{10}}$.

The detailed physical model is used to produce anomaly alarms in two ways: (i) measured signal powers at $z = 0$ and pump powers at both $z = 0$ and $z = L$ are used to predict signal powers at $z = L$, and the predicted values are then compared to measured signal powers at $z = L$; and (ii) a maximum likelihood procedure is used to estimate the connector losses (Δ^S, Δ^R), which are compared to nominal or provisioned values. Discrepancies observed in either (i) or (ii) indicate anomalies.

12.4.1   Calibration Procedure for Detailed Physical Model

The key physical parameters controlling the Raman span behavior are as follows: the attenuation coefficient $\alpha(v)$, the Raman gain coefficient $g(v, \zeta)$, the fiber length L, and the connector losses Δ^S, Δ^R. Values for L, $\alpha(v)$ and total connector loss $(\Delta^S + \Delta^R)$ can be estimated from OTDR (Optical Time Domain Reflectometry) and total span loss measurements, while nominal values for the Raman gain coefficient $g(v, \zeta)$ are typically used.

To illustrate the important role that connector loss estimation plays in fitting field data, the root-mean-squared error (RMSE) in the measured versus simulated output signal powers is plotted in Figure 12.10. The illustrated case has 15 channels propagating on a 103.93 km span of LEAF fiber with 1 forward pump and 5 backward pumps. Note that there is a continuous range of possible values for the connector loss, represented by the dark contours near the diagonal, where the simulated and field data agree to within 0.3 dB. The approximate relation between the S-Office and R-Office connector losses where the best fit (i.e., smallest RMSE) is obtained is

$$(\Delta^R + 0.5\Delta^S) = 1.6 \text{ dB}. \tag{12.11}$$

In Figure 12.11, the field data spectra are compared against two simulated spectra given by (12.11) with two distinctly different connector loss values. Note that both

Fig. 12.10 RMSE between simulated and experimental data as a function of S-Office and R-Office connector losses for 15 channels propagating on 103.93 km of LEAF fiber with both forward and backward pumping

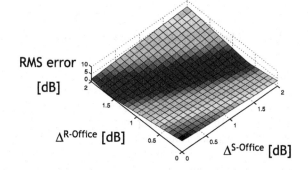

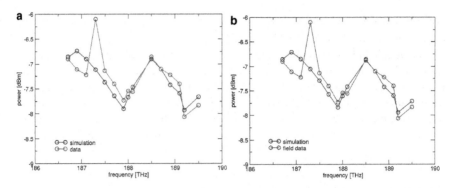

Fig. 12.11 Comparison of simulated versus field data for 15 channels propagating on 103.93 km of LEAF fiber with 1 forward pump and 5 backward pumps: (**a**) $\Delta^S = 1$ dB, $\Delta^R = 1.1$ dB; and (**b**) $\Delta^S = 0$ dB, $\Delta^R = 1.6$ dB. RMS error between simulated and field data is 0.3 dB for (**a**) and (**b**)

Fig. 12.12 Comparison of simulated versus field data for 16 channels propagating on 95.17 km of LEAF fiber with both forward and backward pumping, and $\Delta^{S-Office} = 1$ dB, $\Delta^{R-Office} = 1.2$ dB. RMS error between simulated and field data is 0.9 dB

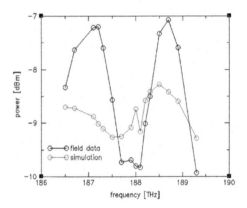

simulated spectra yield nearly identical shapes, suggesting that office loss values given by (12.11) are adequate for estimating expected output signal powers. This result shows that there is a continuum of connector loss values yielding good predictions of the signal gain for this 15-channel configuration.

12.4.2 Detection of Poor Fit to Raman Gain Profile

The detailed physical model can also be used to diagnose anomalies on a Raman span in an optical network. This is illustrated in Figure 12.12, where the predictions of the detailed physical model are compared with field data for the results shown in Figure 12.16 (16 channels propagating on 95.17 km of LEAF fiber on one span of a DWDM link). Note that even though the simulation results shown in Figure 12.12 correspond to a calibrated, best fit to the field data, there is still a significant discrepancy between the simulated and field data – the field data exhibit a different spectral shape in the low frequency range along with significantly larger ripple than the simulations. Furthermore, the RMSE between the simulations and field data is 0.9 dB, significantly larger than the 0.3 dB error observed for the results shown in Figure 12.11. These discrepancies indicate that anomalous behavior is occurring on this span.

12.4.3   Detection of Premature Signal Degradation and Pump Failure

The detailed physical model can also be used to diagnose anomalous behavior not readily captured by the engineering-rule based approaches or the R-beta model. In this section we explore how the detailed physical model can be used to detect the premature degradation and/or failure of a Raman pump.

In Figure 12.13a the predicted output signal spectra are plotted as a function of frequency for the case of 56 channels propagating on 94.04 km of TWRS fiber. The black curve with circles corresponds to the expected output power spectra where all pumps are behaving normally. The other curves correspond to different calibration cases describing the Raman span, and illustrate what the expected output would be if pump 1 was not experiencing the 4 dB degradation of its output power, i.e., pump 1 was actually being launched with +4 dB extra power to compensate for the pump degradation. Note that all of the calibration cases (A–D) show a large expected increase in the total output signal power, along with an increase in the

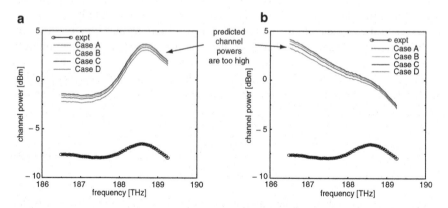

Fig. 12.13 Example of a virtual experiment illustrating a 4 dB counter-pump failure for 56 channels propagating on 94.04 km of TWRS fiber. Black curve with symbols corresponds to non-failure (normal) case, while curves A, B, C, and D correspond to different calibration cases describing the physical span and with the launched pump power for the failed pump being +4 dB too large: (**a**) if the failure is at pump 1; and (**b**) if the failure is at pump 2. Note that the predicted channel powers are approximately 5 dB too large for cases A, B, C, and D, indicating anomalous behavior on the span

signal tilt across the frequency band. The similar spectral shape for the different calibration cases (A–D) suggests that it is not essential to have an absolute fit to the fiber properties to detect anomalous behavior such as a pump failure.

In Figure 12.13b results are plotted illustrating the effect of a 4 dB failure at pump 2 for the same fiber and launch conditions shown in Figure 12.13a. The additional +4 dB in power increases the signal powers, although the tilt (slope) of the signals with respect to frequency has changed sign relative to Figure 12.13a.

These examples show how the detailed physical model can be used to give a precise characterization of the effects of various failures. However, the challenges in calibration leave some uncertainty in identifying the exact reason of the failures. Also, a proper threshold is needed on the similarity measure between the observed and predicted gain profiles in order to flag an anomaly. A good threshold value that is universally useful is often difficult to obtain. In the next section, we describe another method based on using a mathematical model to predict the gain shape and match it with observation. By explicitly introducing a noise model, the method reduces the task of anomaly detection to a standard statistical procedure for outlier detection, where an alarm threshold can be selected in a principled way.

12.5   Anomaly Detection Using the R-Beta Model

In this section, we describe an effective way for modeling the contribution of the physical process and measurement noise to an observed signal. Statistical estimation using the model allows for proper decomposition of an observed signal to the contribution of each. A standard procedure for goodness-of-fit testing gives alarms on the anomaly that the observed signal cannot be explained by the underlying physical process and the expected noise. This may signify a more serious type of anomaly, such as that the measurement has been made at a wrong spot due to equipment installation errors.

The following equation approximates the evolution of the channel power $p(z, \lambda_i)$ at channel wavelength λ_i as a function of distance z along the fiber in a Raman-amplified fiber span

$$\frac{dp(z, \lambda_i)}{dz} \approx -\alpha(\lambda_i)p(z, \lambda_i) + \sum_{j=1}^{N_{pumps}} R(\lambda_i, \lambda_j)p(z, \lambda_i)p(z, \lambda_j). \qquad (12.12)$$

In (12.12), $p(z, \lambda_j)$ denotes the pump power at pump wavelength λ_j, $\alpha(\lambda_i)$ is the fiber attenuation coefficient at wavelength λ_i, $R(\lambda_i, \lambda_j)$ is the Raman gain coefficient between the pump at wavelength λ_j and the signal at wavelength λ_i, and N_{pumps} is the number of pumps. The relationship in (12.12) can be alternatively expressed by dividing by $p(z, \lambda_i)$ and integrating both sides from $z = 0$ to L, the fiber length.

Using $\beta = \{\beta_j\}, \beta_j = \int_0^L p(z, \lambda_j) dz$, for the pump power integrated over the length of the fiber span, R for a $k \times N_{pumps}$ matrix with elements $R_{ij} \equiv R(\lambda_i, \lambda_j)$, and $Y = \{Y_i\}$ for the attenuation-adjusted gain for channel i, the above relationship gives the following model [6]:

$$Y = R\beta + \varepsilon. \tag{12.13}$$

Here, the quantity ϵ measures the gain across the Raman-amplified span that is not captured by the R-Beta model in (12.13). The magnitude of this term, $\|\epsilon\|$, is a measure of how well the actual measured data is described by the R-Beta amplification model, independent of particular pump levels. The residual includes measurement noise, physical effects left out by the R-Beta approximation, and the effects of any potential anomalies (see Figure 12.14a).

Computational experiments comparing the R-Beta model with simulations from the detailed physical model (described in Section 12.4) show that (12.13) captures the essential physics of Raman-amplified spans extremely well. Measurement noises are expected to be small, and, thus, large values for the error norm $\|\varepsilon\|$ are indicative of anomalous behavior present on the Raman-amplified span. In Figure 12.15 the normalized signal gain and the estimated unmodeled gain, defined by $\|\hat{\varepsilon}\| / \|R\hat{\beta}\|$, are plotted for 14 data polls on a fiber span. For these 14 polls, typical values for $\|\hat{\varepsilon}\| / \|R\hat{\beta}\|$ are around 3e-4.

To illustrate how the R-Beta model can be used to detect gain that is not consistent with Raman amplification, consider the data depicted in Figure 12.16, where the normalized signal gain and the error norm are plotted for 14 data polls for span 7 of the same link. In contrast to the data for span 2 (see Figure 12.15), note the more pronounced ripple, or undulations, present in the normalized signal gain. The error

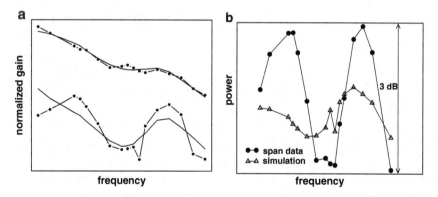

Fig. 12.14 (a) Observed Y (Equation 12.13, dotted lines) and predictions from regression model (solid lines) for two spans on a DWDM link. A large residual vector $\|\varepsilon\|$ in the second span (the lower lines) is indicative of a gain profile that is inconsistent with Raman amplification, and thus triggers an alarm. (b) Observed signal powers (filled circles) and calibrated simulations (hollow triangles). The discrepancies in spectral shape and ripple magnitude are indicative of anomalous behavior

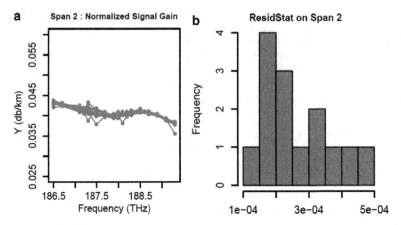

Fig. 12.15 Field data consisting of 14 data polls on span 2 of a 12-span DWDM link: (**a**) normalized signal gain across Raman span; and (**b**) error norm $\|\hat{\varepsilon}\|/\|R\hat{\beta}\|$ in a fit of the R-beta model to field data

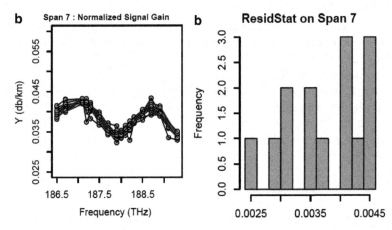

Fig. 12.16 Field data consisting of 14 data polls on span 7 of a 12-span DWDM link: (**a**) Normalized signal gain across Raman span; and (**b**) error norm in a fit of the R-beta model given by (12.13) to field data. Note that the scale of the x-axis in Figure 12.16b is a factor of 10 larger than that of Figure 12.15b

norm shown in Figure 12.16b is an order of magnitude larger than the corresponding values for span 2, and is indicative of anomalous behavior. The large ripple that is observed on this span is likely not due to improper settings of the Raman pumps – if the control algorithm regulating the Raman pumps were to have chosen suboptimal values, i.e., pump values resulting in large ripple, the normalized signal gain would still be expected to lie in the column space of the Raman gain matrix R, and hence the error norm should be of similar magnitude to that shown in Figure 12.15b. This illustrates the usefulness of the R-Beta model as a tool for joint gain-pump analysis to determine anomalous span behavior.

12.6   Conclusions

We have outlined three model-based procedures for detection of anomalous network behavior. The first procedure uses a simulator to generate the baseline distribution of a performance metric under different system configurations (fiber type, fiber length) and operating conditions (connector losses, channel loading). The second procedure uses a detailed physical model that represents a comprehensive description of the important physical phenomena occurring on a Raman span, allowing the direct prediction of output signal powers given input signal and pump powers. Through simulation, this model gives a method for detecting anomalous connector losses and pump failures. Large-scale simulations can be used to establish the expected behavior of the alarms under various failure scenarios. The third procedure uses a simplified (R-Beta) model that accounts for pump-signal amplification. The model represents Raman pump effects via the path-total power β, and can be used to detect gain deviations, here represented by ϵ, that are not explained by Raman physics. Examples of such deviations are those due to power measurement errors, misfibering, monitor failures, and calibration errors. The approximate model has low computational cost and is an attractive choice for real-time anomaly detection.

The proposed model-based alarms can be used in combination with traditional rule-based approaches to provide a diagnostic tool for optically transparent networks that use dynamically controlled Raman amplifiers. Such a tool allows for rapid detection and root cause analysis of network faults, and for proactive detection of anomalous behavior before errors affect transmission quality. As optical networks progress to more transparency and greater complexity, i.e., with mesh architectures and the use of a larger hierarchy of different equipment and components, the need for more sophisticated diagnostic tools will become more important. We have described a step towards meeting this need.

Finally, we note the difference of a model-based approach for anomaly detection from an empirical, data-driven approach. In the examples described in this chapter, it is obvious that much stronger conclusions can be drawn with minimal empirical data, given that the knowledge about the underlying physical process is properly represented in the analysis procedure. The use of the process model has led to substantial advantages in providing more systematic and comprehensive coverage of the variability in operating conditions, alleviating the cost of massive data collection, providing structure and guidance to the analysis, and identifying the potential origins of the anomalies. We believe that this can be the case for anomaly detection in many science and engineering contexts.

Acknowledgements We thank Wonsuck Lee, Lawrence Cowsar, and Roland Freund for early discussions on possible approaches. In identifying useful diagnostic data we were advised by many members of Alcatel-Lucent's Optical Networking Group. Special thanks go to Steve Eichblatt, Sydney Taegar, and Lee Vallone who conceived and developed the transmission diagnostic data retrieval tool. Narasimhan Raghavan, Bill Thompson, Jeff Sutton, and Tom Kissell provided much needed insight into the system engineering, operation, and testing issues. Their help is gratefully acknowledged.

References

1. G. P. Agrawal, *Nonlinear Fiber Optics*, 3rd edition, Academic Press, 2001.
2. J. Fee and M. Bencheck, Optical performance monitoring in the MCI network [invited], *Journal of Optical Networking*, **3**, 7, 2004, 548–556.
3. R. Freund, Simulation of Raman Amplification, Bell Labs Technical Memorandum No. ITD-02-43874P, 2002, http://cm.bell-labs.com/cm/cs/doc/03/4-01.ps.
4. R. Freund, Optimal Pump Control of Broadband Raman Amplifiers via Linear Programming, Bell Labs, Technical Memorandum No. ITD-03-44004F, 2003, http://cm.bell-labs.com/cm/cs/doc/03/raman-tm.pdf.
5. T.K. Ho, T. Salamon, R. Freund, C. White, B. Hillyer, L. Cowsar, C. Nuzman, D. Kilper, Simulation of Power Evolution and Control Dynamics in Optical Transport Systems, *Bell Labs Technical Journal*, **10**, 1, January-March 2005, 119–137.
6. T.K. Ho, T. Bengtsson, T. Salamon, C. White, Monitoring and Diagnostics of Power Anomalies in Transparent Optical Networks, *Technical Digests of Optical Fiber Communications*, Feb 28, 2008, San Diego, CA, USA.
7. M. N. Islam (ed.), *Raman Amplifiers for Telecommunications,* Vols. 1 and 2, Springer-Verlag, New York, 2004.
8. S. V. Kartalopoulos, *Introduction to DWDM Technology: Data in a Rainbow*, IEEE Press, 2000.
9. D. C. Kilper, R. Bach, D. J. Blumenthal, D. Einstein, T. Landolsi, L. Ostar, M. Preiss and A. E. Willner, Optical Performance Monitoring, *Journal of Lightwave Technologies,* **22**, 1, 2004, 119–137.
10. M. Menif, M. Karasek, and L. Rusch, Cross-Gain Modulation in Raman Fiber Amplifier: Experimentation and Modeling, *IEEE Photonics Technology Letters*, **14**, 9, 2002, 1261–1263.
11. D. L. Mills, *Nonlinear Optics*, 2nd edition, Springer-Verlag, Berlin, Germany, 1998.
12. J. Neter, W. Wasserman, *Applied Linear Statistical Models*, Irwin Professional Publishing, U.S., 2nd edition, 1985.
13. K. Rottwitt and A. J. Stentz, Raman Amplification in Lightwave Communication Systems, in *Optical Fiber Telecom., Vol. IV A Components*, I. P. Kaminow, T. Li, eds. (Academic Press, San Diego 2002), pp 213–257.
14. Y. R. Shen, *The Principles of Nonlinear Optics*, John Wiley & Sons, Inc., New York, 1984.

Chapter 13
In-Network Monitoring

Danny Raz, Rolf Stadler, Constantine Elster, and Mads Dam

Abstract Monitoring, i.e., the process of acquiring state information from a network or networked system, is fundamental to system operation. In traditional network and systems management, monitoring is performed on a per-device basis, whereby a centralized management entity polls the devices in its domain for information, which is then analyzed and acted upon.

In this chapter, we describe several monitoring algorithms that utilize a new monitoring paradigm called In-network Monitoring. This paradigm is designed to address the above shortcomings, and we demonstrate how it can be applied to managing highly dynamic networked systems. The main idea of In-network Monitoring is to introduce a small management entity inside each network device, which, in addition to monitoring local parameters, can also perform limited management functions and communicate with peering entities in its proximity. The collection of these entities creates a monitoring layer inside the network, which can perform monitoring and control tasks without involving the centralized entity.

We demonstrate how In-network monitoring can help building better and more efficient systems. We start with a general description of network monitoring

D. Raz (✉)
Computer Science Department, Technion – Israel Institute of Technology,
Haifa 32000, Israel
e-mail: danny@cs.technion.ac.il

R. Stadler
School of Electrical Engineering, KTH Royal Institute of Technology,
SE-100 44 Stockholm, Sweden
e-mail: stadler@ee.kth.se

C. Elster
Qualcomm Israel, Omega Building Matam Postal Agency,
31905, Israel
e-mail: celster@qualcomm.com

M. Dam
School of Computer Science and Communication, KTH Royal Institute of Technology,
SE-100 44 Stockholm, Sweden
e-mail: mfd@kth.se

G. Cormode and M. Thottan (eds.), *Algorithms for Next Generation Networks*,   287
Computer Communications and Networks, DOI 10.1007/978-1-84882-765-3_13,
© Springer-Verlag London Limited 2010

techniques, and then describe two specific cases in which this paradigm generates provably efficient solutions. The first one is in the area of traffic engineering, where there is a need to monitor the aggregated delay of packets along a given network path. The second case deals with the problem of monitoring general aggregated values over the network, with emphasis on computing the values in a distributed way inside the monitoring layer. All together, we believe that this new paradigm presents a promising direction to address the challenges of cost-effective management of future networked systems.

13.1 Introduction

Monitoring, i.e., the process of acquiring state information from a network or a networked system, is fundamental to system operation. In traditional network and systems management, monitoring is performed on a per-device basis, whereby a centralized management entity polls the devices in its domain for information, which is then analyzed and acted upon. Traditional management frameworks and protocols, including SNMP, TMN, and OSI-SM, support this monitoring paradigm [24].

In this approach, the network is oblivious in the sense that the centralized management entity initiates all messages and analyzes all results. Over the past 20 years, this paradigm has proven to be fairly successful for networks of moderate size, whose configuration rarely changes, and whose states evolve slowly and thus do not require intervention within seconds by an outside system. However, the paradigm has two significant weaknesses, which makes it less attractive for today's (and even more so for future) networked systems. To start with, the centralized management approach does not allow for fast reaction to changes, simply because collecting the information, transporting it over the network to the centralized entity, analyzing it, and communicating the control decision back to the managed devices takes time. In addition, in order to check for certain anomalies, the entire system must be monitored continuously, resulting in a high monitoring overhead.

In this chapter, we describe several monitoring algorithms (which we also refer to as monitoring protocols) that utilize a new monitoring paradigm called *In-Network Monitoring*. This paradigm is designed to address the above shortcomings, and we demonstrate how it can be applied to managing highly dynamic networked systems. The main idea of in-network monitoring is to introduce a small management entity inside each network device, which, in addition to monitoring local parameters, can also perform limited management functions and communicate with peering entities in its proximity. The collection of these entities creates a monitoring layer inside the network, which can perform monitoring and control tasks without involving the centralized entity. In-network monitoring is investigated within the EU 4WARD project [1].

Note that the monitoring layer does not replace the centralized management entity, but rather complements it. It is important to understand that computing a global state may require information from all devices, and generating such a global view using the distributed monitoring layer may, in some cases, be more complex and computationally expensive than a centralized solution. Moreover, the centralized management entity is an important reference point for many components in the system and thus must remain part of any management paradigm.

The need for distributing monitoring and management tasks has been recognized before and has been studied in the research community since the mid-1990s. Concepts like management by delegation, mobile agents, and distributed objects have been developed with the goal of making network management systems more efficient, better scalable, and less complex (cf. [21]). Within the same time frame, new engineering concepts in networking and telecommunications, namely active networking and programmable networks, have appeared, aimed at simplifying the introduction of new functionality into a network environment ([19, 27, 35]). In-network monitoring leverages aspects of these efforts as enabling technologies to create the monitoring layer.

In this chapter, we concentrate on the monitoring of parameters in a network setting. We demonstrate how in-network monitoring can help build better and more efficient systems. We start with a general description of network monitoring techniques, and then describe two specific cases in which this paradigm generates provably efficient solutions. The first one is in the area of traffic engineering, where there is a need to monitor the aggregated delay of packets along a given network path. The second case deals with the problem of monitoring general aggregated values over the network, with emphasis on computing the values in a distributed way inside the monitoring layer. All together, we believe that this new paradigm presents a promising direction to address the challenges of cost-effective management of future networked systems.

13.2   Basic Monitoring Techniques and the Cost of Monitoring

We assume that we have a network environment where each network element e can monitor a local variable $f(e)$ (this could be, for example, the delay along link e of a specific flow). We are interested in an aggregated function of these values (e.g., the sum) over a subset of network elements (e.g., the link along a given path in the network), and want to know when this value exceeds a certain predefined threshold.

As described in the Section 13.1 we assume a centralized management entity (CE), together with local monitoring and restricted processing in each of the elements. The CE monitors the value of the function over different sets of elements and determines when these values do not (or soon might not) follow the constraint on the value of the global function f_{global}. Thus the CE only needs to know about sets whose value is too large with respect to their bound.

We distinguish between several basic monitoring techniques that are in practical use today. In the first technique, called *polling* (see, e.g., [28]), the CE polls the Network Elements (NEs) regarding the value associated with each of the relevant sets. Each NE sends this information as requested to the CE, and the CE computes the overall value of each set. This method can be formulated in Figure 13.1.

```
1. for each NE e
2.     if request for report arrived from CE
3.         send report(e, f_e) to CE
```

Fig. 13.1 Polling

```
1. for each NE e
2.     if time to send or local event
3.         send report(e, f_e) to CE
```

Fig. 13.2 Push-based monitoring

A different way to obtain the information is when the monitoring initiative comes from the devices and not from the CE. In this technique, called the push model or *pushing*, the local device decides based on the available local information to send a report to the CE. This push event can be done periodically regardless of the value of the local variables (oblivious pushing) or it can be reactive, triggered by a change in the value of one or more local variables. This is illustrated in Figure 13.2.

The number of control packets sent to the CE is limited from above by the number of nodes N. Taking the average distance to the CE to be B, we get that the network load generated by a single polling event is $O(B \cdot N)$. The computation load of each node is $O(1)$ and the computation load in the CE is $O(N)$. If we have a single push event then the generated network load is $O(B)$, but if we have such an event in each node the cost is similar to the one of polling.

As mentioned before, if monitoring (either push or pull) is done periodically, regardless of the network state, we call it *oblivious monitoring*. Such oblivious monitoring is good to collect full statistics regarding the values of interest. These can then be used off-line to analyze the network performance. However, in many cases, when we need to react to situations where a certain value exceeds its assigned threshold, we can do with much less than the full information delivered by oblivious monitoring. Thus, we can use event-driven monitoring, in which the monitoring is triggered by an event in one of the nodes. In this kind of monitoring – termed *reactive monitoring* – the management station (or the CE) reacts to some anomalous behavior in the network and only then checks whether the global state of the system is illegal (i.e., its aggregated value exceeds the bound).

Reactive monitoring of network elements in general was initially proposed by Dilman and Raz [11]. The basic idea is to partition the global bound associated with a set to small bounds associated with each element (called local thresholds). Once the local threshold in one of the NEs is exceeded, that NE triggers an alarm (i.e., sends a control message) to the CE. The CE responds, according to the deployed monitoring technique, by probing the set, or by polling the NEs in this set. Thus, this general approach yields two reactive monitoring methods. We use these reactive methods, as well as the oblivious ones, as yardsticks for the performance of the monitoring algorithms described in Section 13.3 of this chapter that use the in-network management paradigm.

In Sections 13.4 and 13.5, we present three protocols that rely on the push-based monitoring technique. The protocols – a simple aggregation protocol and two refinements of it – provide two basic capabilities: first, the capability of continuously estimating a global aggregation function, such as SUM, AVERAGE, or MAX, which is computed over local variables associated with NEs; second, the capability of detecting threshold crossings of such global aggregation functions. These protocols create spanning trees that interconnect the NEs and use reactive methods to determine when to send messages towards the root of a tree. They rely on processing capabilities within the NEs that compute the aggregation functions in a decentralized way, using the spanning tree for communication between NEs. The main challenge is to perform such in-network aggregation in a cost-effective way, i.e., with small protocol overhead.

13.3   End-to-End Aggregate QoS Monitoring

With the development of modern Internet applications, such as real-time audio and video, the original "best-effort" design of the Internet Protocol (IP) is no longer sufficient. This has led in the past few years to the development of the Quality of Service (QoS) concept, in which applications can request, and the network can provide the resources needed to guarantee the required service level [39]. This allows Internet Service Providers (ISPs) to offer predictable service levels in terms of data throughput capacity (bandwidth), latency variations (jitter), and propagation latency.

In order to supply a certain level of services and to conform to QoS needs, ISPs need to support a QoS aware mechanism that includes network resource management capability. In this part of the chapter we investigate monitoring of flows' QoS parameters in a network. This is a very influential task essential for the successful provisioning of network services.

Differential Services (DiffServ) [5] is nowadays considered the preferred way of implementing QoS in the Internet. In DiffServ, every packet is classified into one of a small number of possible service classes. DiffServ allows the routers to give different service to different packets according to their QoS class. For example, a router can drop packets of a lower class in order to guarantee that the bandwidth requirements of an upper class are satisfied. Nevertheless, resource allocation remains a big issue; wise planning can dramatically decrease congestion and increase utilization. Moreover, since in DiffServ there is no actual reservation or allocations of resources to specific flows, guaranteeing the end-to-end performance requirements is a very challenging task.

In recent years, reduction in equipment prices has led to the use of the most trivial planning method: over-provisioning. Over-provisioning means that suppliers equip their networks with more resources than they ever expect to consume, and respond to congestion by acquiring more equipment. However, over-provisioning fails to support the new traffic-aware applications; an application may request a significantly large amount of traffic resources at some special period while the network usage is more meager at other times. Thus, an early allocation of these resources to support such kind of turbulence is wasteful, which in turn makes the over-provisioning method ineffective and costly.

An alternative to over-provisioning is dynamic provisioning. Such provisioning is based on a managing authority – the Centralized Entity[1] – which dynamically allocates resources in the network. Like any other controller, the CE must be supported by a monitoring facility [3]. This monitoring facility provides the CE with data that will allow it to make its decisions and judge their results. Needless to say, the more accurate and up to date those data are, the more successful is the resource allocation. Note that this type of approach is not applicable for short timescales (say of several milliseconds). This is due to the fact that the report notification time to the CE is of this short timescale. Thus, the approach aims at events that last longer, and cause the delays in the routers' buffers to increase for timescales of several seconds or minutes. Clearly, no centralized solution can be used for monitoring of very short local congestions.

We focus on end-to-end delay monitoring, which is the critical QoS parameter for popular Internet services such as Voice over IP [29]. To perform the delay monitoring, the CE uses a share of the network resources which in turn reduces the amount of resources available to the users. The challenge in QoS monitoring is twofold. On the one hand, we want to provide the CE with the needed information in order to detect problematic flows, and on the other hand, we want to use as little communication as possible.

In this part of the chapter we describe another approach to the monitoring problem – *autonomous monitoring* that uses the in-network monitoring paradigm. With autonomous monitoring, the network performs all the processing required to detect a congested flow and the CE is only informed about flows which are indeed congested, and thus the network becomes self-monitored. Because congestion detection is fully distributed, the effect of a local congestion, which is due to noise and which does not expand to the whole flow, subsides after just a few messages are exchanged. We concentrate on a protocol, called AMoS – Autonomous Monitoring of Streams – which monitors the end-to-end delay of packets in the flow (see [13]). AMoS requirements from the network are humble. First, each router must be able to monitor its own load, as suggested in [8], and trigger a monitoring message if the local load is greater than a given threshold. Second, upon receiving a monitoring message, a router adds its own load to the accumulated one and makes a simple comparison before deciding if the message should be dropped, forwarded to the next hop, or sent to the CE.

We thoroughly analyze the behavior of AMoS and present extensive simulation results. Our analysis shows that AMoS produces much less traffic than the state-of-the-art protocols either in low or high load network conditions. Similar to reactive monitoring approaches, it poses no monitoring load at all unless there is local congestion. Moreover, because local congestion is dealt with locally, AMoS is robust in the sense that its performance remains almost the same over a wide range of load

---

[1] Sometimes called the Bandwidth Broker.

variations and flow lengths. More specifically, even if a third of the links suffer from a very high load that exceeds their local threshold, AMoS performances are still better than those of any other monitoring algorithm.

13.3.1 Autonomous Monitoring of Streams

In this section we describe the AMoS algorithm. Note that the routers along a path of a flow are the set of nodes, and the function f is the delay along the link going out from this router along the specific path. The algorithm starting point is similar to reactive monitoring, each link along the flow's path receives a local delay threshold; if and only if none of the links exceeds its threshold then the total delay of the flow is within the desired values (as indicated by the SLA) and thus no further actions are needed. However, unlike reactive monitoring, when a local threshold is exceeded on a link, the node attached to this link tries to figure out whether this local event is a global alarm condition (i.e., the total delay of the flow exceeds its threshold) or is a *false alarm*. A false alarm is a situation in which the local threshold has been exceeded but no global event had occurred. The main idea behind AMoS is to allow flows to recover locally from false alarms in a distributed way without involving any CE.

A typical example for a false alarm is a situation in which one of the links of the flow suffers a high load, and thus the delay over a certain QoS class is higher than the local threshold, but the next link on the path experiences a very low load, and therefore the delay of the same class on the same link is much below this link's local threshold. If the total delay over these two links is smaller than the sum of the two local thresholds, they cancel each other out, and there is no need to alert the CE.

Thus, our algorithm uses control messages that are sent along the flow path and contain aggregated delay and aggregated threshold values. Once a message arrives at a node, it checks whether adding its local values (local delay and local threshold) still violates the requirements. If it exceeds the global flow delay it informs the CE immediately. Otherwise, it adds the local delay and threshold to the aggregated ones. If the updated delay exceeds the updated threshold, it forwards the message to the next hop; else the message is dropped.

The formal definition of AMoS is presented in pseudo-code in Figure 13.3 that uses the following notations. For each node, we use (e, s) to indicate that flow s goes over incoming link e. Each node knows the next hop of flow path s, indicated by $next\_hop_s$. The delay of edge e is denoted by $delay_e$ and the local threshold for this edge is given by $threshold_e$. The total threshold of flow s is $total\_threshold_s$. Lines 1 to 9 describe the Initialization Phase of the algorithm. In this part every node examines its local information for every incoming link by comparing the link delay ($delay_e$) to the link threshold ($threshold_e$) for every flow path s. In the case when the local delay exceeds its threshold, the node creates a control message $packet(s, delay_e, threshold_e)$ and addresses it to the next node in the flow path (or to the second node in the path if it is the last node on the path).

AMoS Algorithm

1. for every (e, s)
2.   if $delay_e > threshold_e$
3.   if $delay_e > total\_threshold_s$
4.   send $report(s, delay_e)$ to CE.
5.   else
6.   if $next\_hop_s \neq null$
7.   send $packet(s, delay_e, threshold_e)$ to $next\_hop_s$.
8.   else
9.   send $packet(s, delay_e, threshold_e)$ to $s.origin.next\_hop_s$.
10. if $packet(s, delay, threshold)$ arrives through edge e do
11.   if $delay_e + delay > threshold_e + threshold$
12.   if $delay_e + delay > total\_thresold_s$
13.   send report $(s, delay_e + delay)$ to CE.
14.   else
15.   if $next\_hop_s \neq null$
16.   send $packet(s, delay_e + delay, threshold_e + threshold)$ to $next\_hop_s$.
17.   else
18.   send $packet(s, delay_e + delay, threshold_e + threshold)$ to $s.origin.next\_hop_s$.

Fig. 13.3 Pseudo-code of AMoS

The Work Cycle Phase of the algorithm is described in lines 10–18. If a node receives a message $packet(s, delay, threshold)$, it adds its local information regarding flow s ($delay_e$ and $threshold_e$) to the received message and examines whether the calculated delay violates the new calculated threshold (i.e., $delay + delay_e > threshold + threshold_e$). In such a case, the node updates the received message with the new information and sends it to the next node along flow path s. At any point that a node detects that the flow's global threshold was exceeded it informs the CE and stops the propagation of control messages (see lines 4 and 13 in Figure 13.3).

It is clear from the algorithm that messages are sent to the CE only if the global delay exceeds the global threshold. The more complicated part in proving AMoS correctness is to show that if in some flow the total delay is greater than its threshold, then a report is sent to the CE regarding this flow. Due to space limitations, we do not show the entire proof, yet it can be established based on the observation that no control message can stop its propagation on the path of another control message.

The more interesting question is the performance of AMoS, that is, the number of control messages it uses. Note that if there is no local congestion AMoS sends no messages at all. On the other hand, when the network is congested all over, the delay in all nodes may exceed their local threshold and n messages (assuming n is the flow length) will be sent, resulting in n separate notifications to the CE. In such a situation the message complexity of AMoS could be worst than any of the basic monitoring algorithms described above. It is therefore important to understand the behavior of AMoS with respect to network load.

13.3.1.1   Single Flow Analysis

We focus on analyzing the effect of the probability p of a local congestion event on the expected number of control messages per link that we later denote by E_n for a flow path of length n. We show that if the probability of any link to be congested is p (independent of the state of other links), then as long as $p < 1/3$, the expected number of control messages per link is less than 1, which means AMoS is better than Probing and Polling.

In order to make the analysis possible we use the following model. We consider a single flow of length n, passing through nodes $x_0, \ldots, x_n$ connected by links $e_1, \ldots, e_n$ such that the link e_i connects nodes x_{i-1} and x_i. The delay of each link is 1 (loaded) with probability p, and -1 (not loaded) with probability $1 - p$. The threshold is set to 0. Clearly, as p increases the expected number of control messages sent by AMoS increases as well. In order to characterize this phenomenon we wish to identify the value of p in which AMoS uses the same number of messages as Oblivious Probing. Note that Oblivious Probing sends a single control message along the path of the flow and therefore its average cost per link is one. Hence, we would like to find out the value of p for which the average number of control messages that traverse a link is one. Note that we consider only one monitoring interval and as indicated before we assume that the load parameters are fixed throughout the duration of the interval.

For this analysis, we will need the following definition:

Definition 13.1. For a message $m = packet(s, delay_m, threshold_m)$

$$\Delta_m = delay_m - threshold_m.$$

We try to identify the number of the received messages at a node in a flow path. In order to achieve this goal, we focus on a fixed message and try to recognize the dependency between the examined message (the value Δ) and the number of messages with smaller Δ that were received in this node. We use the following lemma. Note that since the delay can be either 1 or -1 and the threshold is 0, Δ must be an Integer.

Lemma 13.1. *If a node x_k receives a message m with $\Delta_m = \Delta$ then prior to that message it has received exactly $\Delta - 1$ messages.*

This lemma's correctness can be established by focusing on a set of last nodes on the path of message m that increase the value Δ of message m to value d in the interval $[0, \Delta - 1]$.

The following claim follows directly from Lemma 13.1.

Claim 13.3.1.1. The ith message received by a node x_k has $\Delta_m = i$.

As explained before, we try to identify the values of p, for which $E_n < 1$. According to Claim 13.3.1.1, if the expected Δ of a received message is 1, then only one control message is received by this node. Thus, instead of looking at the values Δ_m

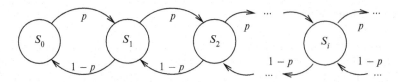

Fig. 13.4 The infinite Markov Chain

at a specific node k, let us examine the value of Δ_m for a fixed message m. When message m moves on an intermediate link l in its path, the value of Δ_m can either increase by the delay of this link, if it is positive, or decrease if negative. Thus, given a value of Δ_m, the probability that Δ_m will be increased by 1 is p, while the probability that Δ_m will be decreased by 1 is $(1-p)$.

We first assume for simplicity that the flow length is infinite. In this case we can build an infinite Markov Chain, where state S_i represents a message with $\Delta_m = i$, for $0 \le i$. The probability of moving from state S_i to state S_{i+1} is p, and the probability of moving from state S_{i+1} to state S_i is $1 - p$ (see Figure 13.4). For $1 - p > p$ (i.e., $p < 0.5$) the system is stable. The following equations describe the relationship between the steady-state probabilities.

$$
\begin{aligned}
Pr[\Delta_m = 0]\, p &= Pr[\Delta_m = 1]\,(1-p), \text{ and for } X \ge 0 \\
Pr[\Delta_m = X] &= Pr[\Delta_m = X - 1]\, p \\
&\quad + Pr[\Delta_m = X + 1]\,(1-p).
\end{aligned}
\tag{13.1}
$$

A well-known solution for this set (using an $M\|M\|1$ queue system with $\rho = \frac{p}{1-p}$) is that

$$
\begin{aligned}
E_\infty &= \sum_{j=0}^{\infty} j Pr[\Delta_m = j] = \sum_{j=0}^{\infty} j \frac{1-2p}{1-p} \left(\frac{p}{1-p}\right)^j \\
&= \frac{1-2p}{1-p} \sum_{j=0}^{\infty} j \left(\frac{p}{1-p}\right)^j = \frac{1-2p}{1-p} \cdot \frac{\frac{p}{1-p}}{\left(1-\frac{p}{1-p}\right)^2} \\
&= \frac{1-2p}{1-p} \cdot \frac{\frac{p}{1-p}}{\left(\frac{1-2p}{1-p}\right)^2} = \frac{\frac{p}{1-p}}{\frac{1-2p}{1-p}} = \frac{p}{1-2p}.
\end{aligned}
\tag{13.2}
$$

Next, we need to evaluate the conditions under which $E_\infty \le 1$.

$$
E_\infty = \frac{p}{1-2p} \le 1 \Rightarrow p \le \tfrac{1}{3}.
\tag{13.3}
$$

We conclude that if the probability of a link being loaded is less than $\frac{1}{3}$, then we expect that less than one message will be received by a node in average. This result is very important, since it allows us to evaluate the conditions under which AMoS performs better than any other algorithm. However, in more realistic cases, network parameters differ from the described binary loaded/not loaded infinite model, yet this result still provides a vision of the performance behavior of AMoS.

Next we turn to analyze the more realistic case where the flow has a finite length n. This case can be treated in a similar way, yielding

$$E_n = \frac{1-2p}{(1-p)\left[1-\left(\frac{p}{1-p}\right)^{n+1}\right]} \cdot \frac{\frac{p}{1-p}-\left(\frac{p}{1-p}\right)^{n+1}\left(n+1-\frac{np}{1-p}\right)}{\left(\frac{1-2p}{1-p}\right)^2}. \qquad (13.4)$$

When $p < 1 - p$ and $n \to \infty$, we get

$$E_n \to \frac{1-2p}{1-p} \cdot \frac{\frac{p}{1-p}}{\left(\frac{1-2p}{1-p}\right)^2} \to \frac{p}{1-2p}. \qquad (13.5)$$

We can use this closed formula. The values for different p and n are plotted in Figure 13.5(a). This figure depicts that as long as we are not too close to the non-stable point, $p = 0.5$, the results match very well the values that were calculated using a recursive formulae we developed.

In this section, we provided the analysis of AMoS performance on a simple network model. Yet, we still need to evaluate the performance of AMoS in more realistic conditions, since the performance measurements of AMoS in these conditions may differ from the examined model. These conditions count different parameters, such as network topology, real-link load functions, node distribution in the network, and more. The next section deals with this problem, and presents the simulation of AMoS in various networks with different properties.

13.3.2   Simulation Results

The theoretical analysis of the previous section indicates that AMoS will perform very well in terms of the number of control messages used. However, one needs to verify that the same holds even without the simplification assumption we made, and in realistic working configuration scenarios. To do so, we examine in this section the performance of AMoS using simulation. Our measurements indicate that in realistic network conditions AMoS outperforms all other algorithms when network utilization is up to 95%. Beyond this point there are too many local alerts, and a simpler algorithm (i.e., Probing or Polling) would perform better.

13.3.2.1   Single Flow Simulations

We first consider a single flow over a path of length n (where n varies from 4 to 20), and we also set up the distance to the CE to be 1 hop from all nodes. (In Section 13.3.2.2 we run simulations on real and simulated ISP networks, there CE is placed in a real network node and we consider the real network distances.) In order to simulate traffic load we used Pareto distribution, and to normalize all the simulations we did, we set up the local threshold value to be 1. In the simulation,

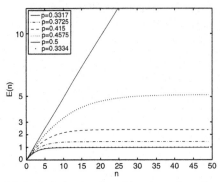

(a) Analytical estimation of the expected number of control messages per link as a function of the flow length, for various probabilities p.

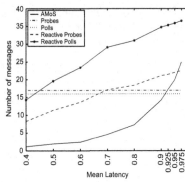

(b) The number of control messages used by the different monitoring algorithms as a function of the load, $n = 16$.

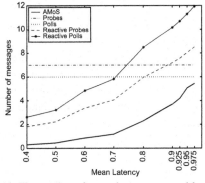

(c) The number of control messages used by the different monitoring algorithms as a function of the load, $n = 6$.

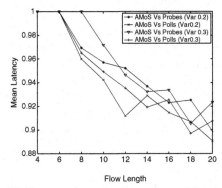

(d) The crossover points for variances 0.2 and 0.3.

Fig. 13.5 The number of control messages used by the different monitoring algorithms. Analytical estimation/single flow simulation

we varied the mean and variance of the Pareto distribution from which the load values are derived. Clearly, as the mean approaches 1, the probability of exceeding a local threshold increases, and the number of control messages used by AMoS will increase. We also expected that the variance will have a similar effect, since when the variance increases, the probability of exceeding a local threshold increases, but as indicated by our results, this effect is very mild and in fact AMoS is not sensitive to the variance.

In order to evaluate the performance of AMoS, we need to compare the number of control messages used by AMoS with common practice and best-known algorithms. This is done by comparing it to the four algorithms described in Section 13.2. For each of these algorithms we simulated the exact flow of control (monitoring) packets, and computed the cost in terms of packets times hops. For the reactive algorithms, we used the same local threshold as for AMoS (i.e., one).

Figure 13.5(b) depicts the average number of control messages used by our algorithm and by the four basic monitoring algorithms for different values of the mean of the Pareto Distribution. Each point in this figure is the average of 500 runs, done on flows of length 16. One can observe that in this region of load, the Polling algorithms outperform the Probing algorithms, and the reactive algorithms do not scale well as load increases. This is due to the fact that even when the load is not very high (the mean is 0.7) and when the path is long enough there is a non-neglectable probability that at least one node will exceed its local threshold. When the load is lower, the reactive monitoring algorithms outperform the oblivious ones.

AMoS, however, scales very well when load increases. One can see that even when the mean of the Pareto distribution is 0.9, it requires fewer messages than Polling. Figure 13.5(c) depicts the same information for a shorter flow of length 6. As expected, the reactive techniques behave much better on short flows since the probability of at least one link to exceed the threshold drops. The performance of AMoS also depends on the path length, yet, we can see that on a flow path of length 6, AMoS outperforms all other algorithms.

The most interesting aspect of the graphs presented in Figure 13.5(b) and Figure 13.5(c) is probably the crossover points. These are the points in which AMoS cost is equal to the next best algorithm, in most cases Polls. We extracted these points for the extensive set of the simulations we ran. The results are depicted in Figure 13.5(d). One can see that for flow length 6 AMoS is superior in any examined mean, and for flow length of 8 AMoS is better than other algorithms up to mean of about 0.96. This value drops gradually when the flow length increases to 20. One can also observe that these points go down when the variance changes from 0.2 to 0.3, but again the drop is very mild, indicating again that AMoS scales well with variance.

13.3.2.2 Multiple Flow Simulations

In the previous section we studied the performance of AMoS on a single flow. As discussed in Section 13.1, the QoS monitoring algorithms we describe here work in an ISP network, where many flows are present. In order to investigate the performance of AMoS and the other monitoring algorithms in such an environment, one needs to consider parameters such as the network topology, the flow source and destination distributions, the number of flows with respect to the network size, etc.

One fundamental issue is the topology of the underlying network. This topology has a critical impact on the performance of any monitoring algorithm as it effects the flow length, the distance messages have to travel when reporting to the CE, and the amount of flows that share the same link. This last parameter is very important since we are primarily interested in the number of control messages, and one message may contain information regarding many flows.

While research regarding the topological structure of the Internet has gained considerable popularity since the fundamental work of Faloutsos et al. [14] (see, e.g.,

[34]) most works deal with the AS structure and not router level topology. Recently, Aiello et al. proposed a technique of creating Power Law Random Graphs (PLRG) [2] that produce more realistic large-scale topologies. Tangmunarunkit et al. (see [34]) examined the properties of the topologies created by different types of generators: random graph generators (see [6, 36]), structural generators that focus on the hierarchical nature of the Internet, and PLRG generators. The authors report that the degree-based generators (such as PLRG) create the most realistic models of the Internet. These topology generators assign degrees to the topology nodes and then uniformly select pairs to form the links in the topology.

Spring et al. created an ISP topology mapping engine called Rocketfuel [33]. They recorded several maps of well-known ISPs, such as AT&T, Sprintlink, and EBONE, and performed a thorough analysis of large-scale topologies. They concluded that router degrees in the network are distributed mostly according to Weibull distribution. In our simulations, we used an AT&T map produced by Rocketfuel for the underlying topology [32].

Another important aspect is the distribution of the flows' endpoints in the network. For person to person phone calls, one can assume that the endpoints are distributed uniformly in the network. However, in many cases, for a specific ISP the endpoints are the connecting points to other ISPs, and thus most traffic concentrate on relatively few points. In such a case the links that are close to this point will be used by many flows. Another factor that affects the number of flows that use a given link is the overall number of QoS enabled flows in the network. While in the current Internet this number may be small, our algorithm should be able to handle a future situation in which this number will be very large when compared to the network size (i.e., the number of nodes or links).

In order to evaluate the performance of AMoS against the other monitoring techniques in the most general setting, we simulated the number of messages times hops they use over a large range of parameters. The network topology we used was, as mentioned before, either a 9,000 node topology of AT&T network from [33], or the synthetic random Weibull distributed PLRG graph with 10,000 nodes. We distributed the source points of the flows either uniformly or using the Zipf Distribution, and varied the overall number of flows between 500 and 50,000. The end points of the flows were distributed uniformly. For combination of the above, we ran our simulation with different load values as in the single flow case; this was done by choosing different mean and variance values for the Pareto Distribution. Each of these simulations was averaged over at least 10 separate runs using the same parameters.

Figure 13.6(a) presents the number of control messages used by the different monitoring algorithms as a function of the mean of the Pareto Distribution used to generate the load. As expected, the oblivious monitoring techniques are not affected by the load, while both the reactive and active techniques generate more monitoring traffic as the average load increases. One can see, however, that there are little fluctuations in the lines of Probes and Polls. These fluctuations are probably the result of the large variance of the control traffic in the Zipf to Uniform model, where the distance of the flow endpoints from the CE changes from one simulation to another.

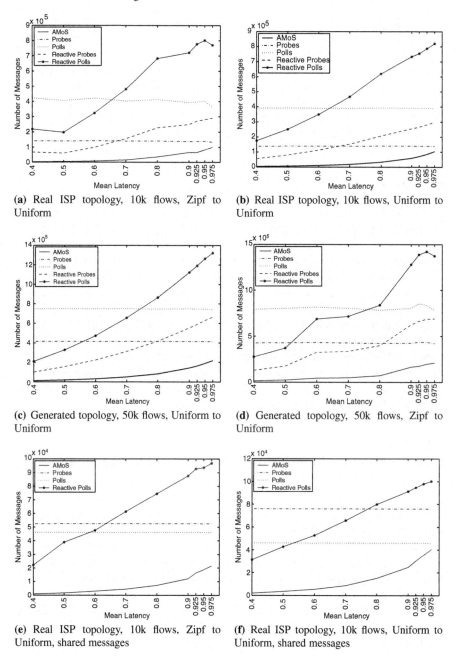

(a) Real ISP topology, 10k flows, Zipf to Uniform

(b) Real ISP topology, 10k flows, Uniform to Uniform

(c) Generated topology, 50k flows, Uniform to Uniform

(d) Generated topology, 50k flows, Zipf to Uniform

(e) Real ISP topology, 10k flows, Zipf to Uniform, shared messages

(f) Real ISP topology, 10k flows, Uniform to Uniform, shared messages

Fig. 13.6 The number of control messages used by the different monitoring algorithms as a function of the load

Nevertheless, while the traffic of both reactive polls and reactive probes increase linearly with the mean, that of AMoS increases slower for small values of the mean. Then, due to the fact that many probes can be sent in parallel, the number of control messages increases dramatically. Still, AMoS outperforms all other algorithms.

The performance of the algorithms depends, of course, on several other parameters such as the number of flows and the flows' endpoint distribution. Surprisingly enough, the endpoint distribution has very little effect on the performance. If we compare the performance of various algorithms in Figure 13.6(a), where one endpoint of each flow is chosen according to Zipf Distribution, to Figure 13.6(b), where both endpoints of the flows are chosen uniformly, we see that there is only a very mild difference.

We also examine the difference between the two endpoint distributions when the overall number of flows is much larger (50k in our case), and we can observe, in Figures 13.6(c) and (d), that the performances are not very affected by the load.

In these simulations all control messages sent by the algorithms hold information regarding one flow. However, for the polling algorithms, a natural approach is to send one control message that contains information about all flows that go through the node. We term such a usage of a single control containing information regarding a number of flows by *message sharing*.

In this part of the chapter we described a novel distributed self-managed algorithm that monitors end-to-end delay of flows using the in-network monitoring paradigm. We have shown, using theoretical analysis and extensive simulation study, that in addition to dramatically reducing the load from the CE, our autonomous monitoring algorithm uses a relatively small amount of network traffic, and it scales very well when the number of flows and the load increase.

13.4   Continuous Monitoring of Network-Wide Aggregates

This section presents GAP (Generic Aggregation Protocol), a protocol for continuous monitoring of network-wide aggregates [9]. GAP is an asynchronous distributed protocol that builds and maintains a BFS (Breadth First Search) spanning tree on an overlay network. The tree is maintained in a similar way as the algorithm that underlies the 802.1d Spanning Tree Protocol (STP). In GAP, each node holds information about its children in the BFS tree, in order to compute the partial aggregate, i.e., the aggregate value of the local variables from all nodes of the subtree where this node is the root. GAP is event-driven in the sense that messages are exchanged as results of events, such as the detection of a new neighbor on the overlay, the failure of a neighbor, an aggregate update, or a change in the local variable.

A common approach to computing aggregates in a distributed fashion involves creating and maintaining a spanning tree (within the monitoring layer) and aggregating state information along that tree, bottom-up from the leaves towards the root (e.g., [10, 20, 26, 30]). GAP is an example of such a tree-based protocol. It builds its spanning tree, also called aggregation tree, in a decentralized, self-stabilizing man-

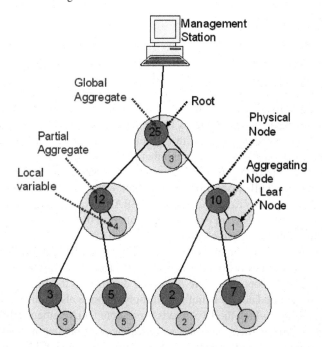

Fig. 13.7 Aggregation tree with aggregation function SUM. The physical nodes in the figure refer to the NEs in Section 13.2, the management station refers to the CE component in Section 13.2

ner, which provides the monitoring protocol with robustness properties. Figure 13.7 shows an example of such an aggregation tree.

A second, less-studied approach to computing aggregates involves the use of gossip protocols, which typically rely on randomized communication to disseminate and process state information in a network (e.g., [4, 16, 17, 37]). This approach will not be further discussed here.

GAP assumes a distributed management architecture, whereby each network device (referred to as NE in Section 13.2) participates in the monitoring task by running a management process, either internally or on an external, associated device. These management processes communicate via a management overlay network for the purpose of monitoring. We also refer to this overlay as the network graph. The topology of the overlay can be chosen independently from the topology of the underlying physical network. The aggregation tree shown in Figure 13.7 spans the management overlay. Each management process contains a leaf node and an aggregating node of this tree. A management station (referred to as CE in Section 13.2) can use any network device as access point for monitoring and invoke the protocol.

13.4.1 The Problem

Formally speaking, we consider a dynamically changing network graph $G(t) = (V(t), E(t))$, in which nodes $n \in V(t)$ and edges/links $e \in E(t) \subseteq V(t) \times V(t)$ appear and disappear over time. Each leaf n has an associated local variable $w_n(t)$, which is an real-valued quantity. The term local variable is used to represent a local state variable or device counter that is being subjected to monitoring. Local variables are updated asynchronously with a given sampling rate. The objective is to engineer a protocol on this network graph that provides a management station with a continuous estimate of $\sum_n w_n(t)$. The symbol $\sum$ denotes an aggregation function, i.e., a function built from a binary function + that is both commutative and associative. SUM, COUNT, MAX, or HISTOGRAM are examples of aggregation functions, and AVERAGE is an example of a function that can be computed using two aggregation functions, namely SUM and COUNT.

Our solution to this problem, GAP, is based upon the BFS algorithm of Dolev et al. [12] which executes in coarsely synchronized rounds during which each node exchanges its beliefs concerning the minimum distance to the root with all of its neighbors and then updates its belief accordingly. A node also maintains a pointer to its parent, through which the BFS tree is represented. GAP amends this basic algorithm in a number of ways. The protocol uses message passing instead of shared registers. Second, each node maintains information about its children in the BFS tree, in order to correctly compute aggregates, and it performs the actual aggregation. Finally, GAP is event-driven. This reduces traffic overhead at the expense of self-stabilization, and it introduces some twists to ensure that topology changes are properly handled.

13.4.2 Data Structures

In GAP each node maintains a neighborhood table T, such as the one pictured in Table 13.1, containing an entry for itself and each of its neighbors on the network graph.

In stable state the table will contain an entry for each live neighbor containing its identity, its status vis-a-vis the current node (*self, parent, child, or peer*), its level in the BFS tree (i.e., distance to root) as a non-negative integer, and its aggregate

Table 13.1 Sample neighborhood table for GAP

Node id	Status	Level	Weight
n_1	child	4	312
n_2	self	3	411
n_3	parent	2	7955
n_4	child	4	33
n_5	peer	4	567

weight (i.e., the aggregate weight of the spanning tree rooted in that particular node). The exception is *self*. In that case, the weight field will contain only the weight of the local node.

Initially, the neighborhood table of all nodes n except the root contains a single entry $(n, self, l_0, w_0)$ where l_0 and w_0 is some initial level, resp. weight. The initial level must be a non-negative integer. The initial neighborhood table of the root contains in addition the entry $(n_{root}, parent, -1, w_{root})$ where n_{root} is a "virtual root" node id used to receive output and w_{root} is arbitrary. This virtual root convention ensures that the same code can be used for the root as for other nodes, unlike [12] where the root is "hardwired" in order to ensure self-stabilization.

13.4.3   The Execution Model

The protocol executes using asynchronous message passing. The execution model assumes a set of underlying services – including failure detection, neighbor discovery, local weight update, message delivery, and timeout – that deliver their output to the process enqueue as messages of the form $(tag, Arg_1, ... , Arg_n)$. The following five message types are considered:

- *(fail, n)* is delivered upon detecting the failure of node n.
- *(new, n)* reports detection of a new neighbor n. At time of initialization, the list of known neighbors is empty, so the first thing done by the protocol after initialization will include reporting the initial neighbors.
- *(update, n, w, l, p)* is the main message, called an update vector, exchanged between neighbors. This message tells the receiving node that the BFS tree rooted in sending node n has aggregate weight w and that n has the level and parent specified. This message is computed in the obvious way from n's neighborhood table using the operation $updatevector(T)$. Observe that the parent field of the update vector is defined only when n's neighborhood table has more than one entry.
- *(weight, w)* is delivered as a result of sampling the local weight. The frequency and precision with which this takes place is not further specified.
- *(timeout)* is delivered upon a timeout.

13.4.4   Ancillary Functions

The algorithm uses the following ancillary functions:

- *newentry(n)* returns n and creates a table entry $T(n) = (n, s, l_0, w_0)$ where $s = peer$, and l_0 and w_0 are suitable default values. If the row $T(n)$ already exists, no change is performed.
- *removeentry(n)* removes the row $T(n)$, if it exists.

- *updateentry(n, w, l, p)* assigns *w* and *l* to the corresponding fields of $T(n)$, if they exist; otherwise the row is first created. If $p = self$ then $T(n).Status$ becomes *child*. This reflects the situation where *n* says that *self()* is *parent*. Otherwise, if $T(n).Status = child$ then $T(n).Status$ becomes *peer*.
- *level(n)* returns the level of *n* in *T*, if it exists, otherwise the return value is undefined.
- *parent()* returns the node id *n* such that $T(n).Status = parent$. If no such node id exists, a special value *nd* representing the undefined node is returned.
- *send(n, v)* sends the update vector *v* to the node *n*.
- *broadcast(v)* sends *v* to all known neighbors, not necessarily in atomic fashion.
- *maxrate()* is a timer service that periodically produces a message (*timeout*) for the purpose of bounding the rate at which a node can send messages to its neighbors.

13.4.5 The Algorithm

The main loop of the algorithm is given in pseudocode in Figure 13.8. Each loop iteration consists of three phases:

```
proc gap() =
    ... initialize data structures and services ...
    Timeout = 0 ;
    New = null ;
    Vector = updatevector();
    ... main loop ...
    while true do
    receive
      {new,From} =>
        NewNode = newentry(From) ;
    | {fail,From} =>
        removeentry(From)
    | {update,From,Weight,Level,Parent} =>
        updateentry(From,Weight,Level,Parent)
    | {updatelocal,Weight} =>
        updateentry(self(),Weight,level(self()),parent())
    | {timeout} => Timeout = 1
    end ;
    restoreTableInvariant() ;
    NewVector = updatevector();
    if NewNode != null
      {send(NewNode,NewVector); NewNode = null} ;
    if NewVector != Vector && Timeout
      { broadcast(NewVector); Vector = NewVector; Timeout = 0 }
    od ;
```

Fig. 13.8 Main loop of GAP

1. Get the next message and update the table accordingly.
2. Update the neighborhood table to take the newly received information into account (the operation *restoreTableInvariant*).
3. Notify neighbors of state changes as necessary. In particular, when a new node has been registered, the update vector must be sent to it to establish connection. Further, when the update vector has changed and sufficient time has elapsed, the new update vector is broadcast to the known neighbors.

Much of the semantics of the GAP protocol is embodied in the operation *restoreTableInvariant*. Part of the tasks of this operation is to ensure a set of basic integrity properties of the neighborhood table, such as:

- Each node is associated with at most one row.
- Exactly one row has status *self* and the node id of that row is *self*( ).
- If the table has more than one entry it has a parent.
- The parent has minimal level among all entries in the neighborhood table.
- The level of the parent is one less than the level of *self*( ).

In addition, an implementation of the *restoreTableInvariant* operation may implement some policy which serves to optimize protocol behavior in some respect such as: optimization of convergence time, or minimization of overshoot/undershoot after faults or during initialization.

Example policies are:

- **Conservative**. Once the parenthood relation changes, all information stored in the neighborhood table – except node identities – becomes in principle unreliable and could be forgotten (e.g., by assigning the undefined value). This policy will ensure that the aggregate is, in some reasonable sense, always a lower approximation of the "real" value.
- **Cache-like**. All information stored in the neighborhood table, except information concerning *self* or status of parent, is left unchanged. This appears to be a natural default policy, as it seems to provide a good compromise between overshoot/undershoot and convergence time.
- **Greedy**. or adaptive policies: Other policies can be envisaged such as policies which attempt to predict changes in neighbor status, such as proactively changing the status of a peer once its level has seen to be 2 or more greater than *self*'s. It is also possible to adapt the tree topology to MAC layer information such as link quality, as is done in [20].

13.5 Refinements of the Generic Protocol for Tree-Based Aggregation

This section outlines two refinements of the GAP protocol, both of which aim at reducing protocol overhead while maintaining certain objectives. The first such refinement, named A-GAP, employs a local filter scheme, whereby a node drops updates when only small changes to its partial aggregate occur. Like the GAP protocol, A-GAP performs continuous monitoring of aggregates, but aims at minimizing protocol overhead while adhering to a configurable accuracy objective. The second refinement of GAP, called TCA-GAP, detects threshold crossings of aggregates. It applies the concepts of local thresholds and local hysteresis, aimed at reducing protocol overhead whenever the aggregate is "far" from the given threshold while ensuring correct detection.

Both protocols, A-GAP and TCA-GAP, operate in an asynchronous and decentralized fashion. They inherit from GAP the functionality of creating and maintaining the aggregation tree (specifically, handling node arrivals, departures, and failures) and that of incremental aggregation. A thorough presentation of A-GAP and TCA-GAP can be found in [26] and [38], respectively.

13.5.1 Continuous Monitoring of Aggregates with Performance Objectives

13.5.1.1 Problem Statement

We consider a dynamically changing network graph $G(t) = (V(t), E(t))$, in which nodes $n \in V(t)$ and edges/links $e \in E(t) \subseteq V(t) \times V(t)$ appear and disappear over time. Each leaf n has an associated local variable $w_n(t)$, which is an integer-valued quantity. Local variables are updated asynchronously with a given sampling rate. The objective is to engineer a protocol on this network graph that provides a management station with a continuous estimate of $\sum_n w_n(t)$ for a given accuracy. The protocol should execute with minimal overhead in the sense that it minimizes the (maximum) processing load over all nodes. The load is expressed as the number of updates per second a node has to process. The accuracy is expressed as the *average error* of the estimate over time. We use here SUM as aggregation function. Other functions can be supported as well [26].

13.5.1.2 Filter Computation

Estimating the aggregate at the root node with minimal overhead for a given accuracy can be formalized as an optimization problem. Let n be a node in the network graph, ω^n the rate of updates received by node n from its children, F^n the filter width of node n, E^{root} the distribution of the estimation error at the root node, and ε the accuracy objective. The problem can then be stated as: Minimize $\max_n\{\omega^n\}$ s.t. $E[|E^{root}|] \leq \varepsilon$, whereby ω^n and E^{root} depend on the filter widths $(F^n)_n$, which are the decision variables.

We developed a stochastic model for the monitoring process, which is based on discrete-time Markov chains and describes individual nodes in their steady state [26]. For each node n, the model relates the error E^n of the partial aggregate of n, the step sizes that indicate changes in the partial aggregate, the rate of updates n sends, and the filter width F^n. In a leaf node, the change of the local variable over time is modeled as a random walk. The stochastic model permits us to compute the distribution E^{root} of the estimation error at the root node and the rate of updates ω_n processed by each node.

To solve the optimization problem, A-GAP employs a distributed heuristic, which maps the global problem into a local problem that each node solves in an asynchronous fashion. This way, each node periodically computes the local filters and (local) accuracy objectives for its children. A-GAP continuously estimates the step sizes in the leaf nodes for the random-walk model using the maximum likelihood estimator (MLE). Note that these step sizes are the only variables that the protocol estimates. All other variables are dynamically computed based on these estimates.

13.5.1.3 Evaluation Results

We evaluated A-GAP through extensive simulations and present here results from only two scenarios, related to (a) controlling the trade-off protocol overhead vs. estimation error and (b) real-time estimation of the error distribution. Both scenarios share the following settings. The management overlay follows the physical topology of Abovenet, an ISP, with 654 nodes and 1332 links. Link speeds in the overlay are 100 Mbps. The communication delay is 4 ms, and the time to process a message at a node is 1 ms. The local management variable represents the number of HTTP flows entering the network at a given node, and thus the monitored aggregate is the current number of HTTP flows in the network. (In the Abovenet scenarios, the aggregate is in the order of 20.000 flows.) The local variables are updated asynchronously, once every second. The evolution of the local variables is simulated based on packet traces that were captured at the University of Twente at two of their network access points and then processed by us to obtain traces for all nodes in the simulation [26].

Figure 13.9 gives a result from the first scenario and shows the protocol overhead (i.e., the maximum number of processed updates across all nodes) as a function of the experienced error. Every point in the graph corresponds to a simulation run. We observe that the overhead decreases monotonically as the estimation error increases. Consequently, the overhead can be reduced by allowing a larger estimation error, and the error objective is an effective control parameter. For example, compared to an error objective of 0 (which results in an experienced error of 4.5), an error objective of 2 flows (experienced error 5) reduces the load by 30%; an error objective of 20 flows (experienced error 21) leads to a 85% reduction in load.

Figure 13.10 relates to the second scenario and shows the predicted error distribution computed by A-GAP and the actual error measured in a simulation run, for an error objective of 8. The vertical bars indicate the average actual error. As one can see, the predicted error distribution is close to the actual distribution. More importantly, the distributions have long tails. While the average error in this measurement period is 8.76, the maximum error during the simulation run is 44 and

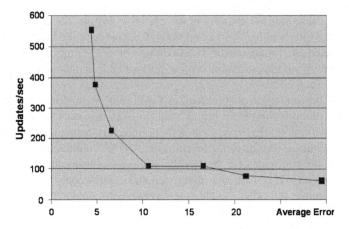

Fig. 13.9 Protocol overhead incurred by A-GAP as a function of the experienced error e

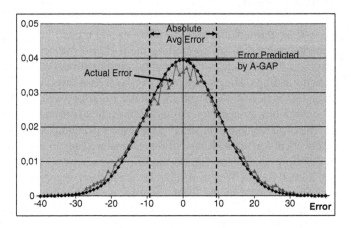

Fig. 13.10 Distribution of the error predicted by A-GAP and the actual error at the root node

the maximum possible error (that would occur in an infinite measurement period) is 70. Based on this observation, we argue that an average error objective is more significant for practical scenarios than a maximum error objective used by other authors [10, 22, 30]. We have implemented A-GAP and deployed it on a testbed of 16 commercial routers where it is used for monitoring IP flows [25]. The testbed measurements are consistent with the simulation studies we performed for different topologies and network sizes, which proves the feasibility of the protocol design, and, more generally, the feasibility of effective and efficient real-time flow monitoring in large network environments.

13.5.1.4 Related Work

Most current research in monitoring aggregates is carried out in the context of wireless sensor networks, where energy constraints are paramount and the objective is to maximize the lifetime of the network. Further, many recent works on monitoring the evolution of aggregates over time focus on n-time queries that estimate the aggregate at discrete times and are realized as periodic snapshots (e.g., [10, 23, 30]).

The trade-off between accuracy and overhead for continuous monitoring of aggregates has been studied first by Olston et al. who proposed a centralized monitoring protocol to control the trade-off [22, 23].

The main differentiator between A-GAP and related protocols is its stochastic model of the monitoring process. This model allows for a prediction of the protocol performance, in terms of overhead and error, and the support of flexible error objectives. In fact, all protocols known to us that allow controlling the trade-off between accuracy and overhead can support only the maximum error as accuracy objective, which, as we and others pointed out, is of limited practical relevance.

13.5.2 Efficient Detection of Threshold Crossing

13.5.2.1 Problem Statement

We are considering a dynamically changing network graph $G(t) = (V(t), E(t))$ in which nodes $i \in V(t)$ and edges/links $e \in E(t) = V(t) \times V(t)$ may appear and disappear over time. To each node i is associated a local state variable $w_i(t)$ that represents the quantity whose aggregate is being subjected to threshold monitoring. We assume here that local variables are *non-negative real-valued* quantities, aggregated using SUM. The objective is to raise an alert on a distinguished root node, when the aggregate $\sum_i w_i(t)$ exceeds a given global threshold T^{g+}, and to clear the alert when the aggregate has decreased below a lower threshold T^{g-} (see Figure 13.11).

13.5.2.2 Local Threshold and Hysteresis Mechanism

A key idea in TCA-GAP is to introduce and maintain local thresholds that apply to each node in the aggregation tree. These local thresholds allow nodes to switch between an *active* state, where the node executes the GAP protocol and sends updates of its partial aggregate to its parent, and a *passive* state, where the node ceases to propagate updates up the aggregation tree. The transition between active and passive state is controlled by a *local threshold* and a *local hysteresis* mechanism.

We restrict the discussion here to the case where the crossing of the upper global threshold is detected. (Detecting a downward crossing of the lower threshold T^{g-} can be achieved in a very similar way [38].) For reason of readability, we do not

Fig. 13.11 Threshold
Crossing Alerts: an alert
is raised when the monitored
variable crosses a given
threshold T^{g+} from below.
The alert is cleared when
the variable crosses a lower
threshold T^{g-} from above

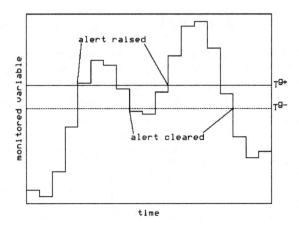

write T^{g+}, but simply T^g. An extension of the discussion to detecting the lower global threshold is straightforward.

Each node has a local threshold, which is set by its parent. For the root node, the local threshold is the same as the global threshold T^g.

Two global parameters $0 \leq k_2 < k_1 \leq 1$ configure the local hysteresis mechanism and control how the node switches between active and passive state. We first explain the transition from active to passive. When a node is active, then all nodes in the subtree rooted at that node are also active (how this is achieved is explained below). The transition from active to passive state takes place whenever the partial aggregate $a_i(t)$ of a node i is less than $k_2 T_i$. When the node turns passive, it assigns a local threshold T_j to each child j, proportionally to the partial aggregate $a_j(t)$ of the child j: $T_j = T_i \frac{a_j}{w_i + \sum_j a_j}$.

Second, a node i in passive state becomes active when it can deduce that its partial aggregate a_i must exceed $k_1 T_i$. It makes this deduction based on the fact that (a) the partial aggregate of each active child is known to the node and (b) the node knows that, for each passive child j, the partial aggregate a_j is below $k_1 T_j$.

When a node i switches to active, it sets the threshold of its children to 0. As a consequence, all nodes in the subtree rooted at node i have their local thresholds recursively set to 0 and, as a result, become active.

The parameters k_1 and k_2 of the hysteresis mechanism control the trade-off between the protocol overhead and the quality of TCA detection. For small values of k_1 and k_2, the protocol tends to make nodes active when the aggregate is relatively far from the threshold, hence increasing the overhead. On the other hand, the larger the number of active nodes, the shorter the detection time tends to become. Values for k_1 and k_2 close to 1 cause the protocol to keep nodes passive unless the aggregate is close to the threshold. Though this decreases the protocol overhead, it generally increases the detection time, since less aggregate updates are reaching the root node.

13.5.2.3 Local Threshold Recomputation

TCA-GAP attempts to reduce the protocol overhead by keeping as many nodes passive as possible while ensuring correct threshold detection. To enable threshold detection at the root node, we introduce *local invariants* that must hold on passive nodes together with *threshold recomputation policies*, which are triggered upon violation of these invariants.

Consider a node i in passive state. There are two conditions under which node i may become active. First, it may be that i's parent reduces the local threshold T_i assigned to i (for the purpose of threshold recomputation; see below). The result may be that T_i becomes strictly smaller than $w_i + \sum_{j \in J} T_j$ with T_j being the threshold assigned to child j and J being the set of children of node i. This can cause the local threshold T_i to be crossed without this being detected at node i, resulting in the possibility of a false negative at the root node. To prevent such a scenario from happening, we introduce the following local threshold rule for node i:

$$(R1) \; T_i \geq w_i + \sum_{j \in J} T_j \, , \text{ where } J \text{ is the set of children of node } i.$$

The second condition under which node i might need to switch to active state concerns the situation where one or more of its children are active. Recall that the local hysteresis mechanism ensures that the actual aggregate of a subtree rooted in a passive child j does not exceed T_j (at least in the approximate sense as computed by the underlying aggregation protocol, GAP). Thus, a sufficient condition for the actual aggregate of i's subtree to not exceed T_i is that the sum of aggregates reported by active children does not exceed the sum of the corresponding local thresholds. This motivates the second local threshold rule:

$$(R2) \; \sum_{j \in J'} T_j \geq \sum_{j \in J' a_j(t)} \, , \text{ where } J' \text{ is the set of active children of node } i.$$

Rules R1 and R2 together ensure that local threshold crossings will be detected [38].

If one of the rules R1 or R2 fails on node i, then the node attempts to reinstate the rule by reducing the threshold of one or more passive children. We call this procedure *threshold recomputation*. Specifically, if (R1) fails, then the protocol reduces the threshold of one or more passive children by $\gamma = w_i + \sum_{j \in J} T_j - T_i$, where J is the set of children of i. Evidently, this may cause one or more passive children to become active.

If (R2) fails, then the protocol reduces the threshold of one or more passive children by $\gamma > \sum_{j \in J'} (a_j - T_j)$ where J' is the set of active children, and, at the same time, increases the assigned threshold of one or more active children by the same amount, which will reinstate (R2). Such a reduction is always possible since the node is passive.

There are many possible policies for threshold recomputation. For instance, there are several ways to choose the set of active children whose threshold is increased. Note though that the amount of threshold increment for child j must not exceed $\frac{a_j}{k_2} - T_j$. If it does, there exists a scenario in which two children alternately borrow threshold space from each other and the system oscillates. In TCA-GAP the protocol identifies the smallest set of active children j^* with the largest values of $\frac{a_j}{k_1} - T_j$ from all $j \in j'$ so that $\sum_{j \in J'} (\frac{a_j}{k_1} - T_j) > \sum_{j \in J'} (a_j - T_j)$. Then γ is chosen such that $\gamma = \sum_{j \in J'} (\frac{a_j}{k_1} - T_j)$ and the threshold of a child j is increased by $\frac{a_j}{k_2} - T_j$ for all $j \in j^*$.

There are also options on how to choose the set of passive children whose threshold is reduced. Here is a policy that is also used in the simulation results below: The child j with the largest threshold T_j is selected. If $\gamma \leq T_j$, then j is the only child whose threshold is reduced. Otherwise, T_j is reduced to 0, and this procedure is applied to the child with the second largest threshold and $\gamma = \gamma - T_j$. This policy attempts to minimize the overhead for threshold updating at the cost of increasing the risk of nodes becoming active.

13.5.2.4 Evaluation Results

We illustrate the efficiency of TCA-GAP for a scenario with a setup very similar to the one given in Section 13.5.1.3, with the major exception that the traces of the local variables in this scenario are obtained by adding a sinusoidal bias to the traces in Section 13.5.1.3 in order to create threshold crossings. (For a detailed description of the scenario and results from a thorough simulation study, see [38].)

Figure 13.12 shows the change of the aggregate and the protocol overhead over time during a simulation run of 45 s. Three threshold crossings occur: at around $t = 9$ s (upper threshold crossing), $t = 23.5$ s (lower threshold crossing) and $t = 39$ sec (upper threshold crossing). Before each threshold crossing, e.g., between $t = 8$ s

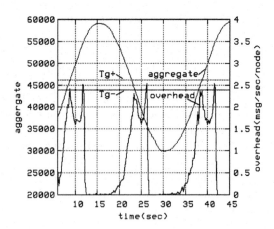

Fig. 13.12 TCA-GAP protocol overhead over time

to $t = 10$ s, we observe a peak in protocol overhead. This can be explained by an increased level of threshold recomputation during those periods, as well as the transition of passive nodes to active state, which includes resetting of thresholds on subtrees. For each of the three threshold crossings, we see a second peak in the protocol overhead, which relates to the root node becoming passive and thus distributing new threshold values to all nodes in a recursive manner.

The conclusions from this and other similar experiments we performed are that the protocol overhead is low whenever the aggregate is far from the threshold. Second, the protocol overhead is highest shortly before a threshold is crossed or for short period after the root node switches from active to passive state. Third, the protocol overhead of TCA-GAP during peak periods is comparable to the average overhead of a tree-based continuous aggregation protocol such as GAP. For this scenario, we measured the protocol overhead for GAP to be 1.7 msgs/s.

13.5.2.5   Related Work

Interest in the problem of detecting network-wide threshold crossings has increased in recent years. All approaches known to us use some type of thresholds or filters on individual nodes to reduce the protocol overhead. Most proposed protocols exhibit low overhead when the aggregate is far from the monitored threshold. The works are generally based on a weakly distributed approach whereby a central coordinator computes local thresholds or filter parameters for all nodes. The coordinator also performs aggregation of the local variables and detects threshold crossings. Results using this approach have been reported in Dilman and Raz [11] for the aggregation function SUM, in Keralapura et al. [18] for COUNT, and in Huang et al. [15] for non-linear aggregation functions. A common drawback of weakly distributed approaches is that the load on the coordinator increases linearly with the system size, which limits the scalability of the protocol. In strongly distributed approaches, such as the one used for the TCA-GAP protocol, local thresholds or filter parameters are computed in a fully distributed manner, and nodes interact with their neighbors on the network graph over which the protocol is running, instead of interacting with a central coordinator. A strongly distributed solution similar to TCA-GAP has been presented by Breitgand et al. in the context of estimating the size of a multicast group [7]. [38] contains a comparative assessment of the protocol in [7] and TCA-GAP. In [31], Sharfman et al. discuss work where threshold crossings are detected for a real-valued function that is computed over the sum of vector-valued local variables. There, the authors present both a weakly distributed version and a strongly distributed version of their approach to the detection of threshold crossing.

Acknowledgements This work has been conducted as part of the EU FP7 Project 4WARD on Future Internet design [1].

References

1. 4WARD Partners. The EU 7th framework project 4WARD. http://www.4ward-project.eu/.
2. W. Aiello, F. Chung, and L. Lu. A random graph model for massive graphs. In *Proceedings of the 32nd Annual Symposium on Theory of Computing*, pages 171–180, 2000.
3. C. Aurrecoechea, A. T. Campbell, and L. Hauw. A survey of QoS architectures. *Multimedia Systems*, 6(3):138–151, 1998.
4. K. Birman. The promise, and limitations, of gossip protocols. *ACM SIGOPS Operating Systems Review*, 41(5):8–13, October 2007.
5. S. Blake, D. Black, M. Carlson, E. Davies, Z. Wang, and W. Weiss. An architecture for differentiated services, RFC 2475, 1998.
6. B. Bollobas. *Random Graphs*. Academic Press, Inc., Orlando, Florida, 1985.
7. D. Breitgand, D. Dolev, and D. Raz. Accounting mechanism for membership size-dependent pricing of multicast traffic. In *NGC '03: Networked Group Communication*, pages 276–286, 2003.
8. T. Chen-Khong and J. Ko. Monitoring QoS distribution in multimedia networks. *International journal of network management*, 10:75–90, 2000.
9. M. Dam and R. Stadler. A generic protocol for network state aggregation. In *RVK 05, Linkping, Sweden, June* 14–16, 2005.
10. A. Deligiannakis, Y. Kotidis, and N. Roussopoulos. Hierarchical in-network data aggregation with quality guarantees. In *In Proc. 9th International Conference on Extending Database Technology (EDBT04), Heraklion Crete, Greece, March* 14–18, 2004.
11. M. Dilman and D. Raz. Efficient reactive monitoring. *IEEE Journal on Selected Areas in Communications (JSAC)*, 20(4):668, 2002.
12. S. Dolev, A. Israeli, and S. Moran. Self-stabilization of dynamic systems assuming only read/write atomicity. *Distributed Computing*, 7:3–16, 1993.
13. C. Elster, D. Raz, and R. Wolff. Autonomous end to end qos monitoring. In *Workshop on End-to-End Monitoring Techniques and Services, 2005.*, pages 1–16, May 2005.
14. M. Faloutsos, P. Faloutsos, and C. Faloutsos. On power-law relationships of the internet topology. In *SIGCOMM*, pages 251–262, 1999.
15. L. Huang, M. Garofalakis, J. Hellerstein, A. Joseph, and N. Taft. Toward sophisticated detection with distributed triggers. In *MineNet '06: Proceedings of the 2006 SIGCOMM workshop on Mining network data*, pages 311–316. ACM Press, 2006.
16. M. Jelasity, A. Montresor, and O. Babaoglu. Gossip-based aggregation in large dynamic networks. *ACM Transactions on Computer Systems*, 23(3):219–252, August 2005.
17. D. Kempe, A. Dobra, and J. Gehrke. Gossip-based computation of aggregate information. In *In Proc. of the 44th Annual IEEE Symposium on Foundations of Computer Science (FOCS03), Cambridge, MA, USA, October* 11–14, 2003.
18. R. Keralapura, G. Cormode, and J. Ramamirtham. Communication-efficient distributed monitoring of thresholded counts. In *SIGMOD '06: Proceedings of the 2006 ACM SIGMOD international conference on Management of data*, pages 289–300. ACM Press, 2006.
19. A.A. Lazar. Programming telecommunication networks. *Network, IEEE*, 11(5):8–18, Sep/Oct 1997.
20. S. Madden, M. Franklin, J. Hellerstein, and W. Hong. TAG: a tiny aggregation service for ad-hoc sensor networks. In *Fifth Symposium on Operating Systems Design and Implementation (USENIX - OSDI '02), Boston, MA, USA, December* 9–12, 2002.
21. J. Martin-Flatin, S. Znaty, and J. Hubaux. A survey of distributed enterprise network andsystems management paradigms. *J. Netw. Syst. Manage.*, 7(1):9–26, 1999.
22. C. Olston, J. Jiang, and J. Widom. Adaptive filters for continuous queries over distributed data streams. In *SIGMOD '03: Proceedings of the 2003 ACM SIGMOD international conference on Management of data*, pages 563–574, New York, NY, USA, 2003. ACM.
23. C. Olston, B. T. Loo, and J. Widom. Adaptive precision setting for cached approximate values. *SIGMOD Rec.*, 30(2):355–366, 2001.

24. G. Pavlou. On the evolution of management approaches, frameworks and protocols: A historical perspective. *J. Netw. Syst. Manage.*, 15(4):425–445, 2007.
25. A. Gonzalez Prieto and R. Stadler. Monitoring flow aggregates with controllable accuracy. In *10th IFIP/IEEE International Conference on Management of Multimedia and Mobile Networks and Services (MMNS 2007), San Jos, California, USA, Oct 31 - Nov 2*, 2007.
26. A.G. Prieto and R. Stadler. A-gap: An adaptive protocol for continuous network monitoring with accuracy objectives. *Network and Service Management, IEEE Transactions on*, 4(1): 2–12, June 2007.
27. D. Raz and Y. Shavitt. Active networks for efficient distributed network management. *Communications Magazine, IEEE*, 38(3):138–143, Mar 2000.
28. K. Salamatian and S. Fdida. Measurement based modeling of quality of service in the internet: A methodological approach. In *IWDC '01: Proceedings of the Thyrrhenian International Workshop on Digital Communications*, pages 158–174, London, UK, 2001. Springer-Verlag.
29. H. Schulzrinne, A. Rao, and R. Lanphier. Real time streaming protocol (RTSP), RFC 2326, 1998.
30. M. A. Sharaf, J. Beaver, A. Labrinidis, and P. K. Chrysanthis. Balancing energy efficiency and quality of aggregate data in sensor networks. *ACM International Journal on Very Large Data Bases*, 13(4):384–403, 2004.
31. Izchak Sharfman, Assaf Schuster, and Daniel Keren. A geometric approach to monitoring threshold functions over distributed data streams. In *SIGMOD '06: Proceedings of the 2006 ACM SIGMOD international conference on Management of data*, pages 301–312. ACM Press, 2006.
32. N. Spring, R. Mahajan, and D. Wetherall. Rocketfuel maps and data. http://www.cs. washington.edu/research/networking/rocketfuel/.
33. N. Spring, R. Mahajan, and D. Wetherall. Measuring ISP topologies with rocketfuel. In *Proceedings of ACM/SIGCOMM '02*, August 2002.
34. H. Tangmunarunkit, R. Govindan, S. Jamin, S. Shenker, and W. Willinger. Network topology generators: Degree-based vs structural. In *ACM SIGCOMM, August*, 2002.
35. David L. Tennenhouse and David J. Wetherall. Towards an active network architecture. *SIGCOMM Comput. Commun. Rev.*, 26(2):5–17, 1996.
36. B. M. Waxman. Routing of multipoint connections. *IEEE Journal of Selected Areas in Communications*, 6(9):1617–1622, December 1988.
37. F. Wuhib, M. Dam, R. Stadler, and A. Clemm. Robust monitoring of network-wide aggregates through gossiping. In *IEEE Transactions on Network and Service Management (TNSM)*, 6(2), June 2009.
38. F. Wuhib, M. Dam, and R. Stadler. Decentralized detection of global threshold crossings using aggregation trees. *Computer Networks*, 52(9):1745–1761, February 2008.
39. X. Xiao and L. M. Ni. Internet QoS: A big picture. *IEEE Network*, 13(2):8–18, March 1999.

Chapter 14
Algebraic Approaches for Scalable End-to-End Monitoring and Diagnosis

Yao Zhao and Yan Chen

Abstract The rigidity of the Internet architecture led to flourish in the research of end-to-end based systems. In this chapter, we describe a linear algebra-based end-to-end monitoring and diagnosis system. We first propose a tomography-based overlay monitoring system (*TOM*). Given n end hosts, TOM selectively monitors a *basis set* of $O(n \log n)$ paths out of all $n(n-1)$ end-to-end paths. Any end-to-end path can be written as a unique linear combination of paths in the basis set. Consequently, by monitoring loss rates for the paths in the basis set, TOM infers loss rates for all end-to-end paths. Furthermore, leveraging on the scalable measurements from the TOM system, we propose the *Least-biased End-to-End Network Diagnosis* (in short, LEND) system. We define a *minimal identifiable link sequence* (MILS) as a link sequence of minimal length whose properties can be uniquely identified from end-to-end measurements. LEND applies an algebraic approach to find out the MILSes and infers the properties of the MILSes efficiently. This also means LEND system achieves the finest diagnosis granularity under the least biased statistical assumptions.

14.1 Introduction

"When something breaks in the Internet, the Internet's very decentralized structure makes it hard to figure out what went wrong and even harder to assign responsibility."

– "Looking Over the Fence at Networks: A Neighbor's View of Networking Research", by Committees on Research Horizons in Networking, US National Research Council, 2001.

The rigidity of the Internet architecture makes it extremely difficult to deploy innovative disruptive technologies in the core. This has led to extensive research into overlay and peer-to-peer systems, such as overlay routing and location, application-

Y. Zhao (✉) and Y. Chen
Tech Institute L359, EECS Department, 2145 Sheridan Road, Northwestern University, Evanston, IL 60208-3118
e-mail: YaoZhao2009@u.northwestern.edu; ychen@cs.northwestern.edu

G. Cormode and M. Thottan (eds.), *Algorithms for Next Generation Networks*, Computer Communications and Networks, DOI 10.1007/978-1-84882-765-3_14, © Springer-Verlag London Limited 2010

level multicast, and peer-to-peer file sharing. These systems flexibly choose their communication paths and targets, and thus can benefit from estimation of end-to-end network distances (e.g., latency and loss rate). Accurate loss rate monitoring systems can detect path outages and periods of degraded performance within seconds. They facilitate management of distributed systems such as virtual private networks (VPN) and content distribution networks; and they are useful for building adaptive overlay applications, like streaming media and multiplayer gaming.

Meanwhile, Internet fault diagnosis is important to end users, overlay network service providers (like Akamai [2]), and Internet service providers (ISPs). For example, with Internet fault diagnosis tools, users can choose more reliable ISPs. Overlay service providers can use such tools to locate faults in order to fix them or bypass them; information about faults can also guide decisions about service provisioning, deployment, and redirection. However, the modern Internet is heterogeneous and largely unregulated, which renders link-level fault diagnosis an increasingly challenging problem. The servers and routers in the network core are usually operated by businesses, and those businesses may be unwilling or unable to cooperate in collecting the network traffic measurements vital for Internet fault diagnosis. Therefore, end-to-end diagnosis approaches attract most of the focus of researchers in this area.

Thus it is desirable to have a scalable end-to-end loss rate monitoring and diagnosis system which is accurate and scalable. We formulate the problem as follows: consider an overlay network of n end hosts; we define a path to be a routing path between a pair of end hosts, and a link to be an IP link between routers. A path is a concatenation of links. We also rely on the two *fundamental* statistical assumptions for any end-to-end network monitoring and diagnosis approaches.

- End-to-end measurement can infer the end-to-end properties accurately.
- The linear system between path- and link-level properties assumes independence between link-level properties.

Therefore, the *monitoring problem* we focus on is to select a minimal subset of paths from the $O(n^2)$ paths to monitor so that the loss rates and latencies of all other paths can be inferred. Also, we aim to only use the above basic assumptions to achieve *the least biased* and, hence, *the most accurate*, diagnosis based on the measurement results of the paths. We define a *minimal identifiable link sequence* (MILS) as a link sequence of minimal length whose properties can be uniquely identified from end-to-end measurements without bias.

In this chapter, we describe a linear algebra-based end-to-end monitoring and diagnosis system. Specifically, the monitoring system we propose is a tomography-based overlay monitoring system (*TOM*) [9] in which we selectively monitor a *basis set* of k paths. Any end-to-end path can be written as a unique linear combination of paths in the basis set. Consequently, by monitoring loss rates for the paths in the basis set, we infer loss rates for all end-to-end paths. This can also be extended to other additive metrics, such as latency. The end-to-end path loss rates can be computed even when the paths contain *unidentifiable links* for which loss rates cannot be computed. Furthermore, based on the measurements from the TOM system, we propose the *Least-biased End-to-end Network Diagnosis* (LEND) system [34], which applies an algebraic approach to find out the MILSes and infers the properties of the MILSes. This also means our LEND system achieves the finest diagnosis granularity under the least biased case.

We describe the following properties of the TOM and LEND systems:

- For reasonably large n (say 100), the basis path set has $k = O(n \log n)$ through linear regression tests on various synthetic and real topologies. We also provide some explanation based on the Internet topology and the AS hierarchy, which shows that the monitoring system TOM is scalable.
- We advocate the unbiased end-to-end diagnosis paradigm and introduce the concept of MILS. However, taking a network as a directed graph, when only topology information is used, we prove that each path is an MILS: no path segment smaller than an end-to-end path has properties which can be uniquely determined by end-to-end measurements. To address the problem, we observe that, in practice, there are many good paths with zero loss rates. Then as a *fact* rather than as a statistical assumption, we know all the links on such paths must also have no losses. Based on such observation, we propose a "good path" algorithm, which uses both topology and measurement snapshots to find MILSes with the finest granularity.
- In an overlay network, end hosts frequently join/leave the overlay and routing changes occur from time to time. For both TOM and LEND systems to adapt to these efficiently, we design incremental algorithms for path addition and deletion with small cost instead of reinitializing the system with high cost. We propose randomized schemes for measurement load balancing as well. The details of these algorithms can be found in [9, 34].

The TOM and LEND systems have been evaluated through extensive simulations and Internet experiments. In both simulations and PlanetLab experiments, path loss rates have been estimated with high accuracy using $O(n \log n)$ measurements, and the lossy links are further diagnosed with fine granularity and accuracy. For the PlanetLab experiments, the average absolute error of path loss rate estimation is only 0.0027, and the average relative error rate is 1.1, even though about 10% of the paths have incomplete or non-existent routing information. Also in the PlanetLab experiments of LEND, the average diagnosis granularity is only four hops for all the lossy paths. This can be further improved with larger overlay networks, as shown through our simulation with a real router-level topology from [20]. In addition, the loss rate inference on the MILSes is highly accurate, as verified through the cross-validation and IP spoof-based validation schemes [34].

For the PlanetLab experiments with 135 hosts, the average setup (monitoring path selection) time of the TOM system is 109.3 s, and the online diagnosis of 18,090 paths, 3,714 of which are lossy, takes only 4.2 s. In addition, we adapt to topology changes within seconds without sacrificing accuracy. The measurement load balancing reduces the load variation and the maximum vs. mean load ratio significantly, by up to a factor of 7.3.

For the rest of the chapter, we first survey related work in the next section. Then we describe the linear algebraic model and the system architecture in Section 14.3, present the monitoring path selection (TOM) in Section 14.4 and the diagnosis algo-rithms (LEND) in Section 14.5. Internet experiments are described in Sections 14.6, while simulations are omitted in the chapter. Finally, we discuss and conclude in Sections 14.7.

14.2 Related Work

14.2.1 End-to-End Monitoring

There are many existing scalable end-to-end latency estimation schemes, which can be broadly classified into clustering-based [10, 18] and coordinate-based sys-tems [23, 28]. Clustering-based systems cluster end hosts based on their network proximity or latency similarity under normal conditions, then choose the centroid of each cluster as the monitor. But a monitor and other members of the same cluster often take different routes to remote hosts. So the monitor cannot detect conges-tion for its members. Similarly, the coordinates assigned to each end host in the coordinate-based approaches cannot embed any congestion/failure information.

Later on, linear algebraic model is introduced into end-to-end monitoring, and many monitoring system designs including TOM use mathematical and statistical approaches to infer the whole network properties from measurements on carefully selected path sets. Ozmutlu et al. select a minimal subset of paths to cover all links for monitoring, assuming link-by-link latency is available via end-to-end measure-ment [24]. But the link-by-link latency obtained from traceroute is often inaccurate. And their approach does not work well for loss rate because it is difficult to estimate link-by-link loss rates from end-to-end measurement. A similar approach was taken for selecting paths to measure overlay network [31]. The minimal set cover selected can only give *bounds* for metrics like latency, and there is no guarantee as to how far the bounds are from the real values. TOM selectively monitor a *basis set* of all paths, and further stimulate several following works. In [11], Chua et al. proposed an SVD (Singular Value Decomposition) based solution, which selects fewer paths than the basis of the path matrix, while all the unmeasured path properties can be inferred without severe degradation of accuracy. More recently, Song et al. [30] in-troduced the Bayesian experimental design framework into network measurement. In [30], the best set of paths that achieves the highest expected estimation accuracy is selected, given the constraint on the total number of selected paths.

14.2.2 End-to-End Diagnosis

Ping and traceroute are the earliest Internet diagnosis tools, and they are still widely used. However, the asymmetry of Internet routing and of link properties makes it difficult to use these tools to infer properties of individual links. The latest work on network diagnosis can be put into two categories: *pure end-to-end approaches* [1,5, 7,12,14,16,25] and *router response-based approaches* [3,21,33].

Most end-to-end tomography tools fall in one of two classes. First, several end-to-end tomography designs are based on temporal correlations among multiple receivers in a multicast-like environment [1,5,7,12,16]. Adams et al. [1] use a single multicast tree and then Bu et al. [5] extend Internet tomography to the general topologies. Meanwhile, Duffield et al. [16] proposed to use back-to-back probing in unicast to mimic multicast and hence get over the multicast barrier in real networks. Second, some other tools [14,25] impose additional statistical assumptions beyond the linear loss model described in Section 14.3.1.

Under certain assumptions, tools in the first class infer a loss rate for each virtual link (*i.e.*, sequence of consecutive links without a branching point) with high probability. Thus, these tools diagnose failures at the granularity of individual virtual links; obviously, this is a bound on the granularity obtainable by the end-to-end tomography system. Typically these systems assume an ideal multicast environment; but since true multicast does not exist in the Internet, they use unicast for approximation. Thus the accuracy of the probe measurements heavily depends on the cross traffic in the network, and there is no guarantee of their accuracy.

As for the second class of tools, the statistically based tools introduced in [14,25] and use only uncorrelated end-to-end measurements to identify lossy network links. One shortcoming of these tools is apparent when studying simple tree topology in Figure 14.1. The numbers in the figure are the loss rates of the corresponding paths or links. In this tree, we can only measure the loss rates of two paths: $A \rightarrow B$ and $A \rightarrow C$. In the Figure 14.1(a) and (b) show two possible link loss rates that lead to the same end-to-end path measurements. The linear programming approach in [25] and SCFS [14] will always obtain the result of (a) because they are biased toward minimizing the number of lossy link predictions; but such results may not be correct. As for the random sampling and Gibbs sampling approaches in [25], either (a) or (b) may be predicted. In fact, none of the loss rates for these three links are identifiable from end-to-end measurements, and the LEND system will determine that none of the individual links are identifiable, and will get MILSes $A \rightarrow N \rightarrow B$ and $A \rightarrow N \rightarrow C$.

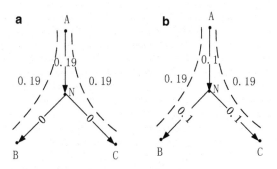

Fig. 14.1 Example of an underconstrained system: (**a**) one possible link loss scenario (**b**) a different link loss scenario with the same end-to-end path measurements

Other than the above two classes, Shavitt et al. use a linear algebraic algorithm to compute some additional "distances" (*i.e.*, latencies of path segments) that are not explicitly measured [29]. The algorithm proposed in [29] has the same function as our link-level diagnosis algorithm in undirected graph model. However, the LEND system incorporates the scalable measurement approach designed in TOM [9] and reuses its outputs to save the computational complexity for link-level diagnosis, and hence our LEND system is both measurement cost-efficient and computation-efficient. More importantly, the Internet should be modeled as a directed graph. The algebraic algorithm in [29] fails to do any link-level diagnosis on directed graphs, shown by Theorem 1 in Section 14.5.3.1.

14.3   Models and Architecture

In this section, we briefly describe the algebraic model and the system architecture of the LEND system. The algebraic model is widely used in Internet tomography and other measurement works [1, 9, 29]. For easy indexing, all the important notations in the paper can be found in Table 14.1.

Table 14.1   Table of notation

Symbols	Symbol meaning
M	Total number of nodes
N	Number of end hosts
n	Number of end hosts on the overlay
$r = O(n^2)$	Number of end-to-end paths
s	# of IP links that the overlay spans
$G \in \{0,1\}^{r \times s}$	Original path matrix
$\bar{G} \in \{0,1\}^{k \times s}$	A basis of G
$k \leq s$	Rank of G
l_i	Loss rate on ith link
p_i	Loss rate on ith measurement path
x_i	$\log(1 - l_i)$
b_i	$\log(1 - p_i)$
v	Vector in $\{0,1\}^s$ (represents path)
p	Loss rate along a path
$\mathscr{R}(G^T)$	Row(path) space of G ($= \mathrm{range}(G^T)$)
$G' \in \{0,1\}^{r' \times s'}$	Reduced G after removing good paths & links
s'	Number of links remaining in G'
r'	Number of bad paths remaining in G'
$k' \leq s'$	Rank of G'
G''	Reduced $\bar{G}$ after removing good paths & links
$\bar{G}'$	A basis of G'', also a basis of G'
Q', R'	QR decomposition of $\bar{G}'^T \cdot \bar{G}'^T = Q'R'$

14.3.1 Algebraic Model

Suppose an overlay network spans s IP links. We represent a path by a column vector $v \in \{0, 1\}^s$, where the jth entry v_j is one if link j is part of the path, and zero otherwise. Suppose link j drops packets with probability l_j; then the loss rate p of a path represented by v is given by

$$1 - p = \prod_{j=1}^{s} \left(1 - l_j\right)^{v_j} . \tag{14.1}$$

Equation (14.1) assumes that packet loss is independent among links. Caceres et al. argue that the diversity of traffic and links makes large and long-lasting spatial link loss dependence unlikely in a real network such as the Internet [6]. Furthermore, the introduction of Random Early Detection (RED) [17] policies in routers will help break such dependence. In addition to [6], formula (14.1) has also been proven useful in many other link/path loss inference works [5, 15, 25, 31]. Our Internet experiments also show that the link loss dependence has little effect on the accuracy of (14.1).

Let us take logarithms on both sides of (14.1). Then by defining a column vector $x \in \mathbb{R}^s$ with elements $x_j = \log\left(1 - l_j\right)$, and writing v^T for the transpose of the column vector v, (14.1) is rewritten as follows:

$$\log\left(1 - p\right) = \sum_{j=1}^{s} v_j \log\left(1 - l_j\right) = \sum_{j=1}^{s} v_j x_j = v^T x. \tag{14.2}$$

There are $r = O(n^2)$ paths in the overlay network, and thus there are r linear equations of the form (14.2). Putting them together, we form a rectangular matrix $G \in \{0, 1\}^{r \times s}$. Each row of G represents a path in the network: $G_{ij} = 1$ when path i contains link j, and $G_{ij} = 0$ otherwise. Let p_i be the end-to-end loss rate of the ith path, and let $b \in \mathbb{R}^r$ be a column vector with elements $b_i = \log\left(1 - p_i\right)$. Then we write the r equations in form (14.2) as

$$Gx = b. \tag{14.3}$$

Normally, the number of paths r is much larger than the number of links s (see Figure 14.2(a)). This suggests that we could select s paths to monitor, use those measurements to compute the link loss rate variables x, and infer the loss rates of the other paths from (14.3).

However, in general, G is rank-deficient, i.e., $k = \text{rank}(G)$ and $k < s$. If G is rank-deficient, we will be unable to determine the loss rate of some links from (14.3). These links are also called *unidentifiable* in network tomography literature [5].

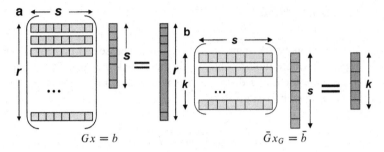

Fig. 14.2 Matrix size representations

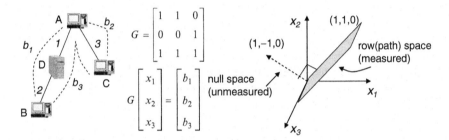

Fig. 14.3 Sample overlay network

Figure 14.3 illustrates how rank deficiency can occur. There are three end hosts (A, B, and C) on the overlay, three links (1, 2, and 3) and three paths between the end hosts. We cannot uniquely solve x_1 and x_2 because links 1 and 2 always appear together. We know their sum, but not their difference.

Figure 14.3 illustrates the geometry of the linear system, with each variable x_i as a dimension. The vectors $\{\alpha \begin{bmatrix} 1 & -1 & 0 \end{bmatrix}^T\}$ comprise $\mathcal{N}(G)$, the *null space* of G. No information about the loss rates for these vectors is given by (14.3). Meanwhile, there is an orthogonal *row(path) space* of G, $\mathcal{R}(G^T)$, which for this example is a plane $\{\alpha \begin{bmatrix} 1 & 1 & 0 \end{bmatrix}^T + \beta \begin{bmatrix} 0 & 0 & 1 \end{bmatrix}^T\}$. Unlike the null space, the loss rate of any vector on the row space can be uniquely determined by (14.3).

To separate the identifiable and unidentifiable components of x, we decompose x into $x = x_G + x_N$, where $x_G \in \mathcal{R}(G^T)$ is its projection on the row space and and $x_N \in \mathcal{N}(G)$ is its projection on the null space (i.e., $G x_N = 0$). The decomposition of $[x_1 \ x_2 \ x_3]^T$ for the sample overlay is shown below.

$$x_G = \frac{(x_1 + x_2)}{2} \begin{bmatrix} 1 \\ 1 \\ 0 \end{bmatrix} + x_3 \begin{bmatrix} 0 \\ 0 \\ 1 \end{bmatrix} = \begin{bmatrix} b_1/2 \\ b_1/2 \\ b_2. \end{bmatrix} \tag{14.4}$$

$$x_N = \frac{(x_1 - x_2)}{2} \begin{bmatrix} 1 \\ -1 \\ 0. \end{bmatrix} \tag{14.5}$$

Thus the vector x_G can be uniquely identified, and contains all the information we can know from (14.3) and the path measurements. The intuition of our scheme is illustrated through *virtual links* in [8].

Because x_G lies in the k-dimensional space $\mathscr{R}(G^T)$, only k-independent equations of the r equations in (14.3) are needed to uniquely identify x_G. We measure these k paths to compute x_G. Since $b = Gx = Gx_G + Gx_N = Gx_G$, we can compute all elements of b from x_G, and thus obtain the loss rate of all other paths.

14.3.2 System Architecture

Suppose n end hosts belong to a single overlay network or to a confederation of overlay networks. They cooperate to share an overlay monitoring and diagnosis service, and are instrumented by a central authority (e.g., an overlay network center (ONC)) to measure the routing topology and path loss rates as needed. First, the end hosts measure the topology and report to the ONC, which selects a small number of paths to measure and instruments the end hosts to execute such measurements. The end hosts periodically report the measured loss rates to the ONC. Then the ONC infers the loss rates of non-measured paths, and locates the congestion/failure points. Applications can query the ONC for the loss rate, or diagnosis of any path, or they can set up triggers to receive alerts when the loss rates of paths/links of interest exceed a certain threshold (see Figure 14.4).

The core part of the monitoring and diagnosis system thus consists of two stages. In the first stage, we select a small number of paths to measure and then infer the loss rates of all end-to-end paths. The first stage is conducted by the TOM system [9], which selects a basis set of paths so that all the path properties can be inferred based on the measurement of the set of paths. The LEND system infers the properties on the *link* level in the second stage, which finds out the minimal identifiable link sequence (MILSes) and computes the properties of MILSes as well.

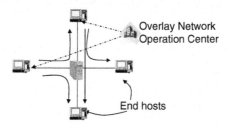

Fig. 14.4 Architecture of a TOM system

14.4 Tomography-Based Overlay Monitoring System (TOM)

Here we describe the basic static monitoring path selection algorithm of TOM; incremental update and load balancing extensions are described in [9]. The basic algorithms involve two steps. First, we select a basis set of k paths to monitor. Such selection only needs to be done once at setup. Then, based on continuous monitoring of the selected paths, we calculate and update the loss rates of all other paths.

14.4.1 Measurement Path Selection

To select k linearly independent paths from G, we use standard rank-revealing decomposition techniques [19], and obtain a reduced system:

$$\bar{G} x_G = \bar{b}, \tag{14.6}$$

where $\bar{G} \in \mathbb{R}^{k \times s}$ and $\bar{b} \in \mathbb{R}^k$ consist of k rows of G and b, respectively. The equation is illustrated in Figure 14.2(b) (compared with $Gx = b$).

As shown below, our algorithm is a variant of the QR decomposition with column pivoting [19, p. 223]. It incrementally builds a decomposition $\bar{G}^T = QR$, where $Q \in \mathbb{R}^{s \times k}$ is a matrix with orthonormal columns and $R \in \mathbb{R}^{k \times k}$ is upper triangular.

In general, the G matrix is very sparse; that is, there are only a few non-zeros per row. We leverage this property for speedup. We further use optimized routines from the LAPACK library [4] to implement Algorithm 7 so that it inspects several rows at a time. The complexity of Algorithm 7 is $O(rk^2)$, and the constant in the bound is modest. The memory cost is roughly $k^2/2$ single-precision floating point numbers for storing the R factor. Notice that the path selection only needs to be executed once for initial setup.

14.4.2 Path Loss Rate Calculations

To compute the path loss rates, we must find a solution to the underdetermined linear system $\bar{G} x_G = \bar{b}$. The vector $\bar{b}$ comes from measurements of the paths. Given

procedure SelectPath(G)
1 **for** *every row(path) v in G* **do**
2      $\hat{R}_{12} = R^{-T} \bar{G} v^T = Q^T v^T$
3      $\hat{R}_{22} = \|v\|^2 - \|\hat{R}_{12}\|^2$
4   **if** $\hat{R}_{22} \neq 0$ **then**
5   Select v as a measurement path
6   Update $R = \begin{bmatrix} R & \hat{R}_{12} \\ 0 & \hat{R}_{22} \end{bmatrix}$ and $\bar{G} = \begin{bmatrix} \bar{G} \\ v \end{bmatrix}$

Algorithm 7: Path (row) selection algorithm

measured values for $\bar{b}$, we compute a solution x_G using the QR decomposition we constructed during measurement path selection [13, 19]. We choose the unique solution x_G with minimum possible norm by imposing the constraint $x_G = \bar{G}^T y$ where $y = R^{-1} R^{-T} \bar{b}$. Once we have x_G, we can compute $b = G x_G$, and from there infer the loss rates of the unmeasured paths. The complexity for this step is only $O(k^2)$ and thus we can update loss rate estimates online.

14.5   Least-Biased End-to-End Network Diagnosis System

In this section, we first give formal definition on MILS and introduce the algorithms to identify and infer the properties of MILSes. For simplicity, we first study link property inference for undirected graphs. We then turn to the more realistic problem of inferring link properties in directed graphs.

14.5.1   Minimal Identifiable Link Sequence

As mentioned before, we know that not all the links (or the corresponding variables in the algebraic model) are uniquely identifiable. Thus our purpose is to find the smallest path segments with loss rates that can be uniquely identified through end-to-end path measurements. We introduce *minimal identifiable link sequence* or *MILS* to define such path sequences. These path sequences can be as short as a single physical link, or as long as an end-to-end path. Our methods are unbiased, and work with any network topology. This provides the *first* lower bound on the granularity at which properties of path segments can be uniquely determined. With this information, we can accurately locate what link (or set of links) causes any congestion or failures.

Figure 14.5 illustrates some examples for undirected graphs. In the top figure, we cannot determine the loss rates of the two physical links separately from one path measurement. Therefore we combine the two links together to form one MILS. In the middle figure, three independent paths traverse three links. Thus each link is identifiable, and is an MILS. In the bottom figure, there are five links and four paths. Each path is an MILS, since no path can be written as a sum of shorter MILSes. But link 3 can be presented as $(2' + 3' - 1' - 4')/2$, which means link 3 is identifiable, and there are *five* MILSes. These examples show three features of the MILS set:

- The MILSes may be linearly dependent, as in the bottom example. We can shrink our MILS set to a basis for the path space by removing such linear dependence, *e.g.*, by removing the MILS c in the bottom example in Figure 14.5. But it is helpful to keep such links for diagnosis.
- Some MILSes may contain other MILSes. For instance, MILS e is contained in MILSes b and c in the bottom example.

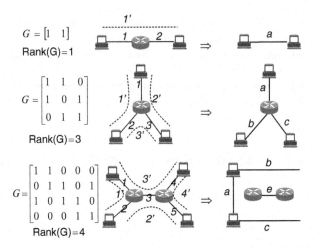

Fig. 14.5 Sample topologies and MILSes

- The MILS is a *consecutive* sequence of links, because for diagnosis purposes we often want to limit the range within the network where congestion/failure happens.

The problem of decomposing a network topology into MILSes is similar to the sparse basis problem in numerical linear algebra. The sparse basis problem is to find a basis for the range of a matrix with as few non-zeros as possible. However, finding MILSes differs from the usual problem of finding a sparse basis for the following reasons:

- The sparse basis problem is an NP-hard problem, and nearly all the heuristic algorithms for this problem are based on a *non-degeneracy* assumption. In particular, these heuristics require that every submatrix of G with the order of rank(G) is non-singular [27], an assumption does not hold for typical network path matrices.
- For Internet diagnosis, we want to locate the possible lossy links in a networking region which is as small as possible. Thus, we want to have vectors which correspond to consecutive link sequences. If we did not make this assumption, there could exist an exponentially large number of MILSes.

An MILS is a path segment and, like a path, it can be represented by a vector in $\{0, 1\}^s$ whose non-zero entries denote the physical links used. Our requirement that the properties of MILSes must be determined by the end-to-end measurements is equivalent to the requirement that the vector v of the MILS is in the path space $\mathscr{R}(G^T)$. Compared to related work [9], of which the goal is to find a basis of $\mathscr{R}(G^T)$ made of end-to-end paths, identifying MILSes is a more challenging task.

14.5.2   *MILSes in Undirected Graphs*

As we have defined them, MILSes satisfy two properties: they are minimal, *i.e.* they cannot be decomposed into shorter MILSes; and they are identifiable, *i.e.* they can be expressed as linear combinations of end-to-end paths. Algorithm 1 finds all possible MILSes by exhaustively enumerating the link sequences and checking each for minimality and identifiability. An identifiable link sequence on a path will be minimal if and only if it does not share an endpoint with a MILS on the same path. Thus as we enumerate the link sequences on a given path in increasing order of size, we can track whether each link is the starting link in some already-discovered MILS, which allows us to check for minimality in constant time. To test whether a link sequence is identifiable, we need only to make sure that the corresponding path vector v lies in the path space. Since Q is an orthonormal basis for the path space, v will lie in the path space if and only if $\|v\| = \|Q^T v\|$.

Now we analyze the computational complexity of identifying MILSes. If a link sequence contains i links, then v will contain only i non-zeros, and it will cost $O(i \times k)$ time to compute $\|Q^T v\|$. This cost dominates the cost of checking for minimality, and so the overall cost to check whether one link subsequence is an MILS will be at worst $O(i \times k)$. On a path of length l, there are $O(l^2)$ link subsequences, each of which costs at most $O(l \times k)$ time to check, so the total time to find all the MILSes on one end-to-end path is at most $O(k \times l^3)$. However, we can further reduce the complexity from $O(k \times l^3)$ to $O(k \times l^2)$ using dynamic programming. If we check every end-to-end path in the network, the overall complexity of Algorithm 1 will then be $O(r \times k \times l^2)$. However, our simulations and Internet experiments show that only a few more MILSes are obtained from scanning all r end-to-end paths than from scanning only the k end-to-end paths which are directly monitored. Furthermore, each physical link used by the network will be used by one of the k monitored paths, so the MILSes obtained from this smaller set of paths do cover every physical link. Therefore, in practice, we scan only the k monitored paths, which costs $O(k^2 \times l^2)$ time, and we accept a slight loss of diagnosis granularity.

Once we have identified all the MILSes, we need to compute their loss rates. We do this by finding a solution to the underdetermined linear system $\bar{G} x_G = \bar{b}$ (see [9]). For example, in Figure 14.6, $x_G = (\frac{2x_1 + x_2 + x_3}{3}, \frac{x_1 + 2x_2 - x_3}{3}, \frac{x_1 - x_2 + 2x_3}{3})^T$. Obviously, x_G shows some identifiable vectors in $\mathscr{R}(G)$; however, they may not be MILSes. Then for each MILS with vector v, the loss rate is $v^T x_G$. The elements of

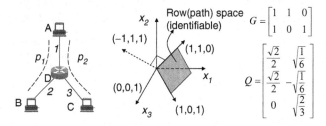

Fig. 14.6 MILSes in undirected graph

x_G need not be the real-link loss rates: only the inner products $v^T x_G$ are guaranteed to be unique and to correspond to real losses. We also note that because loss rates in the Internet remain stable over time scales on the order of an hour [32], the path measurements in $\bar{b}$ need not be taken simultaneously.

14.5.3 MILSes in Directed Graphs

14.5.3.1 Special Properties for Directed Graphs

Surprisingly, our MILS algorithm cannot be simply extended to directed graphs. We found that no path can be decomposed into more than one MILS, *i.e.*, each path itself is an MILS. Figure 14.7 shows a simple star topology as both an undirected graph and a directed graph. In the undirected graph on the left, the loss rate of each link is identifiable from the loss rate of the three paths. In contrast, in the directed graph on the right, rank$(G) = 5$, and none of the six links are identifiable from measurements of the six end-to-end paths. Only the end-to-end paths are identifiable in this case. This is typical of directed networks. In the case illustrated in Figure 14.7, we can explain the lack of identifiable links as follows. We can split G into two submatrices, one containing only incoming links and the other only containing outgoing links of the router N. Thus any vector $v = [v_1, v_2, v_3, v_4, v_5, v_6]^T \in \mathbb{R}^6$ in $\mathscr{R}(G^T)$ satisfies $v_1 + v_2 + v_3 = v_4 + v_5 + v_6$ because any path in G has one incoming link *and* one outgoing link. Vectors like $[1\ 0\ 0\ 0\ 0\ 0]^T$ do not belong to $\mathscr{R}(G^T)$, as they do not satisfy that condition. This example illustrates the intuition of *Theorem 1* which shows that in a directed graph, each path itself is an MILS, *i.e.*, it is the *minimal identifiable consecutive* path segment.

Theorem 14.1. *In a directed graph, no end-to-end path contains an identifiable subpath except loops.*

Proof. For any interior node N in the network, define vectors $u^N \in \{0, 1\}^s$ and $w^N \in \{0, 1\}^s$ such that $u_i^N = 1$ if link i is an incoming link for node i, and $w_i^N = 1$ if link i is an outgoing link for node i. For any path with vector v, $v^T u^N$ is the count of the number of links going into N which appear on the path, and $v^T w^N$ is the

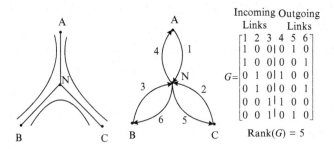

Fig. 14.7 Undirected graph vs directed graph

count of the links exiting N. If v corresponds to an end-to-end routing path, either N is traversed exactly once and $v^T u^N = v^T w^N = 1$, or N is not traversed at all and $v^T u^N = v^T w^N = 0$. Since every row in G represents an end-to-end path, we have $Gu^N = Gw^N$.

Any identifiable link sequence in the network can be represented by a vector x such that $x = G^T z$ for some z; for such a link sequence:

$$x^T u^N = z^T Gu^N = z^T Gw^N = x^T w^N.$$

Therefore, if the link sequence includes an incoming link for node N, it must also include an outgoing link. Thus, no identifiable link sequence may have an endpoint at an interior network node. This means that the only identifiable link sequences are loops and end-to-end paths. □

Routing loops are rare in the Internet, thus given Theorem 1, each path is an MILS and there are no others. This means that there are no individual links or subpaths whose loss rates can be exactly determined from end-to-end measurements. Next, we will discuss some practical methods to get finer level unbiased inference on directed graphs, such as the Internet.

14.5.3.2 Practical Inference Methods for Directed Graphs

Considering the simple directed graph in Figure 14.7, the problem of determining link loss rates is similar to the problem of breaking a deadlock: if any of the individual links can be somehow measured, then loss rates of all other links can be determined through end-to-end measurements. Since link loss rates cannot be negative, for a path with zero loss rate, all the links on that path must also have zero loss rates. This can break the deadlock and help solve the link loss rate of other paths. We call this inference approach the *good path algorithm*. Note that this is a *fact* instead of an extra *assumption*. Our PlanetLab experiments as well as [32] show that more than 50% of paths in the Internet have no loss.

In addition, we can relax the definition of "good path" and allow a negligible loss rate of at most σ (e.g., $\sigma = 0.5\%$, which is the threshold for "no loss" in [32]). Then again it becomes a trade-off between accuracy and diagnosis granularity, as depicted in our framework. Note that although the strict good path algorithm cannot be applied to other metrics such as latency, such bounded inference is generally applicable.

As illustrated in the second stage of Figure 14.8, there are two steps for identifying MILSes under directed graphs. First, we find all the good paths in G and thus establish some good links. We remove these good links and good paths from G to get a submatrix G'. Then we apply Algorithm 8 to G' to find all lossy MILSes and their loss rates in G. For the good links which are in the middle of lossy MILSes identified, we add them back so that MILSes are consecutive. In addition, we apply the following optimization procedures to get Q quickly for the identifiability test (step 10 of Algorithm 8).

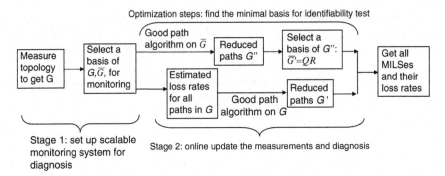

Fig. 14.8 The operational flowchart of the LEND system architecture

procedure Seek_MILS
1 Let Q be an orthonormal basis of $\mathscr{R}(G^T)$ which is pre-computed as in TOM ;
2 **foreach** *path p in G* **do**
3   start_mils := logical array of length(p) ;
4   Clear start_mils to all false ;
5   **for** $i := 1$ *to length(p)* **do**
6   **foreach** *segment $S = p_k \ldots p_l$ of length i* **do**
7   **if** start_mils(k) **then**
8   continue ;
              else
9   Let v be the corresponding vector of S ;
10   **if** $\|Q^T v\| = \|v\|$ **then**
11   start_mils(k) := true ;
12   S is an MILS ;
                  else
13   S is not a MILS ;

Algorithm 8: Seeking all MILSes in an undirected graph

We remove all the good links from $\bar{G}$ and get a smaller submatrix G'' than G'. By necessity, G'' contains a basis of G'. We can then use the small matrix G'' to do QR decomposition and thus get Q'. Since G'' is usually quite small even for G from a reasonably large overlay network, such optimization approach makes the LEND very efficient for online diagnosis. In Figure 14.9, we use a simple topology to show the matrices computed in the whole process. The path from C to B is a good path and thus links 2 and 6 are good links.

14.6 Evaluations

In this section, we mainly describe the scalability of the monitoring selection algorithm in TOM (*e.g.*, the study of rank k) and some real Internet experiments of TOM and LEND using PlanetLab. Meanwhile, a lot of extensive accuracy, load balancing, and other studies in both simulation and real experiments can be found in [9, 34].

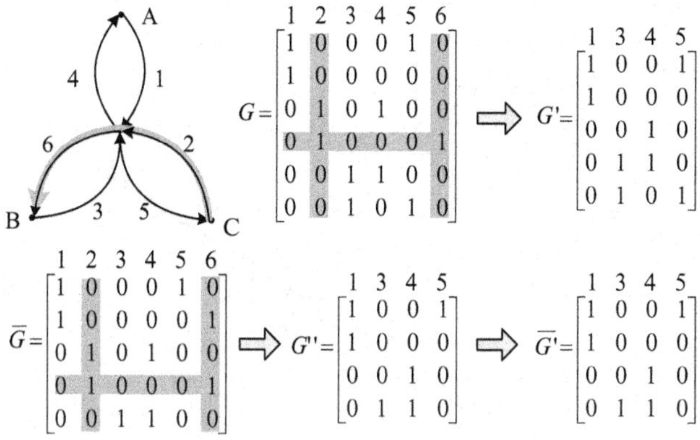

Fig. 14.9 Examples showing all the matrices in the flowchart

14.6.1 Scalability Analysis

We experiment with three types of BRITE [22] router-level topologies – Barabasi-Albert, Waxman, and hierarchical models – as well as with a real router topology with 284,805 nodes [20]. For hierarchical topologies, BRITE first generates an autonomous system (AS) level topology with a Barabasi-Albert model or a Waxman model. Then, for each AS, BRITE generates the router-level topologies with another Barabasi-Albert model or Waxman model. So there are four types of possible topologies. We show one of them as an example because they all have similar trends.

We randomly select end hosts which have the least degree (i.e., leaf nodes) to form an overlay network. We test by linear regression of k on $O(n)$, $O(n \log n)$, $O(n^{1.25})$, $O(n^{1.5})$, and $O(n^{1.75})$. As shown in Figure 14.10, results for each type of topology are averaged over three runs with different topologies for synthetic ones and with different random sets of end hosts for the real one. We find that for Barabasi-Albert, Waxman, and real topologies, $O(n)$ regression has the least residual errors – actually k even grows slower than $O(n)$. The hierarchical models have higher k, and most of them have $O(n \log n)$ as the best fit.

Note that all functions seem to intersect around $n = 800$. This is because that *inherently the growth is subquadratic, and roughly linear for the interested range of problem sizes*. Suppose that we have an exactly linear function x (we use a continuous setting for ease of calculation) and we wish to fit a function of the form $c \times x^a$ to this exactly linear function x over the interval $[0,1]$. The least squares procedure gives a coefficient of the form $c_{ls} = \frac{2+a}{2a+1}$. The data x and the function $c_{ls} \times x^a$ intersect at the following point:

$$x_{intercept} = \left(\frac{2+a}{2a+1} \right)^{\frac{1}{a-1}}. \tag{14.7}$$

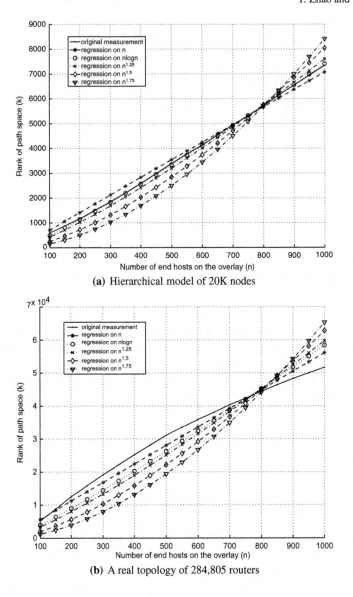

(a) Hierarchical model of 20K nodes

(b) A real topology of 284,805 routers

Fig. 14.10 Regression of k in various functions of n under different router-level topologies

For a between 1.1 and 2.0, $x_{intercept}$ varies between 0.728 and 0.800. That is, the fitted function intersects the data about 3/4 of the way across the domain for a wide range of exponents (including the exponents 1.25, 1.5, and 1.75).

Thus conservatively speaking, we have $k = O(n \log n)$.

14.6.1.1 Explanation from Internet Topology

Note that such trend still holds when the end hosts are sparsely distributed in the Internet, e.g., when each end host is in a different access network. One extreme case is the "star" topology – each end host is connected to the same center router via its own access network. In such a topology, there are only n links. Thus $k = O(n)$. Only topologies with very dense connectivity, like a full clique, have $k = O(n^2)$. Those topologies have little link sharing among the end-to-end paths.

The key observation is that when n is sufficiently large, such dense connectivity is very unlikely to exist in the Internet because of the power-law degree distribution. Tangmunarunkit et al. found that link usage, as measured by the set of node pairs (source–destination pairs) whose traffic traverses the link, also follows a power-law distribution, i.e., there is a very small number of links that are on the shortest paths of the majority of node pairs. So there is a significant amount of link sharing among the paths, especially for backbone links, customer links, and peering links.

14.6.2 Internet Experiments

We deployed and evaluated our TOM and LEND systems on 135 PlanetLab hosts over the world [26]. Each host is from a different institute. About 60% of hosts are in the USA and others are distributed mostly in Europe and Asia. There are altogether $135 \times 134 = 18,090$ end-to-end paths among these end hosts. In our experiments, we measured all the paths for validation. But, in practice, we only need to measure the basis set of on average 5,706 end-to-end paths, determined by the TOM system. The measurement load can be evenly distributed among the paths with the technique in [9] so that each host only needs to measure about 42 paths.

In April 2005, we ran the experiments 10 times, at different times of night and day. Below we report the average results from the 10 experiments (see Table 14.2).

14.6.2.1 Granularity of MILSes and Diagnosis

For the total of $135 \times 134 = 18,090$ end-to-end paths, after removing about 65.5% good paths containing about 70.5% good links, there are only 6450 paths remaining. The average length of lossy MILSes on bad paths is 3.9 links or 2.3 virtual links.

Table 14.2 Internet experiment results. The last two rows are computed using the virtual links. The corresponding length values using physical links are given in the parenthesis

End-to-end path	18,090
Average path length	15.2
Number of MILSes	1009
Average length of MILSes	2.3 (3.9)
Average diagnosis granularity	2.3 (3.8)

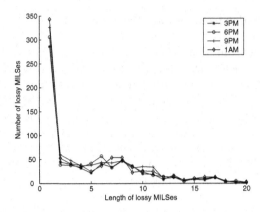

Fig. 14.11 Length distribution of lossy MILSes in physical links

The diagnosis granularity of lossy paths is a little high: 3.8. But we believe it is reasonable and acceptable for the following two reasons. First, in the edge networks, the paths usually have a long link chain without branches. For example, all paths starting from planetlab1.cs.northwestern.edu go through the same five first hops. If we use virtual link as the unit, we find the granularity is reduced to about 2.3 virtual links. This shows our LEND approach can achieve good diagnosis granularity comparable to other more biased tomography approaches, while achieving high accuracy.

Second, we find that there exist some very long lossy MILSes as illustrated in Figure 14.11, which shows the distribution of the length in physical links of lossy MILSes measured in different time periods of a day (US Central Standard Time). For example, some MILSes are longer than 10 hops. Such long lossy MILSes occur in relatively small overlay networks because some paths do not overlap any other paths.

We can further apply Gibbs sampling approach [25] based on the MILSes found and obtain the lower bound on the diagnosis granularity [34], which is 1.9 physical links and obviously one hop with respect to virtual links. However, accuracy will be sacrificed to some extent as shown in [34]. Nevertheless, by combining both statistic approaches and our LEND system, we provide the full flexibility to trade off between granularity and accuracy.

14.7 Conclusions

In this chapter, we design, implement, and evaluate algebraic approaches for adaptive scalable overlay network monitoring (TOM) and diagnosis (LEND).

For an overlay of n end hosts, we selectively monitor a basis set of $O(n \log n)$ paths which can fully describe all the $O(n^2)$ paths. Then the measurements of the basis set are used to infer the loss rates of all other paths. Our approach works in real time, offers fast adaptation to topology changes, distributes balanced load to end hosts, and handles topology measurement errors. Both simulation and Internet implementation yield promising results.

We also advocate the non-biased end-to-end network diagnosis paradigm which gives smooth tradeoff between accuracy and diagnosis granularity when combined with various statistical assumptions. We introduce the concept of minimal identifiable link sequence and propose the good path algorithms to leverage measurement snapshots to effectively diagnose for directed graphs. Both simulation and Planet-Lab experiments show that we can achieve fine level diagnosis with high accuracy in near real time.

References

1. Adams, A., et al.: The use of end-to-end multicast measurements for characterizing internal network behavior. In: IEEE Communications (May, 2000)
2. Akamai Inc.: Technology overview. http://www.akamai.com/en/html/technology/overview.html
3. Anagnostakis, K., Greenwald, M., Ryger, R.: cing: Measuring network-internal delays using only existing infrastructure. In: IEEE INFOCOM (2003)
4. Anderson, E., et al.: LAPACK Users' Guide, third edn. Society for Industrial and Applied Mathematics, Philadelphia, PA (1999)
5. Bu, T., Duffield, N., Presti, F., Towsley, D.: Network tomography on general topologies. In: ACM SIGMETRICS (2002)
6. Caceres, R., Duffield, N., Horowitz, J., Towsley, D.: Multicast-based inference of network-internal loss characteristics. IEEE Transactions in Information Theory **45** (1999)
7. Caceres, R., Duffield, N., Horowitz, J., Towsley, D., Bu, T.: Multicast-based inference of network-internal characteristics: Accuracy of packet loss estimation. In: IEEE INFOCOM (1999)
8. Chen, Y., Bindel, D., Katz, R.H.: Tomography-based overlay network monitoring. In: ACM SIGCOMM Internet Measurement Conference (IMC) (2003)
9. Chen, Y., Bindel, D., Song, H., Katz, R.H.: An algebraic approach to practical and scalable overlay network monitoring. In: ACM SIGCOMM (2004)
10. Chen, Y., Lim, K., Overton, C., Katz, R.H.: On the stability of network distance estimation. In: ACM SIGMETRICS Performance Evaluation Review (PER) (Sep. 2002)
11. Chua, D.B., Kolaczyk, E.D., Crovella, M.: Efficient monitoring of end-to-end network properties. In: IEEE INFOCOM (2005)
12. Coates, M., Hero, A., Nowak, R., Yu, B.: Internet Tomography. IEEE Signal Processing Magazine **19**(3), 47–65 (2002)
13. Demmel, J.: Applied Numerical Linear Algebra. SIAM (1997)
14. Duffield, N.: Simple network performance tomography. In: ACM SIGCOMM Internet Measurement Conference (IMC) (2003)
15. Duffield, N., Horowitz, J., Towsley, D., Wei, W., Friedman, T.: Multicast-based loss inference with missing data. IEEE Journal of Selected Areas of Communications **20**(4) (2002)
16. Duffield, N., Presti, F., Paxson, V., Towsley, D.: Inferring link loss using striped unicast probes. In: IEEE INFOCOM (2001)
17. Floyd, S., Jacobson, V.: Random early detection gateways for congestion avoidance. IEEE/ACM Transactions on Networking **1**(4) (1993)
18. Francis, P., et al.: IDMaps: A global Internet host distance estimation service. IEEE/ACM Trans. on Networking (2001)
19. Golub, G., Loan, C.V.: Matrix Computations. The Johns Hopkins University Press (1989)

20. Govindan, R., Tangmunarunkit, H.: Heuristics for Internet map discovery. In: IEEE INFOCOM (2000)
21. Mahajan, R., Spring, N., Wetherall, D., Anderson, T.: User-level internet path diagnosis. In: ACM SOSP (2003)
22. Medina, A., Matta, I., Byers, J.: On the origin of power laws in Internet topologies. In: ACM Computer Communication Review (2000)
23. Ng, T.S.E., Zhang, H.: Predicting Internet network distance with coordinates-based approaches. In: Proc.of IEEE INFOCOM (2002)
24. Ozmutlu, H.C., et al.: Managing end-to-end network performance via optimized monitoring strategies. Journal of Network and System Management 10(1) (2002)
25. Padmanabhan, V., Qiu, L., Wang, H.: Server-based inference of Internet link lossiness. In: IEEE INFOCOM (2003)
26. PlanetLab: http://www.planet-lab.org/
27. R.A.Brualdi, Pothen, A., Friedland, S.: The sparse basis problem and multilinear algebra. SIAM Journal of Matrix Analysis and Applications 16, 1–20 (1995)
28. Ratnasamy, S., et al.: Topologically-aware overlay construction and server selection. In: Proc. of IEEE INFOCOM (2002)
29. Shavitt, Y., Sun, X., Wool, A., Yener, B.: Computing the unmeasured: An algebraic approach to Internet mapping. In: IEEE INFOCOM (2001)
30. Song, H., Qiu, L., Zhang, Y.: Netquest: A flexible framework for lange-scale netork measurement. In: ACM SIGMETRICS (June 2006)
31. Tang, C., McKinley, P.: On the cost-quality tradeoff in topology-aware overlay path probing. In: IEEE ICNP (2003)
32. Zhang, Y., et al.: On the constancy of Internet path properties. In: Proc. of SIGCOMM IMW (2001)
33. Zhao, Y., Chen, Y.: A suite of schemes for user-level network diagnosis without infrastructure. In: IEEE INFOCOM (2007)
34. Zhao, Y., Chen, Y., Bindel, D.: Towards unbiased end-to-end network diagnosis. In: ACM SIGCOMM (2006)

Part III
Emerging Applications

Chapter 15
Network Coding and Its Applications in Communication Networks

Alex Sprintson

Abstract The *network coding* technique generalizes the traditional routing approach by allowing the intermediate network nodes to create new packets by combining the packets received over their incoming edges. This technique has several important benefits such as an increase in throughput and an improvement in the reliability and robustness of the network. The goal of this chapter is to present a tutorial review of the network coding technique, the practical implementation of network coding, as well as its applications in several areas of networking. We begin by presenting the encoding model and the algebraic framework for network code construction. Next, we discuss efficient deterministic and randomized algorithms for construction of feasible network codes in multicast networks. Next, we present practical implementation schemes and discuss the applications of network coding in content distribution networks, peer-to-peer networks, and wireless networks.

15.1 Introduction

15.1.1 Motivation

Communication networks are designed to deliver information from source to destination nodes. The traditional way of delivering data employs *paths* for *unicast* connections and *trees* for *multicast* connections. When the data is routed over a unicast path, each intermediate node forwards the packets received over its incoming edges to its outgoing edges. In a multicast connection over a tree, the intermediate nodes may duplicate packets and forward them to several outgoing edges. The network coding approach [1] allows the intermediate nodes to generate new packets by combining the packets received on their incoming edges. This technique offers several benefits, such as an increase in throughput and an improvement in reliability and robustness of the network.

A. Sprintson (✉)
Texas A&M University, College Station, TX 77843, Texas
e-mail: spalex@tamu.edu

G. Cormode and M. Thottan (eds.), *Algorithms for Next Generation Networks*,
Computer Communications and Networks, DOI 10.1007/978-1-84882-765-3_15,

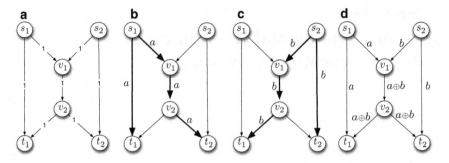

Fig. 15.1 Basic network coding example: (**a**) Original network; (**b**) A multicast tree with a root at node s_1; (**c**) A multicast tree with a root at node s_1; (**d**) A feasible network coding scheme

To demonstrate the advantage of the network coding technique, consider the network depicted in Figure 15.1(a). The network includes two information sources, s_1 and s_2, and two terminals, t_1 and t_2. We assume that all edges of the network are of unit capacity, i.e., each edge can transmit one packet per time unit. With the traditional approach, the packets are forwarded over two Steiner trees,[1] such that the first tree forwards the packets generated by source s_1, while the second tree forwards packets generated by node s_2. However, the network does not contain two edge-disjoint Steiner trees with roots in s_1 and s_2; hence the multicast connection with two information sources cannot be implemented using traditional methods. For example, the trees depicted in Figures 15.1(b) and (c) share the bottleneck edge (v_1, v_2). Figure 15.1(d) shows that this conflict can be resolved by employing the network coding technique. To demonstrate this approach, let a and b be the packets generated by the information sources s_1 and s_2, respectively, at the current communication round. Both packets are sent to the intermediate node v_1, which generates a new packet $a \oplus b$, which is then sent to both nodes t_1 and t_2. It is easy to verify that both terminal nodes can decode the packets a and b from the packets received over their incoming edges.

The network coding technique can also be useful for minimizing the delay of data delivery from the source to the terminal nodes [9]. For example, consider the network depicted in Figure 15.2(a). Suppose that each edge can transmit one packet per time unit and that the delay of each edge is also one time unit. Figures 15.2(b) and (c) show two edge-disjoint Steiner trees that connect s to the terminals t_1, t_2, and t_3. However, one of the trees is of depth three, and, as a result, terminal t_2 will receive one of the packets after a delay of three time units. It can be verified that any scheme that does not employ network coding results in a delay of three time units. Figure 15.2(d) shows a network coding solution which delivers the data with the delay of just two time units.

---

[1] A Steiner tree is a tree that connects the source node with the terminals and may include any number of other nodes.

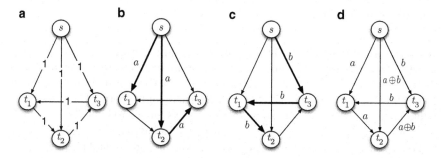

Fig. 15.2 Delay minimization with network coding: (**a**) Original network; (**b**) First Steiner tree with a root at node s; (**c**) Second Steiner tree with a root at node s; (**d**) A network coding scheme

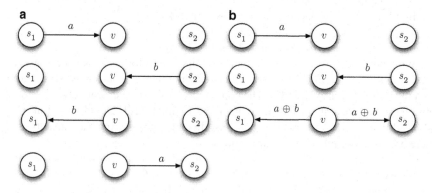

Fig. 15.3 Reducing energy consumption with network coding: (**a**) traditional approach and (**b**) network coding approach

The network coding technique can also be employed to minimize the number of transmissions in wireless networks [36]. For example, consider the wireless network depicted in Figure 15.3. The network contains two nodes s_1 and s_2 that want to exchange packets through an intermediate relay node v. More specifically, node s_1 needs to send packet a to s_2 and node s_2 needs to send packet b to s_1. Figure 15.3(a) shows a traditional routing scheme that requires four transmissions. Figure 15.3(b) shows a network coding scheme in which the intermediate node v first obtains two packets a and b from s_1 and s_2 and then generates a new packet $a \oplus b$ and broadcasts it to both s_1 and s_2. This scheme requires only three transmissions. The example shows that the network coding technique can take advantage of the broadcast nature of wireless spectrum medium to minimize the number of transmissions.

As demonstrated by the above examples, network coding has several benefits for a broad range of applications in both wired and wireless communications networks. The goal of this chapter is to describe the network coding fundamentals as well as to show a broad range of applications of this technique.

15.1.2 Related Work

Network coding research was initiated by a seminal paper by Ahlswede et al. [1] and has since then attracted significant interest from the research community. Many initial works on the network coding technique focused on establishing *multicast* connections. It was shown in [1, 28] that the capacity of the network, i.e., the maximum number of packets that can be sent from the source s to a set T of terminals per time unit, is equal to the minimum capacity of a cut that separates the source s and a terminal $t \in T$. In a subsequent work, Koetter and Médard [25] developed an algebraic framework for network coding and investigated linear network codes for directed graphs with cycles. This framework was used by Ho et al. [18] to show that linear network codes can be efficiently constructed through a randomized algorithm. Jaggi et al. [21] proposed a deterministic polynomial-time algorithm for finding feasible network codes in multicast networks. Network coding for networks with cycles has been studied in [4, 12]. Network coding algorithms resilient to malicious interference have been studied in [20, 24, 35].

While there are efficient polynomial-time algorithms for network code construction in multicast settings, finding efficient network codes in non-multicast scenarios is a more difficult problem [33]. The complexity of several general network coding problems has been analyzed by Lehman and Lehman [27]. Dougherty el al. [11] showed that linear network codes are insufficient for achieving the capacity of a network with multiple unicast connections.

The applications of network coding in wired and wireless communication networks have been the subject of several recent studies. Chou and Wu [9] discussed implementation of network coding in content distribution networks. They discussed several issues such as synchronization, varying delay, and traffic loss. The advantages of network coding in large-scale peer-to-peer content distribution systems have been studied in [14, 15]. Network coding techniques for improving the performance of wireless networks have been studied in [23], [6], and [22].

Comprehensive surveys on the network coding techniques are available in some recent books [13, 19, 37].

15.2 Network Coding Fundamentals

In this section we describe the network model and present the basic definitions of the network coding technique. Then, we present an algebraic framework for multicast connections. Finally, we present deterministic and randomized algorithms for construction of efficient network codes.

15.2.1 Network Model

We model the communication network by a directed graph $G(V, E)$, where V is the set of nodes and E the set of edges in G. The information between network nodes is transmitted in packets. We assume that each packet is an element of some finite field[2] $\mathbf{F}_q = GF(q)$ and can be represented by a binary vector of length $n = \log_2(q)$ bits. We assume that the communication is performed in rounds, such that at each round, every edge of the network can transmit a single packet. Note that this assumption implies that all edges of the network have the same capacity of one unit. This assumption, however, does not result in a loss of generality since edges of larger capacity can be represented by multiple parallel edges of smaller capacity. We define the *multicast coding network* $\mathbb{N}(G, s, T)$ as a triple that includes the graph $G(V, E)$, a source node $s \in V$, and a set $T \subset V$ of terminals.

We define the *capacity* of the multicast coding network $\mathbb{N}(G, s, T)$ to be the tightest upper bound on the amount of information that can be transmitted from the source node s to all destination nodes T per communication round. More specifically, let $h(i)$ be the maximum number of packets that can be delivered from s to all terminals in T in i rounds. Then, the capacity h^* of the network is defined as

$$h^* = \limsup_{i \to \infty} \frac{h(i)}{i}. \tag{15.1}$$

For example, the network depicted in Figure 15.1(a) can deliver two packets per time unit to each terminal; hence its capacity is equal to 2. Indeed, the network coding scheme depicted in Figure 15.1(d) can deliver two new packets at every communication round. For this network, it holds that $h(1) = h^*$, which, in turn, implies that $h^* = \frac{h(i)}{i}$. The last property holds for any acyclic communication network, but it does not necessarily hold for a network that contains cycles. To see this, consider the network $\mathbb{N}(G, s, T)$ depicted in Figure 15.4(a). For this network, it is easy to verify that one round of communication is insufficient for delivering two packets to both terminals t_1 and t_2. Figure 15.4(b) shows a network coding scheme

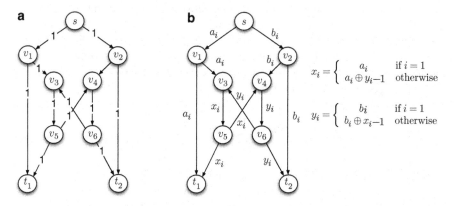

Fig. 15.4 A coding network with cycles: (**a**) Original network (**b**) A feasible network coding scheme

---

[2] For a definition of finite field see, e.g., [31].

that can transmit $2n$ packets over $n+1$ rounds; hence the capacity of the network is equal to 2. In particular, at the first round, node v_3 forwards the packet a_i received over its incoming edge (v_1, v_3), i.e., $x_1 = a_1$. Then, for each round i, $i > 1$, node v_3 generates a new packet by computing bitwise XOR between a_i and y_{i-1}. Node v_4 also generates a new packet by computing bitwise XOR between b_i and x_{i-1}. It is easy to verify that the destination nodes t_1 and t_2 can decode the packets sent by the source node after a delay of one round.

15.2.2 Encoding Model

In this section, we present a formal definition of a linear network code. For clarity, we assume that the underlying network graph $G(V, E)$ is acyclic. As discussed above, such networks are easier to analyze, because we only need to consider a single communication round. We also assume that exactly one packet is sent over each edge and that each node must receive all packets from its incoming edges before sending a packet on its outgoing edges.

Suppose that we would like to transmit h packets $\mathbb{R} = (p_1, p_2, \ldots, p_h)$ over the multicast network $\mathbb{N}(G, s, T)$. We assume that the source node s has exactly h incoming edges, indexed by $e_1, e_2, \ldots, e_h$, and each terminal $t \in T$ has h incoming edges and no outgoing edges. Note that these assumptions can be made without loss of generality. Indeed, suppose that the second assumption does not hold for some terminal $t \in T$. In this case, we can add a new terminal t', connected with t by h parallel edges, resulting in an equivalent network. Figure 15.5(a) depicts an example a network that satisfies these assumptions. For each edge $e \in E$ we denote by p_e the packet transmitted on that edge. Each incoming edge e_i, $1 \le i \le h$, of the source node s transmits original packet p_i.

Let $e(v, u) \in E$ be an edge of the coding network $\mathbb{N}(G, s, T)$ and let $\mathcal{M}_e$ be the set of incoming edges in G of its tail node v, $\mathcal{M}_e = \{(w, v) \mid (w, v) \in E\}$. Then, we associate with each edge $e' \in \mathcal{M}_e$ a *local encoding coefficient* $\beta_{e',e} \in \mathbf{F}_q = GF(q)$. The local encoding coefficients of the edges that belong to $\mathcal{M}_e$ determine the packet p_e transmitted on edge e as a function of packets transmitted on the incoming edges $\mathcal{M}_e$ of e. Specifically, the packet p_e is equal to

$$p_e = \sum_{e' \in \mathcal{M}_e} \beta_{e',e} \cdot p_{e'}, \tag{15.2}$$

where all operations are performed over finite field $\mathbf{F}_q$.

We note that if a node $v \in V$ has in-degree one, then the local encoding coefficient $\beta_{e',e}$ for every pair of edges $e'(u, v)$ and $e(v, w)$ can be set to one.

Definition 15.1 (Linear Network Code). Let $\mathbb{N}(G, s, T)$ be a coding network and let $\mathbf{F}_q = GF(q)$ be a finite field. Then, the assignment of encoding coefficients

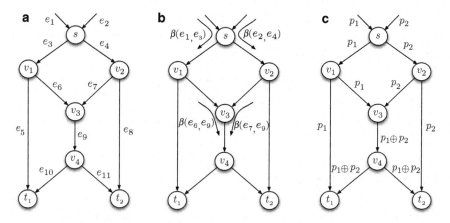

Fig. 15.5 Encoding notation: (**a**) Original network; (**b**) Local encoding coefficients; (**c**) Encoding of transmitted packets

$$\{\beta_{e',e} \in GF(q) \mid e'(v,u), e(u,w) \in E\}$$

is referred to as a *linear network code* for $\mathbb{N}(G, s, T)$.

Figure 15.5(b) demonstrates the local encoding coefficients that form a linear network code for the coding network depicted in Figure 15.5(a).

Our goal is to find a set of network coding coefficients $\{\beta_{e',e}\}$ that allows each terminal to decode the original packets $\mathbb{R}$ from the packets obtained through its incoming edges. The assignment of $\{\beta_{e',e}\}$ that satisfies this condition is referred to as a *feasible network code* for $\mathbb{N}(G, s, T)$. For example, consider the network depicted in Figure 15.5(a) and suppose that all operations are performed over field $\mathbf{F}_2 = GF(2)$. Then, the assignment of encoding coefficients $\beta_{e_1,e_3} = \beta_{e_2,e_4} = \beta_{e_6,e_9} = \beta_{e_7,e_9} = 1$ and $\beta_{e_1,e_4} = \beta_{e_2,e_3} = 0$ results in a feasible network code. The packets transmitted by the edges of the network are shown in Figure 15.5(c).

Note that each packet transmitted over the network is a linear combination of the original packets $\mathbb{R} = \{p_1, p_2, \ldots, p_h\}$ generated by the source node s. Accordingly, for each edge $e \in E$ we define the *global encoding vector* $\Gamma_e = [\gamma_1^e \cdots \gamma_h^e] \in \mathbf{F}_q^h$, that captures the relation between the packet p_e transmitted on edge e and the original packets in $\mathbb{R}$:

$$p_e = \sum_{i=1}^{h} p_i \cdot \gamma_i^e. \tag{15.3}$$

Note that if e_i is an outgoing edge of the source node s, then Γ_e is equal to

$$\Gamma_{e_i} = [\beta_{(e_1,e_i)} \beta_{(e_2,e_i)} \cdots \beta_{(e_h,e_i)}]. \tag{15.4}$$

For any other edge $e_i \in E$, Equation (15.2) implies that

$$\Gamma_{e_i} = \sum_{e' \in \mathcal{M}_{e_i}} \beta_{e',e_i} \cdot \Gamma_{e'}. \tag{15.5}$$

We note that for an edge $e \in E$ each component γ_i^e of Γ_e is a multivariate polynomial on the local encoding coefficients $\{\beta_{e',e}\}$. For example, for the network depicted in Figure 15.5, it holds that

$$\Gamma_{e_3} = \Gamma_{e_5} = \Gamma_{e_6} = [\beta_{e_1,e_3} \quad \beta_{e_2,e_3}];$$
$$\Gamma_{e_4} = \Gamma_{e_7} = \Gamma_{e_8} = [\beta_{e_1,e_4} \quad \beta_{e_2,e_4}];$$
$$\Gamma_{e_9} = \Gamma_{e_{10}} = \Gamma_{e_{11}} = [\beta_{e_1,e_3}\beta_{e_6,e_9} + \beta_{e_1,e_4}\beta_{e_7,e_9} \quad \beta_{e_2,e_3}\beta_{e_6,e_9} + \beta_{e_2,e_4}\beta_{e_7,e_9}].$$
$$(15.6)$$

15.2.3 Coding Advantage

Let $\mathbb{N}(G, s, T)$ be a multicast network. Recall that its capacity h^* is defined by Equation (15.1). Let $\bar{h}$ be the maximum amount of information that can be sent from the source s to the set of terminals T per communication round without network coding, i.e., in a communication model in which each intermediate node can only forward incoming packets. We define the *coding advantage* as the ratio between h^* and $\bar{h}$. The coding advantage captures the benefit of the network coding techniques for increasing the overall throughput of the network. Charikar and Agrawal [7] have shown that the coding advantage for multicast networks can be as large as $\Omega(\frac{\log |V|}{\log \log |V|})$ and $\Omega(\sqrt{|T|})$. For undirected networks, the coding advantage is upper bounded by 2 [29]. For multiple unicast connections in directed networks it is easy to show that the coding advantage can be as large as the number of unicast pairs.

15.3 Algebraic Framework

In this section, we present the algorithmic framework due to [25] for linear network coding in acyclic multicast networks and establish its connection to the min-cut-max-flow theorem.

Let $\mathbb{N}(G, s, T)$ be a coding network and let t be one of the terminals in T. We denote by $E_t = \{e_t^1, \ldots, e_t^h\}$ the set of incoming edges of terminal t. We define the $h \times h$ matrix $\mathbb{M}_t$ as follows:

$$\mathbb{M}_t = \begin{bmatrix} \Gamma_{e_t^1} \\ \Gamma_{e_t^2} \\ \cdots \\ \Gamma_{e_t^h} \end{bmatrix}. \qquad (15.7)$$

That is, each row of $\mathbb{M}_t$ contains the global encoding vector of one of the incoming edges e_t^i of t. We refer to $\mathbb{M}_t$ as the *transfer matrix*. The transfer matrix captures the relation between the original packets $\mathbb{R}$ and the packets received by the terminal node $t \in T$ over its incoming edges. For example, for the network depicted in Figure 15.5(a) the transfer matrix $\mathbb{M}_{t_1}$ for the terminal t_1 is equal to

$$\mathbb{M}_{t_1} = \begin{bmatrix} \beta_{e_1,e_3} & \beta_{e_2,e_3} \\ \beta_{e_1,e_3}\beta_{e_6,e_9} + \beta_{e_1,e_4}\beta_{e_7,e_9} & \beta_{e_2,e_3}\beta_{e_6,e_9} + \beta_{e_2,e_4}\beta_{e_7,e_9} \end{bmatrix}. \quad (15.8)$$

Similarly, the transfer matrix $\mathbb{M}_{t_2}$ for the terminal t_2 is equal to

$$\mathbb{M}_{t_2} = \begin{bmatrix} \beta_{e_1,e_3}\beta_{e_6,e_9} + \beta_{e_1,e_4}\beta_{e_7,e_9} & \beta_{e_2,e_3}\beta_{e_6,e_9} + \beta_{e_2,e_4}\beta_{e_7,e_9} \\ \beta_{e_1,e_4} & \beta_{e_2,e_4} \end{bmatrix}. \quad (15.9)$$

Terminal t can decode the original packets in $\mathbb{R}$ if and only if the transfer matrix $\mathbb{M}_t$ is of full rank, or equivalently, the determinant $\det(\mathbb{M}_t)$ is not zero. Thus, the purpose of the network coding scheme is to find the assignment of the coefficients $\{\beta_{e',e}\}$ that results in a full-rank transfer matrix $\mathbb{M}_t$ for each terminal $t \in T$.

For example, for the network depicted in Figure 15.5(a), the determinant of the transfer matrix $\mathbb{M}_{t_1}$ is equal to

$$\det(\mathbb{M}_{t_1}) = \beta_{e_1,e_3}(\beta_{e_2,e_3}\beta_{e_6,e_9} + \beta_{e_2,e_4}\beta_{e_7,e_9}) \\ -\beta_{e_2,e_3}(\beta_{e_1,e_3}\beta_{e_6,e_9} + \beta_{e_1,e_4}\beta_{e_7,e_9}). \quad (15.10)$$

Similarly, the determinant of the transfer matrix $\mathbb{M}_{t_2}$ is equal to

$$\det(\mathbb{M}_{t_2}) = \beta_{e_2,e_4}(\beta_{e_1,e_3}\beta_{e_6,e_9} + \beta_{e_1,e_4}\beta_{e_7,e_9}) \\ -\beta_{e_1,e_4}(\beta_{e_2,e_3}\beta_{e_6,e_9} + \beta_{e_2,e_4}\beta_{e_7,e_9}). \quad (15.11)$$

It is easy to verify that the assignment $\beta_{e_1,e_3} = \beta_{e_2,e_4} = \beta_{e_6,e_9} = \beta_{e_7,e_9} = 1$ and $\beta_{e_1,e_4} = \beta_{e_2,e_3} = 0$ result in non-zero values of the determinants of both matrix, $\det(\mathbb{M}_{t_1})$ and $\det(\mathbb{M}_{t_2})$.

We observe that the determinant $\det(\mathbb{M}_t)$ of the transfer matrix $\mathbb{M}_t$ is a multivariate polynomial with variables $\{\beta_{e',e}\}$. Let $P = \prod_{t \in T} \det(\mathbb{M}_t)$ be the product of the determinants of the transfer matrices for each terminal $t \in T$. Clearly, if P is identically equal to 0, then there is no feasible linear network code for $\mathbb{N}(G, s, T)$. However, it turns out that if P is not identically equal to 0, then it is possible to find a feasible assignment of coefficients $\{\beta_{e',e}\}$, provided that the field $\mathbf{F}_q$ is sufficiently large. Specifically, the size q of $\mathbf{F}_q$ must be larger than the maximum degree of P with respect to any variable $\beta_{e',e}$.

Figure 15.6 presents a procedure, referred to as Procedure FINDSOLUTION, that finds a non-zero solution for a multivariate polynomial P. The procedure receives, as input, a non-zero polynomial $P(x_1, x_2, \ldots, x_n)$ and a finite field $\mathbf{F}_q = GF(q)$. The procedure iteratively finds the assignments $x_i = \zeta_i$ such that $P(\zeta_1, \zeta_2, \ldots, \zeta_n) \neq 0$. At iteration i, the procedure considers a polynomial P_i obtained from P by substituting $x_j = \zeta_j$ for $1 \leq j \leq i - 1$. Then, we consider P_i to be a multivariate polynomial in $x_{i+1}, \ldots, x_n$ whose coefficients are (univariate) polynomials in x_i. Next, we pick a monomial P' of P_i and consider its coefficient

---

Procedure FINDSOLUTION $(P(x_1, x_2, \ldots, x_n), \mathbf{F}_q)$

    Input:

        $P(x_1, x_2, \ldots, x_n)$ - a non-zero polynomial in variables $x_1, x_2, \ldots, x_n$;

        $\mathbf{F}_q = GF(q)$ - a finite field;

    Output:

        $\zeta_1, \zeta_2, \ldots, \zeta_n \in GF(q)$ such that $P(\zeta_1, \zeta_2, \ldots, \zeta_n) \neq 0$

1   $P_1(x_1, x_2, \ldots, x_n) \leftarrow P(x_1, x_2, \ldots, x_n)$

2   **For each** $i = 1$ to n **do**

3   Consider P_i to be a multivariate polynomial in $x_{i+1}, \ldots, x_n$ whose coefficients are univariate polynomials in $\mathbf{F}_q[x_i]$.

4   Select a monomial P' of P_i which is not identically equal to 0

5   Denote $P^*(x_i)$ be a coefficient of P'.

6   Choose $\zeta_i \in \mathbf{F}_q$ such that $P^*(\zeta_i) \neq 0$

7   Substitute $x_i = \zeta_i$ in P_i and denote the resulting polynomial as $P_{i+1}(x_{i+1}, \ldots, x_n)$

8   **Return** $\zeta_1, \zeta_2, \ldots, \zeta_n$

Fig. 15.6 Procedure FINDSOLUTION

$P^*(x_i)$. Since the size q of the finite field is larger than the maximum degree of variable x_i in $P^*(x_i)$, there exists a value $\zeta_i \in \mathbf{F}_q$, such that $P^*(\zeta_i)$ is not zero. Hence, both $P'|_{x_i = \zeta_i}$ and, in turn, $P_i|_{x_i = \zeta_i}$ are non-zero polynomials.

For example, suppose we would like to find a solution for polynomial $P(x_1, x_2, x_3) = x_1 x_2^2 x_3 + x_1^2 x_2^2 x_3 + x_1^2 x_2^2 x_3^2$ over $\mathbf{F}_3 = GF(3)$. We consider $P_1(x_1, x_2, x_3) = P(x_1, x_2, x_3)$ to be a polynomial in x_2 and x_3 whose coefficients are polynomials in x_1. Specifically, we write

$$P_1(x_1, x_2, x_3) = (x_1 + x_1^2)x_2^2 x_3 + x_1^2 x_2^2 x_3^2 = P'(x_1)x_2^2 x_3 + P''(x_1)x_2^2 x_3^2,$$

where $P'(x_1) = x_1 + x_1^2$ and $P''(x_1) = x_1^2$. Next, we select a monomial $P'(x_1)$ and find $\zeta_1 \in \mathbf{F}_q$ such that $P'(\zeta_1) \neq 0$. Note that $\zeta_1 = 1$ is a good choice for $\mathbf{F}_q = GF(3)$. Next, we set $P_2(x_2, x_3) = P_1(x_1, x_2, x_3)|_{x_1 = 1} = 2x_2^2 x_3 + x_2^2 x_3^2$ and proceed with the algorithm.

The following lemma shows the correctness of Procedure FINDSOLUTION.

Lemma 15.1. *Let P be a non-zero polynomial in variables $x_1, x_2, \ldots, x_n$ over $\mathbf{F}_q = GF(q)$ and let d be the maximum degree of P with respect to any variable. Let $\mathbf{F}_q$ be a finite field of size q such that $q > d$. Then, Procedure FIND-SOLUTION $\{P(x_1, x_2, \ldots, x_n), \mathbf{F}_q\}$ returns $\zeta_1, \zeta_2, \ldots, \zeta_n \in \mathbf{F}_q$ such that $P(\zeta_1, \zeta_2, \ldots, \zeta_n) \neq 0$.*

Proof. (Sketch) We only need to show that at each iteration $i, 1 \le i \le n$, there exists $\zeta_i \in \mathbf{F}_q$ such that $P^*(\zeta_i) \neq 0$. This follows from the fact that $P^*(x_i)$ is a polynomial of maximum degree d, hence it has at most d roots. Since $\mathbf{F}_q$ includes $q > d$ elements, there must be at least one element $\zeta_i \in \mathbf{F}_q$ that satisfies $P^*(\zeta_i) \neq 0$. $\qquad\square$

Theorems 15.1 and 15.2 show the relation between the algebraic properties of the transfer matrices $\mathbb{M}_t, t \in T$, combinatorial properties of $G(V, E)$, and the existence of a feasible network code $\{\beta_{e',e}\}$.

We begin with the analysis of unicast connections, i.e., the case in which T contains a single terminal node.

Theorem 15.1. *Let* $\mathbb{N}(G, s, T)$ *be a coding network, with* $T = \{t\}$, *and h be the number of packets that need to be delivered from s to t. Then, the following three conditions are equivalent:*

1. *There exists a feasible network code for* $\mathbb{N}(G, s, T)$ *and h over* $GF(q)$ *for some finite value of q;*
2. *The determinant* $\det(\mathbb{M}_t)$ *of the transfer matrix* $\mathbb{M}_t$ *is a (multi-variate) polynomial not identically equal to 0;*
3. *Every cut[3] that separates s and t in* $G(V, E)$ *includes at least h edges.*

Proof. (Sketch) (1) → (2) Suppose that there exists a feasible network code $\{\beta_{e',e}\}$ for $\mathbb{N}(G, s, T)$ and h over $GF(q)$. This implies that $\det(\mathbb{M}_t)$ is not zero for $\{\beta_{e',e}\}$, which, in turn, implies that $\det(\mathbb{M}_t)$ as a polynomial in $\{\beta_{e',e}\}$ is not identically equal to 0.

(2) → (1) Lemma 15.1 implies that there exists a non-zero assignment of the local encoding coefficients $\{\beta_{e',e}\}$ for $\mathbb{N}(G, s, T)$ over a sufficiently large field $\mathbf{F}_q$. This assignment constitutes a valid network code for $\mathbb{N}(G, s, T)$.

(1) → (3) Suppose that there exists a feasible network code $\{\beta_{e',e}\}$ for $\mathbb{N}(G, s, T)$ and h over $GF(q)$. By the way of contradiction, assume that there exists a cut C that separates the source s and terminal t that includes $h' < h$ edges. Let $\Gamma_1, \Gamma_2, \ldots, \Gamma_{h'}$ be the set of global encoding vectors for the edges that belong to C. Then, for each incoming edge e of t, it holds that the global encoding vector of e is a linear combination of $\Gamma_1, \Gamma_2, \ldots, \Gamma_{h'}$. This, in turn, implies that the global encoding vectors that correspond to incoming edges of t span a subspace of $\mathbf{F}_q^h$ of dimension h' or smaller. This implies that at least two rows of $\mathbb{M}_t$ are linearly dependent and, in turn, that $\det(\mathbb{M}_t)$ is identically equal to 0, resulting in a contradiction.

(3) → (1) The min-cut-max-flow theorem implies that there exist h edge-disjoint paths that connect s and t. Let $\{\beta_{e',e}\}$ be an assignment of the local encoding coefficients such that $\beta_{e'(v,u),e(u,w)} = 1$ only if both $e'(v, u)$ and $e(u, w)$ belong to the same path. It is easy to verify that this assignment constitutes a feasible network code. □

The next theorem extends these results for multicast connections.

Theorem 15.2. *Let* $\mathbb{N}(G, s, T)$ *be a multicast coding network and let h be the number of packets that need to be delivered from s to all terminals in T. Then, the following three conditions are equivalent:*

---

[3] A cut in a graph $G(V, E)$ is a partition of the nodes of V into two subsets V_1 and $V \setminus V_1$. We say that a cut $C = (V_1, V \setminus V_1)$ separates nodes s and t if $s \in V_1$ and $t \in V \setminus V_1$.

1. *There exists a feasible network code for* $\mathbb{N}(G, s, T)$ *and* h *over* $GF(q)$ *for some finite value of* q.
2. *The product* $\prod_{t \in T} \det(\mathbb{M}_t)$ *of the determinants of the transfer matrices is a (multivariate) polynomial which is not identically equal to 0.*
3. *Every cut that separates* s *and* $t \in T$ *in* $G(V, E)$ *includes at least* h *edges.*

Proof. (Sketch) (1) → (2) Similar to the case of unicast connections, the existence of a feasible network code $\{\beta_{e',e}\}$ for $\mathbb{N}(G, s, T)$ and h over $GF(q)$ implies that the polynomial $\det(\mathbb{M}_t)$ is not identically equal to 0 for each $t \in T$.

(2) → (1) Lemma 15.1 implies that there exists a non-zero assignment of the local encoding coefficients $\{\beta_{e',e}\}$ for $\mathbb{N}(G, s, T)$ over a sufficiently large field q. Since this assignment satisfies $\det(\mathbb{M}_t) \neq 0$ for each $t \in T$, $\{\beta_{e',e}\}$ is a feasible network code for $\mathbb{N}(G, s, T)$.

(1) → (3) Note that a feasible network code for the multicast connection $\mathbb{N}(G, s, T)$ is also feasible for each unicast connection $\mathbb{N}(G, s, \{t\})$, $t \in T$. Then, we can use the same argument as in Theorem 15.1 to show that every cut that separates s and t includes at least h edges.

(3) → (2) The min-cut-max-flow theorem implies that for each $t \in T$ there exist h edge-disjoint paths that connect s and t. The argument similar to that used in Theorem 15.1 implies that for each $t \in T$ the polynomial $\det(\mathbb{M}_t)$ is not identically equal to 0. This, in turn, implies that $\prod_{t \in T} \det(\mathbb{M}_t)$ is also not identically equal to 0.   □

Theorem 15.2 implies that the capacity of undirected multicast network is equal to the minimum size of a cut that separates a source s and a terminal $t \in T$. Algo-

---

Algorithm NETCODE1 ($\mathbb{N}(G, s, T), h$)

    Input:
           $\mathbb{N}(G(V, E), s, T)$ - a coding network;
           h - required number of packets;
    Output:
           A feasible network code $\{\beta_{e',e}\}$ for $\mathbb{N}(G, s, T)$

   1   For each node $v \in V$ in topological order
   2   **For** each outgoing edge $e(v, u)$ of v **do**
   3   Write a global encoding vector Γ_e of e as a function of $\{\beta_{e',e}\}$
   4   **For** terminal $t \in T$ **do**
   5   Write a the transfer matrix $\mathbb{M}_t$ of t as a function of $\{\beta_{e',e}\}$
   6   Identify $\det(\mathbb{M}_t)$ as a multi-variate polynomial in $\{\beta_{e',e}\}$
   7   Identify $\prod_{t \in T} \det(\mathbb{M}_t)$ as a multi-variate polynomial in $\{\beta_{e',e}\}$
   8   Use Procedure FINDSOLUTION to find a set of values of $\{\beta_{e',e}\}$ for which $\prod_{t \in T} \det(\mathbb{M}_t) \neq 0$
   9   **Return** $\{\beta_{e',e}\}$

Fig. 15.7 Algorithm NETCODE1

rithm NETCODE1 depicted in Figure 15.7 summarizes the steps required for finding a feasible network code for a multicast network.

15.4   Required Field Size

One of the most important parameters of a network coding scheme is the minimum required size of a finite field. The field size determines the number of available linear combinations. The number of such combinations, and, in turn, the required field size, is determined by the combinatorial structure of the underlying communication network. For example, consider the network depicted in Figure 15.8. Let $\Gamma_{e_1}, \ldots, \Gamma_{e_4}$ be the global encoding vectors of edges $e_1, \ldots, e_4$. Note that in this network each pair of (v_i, v_j) of the intermediate nodes is connected to a terminal, hence any two of the global encoding vectors $\Gamma_{e_1}, \ldots, \Gamma_{e_4}$ must be linearly independent. Note also that with $GF(2)$ there exist only three non-zero pairwise linearly independent vectors of size two: (1 0), (0 1), and (1 1), hence $\mathbf{F}_2 = GF(2)$ is insufficient for achieving network capacity. However, it is possible to find a network coding solution over $GF(3)$ or a larger field. For example, over $GF(3)$, the following global encoding coefficients are feasible: (1 0), (0 1), (1 1), and (1, 2).

As mentioned in the previous section, a feasible network code can be found by identifying a non-zero solution of a multivariate polynomial $P = \prod_{t \in T} \det(\mathbb{M}_t)$. As shown in Lemma 15.1, such a solution exists if the size q of the finite field $\mathbf{F}_q$ is larger than the maximum degree of any variable β_i of P. In this section, we show that maximum degree of any variable in $P = \prod_{t \in T} \det(\mathbb{M}_t)$ is bounded by $k = |T|$, which implies that a field of size $q \geq k$ is sufficient for finding a feasible solution to the problem.

In our model we assumed that each edge of the network sends a packet only one time when it receives a packet from each incoming edge. In this section, for the purpose of analysis, we assume that the communication is performed in rounds as

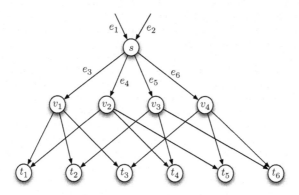

Fig. 15.8 A coding network

follows. Let $e(v, u) \in E$ be an edge in the communication network and let $\mathcal{M}_e$ be the set of parent edges of e. Then, at round i, edge e forwards a linear combination of packets received from edges in $\mathcal{M}_e$ at round $i - 1$. We assume that the original packets $x_1, \ldots, x_h$ are sent over the incoming edges of node s at round 0. For each edge $e \in E$ we denote by Γ_e^i the global encoding coefficients of the packet sent over edge e at round i. Intuitively, Γ_e^i captures the new information delivered to edge e over paths of length i, while the global encoding vector Γ_e summarizes the information available from all communication rounds:

$$\Gamma_e = \sum_{i=0}^{d} \Gamma_e^i, \tag{15.12}$$

where d is the length of the longest path in the network that starts at node s.

We define an $|E| \times |E|$ matrix T that captures the information transfer between different communications rounds. Matrix T is referred to as an *adjacency* matrix.

$$T(i, j) = \begin{cases} \beta_{e_i, e_j} & \text{if } e_i \text{ is a parent edge of } e_j \\ 0 & \text{otherwise.} \end{cases} \tag{15.13}$$

For example, the network depicted in Figure 15.9 has the following adjacency matrix $\mathbf{T}$:

$$\mathbf{T} = \begin{bmatrix} 0 & 0 & \beta_{e_1,e_3} & \beta_{e_1,e_4} & 0 & 0 & 0 \\ 0 & 0 & \beta_{e_2,e_3} & \beta_{e_2,e_4} & 0 & 0 & 0 \\ 0 & 0 & 0 & 0 & \beta_{e_3,e_5} & \beta_{e_3,e_6} & 0 \\ 0 & 0 & 0 & 0 & 0 & 0 & \beta_{e_4,e_7} \\ 0 & 0 & 0 & 0 & 0 & 0 & \beta_{e_5,e_7} \\ 0 & 0 & 0 & 0 & 0 & 0 & 0 \\ 0 & 0 & 0 & 0 & 0 & 0 & 0 \end{bmatrix} \tag{15.14}$$

We also define $h \times |E|$ matrix A and $|E| \times 1$ vector B_e for each $e \in E$ as follows:

$$A(i, j) = \begin{cases} 1 & \text{if } i = j \\ 0 & \text{otherwise,} \end{cases} \tag{15.15}$$

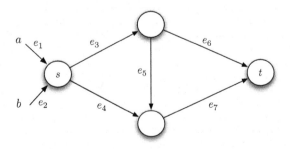

Fig. 15.9 A example of a coding network

$$B_{e_i}(j) = \begin{cases} 1 & \text{if } i = j \\ 0 & \text{otherwise,} \end{cases} \tag{15.16}$$

We note that

$$\Gamma_e^i = AT^i B_e. \tag{15.17}$$

For example, for edge e_3 in Figure 15.9 it holds that

$$\Gamma_{e_3}^1 = \begin{bmatrix} 1\,0\,0\,0\,0\,0\,0 \\ 0\,1\,0\,0\,0\,0\,0 \end{bmatrix} \cdot \begin{bmatrix} 0\,0\,\beta_{e_1,e_3}\,\beta_{e_1,e_4}\,0\,0\,0 \\ 0\,0\,\beta_{e_2,e_3}\,\beta_{e_2,e_4}\,0\,0\,0 \\ 0\,0\,0\,0\,\beta_{e_3,e_5}\,\beta_{e_3,e_6}\,0 \\ 0\,0\,0\,0\,0\,0\,\beta_{e_4,e_7} \\ 0\,0\,0\,0\,0\,0\,\beta_{e_5,e_7} \\ 0\,0\,0\,0\,0\,0\,0 \\ 0\,0\,0\,0\,0\,0\,0 \end{bmatrix} \cdot \begin{bmatrix} 0 \\ 0 \\ 1 \\ 0 \\ 0 \\ 0 \\ 0 \end{bmatrix} = \begin{bmatrix} \beta_{e_1,e_3} \\ \beta_{e_2,e_3}. \end{bmatrix}$$

Note for e_3 it holds that $\Gamma_{e_3}^i$ is non-zero only for $i = 1$. In contrast, edge e_7 has two non-zero vectors, $\Gamma_{e_7}^2$ and $\Gamma_{e_7}^3$.

By substituting Equation (15.17) into Equation (15.12) we obtain

$$\Gamma_e = A \cdot (I + T + T^2 + \cdots + T^d) B_e. \tag{15.18}$$

We observe that matrix T is *nilpotent*,[4] in particular it holds that T^{d+1} is a zero matrix. Thus, it holds that

$$\Gamma_e = A \cdot (I + T + T^2 + \cdots) B_e = A \cdot (I - T)^{-1} B_e. \tag{15.19}$$

Let $t \in T$ be one of the terminals. We define $|E| \times h$ matrix B_t as a concatenation of h vectors B_e that correspond to the incoming edges of t. Then, the transfer matrix $\mathbb{M}_t$ can be written as

$$\mathbb{M}_t = A \cdot (I - T)^{-1} B_t. \tag{15.20}$$

The following theorem shows that the determinant of $\mathbb{M}_t$ is equal to the determinant of another matrix, $\mathbb{M}'_t$, that has a certain structure.

Theorem 15.3. *Let* $\mathbb{N}(G, s, T)$ *be a coding network and let t be a terminal in T. Then the determinant of the transfer matrix* $\mathbb{M}_t = A(I - T)^{-1} B_t$ *of t is equal to*

$$\det(\mathbb{M}_t) = \det(\mathbb{M}'_t),$$

where

$$\mathbb{M}'_t = \begin{bmatrix} A & 0 \\ I - T & B_t^T \end{bmatrix}.$$

The proof of Theorem 15.3 involves basic algebraic manipulations and can be found in [17]. The structure of matrix $\mathbb{M}'_t$ implies that the maximum degree of any local

---

[4] A matrix T called nilpotent if there exists some positive integer n such that T^n is a zero matrix.

encoding coefficient $\beta_{e',e}$ in the multivariate polynomial $\mathbb{M}'_t$, and, in turn, $\mathbb{M}_t$ is equal to 1. As a result, the degree of each encoding coefficient $\beta_{e',e}$ in polynomial $\prod_{t \in T} \det \mathbb{M}_t$ is bounded by $|T|$. Thus, by Lemma 15.1, the field of size $q \geq |T|$ is sufficient for finding a solution for the network coding problem.

We summarize our discussion by the following theorem.

Theorem 15.4. *Let $\mathbb{N}(G, s, T)$ be a multicast coding network. Then, there exists a valid network code $\{\beta_{e',e}\}$ for $\mathbb{N}$ over any field $GF(q)$, where q is greater than the number of terminals.*

15.5 Random Network Coding

One of the important properties of network coding for multicast networks is that a feasible network code can be efficiently identified through a randomized algorithm. A randomized algorithm chooses each encoding coefficient at random with uniform distribution over a sufficiently large field $\mathbf{F}_q$. To see why a random algorithm works, recall that the main goal of the network coding algorithm is to find a set of encoding coefficients $\{\beta_{e',e}\}$ that yield a non-zero value of $P = \prod_{t \in T} \det \mathbb{M}_t$. Theorem 15.5 bounds the probability of obtaining a bad solution as a function of the field size.

Theorem 15.5. *(Schwartz–Zippel). Let $P(x_1, \ldots, x_n)$ be a non-zero polynomial over $\mathbf{F}$ of total degree at most d. Also, let $r_1, \ldots, r_n$ be a set of i.i.d. random variables with uniform distribution over finite field $\mathbf{F}_q$ of size q. Then,*

$$Pr(P(r_1, \ldots, r_n) = 0) \leq \frac{d}{q}.$$

The theorem can be proven by induction on the number of variables. As discussed in the previous section, the degree of each variable $\beta_{e',e}$ in $\prod_{t \in T} \det \mathbb{M}_t$ is at most $|T|$. Let η be the total number of encoding coefficients. Thus, if we use a finite field $\mathbf{F}_q$ such that $q > 2\eta k$, the probability of finding a feasible solution is at least 50%. In [17] a tighter bound of $(1 - \frac{|T|}{q})^\eta$ on the probability of finding a non-zero solution has been shown.

Random network coding has many advantages in practical settings. In particular, it allows each node in the network to choose a suitable encoding coefficient in a decentralized manner without prior coordination with other nodes. Random coding has been used in several practical implementation schemes [10].

Random network coding can also be used to improve the network robustness to failures of network elements (nodes or edges) or to deal with frequently changing topologies. Let $\mathbb{N}(G, s, T)$ be the original coding network and let $\mathbb{N}'(G', s, T)$ be the network topology resulting from a failure of an edge or node in the network. Further, let $P = \prod_{t \in T} \det(\mathbb{M}_t)$ be the product of determinants of the transfer matrices in the $\mathbb{N}(G, s, T)$ and $P' = \prod_{t \in T} \det(\mathbb{M}'_t)$ be a product of determinants of transfer matrices in $\mathbb{N}'(G', s, T)$. The network code $\{\beta_{e',e}\}$ that can be used in both the original network and in the network resulting from the edge failure must be a non-zero solution of the polynomial $P \cdot P'$. Note that degree of $P \cdot P'$ is bounded by $2\eta \cdot |T|$; hence for a sufficiently large field size the random code can be used for both networks, provided that after edge failure the network satisfies the minimum-cut condition. We conclude that with the random network code, the resilience to failure can be achieved by adding redundancy to the network to guarantee that the min-cut condition is satisfied. Then, upon a failure (failures) of an edge or node with high probability the same network code can be used.

15.6 Polynomial-Time Algorithm

In this section we present a polynomial-time algorithm for network code construction due to Jaggi et al. [21]. The algorithm receives, as input, a coding network $\mathbb{N}(G, s, T)$, a number of packets h that need to be delivered to all terminals and outputs a feasible network code $\{\beta_{e',e}\}$ for $\mathbb{N}$. In this section we assume, without loss of generality, that the source node has exactly h outgoing edges. Indeed, if this is not the case, we can always introduce a new source s connected to the original one with h edges. We assume that the outgoing edges of a source node s are indexed by $e_1, \ldots, e_h$.

The algorithm consists of two stages. In the first stage, the algorithm finds, for each terminal $t \in T$, a set of edge-disjoint paths $f^t = \{P_1^t, \ldots, P_h^t\}$ that connect the source node s to that terminal. This stage can be implemented by using a minimum-cost flow algorithm (see, e.g., [2]). Only edges that belong to one of the paths $\{P_i^t \mid t \in T, 1 \le i \le h\}$ are considered in the second stage of the algorithm. Indeed, the minimum-cut condition can be satisfied by edges that belong to $\{P_i^t \mid t \in T, 1 \le i \le h\}$, hence all other edges can be omitted from the network. For each edge $e \in E$ we denote by $T(e)$ the set of sink nodes such that every sink $t \in T(e)$ includes edge e in one of the paths in f^t. For each terminal $t \in T(e)$ we denote by $P^t(e)$ the predecessor of e on the path $P_i^t \in f^t$ that e belongs to.

The goal of the second stage is to assign the local encoding coefficient $\beta_{e',e}$ for each pair of edges $(e(v, u), e'(u, w))$ in E. For this purpose, all nodes in the network are visited in a topological order.[5] Let (V', V'') be a cut in $G(V, E)$, where V' includes a subset of nodes in V already visited by the algorithm and by V'' the set of nodes that were not visited yet. We refer to (V', V'') as the *running cut* of the algorithm. At the beginning of the algorithm, the running cut (V', V'') separates source node s from the rest of the nodes in the graph. At the end of the algorithm, the running cut separates all terminals in T from the rest of the network. At any time during the algorithm, each path $P_i^t, t \in T, 1 \le i \le h$, has exactly one edge that belongs to the cut. We refer to this edge as an *active* edge. For each terminal $t \in T$

---

[5] A topological order is a numbering of the vertices of a directed acyclic graph such that every edge $e(v, u) \in E$ satisfies $v < u$.

Algorithm NETCODE2 $(\mathbb{N}(G, s, T), h)$

    Input:

        $\mathbb{N}(G, s, T)$ - a coding network;

        h - required number of packets;

    Output:

        A feasible network code $\{\beta_{e',e}\}$ for $\mathbb{N}(G, s, T)$

  1   For each terminal $t \in T$ **do**

  2   Find h edge disjoint paths f^t between s and t

  3   For each edge e_i from $i = 1$ to h **do**

  4       $\Gamma(e_i) = [0^{i-1}, 1, 0^{h-i}]^T$

  5   $C_i = \{e_1, \ldots, e_h\}$

  6   $B_t = \{\Gamma(e_1), \ldots, \Gamma(e_h)\}$

  7   For each node $v \in v$ in topological order

  8   **For** each outgoing edge $e(v, u)$ of **do**

  9   Choose the values of local encoding coefficients $\{\beta_{e',e} \mid e' \in \mathcal{M}_e\}$

          such that

 10   For each terminal $t \in T(e)$ the matrix B'_t formed from B_t by

          substituting $\Gamma(P^t(e))$ by $\Gamma(e)$ is of full rank

 11   For each terminal $t \in T(e)$

 12   Substitute $P^t(e)$ by e in C_t

 13   Substitute $\Gamma(P^t(e))$ by $\Gamma(e)$ in B_t

 14 **Return** $\{\beta_{e',e}\}$

Fig. 15.10 Algorithm NETCODE2

we denote by C_t the set of active edges of the disjoint paths $\{P^t_i \mid 1 \leq i \leq h\}$. Also, we denote by B_t the $h \times h$ matrix whose columns are formed by the global encoding vectors of edges in C_t.

The main invariant maintained by the algorithm is that the matrix B_t for each $t \in T$ must be invertible at every step of the algorithm. In the beginning of the algorithm we assign the original packets $\mathbb{R} = (p_1, p_2, \ldots, p_h)$ to h outgoing edges of s. When the algorithm completes, for each terminal $t \in T$ the set of active edges includes the incoming edges in t. Thus, if the invariant is maintained, then each terminal will be able to decode the packets in $\mathbb{R}$. We refer to this algorithm as Algorithm NETCODE2 and present its formal description in Figure 15.10.

An example of the algorithm's execution is presented in Figure 15.11. Figures 15.11(a) and (b) show the original network and two sets of disjoint paths f^{t_1} and f^{t_2} that connect the source node s with terminals t_1 and t_2, respectively. Figures 15.11(c) shows the coding coefficients assigned to edges (s, v_1), (s, v_2), and (s, v_3) after node s has been processed. Note that this is one of several possible assignments of the coefficients and that it satisfies the invariant. Nodes v_1, v_2, and v_3 are processed in a straightforward way since each of those nodes has only one outgoing edge. Figure 15.11(d) shows the processing step for node v_4. This node has one outgoing edge (v_4, v_6) and needs to choose two encoding coefficients $\beta_1 = \beta_{(v_1, v_4), (v_4, v_6)}$ and $\beta_2 = \beta_{(v_2, v_4), (v_4, v_6)}$. In order to satisfy the invariant, the vector $\beta_1[1\ 0\ 0]^T + \beta_2[0\ 1\ 0]^T$ must not belong to the two subspaces, the first

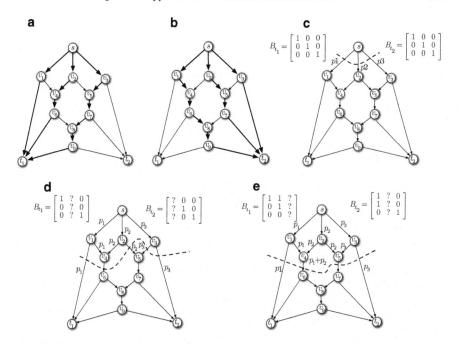

Fig. 15.11 An example of algorithm execution: (**a**) Original network and a set of edge-disjoint paths between s and t_1; (**b**) A set of edge-disjoint path between s and t_2; (**c**) The processing step for node s; (**d**) The processing step for node v_4; (**e**) The processing step for node v_5

subspace defined by vectors $[1\ 0\ 0]^T$ and $[0\ 1\ 0]^T$, and the second subspace is defined by $[0\ 1\ 0]^T$ and $[0\ 0\ 1]^T$. Note that if the finite field $GF(2)$ is used, then the only feasible assignment is $\beta_1 = \beta_2 = 1$. For a larger field, there are several possible assignments of the encoding coefficients. Figure 15.11(e) demonstrates the processing step for node v_5.

The key step of the algorithm is the selection of local encoding coefficients $\{\beta_{e',e} \mid e' \in \mathcal{M}_e\}$ such that the requirement of Line 10 of the algorithm is satisfied. Let e be an edge in E, let $T(e) \subseteq T$ be the set of destination nodes that depend on E, and let $\mathcal{M}_e$ be the set of parent edges of e. Also, consider the step of the algorithm before edge e is processed and let $\{B_t\}$ be the set of matrices for each $t \in T(e)$. Since each matrix B_t is of full rank, there exists an inverse matrix $A_t = B_t^{-1}$. For each $t \in T(e)$, let a_t be a row in A_t that satisfies $a_t \cdot \Gamma(P^t(e)) = 1$, i.e., a_t is a row in A_t that corresponds to column $P^t(e)$ in B_t (see Figure 15.12(a)). We also observe that if the column $P^t(e)$ in B_t is substituted by a column $\Gamma(e)$, the necessary and sufficient condition for B_t to remain full rank is that $a_t \cdot \Gamma(e) \neq 0$ (see Figure 15.12(b)). Thus, we need to select the local encoding coefficients $\{\beta_{e',e} \mid e' \in \mathcal{M}_e\}$ such that the vector $\Gamma(e) = \sum_{e' \in \mathcal{M}_e} \beta_{e',e}\Gamma(e')$ will satisfy $\Gamma(e) \cdot a_t \neq 0$ for each $t \in T(e)$.

The encoding coefficients are selected through Procedure CODING depicted in Figure 15.13. The procedure receives, as input, an edge e for which the encoding coefficients $\{\beta_{e',e} \mid e' \in \mathcal{M}_e\}$ need to be determined. We denote by g the size of

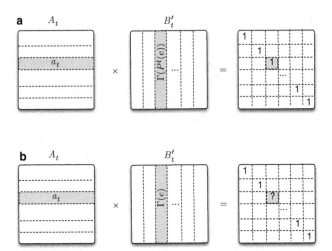

Fig. 15.12 Data structures: (**a**) A row a_t in A_t that satisfies $a_t \cdot \Gamma(P^t(e)) = 1$ (**b**) A condition imposed on $\Gamma(e)$

Procedure CODING $(\mathbb{N}(G, s, T), h)$

    Input:

        $e \in E$ - an edge for which the encoding coefficients need to be determined;

        $\{\Gamma_{e'} \mid e' \in \mathcal{M}_e\}$ - a set of global encoding vectors for parent edges of e;

        $\{a_t \mid t \in T(e)\}$ - set of normals

    Output:

        Coefficients $\{\beta_{e',e} \mid e' \in \mathcal{M}_e\}$ such that $\sum_{e' \in \mathcal{M}_e} \beta_{e',e} \Gamma(e')$ satisfies $\Gamma(e) \cdot a_t \neq 0$

   1 $g \leftarrow |T(e)|$

   2 Index terminals in $T(e)$ by $t^1, t^2, \dots, t^g$

   3 For $i = 1$ to $g - 1$ do

   4      $e^i = P^{t^i}(e)$

   5      $\beta_{e^i,e} \leftarrow 0$

   6 $\beta_{e^1,e} \leftarrow 1$

   7 For $i = 1$ to g **do**

   8      $u^i \leftarrow \sum_{j=1}^{i} \beta_{e^j,e} \Gamma(e^j)$

   9   If $u^i \cdot a_{t^{i+1}} = 1$ then

 10         $\beta_{e^j,e} \leftarrow 0$

 11   else

 12   For each $j, 1 \leq j \leq i$ do

 13            $\alpha^j \leftarrow -\dfrac{\Gamma(e^{i+1}) \cdot a_{t^j}}{u^i \cdot a_{t^j}}$

 14   Choose $\alpha' \in \mathbf{F}_q$ such that $\alpha' \neq \alpha^j$ for $j, 1 \leq j \leq i$

 15   For each $j, 1 \leq j \leq i$ do

 16            $\beta_{e^j,e} \leftarrow \beta_{e^j,e} \cdot \alpha'$

 17      $\beta_{e^j,e} \leftarrow 1$

 18 **Return** $\{\beta_{e',e} \mid e' \in \mathcal{M}_e\}$

Fig. 15.13 Procedure CODING

$T(e)$ and index terminals in $T(e)$ by $t^1, t^2, \ldots, t^g$. Then, we denote $e^i = P^{t^i}(e)$. We also denote by a_{t^i} a row in A_t that satisfies $a_{t^i} \cdot \Gamma(e^i) = 1$. The main idea is to construct a sequence of vectors $u^1, u^2, \ldots, u^g$ such that for all i, j with $1 \leq j \leq i \leq g$ it holds that $u^i \cdot a_{t^j} \neq 0$. The algorithm begins by setting $u^1 = \Gamma(e^1)$. Then, for each i, $1 \leq i \leq g - 1$ we perform the following operations. First, if $u^i \cdot a_{t^{i+1}}$ is not zero, then we set $u^{i+1} = u^i$. Otherwise, we note that for each $\alpha \in \mathbf{F}_q$ it holds that $(\alpha u^i + \Gamma(e^{i+1})) \cdot a_{t^{i+1}} \neq 0$. We also note that for each j, $1 \leq j \leq i$ it holds that $(\alpha u^i + \Gamma(e^{i+1})) \cdot a_{t^j}) = 0$ only if

$$\alpha = \alpha_j = -\frac{\Gamma(e^{i+1}) \cdot a_{t^j}}{u^i \cdot a_{t^j}}.$$

Thus, the set $\mathbf{F}_q \setminus \{\alpha_j \mid 1 \leq j \leq i\}$ is not empty. Thus, we choose $\alpha' \in \mathbf{F}_q$ such that $\alpha' \neq \alpha^j$ for j, $1 \leq j \leq i$ and set $u_{i+1} = \alpha' u_i + \Gamma(e^{i+1})$ (by setting coefficients $\{\beta_{e^j, e}\}$ accordingly). By construction, it holds that $u_{i+1} \cdot a_{t^j} \neq 0$ for $1 \leq j \leq i$.

15.7 Network Coding in Undirected Networks

So far we have considered coding networks represented by directed graphs. In each edge $e(v, u)$ of a directed graph, the data can only flow in one direction, from v to u. In contrast, in undirected networks, that data can be sent in both directions, provided that the total amount of data sent over an edge does not exceed its capacity. Accordingly, to establish a multicast connection in an undirected network, we need first to determine the optimum *orientation* of each edge of the network. The edge orientation is selected in such a way that the resulting directed network has maximum possible multicast capacity. In some cases, to maximize the capacity of the network an undirected edge needs to be substituted by two directed edges with opposite orientation. For example, consider the undirected network depicted in Figure 15.14(a). Figure 15.14(b) shows a possible orientation of the edges in the network, resulting in a directed network of capacity 1. The optimal orientation is shown in Figure 15.14(c). In this orientation, undirected edge (t_1, t_2) is substituted by two bi-directed edges of capacity 0.5, resulting in directed multicast network of capacity 1.5.

For a coding network $\mathbb{N}(G(V, E), s, T)$ we define by $\lambda(\mathbb{N})$ the minimum size of a cut that separates the source node s and one of the terminals. As discussed above, $\lambda(\mathbb{N})$ determines the maximum rate of a multicast coding network over a directed graph. However, in undirected network $\lambda(\mathbb{N})$ can only serve as an upper bound on the transmission rate. For example, for the network $\mathbb{N}(G(V, E), s, \{t_1, t_2\})$ depicted in Figure 15.14(a) it holds that $\lambda(\mathbb{N}) = 2$, while the maximum achievable multicast rate is equal to 1.5. A tighter upper bound can be established by considering the *Steiner strength* of the multicast network [30], defined as follows:

Definition 15.2 (Steiner Strength). Let $\mathbb{N}(G(V, E), s, T)$ be a multicast coding network over an undirected graph G, with the source s and set T of the terminals. Let P be the set of all possible partitions of G, such that each partition includes at least one node in $T \cup \{s\}$. Then, the Steiner strength $\eta(\mathbb{N})$ of $\mathbb{N}$ is defined as

$$\eta(\mathbb{N}) = \min_{p \in P} \frac{|E_p|}{(|p| - 1)},$$

where $|p|$ is the number of components in p and $E_p \subseteq E$ is the set of edges that connect different components of p.

For example, the Steiner strength of the network depicted in Figure 15.14(a) is equal to 1.5, which is a tight bound for this particular case. It turns out that $\eta(\mathbb{N})$ determines the maximum rate of the multicast transmission in the special case in which the set $T \cup \{s\}$ includes all nodes in the network.

The following theorem is due to Li and Li [29].

Theorem 15.6. *Let $\mathbb{N}(G(V, E), s, T)$ be a multicast coding network over an undirected graph G. Let $\pi(\mathbb{N})$ be the maximum rate of multicast connection using traditional methods (Steiner tree packing) and let $\chi(N)$ be the maximum rate achievable by using the network coding approach. Then for the case of $V = T \cup \{s\}$ it holds that*

$$\frac{1}{2}\lambda(N) \leq \pi(N) = \chi(N) \leq \lambda(N).$$

Otherwise it holds that

$$\frac{1}{2}\lambda(N) \leq \pi(N) \leq \chi(N) \leq \lambda(N).$$

Theorem 15.6 shows that the maximum coding advantage of network coding in undirected networks is upper bounded by two. This is in contrast to the case of directed networks, where the coding advantage can be significantly higher.

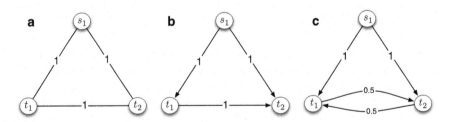

Fig. 15.14 An example of an undirected network: (**a**) Original undirected network; (**b**) An orientation that achieves rate 1; (**c**) An orientation that achieves rate 1.5

15.8 Practical Implementation

As discussed in the previous sections, network coding techniques can offer significant benefits in terms of increasing throughput, minimizing delay, and reducing energy consumption. However, the implementation of network coding in real networks incurs a certain communication and computational overhead. As a result, a thorough cost–benefit analysis needs to be performed to evaluate the applicability of the technique for any given network setting. For example, it is highly unlikely that the network coding technique will be implemented at core network routers due to the high rate of data transmission at the network core. Thus, finding the network setting that can benefit from the network coding technique is a challenging problem by itself. In this section, we discuss the practical implementation of the network coding technique proposed by Chou et al. [9,34]. The principles of this implementation were adopted by many subsequent studies [16] and by real commercial systems such as Microsoft Avalanche.

The content distribution system includes a single information source that generates a stream of bits that need to be delivered to all terminals. The bits are combined into *symbols*. Each symbol typically includes 8 or 16 bits and represents an element of a finite field $GF(q)$. The symbols, in turn, are combined into packets, such that packet p_i is comprised of N symbols $\sigma_1^i, \sigma_2^i, \ldots, \sigma_N^i$. The packets, in turn, are combined into *generations*, each generation includes h packets. In typical settings, the values of h can vary between 20 and 100. Figure 15.15 demonstrates the process of creating symbols and packets from the bit stream.

The key idea of the proposed scheme is to mix the packets that belong to the same generation, the resulting packet is then said to belong to the same generation. Further, when a new packet is generated, the encoding is performed over individual symbols rather than the whole packet. With this scheme, the local encoding coefficients belong to the same field as the symbols, i.e., $GF(q)$. For example, suppose that two packets p_i and p_j are combined into a new packet p_l with local encoding coefficients $\beta_1 \in GF(q)$ and $\beta_2 \in GF(q)$. Then, for $1 \leq y \leq N$, the y's symbol

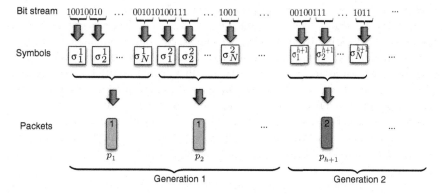

Fig. 15.15 Packetization process: forming symbols from bits and packets from symbols

of p_l is a linear combination of the y's symbol of p_i and y's symbol of p_j, i.e.,

$$\sigma_y^l = \beta_1 \cdot \sigma_y^i + \beta_2 \cdot \sigma_y^j.$$

The scheme is based on the random linear coding technique described in Section 15.5 that chooses local encoding coefficients uniformly over $GF(q)$ (excluding the zero). For each packet sent over the network, it holds that its symbols are linear combinations of the corresponding symbols of the original packets, i.e., the packets generated by the source node. Thus, each packet p_l can be associated with a global encoding vector $\Gamma_l = \{\gamma_1^l, \dots, \gamma_h^l\}$ that captures the dependency between the symbols of p_l and the symbols of the original packets. Specifically, symbol σ_y^l of p_l can be expressed as

$$\sigma_y^l = \sum_{i=1}^{h} \gamma_i^l \cdot \sigma_y^i.$$

Another key idea of this scheme is to attach the global encoding coefficients to the packet. These coefficients are essential for the terminal node to be able to decode the original packets. This method is well suited for settings with random local encoding coefficients. The layout of the packets is shown in Figure 15.16. Note that each packet also includes its generation number.

Attaching global encoding incurs a certain communication overhead. The size of the overhead depends on the size of the underlying finite field. Indeed, the number of bits needed to store the global encoding vectors is equal to $h \cdot q$. In the practical case considered in Chou et al. [9], h is equal to 50 and the field size q is equal to 2 bytes, resulting in a total overhead of 100 bytes for packets. With packet size of 1400 bytes, the overhead constitutes approximately 6% of total size of the packet. If the field size is reduced to 1 byte, then the overhead is decreased to just 3% of the packet size.

Note that the destination node will be able to decode the original packets after it receives h or more linearly independent packets that belong to the same generation. With random network coding, the probability of receiving linearly independent packets is high, even if some of the packets are lost. The major advantage of the proposed scheme is that it does not require any knowledge of the networking topology and efficiently handles dynamic network changes, e.g., due to link failures.

The operation of an intermediate network node is shown in Figure 15.17. The node receives, via its incoming links, packets that belong to different generations. The packets are then stored in the buffer, and sorted according to their generation number. At any given time, for each generation, the buffer contains a set of linearly independent packets. This is accomplished by discarding any packet that belongs to the span of the packets already in the buffer. A new packet transmitted by the node is formed by a random linear combination of the packets that belong to the current generation.

The important design decision of the encoding node is the *flushing policy*. The flushing policy determines when a new generation becomes the current generation.

There are several flushing policies that can be considered. One possibility is to change the current generation as soon as a packet that belongs to a new generation arrives via an incoming link. An alternative policy is to change generation when all incoming links receive packets that belong to the new generation. The performance of different flushing policies can be evaluated by a simulation or an experimental study.

15.8.1 Peer-to-Peer Networks

Network coding can benefit peer-to-peer networks that distribute large files (e.g., movies) among a large number of users [14]. The file is typically partitioned into a large number, say k, of chunks, each chunk is disseminated throughout the network in a separate packet. A target node collects k or more packets from its neighbors and tries to reconstruct the file. To facilitate the reconstruction process, the source node typically distributes parity check packets, generated by using an efficient erasure correction code such as Digital Fountains [5]. With this approach, the target node can decode the original file from any k different packets out of $n > k$ packets sent by the source node.[6]

With the network coding technique each intermediate node forwards linear combinations of the received packets to its neighbors (see Figure 15.18). This approach

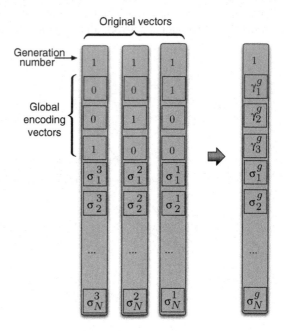

Fig. 15.16   Structure of the packet

---

[6] Some efficient coding schemes require slightly more than k packets to decode the file.

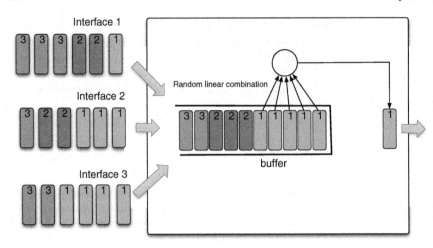

Fig. 15.17 Operation of an intermediate network node

significantly increases the probability of the successful decoding of the file at the target node. For example, consider the network depicted in Figure 15.19. In this example, the file is split into two chunks, a and b. The source node then adds a parity check packet, c, such that any two of the packets a, b, and c are sufficient for reconstructing the original file. Figure 15.19(a) demonstrates a traditional approach in which each intermediate node forwards packets a, b, and c to its neighbors. Since there is no centralized control and the intermediate nodes do not have any knowledge of the global network topology, the routing decision is done at random.

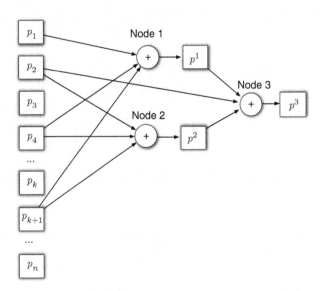

Fig. 15.18 Operation of an intermediate network node

Suppose that two target nodes t_1 and t_2 would like to reconstruct the file. Note that node t_1 obtains two original packets, a and b. However, node t_2 receives two copies of the same packet (b), which are not sufficient for a successful decoding operation. Figure 15.19(b) shows a network coding approach in which the intermediate nodes generate new packets by randomly combining the packets received over their incoming edges. With this approach, the probability that each destination node receives two linearly independent packets, and hence the probability of successful decoding operation, is significantly higher.

15.8.2 Wireless Networks

The distinct property of a wireless medium is the ability of a sender node to broadcast packets to all neighboring nodes that lie within the transmission range. In Section 15.1.1 we presented an example that shows that the network coding technique allows us to take advantage of the broadcast nature of the wireless medium to minimize the number of transmissions. This technique has been exploited at a network scale, in several recent studies. In this section, we will discuss the work of Katti et al. [23] that presents a new forwarding architecture, referred to as COPE, for network coding in wireless networks. The new architecture results in a substantial increase of throughput by identifying coding opportunities and sending encoded packets over the network.

The underlying principle of the COPE architecture is *opportunistic listening*. With this approach, all network nodes are set in a promiscuous mode, snooping on all communications over the wireless medium. The overheard packets are stored at a node for a limited period of time (around 0.5 s). Each node periodically broadcasts reception reports to its neighbors to announce the packets which are stored at this node. To minimize the overhead, the reception reports are sent by annotating the data packets transmitted by the node. However, a node that has no data packets to transmit periodically sends the reception reports in special control packets.

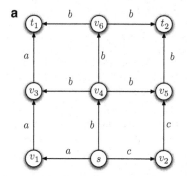
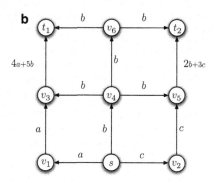

Fig. 15.19 (a) Traditional approach in which intermediate nodes only forward packets received over their incoming edges; (b) Network coding approach

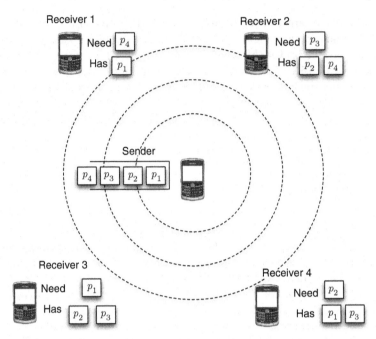

Fig. 15.20 Index coding

Once a sender node knows which overheard packets are stored in its neighbors, it can use this knowledge to minimize the number of transmissions. For example, consider a sender node and a set of its neighbors depicted in Figure 15.20. In this example, the sender node needs to deliver four packets $p_1, \ldots, p_4$ to its neighbors. For each neighbor, we show the packets it requires, as well as the packets stored in its cache. The traditional approach requires four transmissions to deliver all packets, while the network coding approach requires only two transmissions: $p_1 + p_2 + p_3$ and $p_1 + p_4$, all operations are performed over $GF(2^n)$.

This example shows that the network coding technique has the potential to reduce the number of transmissions. The problem of selecting an encoding scheme that minimizes the number of transmissions is referred to as *Index Coding*. It has been studied in several recent works [3, 8, 26, 32].

A practical implementation of this approach needs to overcome several challenges. First, at times of congestion, the reception reports may get lost in collisions. When the traffic is light, the reception reports might arrive too late and the sender might need to guess what overheard packets are available at the neighboring nodes. Further, the destination node might decode packets out of order, which, in turn, might result in a congestion signal issued by the end-to-end protocol such as TCP.

The experimental results of [23] show that network coding is most helpful when the network is moderately loaded. In such situations, the network coding technique can result in a fourfold throughput increase in throughput. The gain is smaller in underloaded networks due to limited coding opportunities at lower demands.

15.9   Conclusion

In this chapter, we discussed the basics of the network coding technique and its applications in several areas of networking. From a theoretical perspective, network coding is a new fascinating research area that requires tools from different disciplines such as algebra, graph theory, and combinatorics. It is rich in challenging problems, many of which are still open. In particular, while multicast problems are well understood, many problems in the general settings are open. From the practical perspective, several potential applications of network coding techniques have been discussed in the literature. The technique has been successfully employed by a commercial product (Microsoft Avalanche). We believe there is a potential for more applications that can benefit from this technique.

References

1. R. Ahlswede, N. Cai, S.-Y. R. Li, and R. W. Yeung. Network Information Flow. *IEEE Transactions on Information Theory*, 46(4):1204–1216, 2000.
2. R. K. Ahuja, T. L. Magnanti, and J. B. Orlin. *Networks Flows*. Prentice-Hall, NJ, USA, 1993.
3. Z. Bar-Yossef, Y. Birk, T. S. Jayram, and T. Kol. Index Coding with Side Information. *In Proceedings of 47th Annual IEEE Symposium on Foundations of Computer Science*, pages 197–206, 2006.
4. A. Barbero and O. Ytrehus. Cycle-logical Treatment for "Cyclopathic Networks". *IEEE/ACM Transactions on Networking*, 14(SI):2795–2804, 2006.
5. J. W. Byers, M. Luby, M. Mitzenmacher, and A. Rege. A Digital Fountain Approach to Reliable Distribution of Bulk Data. *SIGCOMM Comput. Commun. Rev.*, 28(4):56–67, 1998.
6. S. Chachulski, M. Jennings, S. Katti, and D. Katabi. MORE: Exploiting Spatial Diversity with Network Coding. In *MIT CSAIL Technical Report*, 2006.
7. M. Charikar and A. Agarwal. On the Advantage of Network Coding for Improving Network Throughput. In *Proceedings of IEEE Information Theory Workshop, San Antonio*, 2004.
8. M. Chaudhry and A. Sprintson. Efficient Algorithms for Index Coding. *Computer Communications Workshops, 2008. INFOCOM. IEEE Conference on*, pages 1–4, April 2008.
9. P. Chou and Y. Wu. Network Coding for the Internet and Wireless Networks. *Signal Processing Magazine, IEEE*, 24(5):77–85, Sept 2007.
10. P. A. Chou, Y. Wu, and K. Jain. Practical Network Coding. In *Proceedings of Allerton Conference on Communication, Control, and Computing*, Monticello, IL, October 2003.
11. R. Dougherty, C. Freiling, and K. Zeger. Insufficiency of Linear Coding in Network Information Flow. *IEEE Transactions on Information Theory*, 51(8):2745–2759, 2005.
12. E. Erez and M. Feder. Convolutional Network Codes. In *IEEE International Symposium on Information Theory*, 2004.
13. C. Fragouli and E. Soljanin. *Network Coding Fundamentals*. Now Publishers, Inc, 2007.
14. C. Gkantsidis, J. Miller, and P. Rodriguez. Anatomy of a P2P Content Distribution System with Network Coding. In *IPTPS'06*, February 2006.
15. C. Gkantsidis, J. Miller, and P. Rodriguez. Comprehensive View of a Live Network Coding P2P System. In *IMC '06: Proceedings of the 6th ACM SIGCOMM conference on Internet measurement*, pages 177–188, 2006.
16. C. Gkantsidis and P. Rodriguez. Network Coding for Large Scale Content Distribution. *INFOCOM 2005. 24th Annual Joint Conference of the IEEE Computer and Communications Societies. Proceedings IEEE*, 4:2235–2245 vol. 4, March 2005.

17. T. Ho. *Networking from a Network Coding Perspective*. Dissertation, Massachusetts Institute of Technology, 2004.
18. T. Ho, R. Koetter, M. Medard, D. Karger, and M. Effros. The Benefits of Coding over Routing in a Randomized Setting. In *Proceedings of the IEEE International Symposium on Information Theory*, 2003.
19. T. Ho and D. S. Lun. *Network Coding: An Introduction*. Cambridge University Press, Cambrige, UK, 2008.
20. S. Jaggi, M. Langberg, S. Katti, T. Ho, D. Katabi, M. Medard, and M. Effros. Resilient Network Coding in the Presence of Byzantine Adversaries. *IEEE Transactions on Information Theory*, 54(6):2596–2603, June 2008.
21. S. Jaggi, P. Sanders, P. A. Chou, M. Effros, S. Egner, K. Jain, and L. Tolhuizen. Polynomial Time Algorithms for Multicast Network Code Construction. *IEEE Transactions on Information Theory*, 51(6):1973–1982, June 2005.
22. S. Katti, D. Katabi, W. Hu, H. S. Rahul, and M. Médard. The Importance of Being Opportunistic: Practical Network Coding for Wireless Environments. In *43rd Annual Allerton Conference on Communication, Control, and Computing*, Allerton, 2005.
23. S. Katti, H. Rahul, D. Katabi, W. H. M. Médard, and J. Crowcroft. XORs in the Air: Practical Wireless Network Coding. In *ACM SIGCOMM*, Pisa, Italy, 2006.
24. R. Koetter and F. Kschischang. Coding for Errors and Erasures in Random Network Coding. *Information Theory, IEEE Transactions on*, 54(8):3579–3591, Aug. 2008.
25. R. Koetter and M. Medard. An Algebraic Approach to Network Coding. *IEEE/ACM Transactions on Networking*, 11(5):782 – 795, 2003.
26. M. Langberg and A. Sprintson. On the Hardness of Approximating the Network Coding Capacity. *Information Theory, 2008. ISIT 2008. IEEE International Symposium on*, pages 315–319, July 2008.
27. A. Lehman and E. Lehman. Complexity Classification of Network Information Flow Problems. In *Proceedings of SODA*, 2004.
28. S.-Y. R. Li, R. W. Yeung, and N. Cai. Linear Network Coding. *IEEE Transactions on Information Theory*, 49(2):371 – 381, 2003.
29. Z. Li and B. Li. Network Coding in Undirected Networks. In *Proceedings of 38th Annual Conference on Information Sciences and Systems (CISS)*, Princeton, NJ, USA, 2004.
30. Z. Li, B. Li, D. Jiang, and L. C. Lau. On Achieving Optimal Throughput with Network Coding. *INFOCOM 2005. 24th Annual Joint Conference of the IEEE Computer and Communications Societies. Proceedings IEEE*, 3:2184–2194 vol. 3, March 2005.
31. R. Lidl and H. Niederreiter. *Finite Fields*. Cambridge University Press, 2nd edition, 1997.
32. E. Lubetzky and U. Stav. Non-linear Index Coding Outperforming the Linear Optimum. *In Proceedings of 48th Annual IEEE Symposium on Foundations of Computer Science*, pages 161–168, 2007.
33. M. Médard, M. Effros, T. Ho, and D. Karger. On Coding for Non-multicast Networks. In *41st Annual Allerton Conference on Communication Control and Computing*, Oct. 2003.
34. Y. W. P. A. Chou and K. Jain. Network Coding for the Internet. In *IEEE Communication Theory Workshop*, Capri, Italy, 2004.
35. D. Silva, F. Kschischang, and R. Koetter. A Rank-Metric Approach to Error Control in Random Network Coding. *Information Theory, IEEE Transactions on*, 54(9):3951–3967, Sept. 2008.
36. Y. Wu, P. Chou, and S.-Y. Kung. Minimum-Energy Multicast in Mobile Ad Hoc Networks Using Network Coding. *IEEE Transactions on Communications*, 53(11):1906–1918, Nov. 2005.
37. R. Yeung. *Information Theory and Network Coding*. Springer, 2008.

Chapter 16
Next Generation Search

Debora Donato and Aristides Gionis

Abstract Searching for information is one of the most common tasks that users of any computer system perform, ranging from searching on a local computer, to a shared database, to the Internet. The growth of the Internet and the World Wide Web, the access to an immense amount of data, and the ability of millions of users to freely publish their own content has made the search problem more central than ever before. Compared to traditional information-retrieval systems, many of the emerging information systems of interest, including peer-to-peer networks, blogs, and social networks among others, exhibit a number of characteristics that make the search problem considerably more challenging. We survey algorithms for searching information in systems that are characterized by a number of such features: the data are linked in an underlying graph structure, they are distributed and highly dynamic, and they contain social information, tagging capabilities, and more. We call such algorithms next-generation search algorithms.

16.1 Introduction

The problem of searching for information in large volumes of data involves dealing with two main challenges: (i) identifying the information need of the users and designing models that provide an estimate of the relevance of each data item with respect to the user queries, and (ii) designing efficient algorithms that make it possible to locate the relevant information without having to visit all items in the available data.

The growth of the Internet and the World Wide Web, the access to an immense amount of data, and the ability of millions of users to freely publish their own content has made the search problem more difficult than ever before. The growth of the available information has an impact on both of the above-mentioned search challenges. First, the overwhelming wealth of information, which often is very noisy

D. Donato (✉) and A. Gionis
Yahoo! Research, Avd. Diagonal 177, 08018, Barcelona, Spain
e-mail: debora@yahoo-inc.com; gionis@yahoo-inc.com

G. Cormode and M. Thottan (eds.), *Algorithms for Next Generation Networks*,
Computer Communications and Networks, DOI 10.1007/978-1-84882-765-3_16,
© Springer-Verlag London Limited 2010

and of low quality, makes it extremely difficult to find relevant items, and even more difficult to distinguish the items of the highest quality among all the relevant ones. Second, due to the formidable size and the distributed nature of the data there is imperative need for efficient search algorithms, especially for those search systems that are designed to work in an online mode – such as web search engines.

Information retrieval is a well-established area that deals with many different aspects of the information-search problem. In the typical scenario of an information-retrieval system, users search for information in a collection of documents, which is assumed to be "static" and "flat." In contrast, many of the emerging information systems of interest, such as peer-to-peer networks, blogs, social networks, and social tagging systems among others, exhibit additional structure and have a number of properties that make the search problem very different than in the typical information-retrieval setting of plain document collections.

A very important and almost ubiquitous characteristic of emerging information systems is that the data can be abstracted by considering an underlying *graph* and assuming that content is residing on the nodes of this graph. The most typical example is the web graph, which is formed by hyperlinks between web documents. Another example is a social-network graph, the users of which are implicitly or explicitly connected to each other. In the case of a social network the content information consists of the user profiles, the actions of the users in the network, etc. When a user of a social network searches for information in the network, we would like to take into account the underlying graph structure, as well as the content (profile) of the user and his/her neighbors. Using such additional information the search results can be fine-tuned to the preferences and information needs of the users. As another example, in a peer-to-peer network, the data are distributed in an overlay network of autonomous users who may join or quit the network at will. As the available information is prone to adversarial manipulation, identifying authoritative sources of information is very important, as well as building mechanisms that quantify the reputation of the data publishers. In cases such as blogs and news, the available information is highly dynamic and becomes obsolete very fast. In other cases, in addition to the document structure and graph structure of the data, *tags* are also available and can be used to guide the search process.

In this chapter we survey algorithms for searching information in systems characterized by the features we described above: presence of additional graph structure, availability of social or other context, social tagging systems, vulnerability to adversarial manipulation, high dynamicity, and more. We call such algorithms algorithms for next-generation search.

Our survey is organized as follows. We start by reviewing traditional information-retrieval and web-retrieval systems. We provide a brief description of the now classic PageRank and HITS algorithms that are used for ranking information by determining authoritativeness scores. We then discuss distributed search algorithms and how to obtain ranking scores for the case of peer-to-peer networks. We next turn into searching in social networks; we review the seminal work of Kleinberg on navigating in small-world graphs, as well as searching in social tagging systems. We conclude our survey with additional topics, such as searching in highly dynamic information systems, and searching with context information.

16.2 Search in the Web

Early web-search engines retrieved documents only on the basis of text. As more information was accumulated in the web, text-based retrieval became ineffective due to what Jon Kleinberg called "the abundance problem" [46]. The "abundance problem" occurs when a search for a query returns millions of documents all containing the appropriate text, and one has to select the documents of highest quality and the ones that will better address the information needs of a user. Search engine algorithms had to evolve in complexity to handle the problem of over abundance.

16.2.1 Text-Based Web Search

The first generation of web-search engines, which appeared in the mid-1990s, were based solely on traditional information-retrieval methods. A formal characterization of information-retrieval models is given by Baeza-Yates and Ribeiro-Nieto [9].

Definition 16.1. An information-retrieval model is a quadruple $[D, Q, \mathscr{F}, R(q_i, d_j)]$ where

1. D is a set composed of logical views (or representations) for the documents in the collection.
2. Q is a set composed of logical views (or representations) for the user information needs. Such representations are called queries.
3. $\mathscr{F}$ is a framework for modeling document representations, queries, and their relationships.
4. $R(q_i, d_j)$ is a ranking function which associates a real number with a query $q_i \in Q$ and a document representation $d_j \in D$. Such ranking defines an ordering among the documents with regard to the query q_i.

Roughly speaking a model includes (i) a representation of documents in a document collection; (ii) a representation of user queries; (iii) a framework to relate documents to queries; and (iv) a ranking function that provides an ordering of documents for a particular query.

Perhaps the most common document-representation model is the *bag-of-words model*. According to this model, a document d is represented as the *multi-set* of the terms that it contains: for each term t contained in document d we only maintain the count of how many times each term t appears in the document d, and we ignore any other linguistic or structural information about the document. The latter count tf_{dt} is known as the *document frequency* of the term t in the document d. The intuition behind document frequency is that the more times a term appears in a document, the more important is this term for that document. However, for defining importance of a term with respect to a document, we also want to account for very common terms (like articles and other stop words) that are not specific to any document. This "normalization" is achieved by the concept of *inverse document frequency (idf)*:

assuming that a document collection consists of N documents, the inverse document frequency of a term t is defined to be

$$\text{idf}_t = \log \frac{N}{\text{df}_t},$$

where df_t is the *document frequency* of t, that is, the number of documents in the collection that t appears at least one time. As a result, the idf of a rare term is high, whereas the idf of a frequent term is low. The two factors, tf_{dt} and idf_t, are combined in the tf-idf *weighting scheme* in order to obtain a measure of the importance of a term in a document:

$$\text{tf-idf}_{dt} = \text{tf}_{dt} \times \text{idf}_t.$$

The above weighting scheme can be used to obtain the well-known tf-idf *ranking function*. Assuming that a user query q consists of a number of terms and the task is to rank documents in order of their relevance to the query, the tf-idf *ranking score* of a document d with respect to q is defined to be the sum of the tf-idf scores of the query terms

$$\text{score}(d, q) = \sum_{t \in q} \text{tf-idf}_{dt}.$$

The higher the score of a document, the more relevant the document is considered as an answer to the user query, and the final ranking to the query is produced by ordering the documents in descending score order.

Many variants of tf-idf, involving numerous normalization and scaling schemes for documents and queries, have been proposed in the literature [9]. In recent years, with the increased importance of the web-search problem, researchers have put a lot of emphasis in learning ranking functions using machine-learning algorithms [20, 32, 61]. Such machine-learning algorithms fit ranking functions on training data that contain relevance assessments provided by human editors. The benefit of the machine-learning approach is that it can be used to obtain functions over an extensive number of features that go well beyond tf and idf. Such features may include link-structure information, as explained in the next sections, anchor-text information, linguistic characterization of terms, importance of the domain name of a document, spam scores, and possibly more. Combining such a large number of features with a ranking function with ad hoc methods is a daunting task.

A query typically represents an information need of the user. A document is considered *relevant* to the user query, if the user perceives it as containing information of value with respect to their information need. To assess the effectiveness of an IR model, the measures of *precision* and *recall* are the ones most typically used.

Precision: The fraction of documents returned from the IR model that are considered relevant.

Recall: The fraction of the relevant documents in the whole collection that are returned from the IR model.

The goal is to build an IR system that has both precision and recall as close to 1 as possible. Notice the trade-off between the two measures: higher score for one measure can be achieved at the expense of the other. For instance, a recall value of 1 can be achieved by returning all the documents in the collection, but obviously such a method will have extremely low precision.

The measures of precision and recall, as defined above, are used for evaluating unranked sets. For evaluating ranked sets many other measures are used, such as *mean average precision* (MAP), *precision at* k, *the Receiver Operating Character-istic* (ROC) curve, *discounted cumulative gain* (DCG), and *normalized discounted cumulative gain* (NDCG). For definitions and detailed discussion the interested reader is referred to the Information Retrieval textbook of Manning, Raghavan, and Schütze [56].

16.2.2   Link-Based Web Search

Metrics and models that are based on estimating the relevance of a document to the query using only the text of the documents are not sufficient to address the abun-dance problem. An elegant solution to the abundance problem is to favor documents that are considered to be authoritative. One way to estimate the authoritativeness of each document in the collection is to use the link-structure of the web graph: in par-ticular, every hyperlink between two pages in the web graph can be considered as an implicit endorsement of authority from the source document toward the target doc-ument. Two different applications of this idea have led to two seminal algorithms in web-search literature: the PageRank algorithm by Page and Brin [19], and the HITS algorithm by Jon Kleinberg [46].

16.2.2.1   PageRank

The PageRank algorithm models the behavior of a "random surfer" on the web graph, which is the graph that has as nodes the web documents, and has a di-rected edge between two nodes if there is a hyperlink between the corresponding documents. The surfer essentially browses the documents by following hyperlinks randomly. More specifically, the surfer starts from some node arbitrarily. At each step the surfer proceeds as follows:

- With probability c an outgoing hyperlink is selected randomly from the current document, and the surfer moves to the document pointed by the hyperlink.
- With probability $1 - c$ the surfer jumps to a random page chosen according to some distribution, typically the uniform distribution.

The value Rank(i) of a node i (called the PageRank value of node i) is the fraction of time that the surfer spends at node i. Intuitively, Rank(i) is considered to be a measure of importance of node i.

PageRank is expressed in matrix notation as follows. Let N be the number of nodes of the graph and let $n(j)$ be the out-degree of node j. Denote by M the square matrix whose entry M_{ij} has value $\frac{1}{n(j)}$ if there is a link from node j to node i. Denote by $\left[\frac{1}{N}\right]$ the square matrix of size $N \times N$ that has all entries equal to $\frac{1}{N}$ and which models the uniform distribution of jumping to a random node in the graph. The vector Rank stores the PageRank values that are computed for each node in the graph. A matrix M' is then derived by adding transition edges of probability $\frac{1-c}{N}$ between every pair of nodes to include the case of jumping to a random node of the graph.

$$M' = cM + (1 - c)\left[\frac{1}{N}\right]$$

Since the PageRank process corresponds to computing the stationary distribution of the random surfer, we have $M'\text{Rank} = \text{Rank}$. In other words, Rank is the principal eigenvector of the matrix M', and thus it can be computed by the power-iteration method [19].

The notion of PageRank has inspired a large body of research on many different aspects, both on designing improved algorithms for more efficient computation of PageRank [25, 44, 55] and for providing alternative definitions that can be used to address specific issues in search, such as personalization [29], topic-specific search [16, 36], and spam detection [12, 35].

One disadvantage of PageRank is that it is prone to adversarial manipulation. For instance, one of the methods that owners of spam pages use to boost the ranking of their pages is to create a large number of auxiliary pages and hyperlinks among them, called *link-farms*, which result in boosting the PageRank score of certain target spam pages [12].

16.2.2.2 HITS

The HITS algorithm, proposed by Jon Kleinberg [46], introduced the paradigm of *hubs* and *authorities*. In the HITS framework, every page can be thought of as having a hub and an authority identity. There is a mutually reinforcing relationship between the two: a good hub is a page that points to many good authorities, while a good authority is a page that is pointed to by many good hubs.

In order to quantify the quality of a page as a hub and as an authority, Kleinberg associated every page with a hub and an authority *score*, and he proposed the following iterative algorithm: Assuming n pages with hyperlinks among them, let h and a denote n-dimensional hub and authority score vectors. Let also W be an $n \times n$ matrix, whose (i, j)-th entry is 1 if page i points to page j and 0 otherwise. Initially, all scores are set to 1. At each iteration the algorithm updates sequentially the hub and authority scores. For a node i, the authority score of node i is set to be the sum of the hub scores of the nodes that point to i, while the hub score of node i is the authority score of the nodes pointed by i. In matrix-vector terms this is equivalent to setting $h = Wa$ and $a = W^T h$. A normalization step is then applied, so that the vectors h and a become unit vectors. The vectors a and h converge to the principal eigenvectors of the matrices $W^T W$ and $W W^T$, respectively. The vectors a and h correspond to the right and left *singular vectors* of the matrix W.

Given a user query, the HITS algorithm determines a set of relevant pages for which it computes the hub and authorities scores. Kleinberg suggested to obtain such a set of pages by submitting the query to a text-based search engine. The pages returned by the search engine are considered as a root set, which is consequently expanded by adding other pages that either point to a page in the root set or are pointed by a page in the root set.

Kleinberg showed that additional information can be obtained by using more eigenvectors, in addition to the principal ones. Those additional eigenvectors correspond to clusters or distinct topics associated with the user query. One important characteristic of the HITS algorithm is that it computes page scores that depend on the user query: one particular page might be highly authoritative with respect to one query, but not such an important source of information with respect to another query. On the negative side, having to compute eigenvectors for each query makes the algorithm computationally demanding. In contrast, the authority scores computed by the PageRank algorithm are non-query-sensitive, and thus, they can be computed in a preprocessing stage.

16.3   Distributed Search

With the extremely fast pace that characterizes the growth in the web, a key challenge in modern information retrieval is the development of distributed tools that are able to allocate the computational load and divide the storage requirements among different machines. The benefits of such a distributed framework are straightforward: more computational power devoted to each single task, availability of larger storage, and the ability to scale down operational costs.

Peer-to-Peer (P2P) networks have recently been a niche paradigm for distributed computation and file sharing. In P2P networks a large amount of peers are acting as both clients and servers. In addition to all advantages of distributed systems, P2P networks ensure a number of further features such as self-organization, symmetric communication, distributed control, and robustness. Search algorithms for P2P methods have been the subject of an increasing number of research work. Topics of interest include P2P indexing methods, distributed hash tables, distributed ranking, query optimization over P2P indexes, and more. A good survey of P2P search methods can be found in [63].

Algorithms for distributed search are also very important for designing centralized web-search engines. In the case of web-search engines, distributed information retrieval tasks are accomplished using a number of modules devoted to crawling the web, indexing the collected data, computing page-quality assessment scores, and processing the user queries. The centralized approach presents several disadvantages in terms of scalability, updating speed, capacity, and maintenance costs [8,69]. Recently Baeza-Yates et al. [8] provided an in-depth discussion regarding the main characteristics and the key issues concerning the three search modules: crawling, indexing, and querying. The authors of [8] emphasize the main challenges and open problems that modern search engines are facing in order to cope with the immense amount of data generated continuously by users and in order to guarantee high quality of results, fast response time, and high query throughput.

In this section we concentrate on the problem of assigning a quality-assessment value to each page in a distributed environment. The challenge to this problem arises from the fact that relevance-based measures, such as PageRank, depend on the overall structure of the underlying graph, while in a distributed setting each module accesses only a subset of the data. For instance, the PageRank value of a particular node collects the authority contributions of the nodes along all the paths ending in this particular node [7]. Therefore, the computation of PageRank is typically accomplished by a central server that has access to the whole underlying graph. This constraint for centralized access poses a potential bottleneck for the performance of search engines and performing the PageRank computation in a distributed fashion is a very interesting research problem.

All the solutions proposed so far for the problem of computing PageRank in a distributed fashion follow two main directions:

- Decentralized algorithms [69, 71] that start from the assumption that the underlying web graph is characterized by a block structure of the corresponding adjacency matrix. All these method are inspired by the work of Kamvar et al. [44] that propose to exploit the topology of the web graph in order to speed up PageRank computation.
- Approximation algorithms that estimate the actual PageRank scores by performing the computations locally to a small subgraph [22] or at peer level [64, 72] and using message exchange to update scores through the network.

Next we present the BlockRank algorithm [44] that inspired many of the following work on the topic and we review some of the distributed ranking algorithms that recently appeared in literature.

16.3.1 BlockRank

Web pages are organized in web sites that are usually stored on web hosts. Empirical analysis of portions of the web has shown that pages in the same site and the same host are highly interconnected and loosely linked to external pages [15, 44, 69]. This means that the number of intra-host and intra-domain links is much higher than the number of inter-host and inter-domain links. As a result, ordering the URLs of the pages (for instance, lexicographically) leads to a block structure of the adjacency web matrix. This observation motivated Kamvar et al. to propose the BlockRank algorithm, which is based on aggregation/disaggregation techniques [23, 66], and domain-decomposition techniques [31]. Even though in its original formulation the BlockRank algorithm was not intended to work in a distributed manner, its simple idea inspired many distributed ranking methods.

The BlockRank algorithm is summarized as follows. The details of each step are discussed subsequently.

1. Split the web pages into blocks by domain.
2. Compute the local PageRank vector $\mathbf{l}_J$ for the pages within each block J.
3. Estimate the relative importance scores, or BlockRank scores, for each block.
4. Weight the Local PageRank of a page in each block by the BlockRank of the corresponding block and aggregate the weighted Local PageRank to form an approximate Global PageRank vector $\mathbf{z}$.
5. Use $\mathbf{z}$ as a starting vector for standard PageRank.

The local PageRank vector $\mathbf{l}_J$ is computed by considering only the links within the block J. It has been empirically observed that local PageRank preserves the relative ranking with respect to the global one. This observation suggests using as stopping criteria the Kendall's τ [45] between the rankings obtained in two consecutive iterations of the algorithm. The computation ends when the Kendall's τ residual is equal to 1.[1]

The relative importance of each block is computed using the standard PageRank algorithm over the *block graph B*, a weighted directed graph, whose nodes correspond to blocks and an edge between two nodes is present if there is a link between two pages in the corresponding blocks. The edges from a block I to a block J are weighted by the sum of the local PageRank values of the pages of I pointing to J. Formally, the block matrix B is the $k \times k$ matrix

$$\mathbf{B} = \mathbf{L}^T \mathbf{A} \mathbf{S},$$

where $\mathbf{L}$ is the $n \times k$ matrix whose columns are the local PageRank vectors $\mathbf{l}_J$, $\mathbf{A}$ is the adjacency matrix of the global graph, and $\mathbf{S}$ is a $k \times n$ matrix with the same structure of $\mathbf{L}$, but whose nonzero entries are replaced by 1.

The global PageRank value of a page $j \in J$ is approximated by its local PageRank score, weighted by the BlockRank value of the block J that the page belongs to.

The main advantage of the BlockRank algorithm is that the majority of the host blocks can fit in main memory with an effective speed up of the overall performance. The extension of the algorithm to distributed environments is straightforward. The main limitation is clearly due to the need of knowing the overall structure of the network for the BlockRank computation.

---

[1] We remind the reader that the Kendall's τ distance between two rankings r_1 and r_2 on n items is defined to be the fraction of item pairs (i, j) for which the two rankings disagree

$$KDist = \frac{\sum_{i,j} K_{\{i,j\}}(r_1, r_2)}{n(n-1)/2}$$

where $K_{\{i,j\}}(r_1, r_2)$ is equal to 1 if i and j are in different order in r_1 and r_2 and 0 otherwise.

16.3.2 Distributed Computation of Ranking Scores

Next we discuss some of the algorithms that have been recently proposed in the literature for computing PageRank scores in a distributed setting. Far from being an exhaustive survey of the topic, this section aims to illustrate some of the current research directions.

16.3.2.1 ServerRank

The BlockRank algorithm, as presented in the previous section, is a more efficient method for computing global PageRank scores. Wang and DeWitt [69] applied the main ideas of BlockRank to a distributed search environment. They called their algorithm *ServerRank*. Their main objective was to define high-quality local ranking functions within each server without requiring from the servers to perform global PageRank computations. In their framework, a local web-search engine is hosted on each web server, and it is responsible only for the queries related to data stored locally. The overall query process is organized in three steps: first the submitted query is routed to the web servers that host relevant data. Then the query is locally processed and a list of ranked results is returned. Finally, the results obtained from different servers are merged into a single ranked list of URLs.

ServerRank, as the BlockRank algorithm, computes (i) the local PageRank scores within each block, (ii) the ServerRank score of each server, which is the result of running the PageRank algorithm on the server-link graph, and then (iii) weights the local PageRank score of each page by the ServerRank score of the server that the page belong to. The main difficulty is that none of the web servers has complete information about the global structure of the server-link graph. Therefore, the weight values for each outgoing link have to be communicated to all the other servers through message exchange. Note that each server has to broadcast just one message with the list of all the servers with which it is connected to.

16.3.2.2 SiteRank

Wu and Aberer [71] propose to study the web graph at the granularity of web sites, instead of considering web pages. Their algorithm, which they called *SiteRank*, works in a similar way to ServerRank but the motivation behind the two algorithms is different. ServerRank is proposed as a solution to the problem of ranking in a distributed fashion sets of pages that are physically stored on different servers. SiteRank, instead, studies the rank of each single web site whose pages might belong or not to different servers. The algorithm performs the traditional PageRank computation on the *site graph*, i.e., the graph whose nodes are sites and edges are hyperlinks among them.

One of the interesting results of Wu and Aberer is that the SiteRank distribution still follows a power law with coefficient equal to 0.95. Moreover their experiments verify the existence of a mutual reinforcement relationship between SiteRank and PageRank:

1. Most pages of important web sites are also important.
2. If a web site has many important pages, it is highly probable that it is an important site.

This empirical observation justifies the choice of algorithms in this family to weight local PageRank scores with block/server/site PageRank scores in order to obtain global authority scores for web pages. As in the case of ServerRank, the computation of a global ranking for web documents using a decentralized architecture for search systems [64] requires three steps:

1. The computation of the SiteRank vector $\mathbf{r_S}$.
2. The computation of a local score vector $\mathbf{r_L}$ is given by the sum of local PageRank score $\mathbf{r_I}$ and a correction vector $\mathbf{r_E}$. The coordinate of the vector $\mathbf{r_E}$ that corresponds to document d is defined as

$$r_E^d = \sum_{I(d)} \frac{out_d(I_i(d))}{N_{I(d)}} r_S(v_d),$$

where $I(d)$ is the set of sites with at least one page pointing to d, $out_d(I_i(d))$ is the number of pages that point to d within the site $I_i(d) \in I(d)$, $N_{I(d)}$ is equal to $\sum_{I(d)} out_d(I_i(d))$, and $r_S(v_d)$ is the rank value the web site that the document d belongs to.

The local score for each document is given by $\mathbf{r_L} = w_I \cdot \mathbf{r_I} + w_E \cdot \mathbf{r_E}$. In [71], the authors choose $(w_I, w_E) = (0.2, 0.8)$ in order to give more importance to external links as opposed to internal due to the relatively low number of links across web sites as compared to the number of links within the same web site.
3. The application of a new operator, i.e., the *Folding Operator* [1], to combine both rankings into a global authority score.

16.3.3   The JXP Method for Robust PageRank Approximation

Most of the techniques proposed in literature are based on the assumption that the web can be partitioned in almost-disjoint partitions that correspond to pages belonging to the same hosts or domains. In this case, the link matrix has a block structure that can be exploited to speed up PageRank computation: PageRank scores are computed locally within each block and the results are combined.

In a P2P scenario, the above assumption that the link matrix has a block structure does not hold. The reason is that peers crawl portions of the web in a completely decentralized way without any control over overlaps between local graphs. As a consequence pages might link to or be linked by pages at other peers. Moreover, peers have only local (incomplete) information about the global structure of the graph and this makes it impossible to merge local scores into global ones.

The *JXP* algorithm [72] is a distributed algorithm that addresses the two main limitations described above: it allows overlap among the local networks of peers and it does not require any a priori knowledge of the content of the other peers. It runs locally at every peer, and combines these local authority scores with the information obtained from other peers during randomly occurring meetings. It has been proved that the scores computed by the JXP algorithm, called JXP scores, converge to the true global PageRank scores.

As mentioned before, peers know exclusively the pages in their local crawl, nevertheless these pages might link to or be linked by external pages belonging to other peers' networks. In order to perform local computation taking into account external links, a special node, called *World Node*, is added to each local graph. The world node represents all the pages in the network that do not belong to local graph, and all the links from local pages to external pages point to the world node. In the first iteration of the algorithm, each peer knows only the links that point to the world node, but it does not have any information about links from external nodes and, hence, from the world node. The main phase of the algorithm consists of two iterative steps: (i) the local computation of PageRank scores over the local graph with the addition of the world node; (ii) a meeting phase between pairs of peers in which the local graphs are merged into a new one.

During the first step of local PageRank computation the authority score of the world node represents the sum of all the scores of the external nodes. In the second step, i.e., the meeting phase, each peer exchanges the local authority scores and discovers external links that point to its internal pages. After the meeting phase all the information related to the other peers is discarded with the only exception of the transition probabilities from external incoming links that are stored in the link matrix. In this way, the outgoing links of the world node are weighted to reflect the score mass given by the original links. It is worth noting that the transitions among external pages have to be taken into account during the PageRank computation. For this reason a self-loop link is added at the world node.

The two phases, described before, are summarized as follows:

Initialization Phase

1. Extend the local graph by adding the world node.
2. Compute the PageRank in the extended graph.

Main Algorithm (for every $peer_i$ in the network)

1. Choose $peer_j$ at random.
2. Merge the local graphs by forming the union of pages in the two peers and the edges among them (world nodes are combined as well).
3. Compute PageRank in the merged graph.
4. Use the PageRank scores in the merged graph to update the JXP scores of the pages in the two peers.
5. Update the local graphs: Reconstruct world nodes for the two peers based on what was learned in the meeting phase.

16.3.3.1   Optimization: Light-Weight Merging of Local Graphs

At a peer meeting, instead of merging the graphs and world nodes, one can simply add relevant information received from the other peers into the local world node, and perform the PageRank computation on the extended local graph. It can be proved that the JXP scores still converge to the global PageRank scores.

16.3.3.2   Convergence Analysis

The JXP authority vector is proved to converge to the global PageRank, i.e., to the global stationary distribution vector π associated to the global transition matrix $\mathbf{C}_{N \times N}$. The analysis is accomplished on the light-weight merging version of the algorithm and it is based on the assumption that the number of nodes N in the graph is fixed.

The proof builds on the theory of state aggregation in Markov chains [23, 58]. Let

$$
\mathbf{P} = \left(\begin{array}{ccc|c}
p_{11} & \cdots & p_{1n} & p_{1w} \\
\vdots & \cdots & \vdots & \vdots \\
p_{n1} & \cdots & p_{nn} & p_{nw} \\
\hline
p_{w1} & \cdots & p_{wn} & p_{ww}
\end{array} \right)
$$

be the local transition matrix associated with each extended local graph G (that is, the last row and last column correspond to the world node), where:

$$
p_{ij} = \begin{cases} \frac{1}{out(i)} & \text{if there exists a transition from } i \text{ to } j \\ 0 & \text{otherwise} \end{cases}
$$

and

$$
p_{iw} = \sum_{\substack{i \to r \\ r \notin G}} \frac{1}{out(i)}
$$

for every $i, j, 1 \le i, j \le n$.

The transition probabilities from the world node, p_{wi} and p_{ww}, change during the computation, so they are defining according to the current meeting t

$$
p_{wi}^t = \sum_{\substack{r \to i \\ r \in W^t}} \frac{\alpha(r)^t}{out(r)} \cdot \frac{1}{\alpha_w^{t-1}} \tag{16.1}
$$

$$
p_{ww}^t = 1 - \sum_{i=1}^{n} p_{wi}^t \tag{16.2}
$$

Moreover let

$$\alpha = \left(\alpha_1 \; \ldots \; \alpha_n \middle| \alpha_w \right)^T$$

be the local stationary distribution, i.e., the JXP scores.

The following two theorems describe important properties of the JXP scores.

Theorem 16.1 ([72]). *The JXP score of the world node, at every peer in the network, is monotonically non-increasing.*

Theorem 16.2 ([72]). *The sum of scores over all pages in a local graph, at every peer in the network, is monotonically non-decreasing.*

These above-mentioned properties allow to relate JXP scores with the global PageRank scores. The next Theorem states that the global PageRank values are an upper bound for the JXP scores.

Theorem 16.3 ([72]). *Consider the true stationary probabilities (PageRank scores) of pages $i \in G$ and the world node w, π_i and π_w, and their JXP scores after t meetings α_i^t and α_w^t. The following holds throughout all JXP meetings: $0 < \alpha_i^t \leq \pi_i$ for $i \in G$ and $\pi_w \leq \alpha_w^t < 1$.*

Theorem 16.3 shows that the algorithm never overestimate the correct global PageRank scores and, as direct consequence, using the notion of fairness [54] the convergence of JXP toward the true PageRank scores can be proved:

Theorem 16.4 ([72]). *In a fair series of JXP meetings, the JXP scores of all nodes converge to the true global PageRank scores.*

16.4 Social Search

Services of social networking, which are also known as social media, are based on people forming a network with their friends and their acquaintances and publishing their own content. Nowadays the web is dominated by a large number of applications tailored for social interaction including, blogs, wikis, social bookmarking, peer-to-peer networks, and photo/video sharing. The dramatic growth in popularity of such social networking sites is changing radically the way people communicate and exchange information. Naturally, the study of social networks is drawing a lot of attention in the research community; since the existing web-search algorithms are not designed for these social environments, searching and ranking information in social networks is an emerging area of research, too.

Social search is motivated by searching for information relevant to one's social interactions, profile, preferences, or communities of interest. In some cases, users are searching in order to find the right person for a professional collaboration, for file sharing, or just for chatting. In other cases, users are searching for an expert who can solve a practical problem or give an opinion on different questions, ranging from product reviews to personal relationships.

With respect to the "first generation" web content, social media is characterized by more heterogeneous data integrating user-generated content, user connections, ratings, comments, and more. As mentioned by Amer-Yahia et al. [6] all the activities that users perform in social-content sites can be seen as "filtering of resources in communities by various search criteria". Thus, services of social networking may help users in creating and expanding their social circle, and for such a task, effective algorithms for social search can be essential.

An idea related to social search is the concept of *social web search*, which is based on *social tagging*, a paradigm that lets users rate and tag web pages or other web content. Social web search is motivated by the intuition that users could find more easily what they were looking for, based on the collective judgment of all other users. This idea has inspired sites such as MySpace, and del.icio.us that allow users to discover, organize, and share web content.

16.4.1 Structure of Social Networks

As the Internet has enabled social-networking services to emerge as a new mode of interaction and communication, the study of the structure of social networks has increasingly received a lot of attention. Important research questions include characterizing social networks in terms of their properties and developing generative models that capture those properties. Among the properties of social networks that research has focused on are the following:

- *Degree distribution* of the nodes of the network, which typically follows a power law distribution [4, 17, 60, 62].
- *Short paths* among the nodes of the network [21, 62]: in social networks there are very short paths between arbitrary pairs of nodes. A few different measures have been proposed in order to capture the short-path effect, such as diameter, effective diameter, and characteristic path length, which is the median of average path-length of a node to all other nodes in the network.
- *Community structure* [21, 62]. A local measure of community structure can be quantified by the *clustering coefficient*, which estimates the probability that two nodes with a common neighbor are connected. The clustering coefficient measure captures the "transitivity" between acquaintances and friends that one expect to find among people.

The first and the simplest random-graph model, originating from the pioneering work of Erdős and Rényi [27] that initiated the study of random graphs, states that for each pair of nodes u and v in the graph, the edge (u, v) is present with probability p. Random graphs have indeed short paths (e.g., see [18]), however, neither do they exhibit power-law behavior on the distribution of their degrees nor do they have community structure, i.e., they have small clustering coefficient.

As early as in the mid-1950s Simon [65] showed that power-law distributions arise when there is a rich-gets-richer phenomenon, and later de Solla Price [24] showed how to apply this idea in order to obtain networks with power-law degree distribution by adding nodes over time. A similar model is proposed by Barabasi and Albert [11] and inspired many researchers for further work. The idea of the Barabasi and Albert model, also known as *preferential attachment* model, is to grow the network by adding nodes over time. Each node gets a certain out-degree, and when adding a new node each outgoing edge connects to an old node with a probability proportional to the in-degree of the old node. The preferential attachment model yields indeed networks with power-law degree distribution and short paths but with no community structure.

In reality, people do not form connections randomly, or just based on their current number of acquaintances, but rather based on geographical proximity, going to the same school, having the same workplace, etc. Thus, existence of latent clusters leads to networks with community structure and high clustering coefficient. Watts and Strogatz [70] propose a model that has low diameter but high clustering coefficient. Their idea involves a superposition of networks: a highly structured network, which has large diameter, with a small number of random links added in. The highly structured network is responsible for the high clustering coefficient and the random links serve as shortcuts to obtain small diameter. An instantiation of this idea is a network, in which the nodes are arranged in a ring; each node is connected to its k-nearest neighbors in the ring ($k/2$ on each side), and then each edge is "rewired" randomly with probability p.

16.4.2 Navigating in Small-World Graphs

In 1967, Milgram [59] tested the existence of short paths inside a social network. In the famous experiment he conducted, he asked randomly chosen individuals in the USA to pass a chain letter to one particular person living in a suburb of Boston. The participants of the experiment had to forward the letter they received to a single acquaintance whom they knew on a first-name basis. While only around 29% of the initial number of letters found their target, the median length of the completed paths was only six. In fact, one can observe that not only short paths exist in social networks among essentially arbitrary pairs of nodes, but also, perhaps even more surprisingly, that people were able to discover and navigate through those short paths.

Kleinberg took up the challenge to study the design of decentralized search algorithms that can be used to find so effectively a target in a social network [47, 48]. He suggests a simple model, a variant of the small-world model of Watts and Strogatz [70], in which n nodes are arranged in a regular square lattice (of side $\sqrt{n}$). However, instead of adding long-range links uniformly at random, Kleinberg suggests to add a link between two nodes u and v with probability proportional to $r^{-\alpha}$, where r is the distance between u and v in the square lattice. The parameter α controls the extent to which the long-range links are correlated with the geometry of the underlying lattice. For $\alpha = 0$ the long-range links are random, while as α increases there is stronger bias for linking to nearby nodes. The case of $\alpha = 2$, matching the dimension of the lattice, is important because it produces a number of links within an area from a source node that are approximately proportional to the radius of the area.

Given the coordinates of a target node in the above lattice-based network, a natural decentralized algorithm for passing a message to that node is the following: each node forwards the message to a neighbor – long-range or local – whose lattice distance is as close to the target node as possible. Kleinberg showed that there is a unique value of α for which the above "greedy" algorithm achieves a polylogarithmic delivery time.

Theorem 16.5 ([47, 48]).

(a) For $0 \leq \alpha < 2$ the delivery time of any decentralized algorithm is $\Omega(n^{(2-\alpha)/3})$.
(b) For $\alpha = 2$ the delivery time of above greedy algorithm is $O(\log^2 n)$.
(c) For $\alpha > 2$ the delivery time of any decentralized algorithm is $\Omega(n^{(\alpha-2)/(\alpha-1)})$.

The theorem shows a threshold phenomenon in the behavior of the algorithm with respect to the value of the parameter α. For values $\alpha < 2$ the long-range links are too random while for $\alpha > 2$ they are too short to guarantee creating a small world. More generally, for networks built on an underlying lattice in d dimensions, the optimal performance of the greedy algorithm occurs for the value of the parameter $\alpha = d$.

Kleinberg generalizes the decentralized search algorithm for other models, including a hierarchical variant of a small-world graph [49]. According to this model, the nodes of the network are organized on a complete b-ary tree. A motivation for this abstraction can be derived by thinking about professions or interests of people, or about the organization within a company.

In this hierarchical model, the distance between two nodes u and v is defined to be the height $h(u, v)$ of their lowest common ancestor. The construction of the random long-range links is controlled by two parameters k and β: for each node u in the tree, outgoing edges are added by selected k other nodes v, where each such node v is selected with probability proportional to $b^{-\beta h(u,v)}$. As in the lattice case, the model adds long-range links in a way that nearby nodes are favored. As before, the case of $\beta = 0$ corresponds to uniformly random links, and larger values of β favor more nearby nodes.

The search algorithm for locating a target node at a given position in the graph is as before: each node selects the node among its neighbors that is the nearest to the target node. As an analogue of Theorem 16.5, Kleinberg showed that there is a unique value of the parameter β that polylogarithmic delivery time can be achieved.

Theorem 16.6 ([49]).

(a) In the hierarchical model with exponent $\beta = 1$ and out-degree $k = O(\log^2 n)$,
there is a decentralized algorithm with polylogarithmic delivery time.

(b) For every β ≠ 1 and every polylogarithmic function k(n) there is no decentral-
ized algorithm in the hierarchical model with exponent β and out-degree k(n)
that achieves polylogarithmic delivery time.

A more extensive discussion on decentralized search algorithms and additional results on more general graph models and can be found in the excellent paper of
Kleinberg [51].

Adamic and Adar [2] experiment with decentralized search algorithms on real
datasets. They use a graph derived from the email network of HP Labs, by considering an edge between two individuals if they have exchanged more than a certain
number of email messages. They also consider a friendship network dataset from
a community web site, where nodes represented students within a University cam-
pus. The average distance between all pairs of nodes in the email network was three
links, while for the friendship network it was around 3.5.

For both datasets the task was to find specific individuals in the network, by
following links. For the email network, Adamic and Adar consider three different
search strategies, described as follows: at each step the current node is contacting
its neighbor who is (i) best connected, (ii) closest to the target in the organizational
hierarchy, (iii) located in the closest physical proximity to the target. Among the
three strategies, following links in the organizational hierarchy is proven to be the
best, yielding an average path length of size 5. Adamic and Adar speculated that the
best-connected (highest degree) strategy did not work well (average path length 43)
because the actual degree distribution of the email network was Poisson and not a
power law, and in their previous work [3] they showed that the high-degree strategy
performs poorly for such networks.

The strategy of contacting the neighbor with the closest physical proximity to the
target gave an average path length of 11.7. Adamic and Adar explained this high path
length by computing the probability of two individuals being connected in the email
network as a function of their physical distance r. They found that the probability
of being connected was proportional to r^{-1}, instead of r^{-2}, which would have been
the optimal according to Theorem 16.5.

16.4.3 Search in Social Tagging Systems

Social tagging systems, such as del.icio.us and flickr, allow users to annotate particular resources, such as web pages or images, with freely chosen sets of keywords,
also known as "tags." Tagging can be seen as personal bookmarking, allowing the
users to keep organized and locate fast what they have already encountered, as well
as a form of social interaction, since users can be implicitly connected based on their
tagging activity and the resources they have shared.

Marlow et al. [57] discuss tagging systems with respect to their characteristic and
their possible benefits. In a recent study, Heymann et al. [37] investigated how social
tagging systems can be used to improve web search. Based on data obtained by
crawling the del.icio.us site over many months, they concluded that socially tagged

URLs are full of fresh information, and also that tags are appropriate and objective. On the negative side, they showed that tags on URLs are often redundant given title, domain, and page text, and that the coverage of tags is still small to have a big impact on web search.

Gulli et al. [34] present a link-based algorithm, called TC-SocialRank, which leverages the importance of users in the social community, the importance of the bookmarks/resource they share, additional temporal information, and clicks, in order to perform ranking in folksonomy systems.

Amer Yahia et al. [6] provide a survey of search tasks in social tagging systems and they discuss the challenges in making such systems applicable. They consider many features of social tagging systems that can be used to improve the relevance of search tasks. Those features, in addition to the traditional features of text content, timeliness, freshness, and incoming links, they also include tags, popularity, social distance, and relevance to people's interest.

Following on the ideas discussed in [6], Benedikt et al. [13] have recently presented an in-depth study of a top-k search problem for social tagging systems. The problem formulation in [13] is as follows. Users have the dual role of taggers and seekers: taggers are tagging items (resources) and seekers are searching for those items using keyword search. A social network is defined among users, which can be based on explicitly declared contacts or on evaluating a similarity measure among the users. Thus, for a user u we define by $N(u)$ to be the set of neighbors of u in the social network. A seeker u searches for information, and the score of an item i for the user u depends on the keyword-search of u and the number of users in $N(u)$ who have tagged item i. Therefore, the score of each item can be different for each user based on the social connections of u and the tagging activity of the neighbors of u. The problem is to find the top-k items to return to a user query.

Solving the above top-k search problem can be a very inefficient process. First, if inverted indices are to be used, as in the classic paradigm of information retrieval, one inverted index is needed for each (tag, seeker) pair (instead of one inverted index per tag). This is because the score of each item with respect to a tag depends on the particular seeker who searchers for this tag. Such a solution, however, requires a prohibitively large amount of space. Benedikt et al. [13] show how to obtain an efficient solution for this top-k search problem while keeping the amount of space required manageable. The idea is to use a rank combination algorithm, such as the threshold algorithm (TA) [28]. The difference with the standard application of the TA algorithm, is that instead of maintaining exact scores for each item in the inverted list of a tag, we need to keep an upper bound that depends on all possible seekers. The tighter the upper bound the more efficient the rank combination algorithm will be. Benedikt et al. [13] propose clustering the users based on their behavior (either as seekers or as taggers), in order to obtain tighter upper bounds and, thus, improving the performance of their top-k algorithm.

16.5 Other Topics

16.5.1 Searching the Live Web

A large part of the web can be described as a *static* set of pages that contain information, which does not change so often. Such a view of the web resembles an encyclopedia or a University library. In addition to this static component, however, there is a large volume of activity in the web that is described by a very large degree of dynamicity: new information is posted continuously, people discuss at real time and exchange opinions, and information becomes obsolete very rapidly. This part of the web is referred to as the *live web*, and two of its most important aspects are *blogs* and *News*.

16.5.1.1 Blog Search

The large volume of user-generated content has significantly changed the web paradigm in the last 5 years: users do not simply consume content produced by professional publishers or other users but they constantly offer their own contribution in the form of opinions, comments, and feedback, building an extremely complex network of social interactions. An important role in this radical change has been played by Blogs (an abbreviation for weblogs). Blogs are online journals regularly updated by users in order to share ideas and comment on topics of interest for them. The key to their success has been the immediate accessibility to a large audience. The last item, inserted by the blog owner, is visualized at the top of the page, capturing the attention of readers who are allowed to post comments and feedback. The type of content posted is extremely rich and vary from text to multimedia, with a high number of links toward external pages and other blogs. The term Blogosphere indicates the totality of blogs and the interconnections among them. The blogosphere has been continuously growing as reported in *Technorati* [43] in its quarterly *State of the Blogosphere* reports [42]. In April 2007, Technorati was tracking 70 million blogs and observed a rate of 120,000 new blogs created worldwide each day. With respect to posting volume the measure is about 1.5 million postings per day, even though, the rate of growth of postings is not as fast as the rate of growth of new blogs created.

With respect to search algorithms, there are a number of factors that make searching the Blogosphere different than traditional web search:

Temporal Connotation Each post is associated with the date and the time it was created.

Geographical Locality Each blog should be placed in the context of the geographical location of its author.

Heterogeneous Information The utility of the information in the blogosphere can be significantly increased if it is cross-referenced with public information in other information networks, such as the web, user profiles, and social networks, for example, Bhagat et al. [14] present a study on how different networks collide and interact with each other.

High Dynamics Blog posts attract comments of other bloggers, leading to discussions among different members of the Blogosphere.

The previous considerations propel the need for focused technology and specialized search engines as Technorati [43], Ice Rocket Blog Search [40], BlogPulse [41], Ask Blog Search [38], and Google Blog search [39].

Applying standard web-search engines for searching the Blogosphere can be extremely ineffective, since standard web-search engines are not designed to cope with the characteristics of blogs. Algorithms for searching blogs should be able to exploit the temporal and geographical dimensions in order to discover valuable information not directly associated with search keywords. As suggested by Bansal and Koudas [10], such additional information is easily inferable from keywords whose popularity is strongly correlated to the search term popularity along the time axis. This objective requires integrating search engines with methods and algorithms for (i) temporal burst detection of term popularity, (ii) efficient discovery of correlated set of keywords, and (iii) monitoring hot keywords.

Temporal Burst Detection It has been observed that many forms of temporal data that reflect human-generated content, including emails [50], blogs posts [10, 53], and news streams [26], are characterized by a bursty structure.

Kleinberg [50] studied the problem of modeling the temporal behavior of an email containing particular keywords (such as "NSF grant"). He observed that such behavior can be characterized by bursty activity: fragments of *low* and *high* activity are interleaved. In fact, a more accurate description can be obtained by a hierarchical model: fragments of *high* activity contain other fragments of even *higher* activity, and so on. Kleinberg described a generative model that generates such bursty activity and given an input sequence described a dynamic programming algorithm that finds the maximum-likelihood parameters of the model that describe the data. A sequence of events is considered bursty if the fraction of relevant events alternates between periods in which it is large and long periods in which it is small. Kleinberg defines a measure of weight associated with each such burst and solves the problem of enumerating all the bursts by order of weight.

Another model for detecting bursty activity is described by Bansal and Koudas [10], who apply their model on queries submitted to blog sites. Bansal and Koudas express the popularity x of a query as the sum $x = \mu + N(0, \sigma^2)$ where μ is a base popularity and a $N(0, \sigma^2)$ is a Gaussian random variable with zero mean and variance σ^2.

Given a temporal window of the last w days, the popularity values $x_1, x_2, \ldots, x_w$ for each query x are monitored. These values are then used to estimate the parameters μ and σ of the model via the maximum likelihood estimation [5]:

$$\mu = \frac{1}{w} \sum_{i=1}^{w} x_i, \text{ and } \sigma^2 = \frac{1}{w} \sum_{i=1}^{w} (x_i - \mu)^2.$$

Since Bansal and Koudas [10] observe that less than the 5% of the x_i values are greater than $\mu + 2\sigma$, such a value is taken as threshold for burst detection: the ith day is a burst if the popularity value is greater than $\mu + 2\sigma$.

Discovery of Correlated Keywords Potential correlation between blog posting terms and blog query terms may provide an explanation for the observed similarities of bursty activity between the two. However, finding all the terms correlated to the query q is not a simple task. One of the possible definitions of correlation $c(t, q)$ between a term t and a query q is by using the conditional probability of having a term t in a particular document d, given the query q, across several temporal granularities.

$$c(t, q) = \frac{P(t \in D \mid q \in D)}{P(t \in D)}.$$

An efficient solution to this problem was proposed recently by Bansal and Koudas [10]. Here the correlation $c(t, q)$ between the term t and the query q is measured in terms of the *score* $s(t, q)$ of term t with respect to the query q, which is defined as follows:

$$s(t, q) = |\{D \mid D \in \mathcal{D}_q \text{ and } t \in D\}| \cdot \text{idf}(t),$$

where D is a document in the set $\mathcal{D}_q$ of all the documents that contain the query q and $\text{idf}(t)$ is the *inverse document frequency* of t in all documents $\mathcal{D}$. That is, the score $s(t, q)$ is the number of the documents that contain the term t among the set of documents that are relevant to the query q. The factor $\text{idf}(t)$ is used, as usual, to decrease the score of very frequent words such as articles, prepositions, and adverbs. The top-k terms in $\mathcal{D}_q$ are returned as correlated terms with respect to q.

Computing the above measure requires a single scan on the set of documents $\mathcal{D}_q$; however, this can still be too expensive if the total number of documents in $\mathcal{D}_q$ is large. To avoid this computational overhead a solution proposed by [10] was to approximate the score $s(t, q)$ on a sample of documents.

It can be observed that $s(t, q)$ is proportional to $c(t, q)$ in expectation, since, taking as $\text{idf}(t)$ the ratio between the total number of documents $\mathcal{D}$ and the set of documents $\mathcal{D}_t$ that contains t

$$s(t, q) = \frac{|\{D \mid D \in \mathcal{D}_q \text{ and } t \in D\}| \cdot |\mathcal{D}|}{|\mathcal{D}_t|} \propto \frac{\hat{P}(q \in D \text{ and } t \in D)}{P(t \in D)P(q \in D)},$$

where $\hat{P}(q \in D \text{ and } t \in D)$ is the estimate of $P(q \in D \text{ and } t \in D)$ restricted to the set of sampled documents.

Monitoring Hot Keywords The key factors that lead a particular term to become popular are many and are often related to the particular group of users that read and post on the blog. Bansal and Koudas [10] present a measure of interest for the top daily keywords essentially given by the weighted sum of two ranking factors: the *burstiness* and the *surprise*.

Burstiness measures the deviation from the mean value μ_t of the popularity x_i observed over a temporal window of w days before the current one. Given the term t, the burstiness can be computed as $\frac{x_t - \mu_t}{\sigma_t}$.

Surprise measures the deviation of popularity from the expected value $r(x^t)$ computed by a regression model over a temporal window of w days. It is given by $\frac{|r(x^t) - x^t|}{\mu^t}$. The global ranking can be efficiently computed, maintaining a pre-computed list of the term frequencies.

The EigenRumor Algorithm Fujimura et al. [30] observe that the number of in-links to individual blog entries is very small in general, and a large amount of time is needed to acquire inlinks. Such a lack of inlinks makes it difficult for blog posts to acquire meaningful authority values. To overcome this problem and to obtain better authority scores for ranking blog postings, they propose the EigenRumor algorithm, which is a variant of the HITS algorithm [46].

Fujimura et al. [30] consider a graph $G = (V_a \cup V_p, E_a \cup E_c)$, where V_a is the set of vertices representing users (or agents), and V_p is the set of vertices representing posts (or items, in general). The set of edges include $E_a \subseteq V_a \times V_p$, that capture the authorship relation, so that $(a, p) \in E_a$ if a is the author of the post p. The edges in graph G also include $E_c \subseteq V_p \times V_p$, that captures every comment or evaluation of a previous published item, so that $(p_1, p_2) \in E_c$ if post p_1 is a comment to post p_2. E_a and E_p are denoted in the framework of Fujimura and Tanimoto [30] as *information provisioning* and *information evaluation*, respectively.

The model in [30] consists of two different matrices: the *provisioning matrix* P, whose nonzero entries correspond to edges of E_a, and the *evaluation matrix* E whose nonzero entries correspond to edges in E_c.

The reputation score $\mathbf{r}_p$ of an item p and the authority score $\mathbf{a}_a$ and hub score $\mathbf{h}_a$ of the author/agent a are computed as follows:

$$\mathbf{r} = \alpha P^T \mathbf{a} + (1 - \alpha) E^T \mathbf{h},$$

$$\mathbf{a} = P\mathbf{r},$$

$$\mathbf{h} = E\mathbf{r}.$$

The above equations model the following mutually reinforcing relations: (i) posts that acquire good reputation are written by authoritative authors and are commented by authors of good hub score, (ii) authoritative authors write posts of good rep-utation, and (iii) authors of good hub score comment on posts that acquire good reputation. As in the HITS algorithm, the above system of equation is solved by considering an arbitrary initial solution and iteratively apply the formulas until the vectors $\mathbf{r}$, $\mathbf{a}$, and $\mathbf{h}$ converge.

16.5.1.2   News Search

Searching news articles is one of the most important online activities. According to a recent survey of *Nielsen Online*, the online reach of newspapers in July 2008 increased to 40.2% of total web users, up from 37.3% the previous year.

The problems related to news searching are similar to the ones discussed in the previous section and, in particular, derive from the fact that news articles are generated in a stream fashion and usually have a quick expiring time. The principal news search engines (Yahoo! news, Ask news, Google news, Topix) collect news articles coming from many different news sources, automatically assign them to one or more categories and rank them according to many factors, like freshness, authoritativeness of the source, number of difference sources that cite such a news article, and so on. Gulli [33] introduces a general framework for building a News search engine, describing the architecture and the various components.

Del Corso et al. [26] propose a ranking framework which models many of the characteristics of a stream of news articles. Their approach is the first attempt to tackle the main aspects that make news search completely different from classical web search. Their ranking algorithm has the following characteristics:

- Using two ranking score vectors for news posting and news sources.
- Detecting clusters of postings that "tell the same story." The dimension of the cluster centered around a single story is an indirect measure of the relevance of the story itself.
- Capturing the mutual reinforcement between news articles and news sources: *good* news articles are issued by *authoritative* news sources, i.e., press agencies, and vice versa.
- Taking directly into account the time of each news article as an inherent indicator of the freshness of the article: fresh news articles should be considered more important than old ones.
- Ensuring low time and space complexity to allow online computation over the continuously incoming news stream.

Consider a news article n_i appearing in time t_i from a news site $S(n_i)$. The ranking algorithm assigns a ranking score value $R(n_i, t_i)$ to that news article, and a ranking score article $R(S(n_i), t_i)$ to the site $S(n_i)$. The decay of news importance over time is modeled by an exponentially decreasing function: at any instance $t > t_i$, the news article ranking score is given by $R(n_i, t) = e^{-\alpha(t-t_i)} R(n_i, t_i)$, where α is a parameter of the algorithm that depends on the category which the news belongs to. The initial news article ranking score $R(n_i, t_i)$ takes into account two main factors:

- The authoritativeness of its source $S(n_i)$ at the instant immediately before the emission time t_i
- The ranking scores of similar news articles previously emitted whose importance has already been multiplied by the exponential factor

The global formula for the initial rank value of a news is given by:

$$R(n_i, t_i) = \left[\lim_{\tau \to 0+} R(S(n_i), t_i - \tau) \right]^\beta + \sum_{n_j | t_j < t_i} e^{-\alpha(t_i - t_j)} \sigma_{ij} R(n_j, t_j)^\beta,$$

where $0 < \beta < 1$ is a parameter introduced to put the source rank in relation with its emission frequency (see [26] for further details) and σ_{ij} is a similarity measure of the news articles n_i and n_j that depends on the clustering algorithm used.

The ranking score of a news source s_k is then given by the ranking scores of the articles generated in the past from this source, plus a term of the ranking scores of news articles similar to those issued from s_k and posted later on by other sources. Following the same intuition that holds for the ranking scores of news article, both these factors are weighted by the decay factor $e^{-\alpha(t-t_i)}$. The final equation for news sources is as follows:

$$R(s_k, t) = \sum_{S(n_i)=s_k} e^{-\alpha(t-t_i)} R(n_i, t) + \sum_{S(n_i)=s_k} e^{-\alpha(t-t_i)} \sum_{\substack{t_j > t_i \\ S(n_j) \neq s_k}} \sigma_{ij} R(n_j, t_j)^\beta.$$

The complexity of the algorithm is linear in the number of articles whose ranking score by time t is still high enough to be considered. This allows a continuous on-line process of computing ranking scores. Moreover the set of experiments described in [26] show the robustness of this approach with respect to the range of variability of the parameters α and β.

16.5.2   Searching with Context

Consider the scenario in which a user reads or browses a particular web page and she wants to find more information about a particular term or a phrase in the page. For instance, a user wants to find more information about "chili peppers" while reading a page, and the answer might depend on whether this page is about music or about food. In other words, the information about the current page provides the *context* to the user query.

Von Brzeski et al. [68] and Kraft et al. [52] introduce the problem of searching the web with contextual information. In [52], they propose three algorithms that leverage existing technology of search engines. The first algorithm identifies infor-mative terms from the context page and adds those terms in the query, and then it submits the rewritten query to a search engine. The second algorithm is a "softer" version of the first algorithm, in which the terms of the context are not just added to the query but they are used to bias the query result. The third algorithm is based on the idea of rank aggregation: the context page is used to rewrite many queries and the results of those queries are combined by using rank aggregation.

Ukkonen et al. [67] describe a framework for context-sensitive search, in which the underlying link structure of pages is taken into account. In their framework a graph $G = (V, E)$ is used to represent entities containing textual information and links among the entities. For example, nodes can represent document and edges can represent hyperlinks among the documents, however, other interpretations are possible depending on the application. A query is defined by a pair $\langle q, p \rangle$, where q is a set of terms and $p \in V$ is a node of G that defines the *context* of the query. They suggest a number of text-based features from the query node p that can be used for learning a ranking function, as well as features that are based on the structure of the graph G.

Graph-based features in [67] include in-degree and PageRank, as well as a *graph-based distance* and a *spectral distance* between the query node and the target node to be ranked. They also use a version of personalized PageRank score with teleportation at the query page p. Intuitively, this corresponds to a random walk that favors nodes of G that are easily accessible from the query page p. However, computing such context-sensitive PageRank scores is infeasible at query time, and extremely space-consuming to store at a preprocessing stage. To make it feasible Ukkonen et al. propose a clustering approach: the nodes in the graph are partitioned into clusters and a single personalization vector is used for all the nodes in the same cluster.

The algorithm of Ukkonen was tested on the Wikipedia dataset and their experiments indicate that taking into account the context of the query improves the results compared with the results obtained by a traditional approach that does not take the context into account.

16.6 Conclusions

Search algorithms are continuously adapting to engage the challenges that have been posed by the web evolution. Scientists are called to address the research questions that has recently been created by the transition from web 1.0 to web 2.0, with users more and more active in delivering content. Search engines are forced to cope with the extremely rich and heterogeneous datasets that are being created by blogs, tagging systems, social communities, media-sharing sites, and news. Such heterogeneity has caused the proliferation of special-purpose search engines, such as blogs and news search engines that require ad hoc algorithms for collecting, indexing, and ranking different items.

There are still many open problems to be addressed in next-generation search algorithms, and furthermore new paradigms and alternate forms of communication (e.g., mobile networks) are emerging, which will create more research directions. At this point it is very difficult to predict which issues will be posed by the new paradigms of web 3.0 (with type-sensitive links pointing to focused search engines depending on the topological category to which the anchor text belongs to) or web 4.0 (with personalized-links, dynamically constructed to redirect to the focus search engine of that the user specify for the particular link type).

References

1. K. Aberer and J. Wu. A framework for decentralized ranking in web information retrieval. In X. Zhou, Y. Zhang, and M.E. Orlowska, editors, *APWeb*, volume 2642 of *Lecture Notes in Computer Science*, pages 213–226. Springer, 2003.
2. L. Adamic and E. Adar. How to search a social network. *Social Neworks*, 27(3):187–203, July 2005.
3. L. Adamic, R. Lukose, A. Puniyani, and B. Huberman. Search in power-law networks. *Physical Review E*, 64, 2001.

4. R. Albert and A.-L. Barabasi. Statistical mechanics of complex networks. *Reviews of Modern Physics*, 74(47), 2002.

5. J. Aldrich. R.A. Fisher and the making of maximum likelihood 1912-1922. *Statist. Sci.*, (3):162–176, 1997.

6. S. Amer Yahia, M. Benedikt, and P. Bohannon. Challenges in searching online communities. *Bulletin of the IEEE Computer Society Technical Committee on Data Engineering*, pages 1–9, 2007.

7. R. Baeza-Yates, P. Boldi, and C. Castillo. Generalizing pagerank: damping functions for link-based ranking algorithms. In *Procs. of the ACM Conference on Research and Development in Information Retrieval (SIGIR)*, 2006.

8. R. Baeza-Yates, C. Castillo, F. Junqueira, V. Plachouras, and F. Silvestri. Challenges on distributed web retrieval. In *Procs. of the IEEE 23rd International Conference on Data Engineering (ICDE)*, 2007.

9. R. Baeza-Yates and B. Ribeiro-Neto. *Modern Information Retrieval*. Addison Wesley, May 1999.

10. N. Bansal and N. Koudas. Searching the blogosphere. In *Procs. of the International Workshop on the Web and Databases (WebDB)*, 2007.

11. A.-L. Barabasi and R. Albert. Emergence of scaling in random networks. *Science*, 286, 1999.

12. L. Becchetti, C. Castillo, D. Donato, R. Baeza-Yates, and S. Leonardi. Link analysis for web spam detection. *ACM Transactions on the Web (TWEB)*, 2(1):1–42, February 2008.

13. M. Benedikt, S. Amer Yahia, L. Lakshmanan, and J. Stoyanovich. Efficient network-aware search in collaborative tagging sites. In *Procs. of the 34th International Conference on Very Large Databases (VLDB)*, 2008.

14. S. Bhagat, I. Rozenbaum, G. Cormode, S. Muthukrishnan, and H. Xue. No blog is an island — analyzing connections across information networks. In *Intlernational Conference on Weblogs and Social Media (ICWSM)*, 2007.

15. K. Bharat, B.W. Chang, M. R. Henzinger, and M. Ruhl. Who links to whom: Mining linkage between web sites. In *Procs. of the IEEE International Conference on Data Mining (ICDM)*, 2001.

16. P. Boldi, R. Posenato, M. Santini, and S. Vigna. Traps and pitfalls of topic-biased pagerank. In *Fourth International Workshop on Algorithms and Models for the Web-Graph (WAW)*, 2008.

17. B. Bollobás. Mathematical results on scale-free random graphs. *Handbook of Graphs and Networks*, 2002.

18. B. Bollobás and W. F. de la Vega. The diameter of random regular graphs. *Combinatorica*, 2(2), 1982.

19. S. Brin and L. Page. The anatomy of a large-scale hypertextual web search engines. *Computer Networks and ISDN Systems*, 30(1–7):107–117, 1998.

20. Y. Cao, J. Xu, T.-Y. Liu, H. Li, Y. Huang, and H.-W. Hon. Adapting ranking SVM to document retrieval. In *Procs. of the ACM Conference on Research and Development in Information Retrieval (SIGIR)*, 2006.

21. D. Chakrabarti and C. Faloutsos. Graph mining: Laws, generators, and algorithms. *ACM Computer Surveys*, 38(1), 2006.

22. Y.-Y. Chen, Q. Gan, and T. Suel. Local methods for estimating pagerank values. In *Procs. of the 13nd ACM Conference on Information and Knowledge Management (CIKM)*, pages 381–389, New York, NY, USA, 2004.

23. P. J. Courtois. *Queueing and Computer System Applications*. Academic Press, 1997.

24. D. De Solla Price. A general theory of bibliometric and other cumulative advantage processes. *Journal of the American Society for Information Science and Technology*, 27, 1976.

25. G. M. Del Corso, A. Gulli, and F. Romani. Fast pagerank computation via a sparse linear system. *Internet Mathematics*, 2(3), 2005.

26. G.M. Del Corso, A. Gulli, and F. Romani. Ranking a stream of news. In *Procs. of the 14th International Conference on World Wide Web (WWW)*, pages 97–106, 2005.

27. P. Erdős and A. Rényi. On the evolution of random graphs. *Publ. Math. Inst. Hung. Acad. Sci*, 5, 1960.

28. R. Fagin, A. Lotem, and M. Naor. Optimal aggregation algorithms for middleware. In *Procs. of the 12th ACM Symposium on Principles of database systems (PODS)*, 2001.

29. D. Fogaras, B. Rácz, K. Csalogány, and T. Sarlós. Towards scaling fully personalized pageRank: algorithms, lower bounds, and experiments. *Internet Math.*, 2(3):333–358, 2005.

30. K. Fujimura and N. Tanimoto. The eigenrumor algorithm for calculating contributions in cyberspace communities. *Trusting Agents for Trusting Electronic Societies*, pages 59–74, 2005.

31. Gene H. Golub and Charles F. Van Loan. *Matrix Computations*. The Johns Hopkins University Press, October 1996.

32. F. Grey. Inferring probability of relevance using the method of logistic regression. In *Procs. of the ACM Conference on Research and Development in Information Retrieval (SIGIR)*, 1994.

33. A. Gulli. The anatomy of a news search engine. In *WWW*, 2005.

34. A. Gulli, S. Cataudella, and L. Foschini. Tc-socialrank: Ranking the social web. In *Proceedings of the 6th International Workshop on Algorithms and Models for the Web-Graph (WAW)*, 2009.

35. Z. Gyöngyi, H. Garcia-Molina, and J. Pedersen. Combating Web spam with TrustRank. In *Procs. of the 30th International Conference on Very Large Data Bases (VLDB)*, pages 576–587, Toronto, Canada, August 2004. Morgan Kaufmann.

36. T.H. Haveliwala. Topic-sensitive pagerank. In *Procs. of the 11th International World Wide Web Conference (WWW)*, Honolulu, Hawaii, May 2002.

37. P. Heymann, G. Koutrika, and H. Garcia-Molina. Can social bookmarking improve web search? In *Procs. of the International Conference on Web Search and Web Data Mining (WSDM)*, 2008.

38. Ask blog search. http://blog.ask.com/.

39. Google blog search. http://blogsearch.google.com/.

40. Ice rocket blog search. http://blogs.icerocket.com.

41. Blogpulse. http://www.blogpulse.com/.

42. The state of the live web, april 2007. http://www.sifry.com/alerts/archives/000493.html.

43. Technorati. whats percolating in blogs now. http://www.technorati.com.

44. S. Kamvar, T. Haveliwala, C. Manning, and G. Golub. Exploiting the block structure of the web for computing pagerank. Technical report, Stanford University, 2003.

45. M. Kendall and J.D. Gibbons. *Rank Correlation Methods*. Edward Arnold, 1990.

46. J.M. Kleinberg. Authoritative sources in a hyperlinked environment. *Journal of the ACM*, 46(5):604–632, 1999.

47. J.M. Kleinberg. Navigation in a small world. *Nature*, 6798, 2000.

48. J.M. Kleinberg. The Small-World Phenomenon: An Algorithmic Perspective. In *Procs. of the 32nd ACM Symposium on Theory of Computing (STOC)*, 2000.

49. J.M. Kleinberg. Small-world phenomena and the dynamics of information. In *Advances in Neural Information Processing Systems (NIPS)*, 2001.

50. J.M. Kleinberg. Bursty and hierarchical structure in streams. In *Procs. of the 8th ACM SIGKDD International Conference on Knowledge Discovery and Data Mining (KDD)*, pages 91–101, New York, NY, USA, 2002. ACM Press.

51. J.M. Kleinberg. Complex networks and decentralized search algorithms. In *International Congress of Mathematicians (ICM)*, 2006.

52. R. Kraft, C.C. Chang, F. Maghoul, and R. Kumar. Searching with context. In *Procs. of the 15th International Conference on World Wide Web (WWW)*, 2006.

53. R. Kumar, J. Novak, P. Raghavan, and A. Tomkins. On the bursty evolution of blogspace. In *Procs. of the 12th International Conference on World Wide Web (WWW)*, pages 568–576. ACM Press, 2003.

54. L. Lamport. *Specifying Systems: The TLA+ Language and Tools for Hardware and Software Engineers*. Addison-Wesley Professional, July 2002.

55. A.N. Langville and C.D. Meyer. Updating pagerank with iterative aggregation. In *Procs. of the 13th International World Wide Web Conference on Alternate track papers & posters (WWW)*, pages 392–393, New York, NY, USA, 2004. ACM Press.

56. C. Manning, P. Raghavan, and H. Schütze. *Introduction to Information Retrieval*. Cambridge University Press, 2008.

57. C. Marlow, M. Naaman, D. Boyd, and M. Davis. Ht06, tagging paper, taxonomy, flickr, academic article, to read. In *Procs. of the 17th Conference on Hypertext and hypermedia (HYPERTEXT)*, 2006.
58. C.D. Meyer. *Matrix Analysis and Applied Linear Algebra*. SIAM, 2000.
59. S. Milgram. The small world problem. *Psychology Today*, 2:60–67, 1967.
60. M. Mitzenmacher. A brief history of generative models for power law and lognormal distributions. *Internet Mathematics*, 1(2), 2003.
61. R. Nallapati. Discriminative models for information retrieval. In *Procs. of the ACM Conference on Research and Development in Information Retrieval (SIGIR)*, 2004.
62. M. Newman. The structure and function of complex networks. *SIAM Review*, 45(2), 2003.
63. J. Risson and T. Moors. Survey of research towards robust peer-to-peer networks: Search methods. Technical report, Univ of New South Wales, Sydney Australia, 2006.
64. K. Sankaralingam, S. Sethumadhavan, and J.C. Browne. Distributed pagerank for p2p systems. pages 58+. IEEE Computer Society, 2003.
65. H. Simon. On a class of skew distribution functions. *Biometrica*, 42(4/3), 1955.
66. H.A. Simon and A. Ando. Aggregation of variables in dynamic systems. *Econometrica*, 29:111–138, 1961.
67. A. Ukkonen, C. Castillo, D. Donato, and A. Gionis. Searching the wikipedia with contextual information. In *Procs. of the 17th ACM Conference on Information and knowledge management (CIKM)*, 2008.
68. V. Von Brzeski, U. Irmak, and R. Kraft. Leveraging context in user-centric entity detection systems. In *Procs. of the 16th ACM Conference on Information and knowledge management (CIKM)*, 2007.
69. Y. Wang and D. J. Dewitt. Computing pagerank in a distributed internet search system. In *Procs. of the 30th International Conference on Very Large Databases (VLDB)*, 2004.
70. D. Watts and S.H. Strogatz. Collective dynamics of 'small-world' networks. *Nature*, 6684, 1998.
71. J. Wu and K. Aberer. Using siterank for P2P web retrieval. Technical Report IC/2004/31, Swiss Federal Institute of Technology, Lausanne, Switzerland, 2004.
72. J. Xavier-Parreira, C. Castillo, D. Donato, S. Michel, and G. Weikum. The JXP method for robust pagerank approximation in a peer-to-peer web search network. *VLDB Journal*, 17(2):291–313, 2008.

Chapter 17
At the Intersection of Networks and Highly Interactive Online Games

Grenville Armitage

Abstract The game industry continues to evolves its techniques for extracting the most realistic 'immersion' experience for players given the vagaries on best-effort Internet service. A key challenge for service providers is understanding the characteristics of traffic imposed on networks by games, and their service quality requirements. Interactive online games are particularly susceptible to the side effects of other non-interactive (or delay- and loss-tolerant) traffic sharing next- generation access links. This creates challenges out toward the edges, where high-speed home LANs squeeze through broadband consumer access links to reach the Internet. In this chapter we identify a range of research work exploring many issues associated with the intersection of highly interactive games and the Internet, and hopefully stimulate some further thinking along these lines.

17.1 Introduction

Over the past decade online multiplayer computer games have emerged as a key driver of consumer demand for higher-quality end-to-end Internet services. Early adoption of 'broadband' last-mile technologies (such as cable modems or ADSL) was driven as much by game players demanding better quality of service (QoS) as it was by computer enthusiasts and telecommuters desiring quicker access to 'the web' and corporate networks. By the early 2000s, online game players were sometimes even alerting network service providers of outages before the providers' own monitoring systems. Multiplayer games range from handfuls of players on individual servers run by enthusiasts to tens of thousands of players linked by geographically distributed and commercially operated server clusters. The games themselves vary widely – from highly interactive 'first-person shooter' and car-racing games to more sedate role-playing and strategy games, or even modern re-interpretations of traditional card games and board games [10]. A common attribute of online

G. Armitage (✉)
Centre for Advanced Internet Architectures, Swinburne University of Technology, PO Box 218, John Street, Hawthorn, Victoria 3122, Australia
e-mail: garmitage@swin.edu.au

G. Cormode and M. Thottan (eds.), *Algorithms for Next Generation Networks*, Computer Communications and Networks, DOI 10.1007/978-1-84882-765-3_17,
© Springer-Verlag London Limited 2010

games is creation of a shared, virtual environment (or virtual world) within which players 'immerse' themselves. Realistic immersion depends on timely exchange of up-to-date information between participants in the virtual world. Consequently, understanding and supporting the needs of multiplayer online games is one of the many interesting challenges facing next-generation networks. Online games are particularly susceptible to the side effects of other non-interactive (or delay- and loss-tolerant) traffic sharing next-generation access links.

17.1.1 Game Genres

A single taxonomy of game types or genres has yet to emerge from the game industry or academia. For the purpose of this chapter we will classify games by their different requirements for interactivity, using names that are relatively common in today's online forums.

First-person shooter (FPS) games are arguably the most network-intensive, multiplayer online game genre.[1] FPS games typically involve players moving around a virtual world where the goal of the game is to shoot as many 'enemy' players (or monsters, as the game story line dictates) as possible as quickly as possible. As the name suggests, a player's viewpoint is rendered in the first person and winning usually depends on your speed at accumulating kills (often known as 'frags'). Because success relies so much on reaction times FPS games are sometimes referred to as 'twitch games,' and players are often intolerant of network disturbances that last beyond tens of milliseconds [4, 9, 13, 27, 32, 53].

Networked, multiplayer forms of *role-playing games* (RPGs) and *real-time strategy* (RTS) games also emerged during the 1990s.[2] The game environment is often presented in a third-person or top-down view, where the human player controls one or more characters within a virtual world. The concept of 'winning' in such games is usually tied to solving puzzles, mapping out strategies, exploring the virtual world, and negotiating (or collaborating) with other players. Unlike FPS games, frenetic real-time interactions are relatively rare. Consequently, players will often tolerate network-induced disruptions lasting for multiple seconds [26, 45]. However, during brief periods of highly interactive play (if the game supports or requires real-time fighting scenes) the players may exhibit FPS-like intolerance of network disturbances.

---

[1] In 1996, idSoftware's *Quakeworld* (a variant of their single-player FPS game *Quake*) was one of the earliest FPS games developed specifically to support highly interactive multiplayer operation over a wide-area network. Prior to Quakeworld, idSoftware's Doom had been modified for LAN-based games, but was suboptimal for wide-area (Internet-based) play. Modern examples include Counterstrike:Source, Unreal Tournament 2007, and Enemy Territory:Quake Wars.

[2] Massively multiplayer online games (MMORPGs) were first popularized in their modern form by Ultima Online in 1997. Modern examples include World of Warcraft, Everquest II, and Eve Online. Modern examples of multiplayer RTS games include Warcraft 3, Company of Heros, and World in Conflict. Such games are usually built to support tens of thousands of concurrent players.

Other interactive genres exist (such as multiplayer car racing, or team-based sports games), but it is sufficient to observe that they too exhibit varying degrees of intolerance to network-induced packet latency and loss [41].

For the purpose of this chapter we will not consider turn-based games (such as online versions of chess, etc.) or any games where player thinking time is likely to be measured in multiples of seconds (or longer). Such games are sufficiently supported by typical 'best-effort' Internet service.

17.1.2   Communication Models

The front line of all online games comprises human players interacting with game clients, software coupled to an underlying hardware platform (loosely in the case of general purpose PCs, or tightly in the case of consoles or hand-held game devices). Game clients are responsible for establishing the immersive in-game experience for their players, and communicating with other clients to keep the shared virtual environment up to date. Typically, this involves sending and receiving regular *updates*, informing other clients what your player is doing, and learning from other clients what their player is (or players are) doing.

Conceptually, a game could operate in a pure *peer-to-peer* mode, with every client exchanging information with every other client to maintain a common, shared view of the virtual environment. However, the traffic mesh resulting from pure peer-to-peer communication is problematic at the network layer. Consider a game with N clients. All N clients must have sufficient in-bound network capacity to handle the traffic from $(N-1)$ other clients, and out-bound capacity to support the traffic sent to $(N-1)$ other clients. Every client's messages are likely to be short (a few tens of bytes indicating that, for example, a player is moving, or just triggered a weapon) and of very similar size. Short messages mean each IP packet contains very little information. Furthermore, each time a client updates their peers they will emit $(N-1)$ identical messages, and N will be constrained by the outbound capacity of (typically asymmetric) consumer access links.[3] Finally, shared knowledge of everyone's IP address allows malicious players to launch direct IP-layer denial of service (DoS) attacks on other players (overloading the target's network link and disrupting the target's game play).

A *client server* alternative involves clients communicating indirectly through a central server. The simplest approach is to emulate network layer multicast – clients unicast each game update message to the server, which unicasts copies of the update messages back out to every other client. Each client now sends only one message per update (rather than $N-1$ messages), and clients no longer know each others' IP

---

[3] It would be advantageous to use multicast rather than unicast, yet network layer multicast is largely theoretical in consumer environments.

addresses (reducing the risk of IP-layer DoS attacks).[4] However, most online games take this one step further and implement game-logic in the server to make it a central arbiter of all events and activities occurring inside the game world. Update messages arriving from individual clients are interpreted and vetted by the game server to ensure each player's actions are consistent with the game world's rules. At regular time intervals the game server unicasts aggregate update messages (*snapshots*) to all clients, informing them of events and actions occurring since the last snapshot.[5] A single snapshot replaces $(N-1)$ update messages from individual clients, reducing the number of packets per second required to support N clients.[6]

Client server is usually preferred over peer-to-peer because it reduces the client-side bandwidth requirements and centralizes cheat-mitigation and game rule enforcement in a (relatively) trusted third party [10]. However, servers can come under significant pressure for networking and computational resources, particularly for games that create a single environment for thousands or tens of thousands of players. Large-scale games will often use a hybrid scheme, where the 'game server' is really a cluster of physically separate servers using a peer-to-peer mesh amongst themselves to create an illusion of coordinated game state processing.

Both UDP (user datagram protocol) [42] and TCP (transmission control protocol) [28, 43] have been used for sending update and snapshot messages over IP. The choice tends to depend on a game's particular trade-off between timeliness and reliability of sending messages. TCP will transfer messages reliably yet introduce multisecond delays in the face of short-term network degradation. UDP will either get messages through or lose them completely, without causing any additional delays to subsequent messages.

17.1.3 Potential for Collateral Damage

Unlike relatively delay- and loss-tolerant applications (such as email, instant messaging, peer-to-peer file transfer, and streaming non-interactive multimedia content), online games make consumers intimately aware of degradations to network service. Unfortunately, today's consumer broadband access links tend to lump all traffic together at the home–Internet boundary. A game player's experience may become collateral damage as other applications push and shove their way across the consumer's home link.

---

[4] From the perspective of each client's game logic this model is still peer-to-peer, as the server simply repeats and replicates messages at the network level.

[5] Snapshots typically occur tens of times per second to ensure smooth approximation to real-time updates of player movements and actions.

[6] A common optimization is for the server to send client X a snapshot that excludes information on events and avatars not visible to the player controlling client X (e.g., because the player's view is obscured by a wall). This limits the potential for a hacked client to reveal information about other players who believe themselves to be hidden behind some in-game obstruction.

A typical scenario involves multiple home computers (and/or network-enabled game consoles) sharing a broadband access link to the outside world. The access link is usually far slower than the home network's LAN (e.g., a common broadband service in many parts of the world offers 256 Kbps upstream and 1.5 Mbps downstream, whereas the home LAN is often 100 Mbps or 1 Gbps Ethernet). It is already well understood that TCP exhibits cyclical expansion and contraction of its congestion window as it probes the network path for capacity. Online game players are already well aware that sharing a home broadband connection usually leads to noticeable degradation in their game-play experience when someone else begins bulk data transfers using TCP (such as sending large emails or serving files over peer-to-peer networks). The non-game TCP traffic can repeatedly congest one's home gateway[7] every few seconds, causing fluctuations in the latency experienced by everyone sharing the home broadband link[8].

Society's perception of next-generation network services will be strongly influenced by how well we engineer the network's edges to 'play nice' with multiplayer games. Today's consumer-grade home gateways often come with rudimentary, user-configured QoS capabilities. The home user manually configures their gateway to identify (classify) certain IP packets as being of higher priority than others. Then, whenever two or more packets are waiting (in a queue within the gateway) to be transmitted upstream, the gateway chooses (schedules) packets for transmission according to each packet's priority. A game player might classify as 'high-priority' all UDP packets to and from a known (remote) game server's IP address. These high priority UDP packets 'jump ahead' of other TCP packets queued up at the gateway, reducing the latency experienced by game packets due to non-game TCP packets.

Unfortunately, the current QoS mechanisms are unwieldy. The home user must know particular information in each IP packet header than can be used to differentiate between game and non-game traffic. They must manually configure such information into their local gateway, and may be required to change the configuration when playing different games. An important consideration for network designers is how to evolve home gateways (and broadband services as a whole) to protect game traffic from bulk TCP transfers in a more transparent manner. However, it is beyond the scope of this chapter to review all possible solutions in this space.

17.1.4 Chapter Outline

This chapter's main focus will be FPS games – due to their significantly interactive nature they provide a good illustration of games that are intolerant of fluctuations

---

[7] Typically a small router or switch integrated with a broadband ADSL or Cable modem.

[8] Variants of traditional 'NewReno' TCP have also emerged in the past decade – such as HTCP (available for Linux and FreeBSD), CUBIC (now the default in Linux), and Compound TCP (an option for Windows Vista). Experimental trials with CUBIC and HTCP revealed that TCP sessions using either algorithm cause faster cycling of the latency through a congested router than NewReno sessions. They also generally induced higher latencies than NewReno [12, 46].

in, and degradations of, network service. We will consider how FPS games operate, summarize their latency sensitively, and review the traffic they impose on networks over short and long time frames. We will then review recent work on simulating FPS game traffic (for ISP network engineering), techniques for connecting clients together with servers who are 'close enough,' and conclude with emerging techniques for detecting game traffic running across an ISP network.

17.2   Phases of Network Activity Caused by First-Person Shooter Games

Internet-based FPS games generally operate in a client server mode, with game servers being hosted by Internet service providers (ISPs), dedicated game hosting companies, and individual enthusiasts. Although individual FPS game servers typically host only from 4 to around 30+ players, there are usually many thousands of individually operated game servers active on the Internet at any time.

Different publishing models also exist. PC-based FPS games commonly (and traditionally) utilize a rendezvous service – game servers are explicitly established by end-users, and announced on a master server (funded by the game publisher) that clients then query. More recently, some console-based games (such as Ghost Recon and Halo on XBox Live [35]) utilize a central server for 'matchmaking' – dynamically allocating one of a group of peer consoles to be the game server for individual game-play sessions.

FPS games utilize the network in three distinct ways: *server discovery*, *game play*, and *content downloads*. Each of these impose different requirements on the network, and create a different aspect to the player's overall experience.

17.2.1   Server Discovery

In this chapter we will focus on the traditional model of hosting and discovering game servers that originated with PC-based games. Players trigger *server discovery* to populate or refresh their game client's on-screen 'server browser' (a list of available game servers). Clients first query a well-known master server, which returns a list of all registered game servers (usually broken over multiple reply packets, as the lists can be quite long). Clients then probe each game server in turn for information (such as the current map type, game type, and players already on the server). The probe is typically a brief UDP packet exchange, which allows the client to also estimate the round trip time (RTT)[9] between itself and each game server. Players are presented with this information as it is gathered, and then select a game server to join.

---

[9] Network latency, also colloquially known as 'lag' or 'ping' in online game communities (the latter due to *ping* being the name of a common tool for measuring RTT).

A given client will send out hundreds or thousands of probe packets to find and join only one game server. Consequently, individual game servers end up receiving, and responding to, tens of thousands of probe packets unrelated to the number of people actually playing (or likely to play) at any given time. The 'background noise' due to probe traffic fluctuates over time as game clients around the Internet startup and shutdown [52].

17.2.2   Game Play

Game play begins once a suitable server has been selected. This represents the primary period throughout which the FPS game players are most sensitive to fluctuations or degradation in network service. Client(s) send regular (although not necessarily consistently spaced) update messages to the server and the server will send regular snapshot messages back. The traffic flowing between client and server is usually asymmetric – client-to-server packets are often under 100 bytes long, whereas server-to-client packets will often range from 80 to 300+ bytes long. Update and snapshot messages are sent tens of times per second to ensure that events within the virtual world are propagated among all players in a timely and believable fashion. Messages are sent in UDP packets, with the FPS game engines providing their own mechanisms above UDP for packet loss detection and mitigation.

17.2.3   Content Download

Online games often evolve new characters, virtual worlds, items inside the virtual worlds, and software patches long after the original game software is released (or sold) to the public. Most FPS games now have mechanisms for downloading new or updated in-game content, and some are even capable of automatically updating their executable code. Depending on the game's design, content download may occur before, during, or after game play. It may be triggered by connecting to a server that's running a virtual environment ('map') not previously seen by the client, or be a scheduled update initiated by the game client.

Some content (such as new 'skins' for player avatars) may be downloaded while the game is in progress, in parallel with the network traffic associated with game play. Other content updates (such as new maps) must be completed before the client may begin a new game. Depending on how the content update is triggered, new content may come directly from the game server, or the game server may redirect the client to pull updated content from an entirely separate server.

Regardless of origin, content updates are infrequent events (days, weeks, or months apart) and usually designed not to interfere with game play. Consequently we will not discuss them in further detail.

17.3   Sensitivities of Game Players to Network Latency

Real-world communication latency is a significant impediment to realism in highly interactive games. When players 'see' their avatars only metres apart, the sense of immersion is diluted if in-game interactions are noticeably delayed by many tens or hundreds of milliseconds. Player tolerance to latency will vary depending on the style of game being played, and mechanisms deployed by the game designers to hide latency-induced inconsistencies into the flow of in-game events.

17.3.1   Observed Impact of Latency

Due to the fast-pace and highly interactive nature of FPS games, players prefer game servers that exhibit low RTT. For example, in a typical FPS 'death match' game players win by having the highest total kills (or 'frags') after a certain time period (typically tens of minutes), or by being the first to reach a particular number of frags. Figure 17.1 (from [4, 9]) shows the general impact of network latency on frag rate for Quake III Arena (Q3A) players in 2001. Over a period of minutes the cumulative benefit of being 50ms rather than 150ms from the game server can be significant.[10]

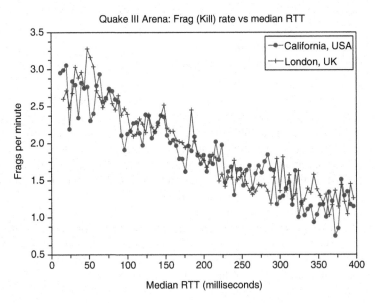

Fig. 17.1 Success (measured in 'frags' per minute) of Quake III Arena players in 2001 as a function of the player's median RTT from a server [4]

---

[10] In Figure 17.1 identical Q3A servers were based in California and London over a period of months. The set of players on each server only partially overlapped, yet a similar trend is evident in each case.

Published literature suggests that competitive online FPS game play requires latencies below 150–200 ms [10, 35]. Sports and strategy games have also demonstrated some latency intolerance, but less so than FPS overall as the game play is not always frenetic [13, 27, 41].

Given an intolerance for RTT over roughly 150-200ms, it is easy to see why online gamers abhor RTT fluctuations induced by transient queuing delays along their network paths. Service providers who can stabilize the RTT experienced by game players will likely gain an appreciative market.

17.3.2 Mitigating Latency

FPS game developers utilize a number of client- and server-side techniques to circumvent the time-line inconsistencies introduced when multiple clients have non-negligible and different RTT to the game server. The full range is outside the scope of this chapter, but one illustrative example should suffice.

Consider the case of Player 1 firing a weapon, such as a hand gun, at Player 2 who is about 5 m away and moving perpendicular to Player 1 at 4 m/s. Assume Player 1's RTT to the game server is 100 ms. Activating the gun's trigger causes the next update message from client-to-server to indicate that a shot has been fired. Rather than waiting for confirmation in a later snapshot message from the server, a client will immediately begin rendering on screen the predicted consequences of the shot being fired (such as muzzle flash followed almost immediately by bullet impact).

However, in-game events are only 'real' when announced by the game server in a subsequent snapshot message to all affected clients. A potential discrepancy arises as the game server receives the 'shoot' message at least 50 ms after Player 1's client begins rendering the shot's consequences. From the game server's perspective, in 50 ms Player 2 would have moved 20 cm from the position observed by Player 1 when the shot was fired. To compensate for latency, the game server will 'roll back time' and calculate the bullet's hit (or miss) based on where everyone's avatars were 50 ms in the past.[11]

The combination of client side prediction (to ensure smooth animation) and server-side roll back (to correctly adjudicate hits and misses) is an imperfect solution. Player 2 may be surprised to learn that they have been shot if (according to their own client's rendering of the scene) they perceived themselves to have moved out of range or hidden behind a physical obstruction. Player 2's client is then forced to 'snap back' the rendered scene and play out a brief death animation. Conversely, Player 1's client may have incorrectly predicted a hit on Player 2. When the game server's next snapshot message indicates Player 2 is still alive and running, Player 1's client will need to re-render the scene and move on.

---

[11] Game servers track RTT to each client so that they know how much roll back is required for events involving different players.

17.4 Server Discovery Protocols

As noted in Section 17.2.1, server discovery is the process by which FPS game
clients locate up-to-date information about active game servers so that a player can
select a suitable server on which to play. Server discovery can trigger mega bytes of
network traffic per client and take multiple minutes to complete. Network devices
that keep per-flow state (such as NAT-enabled home routers) can experience bursts
of thousands of dynamically created state entries, tying up memory for minutes
simply to enable a sub-second packet exchange. Finding servers with low RTT is
a common goal, and optimizing this process is an active area of research [5, 6, 11,
24, 25, 35]. In this section, we will briefly review the server discovery techniques
of Valve Corporation's Counterstrike:Source (CS:S) [47], then summarize a recent
idea for reducing the number of probe flows generated during FPS server discovery.

17.4.1 Counterstrike:Source Server Discovery

Counterstrike:Source (CS:S) was first released in late 2004 by Valve Corporation
through their Steam online game delivery system. Public CS:S game servers register themselves with Steam's *master server* at hl2master.steampowered.com. Players
initiate server discovery through their Steam client's game *server browser*. As illustrated in Figure 17.2, a Steam client will:

- Issue a *getservers* query to UDP port 27011 on the Steam master server, then
  receive a *getserversResponse* packet containing the ⟨IP address:port⟩ pairs of up
  to 231 active game servers.[12]

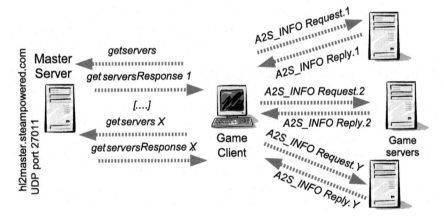

Fig. 17.2 A Steam client discovering Counterstrike:Source game servers

---

[12] Valve has no specific names for the messages between master server and client, so *getservers*,
and *getserversResponse* have been chosen for clarity. UDP/IP packet formats for server discovery
are available online [48].

- Send one *A2S_INFO Request* probe packet to each game server in order, eliciting an *A2S_INFO Reply* packet from every active game server.
- Repeat the previous steps until the Steam master server has no more game server details to return.

Each game server's RTT is estimated from the time between the client sending an *A2S_INFO Request* and receiving the *A2S_INFO Reply*. Server-specific information in each *A2S_INFO Reply* is used to update the Steam client's on-screen server browser, enabling players to select their preferred server for game play.

Third-party server browsers may use a different sequence. Qstat [1] (an open-source server browser) retrieves all registered servers first (using back-to-back *getserver* queries) before issuing *A2S_INFO Request* probes. They achieve a similar result – information (including RTT) is collected about all active servers and presented for player selection.

In late 2007, the master server would return between 28 and 31 K servers, of which roughly 27 K responded to probes [6]. A single server discovery sequence would result in roughly 5 Mbytes of traffic,[13] and show quite different RTT distributions depending on the client's location.

Figures 17.3 and 17.4 (from [6]) show the game server RTTs versus time measured by German and Taiwanese clients during server discovery. At a nominal rate

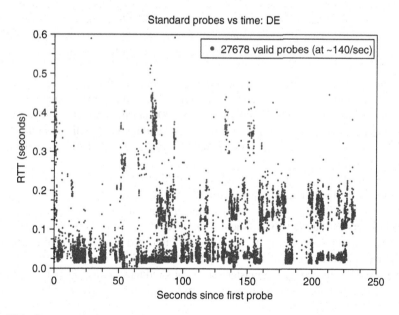

Fig. 17.3 Counterstrike:Source game server RTTs vs time as seen from Germany in Nov'07

---

[13] Outbound *A2S_INFO Request*s (53-byte UDP/IP packets) account for about 30%, with the remainder (inbound) made up of variable-length *A2S_INFO Replies*.

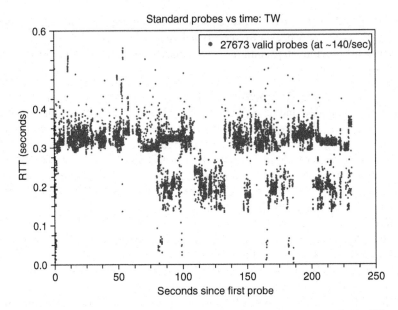

Fig. 17.4 Counterstrike:Source game server RTTs vs time as seen from Taiwan in Nov'07

of 140 probes/s[14] server discovery takes roughly 230 s to complete. As measured game server RTTs vary throughout the discovery period players must wait for all game servers to be probed before they can presume to have seen all those with 'playable' RTT.

Figure 17.5 (also from [6]) contrasts the RTT distributions experienced by clients in six different locations. CS:S has many game servers in Europe, some in the USA and few in Asia. Game servers with RTT under 200 ms are scarce for clients in AU, TW, and JP, and common for clients in DE, UK, and the USA. Clients in the Asia-pacific region end up probing many game servers that are, realistically, unsuitable for competitive play.

CS:S supports both server- and client-side filtering to deal with the deluge of information generated during server discovery.

Server-side filtering occurs when a player's initial *getservers* query requests game servers of a certain type (such as "only CS:S game servers") or servers be-lieved (by the master server) to be in one of eight broad geographical regions of the planet (such as "US-West", "Europe", and "Asia"). Reducing the number of game servers returned by the master server thus reduces the number of *A2S_INFO Request/Reply* probes and the time spent probing.[15] Server-side filtering currently

---

[14] Approximating a Steam client configured for 'DSL > 256K' network access.

[15] This also reduces the level of transient per-flow state created in network devices such as NAT-enabled home routers (which often retain new UDP flow mapping state for minutes after each sub-second *A2S_INFO Request/Reply* transaction).

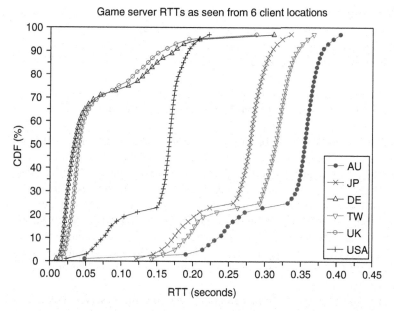

Fig. 17.5 Distribution of RTTs measured to all Counterstrike:Source game servers from six client locations

relies on individual game servers self-identifying as being in a particular geographic region, and on clients explicitly requesting servers from that region. This is not particularly robust.

Client-side filtering (such as not showing servers that are full or empty, or ranking the servers in order of ascending RTT) simplifies the server browser's presentation of information. However, it occurs during or after each active probe and has limited impact on the traffic generated during server discovery.

17.4.2 Reducing Probe Traffic during Counterstrike: SourceServer Discovery

The challenge of finding FPS servers with low enough RTT is well recognized [25]. Early research focused on relocating clients to optimally placed servers (e.g., [24]), rather than optimizing the server discovery process itself. Ideally, we would like to reduce the tens of thousands of short-lived UDP probe flows generated by current server discovery. This can be achieved by probing closer servers before those of more distant servers, and automatically terminating the search sequence once it no longer seems likely the client will find any more game servers with 'playable' RTT.

As noted in [5, 6] the problem appears contradictory: we wish to probe game servers in order of ascending RTT before we have probed them to establish their

RTT. A master server cannot pre-sort the list of game servers in order of ascending RTT because it cannot know the network conditions existing between any given client and every game server.[16] Every client must emit active probes to establish their RTT to individual game servers.

17.4.2.1 Clustering, Calibration, and Optimized Probing

There are three key steps to optimized server discovery: clustering, calibration, and optimized probing. In 2006, the author hypothesized that a client might locally re-order the probe sequence so that game servers in countries 'closer' to the client would be probed before those 'further away' [11]. First, game servers returned by the master server would be *clustered* in such a way that members of a cluster were likely to share similar RTT from the client. *Calibration* involves probing a subset of servers in each cluster, providing an estimate of the RTT to each cluster relative to the client's current location. Finally, the clusters would be ranked in ascending order of estimated RTT, and all remaining game servers probed in order of their cluster's rank (*optimized probing*).

Clustering by country codes[17] and high-order bits of the server IP addresses was proposed in [11] and explored in [5]. Unfortunately, country codes are a very coarse indicator of topological locality and the estimated RTT for particular countries often bore little relation to the spread of RTTs of individual servers falling under the same country code. An alternative approach clustered game servers by the Autonomous System[18] (AS) to which each game server's IP address belongs (its *origin AS*) [6]. Game servers sharing a common origin AS are likely to share a similar distance (and hence RTT) from any given client.[19]

During the optimized probing phase, successive RTT estimates tend to trend upwards (although the trend will fluctuate due to variability of RTT to individual game servers in each cluster). Nevertheless [6] illustrates that a client can implement early termination of server discovery when recent RTT estimates exceed some player-specified threshold. Early termination reduces the number of probes emitted, the number of UDP flows generated, and the player's time waiting to know if all *playable* servers have been probed. (The latter is particularly relevant for clients a long way from many servers.)

---

[16] A master server also cannot trust other clients to accurately report such information from different parts of the Internet. A few misbehaving players injecting corrupt RTT information could easily disrupt such a system.

[17] For example, using MaxMind's free GeoLite Country database [36].

[18] AS numbers are used in inter-domain routing (by the Border Gateway Protocol, BGP [44]) to identify topologically distinct regions of the Internet.

[19] Reference [6] further refines the definition of a cluster to catch origin ASes covering a wide geographical area (and hence a potentially wide spread of RTTs). However, the details are beyond the scope of this chapter.

17.4.2.2   Illustrating AS-Based Optimization

Figure 17.6 (from [6]) illustrates the impact on CS:S clients located in Taiwan. For each client the optimized probe sequence generates traffic in two phases – 'calibration probes' and 'reordered probes.' It takes roughly 23 s (approximately 3,200 probes at 140/s) to calibrate before issuing reordered probes. Early termination occurs when the 'auto-stop estimator' exceeds the player RTT tolerance (set to 200 ms for this example), and the estimated auto-stop time is indicated by a dashed vertical line. Reordered probes are plotted beyond auto-stop to illustrate the effectiveness of reordering.

Taiwanese clients see a distinct improvement – auto-stop causes the probing to terminate well before the roughly 230 s period taken by regular server discovery. A similar improvement is seen in [6] for Australian and Japanese clients too.

Because they are close to large concentrations of game servers under 200 ms, clients based in the UK (Figure 17.7 from [6]) see a fairly neutral impact. Some servers over 200 ms are seen toward the end of the probe sequence, but even with auto-stop such the clients ultimately probe almost all active servers. Similar results are seen in [6] for clients based in the USA, and Germany.

With an optimized search order and auto-stop, clients far away from most game servers see significant reduction in the number of probes emitted by their clients before concluding that all playable servers have been seen. This reduces the player's wait time, the number of transient UDP flows in the network and the number of bytes sent or received.

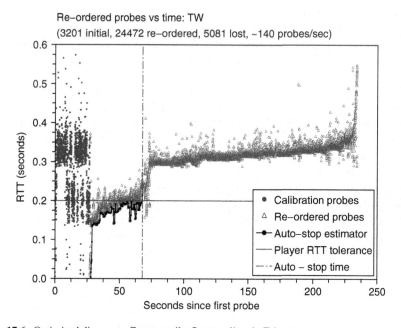

Fig. 17.6 Optimized discovery, Counterstrike:Source client in Taiwan

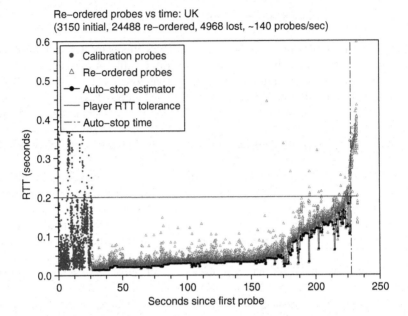

Re-ordered probes vs time: UK
(3150 initial, 24488 re-ordered, 4968 lost, ~140 probes/sec)

Fig. 17.7 Optimized discovery, Counterstrike:Source client in the UK

17.4.2.3 Implementation Issues for AS-Based Optimization

[6] proposes that integration of an open-source tool (such as Quagga [2]) into the
Steam master server could allow mapping of game server IP addresses to origin
AS numbers to occur at the master server.[20] Currently, the master server returns an
unordered list S_1, S_2, ... S_N where S_x is a 6-byte ⟨IP addr:port⟩ pair. AS numbers
may be embedded by instead returning a list of the form AS_1, S_{11}, S_{12}, ..., S_{1N} ,
AS_2, S_{21}, S_{22}, ..., S_{2N} ..., and so on. Each AS_x indicates the origin AS to which
the following game servers belong. The AS_x is encoded as 6-byte S_x field with the
'port' field set to zero (an otherwise invalid port for a genuine game server) and the
nonzero AS number encoded in the 4-byte 'IP addr' field. (New AS numbers take
4 bytes. Traditional 2-byte AS numbers would be encoded as 4-byte numbers with
the top 2 bytes zeroed.)

Embedding AS numbers will increase the typical master server reply list by
roughly 4% (roughly 1,200 additional 6-byte AS_x markers, or 7 Kbytes). However,
there is a net gain to the client if auto-stop eliminates roughly 55 or more *A2S_INFO
Reply* packets (which are often over 135 bytes long). For many clients auto-stop will
eliminate hundreds or thousands of *A2S_INFO Request/Reply* probes.

---

[20] In principle clustering might also be performed at the client, but this would require all clients
have access to up-to-date BGP routing information (impractical) and create additional network
traffic for limited return.

Retrieving all game servers (and AS_x markers) from the master server before initiating calibration and reordered probing would be a change for Steam clients, but represents no change to server browsers such as Qstat.

There is still room for improvement in [6], particularly in the trade-off between the number (and distribution) of probes sent during calibration and the accuracy of subsequent cluster rankings. Nevertheless, this technique may be applied to other FPS games that use a similar server discovery process.

17.4.3   Impact of Access Links on Server RTT Estimation

Leaving aside certain innovative Asian markets, most game players today utilize consumer 'broadband' access links with upstream rates between 128 Kbps and 1+Mbps. This places a practical upper bound on the speed with which server discovery probes may be sent. Another issue is the mismatch between home LAN speeds and the access link. Game clients must shape their probe traffic to minimize inflation of subsequent RTT estimates.

For example, Valve's Steam client's bursty emission of *A2S_INFO Request* probes has been shown to inflate RTT estimates even when the average rate would appear acceptable [7]. CS:S players may influence their *A2S_INFO Requests* emission rate by configuring their Steam client to assume a network connection of "Modem-56 K", "DSL > 256K", etc. In [7] a Steam client in Australia was connected to the Internet in early 2008 via an 100 Mbps LAN and ADSL2+ link.[21] Figures 17.8 and 17.9 (taken from [7]) illustrate the different spread of RTTs experienced when the Steam client was configured for "modem-56K" (measured at 35 probes/second) and "DSL/Cable > 2M" (measured at 319 probes/s) modes, respectively. Relative to Figure 17.8, Figure 17.9 showing a noticeable 'smearing upwards' of estimated RTTs belonging to servers in different regions of the planet.

Closer inspection of the Steam client's traffic revealed that probes were being sent in bursts at LAN line-rate, causing additional queuing delays along the outbound link. Figure 17.10 compares (as cumulative distribution of measured RTTs) the Steam client's results to those obtained using Qstat 2.11 with default settings (measured as 54 probes/s).[22] Steam's burstiness when configured for "DSL/Cable > 2M" has clear impact. Interestingly, when configured for "modem - 56K" the

---

[21] Steam client built: Jan 9 2008, at 15:08:59, Steam API: v007, Steam package versions: 41/457. ADSL2 + link synchronized at 835 Kbps up and 10866 Kbps down.

[22] Figure 17.10 reveals, a small number of servers are within Australia or Asia (roughly 20ms to 140ms), a moderate number of servers are in North America (the 200ms+ range), and a far larger community of game servers are in Europe (330ms+). The need to jump oceans to reach Asia, North America, and then Europe leads to the distinctly non-uniform distribution of RTTs.

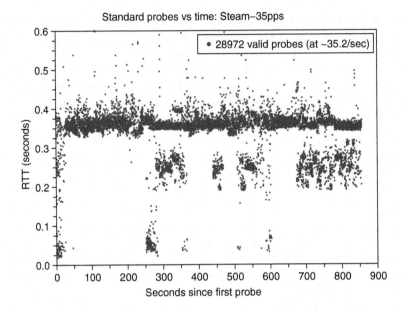

Fig. 17.8 Estimated RTT versus time – Steam client at low speed ("modem-56 K") setting

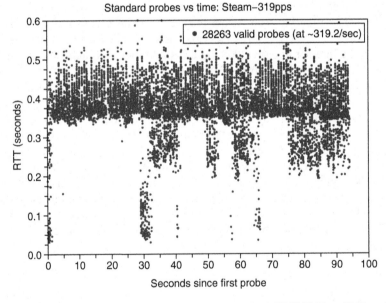

Fig. 17.9 Estimated RTT versus time – Steam client at low speed ("DSL/Cable > 2M") setting

Steam client's burstiness still caused a slight inflation of RTT estimates relative to Qstat (despite Qstat probing faster on average).[23]

---

[23] When running in "DSL/Cable > 2M" mode, over 90% of the probes emitted by the Steam client are less than 1ms apart. In "modem - 56K" mode the Steam client emits 70% of its probe packets less than 1ms apart. Qstat makes a modest attempt to 'pace' the transmission of probe packets.

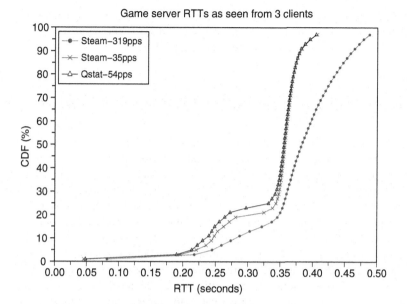

Fig. 17.10 Distribution of estimated RTTs for each test scenario

Traffic between an online game client and remote servers will encounter packet queues in any locations – such as routers, switches, bridges, and modems. A good FPS client should attempt to smoothly pace out the transmission of probe packets, in addition to ensuring, the average probe packet rate does not exceed the player's available upstream network capacity.

17.5   Measuring and Synthesizing Long- and Short-Term Traffic Patterns

Traffic patterns are of interest when investigating the sharing of network infrastructure between online games and more traditional, non-interactive services. For trend analysis and capacity planning, aggregate patterns over long-timescale (hours, days, and weeks) are of interest. Short-timescale traffic characteristics (such as geographic/topological diversity of participating network endpoints, inter-packet arrival times, and packet size distributions) are important when evaluating IP quality of service (QoS) implications during game play.

Whether long or short timescale, traffic is easily monitored using conventional packet capture tools (such as tcpdump) and post-analysis scripts. Predicting traffic from direct inspection of an FPS game's source code cannot replace actual measurements. First, most games do not release their source code. Second, the common use of delta compression (to keep packets small) means the actual distribution of traffic depends on how players actually tend to interact in each virtual world.

The next step is to create synthetic models of typical game traffic so, as network engineers, we may simulate the impact of game traffic under circumstances different to those we can measure empirically [14–19, 23, 29–31, 33, 34].

17.5.1 Long-Timescale Game-Play and Server-Discovery Traffic

Long-timescale traffic is most interesting near individual game servers. Networks near FPS game servers experience two distinct types of traffic game play update and snapshot messages from actual players, and server discovery messages triggered by potential players (and automated game server monitoring systems such as ServerSpy [3]). Both types of traffic exhibit diurnal variation when broken down by geographic origin (as people tend to play in the afternoon and evening of their local timezone) [8, 30, 32, 35, 52]. However, game-play traffic originates primarily from regions 'close enough' to a server for competitive play whilst server-discovery traffic originates from wherever there are potential players. Observation of such diurnal patterns provide insight into where potential players are most densely populated, and how well positioned a game server is relative to players who use it most frequently.

By limiting the number of concurrent players, an FPS game server can constrain the number of concurrent game-play UDP flows at any given time. However, an individual game server has no control on the number of UDP flows generated at any point in time by short-lived server discovery probes. A game server will attract server discovery traffic simply by virtue of being registered with that particular game's master server, even if the game server is unpopular and a long way from most potential players.

The difference is illustrated by Figures 17.11 and 17.12, from a 2005 analysis of traffic impacting a Wolfenstein Enemy Territory (ET) game server in Australia [52]. Figure 17.11 reveals that a majority of potential players (ET clients doing server discovery) were based in Europe (and the "Europe" server discovery traffic peaks during afternoon and evening in Europe). Yet Figure 17.12 reveals that actual game play was dominated by Australian clients, in the afternoon and evening in Australia.

Network-monitoring equipment placed near a game server should bear in mind that the potential number of unique UDP flows are generated by server discovery traffic. Game hosts should keep in mind that they will experience significant, long-term traffic due to short-lived flows even if their server is distant and unpopular.[24] Similar traffic patterns have been seen with newer FPS games (such as Counter-strike:Source).

---

[24] Two ET servers were observed in [52]. Game player accounted for 116GB of traffic on one server and 14GB on the other over 20 weeks. Yet over the same period both servers were equally impacted by server discovery, experiencing 19 million short-lived flows totalling 8GB of traffic each.

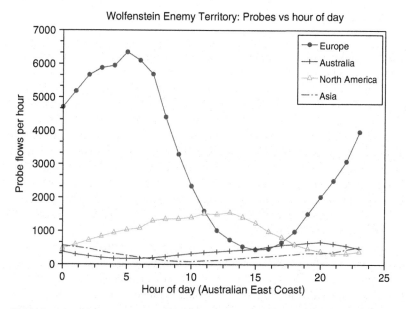

Fig. 17.11 Density of server discovery traffic over time experienced by a Wolfenstein Enemy Territory server in 2005

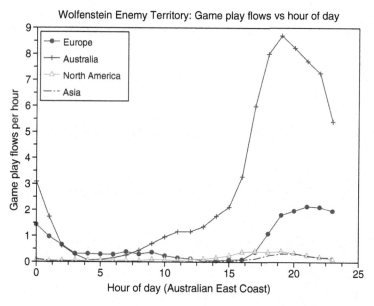

Fig. 17.12 Density of game-play traffic over time experienced by a Wolfenstein Enemy Territory server in 2005

17.5.2 Short-Timescale Game-Play Traffic

Game play is the period when interactions between game traffic and non-game traffic are most important. During game play, and over short timescales, most FPS games exhibit limited variation in packet size from client-to-server and larger variation from server to client.

Figures 17.13 (from [33]) and 17.14 (from [51]) illustrate the client-to-server packet size distributions of Half Life and Halo 2, respectively (both during deathmatch games). Many FPS games tend to send client-to-server updates varying from 10 to 50 ms apart, so there is not too much to report in any given update message. In Half Life there is only one player per client, and Figure 17.13 illustrates that packet sizes are not influenced by particular choice of map. The Halo 2 client is Microsoft's XBox game console, which supports up to four players and leads to Figure 17.14's four different packet distributions.[25]

Traffic in the server-to-client direction is typically emitted as regular bursts of back-to-back snapshot packets, one to each of the clients attached to the game server at any given time.[26] The precise interval between snapshots depends on the FPS game itself and local configuration, but typically ranges from 15 to 50 ms (Chapter 10, [10]). Figures 17.15 (from [33]) and 17.16 (from [51]) use Half Life and Halo 2, respectively (both during deathmatch games) to illustrate the influence on snapshot sizes of the number of players and type of map (as they reflect all changes in game

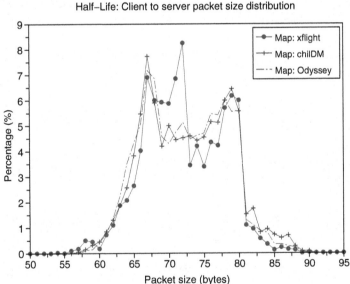

Fig. 17.13 Client-to-server packet sizes for Half Life (original) with three different game maps

---

[25] Figure 17.14 also reflects the fact that Halo 2's client update messages increment in 8 byte jumps.

[26] Snapshots are sent in bursts to minimize any unfairness between clients receiving their individual snapshots at different times.

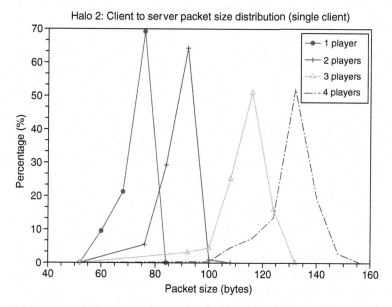

Fig. 17.14 Client-to-server packet sizes for Halo 2 (Xbox) with varying numbers of players on one client (console) and the same map

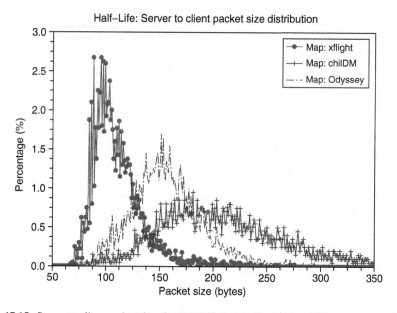

Fig. 17.15 Server-to-client packet sizes for Half Life (original) with three different game maps

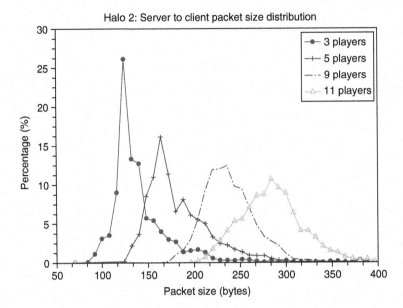

Fig. 17.16 Server-to-client packet sizes for Halo 2 (Xbox) with varying total numbers of players and the same map

state each client needs to see).[27] For a given number of players the type of map can influence how often individual players see or interact with each other – longer snapshots occur when more player interactions occur per unit time (Figure 17.15). Similarly, for a given map we see more player interactions per unit time as the total number of players increases (Figure 17.16).

Snapshot burstiness drives up the bandwidth required of network links close to a game server. For example, an FPS game server serving 30 clients at 20 snapshots per second will emit 30 snapshots back-to-back once every 50 ms. A game server link provisioned for a smooth flow of 600 snapshots per second will become congested every 50 ms, queuing (and delaying) most snapshots in the burst. This creates a slight bias against the client whose snapshot is transmitted last. Network links carrying traffic away from a server must be overprovisioned to minimize queuing delays during each burst of snapshots.

17.5.3 Synthesizing Large Numbers of Players

Client-to-server traffic appears largely independent of the game's map selection or the total number of players. Controlled, empirical measurements of FPS

---

[27] Most FPS games minimize bandwidth requirements by using delta compression to avoid sending updates about entities whose state has not changed since the previous snapshot.

server-to-client traffic with more than ten (or so) players can be a practical challenge to set up and manage. However, it appears that reasonable approximations of many-player FPS server-to-client traffic may be synthesized from traffic captured with small numbers of players (such as two- and three-player games) [15–19].

Two assumptions underly a simple synthesis technique [15]. First, assume that the nature of game play for individual players does not significantly change regardless of the number of players. (Each player spends similar amounts of time involved in exploring the map, collecting useful items, and engaging in battles regardless of the number of players.) Second, assume that players have similar behavior. (They may not be of similar ability but will engage in similar activities in much the same way as each other.) Consequently, the random variable describing the packet length of an N-player game can be constructed through adding together the random variables of smaller player games. We can thus construct the server-to-client packet size probability mass function (PMF)[28] of an N-player game by suitable convolutions of the (measured) PMFs of two- and three-player games.

Figures 17.17 and 17.18 (both from [15]) compare a synthesized PMF with empirically measured PMF of server-to-client packet size for five- and nine-player Half Life 2 Deathmatch games. The synthesized five-player PMF involved convolving a two-player PMF and three-player PMF together. The synthesized nine-player PMF involved convolving a three-player PMF three times. On the right of each PMF is a Q-Q plot whose 45-degree diagonal indicates reasonably good match between the measured and synthesized distributions.

As N increases there is increased divergence between reality and the synthesized PMFs. The scheme's utility can be extended by starting with larger empirically measured PMFs (e.g., synthesizing an 18-player PMF by convolving a measured nine-player PMF with itself).

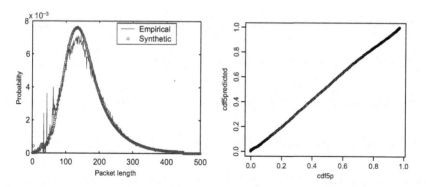

Fig. 17.17 Measured and synthesized server-to-client packet sizes for Half Life 2 Deathmatch for five-player match

---

[28] A probability density function (PDF) for variables, such as packet sizes, that take on discrete values.

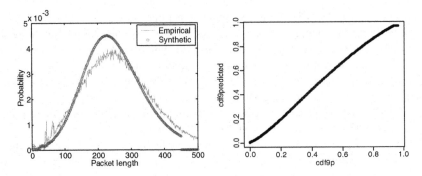

Fig. 17.18 Measured and synthesized server-to-client packet sizes for Half Life 2 Deathmatch for nine-player match

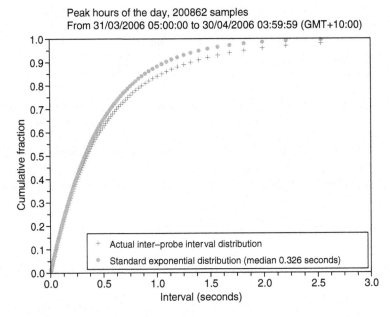

Fig. 17.19 Distribution of intervals between incoming server discovery probes during busiest hours (Wolfenstein Enemy Territory in April 2006)

17.5.4 Short-Timescale Server Discovery Traffic

A typical FPS game server experiences server discovery traffic as a 24-h per day background noise. Arrivals of Wolfenstein Enemy Territory server discovery probes have been seen to be uncorrelated and exhibit exponentially distributed inter-probe intervals during both busiest and least-busy hours of the 24-hour cycle [8]. Figure 17.19 (from [8]) shows how inter-probe intervals closely resemble an exponential distribution (using the median inter-probe interval at any given time). The measured distribution is based on arrivals during the busiest hour of each day in

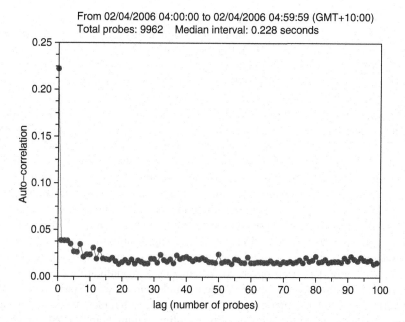

Fig. 17.20 Auto-correlation of intervals between incoming server discovery probes during busiest hours (Wolfenstein Enemy Territory in April 2006)

April 2006. Figure 17.20 (also from [8]) shows the probe arrivals are uncorrelated (using samples from a particular 'busy hour').

The author has seen similar patterns for Counterstrike:Source server discovery probes. As server discovery is triggered by independent human behavior across the planet, it seems reasonable to expect uncorrelated and exponentially distributed inter-probe intervals for many (if not all) FPS games.

17.6   Detection of Live Game Traffic

Service providers may chose to detect and/or track game traffic for reasons such as network performance monitoring, auditing customer usage, automated network re-configuration, and market research. However, isolating (or merely identifying) game traffic flows amongst the hundreds of thousands of flows seen in a service providers core network is non-trivial.

It would be challenging to track the many 'well-known' UDP or TCP port numbers associated with every existing and future online game, and existing games are not always run on their 'official' ports [50]. Packets might be classified by inspecting UDP or TCP payloads, looking for evidence of game protocols in use. However, keeping track of every future permutation of online game protocols would be problematic at best. Furthermore, in some jurisdictions the legality of inspecting the payloads of packets without appropriate authorization is in doubt.

Consequently, there is increasing interest in classifying traffic by looking at each flow's statistical properties[29] over time – in particular by the application of Machine Learning (ML) techniques to IP traffic classification [39, 49]. Recent work on detecting FPS game traffic has been promising [21, 37, 38, 40]. Given the design goals described earlier in this chapter, FPS games tend to exhibit similar combinations of client server and server-client traffic statistics (known as *features* in ML terminology) regardless of the precise payload encoding used by a particular FPS game. For example, consider Figures 17.21 and 17.22 (taken from [40]). They reveal the distribution of two features (mean packet length and standard deviation of packet length) calculated during four different periods of time – probing for the server, connecting to server, actual game play (In game), and over the entire duration of the game. (Figure 17.21 illustrates features calculated in the client-to-server direction, whilst Figure 17.22 shows the server-to-client direction.) Distinct clusters of feature values allows ML algorithms to be trained to differentiate between online game traffic and conventional non-game (e.g., HTTP, SMTP, etc.) applications.

In addition to merely counting how much traffic is consumed by game players, ML classification has been proposed for automated reconfiguration of consumer devices. The author was involved in one example, known as ANGEL (automated network games enhancement layer), that used ML techniques to identify which flows should be provided with priority handling within home ADSL or cable-modem gateways [20–22]. A key part of the ANGEL architecture was decoupling

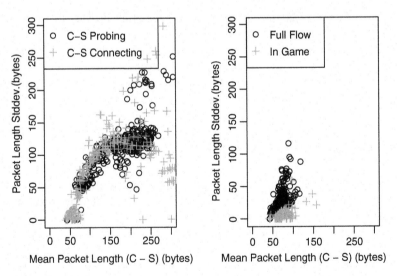

Fig. 17.21 Distribution of two ML features during four different periods of time for Wolfenstein Enemy Territory client-to-server traffic

---

[29] Statistics such as the distribution of packet sizes or inter-packet arrival times are attractive because they can be measured by observing 'external' attributes of packets (timestamps and length fields), side-stepping any need to 'look inside' the packets.

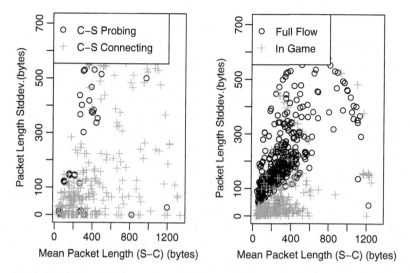

Fig. 17.22 Distribution of two ML features during four different periods of time for Wolfenstein Enemy Territory server-to-client traffic

classification (which would occur inside the ISP's own network, on one or more dedicated traffic-monitoring boxes) from instantiation of the priority game traffic handling (typically on the uplink side of the consumer's home router). The decoupling ensured that the low-power consumer devices would not be burdened with execution of the ML algorithms, and allows ISPs to provide a 'value-added' service to owners of suitably 'ANGEL-aware' home routers or gateways. In early testing the system would identify Wolfenstein Enemy Territory traffic with less than a second of game-play traffic, and successfully reconfigure an otherwise-congested home router. Within seconds of the game-play traffic ceasing, ANGEL would remove the previously installed rules for prioritization of a particular UDP flow.

Statistical classification of game traffic is still in its early days. The likely scalability and utility of this technique remain to be seen.

17.7 Conclusion

The game industry continues to evolves its techniques for extracting the most realistic 'immersion' experience for players given the vagaries on best-effort Internet service. A key challenge for service providers is understanding the characteristics of traffic imposed on networks by games, and their service quality requirements. Interactive online games are particularly susceptible to the side effects of other non-interactive (or delay- and loss-tolerant) traffic sharing next-generation access links. This creates challenges out toward the edges, where high-speed home LANs squeeze through broadband consumer access links to reach the Internet. We have identified a range of research work exploring many issues associated with the intersection of highly interactive games and the Internet, and hopefully stimulated some further thinking along these lines.

Of course, space does not allow this chapter to represent the full spectrum of issues associated with development and deployment of multiplayer online games. Interested readers will find numerous relevant papers published in a number of conferences whose scopes have expanded to include multiplayer online games in recent years. Two notable examples are Netgames (Workshop on Network and System Support for Games, http://www.netgames-conf.org/), and ACM NOSS-DAV (Network and Operating System Support for Digital Audio and Video, http://www.nossdav.org/). Most data-networking and multimedia systems conferences run by the ACM or IEEE have begun attracting games-related papers, which can be found in the ACM Digital Library (http://portal.acm.org) and IEEEXplore (http://www.ieee.org/web/publications/xplore/). The ACM in particular has a number of Special Interest Groups (SIGs) whose scopes overlap the area of networking and online games. Of particular interest are SIGCHI (Computer Human Interaction, http://www.sigchi.org/), SIGCOMM (Data Communications, http://www.sigcomm.org/), and SIGGRAPH (Graphics and Interactive Techniques, http://www.siggraph.org).

References

1. *QStat.* http://www.qstat.org/, accessed February 8th 2008.
2. *Quagga Software Routing Suite.* http://www.quagga.net/, accessed February 8th 2008.
3. *ServerSpy - Online PC Gaming Statistics.* http://www.serverspy.net/, as of July 30th 2008.
4. G. Armitage. Sensitivity of Quake3 players to network latency (poster). In *SIGCOMM Internet Measurement Workshop*, November 2001.
5. G. Armitage. Client-side Adaptive Search Optimisation for Online Game Server Discovery. In *Proceedings of IFIP/TC6 NETWORKING 2008*, Singapore, May 2008.
6. G. Armitage. Optimising Online FPS Game Server Discovery through Clustering Servers by Origin Autonomous System. In *Proceedings of ACM NOSSDAV 2008*, Braunschweig, Germany, May 2008.
7. G. Armitage. Over-estimation of game server RTT during FPS server discovery. CAIA Technical Report 080222B, February 2008.
8. G. Armitage. A packet arrival model for wolfenstein enemy territory online server discovery traffic. In *Proceedings of 15th IEEE International Conference on Networks (ICON)*, Adelaide, Australia, November 2007.
9. G. Armitage. An Experimental Estimation of Latency Sensitivity in Multiplayer Quake3. In *Proceedings of 11th IEEE International Conference on Networks (ICON)*, Sydney, Australia, September 2003.
10. G. Armitage, M. Claypool, and P. Branch. *Networking and Online Games - Understanding and Engineering Multiplayer Internet Games.* John Wiley & Sons, Ltd., United Kingdom, June 2006.
11. G. Armitage, C. Javier, and S. Zander. Topological optimisation for online first person shooter game server discovery. In *Proceedings of Australian Telecommunications and Network Application Conference (ATNAC)*, Sydney, Australia, December 2006.
12. Grenville Armitage, Lawrence Stewart, Michael Welzl, and James Healy. An independent H-TCP implementation under FreeBSD 7.0: description and observed behaviour. *SIGCOMM Comput. Commun. Rev.*, 38(3), July 2008.

13. Tom Beigbeder, Rory Coughlan, Corey Lusher, John Plunkett, Emmanuel Agu, and Mark Clay-pool. The effects of loss and latency on user performance in Unreal Tournament 2003. In *NetGames '04: Proceedings of 3rd ACM SIGCOMM workshop on Network and system support for games*, pages 144–151, New York, NY, USA, 2004. ACM.
14. M. Borella. Source models of network game traffic. *Computer Communications*, 23(3): 403–410, February 2000.
15. P. Branch and G. Armitage. Extrapolating server to client IP traffic from empirical measurements of first person shooter games. In *5th Workshop on Network System Support for Games 2006 (Netgames2006)*, October 2006.
16. P. Branch and G. Armitage. Measuring the auto-correlation of server to client traffic in first person shooter games. In *Australian Telecommunications, Network and Applications Conference (ATNAC)*, December 2006.
17. P. Branch, G. Armitage, and T. Cricenti. Time-series Modelling of Server to Client IP Packet Length in First Person Shooter Games. In *Proceedings of 15th IEEE International Conference on Networks (ICON)*, Adelaide, Australia, November 2007.
18. P. Branch and T. Cricenti. ARMA(1,1) Modeling of Quake4 Server to Client Game Traffic. In *6th Workshop on Network System Support for Games 2007 (Netgames2007)*, September 2007.
19. P. Branch, T. Cricenti, and G. Armitage. A Markov Model of Server to Client IP traffic in First Person Shooter Games. In *Proceedings of 2008 IEEE International Conference on Communications (ICC2008)*, Beijing, China, May 2008.
20. J. But, T.T.T. Nguyen, L. Stewart, N. Williams, and G. Armitage. Peformance Analysis of the ANGEL System for Automated Control of Game Traffic Prioritisation. In *Proceedings of 6th Annual Wokshop on Network and Systems Support for Games (Netgames 2007)*, Melbourne, Australia, September 2007.
21. J. But, N. Williams, S. Zander, L. Stewart, and G. Armitage. ANGEL - Automated Network Games Enhancement Layer. In *Proceedings of Netgames 2006*, Singapore, October 2006.
22. Centre for Advanced Internet Architectures. *ANGEL - Automated Network Games Enhancement Layer*. http://caia.swin.edu.au/sitcrc/angel/, as of July 30th 2008.
23. C. Chambers, W.-C. Feng, S. Sahu, and D. Saha. Measurement based characterization of a collection of on-line games. In *Internet Measurement Conference 2005 (IMC2005)*, October 2005.
24. C. Chambers, W.-C. Feng, W.-C. Feng, and D. Saha. A geographic, redirection service for on-line games. In *ACM Multimedia 2003 (short paper)*, November 2003.
25. M. Claypool. Network characteristics for server selection in online games. In *ACM/SPIE Multimedia Computing and Networking (MMCN)*, January 2008.
26. Mark Claypool. The effect of latency on user performance in real-time strategy games. *Comput. Netw.*, 49(1):52–70, 2005.
27. Mark Claypool and Kajal Claypool. Latency and player actions in online games. *Commun. ACM*, 49(11):40–45, 2006.
28. M. Duke, R. Braden, W. Eddy, and E. Blanton. A Roadmap for Transmission Control Protocol (TCP) Specification Documents. RFC 4614 (Informational), September 2006.
29. J. Farber. Traffic modelling for fast action network games. *Multimedia Tools and Applications*, 23:31–46, December 2004.
30. W.-C. Feng, F. Chang, W.-C. Feng, and J. Walpole. Provisioning on-line games: A traffic analysis of a busy Counter-Strike server. In *SIGCOMM Internet Measurement Workshop*, 2002.
31. W.-C. Feng, F. Chang, W.-C. Feng, and J. Walpole. A traffic charaterization of popular on-line games. *IEEE/ACM Transactions on Networking (TON)*, 13:488–500, June 2005.
32. T. Henderson and S. Bhatti. Modelling user behaviour in networked games. In *9th ACM International Conference on Multimedia (ACM Multimedia)*, 2001.
33. T. Lang, G. Armitage, P. Branch, and H.-Y. Choo. A synthetic traffic model for Half-Life. In *Australian Telecommunications, Networks and Applications Conference (ATNAC)*, December 2003.
34. T. Lang, P. Branch, and G. Armitage. A synthetic model for Quake III traffic. In *Advances in Computer Entertainment (ACE2004)*, June 2004.

35. Youngki Lee, Sharad Agarwal, Chris Butcher, and Jitu Padhye. Measurement and Estimation of Network QoS Among Peer Xbox 360 Game Players. In *Proc. 9th Passive and Active Network Measurement Conference (PAM 2008)*, pages 41–50. Springer Berlin/Heidelberg, April 2008.

36. MaxMind. *GeoLite Country*. http://www.maxmind.com/app/geoip_country, accessed February 8th 2008.

37. T.T.T. Nguyen and G. Armitage. Synthetic Sub-flow Pairs for Timely and Stable IP Traffic Identification. In *Proc. Australian Telecommunication Networks and Application Conference*, Melbourne, Australia, December 2006.

38. T.T.T. Nguyen and G. Armitage. Training on multiple sub-flows to optimise the use of Machine Learning classifiers in real-world IP networks. In *Proc. IEEE 31st Conference on Local Computer Networks*, Tampa, Florida, USA, November 14–16 2006.

39. T.T.T. Nguyen and G. Armitage. A Survey of Techniques for Internet Traffic Classification using Machine Learning. *IEEE Communications Surveys & Tutorials*, 10(4), October 2008.

40. T.T.T. Nguyen and G. Armitage. Clustering to Assist Supervised Machine Learning for Real-Time IP Traffic Classification. In *IEEE International Conference on Communications (ICC 2008)*, Beijing, China, May 2008.

41. James Nichols and Mark Claypool. The effects of latency on online madden NFL football. In *NOSSDAV 04: Proceedings of the 14th international workshop on Network and operating systems support for digital audio and video*, pages 146–151, New York, NY, USA, 2004. ACM Press.

42. J. Postel. User Datagram Protocol. RFC 768 (Standard), August 1980.

43. J. Postel. Transmission Control Protocol. RFC 793 (Standard), September 1981. Updated by RFC 3168.

44. Y. Rekhter, T. Li, and S. Hares. RFC 4271: A Border Gateway Protocol 4 (BGP-4), January 2006.

45. Nathan Sheldon, Eric Girard, Seth Borg, Mark Claypool, and Emmanuel Agu. The effect of latency on user performance in Warcraft III. In *NetGames '03: Proceedings of the 2nd workshop on Network and system support for games*, pages 3–14, New York, NY, USA, 2003. ACM.

46. Lawrence Stewart, Grenville Armitage, and Alana Huebner. Collateral Damage: The Impact of Optimised TCP Variants On Real-time Traffic Latency in Consumer Broadband Environments. In *IFIP/TC6 NETWORKING 2009*, Aachen, Germany, May 2009.

47. Valve Corporation. *CounterStrike: Source*. http://counter-strike.net/, accessed February 8th 2008.

48. Valve Corporation. *Server Queries*. http://developer.valvesoftware.com/wiki/Server_Queries, as of February 7th 2008.

49. Nigel Williams, Sebastian Zander, and Grenville Armitage. A preliminary performance comparison of five machine learning algorithms for practical IP traffic flow classification. *SIGCOMM Comput. Commun. Rev.*, 36(5):5–16, 2006.

50. S. Zander. Misclassification of game traffic based on port numbers: A case study using enemy territory. CAIA Technical Report 060410D, April 2006.

51. S. Zander and G. Armitage. A traffic model for the XBOX game Halo 2. In *15th ACM International Workshop on Network and Operating System Support for Digital Audio and Video (NOSSDAV2005)*, June 2005.

52. S. Zander, D. Kennedy, and G. Armitage. Dissecting server-discovery traffic patterns generated by multiplayer first person shooter games. In *Proceedings of ACM Networks and System Support for Games (NetGames) Workshop*, New York, USA, October 2005.

53. Sebastian Zander, Ian Leeder, and Grenville Armitage. Achieving fairness in multiplayer network games through automated latency balancing. In *ACE '05: Proceedings of the 2005 ACM SIGCHI International Conference on Advances in computer entertainment technology*, pages 117–124, New York, NY, USA, 2005. ACM.

Chapter 18
Wayfinding in Social Networks

David Liben-Nowell

Abstract With the recent explosion of popularity of commercial social-networking sites like Facebook and MySpace, the size of social networks that can be studied scientifically has passed from the scale traditionally studied by sociologists and anthropologists to the scale of networks more typically studied by computer scientists. In this chapter, I will highlight a recent line of computational research into the modeling and analysis of the *small-world phenomenon* – the observation that typical pairs of people in a social network are connected by very short chains of intermediate friends – and the ability of members of a large social network to collectively find efficient routes to reach individuals in the network. I will survey several recent mathematical models of social networks that account for these phenomena, with an emphasis on both the provable properties of these social-network models and the empirical validation of the models against real large-scale social-network data.

18.1 Introduction

An intrepid graduate student at a university in Cambridge, MA, leaves his department on a quest for cannoli in the North End, a largely Italian neighborhood of Boston. This mission requires him to solve a particular navigation problem in the city: from his background knowledge (his own "mental map" of Boston, including what he knows about the proximity of particular landmarks to his destination pastry shop, how he conceives of the margins of the North End district, and where he thinks his office is) and what he gathers at his initial location (street signs, perhaps the well-trodden routes scuffed into the grass outside his office that lead to the nearest subway station, perhaps the smell of pesto), he must begin to construct a path toward his destination. *Wayfinding*, a word coined by the urban planner Kevin Lynch in the 1960s [33], refers to the processes by which a person situates himself or herself in an urban environment and navigates from point to point in that setting.

D. Liben-Nowell (✉)
Department of Computer Science, Carleton College, Northfield, MN 55057
e-mail: dlibenno@carleton.edu

G. Cormode and M. Thottan (eds.), *Algorithms for Next Generation Networks*,   435
Computer Communications and Networks, DOI 10.1007/978-1-84882-765-3_18,
© Springer-Verlag London Limited 2010

(Incidentally, wayfinding is particularly difficult in Boston, with its often irregular angles and patterns: one may become confused about directions – the North End is almost due east of the West End – or encounter impermeable boundaries like rivers or highways even while heading in the right cardinal direction.)

This chapter will be concerned with wayfinding in networks – specifically in *social networks*, structures formed by the set of social relationships that connect a set of people. The issues of navigability of a social network are analogous to the issues of navigability of a city: can a source person s reliably identify a step along an efficient path "toward" a destination person t from her background knowledge (a "mental map" of the social network) plus whatever information she gathers from her immediate proximity? How does one find routes in a social network, and how easy is it to compute those routes? To borrow another term from Kevin Lynch, is the "legibility" of a real social network more like Manhattan – a clear grid, easy navigation – or like Boston?

In later sections, I will describe a more formal version of these notions and questions, and describe some formal models that can help to explain some of these real-world phenomena. (The interested reader may also find the recent surveys by Kleinberg [25] and Fraigniaud [17] valuable.) I will begin with a grid-based model of social networks and social-network routing due to Jon Kleinberg [23, 26], under which Kleinberg has fully characterized the parameter values for which the resulting social network supports the construction of short paths through the network in a decentralized, distributed fashion. Geography is perhaps the most natural context in which to model social networks via a regular grid, so I will next turn to empirical observations of geographic patterns of friendship in real large-scale online social networks. I will then describe some modifications to Kleinberg's model suggested by observed characteristics of these real-world networks, most notably the widely varying population density across geographic locations. Finally, I will turn to other models of social networks and social-network routing, considering both network models based on notions of similarity that are poorly modeled by a grid (e.g., occupation) and network models based simultaneously on multiple notions of person-to-person similarity.

18.2 The Small-World Phenomenon

Although social networks have been implicit in the interactions of humans for millennia, and social interactions among humans have been studied by social scientists for centuries, the academic study of social networks *qua* networks is more recent. Some of the early foundational contributions date from the beginning of the twentieth century, including the "web of group affiliations" of Georg Simmel [45], the "sociograms" of Jacob Moreno [40], and the "topological psychology" of Kurt Lewin [31]. In the 1950s, Cartwright and Zander [9] and Harary and Norman [20] described an explicitly graph-theoretic framework for social networks: nodes represent individuals and edges represent relationships between pairs of individuals. We will use this graph-theoretic language throughout the chapter.

The line of social-network research that is the focus of this chapter can be traced back to an innovative experiment conceived and performed by the social psychologist Stanley Milgram in the 1960s [38]. Milgram chose 100 "starter" individuals in Omaha, NE, and sent each one of them a letter. The accompanying instructions said that the letter holder s should choose one of his or her friends to whom to forward the letter, with the eventual goal of reaching a target person t, a stockbroker living near Boston. (For Milgram's purposes, a "friend" of s was anyone with whom s was on a mutual first-name basis.) Each subsequent recipient of the letter would receive the same instructions, and, presumably, the letter would successively home in on t with each step. What Milgram found was that, of the chains that reached the stockbroker, on average they took about six hops to arrive. That observation was the origin of the phrase "six degrees of separation." Of course, what this careful phrasing glosses over is the fraction of chains – about 80% – that failed to reach the target; Judith Kleinfeld has raised an interesting and compelling set of critiques about the often overbroad conclusions drawn from these limited data [27]. Still, Milgram's small-world results have been replicated in a variety of settings – including a recent large-scale email-based study by Dodds, Muhamad, and Watts [13] – and Milgram's general conclusions are not in dispute.

The *small-world problem* – why is it that a random resident of Omaha should be only a few hops removed from a stockbroker living in a suburb of Boston? – was traditionally answered by citing, explicitly or implicitly, the voluminous body of mathematical literature that shows that random graphs have small diameter. But that explanation suffers in two important ways: first, social networks are poorly modeled by random graphs; and, second, in the language of Kevin Lynch, Milgram's observation is much more about wayfinding than about diameter. The first objection, that social networks do not look very much like random graphs, was articulated by Duncan Watts and Steve Strogatz [49]. Watts and Strogatz quantified this objection in terms of the high *clustering* in social networks: many pairs of people who share a common friend are also friends themselves. The second objection, that the Milgram experiment says something about the efficiency of wayfinding in a social network and not just something about the network's diameter, was raised by Jon Kleinberg [23, 26]. Kleinberg observed that Milgram's result is better understood not just as an observation about the existence of short paths from source to target, but rather as an observation about distributed algorithms: somehow people in the Milgram experiment have collectively managed to *construct* short paths from source to target.

How might people be able to accomplish this task so efficiently? In a social network – or indeed in any network – finding short paths to a target t typically hinges on making some form of measurable progress toward t. Ideally, this measure of progress in a social network would simply be graph distance: at every step, the path would move to a node with smaller graph distance to t, i.e., along a shortest path to t. But the highly decentralized nature of a social network means that only a handful of nodes (the target t himself, the neighbors of t, and perhaps a few neighbors of the neighbors of t) genuinely know their graph distance to t. Instead one must use some guide other than graph distance to home in on t.

The key idea in routing in this context – frequently cited by the participants in real small-world experiments as their routing strategy [13, 21] – is to use similarity of characteristics (geographic location, hobbies, occupation, age, etc.) as a measure of progress, a proxy for the ideal but unattainable graph-distance measure of proximity. The success of this routing strategy hinges on the sociological observation of the crucial tendency toward *homophily* in human relationships: the friends of a typical person x tend to be similar to x. This similarity tends to occur with respect to race, occupation, socioeconomics, and geography, among other dimensions. See the survey of McPherson, Smith-Lovin, and Cook [36] for an excellent review of the literature on homophily. Homophily makes characteristic-based routing reasonable, and in fact it also gives one explanation for the high clustering of real social networks: if x's friends tend to be similar to x, then they also tend to be (somewhat less) similar to each other, and therefore they also tend to know each other directly with a (somewhat) higher probability than a random pair of people.

Homophily suggests a natural *greedy algorithm* for routing in social networks. If a person s is trying to construct a path to a target t, then s should look at all of his or her friends $\Gamma(s)$ and, of them, select the friend in $\Gamma(s)$ who is "most like" the target t. This notion is straightforward when it comes to geography: the source s knows both where his her friends live and where t lives, and thus s can just compute the geographic distance between each $u \in \Gamma(s)$ and t, choosing the u minimizing that quantity. Routing greedily with respect to occupation is somewhat murkier, though one can imagine s choosing u based on distance within an implicit hierarchy of occupations in s's head. (Milgram's stockbroker presumably falls into something like the service industry $\rightarrow$ financial services $\rightarrow$ investment $\rightarrow$ stocks.) Indeed, the greedy algorithm is well founded as long as an individual has sufficient knowledge of underlying person-to-person similarities to compare the distances between each of his or her friends and the target.

18.3   Kleinberg's Small-World Model: the Navigable Grid

Although homophily is a key motivation for greedy routing, homophily alone does not suffice to ensure that the greedy algorithm will find short paths through a social network. As a concrete example, suppose that every sociologist studying social networks knows every other such sociologist and nobody else, and every computer scientist studying social networks knows every other such computer scientist and nobody else. This network has an extremely high degree of homophily. But the network is not even connected, let alone navigable by the greedy algorithm. For the greedy algorithm to succeed, the probability of friendship between people u and v should somehow vary more smoothly as the similarity of u and v decreases. Intuitively, there is a tension between having "well-scattered" friends to reach faraway targets and having "well-localized" friends to home in on nearby targets. Without the former, a large number of steps will be required to span the large gap from a source s to an especially dissimilar target t; without the latter, similarity will be only vaguely related to graph-distance proximity, and thus the greedy algorithm will be a poor approximation to a globally aware shortest-path algorithm.

A rigorous form of this observation was made by Jon Kleinberg [23,26], through formal analysis of this trade-off in an elegant model of social networks. Here is Kleinberg's model, in its simplest form (see Section 18.6 for generalizations). Consider an n-person population, and arrange these people as the points in a regular k-dimensional grid. Each person u in the network is connected to $2k$ "local neighbors," the people who live one grid point above and below u in each of the k cardinal directions. (People on the edges of the grid will have fewer local neighbors, or we can treat the grid as a torus without substantively affecting the results.) Each person u will also be endowed with a "long-range link" to one other person v in the network. That person v will be chosen probabilistically with $\Pr[u \rightarrow v] \propto d(u, v)^{-\alpha}$, where $d(\cdot, \cdot)$ denotes Manhattan distance in the grid and $\alpha \geq 0$ is a parameter to the model. (Changing the model to endow each person with any constant number of long-range links does not qualitatively change the results.) See Figure 18.1 for an example network, with $k = \alpha = 2$. Notice that the parameter α operationalizes the trade-off between highly localized friends and highly scattered friends: setting $\alpha = 0$ yields links from each person u to a person v chosen uniformly from the network, while letting $\alpha \rightarrow \infty$ yields links from u to v only if $d(u, v) = 1$.

A *local-information algorithm* is one that computes a path to a target without global knowledge of the graph. When a person u chooses a next step v in the path to the target t, the person u has knowledge of the structure of the grid, including the grid locations of u herself, u's local neighbors, u's long-range contact, and the

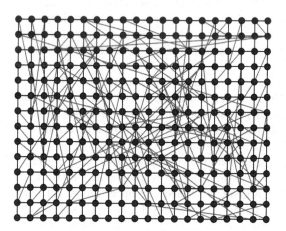

Fig. 18.1 Kleinberg's small-world model [23, 26]. A population of n people is arranged on a k-dimensional grid, and each person u is connected to her immediate neighbors in each direction. Each person u is also connected to a long-range friend v, chosen with probability $\propto d(u, v)^{-\alpha}$, where $d(\cdot, \cdot)$ denotes Manhattan distance and $\alpha \geq 0$ is a parameter to the model. The example two-dimensional network here was generated with $\alpha = 2$

target t. However, the remaining structure of the graph – that is, the long-range links for nodes other than u – are not available to u when she is making her routing choice. (The results are not affected by expanding the knowledge of each node u to include the list of all people previously on the path from the original source s to u, or even the list of long-range links for each of those people.)

Kleinberg was able to give a complete characterization of the navigability of these networks by local-information algorithms:

Theorem 18.1 (Kleinberg [23, 26]). *Consider an n-person network with people arranged in a k-dimensional grid, where each person has $2k$ local neighbors and one long-range link chosen with parameter $\alpha \geq 0$, so that $\Pr[u \rightarrow v] \propto d(u,v)^{-\alpha}$. For an arbitrary source person s and an arbitrary target person t:*

- *If $\alpha \neq k$, then there exists some constant $\varepsilon > 0$, where ε depends on α and k but is independent of n, such that the expected length of the path from s to t found by any local-information algorithm is $\Omega(n^\varepsilon)$.*
- *If $\alpha = k$, then the greedy algorithm – i.e., the algorithm that chooses the next step in the path as the contact closest to the target t under Manhattan distance in the grid – finds a path from s to t of expected length $O(\log^2 n)$.*

The proof that greedy routing finds a path of length $O(\log^2 n)$ when $\alpha = k$ proceeds by showing that the probability of halving the distance to the target at any step of the path is $\Omega(1/\log n)$. Thus, in expectation, the distance to the target is halved every $O(\log n)$ steps. The path reaches the target after the distance is halved $\log n$ times, and therefore $O(\log^2 n)$ total steps suffice to reach the target in expectation.

For our purposes, we will broadly treat paths of length polynomial in the logarithm of the population size as "short," and paths of length polynomial in the population size as "long." (We will use standard terminology in referring to these "short" paths as having *polylogarithmic* length – that is, length $O(\log^c n)$ for some constant exponent c, in a population of size n.) There has been significant work devoted to tightening the analysis of greedy routing in Kleinberg's networks – for example, [7, 35] – but for now we will focus on the existence of algorithms that find paths of polylogarithmic length, without too much concern about the precise exponent of the polynomial. A network in which a local-information algorithm can find a path of polylogarithmic length is called *navigable*. Theorem 18.1, then, can be rephrased as follows: a k-dimensional grid-based social network with parameter α is navigable if and only if $k = \alpha$.

Note that this definition of navigability, and hence Kleinberg's result, describes routing performance asymptotically in the population size n. Real networks, of course, are finite. Aaron Clauset and Cristopher Moore [11] have shown via simulation that in finite networks greedy routing performs well even under what Theorem 18.1 identifies as "non-navigable" values of α. Following [11], define α_{opt} as the value of α that produces the network under which greedy routing achieves the shortest path lengths. Clauset and Moore's simulations show that α_{opt} is somewhat less than k in large but finite networks; furthermore, although α_{opt} approaches k as the population grows large, this convergence is relatively slow.

18.4   Geography and Small Worlds

Now that we have formal descriptions of mathematical models of social networks, we can turn to evaluating the correspondence between these models' predictions and real social-network data. To begin with, consider physical-world geographic proximity as the underlying measure of similarity between people. Geographic distance is a natural metric on which to focus both because of its simplicity and its observed importance in empirical studies: participants in real-world Milgram-style experiments of social-network routing frequently cite geographic proximity as the reason that they chose a particular friend as the next step in a chain [13, 21]. (Typically, people who were early in these chains cited geography as a principal reason for their choice, and those who appeared later in the chains more frequently reported that their choice was guided by similarity of occupation.)

Although the description of Kleinberg's model in Section 18.3 was couched in abstract terms, there is a very natural geographic interpretation to the model's underlying grid. Geographic distance on the surface of the earth is well modeled by a two-dimensional grid under Manhattan distance, where we imagine grid points as the intersections of evenly spaced lines of longitude and latitude. The grid is of course a simplification of real proximity in the real world, but it is plausible as a first approximation. Thus, we have a mathematical model of social-network routing based on geographic proximity, and real-world evidence that people who (at least partially) successfully route through social networks do so (at least partially) based on geographic proximity. We are now in a position to test the mathematical model against real social networks.

Much of the empirical work described here will be based on data from the Live-Journal blogging community, found online at livejournal.com. LiveJournal is an appealing domain for study in part because it contains reasonably rich data about its users, even if one ignores the detailed accounts of users' personal lives frequently found in their blog posts. LiveJournal users create profiles that include demographic information such as birthday, hometown, and a list of interests/hobbies. Each user's profile also includes an explicit list of other LiveJournal users whom that user considers to be a friend. The analysis that follows – performed in joint work with Jasmine Novak, Ravi Kumar, Prabhakar Raghavan, and Andrew Tomkins [32] – was based on a crawl of LiveJournal performed in February 2004, comprising about 1.3 million user profiles. (As of this writing, there are slightly more than 17 million LiveJournal accounts.) Of those 1.3 million users, approximately 500,000 users declared a hometown that we were able to locate in a database of longitudes and latitudes in the continental USA. These data yield a large-scale social network with geographic locations, using the explicitly listed friendships to define connections among this set of 500,000 people. Figure 18.2 contains a visual representation of this social network.

Using this 500,000-person network, we can simulate the Milgram experiment, using the purely geographic greedy routing algorithm. There is some subtlety in setting up this simulation – for example, what happens if the simulated chain reaches a person u who has no friends closer to the target than u herself? – and, because

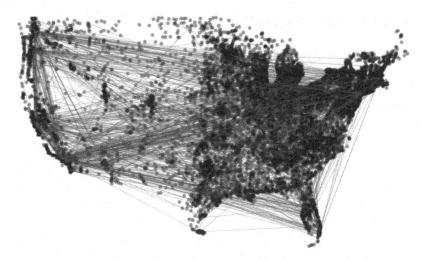

Fig. 18.2 The LiveJournal social network [32]. A dot is shown for each geographic location that was declared as the hometown of at least one of the ≈500,000 LiveJournal users whom we were able to locate at a longitude and latitude in the continental USA. A random 0.1% of the friendships in the network are overlaid on these locations

the resolution of geographic locations is limited to the level of towns and cities, we try only to reach the city of the target t rather than t herself. We found that, subject to these caveats, the geographic greedy algorithm was able to find short paths connecting many pairs of people in the network (see [32] for more detail).

With the above observations (people are arranged on a two-dimensional geographic grid; greedy routing based on geography finds short paths through the network) and Theorem 18.1, we set out – in retrospect, deeply naïvely – to verify that the probability of friendship between people u and v grows asymptotically as $d(u, v)^{-2}$ in the LiveJournal network. In other words, in the language of Kleinberg's theorem, we wanted to confirm that $\alpha = 2$. The results are shown in Figure 18.3, which displays the probability $P(d)$ of friendship between two people who live a given distance d apart – i.e., the fraction of pairs separated by distance d who declare a friendship in LiveJournal.

One immediate observation from the plot in Figure 18.3 is that the probability $P(d)$ of friendship between two people in LiveJournal separated by distance d really does decrease smoothly and markedly as d increases. This relationship already reveals a nonobvious fact about LiveJournal; there was no particular reason to think that geographic proximity would necessarily play an important role in friendships in a completely virtual community like this one. Section 18.7 includes some discussion of a few possible reasons why geography remains so crucial in this virtual setting, but for now it is worth noting that the "virtualization" of real-world friendships (i.e., the process of creating digital records of existing physical-world friendships) seems to explain only some of the role of geography. For example, it seems hard for

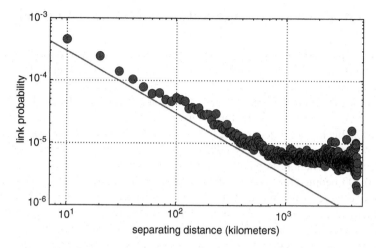

Fig. 18.3 The probability $P(d)$ of a friendship between two people in LiveJournal as a function of the geographic distance d between their declared hometowns [32]. Distances are rounded into 10-km buckets. The solid line corresponds to $P(d) \propto 1/d$. Note that Theorem 18.1 requires $P(d) \propto 1/d^2$ for a network of people arranged in a regular two-dimensional grid to be navigable

this process to fully account for the marked difference in link probability between people separated by 300 versus 500 km, a range at which regular physical-world interactions seem unlikely.

A second striking observation from the plot in Figure 18.3 is that the probability $P(d)$ of friendship between people separated by distance d is very poorly modeled by $P(d) \propto 1/d^2$, the relationship required by Theorem 18.1. This probability is better modeled as $P(d) \propto 1/d$, and in fact is even better modeled as $P(d) = \varepsilon + \Theta(1/d)$, for a constant $\varepsilon \approx 5.0 \times 10^{-6}$. Apropos the discussion in the previous paragraph, this additive constant makes some sense: the probability that people u and v are friends can be thought of as the sum of two probabilities, one that increases with their geographic proximity, and one that is independent of their geographic locations. But, regardless of the presence or absence of the additive ε, the plot in Figure 18.3 does not match – or even come close to matching – the navigable exponent required by Kleinberg's theorem.

Similar results have also been observed in another social-networking context. In a study of email-based social links among about 450 members of Hewlett–Packard Research Labs [1], Lada Adamic and Eytan Adar found that the link probability $P(d)$ between two HP Labs researchers was also closely matched by $P(d) \propto 1/d$, where d measures the Manhattan distance between the cubicle locations of the employees. In this setting, too, geographic greedy routing found short paths to most targets – though not as short as those found by routing greedily according to proximity in the organizational hierarchy of the corporation (see Sections 18.6 and 18.7) – again yielding a greedily navigable network that does not match Theorem 18.1.

18.5   Variable Population Density and Rank-Based Friendship

The observations from the previous section lead to a seeming puzzle: a navigable two-dimensional grid, which must have link probabilities decaying as $1/d^2$ to be navigable according to Theorem 18.1, has link probabilities decaying as $1/d$. But another look at Figure 18.2 reveals an explanation – and reveals the naïvete of looking for $P(d) \propto 1/d^2$ in the LiveJournal network. Although a two-dimensional grid is a reasonable model of geographic location, a *uniformly distributed* population on a two-dimensional grid is a very poor model of the geographic distribution of the LiveJournal population. Population density varies widely across the USA – from over 10,000 people/km^2 in parts of Manhattan to approximately 1 person/km^2 in places like Lake of the Woods County, in the far northern reaches of Minnesota. Two Manhattanites who live 500 m apart have probably never even met; two Lake of the Woods residents who live 500 m apart are probably next-door neighbors, and thus they are almost certain to know each other. This wide spectrum suggests that distance cannot be the whole story in any reasonable geographic model of social networks: although $\Pr[u \rightarrow v]$ should be a decreasing function of the geographic distance between u and v, intuitively the rate of decrease in that probability should reflect something about the population in the vicinity of these people.

One way to account for variable population density is *rank-based friendship* [6, 28, 32]. The grid-based model described here is the simplest version of rank-based friendship; as with Kleinberg's distance-based model, generalizations that do not rely on the grid have been studied (see Section 18.6). We continue to measure person-to-person distances using Manhattan distance in a k-dimensional grid, but we will now allow an arbitrary positive number of people to live at each grid point. Each person still has $2k$ local neighbors, one in each of the two directions in each of the k dimensions, and one long-range link, chosen as follows. Define the *rank* of a person v with respect to u as the number of people who live at least as close to u as v does, breaking ties in some consistent way. (In other words, person u sorts the population in descending order of proximity to u; the rank of v is her index in this sorted list.) Now each person u chooses her long-range link according to rank, so that $\Pr[u \rightarrow v]$ is inversely proportional to the rank of v with respect to u. See Figure 18.4 for an example rank-based network.

Rank-based friendship generalizes the navigable $\alpha = k$ setting in the distance-based Theorem 18.1: in a k-dimensional grid with constant population at each point, the rank of v with respect to u is $\Theta(d(u, v)^k)$. But even under nonuniform population densities, social networks generated according to rank-based friendship are navigable by the greedy algorithm:

Theorem 18.2 (Liben-Nowell, Novak, Kumar, Raghavan, Tomkins [28, 32]). *Consider an n-person network where people are arranged in a k-dimensional grid so that at least one person lives at every grid point x. Suppose each person has $2k$ local neighbors and one long-range link chosen via rank-based friendship. Fix any source person s and choose a target person t uniformly at random from the population. Then under greedy routing the expected length of the path from s to the point x_t in which t lives is $O(\log^3 n)$.*

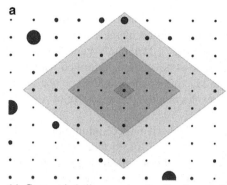

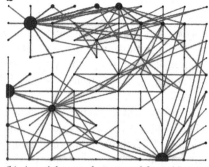

(a) Concentric balls around a city C, where each ball's population increases by a factor of four. A resident of C choosing a rank-based friend is four times more likely to choose a friend at the boundary of one ball than a friend at the boundary of the next-larger ball.

(b) A social network generated from this population distribution via rank-based friendship. For visual simplicity, edges are depicted as connecting cities; the complete image would show each edge connecting one resident from each of its endpoint cities.

Fig. 18.4 Two images of a sample rank-based social network with variable population density. Each blue circle represents a city with a population whose size is proportional to the circle's radius. Distances between cities, and hence between people, are computed using Manhattan distance. A rank-based friendship for each person u is formed probabilistically, where $\Pr[u \to v]$ is inversely proportional to the number of people who live closer to u than v is, breaking ties consistently. The local neighbors – for each person u, one friend in the neighboring city in each cardinal direction – are not shown

A few notes about this theorem are in order. First, relative to Theorem 18.1, rank-based friendship has lost a logarithmic factor in the length of the path found by greedy routing. Recently, in joint work with David Barbella, George Kachergis, Anna Sallstrom, and Ben Sowell, we were able to show that a "cautious" variant on greedy routing finds a path of expected length $O(\log^2 n)$ in rank-based networks [6], but the analogous tightening for greedy routing itself remains open.

Second, Theorem 18.2 makes a claim about the expected length of the path found by the greedy algorithm for a randomly chosen target t, where the expectation is taken over both the random construction of the network *and* the random choice of the target. In contrast, Theorem 18.1 makes a claim about the expected length of the path found by the greedy algorithm for *any* target, where the expectation is taken only over the random construction of the network. Intuitively, some targets in a rank-based network may be very difficult to reach: if a person t lives in a region of the network that has a comparatively very sparse population, then there will be very few long-range links to people near t. Thus making progress toward an isolated target may be very difficult. However, the difficulty of reaching an isolated target like t is offset by the low probability of choosing such a target; almost by definition, there cannot be very many people who live in regions of the network that have unusually low density. The proof of Theorem 18.2 formalizes this intuition [28, 32].

This technical difference in the statements of Theorems 18.1 and 18.2 in fact echoes points raised by Judith Kleinfeld in her critique of the overly expansive interpretation of Milgram's experimental results [27]. Milgram's stockbroker was a socially prominent target, and other Milgram-style studies performed with less prominent targets – e.g., the wife of a Harvard Divinity School student, in one study performed by Milgram himself – yielded results much less suggestive of a small world.

It is also worth noting that, although the "isolated target" intuition suggests why existing proof techniques are unlikely to yield a "for all targets" version of Theorem 18.2, there are no known population distributions in which greedy routing fails to find a short path to any particular target in a rank-based network. It is an interesting open question to resolve whether there are population distributions and source–target pairs for which greedy routing fails to find a path of short expected length in rank-based networks (where, as in Theorem 18.1, the expectation is taken only over the construction of the network).

These two ways in which Theorem 18.2 is weaker than Theorem 18.1 are counterbalanced by the fact that Theorem 18.2 can handle varying population densities, but the real possible benefit is the potential for a better fit with real data. Figure 18.5 is the rank analogue of Figure 18.3: for any rank r, the fraction of LiveJournal users who link to their rth-most geographically proximate person is displayed. (Some averaging has been done in Figure 18.5: because a random person in the LiveJournal network lives in a city with about 1,300 residents, the data do not permit us to adequately distinguish among ranks that differ by less than this number.)

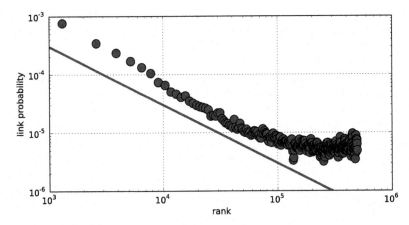

Fig. 18.5 The probability $P(r)$ of a friendship between two people u and v in LiveJournal as a function of the rank r of v with respect to u [32]. Ranks are rounded into buckets of size 1,300, which is the average LiveJournal population of the city for a randomly chosen person in the network, and thus 1,300 is in a sense the "rank resolution" of the dataset. (The unaveraged data are noisier, but follow the same trend.) The solid line corresponds to $P(r) \propto 1/r$. Note that Theorem 18.2 requires $P(r) \propto 1/r$ for a rank-based network to be navigable

As it was with distance, the link probability $P(r)$ between two people is a smoothly decreasing function of the rank r of one with respect to the other. And just as before, link probability levels off to about $\varepsilon = 5.0 \times 10^{-6}$ as rank gets large, so $P(r)$ is well modeled by $P(r) = \Theta(1/r) + \varepsilon$. But unlike the distance-based model of Figure 18.3 and Theorem 18.1, the fit between Figure 18.5 and Theorem 18.2 is notable: people in the LiveJournal network really have formed links with a geographic distribution that is a remarkably close match to rank-based friendship.

18.6 Going Off the Grid

Until now, our discussion has concentrated on models of proximity that are based on Manhattan distance in an underlying grid. We have argued that these grid-based models are reasonable for geographic proximity. Even in the geographic context, though, they are imperfect: the two-dimensional grid fails to account for real-world geographic features like the third dimension of a high-rise apartment complex or the imperfect mapping between geographic distance and transit-time distance between two points. But in a real Milgram-style routing experiment, there are numerous other measures of proximity that one might use as a guide in selecting the next step toward a target: occupation, age, hobbies, and alma mater, for example. The grid is a very poor model for almost all of these notions of distance. In this section, we will consider models of social networks that better match these non-geographic notions of similarity. Our discussion will include both non-grid-based models of social networks and ways to combine multiple notions of proximity into a single routing strategy.

18.6.1 Non-Grid-Based Measures of Similarity

Excluding geographic proximity to the target, similarity of occupation is the most-cited reason for the routing choices made by participants in Milgram-style routing experiments [13,21]. Consider, then, modeling person-to-person proximity according to occupation. A hierarchical notion of similarity is natural in this context: imagine a tree T whose leaves correspond to particular occupations ("cannoli chef" or "urban planner," perhaps), where each person u "lives" at the leaf ℓ_u that represents her occupation. The occupational proximity of u and v is given by the height of the least common ancestor (LCA) of ℓ_u and ℓ_v in T, which will be denoted by $\mathsf{lca}(u,v)$.

Hobbies can be modeled in a similar hierarchical fashion, though modeling hobby-based proximity is more complicated: a typical person has many hobbies but only one occupation. Measuring the similarity of two alma maters is more complicated still. There are many ways to measure the similarity of two schools, paralleling the many ways to measure the similarity of two people: geography, "type of

school" like liberal arts college or research university, athletic conference, strength
of computer science department, etc. But even with these complications, similarity
of occupation, hobbies, or alma mater is more naturally modeled with a hierarchy
than with a grid.

Navigability in social networks derived from a hierarchical metric has been explored through analysis, simulation, and empirical study of real-world interactions.
Kleinberg has shown a similar result to Theorem 18.1 for the tree-based setting,
characterizing navigable networks in terms of a single parameter that controls how
rapidly the link probability between people drops off with their distance [24]. As in
the grid, Kleinberg's theorem identifies an optimal middle ground in the trade-off
between having overly parochial and overly scattered connections: if T is a regular
b-ary tree and $\Pr[u \to v] \propto b^{-\beta \cdot \mathrm{lca}(u,v)}$, then the network is navigable if and only
if $\beta = 1$. Watts, Dodds, and Newman [48] have explored a similar hierarchical
setting, finding the ranges of parameters that were navigable in simulations. (Their
focus was largely on the combination of multiple hierarchical measures of proximity, an issue to which we will turn shortly.) Routing in the hierarchical context has
also been studied empirically by Adamic and Adar, who considered the role of proximity in the organizational structure of Hewlett–Packard Labs in social links among
HP Labs employees [1]. (Because a company's organizational structure forms a tree
where people more senior in the organization are mapped to internal nodes instead of
to leaves, Adamic and Adar consider a minor variation on LCA to measure person-
to-person proximity.) Adamic and Adar found that, as with geography, there is a
strong trace of organizational proximity in observed connections, and that, again as
with geography, greedily routing toward a target based on organizational proximity
was generally effective (see Section 18.7 for some discussion).

The question of navigability of a social network derived from an underlying
measure of distance has also been explored beyond the contexts of the grid and
the tree. Many papers have considered routing in networks in which person-to-
person distances are measured by shortest-path distances in an underlying graph that
has some special combinatorial structure. These papers then typically state bounds
on navigability that are based on certain structural parameters of the underlying
graph; examples include networks that have low treewidth [16], bounded growth
rate [14, 15, 42], or low doubling dimension [19, 47]. The results on rank-based
friendship, including generalizations and improvements on Theorem 18.2, have also
been extended to the setting of low doubling dimension [6,28]. However, a complete
understanding of the generality of these navigability results in terms of properties
of the underlying metric remains open.

Another way to model person-to-person proximity – and also to model variation in population density, in a different way from rank-based friendship – is the
very general *group-structure model* of Kleinberg [24]. Each person in an n-person
population is a member of various groups (perhaps defined by a shared physical
neighborhood, an employer, a hobby), and $\Pr[u \to v]$ is a decreasing function of
the size of the smallest group containing both u and v. Kleinberg proved that the
resulting network is navigable if $\Pr[u \to v]$ is inversely proportional to the size of
the smallest group including both u and v, subject to two conditions on the groups.

Informally, these conditions are the following. First, every group g must be "covered" by relatively large subgroups (so that once a path reaches g it can narrow in on a smaller group containing any particular target t). Second, groups must satisfy a sort of "bounded growth" condition (so that a person u has only a limited number of people who are in a group of any particular size with u, and thus u has a reasonable probability of "escaping" from small groups to reach a faraway target t).

18.6.2   Simultaneously Using Many Different Notions of Similarity

One of the major advantages of the group-structure model is that it allows us to model proximity between two people based on many "dimensions" of similarity, simply by defining some groups in terms of each of these multiple dimensions. Combining knowledge of various measures of the proximity of one's friends to the target – age, geography, and occupation, say – is natural, and, indeed, something that real-world participants in small-world studies do [13, 21, 38]. Identifying plausible models for social networks and good routing algorithms to find short paths when there are many relevant notions of similarity remains an interesting and fertile area for research.

We have already implicitly considered one straightforward way of incorporating additional dimensions of similarity by modeling proximity in a k-dimensional grid for $k > 2$. (Even $k = 2$ uses two types of similarity – for geography, longitude and latitude – and computes person-to-person similarity by the combination of the two.) Because the grid-based model uses Manhattan distance, here the various dimensions of proximity are combined simply by summing their measured distances. Martel and Nguyen [35, 41], Fraigniaud, Gavoille, and Paul [18], and Barrière et al. [7] have performed further work in analyzing the grid-based setting for general k. These authors have shown that if people are given a small amount of additional information about the long-range links of their friends, then k-dimensional grids result in shorter paths as k increases. (Theorem 18.1 implies that we must have $\Pr[u \to v] \propto d(u, v)^{-k}$ to achieve polylogarithmic path lengths; these results establish improvements in the polylogarithmic function as k increases, for a slightly souped-up version of local-information routing.)

Watts, Dodds, and Newman have explored a model of person-to-person similarity based on multiple hierarchies [48]. They consider a collection of k different hierarchies, where each is a regular b-ary tree in which the leaves correspond to small groups of people. The similarity of people u and v is given by their most similar similarity: that is, if $\mathsf{lca}_i(u, v)$ denotes the height of the LCA of u and v in the ith hierarchy, then we model $d(u, v) := \min_i \mathsf{lca}_i(u, v)$. People are mapped to each hierarchy so that a person's position in each hierarchy is determined independently of positions in other hierarchies. Watts, Dodds, and Newman show via simulation that using $k > 1$ hierarchies yields better performance for greedy routing than using just one. In particular, using $k \in \{2, 3\}$ hierarchies gave the best performance.

These simulations show that, for these values of k, the resulting network appears to be searchable under a broader range of parameters for the function giving friendship probability as a function of distance. As with Theorem 18.1, there is provably a single exponent $\beta = 1$ under which greedy routing produces polylogarithmic paths when there is one hierarchy; for two or three hierarchies, these simulations showed a wider range of values of β that yield navigable networks.

The results in the Watts–Dodds–Newman setting are based on simulations, and giving a fully rigorous theoretical analysis of routing in this context remains an interesting open challenge. So too do a variety of generalizations of that setting: dependent hierarchies, a combination of grid-based and hierarchy-based measures of proximity, or the incorporation of variable population density into the multiple-hierarchy setting. Broader modeling questions remain open, too. One can conceive of subtler ways of combining multiple dimensions of similarity that seem more realistic than just the sum or the minimum. For example, it seems that making significant progress toward a target in one dimension of similarity at the expense of large decreases in similarity in several other dimensions is a routing mistake, even if it reduces the minimum distance to the target over all the dimensions. Realistically modeling these multidimensional scenarios is an interesting open direction.

18.6.3   From Birds of a Feather to Social Butterflies (of a Feather)

The generalizations that we have discussed so far are based on extending greedy routing to broader and more realistic notions of proximity, but one can also consider enriching the routing algorithm itself. For example, algorithms that endow individuals with additional "semi-local" information about the network, such as awareness of one's friends' friends, have also been studied (e.g., [18, 30, 34, 35, 47]). But there is another natural and simple consideration in Milgram-style routing that we have not mentioned thus far: some people have more friends than others. This is a significant omission of the models that we have discussed; people in these models have a constant or nearly constant number of friends. In contrast, degrees in real social networks are usually well modeled by a *power-law distribution*, in which the proportion of the population with f friends is approximately $1/f^\gamma$, where γ is a constant typically around 2.1–2.4 in real networks (see, e.g., [5, 8, 12, 29, 39]). In the routing context, a popular person can present a significant advantage in finding a shorter path to the target. A person with more friends has a higher probability of knowing someone who is significantly closer to any target – in virtue of having drawn more samples from the friendship distribution – and thus a more popular person will be more likely to find a shorter path to a given target.

Strategies that choose high-degree people in routing have been studied in a number of contexts, and, largely through simulation, these strategies have been shown to perform reasonably well [1–3, 22, 46]. Of these, perhaps the most promising algorithm for homophilous power-law networks is the *expected-value navigation (EVN)* algorithm of Şimşek and Jensen [46], which explicitly combines popularity and proximity in choosing the next step in a chain. Under EVN, the current node u chooses as the next node in the path its neighbor v whose probability of a direct link to the target is maximized. The node u computes this probability using the knowledge of v's proximity to t as well as v's outdegree δ_v. An underlying model like the grid, for example, describes the probability p_v that a particular one of v's friendships will connect v to t; one can then compute the probability $1 - (1 - p_v)^{\delta_v}$ that one of the δ_v friendships of v will connect v to t. EVN chooses the friend maximizing this probability as the next step in the chain. Although Şimşek and Jensen give empirical evidence for EVN's success, no theoretical analysis has been performed. Analyzing this algorithm – or other similar algorithms that incorporate knowledge of node degree in addition to target proximity – in a formal setting is an important and open problem. Although a precise rigorous account of EVN has not yet been given, it is clear that EVN captures something crucial about real routing: the optimal routing strategy is some combination of getting close to a target in terms of similarity (the people who are more likely to know others most like the target) and of getting to popular intermediate people who have a large social circle (the people who are more likely to know many others in general). The interplay between popularity and proximity – and incorporating richer notions of proximity into that understanding – is a rich area for further research.

18.7 Discussion

It is clear that the wayfinding problem for real people in real social networks is only approximated by the models of social networks and of social-network routing discussed in this chapter. In many ways, real wayfinding is easier than it is in these models: we know which of our friends lived in Japan for a year, or tend to be politically conservative, or have a knack for knowing people in many walks of life, and we also have some intuitive sense of how to weight these considerations in navigating the network toward a particular target person. But real wayfinding is harder for real people in many ways, too: for example, even seemingly simple geography-based routing is, at best, a challenge for the third of college-age Americans who were unable to locate Louisiana on a map of the USA, even after the extensive press coverage of Hurricane Katrina [43].

The models of similarity and network knowledge that we have considered here are simplistic, and studying more realistic models – models with richer notions of proximity, or models of the errors or inconsistencies in individuals' mental maps of these notions of proximity, for example – is very interesting. But there is, of course, a danger of trying to model "too well": the most useful models do not reproduce all of the fine-grained details of a real-world phenomenon, but rather shed light on that phenomenon through some simple and plausible explanation of its origin.

With this perspective in mind, I will highlight just one question here: why and how do social networks become navigable? A number of models of the evolution of social networks through the "rewiring" of long-range friendships in a grid-like setting have been defined and analyzed [10, 11, 44]; these authors have shown that navigability emerges in the network when this rewiring is done appropriately. We have seen here that rank-based friendship is another way to explain the navigability of social networks, and we have seen that friendships in LiveJournal, viewed geographically, are well approximated by rank-based friendship. One piece is missing from the rank-based explanation, though: why is it that rank-based friendship should hold in a real social network, even approximately? Figure 18.3 shows that geography plays a remarkably large role in friendships even in LiveJournal's purely virtual community; friendship probability drops off smoothly and significantly as geographic proximity decreases. Furthermore, Figure 18.5 shows that rank-based friendship is a remarkably accurate model of friendship in this network. But are there natural processes that can account for this behavior? Why should geographic proximity in the flesh-and-blood world resonate so much in the virtual world of LiveJournal? And why should this particular rank-based pattern hold?

One explanation for the important role of geography in LiveJournal is that a significant number of LiveJournal friendships are online manifestations of existing physical-world friendships, which crucially rely on geographic proximity for their formation. This "virtualization" is undoubtedly an important process by which friendships appear in an online community like LiveJournal, and it certainly explains some of geography's key role. But accounting for the continued slow decay in link probability as geographic separation increases from a few hundred kilometers to a thousand kilometers, beyond the range of most spontaneous physical-world interactions, seems to require some additional explanation. Here is one speculative possibility: many interests held by LiveJournal users have natural "geographic centers" – for example, the city where a professional sports team plays, or the town where a band was formed, or the region where a particular cuisine is popular. Shared interests form the basis for many friendships. The geographic factor in LiveJournal could perhaps be explained by showing that the "mass" of u and v's shared interests (appropriately defined) decays smoothly as the geographic distance between u and v increases. Recent work of Backstrom et al. [4] gives some very intriguing evidence related to this idea. These authors have shown results on the geographic distribution of web users who issue various search queries. They characterize both the geographic "centers" of particular search queries and the "spread" of those queries, in terms of how quickly searchers' interest in that query drops off with the geographic distance from the query's center. Developing a comprehensive model of friendship formation on the basis of this underlying geographic nature of interests is a very interesting direction for future work.

To close, I will mention one interesting perspective on the question of an underlying mechanism by which rank-based friendship might arise in LiveJournal. This perspective comes from two other studies of node-linking behavior as a function of node-to-node similarity, in two quite different contexts. Figure 18.6(b) shows the results of the study by Adamic and Adar [1] of the linking probability between HP Labs employees as a function of the distance between them in the corporate hierarchy. Their measure of similarity is a variant of LCA, modified to allow the calculation of distances to an internal node representing a manager in the organization.

LCA distance is in a sense implicitly a logarithmic measure: for example, in a uniformly distributed population in the hierarchy, the number of people at distance d grows exponentially with d. Thus, this semilog plot of link probabilities is on the same scale as the other log–log plots in Figure 18.6. Figure 18.6(c) shows the analogous plot from a study by Filippo Menczer [37] on the linking behavior between pages on the web. Here the similarity between two web pages is computed

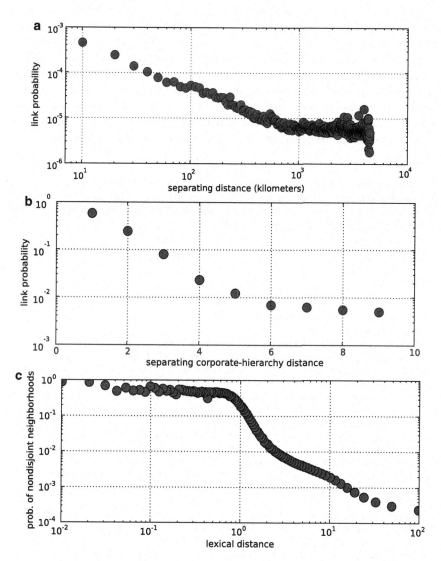

Fig. 18.6 Three plots of distance versus linking probability: (**a**) the role of geographic distance between LiveJournal users [32], a reproduction of Figure 18.3; (**b**) the role of corporate-hierarchy distance between HP Labs employees, from a study by Lada Adamic and Eytan Adar [1]; and (**c**) the role of lexical distance between pages on the web, from a study by Filippo Menczer [37]

based on the lexical distance of the pages' content. Because the raw link probabilities are so small, the plot shows the probability that the neighborhoods of two pages have nonempty overlap, where a page p's neighborhood consists of the page p itself, the pages to which p has a hyperlink, and pages that have a hyperlink to p.

Intriguingly, the LiveJournal linkage pattern, reproduced as Figure 18.6(a), and the HP Labs plot in Figure 18.6(b) show approximately the same characteristic shape in their logarithmic plots: a linear decay in link probability for comparatively similar people, leveling off to an approximately constant link probability for comparatively distant pairs. Figure 18.6(c) shows the opposite pattern: the probability of connection between two comparatively similar web pages is roughly constant, and then begins to decay linearly (in the log–log plot) once the pages' similarity drops beyond a certain level. Figure 18.6(a) and (b) both plot link probability between people in a social network against their (geographic or corporate) distance; Figure 18.6(c) plots link probability for web pages. Understanding why linking patterns in social networks look different from the web – and, more generally, making sense of what might be generating these distributions – remains a fascinating open question.

Acknowledgements Thanks to Lada Adamic and Filippo Menczer for helpful discussions and for providing the data used to generate Figure 18.6(b) and (c). I would also like to thank the anonymous referees for their very helpful comments. This work was supported in part by NSF grant CCF-0728779 and by grants from Carleton College.

References

1. Lada A. Adamic and Eytan Adar. How to search a social network. *Social Networks*, 27(3): 187–203, July 2005.
2. Lada A. Adamic, Rajan M. Lukose, and Bernardo A. Huberman. Local search in unstructured networks. In *Handbook of Graphs and Networks*. Wiley-VCH, 2002.
3. Lada A. Adamic, Rajan M. Lukose, Amit R. Puniyani, and Bernardo A. Huberman. Search in power-law networks. *Physical Review E*, 64(046135), 2001.
4. Lars Backstrom, Jon Kleinberg, Ravi Kumar, and Jasmine Novak. Spatial variation in search engine queries. In *Proceedings of the 17th International World Wide Web Conference (WWW'08)*, pages 357–366, April 2008.
5. Albert-László Barabási and Eric Bonabeau. Scale-free networks. *Scientific American*, 288: 50–59, May 2003.
6. David Barbella, George Kachergis, David Liben-Nowell, Anna Sallstrom, and Ben Sowell. Depth of field and cautious-greedy routing in social networks. In *Proceedings of the 18th International Symposium on Algorithms and Computation (ISAAC'07)*, pages 574–586, December 2007.
7. Lali Barrière, Pierre Fraigniaud, Evangelos Kranakis, and Danny Krizanc. Efficient routing in networks with long range contacts. In *Proceedings of the 15th International Symposium on Distributed Computing (DISC'01)*, pages 270–284, October 2001.
8. Béla Bollobás, Oliver Riordan, Joel Spencer, and Gábor Tusnády. The degree sequence of a scale-free random graph process. *Random Structures and Algorithms*, 18(3):279–290, May 2001.
9. Dorwin Cartwright and Alvin Zander. *Group Dynamics: Research and Theory*. Row, Peterson, 1953.

10. Augustin Chaintreau, Pierre Fraigniaud, and Emmanuelle Lebhar. Networks become navigable as nodes move and forget. In *Proceedings of the 35th International Colloquium on Automata, Languages and Programming (ICALP'08)*, pages 133–144, July 2008.

11. Aaron Clauset and Cristopher Moore. How do networks become navigable? Manuscript, 2003. Available as cond-mat/0309415.

12. Aaron Clauset, Cosma Rohilla Shalizi, and M. E. J. Newman. Power-law distributions in empirical data. Manuscript, 2007. Available as arXiv:0706.1062.

13. Peter Sheridan Dodds, Roby Muhamad, and Duncan J. Watts. An experimental study of search in global social networks. *Science*, 301:827–829, 8 August 2003.

14. Philippe Duchon, Nicolas Hanusse, Emmanuelle Lebhar, and Nicolas Schabanel. Could any graph be turned into a small world? *Theoretical Computer Science*, 355(1):96–103, 2006.

15. Philippe Duchon, Nicolas Hanusse, Emmanuelle Lebhar, and Nicolas Schabanel. Towards small world emergence. In *Proceedings of the 18th ACM Symposium on Parallelism in Algorithms and Architectures (SPAA'06)*, pages 225–232, August 2006.

16. Pierre Fraigniaud. Greedy routing in tree-decomposed graphs. In *Proceedings of the 13th Annual European Symposium on Algorithms (ESA'05)*, pages 791–802, October 2005.

17. Pierre Fraigniaud. Small worlds as navigable augmented networks: Model, analysis, and validation. In *Proceedings of the 15th Annual European Symposium on Algorithms (ESA'07)*, pages 2–11, October 2007.

18. Pierre Fraigniaud, Cyril Gavoille, and Christophe Paul. Eclecticism shrinks even small worlds. In *Proceedings of the 23rd Symposium on Principles of Distributed Computing (PODC'04)*, pages 169–178, July 2004.

19. Pierre Fraigniaud, Emmanuelle Lebhar, and Zvi Lotker. A doubling dimension threshold $\theta(\log \log n)$ for augmented graph navigability. In *Proceedings of the 14th Annual European Symposium on Algorithms (ESA'06)*, pages 376–386, September 2006.

20. Frank Harary and Robert Z. Norman. *Graph Theory as a Mathematical Model in Social Science*. University of Michigan, 1953.

21. P. Killworth and H. Bernard. Reverse small world experiment. *Social Networks*, 1:159–192, 1978.

22. B. J. Kim, C. N. Yoon, S. K. Han, and H. Jeong. Path finding strategies in scale-free networks. *Physical Review E*, 65(027103), 2002.

23. Jon Kleinberg. The small-world phenomenon: An algorithmic perspective. In *Proceedings of the 32nd Annual Symposium on the Theory of Computation (STOC'00)*, pages 163–170, May 2000.

24. Jon Kleinberg. Small-world phenomena and the dynamics of information. In *Advances in Neural Information Processing Systems (NIPS'01)*, pages 431–438, December 2001.

25. Jon Kleinberg. Complex networks and decentralized search algorithms. In *International Congress of Mathematicians (ICM'06)*, August 2006.

26. Jon M. Kleinberg. Navigation in a small world. *Nature*, 406:845, 24 August 2000.

27. Judith Kleinfeld. Could it be a big world after all? The "six degrees of separation" myth. *Society*, 39(61), April 2002.

28. Ravi Kumar, David Liben-Nowell, and Andrew Tomkins. Navigating low-dimensional and hierarchical population networks. In *Proceedings of the 14th Annual European Symposium on Algorithms (ESA'06)*, pages 480–491, September 2006.

29. Ravi Kumar, Prabhakar Raghavan, Sridhar Rajagopalan, D. Sivakumar, Andrew Tomkins, and Eli Upfal. Stochastic models for the web graph. In *Proceedings of the 41st IEEE Symposium on Foundations of Computer Science (FOCS'00)*, pages 57–65, November 2000.

30. Emmanuelle Lebhar and Nicolas Schabanel. Close to optimal decentralized routing in long-range contact networks. In *Proceedings of the 31st International Colloquium on Automata, Languages and Programming (ICALP'04)*, pages 894–905, July 2004.

31. Kurt Lewin. *Principles of Topological Psychology*. McGraw Hill, 1936.

32. David Liben-Nowell, Jasmine Novak, Ravi Kumar, Prabhakar Raghavan, and Andrew Tomkins. Geographic routing in social networks. *Proceedings of the National Academy of Sciences*, 102(33):11623–11628, August 2005.

33. Kevin Lynch. *The Image of the City*. MIT Press, 1960.
34. Gurmeet Singh Manku, Moni Naor, and Udi Wieder. Know thy neighbor's neighbor: the power of lookahead in randomized P2P networks. In *Proceedings of the 36th ACM Symposium on Theory of Computing (STOC'04)*, pages 54–63, June 2004.
35. Chip Martel and Van Nguyen. Analyzing Kleinberg's (and other) small-world models. In *Proceedings of the 23rd Symposium on Principles of Distributed Computing (PODC'04)*, pages 179–188, July 2004.
36. Miller McPherson, Lynn Smith-Lovin, and James M. Cook. Birds of a feather: Homophily in social networks. *Annual Review of Sociology*, 27:415–444, August 2001.
37. Filippo Menczer. Growing and navigating the small world web by local content. *Proceedings of the National Academy of Sciences*, 99(22):14014–14019, October 2002.
38. Stanley Milgram. The small world problem. *Psychology Today*, 1:61–67, May 1967.
39. Michael Mitzenmacher. A brief history of lognormal and power law distributions. *Internet Mathematics*, 1(2):226–251, 2004.
40. Jacob L. Moreno. *Who Shall Survive? Foundations of Sociometry, Group Psychotherapy and Sociodrama*. Nervous and Mental Disesase Publishing Company, 1934.
41. Van Nguyen and Chip Martel. Analyzing and characterizing small-world graphs. In *Proceedings of the 16th ACM–SIAM Symposium on Discrete Algorithms (SODA'05)*, pages 311–320, January 2005.
42. Van Nguyen and Chip Martel. Augmented graph models for small-world analysis with geographical factors. In *Proceedings of the 4th Workshop on Analytic Algorithms and Combinatorics (ANALCO'08)*, January 2008.
43. Roper Public Affairs and National Geographic Society. 2006 geographic literacy study, May 2006. http://www.nationalgeographic.com/roper2006.
44. Oskar Sandberg and Ian Clarke. The evolution of navigable small-world networks. Manuscript, 2006. Available as cs/0607025.
45. Georg Simmel. *Conflict And The Web Of Group Affiliations*. Free Press, 1908. Translated by Kurt H. Wolff and Reinhard Bendix (1955).
46. Özgür Şimşek and David Jensen. Decentralized search in networks using homophily and degree disparity. In *Proceedings of the 19th International Joint Conference on Artificial Intelligence (IJCAI'05)*, pages 304–310, August 2005.
47. Aleksandrs Slivkins. Distance estimation and object location via rings of neighbors. In *Proceedings of the 24th Symposium on Principles of Distributed Computing (PODC'05)*, pages 41–50, July 2005.
48. Duncan J. Watts, Peter Sheridan Dodds, and M. E. J. Newman. Identity and search in social networks. *Science*, 296:1302–1305, 17 May 2002.
49. Duncan J. Watts and Steven H. Strogatz. Collective dynamics of 'small-world' networks. *Nature*, 393:440–442, 1998.

Index